WEBSTER'S
UNIVERSAL

SPANISH-ENGLISH
DICTIONARY

GEDDES&
GROSSET

List of Abbreviations/
Lista de Abreviaturas

abbrev	abbreviation	abreviatura
adj	adjective	adjectivo
adv	adverb	adverbio
art	article	artículo
auto	automobile	automóvil
aux	auxiliary	auxiliar
bot	botany	botánica
chem	chemistry	química
col	colloquial term	lengua familiar
com	commerce	comercio
compd	in compounds	usada en palabras compuestas
comput	computers	informática
conj	conjunction	conjunción
excl	exclamation	exclamación
f	feminine noun	sustantivo femenino
fig	figurative use	uso figurado
gr	grammar	gramática
interj	interjection	interjección
invar	invariable	invariable
Lat Am	Latin American	latinoamericano
law	law term	jurisprudencia
ling	linguistics	lingüística
m	masculine noun	sustantivo masculino
math	mathematics	matemáticas
med	medicine	medicina
mil	military term	lo militar
mus	music	música
n	noun	sustantivo
npl	plural noun	sustantivo plural
pej	pejorative	peyorativo
pl	plural	plural
pn	pronoun	pronombre
poet	poetical term	vocablo poético
pref	prefix	prefijo
prep	preposition	preposición
rad	radio	radio
rail	railway	ferrocarilero
theat	theater	teatro
tec	technology	téchnica, tecnologia
TV	television	televisión
vi	intransitive verb	verbo intransitivo
vr	reflexive verb	verbo reflexivo
vt	transitive verb	verbo transitivo

First published in this edition 2004

Copyright © 2004 Geddes & Grosset,
David Dale House, New Lanark, Scotland, ML11 9DJ

ISBN 1 84205 443 0

Printed and bound in Canada

Spanish–English

A

a *prep* to; in; at; according to; on; by; for; of.

abacería *f* grocery.

abacero *m* grocer.

ábaco *m* abacus.

abad *m* abbot.

abadejo *m* cod.

abadesa *f* abbess.

abadía *f* abbey.

abajo *adv* under; underneath; below; ~ **de** *prep* under, below.

abalanzarse *vr* to rush forward.

abalorio *m* glass bead.

abanderado *m* (*mil*) ensign; standard bearer.

abandonado/da *adj* derelict; abandoned; neglected.

abandonar *vt* to abandon; to leave; ~**se** *vr* ~ **a** to give oneself up to.

abandono *m* desertion; neglect; retirement.

abanicar *vt* to fan.

abanico *m* fan.

abaratar *vt* to lower the price of.

abarca *f* sandal.

abarcar *vt* to include.

abarrancarse *vr* to get into difficulties.

abarrotado/da *adj* packed.

abarrotar *vt* to tie down.

abastecedor/ra *m/f* supplier, purveyor.

abastecer *vt* to supply, provide.

abastecimiento *m* supplying; provisions.

abasto *m* supply of provisions.

abate *m* French abbot.

abatido/da *adj* dejected, low-spirited.

abatimiento *m* low spirits *pl*; depression.

abatir *vt* to knock down; to humble.

abdicación *f* abdication.

abdicar *vt* to abdicate.

abdomen *m* abdomen.

abdominal *adj* abdominal.

abecé *m* alphabet.

abecedario *m* alphabet; spelling book, primer.

abedul *m* birch tree.

abeja *f* bee; ~ **reina** queen bee.

abejar *m* beehive.

abejarrón *m* bumblebee.

abejón *m* drone; hornet.

abejorro *m* bumblebee.

aberración *f* aberration.

abertura *f* aperture, chink, opening.

abeto *m* fir tree.

abetunado/da *adj* dark-skinned.

abierto/ta *adj* open; sincere; frank.

abigarrado/da *adj* multicolored.

abintestato *adj* intestate.

abismal *adj* abysmal.

abismo *m* abyss; gulf; hell.

abjuración *f* abjuration.

abjurar *vt* to abjure, to recant; * *vi*: ~ **de** to abjure, to recant.

ablandamiento *m* softening.

ablandar *vt, vi* to soften.

ablativo *m* (*gr*) ablative.

ablución *f* ablution.

abnegación *f* self-denial.

abnegado/da *adj* selfless.

abnegar *vt* to renounce.

abobado/da *adj* silly.

abobamiento *m* stupefaction.

abobar *vt* to stupefy.

abocado/da *adj* light (wine).

abocar *vt* to seize with the mouth; ~**se** *vr* to meet by agreement.

abochornar *vt* to swelter; ~**se** *vr* to shame.

abofetear *vt* to slap.

abogacía *f* legal profession.

abogado/a *m/f* attorney-at-law, counsel.

abogar *vi* to intercede; ~ **por** to advocate.

abolengo *m* ancestry; inheritance from ancestors.

abolición *f* abolition, abrogation.

abolir *vt* to abolish.

abolladura *f* dent.

abollar *vt* to dent.

abominable *adj* abominable, cursed.

abominación *f* abomination.

abominar *vt* to detest.

abonado/da *adj* ready; prepared; * *m/f* subscriber; season ticket holder.

abonar *vt* to settle; to fertilize; to endorse; ~**se** *vr* to subscribe; * *vi* to clear up.

abono *m* payment; subscription; dung, manure.

abordaje *m* boarding.

abordar *vt* (*mar*) to board; to broach.

aborigen *m* aborigine.

aborrecer *vt* to hate, to abhor.

aborrecible *adj* hateful, detestable.

aborrecimiento *m* abhorrence, hatred.

abortar *vi* to miscarry; to have an abortion.

abortivo/va *adj* abortive.

aborto *m* miscarriage; abortion; monster.

abortón *m* abortion (in animals).

abotagado/da *adj* swollen.

abotinado/da *adj* tied up.

abotonar *vt* to button.

abovedado/da *adj* vaulted.

abrasar *vt* to burn; to parch; ~**se** *vr* to burn oneself.

abrazadera f bracket; clasp.
abrazar vt to embrace; to surround.
abrazo m embrace.
abrebotellas m invar bottle opener.
abrecartas m invar letter opener.
abrelatas m invar can opener.
abrevadero m watering place.
abrevar vt to water (cattle).
abreviación f abbreviation, abridgement; shortening.
abreviar vt to abridge, to cut short.
abreviatura f abbreviation.
abridor m opener.
abrigar vt to shelter; to protect; ~se vr to take shelter.
abrigo m coat; shelter; protection; aid.
abril m April.
abrillantar vt to polish.
abrir vt to open; to unlock; ~se vr to open up; to clear the way; to be open.
abrochador m buttonhook.
abrochar vt to button; to do up.
abrogar vt to abrogate.
abrumador/ra adj overwhelming; annoying.
abrumar vt to overwhelm.
abrupto/ta adj abrupt; steep.
absceso m abscess.
absentismo m absenteeism.
absolución f forgiveness, absolution.
absoluto/ta adj absolute.
absolutorio/a adj absolutely.
absolver vt to absolve.
absorbente adj absorbent.
absorber vt to absorb.
absorción f absorption; takeover.
absorto adj engrossed.
abstemio adj teetotal.
abstención f abstention.
abstenerse vr to abstain.
abstinencia f abstinence.
abstinente adj abstinent, abstemious.
abstracción f abstraction.
abstracto/ta adj abstract.
abstraer vt to abstract; ~se vr to be absorbed.
abstraído adj absent-minded.
absuelto/ta adj absolved.
absurdidad f, **absurdo** m absurdity.
absurdo adj absurd.
abuela f grandmother.
abuelo m grandfather.
abulia f lethargy.
abultado/da adj bulky, large, massive.
abultar vt to increase, to enlarge; * vi to be bulky.
abundancia f abundance.
abundante adj abundant, copious.
abundar vi to abound.
aburrido/da adj boring, dull.
aburridor/ra adj Lat Am boring, dull.
aburrimiento m boredom.
aburrir vt to bore.
abusador/ra adj Lat Am greedy.

abusar vt to abuse.
abusivo/va adj abusive.
abuso m abuse.
abyección f abjectness.
abyecto/ta adj abject, wretched.
acá adv here.
acabado/da adj perfect, accomplished.
acabar vt to finish, to complete; to achieve; ~se vr to finish; to be over; to run out; * vi to finish; to die, to expire.
acabose m: el ~ the last straw.
acacia f acacia.
academia f academy.
académico/ca m/f academician; * adj academic.
acaecer vi to happen.
acallar vt to quiet, to hush; to soften, to appease.
acalorado/da adj heated.
acalorarse vr to become heated.
acampar vt to camp.
acanalado/da adj grooved; fluted.
acanalar vt to corrugate.
acanto m acanthus.
acantonamiento m cantonment.
acantonar vt to billet.
acaparar vt to monopolize; to hoard.
acápite m Lat Am paragraph.
acariciar vt to fondle, to caress.
acarrear vt to transport; to occasion.
acarreo m carriage, transportation.
acaso m chance; * adv perhaps.
acatarrarse vr to catch (a) cold.
acaudalado/da adj rich, wealthy.
acaudalar vt to hoard.
acaudillar vt to command.
acceder vi to agree; ~ a to have access to.
accesible adj attainable; accessible.
acceso m access; fit.
accesorio/ria adj, m accessory.
accidentado/da adj uneven; hilly; eventful.
accidental adj accidental; casual.
accidentarse vr to have an accident.
accidente m accident.
acción f action, operation; share.
accionar vt to work; Lat Am to bring a suit against.
accionista m shareholder.
acebo m holly tree.
acebuche m wild olive tree.
acechador/ra m/f spy, observer.
acechar vt to lie in wait for; to spy on, observe.
acecho m spying, watching; ambush.
aceitar vt to oil.
aceite m oil.
aceitera f oilcan.
aceitoso/sa adj oily.
aceituna f olive.
aceitunado/da adj olive-green.
aceitunero m olive seller.
aceituno m olive tree.
aceleración f acceleration.
acelerada f Lat Am acceleration.

aceleradamente *adv* swiftly, hastily.

acelerador *m* gas pedal.

acelerar *vt* to accelerate; to hurry.

acelga *f* (*bot*) chard (a variety of beet).

acento *m* accent.

acentuación *f* accentuation.

acentuar *vt* to accentuate.

aceña *f* water mill.

acepción *f* acceptation.

aceptable *adj* acceptable.

aceptación *f* acceptance; approval.

aceptar *vt* to accept, to admit.

acequia *f* canal, channel; drain.

acera *f* sidewalk.

acerado/da *adj* steel *compd*, made of steel; sharp; steely.

acerbo/ba *adj* rigorous, harsh; cruel.

acerca *prep* about, relating to.

acercar *vt* to move nearer; ~**se** *vr* ~ **a** to approach.

acerico *m* pincushion.

acero *m* steel.

acérrimo/ma *adj* staunch; bitter.

acertado/da *adj* correct, proper; prudent.

acertar *vt* to hit; to guess right; * *vi* to get it right; to turn out true.

acertijo *m* riddle.

acervo *m* heap, pile.

acetato *m* (*chem*) acetate.

achacar *vt* to impute.

achacoso/sa *adj* sickly, unhealthy.

achantar *vt* (*col*) to scare; ~**se** *vr* to back down.

achaparrado/da *adj* stunted; stocky.

achaque *m* ailment; excuse; subject, matter.

achicar *vt* to diminish; to humiliate; to bale (out).

achicharrar *vt* to scorch; to overheat.

achicoria *f* (*bot*) chicory.

achiquitar *vt Lat Am* to make smaller.

achisparse *vr* to get tipsy.

aciago/ga *adj* unlucky; ominous.

acíbar *m* aloes; (*fig*) bitterness; displeasure.

acicalar *vt* to polish; ~**se** *vr* to dress in style.

acicate *m* spur.

acidez *f* acidity.

ácido *m* acid; * ~/**da** *adj* acid, sour.

acierto *m* success; solution; dexterity.

aclamación *f* acclamation.

aclamar *vt* to applaud, to acclaim.

aclaración *f* clarification.

aclarar *vt* to clear; to brighten; to explain; to clarify; ~**se** *vr* to understand; * *vi* to clear up.

aclimatar *vt* to acclimatize; ~**se** *vr* to become acclimatized.

acne *m* acne.

acobardar *vt* to intimidate.

acodarse *vr* to lean.

acogedor/ra *adj* welcoming.

acoger *vt* to receive; to welcome; to harbor; ~**se** *vr* to take refuge.

acogida *f* reception; asylum.

acolchar *vt* to quilt; to cushion.

acólito *m* acolyte; assistant.

acometer *vt* to attack; to undertake.

acometida *f* attack, assault.

acomodadizo *adj* accommodating.

acomodado/da *adj* suitable, convenient, fit; wealthy.

acomodador/ra *m/f* usher, usherette.

acomodar *vt* to accommodate, to arrange; ~**se** *vr* to comply.

acomodaticio/cia *adj* accommodating; pliable.

acompañamiento *m* (*mus*) accom-paniment.

acompañar *vt* to accompany; to join; (*mus*) to accompany.

acompasado/da *adj* measured; well-proportioned.

acondicionado/da *adj* conditioned.

acondicionar *vt* to arrange; to condition.

acongojar *vt* to distress.

aconsejable *adj* advisable.

aconsejar *vt* to advise; ~**se** *vr* to take advice.

acontecer *vi* to happen.

acontecimiento *m* event, incident.

acopio *m* gathering, storing.

acopiar *vt* to gather, to store up.

acoplamiento *m* coupling.

acoplar *vt* to couple; to fit; to connect.

acorazado/da *adj* armored; * *m* battle-ship.

acordado/da *adj* agreed.

acordar *vt* to agree; to remind; *Lat Am* to award; ~**se** *vr* to agree; to remember.

acorde *adj* harmonious; * *m* chord.

acordeón *m* accordion.

acordonado/da *adj* cordoned-off.

acordonar *vt* to tie up; to cordon off.

acorralar *vt* to round up, corral, -corner.

acortar *vt* to abridge, to shorten; ~**se** *vr* to become shorter.

acosar *vt* to pursue closely; to pester.

acostado/da *adj* in bed; lying down.

acostar *vt* to put to bed; to lay down; ~**se** *vr* to go to bed; to lie down.

acostumbrado/da *adj* usual.

acostumbrar *vi* to be used to; ~**se** *vr* ~ **a** to get used to; * *vt* to accustom.

acotación *f* boundary mark; quotation in the margin; stage direction.

acotar *vt* to set bounds to; to annotate.

ácrata *m/f* anarchist.

acre *adj* acid; sharp; * *m* acre.

acrecentamiento *m* increase.

acrecentar *vt* to increase, to augment.

acreditar *vt* to guarantee; to assure, to affirm; to authorize; to credit; ~**se** *vr* to become famous.

acreedor *m* creditor.

acribillar *vt* to riddle with bullets; to molest, to torment.

acriminar *vt* to incriminate; to accuse.

acrimonia *f* acrimony.

acriollado/da *adj Lat Am* integrated.

acrisolar vt to refine, to purify.

acritud f acrimony.

acróbata m/f acrobat.

acta f act; ~s fpl records pl.

actitud f attitude; posture.

activar vt to activate; to speed up.

actividad f activity; liveliness.

activo/va adj active; diligent.

acto m act, action; act of a play; ceremony.

actor m actor; plaintiff.

actriz f actress.

actuación f action; behavior; proceedings pl.

actual adj actual, present.

actualidad f present time; ~es fpl current events pl.

actualizar vt to update.

actualmente adv at present.

actuar vt to work; to operate; * vi to work; to act.

acuarela f watercolor.

acuariano/na adj Lat Am Aquarian (zodiac sign).

acuario m tank.

Acuario m Aquarius (zodiac sign).

acuartelamiento m quartering of troops.

acuartelar vt (mil) to quarter (troops).

acuático/ca adj aquatic.

acuchillar vt to cut; to plane.

acuciar vt to urge on.

acuclillarse vr to crouch.

acudir vi to go to; to attend; to assist.

acueducto m aqueduct.

acuerdo m agreement; de ~ (col) OK, all right.

acumular vt to accumulate, to collect.

acuñación f coining.

acuñar vt to coin, to mint; to wedge in.

acuoso/sa adj watery.

acupuntura f acupuncture.

acurrucarse vr to squat; to huddle up.

acusación f accusation.

acusador/ra m accuser; * adj accusing.

acusar vt to accuse; to reveal; to denounce; ~se vr to confess.

acusativo m (gr) accusative.

acuse m: ~ de recibo acknowledgement of receipt.

acústica f acoustics pl.

acústico/ca adj acoustic.

adagio m adage, proverb; (mus) adagio.

adalid m chief, commander.

adamascado/da adj damask.

adaptable adj adaptable.

adaptación f adaptation.

adaptador m adapter.

adaptar vt to adapt.

adecuado/da adj adequate, fit; appropriate.

adecuar vt to fit, to accommodate, to proportion.

adefesio m folly, nonsense.

adelantado/da adj advanced; fast.

adelantamiento m progress, improvement, advancement; overtaking.

adelantar vt, vi to advance, to accelerate; to pass; to ameliorate, to improve; ~se vr to advance; to outdo.

adelante adv forward(s); de hoy en ~ from now on; más ~ later on; further on; ~ de Lat Am in front of; * excl come in!

adelanto m advance; progress; improvement.

adelfa f (bot) rosebay.

adelgazar vt to make thin/slender; * vi to lose weight.

ademán m gesture; attitude.

además adv moreover, besides; ~ de besides.

adentrarse vr to get inside; to penetrate.

adentro adv in; inside; ~ de Lat Am inside.

adepto/ta m/f supporter.

aderezar vt to dress, to adorn; to prepare; to season.

aderezo m adorning; seasoning; arrangement.

adeudado adj in debt.

adeudar vt to owe; ~se vr to run into debt.

adherencia f adhesion, cohesion; alliance.

adherente adj adhering to, cohesive.

adherir vi: ~ a to adhere to; to espouse.

adhesión f adhesion; cohesion.

adición f addition.

adicionar vt to add.

adicto/ta adj: ~ a addicted to; devoted to; * m supporter; addict.

adiestrar vt to guide; to teach, to instruct; ~se vr to practice.

adinerado/da adj wealthy, rich.

adiós excl goodbye; hello.

aditivo m additive.

adivinanza f enigma; riddle.

adivinar vt to foretell; to guess.

adivino/na m/f fortune-teller.

adjetivo m adjective.

adjudicación f adjudication.

adjudicar vt to adjudge; ~se vr to appropriate.

adjuntar vt to endorse.

adjunto/ta adj united, joined, annexed; * m/f assistant.

administración f administration.

administrador/a m/f administrator.

administrar vt to administer.

administrativo/va adj administrative.

admirable adj admirable, marvelous.

admiración f admiration; wonder; (gr) exclamation mark.

admirar vt to admire; to surprise; ~se vr to be surprised.

admisible adj admissible.

admisión f admission, acceptance.

admitir vt to admit; to let in; to concede; to permit.

admonición f warning.

adobado m pickled pork.

adobar vt to dress; to season.

adobe m adobe, sun-dried brick.

adobo m dressing; pickle sauce.

adoctrinar vt to indoctrinate; to teach.

adolecer *vi* to suffer from.

adolescencia *f* adolescence.

adolescente *adj, m/f* adolescent.

adonde *adv* (to) where.

adónde *adv* where.

adopción *f* adoption.

adoptar *vt* to adopt.

adoptivo/va *adj* adoptive; adopted.

adoquín *m* paving stone.

adoración *f* adoration, worship.

adorar *vt* to adore; to love.

adormecer *vt* to put to sleep; **~se** *vr* to fall asleep.

adormidera *f* (*bot*) poppy.

adornar *vt* to embellish, to adorn.

adorno *m* adornment; ornament, decoration.

adosado/da *adj* semidetached, joined to another building by a common wall.

adquirir *vt* to acquire.

adquisición *f* acquisition.

adrede *adv* on purpose.

adscribir *vt* to appoint.

aduana *f* customs *pl.*

aduanero *m* customs officer; **~/ra** *adj* customs *compd.*

aducir *vt* to adduce.

adueñarse *vr:* **~ de** to take possession of.

adulación *f* adulation.

adulador/ra *m/f* flatterer.

adular *vt* to flatter.

adulterar *vt* to adulterate; * *vi* to commit adultery.

adulterio *m* adultery.

adúltero/ra *m/f* adulterer, adulteress.

adulto/ta *adj, m/f* adult, grown-up.

adusto/ta *adj* gloomy; stern.

advenedizo *m* upstart.

advenimiento *m* arrival; accession.

adverbio *m* adverb.

adversario *m* adversary; antagonist.

adversidad *f* adversity; setback.

adverso/sa *adj* adverse.

advertencia *f* warning, foreword.

advertido/da *adj* sharp.

advertir *vt* to notice; to warn.

Adviento *m* Advent.

adyacente *adj* adjacent.

aéreo/rea *adj* aerial.

aerobic *m* aerobics *pl.*

aerobismo *m Lat Am* aerobics *pl.*

aerodeslizador *m* hovercraft.

aerodeslizante *m* hovercraft.

aerogenerador *m* wind turbine.

aeromozo/za *m/f Lat Am* air steward/ess.

aeronauta *m* aeronaut.

aeronáutica *f* aeronautics.

aeronave *f* spaceship.

aeroplano *m* airplane.

aeropuerto *m* airport.

aerosol *m* aerosol.

aerostática *f* aerostatics.

afabilidad *f* affability.

afable *adj* affable.

afán *m* hard work; desire.

afanar *vt* to harass; (*col*) to pinch; **~se** *vr* to strive.

afanoso/sa *adj* hard, industrious.

afear *vt* to deform, to misshape.

afección *f* affection; fondness, attachment; disease.

afectación *f* affectation.

afectadamente *adv* affectedly.

afectado/da *adj* affected.

afectar *vt* to affect, to feign.

afectísimo/ma *adj* affectionate; **~ suyo** yours truly.

afectivo/va *adj* fond, tender.

afecto *m* affection; passion; **~/ta** *adj* affectionate; disposed; reserved.

afectuoso/sa *adj* affectionate; moving; tender.

afeitada *f Lat Am* shave.

afeitar *vt,* **~se** *vr* to shave.

afeite *m* make-up, rouge.

afeminado/da *adj* effeminate.

afeminar *vt* to make effeminate.

aferrado/da *adj* stubborn.

aferrar *vt* to grapple, to grasp, to seize.

afianzamiento *m* strengthening.

afianzar *vt* to strengthen; to prop up; **~se** *vr* to become established.

afiche *m Lat Am* poster.

afición *f* affection; hobby; fans *pl.*

aficionado/da *adj* keen; * *m/f* lover, fan; amateur.

aficionar *vt* to inspire affection; **~se** *vr* **~ a** to grow fond of.

afiebrado/da *adj Lat Am* feverish.

afiladera *f* grindstone.

afilado *adj* sharp.

afilar *vt* to sharpen, to grind.

afín *m* related; similar.

afinar *vt* to tune; to refine.

afincarse *vr* to settle.

afinidad *f* affinity; analogy; relationship.

afirmación *f* affirmation.

afirmado *m* road surface.

afirmar *vt* to secure, to fasten; to affirm, to assure.

afirmativo/va *adj* affirmative.

aflicción *f* affliction, grief.

aflictivo/va *adj* distressing.

afligir *vt* to afflict, to torment.

aflojar *vt* to loosen, to slacken, to relax; * *vi* to grow weak; to abate; to relent; **~se** *vr* to relax.

aflorar *vi* to emerge.

afluente *adj* flowing; * *m* tributary.

afluir *vi* to flow.

afónico/ca *adj* hoarse; voiceless.

aforismo *m* aphorism.

afortunado/da *adj* fortunate, lucky.

afrancesado/da *adj* Frenchified.

afrenta *f* outrage; insult.

afrentar *vt* to affront; to insult.

afroamericano/na *adj, m/f* African-American.

afrontar *vt* to confront; to bring face to face.

afuera *adv* out, outside; **~ de** *Lat Am* outside.

afueras *fpl* outskirts *pl*.

agacharse *vr* to stoop, to squat.

agalla *f* gill; **~s** *pl* pluck, guts; tonsils *pl*; tonsillitis.

agarradera *f Lat Am* handle.

agarradero *m* handle.

agarrado/da *adj* miserly, stingy.

agarrar *vt* to grasp, to seize; **~se** *vr* to hold on tightly.

agarrón *m Lat Am* fight.

agarrotar *vt* to tie down; to squeeze tightly; to garrote.

agasajar *vt* to receive and treat kindly; to regale.

agasajo *m* graceful reception; kindness.

ágata *f* agate.

agazaparse *vr* to crouch.

agencia *f* agency.

agenciarse *vr* to obtain.

agenda *f* diary.

agente *m* agent; police officer.

ágil *adj* agile.

agilidad *f* agility, nimbleness.

agitación *f* shaking; stirring; agitation.

agitanado/da *adj* Gypsy-like.

agitar *vt* to wave; to move; **~se** *vr* to become excited; to become worried.

aglomeración *f* crowd; **~ de tráfico** traffic jam.

aglomerar *vt*, **~se** *vr* to crowd together.

agnóstico/ca *adj*, *m/f* agnostic.

agobiar *vt* to weigh down; to oppress; to burden.

agolparse *vr* to assemble in crowds.

agonía *f* death throes *pl*.

agonizante *adj* dying.

agonizar *vi* to be dying.

agorar *vt* to predict.

agostar *vt* to parch.

agosto *m* August.

agotado/da *adj* exhausted; finished; sold out.

agotador/ra *adj* exhausting.

agotamiento *m* exhaustion.

agotar *vt* to exhaust; to drain; to misspend.

agraciado/da *adj* attractive; lucky.

agraciar *vt* to pardon; to reward.

agradable *adj* pleasant; lovely.

agradar *vt* to please, to gratify.

agradecer *vt* to be grateful for; to thank.

agradecido/da *adj* thankful.

agradecimiento *m* gratitude, gratefulness, thanks *pl*.

agrado *m* agreeableness, courteousness; will, pleasure; liking.

agrandar *vt* to enlarge; to exaggerate; to aggrandize; **~se** *vr* to get bigger.

agrario/ria *adj* agrarian; agricultural.

agravante *f* further difficulty.

agravar *vt* to oppress; to aggrieve; to aggravate; to exaggerate; **~se** *vr* to get worse.

agraviar *vt* to wrong; to offend; **~se** *vr* to be aggrieved; to be piqued.

agravio *m* offence; grievance.

agredir *vt* to attack.

agregado *m* aggregate; attaché.

agregar *vt* to aggregate, to heap together; to collate; to appoint.

agremiado/da *adj Lat Am* unionized.

agresión *f* aggression, attack.

agresivo/va *adj* aggressive.

agresor *m* aggressor, assaulter.

agreste *adj* rustic, rural.

agriar *vt* to sour; to exasperate.

agrícola *adj* farming *compd*.

agricultor/ra *m/f* farmer.

agricultura *f* agriculture; **~ biológica** organic farming.

agridulce *adj* sweet and sour.

agrietarse *vr* to crack.

agrimensor *m* surveyor.

agrimensura *f* surveying.

agrio *adj* sour, acrid; rough, sharp, rude, unpleasant.

agronomía *f* agronomy.

agropecuario/ria *adj* farming *compd*.

agrupación *f* group(ing).

agrupar *vt* to group, to cluster; to crowd.

agua *f* water; slope of a roof; **~ fuerte** etching; **~ bendita** holy water; **~s** *fpl* waters *pl*.

aguacate *m* avocado pear.

aguacero *m* short, heavy shower of rain.

aguachento/ta *adj Lat Am* watery.

aguachirle *f* slops *pl*.

aguado/da *adj* watery; *Lat Am* weak.

aguador *m* water carrier.

aguafuerte *m* etching.

aguamarina *f* aquamarine (precious stone).

aguanieve *f* sleet.

aguantador/ra *adj Lat Am* patient.

aguantar *vt* to bear, to suffer; to hold up.

aguante *m* firmness; patience.

aguar *vt* to water down.

aguardar *vt* to wait for.

aguardiente *m* brandy.

aguarrás *f* turpentine.

aguatero/ra *m/f Lat Am* water seller.

agudeza *f* keenness, sharpness; acuteness; acidity; smartness.

agudizar *vt* to make worse; **~se** *vr* to get worse.

agudo/da *adj* sharp; keen-edged; smart; fine; acute; witty; brisk.

agüero *m*: **buen/mal ~** good/bad omen.

aguijar *vt* to prick, to spur, to goad; to stimulate.

aguijón *m* sting of a bee, wasp etc; stimulation.

aguijonear *vt* to prick; to spur; to stimulate.

águila *f* eagle; genius.

aguileño/ña *adj* aquiline; sharp-featured.

aguilucho *m* eaglet.

aguinaldo *m* Christmas box, New Year gift, tip.

aguja *f* needle; spire; hand; magnetic needle; (*rail*) points *pl*.

agujerear *vt* to pierce, to bore.

agujero *m* hole.

agujetas *fpl* stitch; stiffness; pains *pl* from fatigue.

agustino *m* monk of the order of St Augustine.

aguzar *vt* to whet, to sharpen; to stimulate.

ahí *adv* there.

ahijada *f* goddaughter.

ahijado *m* godson.

ahijar *vt* to adopt (as one's own child).

ahínco *m* earnestness; eagerness.

ahogar *vt* to smother; to drown; to suffocate; to oppress; to quench; **~se** *vr* to drown; to suffocate.

ahogo *m* breathlessness; financial difficulty.

ahondar *vt* to deepen; to study deeply; * *vi:* **~ en** to penetrate into.

ahora *adv* now, at present; just now.

ahorcar *vt* to hang; **~se** *vr* to hang oneself.

ahorrar *vt* to save; to avoid.

ahorrativo/va *adj* thrifty, careful with money.

ahorro *m* saving; thrift.

ahuecar *vt* to hollow, to scoop out; **~se** *vr* to get pig-headed.

ahumar *vt* to smoke, to cure (in smoke); **~se** *vr* to fill with smoke.

ahuyentar *vt* to drive off; to dispel.

airado/da *adj* angry.

airarse *vr* to get angry.

airbag *m* airbag.

aire *m* air; wind; aspect; musical composition.

airearse *vr* to take the air.

airoso/sa *adj* airy; windy; graceful; successful.

aislado/da *adj* insulated; isolated.

aislar *vt* to insulate; to isolate.

ajar *vt* to spoil; to abuse.

ajardinado/da *adj* landscaped.

ajedrez *m* chess.

ajedrezado/da *adj* checkered.

ajenjo *m* wormwood, absinth.

ajeno/na *adj* someone else's; foreign; ignorant; improper.

ajetrearse *vr* to exert oneself; to bustle; to toil; to fidget.

ajetreo *m* activity; bustling.

ají *m* red pepper.

ajo *m* garlic.

ajorca *f* bracelet.

ajuar *m* household furniture; trousseau.

ajustado/da *adj* tight; right; close.

ajustar *vt* to regulate, to adjust; to settle (a balance); to fit; to agree on; * *vi* to fit.

ajuste *m* agreement; accommodation; settlement; fitting.

ajusticiar *vt* to execute.

al = a el.

ala *f* wing; aisle; row, file; brim; -winger.

alabanza *f* praise; applause.

alabar *vt* to praise; to applaud.

alabastro *m* alabaster.

alacena *f* cupboard, closet.

alacrán *m* scorpion.

alado/da *adj* winged.

alambique *m* still.

alambrada *f* wire fence; wire netting.

alambrado *m* *Lat Am* wire fence; wire netting.

alambre *m* wire.

alambrista *m/f* tightrope walker.

alameda *f* avenue; poplar grove.

álamo *m* poplar.

alano *m* mastiff.

alarde *m* show.

alargador *m* extension lead.

alargar *vt* to lengthen; to extend; to hasten; to stretch out; to spin out; **~se** *vr* to get longer; to drag on.

alarido *m* outcry, shout; **dar ~s** to howl.

alarma *f* alarm.

alarmante *adj* alarming.

alarmar *vt* to alarm.

alarmista *m* alarmist.

alazán *m* sorrel.

alba *f* dawn.

albacea *m* executor.

albahaca *f* (*bot*) basil.

albañil *m* bricklayer.

albañilería *f* bricklaying.

albarán *m* invoice.

albarda *f* saddle.

albaricoque *m* apricot.

albedrío *m* free will.

alberca *f* reservoir; swimming pool.

albergar *vt* to lodge, to harbor; **~se** *vr* to shelter.

albergue *m* shelter; **~ de juventud** youth hostel.

albóndiga *f* meatball.

albor *m* dawn; whiteness.

alborada *f* dawn; reveille.

alborear *vi* to dawn.

albornoz *m* dressing gown.

alborotado/da *adj* restless, turbulent.

alborotar *vi* to make a row; * *vt* to stir up; **~se** *vr* to get excited; to get rough.

alboroto *m* noise; disturbance, riot.

alborozar *vt* to exhilarate; **~se** *vr* to rejoice.

alborozo *m* joy.

albricias *fpl* good news *pl*.

albufera *f* lagoon.

álbum *m* album.

albumen *m* egg white.

alcachofa *f* artichoke.

alcahuete/ta *m/f* pimp, bawd.

alcalde *m* mayor.

alcaldesa *f* mayoress.

alcaldía *f* office and jurisdiction of a mayor; mayor's office.

alcalino/na *adj* alkaline.

alcance *m* reach; bad balance.

alcancía *f* *Lat Am* money box.

alcanfor *m* camphor.

alcantarilla *m* sewer; gutter.

alcanzar *vt* to reach; to get, to obtain; to hit; * *vi* to suffice; to reach.

alcaparra *f* caper.

alcatraz *m* gannet.

alcayata *f* hook.

alcázar *m* castle, fortress.

alcoba *f* bedroom.

alcohol *m* alcohol.

alcohólico/ca *adj, m/f* alcoholic.

alcoholismo *m* alcoholism.

alcornoque *m* cork tree.

aldaba *f* knocker.

aldea *f* village.

aldeano/na *m/f* villager; * *adj* rustic.

ale *excl* come on!

aleación *f* alloy.

aleatorio/ria *adj* random.

aleccionar *vt* to instruct; to train.

alegación *f* allegation.

alegar *vt* to allege; to quote; * *vi Lat Am* to argue; to complain.

alegato *m* allegation; argument.

alegoria *f* allegory.

alegórico/ca *adj* allegorical.

alegrar *vt* to cheer; to poke; to liven up; ~**se** *vr* to get merry.

alegre *adj* happy; merry, joyful; content.

alegría *f* happiness; merriment.

alegrón *m* sudden joy; flicker.

alejamiento *m* remoteness; removal.

alejar *vt* to remove; to estrange; ~**se** *vr* to go away.

aleluya *f* hallelujah.

alemán/ana *adj, m/f* German; * *m* German language.

alentador/ra *adj* encouraging.

alentar *vt* to encourage.

alergia *f* allergy.

alero *m* gable-end; eaves *pl*.

alerta *adj, f* alert.

alertar *vt* to alert.

aleta *f* fin; wing; flipper; fender.

aletargarse *vr* to get drowsy.

aletazo *m* flap.

aletear *vi* to flutter.

aleteo *m* fluttering.

alevosía *f* treachery.

alevoso/sa *adj* treacherous.

alfabéticamente *adv* alphabetically.

alfabético/ca *adj* alphabetical.

alfabeto *m* alphabet.

alfalfa *f* (*bot*) lucerne.

alfarería *f* pottery.

alfarero *m* potter.

alféizar *m* window sill.

alférez *m* second lieutenant; (US navy) ensign.

alfil *m* bishop (at chess).

alfiler *m* pin; clip; clothes peg.

alfiletero *m* pincushion.

alfombra *f* carpet; rug.

alfombrar *vt* to carpet.

alfombrilla *f* mouse mat.

alforja *f* saddlebag; knapsack.

alga *f* (*bot*) seaweed.

algarabía *f* gabble, gibberish.

algarroba *f* (*bot*) carob.

algarrobo *m* (*bot*) carob tree.

algazara *f* din.

álgebra *f* algebra.

álgido/da *adj* chilly; crucial.

algo *pn* something; anything; * *adv* somewhat.

algodón *m* cotton; cotton plant; cotton wool; ~ **azucarado** *m* cotton candy.

algodonero *m* cotton plant; dealer in cotton.

alguacil *m* bailiff; mounted official.

alguien *pn* someone, somebody; anyone, anybody.

alguno/na *adj* some; any; no; * *pn* someone, somebody.

alhaja *f* jewel.

alhajera *f Lat Am* jewelry box.

alhelí *m* wallflower.

aliado/da *adj* allied.

alianza *f* alliance, league; wedding ring.

aliar *vt* to ally; ~**se** *vr* to form an alliance.

alias *adv* alias.

alicaído/da *adj* weak; downcast.

alicates *mpl* pincers *pl*, nippers *pl*.

aliciente *m* attraction; incitement.

alienación *f* alienation.

aliento *m* breath; respiration.

aligerar *vt* to lighten; to alleviate; to hasten; to ease.

alijo *m* lightening of a ship; alleviation; cache.

alimaña *f* pest.

alimentación *f* nourishment; food; grocery.

alimentar *vt* to feed, to nourish; ~**se** *vr* to feed.

alimenticio/cia *adj* food *compd*; nutritious.

alimento *m* food; ~**s** *mpl* alimony.

alineación *m* alignment; line-up.

alinear *vt* to arrange in line; ~**se** *vr* to line up.

aliñar *vt* to adorn; to season.

aliño *m* dressing; ornament, decoration.

alisar *vt* to plane; to polish; to smooth.

alistarse *vr* to enlist, to enroll; *Lat Am* to get ready.

aliviar *vt* to lighten; to ease; to relieve, to mollify.

alivio *m* alleviation; mitigation; relief; comfort.

aljibe *m* cistern.

allá *adv* there; over there; then.

allanamiento *m*: ~ **de morada** burglary.

allanar *vt* to level, to flatten; to overcome difficulties; to pacify; to subdue; to burgle; *Lat Am* to raid; ~**se** *vr* to submit; to tumble down.

allegado/da *adj* near; * *m/f* follower.

allí *adv* there, in that place.

alma *f* soul; human being.

almacén *m* warehouse, store; magazine.

almacenaje *m* storage.

almacenar *vt* to store (up).

almanaque *m* almanac.

almeja *f* clam.

almena *f* battlement.

almendra *f* almond.

almendrado/da *adj* almond-shaped; * *m* macaroon.

almendro *m* almond tree.

almiar *m* haystack.

almíbar *m* syrup.

almidón *m* starch.

almidonado/da *adj* starched; affected; spruce.

almidonar *vt* to starch.

almirantazgo *m* admiralty.

almirante *m* admiral.

almirez *m* mortar.

almizcle *m* musk.

almohada *f* pillow; cushion.

almohadilla *f* small pillow; pad; pincushion.

almohadón *m* large cushion.

almorranas *fpl* hemorrhoids *pl.*

almorzar *vt* to have for lunch; * *vi* to have lunch.

almuerzo *m* lunch.

alocado/da *adj* crazy; foolish; inconsiderate.

alocución *f* allocution.

áloe *m* (*bot*) aloes.

alojamiento *m* lodging; housing.

alojar *vt* to lodge; ~**se** *vr* to stay.

alondra *f* lark.

alpargata *f* rope-soled shoe.

alpinismo *m* mountaineering.

alpinista *m/f* mountaineer.

alpiste *m* canary seed.

alquería *f* farmhouse.

alquilar *vt* to let, to rent; to hire.

alquiler *m* renting, letting; hiring; rent; hire.

alquimia *f* alchemy.

alquimista *m* alchemist.

alquitrán *m* tar, liquid pitch.

alquitranado/da *adj* tarred.

alrededor *adv* around.

alrededores *mpl* surroundings *pl.*

alta *f* discharge from hospital.

altanería *f* haughtiness.

altanero/ra *adj* haughty, arrogant, vain, proud.

altar *m* altar; ~ **mayor** high altar.

altavoz *m* loudspeaker.

alterable *adj* changeable.

alteración *f* alteration; disturbance, tumult.

alterar *vt* to alter, to change; to disturb; ~**se** *vr* to get upset.

altercado *m* altercation, controversy; quarrel.

alternar *vt, vi* to alternate.

alternativa *f* alternative.

alternativo/va *adj* alternate.

alterno/na *adj* alternate; alternating.

Alteza *f* Highness (title).

altibajos *mpl* ups and downs *pl.*

altillo *m* hillock.

altiplanicie *f* high plateau.

altísimo/ma *adj* extremely high, most high; * *m* **el A~** the Most High, God.

altisonante, **altísono/na** *adj* high-sounding, pompous.

altitud *f* height; altitude.

altivez *f* haughtiness.

altivo/va *adj* haughty, proud, high-flown.

alto/ta *adj* high; elevated; tall; sharp; arduous;

difficult; eminent; enormous; * *m* height; story; highland; (*mil*) halt; (*mus*) alto; **i~!, i~ ahí!** *interj* stop!

altoparlante *m Lat Am* loudspeaker.

altramuz *m* (*bot*) lupin.

altura *f* height; depth; mountain summit; altitude; ~**s** *pl*: **las ~s** the heavens.

alubia *f* bean.

alucinación *f* hallucination.

alucinar *vt* to blind, to deceive; * *vi* to hallucinate; ~**se** *vr* to deceive oneself, to labor under a delusion.

aludir *vi* to allude.

alumbrado *m* lighting; illumination.

alumbramiento *m* lighting; illumination; childbirth.

alumbrar *vt* to light; * *vi* to give birth.

aluminio *m* aluminum.

alumno/na *m/f* student, pupil.

alunizar *vi* to land on the moon.

alusión *f* allusion; hint.

alusivo/va *adj* allusive.

aluvión *f* alluvium; flood.

alvéolo *m* socket; cell of a honeycomb.

alza *f* rise; sight.

alzacuello *m* dog collar.

alzada *f* height; appeal.

alzamiento *m* rise; elevation; higher bid; uprising.

alzar *vt* to raise, to lift up; to construct, to build; to gather (in); ~**se** *vr* to get up; to rise in rebellion; ~**se** *vr*: ~ **con algo** to make off with something.

ama *f* mistress, owner; housewife; foster mother; ~ **de llaves** housekeeper; ~ **de leche** nurse.

amabilidad *f* kindness, niceness.

amable *adj* kind, nice.

amaestrado/da *adj* performing.

amaestrar *vt* to teach; to instruct; to train.

amagar *vt* to threaten; to shake one's fist at; * *vi* to feint.

amago *m* threat; indication; symptom.

amalgama *f* amalgam.

amalgamar *vt* to amalgamate.

amamantar *vt* to suckle.

amanecer *vi* to dawn; **al ~** at daybreak.

amanerado/da *adj* affected.

amansar *vt* to tame; to soften; to subdue; ~**se** *vr* to calm down.

amante *m/f* lover.

amanuense *m* amanuensis, clerk, copyist.

amapola *f* (*bot*) poppy.

amar *vt* to love.

amargar *vt* to make bitter; to exasperate; ~**se** *vr* to be bitter.

amargo/ga *adj* bitter, acrid; painful; * *m* bitterness.

amargor *m* bitterness; sorrow, distress.

amargura *f* bitterness; sorrow.

amarillear *vi* to turn yellow.

amarillento/ta *adj* yellowish.

amarillo/lla *adj* yellow; * *m* yellow.

amarra *f* mooring rope.

amarrar *vt* to moor; to tie, to fasten.

amartelar *vt* to court, to woo; ~**se** *vr* to fall in love with.

amartillar *vt* to hammer; to cock (a gun/pistol).

amasar *vt* to knead; (*fig*) to arrange, to settle; to prepare.

amasijo *m* dough; mixed mortar; medley.

amateur *m/f* amateur.

amatista *f* amethyst.

amatorio/ria *adj* relating to love.

amazona *f* amazon; masculine -woman.

ambages *mpl*: **sin ~** in plain language.

ámbar *m* amber.

ambición *f* ambition.

ambicionar *vt* to crave, to covet.

ambicioso/sa *adj* ambitious.

ambidextro/tra *adj* ambidextrous.

ambientación *f* setting; sound effects *pl*.

ambiente *m* atmosphere; environment.

ambigüedad *f* ambiguity.

ambiguo/gua *adj* ambiguous; doubtful, equivocal.

ámbito *m* circuit, circumference; field; scope.

ambos/bas *adj, pn* both.

ambrosía *f* ambrosia.

ambulancia *f* ambulance.

ambulante *adj* traveling.

ambulatorio *m* state-run clinic.

ameba *f* ameba.

amedrentar *vt* to frighten, to terrify; to intimidate.

amén *f* amen; so be it; ~ **de** besides; except.

amenaza *f* threat.

amenazar *vt* to threaten.

amenizar *vt* to make pleasant.

ameno/na *adj* pleasant; delicious; flowery (of language).

América *f* America; ~ **del Norte/del Sur** North/ South America.

americano/na *adj, m/f* (Latin) American.

ameritar *vt Lat Am* to deserve.

ametralladora *m* machine gun.

amianto *m* asbestos.

amiga *f* (female) friend.

amigable *adj* amicable, friendly; suitable.

amigo *m* friend; comrade; lover; ~/**ga** *adj* friendly.

amilanar *vt* to frighten, to terrify; ~**se** *vr* to get scared.

aminorar *vt* to diminish; to reduce.

amistad *f* friendship.

amistoso/sa *adj* friendly, cordial.

amnesia *f* amnesia.

amnistía *f* amnesty.

amo *m* owner; boss.

amoblar *vt Lat Am* to furnish.

amodorrarse *vr* to grow sleepy.

amohinar *vt* to annoy; ~**se** *vr* to sulk.

amoldar *vt* to mold; to adapt; ~**se** *vr* to adapt oneself.

amonestación *f* advice; admonition; ~**ones** *fpl* publication of marriage banns.

amonestar *vt* to advise; to admonish; to publish banns of marriage of.

amoníaco *m* ammoniac.

amor *m* love; fancy; lover; ~ **mío** my love; **por ~ de Dios** for God's sake; ~ **propio** self-love.

amoratado *adj* livid.

amordazar *vt* to muzzle; to gag.

amorfo/fa *adj* shapeless.

amorío *m* love affair.

amoroso/sa *adj* affectionate, loving; lovely.

amortajar *vt* to shroud.

amortiguador *m* shock absorber.

amortiguadores *mpl* suspension.

amortiguar *vt* to mortify; to deaden; to temper; to muffle.

amortización *f* repayment; redemption.

amortizar *vt* to entail (an estate), to render inalienable; to pay, to liquidate, to discharge (a debt).

amotinamiento *m* mutiny.

amotinar *vt* to incite rebellion; ~**se** *vr* to mutiny.

amparar *vt* to shelter, to protect; to favor; ~**se** *vr* to claim protection.

amparo *m* protection, support; help; refuge, asylum.

amperio *m* amp.

ampliación *f* amplification, enlargement.

ampliar *vt* to amplify; to enlarge; to extend; to expand.

amplificación *f* enlargement.

amplificador *m* amplifier.

amplificar *vt* to amplify.

amplio/lia *adj* ample, extensive.

amplitud *f* amplitude, extension, largeness.

ampolla *f* blister; ampoule.

ampuloso/sa *adj* pompous.

amputación *f* amputation.

amputar *vt* to amputate.

amueblar *vt* to furnish.

amuleto *m* amulet.

amurallar *vt* to surround with walls.

anacoreta *m* anchorite, hermit.

anacronismo *m* anachronism.

ánade *m/f* duck.

anadear *vi* to waddle.

anagrama *f* anagram.

anales *mpl* annals *pl*.

analfabetismo *m* illiteracy.

analfabeto/ta *adj* illiterate.

analgésico *m* painkiller.

análisis *m* analysis.

analista *m/f* analyst.

analítico/ca *adj* analytical.

analizar *vt* to analyze.

analogía *f* analogy.

analógico/ca, análogo/ga *adj* analogous.

ananá *m* pineapple.

anaquel *m* shelf (in a bookcase).

anaranjado/da *adj* orange-colored.

anarquía *f* anarchy.

anárquico/ca *adj* anarchic, chaotic.

anarquismo *m* anarchism.

anarquista *m/f* anarchist.

anatema *f* anathema.

anatomía *f* anatomy.

anatómico/ca *adj* anatomical.

anca *f* rump.

ancho/cha *adj* broad, wide, large; * *m* breadth, width.

anchoa *f* anchovy.

anchura *f* width, breadth.

anciano/na *adj* old; * *m/f* old man/woman.

ancla *f* anchor.

ancladero *m* anchorage.

anclaje *m* anchorage.

anclar *vi* to anchor.

andaderas *fpl* baby walker.

andadura *f* walk; pace; amble.

andamio *m* scaffold.

andamiaje *m* scaffolding.

andanada *f* (*mar*) broadside.

andar *vi* to go, to walk; to fare; to act, to proceed, to work; to behave; to elapse; to move; * *vt* to go, to travel; * *m* walk, pace.

andariego/ga *adj* wandering.

andarín *m* fast walker.

andas *fpl* stretcher.

andén *m* sidewalk; (*rail*) platform; quayside.

andinismo *m Lat Am* mountaineering.

andinista *m/f Lat Am* mountaineer.

andrajo *m* rag.

andrajoso/sa *adj* ragged.

andurriales *mpl* byways *pl*.

anécdota *f* anecdote.

anegar *vt* to inundate, to submerge; **~se** *vr* to drown; to sink.

anejo/ja *adj* attached.

anemia *f* anemia.

anestésico *m* anesthetic.

anexar *vt* to annex; to join.

anexión *f* annexation.

anexionamiento *m* annexation.

anexo/xa *adj* annexed.

anfibio/bia *adj* amphibious.

anfiteatro *m* amphitheater.

anfitrión/ona *m/f* host/ess.

ángel *m* angel.

angelical *adj* angelic, heaven-born.

angélico/ca *adj* angelic.

angina *f* angina.

anglicano/na *adj*, *m/f* Anglican.

anglicismo *m* Anglicanism.

angosto/ta *adj* narrow, close.

anguila *f* eel.

angula *f* elver.

angular *adj* angular; **piedra ~** *f* cornerstone.

ángulo *m* angle, corner.

anguloso/sa *adj* angled, cornered.

angurria *f Lat Am* hunger; greed.

angurriento/ta *adj Lat Am* hungry; greedy.

angustia *f* anguish; heartache.

angustiar *vt* to cause anguish.

anhelante *adj* eager; longing.

anhelar *vi* to gasp; * *vt* to long for.

anhelo *m* desire, longing.

anidar *vi* to nestle, to make a nest; to dwell, to inhabit.

anillo *m* ring.

ánima *f* soul.

animación *f* liveliness; activity.

animado/da *adj* lively.

animador/ora *m/f* host(ess).

animadversión *f* ill-will.

animal *adj*, *m* animal.

animar *vt* to animate, to liven up; to comfort; to revive; **~se** *vr* to cheer up.

ánimo *m* soul; courage; mind; intention, meaning; will; thought; * *excl* come on!

animosidad *f* valor, courage; boldness.

animoso/sa *adj* courageous, spirited.

aniñarse *vr* to act in a childish manner.

aniquilar *vt* to annihilate, to destroy; **~se** *vr* to decline, to decay.

anís *m* aniseed; anisette.

aniversario/ria *adj* annual; * *m* anniversary.

ano *m* anus.

anoche *adv* last night.

anochecer *vi* to grow dark; * *m* nightfall.

anodino/na *adj* (*med*) anodyne.

anomalía *f* anomaly.

anómalo/la *adj* anomalous.

anonadar *vt* to annihilate; to lessen; **~se** *vr* to humble oneself.

anonimato *m* anonymity.

anónimo/ma *adj* anonymous.

anormal *adj* abnormal.

anotación *f* annotation, note.

anotar *vt* to comment, to note.

anquilosamiento *m* paralysis.

ánsar *m* goose.

ansia *f* anxiety, eagerness, hankering.

ansiar *vt* to desire.

ansiedad *f* anxiety.

ansioso/sa *adj* anxious, eager.

antagónico/ca *adj* antagonistic; -opposed.

antagonista *m* antagonist.

antaño *adv* formerly.

antártico/ca *adj* Antarctic; * *m*: **el A~** the Antarctic.

ante *m* suede; * *prep* before; in the presence of; faced with.

anteanoche *adv* the night before last.

anteayer *adv* the day before yesterday.

antebrazo *m* forearm.

antecámara *f* antechamber.

antecedente *adj*, *m* antecedent.

anteceder *vt* to precede.

antecesor/ra *m/f* predecessor; * *m* forefather.

antedicho/cha *adj* aforesaid.

antelación *f*: **con ~** in advance.

antemano *adv*: **de ~** beforehand.

antena *f* feeler, antenna; aerial; **~ parabólica** satellite dish.

antenoche *adv Lat Am* the night before last.

anteojo *m* eyeglass; **~ de larga vista** telescope; **~s** *mpl Lat Am* glasses *pl*.

antepasado/da *adj* passed, elapsed; **~s** *mpl* ancestors *pl*.

antepecho *m* (*mil*) parapet; ledge.

anteponer *vt* to place in front; to prefer.

anteproyecto *m* sketch; blueprint.

anterior *adj* preceding; former.

anterioridad *f* priority; preference.

antes *prep*, *adv* before; * *conj* before.

antesala *f* antechamber.

antiaéreo/rea *adj* anti-aircraft.

antibalas *adj* bullet-proof.

antibiótico *m* antibiotic.

anticición *m* anticyclone.

anticipación *f* anticipation.

anticipado/da *adj* advance.

anticipar *vt* to anticipate; to forestall; to advance.

anticipo *m* advance.

anticonceptivo *m* contraceptive.

anticongelante *m* antifreeze.

anticuado/da *adj* antiquated.

anticuario *m* antiquary, antiquarian.

anticuerpo *m* antibody.

antídoto *m* antidote.

antífona *f* antiphony; anthem.

antiestético/ca *adj* unsightly.

antifaz *m* mask.

antigualla *f* monument of antiquity; antique.

antiguamente *adv* in ancient times, of old.

antigüedad *f* antiquity, oldness.

antiguo/gua *adj* antique, old, ancient; * *m* senior; **~s** *mpl*: **los ~s** the ancients.

antílope *m* antelope.

antinatural *adj* unnatural.

antimonio *m* antimony.

antipatía *f* antipathy.

antipático/ca *adj* unpleasant.

antipasto *m Lat Am* antipasto.

antípodas *mpl* antipodes.

antirrobo *adj* anti-theft.

antisemita *adj* anti-Semitic.

antiséptico/ca *adj* antiseptic.

antítesis *f* (*gr*) antithesis.

antojadizo/za *adj* capricious, fanciful.

antojarse *vr* to long, to desire; to itch.

antojo *m* whim, fancy; longing.

antología *f* anthology.

antorcha *f* torch; taper.

antro *m* (*poet*) cavern, den, grotto.

antropófago *m* cannibal.

antropología *f* anthropology.

antropólogo/ga *m/f* anthropologist.

anual *adj* annual.

anualidad *f* annuity.

anublar *vt* to cloud, to obscure; **~se** *vr* to become clouded.

anudar *vt* to knot; to join; **~se** *vr* to get into knots.

anulación *f* annulment; cancellation.

anular *vt* to annul; to revoke; to cancel; * *adj* annular.

anunciación *f* announcement.

anunciante *m/f* advertiser.

anunciar *vt* to announce; to advertise.

anuncio *m* advertisement.

anverso *m* obverse.

anzuelo *m* hook; allurement.

añadidura *f* addition.

añadir *vt* to add.

añejo/ja *adj* old; stale, musty.

añicos *mpl* bits *pl*, small pieces *pl*; **hacer ~** to shatter.

añil *m* indigo plant; indigo.

año *m* year.

añojo *m* yearling calf.

añoranza *f* longing.

aorta *f* aorta.

aovar *vi* to lay eggs.

apabullar *vt* to squash.

apacentar *vt* to graze.

apacible *adj* affable; gentle; placid, quiet.

apaciguar *vt* to appease; to pacify, to calm.

apadrinar *vt* to support, to favor; to be godfather to.

apagado/da *adj* dull; quiet; muted; listless.

apagar *vt* to put out; to turn off; to quench, to extinguish; to damp; to destroy; to soften.

apagón *m* power cut, outage.

apalabrar *vt* to agree to; to engage.

apalancar *vt* to lever.

apalear *vt* to cane, to drub; to winnow.

apañado/da *adj* skillful; suitable.

apañar *vt* to grasp; to pick up; to patch; **~se** *vr* to manage.

aparador *m* sideboard; shop/store window.

aparato *m* apparatus; machine; ostentation, show.

aparatoso/sa *adj* showy; spectacular.

aparcamiento *m* parking lot.

aparcar *vt*, *vi* to park.

aparcería *f* partnership in a farm/other business.

aparcero/ra *m/f* partner; associate.

aparecer *vi* to appear; **~se** *vr* to appear.

aparecido/da *m/f* ghost.

aparejar *vt* to prepare; to harness (horses); to rig (a ship).

aparejo *m* preparation; harness, gear; (*mar*) tackle, rigging; **~s** *mpl* tools *pl*, implements *pl*.

aparentar *vt* to look; to pretend; to deceive.

aparente *adj* apparent; convenient.

aparición *f* apparition; appearance.

apariencia *f* outward appearance.

apartadero *m* (*rail*) siding.

apartado *m* paragraph; **~ de correos/postal** PO Box.

apartamento *m* apartment.

apartamiento *m* isolation; separation; apartment.

apartar *vt* to separate, to divide; to remove; to sort; **~se** *vr* to go away; to be divorced; to desist.

aparte *m* aside; new paragraph; * *adv* apart, separately; besides; aside.

apasionado/da *adj* passionate; devoted; fond; biased.

apasionar *vt* to excite; **~se** *vr* to get excited.

apatía *f* apathy.

apático/ca *adj* apathetic, indifferent.

apeadero *m* halt, stopping place; station.

apearse *vr* to dismount; to get down/out/off.

apechugar *vt* to face up to.

apedrear *vt* to stone; * *vi* to hail.

apegarse *vr*: **~ a** to become fond of.

apego *m* attachment, fondness.

apelación *f* (*law*) appeal.

apelar *vi* (*law*) to appeal; **~ a** to have recourse to.

apelativo *adj* (*gr*): **nombre ~** *m* generic name.

apellidar *vt* to call by name; to proclaim; **~se** *vr* to be called.

apellido *m* surname; family name; epithet.

apelmazar *vt* to compress.

apenar *vt* to grieve; to embarrass; **~se** *vr* to grieve; to be embarrassed.

apenas *adv* scarcely, hardly; * *conj* as soon as.

apéndice *m* appendix, supplement.

apendicitis *f* appendicitis.

apercibido/da *adj* provided; ready.

apercibirse *vr* to notice.

aperitivo *m* aperitif; appetizer.

apero *m* agricultural implement.

apertura *f* aperture, opening, chink; cleft.

apesadumbrar *vt* to sadden.

apestar *vt* to infect; * *vi*: **~ a** to stink of.

apetecer *vt* to fancy.

apetecible *adj* desirable; appetizing.

apetito *m* appetite.

apetitoso/sa *adj* pleasing to the taste, appetizing; tempting.

apiadarse *vr* to take pity.

apiario *m Lat Am* apiary.

ápice *m* summit, point; smallest part of a thing.

apilar *vt* to pile up; **~se** *vr* to pile up.

apiñado/da *adj* crowded; pyramidal; pine-shaped.

apiñarse *vr* to clog, to crowd.

apio *m* (*bot*) celery.

apisonadora *f* steamroller, roadroller.

apisonar *vt* to ram down.

aplacar *vt* to appease, to pacify; **~se** *vr* to calm down.

aplanadora *f Lat Am* roadroller, steamroller.

aplanar *vt* to level, to flatten.

aplastar *vt* to flatten, to crush.

aplatanarse *vr* to get weary.

aplaudir *vt* to applaud; to extoll.

aplauso *m* applause; approbation, praise.

aplazamiento *m* postponement.

aplazar *vt* to postpone.

aplicable *adj* applicable.

aplicación *f* application; effort.

aplicado/da *adj* studious; industrious.

aplicar *vt* to apply; to clasp; to attribute; **~se** *vr*: **~ a** to devote oneself to.

aplique *m* wall light.

aplomo *m* self-assurance.

apocado/da *adj* timid.

Apocalipsis *m* Apocalypse.

apocamiento *m* timidity; depression.

apocar *vt* to lessen, to diminish; to contract; **~se** *vr* to feel humiliated.

apócrifo/fa *adj* apocryphal; fabulous.

apodar *vt* to nickname.

apoderado/da *m/f* proxy, attorney; agent.

apoderar *vt* to authorize; to give the power of attorney to; **~se** *vr*: **~ de** to take possession of.

apodo *m* nickname, sobriquet.

apogeo *m* peak.

apolillar *vt* to gnaw/eat (clothes); **~se** *vr* to be moth-eaten.

apología *f* eulogy; defense.

apoltronarse *vr* to grow lazy; to loiter.

apoplejía *f* apoplexy.

apoplético/ca *adj* apoplectic.

apoquinar *vt* (*col*) to fork out.

aporrear *vt* to beat up.

aportar *vi* to arrive at a port; to arrive; * *vt* to contribute.

aposentar *vt* to harbor; to put up.

aposento *m* room.

aposición *f* (*gr*) apposition.

apósito *m* (*med*) external dressing.

aposta *adv* on purpose.

apostar *vt* to bet, to wager; to post soldiers; * *vi* to bet.

apostasía *f* apostasy.

apóstata *m* apostate.

apostatar *vi* to apostatize.

apostilla *f* marginal note; postscript.

apóstol *m* apostle.

apostolado *m* apostleship.

apostólico/ca *adj* apostolic(al).

apostrofar *vt* to apostrophize.

apóstrofe *m* apostrophe.

apóstrofo *m* (*gr*) apostrophe.

apostura *f* neatness.

apoteosis *f* apotheosis.

apoyar *vt* to rest; to favor, to patronize, to support; **~se** *vr* to lean.

apoyo *m* support; protection.

apreciable *adj* appreciable; valuable; respectable.

apreciar *vt* to appreciate; to estimate, to value.

aprecio *m* appreciation; esteem.

aprehender *vt* to apprehend, to seize.

aprehensión *f* apprehension, seizure.

apremiante *adj* urgent.

apremiar *vt* to press; to compel.

apremio *m* pressure, constriction; judicial compulsion.

aprender *vt* to learn; ~ **de memoria** to learn by heart.

aprendiz/za *m/f* apprentice.

aprendizaje *m* apprenticeship.

aprensión *f* apprehension.

aprensivo/va *adj* apprehensive.

apresar *vt* to seize, to grasp.

apresurado/da *adj* hasty.

apresuramiento *m* hurry.

apresurar *vt* to accelerate, to hasten, to expedite; ~**se** *vr* to hurry.

apretado/da *adj* tight; cramped; difficult.

apretar *vt* to compress, to tighten; to constrain; to distress; to urge earnestly; * *vi* to be too tight.

apretón *m* squeeze.

apretura *f* squeeze.

aprieto *m* conflict; tight spot.

aprisa *adv* quickly, swiftly; promptly.

aprisco *m* sheepfold.

aprisionar *vt* to imprison.

aprobación *f* approbation, approval.

aprobar *vt* to approve; to pass; * *vi* to pass.

apropiación *f* appropriation, assumption.

apropiado/da *adj* appropriate.

apropiarse *vr* to appropriate.

aprovechable *adj* profitable.

aprovechado/da *adj* industrious; thrifty; selfish.

aprovechamiento *m* use; exploitation.

aprovechar *vt* to use; to exploit; to profit from; to take advantage of; * *vi* to be useful; to progress; ~**se** *vr*: ~ **de** to use; to take advantage of.

aproximación *f* approximation; closeness.

aproximado/da *adj* approximate.

aproximar *vt* to approach; ~**se** *vr* to approach.

aptitud *f* aptitude, fitness, ability.

apto/ta *adj* apt; fit, able; clever.

apuesta *f* bet, wager.

apuesto/ta *adj* neat.

apuntado/da *adj* pointed.

apuntador *m* prompter.

apuntalar *vt* to prop up.

apuntar *vt* to aim; to level, to point at; to mark; * *vi* to begin to appear/show itself; to prompt (theater); ~**se** *vr* to score; to enroll.

apunte *m* annotation; prompting (theater).

apuñalar *vt* to stab.

apurado/da *adj* poor, destitute of means; exhausted; hurried.

apurar *vt* to purify; to clear up, to verify; to exhaust; to tease and perplex; ~**se** *vr* to worry, to hurry.

apuro *m* want; pain, affliction; haste; jam.

aquejado/da *adj* afflicted.

aquel/~la *adj* that; ~**los/~las** *pl* those.

aquél/~ la; *pn* that (one); ~ **los/~ las** *pl* those (ones).

aquello *pn* that.

aquí *adv* here; now.

aquietar *vt* to quiet, to appease.

aquilino *adj* aquiline.

aquilón *m* north wind.

ara *f* altar.

árabe *adj*, *m/f*, *m* (*ling*) Arabic.

arabesco *m* arabesque.

arado *m* plow.

arancel *m* tariff.

arándano *m* bilberry; blueberry.

arandela *f* washer.

araña *f* spider; chandelier.

arañar *vt* to scratch; to scrape; to corrode.

arar *vt* to plow.

arbitraje *m* arbitration.

arbitrar *vt*, *vi* to arbitrate; to referee.

arbitrariedad *f* arbitrariness.

arbitrario/ria *adj* arbitrary.

arbitrativo/va *adj* arbitrary.

arbitrio *m* free will; arbitration.

árbitro *m* arbitrator; referee; umpire.

árbol *m* tree; (*mar*) mast; shaft.

arbolado/da *adj* forested; wooded; * *m* woodland.

arboladura *f* rigging; masts *pl*.

arbolar *vt* to hoist, to set upright.

arboleda *f* grove.

arbusto *m* shrub.

arca *f* chest, wooden box.

arcada *f* arch; arcade; ~**s** *fpl* retching.

arcaico/ca *adj* archaic.

arcaísmo *m* archaism.

arcángel *m* archangel.

arce *m* maple tree.

archipiélago *m* archipelago.

archivador *m* filing cabinet.

archivar *vt* to file.

archivero, archivista *m* keeper of records, archivist.

archivo *m* file(s) (*pl*); archives *pl*.

arcilla *f* clay.

arcilloso/sa *adj* clayey.

arcipreste *m* archpriest.

arco *m* arc; arch; fiddle bow; hoop; *Lat Am* goalmouth; ~ **iris** rainbow.

arder *vi* to burn, to blaze.

ardid *m* stratagem, artifice; cunning.

ardiente *adj* burning; ardent, passionate; active; fiery.

ardilla *f* squirrel.

ardor *m* heat; valor; vivacity; fieriness, fervor.

ardoroso/sa *adj* fiery; restless.

arduo/dua *adj* arduous, difficult; high.

área *f* area.

arena *f* sand; grit; arena.

arenal *m* sandy ground.

arenga *f* harangue; speech.

arengar *vi* to harangue.

arenisca *f* sandstone; grit.

arenoso/sa *adj* sandy.

arenque *m* herring; **~ ahumado** smoked herring, kipper.

argamasa *f* mortar.

argamasar *vi* to mix mortar.

argolla *f* large ring.

argot *m* slang.

argucia *f* subtlety.

argüir *vi* to argue, to dispute; * *vt* to deduce; to argue; to imply.

argumentación *f* argumentation.

argumentar *vt, vi* to argue, to dispute; to conclude.

argumento *m* argument.

aria *f* (*mus*) aria; tune, air.

ariano/na *adj Lat Am* Arien (zodiac sign).

aridez *f* drought, want of rain.

árido/da *adj* dry; barren.

Aries *m* Aries (sign of the zodiac).

ariete *m* battering ram.

ario/a *adj* Aryan.

arisco/ca *adj* fierce; rude; intractable.

aristocracia *f* aristocracy.

aristócrata *m* aristocrat.

aristocrático/ca *adj* aristocratic.

aritmética *f* arithmetic.

arlequín *m* harlequin, buffoon.

arma *f* weapon, arm.

armada *f* fleet, armada.

armadillo *m* armadillo.

armado/da *adj* armed; reinforced.

armador *m* ship owner; privateer; jacket, jerkin.

armadura *f* armor; framework; skeleton; armature.

armamento *m* armament.

armar *vt* to man; to arm; to fit; **~la** to kick up a fuss.

armario *m* wardrobe; cupboard.

armatoste *m* hulk; contraption.

armazón *f* chassis; skeleton; frame.

armería *f* arsenal; heraldry; gunsmith's (premises).

armero *m* gunsmith.

armiño *m* ermine.

armisticio *m* armistice.

armonía *f* harmony.

armonioso/sa *adj* harmonious.

armonizar *vt* to harmonize; to reconcile.

arnés *m* harness; **~eses** *mpl* gear, trappings *pl*.

aro *m* ring; earring.

aroma *m* aroma, fragrance.

aromaterapia *f* aromatherapy.

aromático/ca *adj* aromatic.

arpa *f* harp.

arpegio *m* (*mus*) arpeggio.

arpía *f* (*poet*) shrew.

arpillera *f* sackcloth.

arpón *m* harpoon.

arqueado/da *adj* arched, vaulted.

arquear *vt* to arch; to bend.

arqueo *m* arching; tonnage, capacity (of a ship).

arqueología *f* archeology.

arqueólogo/ga *m/f* archeologist.

arquero *m* archer; *Lat Am* goalkeeper.

arqueta *f* small trunk.

arquetipo *m* archetype.

arquitecto *m* architect.

arquitectónico/ca *adj* architectural.

arquitectura *f* architecture.

arrabal *m* suburb; slum.

arrabalero *m* suburbanite.

arraigado/da *adj* deep-rooted; established.

arraigar *vi* to root; to establish; * *vt* to establish; **~se** *vr* to take root; to settle.

arrancar *vt* to pull up by the roots; to pull out; to wrest; to extract; * *vi* to start; to move.

arranque *m* sudden start; start; outburst.

arras *fpl* security.

arrasar *vt* to demolish, to destroy.

arrastrado/da *adj* miserable; painstaking; servile.

arrastrar *vt* to drag; * *vi* to creep, to crawl; to lead a trump at cards; **~se** *vr* to crawl; to grovel.

arrastre *m* dragging.

¡arre! *excl* gee!, go on!

arrear *vt* to drive on; * *vi* to hurry along.

arrebañar *vt* to scrape together; to pick up.

arrebatado/da *adj* rapid; violent, impetuous; rash, inconsiderate.

arrebatar *vt* to carry off, to snatch; to enrapture.

arrebato *m* fury; rapture.

arrebol *m* rouge.

arrebujar *vt* to crumple; to wrap up.

arrecife *m* reef.

arrecirse *vr* to grow stiff with cold.

arreglado/da *adj* neat; regular, moderate.

arreglar *vt* to regulate; to tidy; to adjust; **~se** *vr* to come to an understanding.

arreglo *m* rule, order; agreement; arrangement.

arrellanarse *vr* to sit at ease; to make oneself comfortable.

arremangar *vt* to roll up; **~se** *vr* to roll up one's sleeves.

arremeter *vi* to attack; to seize suddenly.

arremetida *f* attack, assault.

arrendador *m* landlord.

arrendamiento *m* leasing; hire; lease.

arrendar *vt* to rent, to let out, to lease.

arrendatario/ria *m/f* tenant.

arreo *m* dress, ornament; **~s** *mpl* harness.

arrepentido/da *adj* repentant.

arrepentimiento *m* repentance, penitence.

arrepentirse *vr* to repent.

arrestar *vt* to arrest; to imprison.

arresto *m* boldness; prison; arrest.

arriada *f* flood, overflowing.

arriar *vt* (*mar*) to lower, to strike; to pay out.

arriate *m* bed; causeway.

arriba *adv* above, over, up; high, on high, overhead; aloft; **~ de** *Lat Am* above.

arribada *f* (*mar*) arrival (of a vessel) in port.

arribar *vi* (*mar*) to put into harbor.

arribeño/ña *m/f Lat Am* highlander.

arribista *m/f* upstart.

arriendo *m* lease; farm rent.

arriero *m* muleteer.

arriesgado/da *adj* risky; daring.

arriesgar *vt* to risk, to hazard; to expose to danger; **~se** *vr* to take a chance.

arrimar *vt* to approach, to draw near; (*mar*) to stow (cargo); **~se** *vr* to side up; to lean.

arrinconar *vt* to put in a corner; to lay aside.

arrobado/da *adj* enchanted.

arrobamiento *m* rapture; amazement.

arrobarse *vr* to be totally amazed; to be out of one's senses.

arrocero/ra *adj* rice-producing.

arrodillarse *vr* to kneel down.

arrogancia *f* arrogance, haughtiness.

arrogante *adj* arrogant; haughty, proud; stout.

arrojadizo/za *adj* easily thrown.

arrojar *vt* to throw, to fling; to dash; to emit; to shoot, to sprout; **~se** *vr* to hurl oneself.

arrojo *m* boldness, fearlessness.

arrollador/ra *adj* overwhelming.

arrollar *vt* to run over; to defeat heavily.

arropar *vt* to clothe, to dress; **~se** *vr* to wrap up.

arrostrar *vt* to face (up to).

arroyo *m* stream; gutter.

arroz *m* rice.

arrozal *m* paddy, paddy field, rice field.

arruga *f* wrinkle; rumple.

arrugar *vt* to wrinkle; to rumple; to fold; **~ la frente** to frown; **~se** *vr* to shrivel.

arruinar *vt* to demolish; to ruin; **~se** *vr* to go bankrupt.

arrullador/ra *adj* flattering, cajoling.

arrullar *vt* to lull; * *vi* to coo.

arrullo *m* cooing (of pigeons); lullaby.

arrumaco *m* caress.

arsenal *m* arsenal; dockyard.

arsénico *m* arsenic.

arte *m/f* art; skill; artfulness.

artefacto *m* appliance.

arteria *f* artery.

artero/ra *adj* dexterous, cunning, artful.

artesa *f* trough; kneading trough.

artesanía *f* craftsmanship.

artesano *m* artisan, workman.

ártico/ca *adj* arctic; * *m*: **el A~** the Arctic.

articulación *f* articulation; joint.

articulado/da *adj* articulated; jointed.

articular *vt* to articulate; to joint.

artículo *m* article; clause; point; (*gr*) article; condition.

artífice *m* artisan; artist.

artificial *adj* artificial.

artificio *m* workmanship, craft; artifice, cunning trick.

artificioso/sa *adj* skillful, ingenious; artful, cunning.

artillería *f* gunnery; artillery.

artillero *m* artillery man.

artimaña *f* trap; cunning.

artista *m* artist; craftsman.

artístico/ca *adj* artistic.

artritis *f* arthritis.

arzobispado *m* archbishopric.

arzobispo *m* archbishop.

as *m* ace.

asa *f* handle; lever.

asado *m* roast meat; barbecue.

asador *m* spit.

asadura *f* offal.

asalariado/da *adj* salaried.

asaltador/a *m/f* assailant.

asaltante *m/f* assailant.

asaltar *vt* to assault; to storm (a position); to assail.

asalto *m* assault, attack; stick-up.

asamblea *f* assembly, meeting.

asar *vt* to roast.

asbesto *m* asbestos.

ascendencia *f* ascendancy; ancestry.

ascendente *adj* ascending; (*rail*) **tren ~** *m* up train.

ascender *vi* to be promoted; to rise; * *vt* to promote.

ascendiente *m* forefather; influence.

Ascensión *f* feast of the Ascension.

ascenso *m* promotion; ascent.

ascensor *m* elevator.

asceta *m* ascetic.

ascético/ca *adj* ascetic.

asco *m* nausea; loathing.

ascua *f* red-hot coal.

aseado/da *adj* clean; elegant; neat.

asear *vt* to clean; to tidy.

asediar *vt* to besiege; to chase.

asedio *m* siege.

asegurado/da *adj* insured.

asegurador *m* insurer.

asegurar *vt* to secure; to insure; to affirm; to bail; **~se** *vr* to make sure.

asemejarse *vr* to be like, to resemble.

asentado/da *adj* established.

asentar *vt* to sit down; to affirm, to assure; to note; * *vi* to suit.

asentir *vi* to acquiesce, to concede.

aseo *m* cleanliness; neatness; **~s** *mpl* bathroom facilities *pl*.

aséptico/ca *adj* germ-free.

asequible *adj* attainable; obtainable.

aserción *f* assertion, affirmation.

aserradero *m* sawmill.

aserrar *vt* to saw.

aserrín *m* sawdust.

asertivo/va *adj* affirmative.

asesinar *vt* to assassinate; to murder.

asesinato *m* assassination; murder.

asesino *m* assassin; murderer.

asesor *m* counselor, adviser, consultant.

asesorar *vt* to advise; to act as consultant to; **~se** *vr* to consult.

asestar *vt* to aim, to point; to strike.

aseverar *vt* to affirm.

asfalto *m* asphalt.

asfixia *f* suffocation.

asfixiar *vt* to suffocate; **~se** *vr* to suffocate.

así *adv* so, thus, in this manner; like this; therefore; so that; also; **~ que** so that; therefore; **así, así** so-so; middling.

asidero *m* handle.

asiduidad *f* assiduousness.

asiduo/dua *adj* assiduous.

asiento *m* chair; bench, stool; seat; contract; entry; residence.

asignación *f* assignation; destination.

asignar *vt* to assign, to attribute.

asignatario/a *m/f Lat Am* heir.

asignatura *f* subject; course.

asilado/da *m/f* inmate; refugee.

asilo *m* asylum, refuge; **~ político** political asylum.

asimilación *f* assimilation.

asimilar *vt* to assimilate.

asimismo *adv* similarly, in the same manner.

asir *vt* to grasp, to seize; to hold, to grip; * *vi* to take root.

asistencia *f* audience; presence; assistance, help.

asistente *m* assistant, helper.

asistir *vi* to be present; to assist; * *vt* to help.

asma *f* asthma.

asmático/ca *adj* asthmatic.

asno *m* ass.

asociación *f* association; partnership.

asociado *m* associate.

asociar *vt* to associate; **~se** *vr* to associate.

asolar *vt* to destroy; to devastate.

asolear *vt* to expose to the sun; **~se** *vr* to sunbathe.

asomar *vi* to appear; **~se** *vr* to appear, to show up.

asombrar *vt* to amaze; to astonish; **~se** *vr* to be amazed; to get a fright.

asombro *m* dread, terror; astonishment.

asombroso/sa *adj* astonishing, marvelous.

asomo *m* mark, token, indication; conjecture.

asonancia *f* assonance; harmony.

aspa *f* cross; sail.

aspaviento *m* astonishment; fuss.

aspecto *m* appearance; aspect.

aspereza *f* roughness; surliness.

áspero/ra *adj* rough, rugged; craggy, knotty; horrid; harsh, hard; severe, austere; gruff.

asperón *m* grindstone.

aspersión *f* sprinkling; aspersion.

áspid *m* asp.

aspiración *f* breath; pause.

aspirante *m* aspirant, aspirer.

aspirar *vt* to breathe; to aspire; (*gr*) to aspirate.

aspirina *f* aspirin.

asquear *vt* to sicken; * *vi* to be sickening; **~se** *vr* to feel disgusted.

asqueroso/sa *adj* disgusting.

asta *f* lance; horn; handle.

astado/da *adj* horned.

asterisco *m* asterisk.

astilla *f* chip (of wood), splinter.

astillero *m* dockyard.

astral *adj* astral.

astringente *adj* astringent.

astro *m* star.

astrología *f* astrology.

astrológico/ca *adj* astrological.

astrólogo/ga *m/f* astrologer.

astronauta *m/f* astronaut.

astronave *f* spaceship.

astronomía *f* astronomy.

astronómico/ca *adj* astronomical.

astrónomo/ma *m/f* astronomer.

astucia *f* cunning, slyness.

astuto/ta *adj* cunning, sly; astute.

asueto *m* time off; vacation, holiday.

Asunción *f* Assumption.

asunto *m* subject, matter; affair, business.

asustar *vt* to frighten; **~se** *vr* to be frightened.

atacar *vt* to attack.

atajada *f Lat Am* (*sport*) save.

atajo *m* short cut.

atalaya *f* watchtower.

atañer *vi*: **~ a** to concern.

ataque *m* attack.

atar *vt* to tie; to fasten.

atardecer *vi* to get dark; * *m* dusk; evening.

atareado/da *adj* busy.

atascar *vt* to jam; to hinder; **~se** *vr* to become bogged down.

atasco *m* traffic jam.

ataúd *m* coffin.

ataviar *vt* to dress up, to trim, to adorn.

atavío *m* dress; ornament; **~s** *mpl* finery.

ateísmo *m* atheism.

atemorizar *vt* to frighten; **~se** *vr* to get scared.

atenazar *vt* to grip; to torment.

atención *f* attention, heedfulness; civility; observance, consideration.

atender *vi* to be attentive; * *vt* to attend to; to heed, to expect, to wait for; to look at.

atenerse *vr*: **~ a** to adhere to.

atentado *m* terrorist attack; transgression, offence.

atentamente *adv* observantly; **le saluda ~** yours faithfully.

atentar *vt* to attempt; to commit.

atento/ta *adj* attentive; heedful; observing; mindful; polite, courteous, mannerly.

atenuante *adj* extenuating.

atenuar *vt* to diminish; to lessen.

ateo/a *adj*, *m/f* atheist.

aterciopelado/da *adj* velvety.

aterido/da *adj* frozen stiff.

aterirse *vr* to grow stiff with cold.

aterrador/a *adj* frightening.

aterrar *vt* to terrify; **~se** *vr* to be terrified.

aterrizaje *m* landing.

aterrizar *vi* to land.

aterrorizar *vt* to frighten, to terrify.

atesorar *vt* to treasure/hoard up (riches).

atestación *f* testimony, evidence.

atestado/da *adj* packed; * *m* affidavit.

atestar *vt* to cram, to stuff; to attest, to witness.

atestiguar *vt* to witness, to attest.

atiborrar *vt* to stuff; **~se** *vr* to stuff oneself.

ático *m* attic.

atildar *vt* to punctuate with a tilde; to censure.

atinado/da *adj* wise; correct.

atisbar *vt* to pry into; to examine closely.

atizar *vt* to stir (the fire) with a poker; to stir up.

atlántico/ca *adj* Atlantic; * *m*: **el A~** the Atlantic.

atlas *m* atlas.

atleta *m/f* athlete.

atlético/ca *adj* athletic.

atletismo *m* athletics.

atmósfera *f* atmosphere.

atmosférico/ca *adj* atmospheric.

atolladero *m* bog; obstacle; impediment.

atollar *vi* to stick; **~se** *vr* to get stuck.

atolondramiento *m* stupefaction, consternation.

atolondrar *vt* to stun, to stupefy; **~se** *vr* to be stupefied.

atómico/ca *adj* atomic.

atomizador *m* spray.

átomo *m* atom.

atónito/ta *adj* astonished, amazed.

atontado/da *adj* stunned; silly.

atontar *vt* to stun, to stupefy; **~se** to grow stupid.

atormentar *vt* to torture; to harass; to torment.

atornillar *vt* to screw on; to screw down.

atosigar *vt* to poison; to harass; to oppress.

atracadero *m* landing-place.

atracador/a *m/f* robber.

atracar *vt* to moor; to rob; **~se** *vr*: **~ (de)** to stuff oneself (with).

atracción *f* attraction.

atraco *m* stick-up, robbery.

atractivo/va *adj* attractive; magnetic; * *m* charm.

atraer *vt* to attract, to allure.

atragantarse *vr* to stick in the throat, to choke.

atrancar *vt* to bar (a door).

atrapar *vt* to trap; to nab; to deceive.

atrás *adv* backward(s); behind; previously, **hacia ~** backward(s); **~ de** *Lat Am* behind.

atrasado/da *adj* slow; backward; in arrears.

atrasar *vi* to be slow; * *vt* to postpone; **~ el reloj** to put back a watch; **~se** *vr* to stay behind; to be late.

atraso *m* backwardness; slowness; delay.

atravesado/da *adj* oblique; cross; perverse; mongrel; degenerate.

atravesar *vt* to cross; to pass over; to pierce; to go through; **~se** *vr* to get in the way; to meddle.

atrayente *adj* attractive.

atreverse *vr* to dare, to venture.

atrevido/da *adj* bold, audacious, -daring.

atrevimiento *m* boldness, audacity.

atribución *f* attribution, imputation.

atribuir *vt* to attribute, to ascribe; to impute.

atribular *vt* to vex, to afflict.

atributivo/va *adj* attributive.

atributo *m* attribute.

atrición *f* attrition.

atril *m* lectern; music stand.

atrio *m* porch; portico.

atrocidad *f* atrocity.

atrochar *vi* to take a short cut.

atropellado/da *adj* hasty, precipitate.

atropellar *vt* to trample; to run down; to hurry; to insult; **~se** *vr* to hurry.

atropello *m* accident; push; outrage.

atuendo *m* attire.

atroz *adj* atrocious, heinous; cruel.

atufar *vt* to vex, to plague; **~se** *vr* turn sour; to get mad.

atún *m* tuna.

aturdido/da *adj* hare-brained.

aturdimiento *m* stupefaction; astonishment; dullness.

aturdir *vt* to stun, to confuse; to -stupefy.

atusar *vt* to smooth.

audacia *f* audacity, boldness.

audaz *adj* audacious, bold.

audible *adj* audible.

audiencia *f* audience.

audífonos *mpl* *Lat Am* headphones.

auditivo/va *adj* auditory.

auditor *m* auditor.

auditoría *f* audit.

auditorio *m* audience; auditorium.

auge *m* boom; climax.

augurar *vt* to predict.

augurio *m* omen.

aula *f* lecture room.

aullar *vi* to howl.

aullido/aullo *m* howling.

aumentar *vt* to augment, to increase; to magnify; to put up; * *vi* to increase; to grow larger.

aumento *m* increase; promotion, advancement.

aún *adv* even; **~ así** even so.

aun *adv* still; yet.

aunar *vt* to unite, to assemble.

aunque *adv* though, although.

¡aúpa! *excl* come on!

aura *f* *Lat Am* turkey vulture/buzzard.

áureo/rea *adj* golden, gilt *compd*.

aureola *f* glory; nimbus.

auricular *m* receiver; **~es** *mpl* headphones *pl*.

aurora *f* dawn.

auscultar *vt* to sound.

ausencia *f* absence.

ausentarse *vr* to go out.

ausente *adj* absent.

auspicio *m* auspice; prediction; protection.

austeridad *f* austerity.

austero/ra *adj* austere, severe.

austral *adj* southern.
autenticar *vt* to authenticate.
autenticidad *f* authenticity.
auténtico/ca *adj* authentic.
autillo *m* brown owl.
auto *m* judicial sentence; car; edict, ordinance; ~ **de fe** auto-da-fé.
autoadhesivo/va *adj* self-adhesive.
autobiografía *f* autobiography.
autobús *m* bus.
autocar *m* bus.
autocracia *f* autocracy.
autócrata *m* autocrat.
autóctono/na *adj* native.
autodefensa *f* self-defense.
autodeterminación *f* selfdetermina-tion.
autoedición *f* desktop publishing.
autoescuela *f* driving school.
autoestop, autostop *f* hitchhiking; **hacer** ~ to hitchhike.
autoestopista, autostopista *m/f* hitchhiker.
autógrafo *m* autograph.
autómata *m* automaton.
automático/ca *adj* automatic.
automatización *f* automation.
automedicación *f* self-medication.
automotor *m* diesel train.
automóvil *m* automobile.
automovilismo *m* motoring; motor racing.
automovilista *m/f* motorist, driver.
automovilístico/ca *adj* car *compd*.
autonomía *f* autonomy.
autónomo/ma *adj* autonomous.
autonómico/ca *adj* autonomous.
autopista *f* highway, superhighway, expressway; ~ **de la información** information superhighway; ~ **de peaje** turnpike.
autopsia *f* post mortem, autopsy.
autor/ra *m/f* author; maker; writer.
autoridad *f* authority.
autorización *f* authorization.
autorizar *vt* to authorize.
autorradio *m* car radio.
autorretrato *m* self-portrait.
autoservicio *m* self-service store; self-service restaurant.
autosuficiencia *f* self-sufficiency.
autovía *f* state highway.
auxiliar *vt* to aid, to help, to assist; to attend; * *adj* auxiliary.
auxilio *m* aid, help, assistance.
aval *m* guarantee; guarantor.
avalancha *f* avalanche.
avaluar *vt Lat Am* to value.
avance *m* advance; attack; trailer (for a film).
avanzada *f* (*mil*) vanguard.
avanzar *vt, vi* to advance.
avaricia *f* avarice.
avaricioso/sa *adj* avaricious, covetous.
avaro/ra *adj* miserly; * *m/f* miser.
avasallar *vt* to subdue; to enslave.

ave *f* bird; fowl.
avecinarse *vr* to be on the way.
avellana *f* hazelnut.
avellano *m* hazelnut tree.
ave maría *f* Hail Mary.
avena *f* oats *pl*.
avenencia *f* agreement, bargain; union.
avenida *f* avenue.
avenido/da *adj* agreed.
avenir *vt* to reconcile; ~**se** *vr* to reach a compromise.
aventajado/da *adj* advantageous, profitable; beautiful; excellent.
aventajar *vt* to surpass, to excel.
aventar *vt* to fan; to expel.
aventura *f* adventure; event, incident.
aventurado/da *adj* risky.
aventurar *vt* to venture, to risk.
aventurero/ra *adj* adventurous.
avergonzar *vt* to shame, to abash; ~**se** *vr* to be ashamed.
avería *f* breakdown.
averiado/da *adj* broken down; out of order.
averiarse *vr* to break down.
averiguación *f* discovery; investigation.
averiguar *vt* to inquire into; to investigate, to explore.
aversión *f* aversion, dislike; abhorrence.
avestruz *m* ostrich.
aviación *f* aviation; air force.
aviador/a *m/f* aviator.
avicultura *f* poultry farming.
avidez *f* covetousness.
ávido/da *adj* (*poet*) greedy, covetous.
avieso/sa *adj* irregular, out of the way; mischievous, perverse.
avinagrado/da *adj* sour.
avinagrarse *vr* to go sour.
avío *m* preparation, provision.
avión *m* airplane.
avioneta *f* light aircraft.
avisado/da *adj* prudent, cautious; **mal** ~ ill-advised.
avisar *vt* to inform; to warn; to advise.
aviso *m* notice; warning; hint; *Lat Am* advertisement.
avispa *f* wasp.
avispado/da *adj* lively, brisk; vivacious.
avisparse *vr* to worry.
avispero *m* wasp's nest.
avispón *m* hornet.
avistar *vt* to sight.
avituallar *vt* (*mil*) to supply (with food).
avivar *vt* to quicken, to enliven; to encourage.
avutarda *f* bustard.
axioma *m* axiom, maxim.
¡ay! *excl* ouch!; ow! **¡~ de mí!** alas!, poor me!
aya *f* governess, instructress.
ayer *adv* yesterday.
ayuda *f* help, aid; support; * *m* deputy, assistant.
ayudante *m* (*mil*) adjutant; assistant.

ayudar vt to help, to assist; to further.

ayunar vi to fast, to abstain from food.

ayuno m fasting, abstinence from food.

ayuntamiento m town/city hall.

azabache m jet.

azada f spade; hoe.

azafata f air stewardess.

azafrán m saffron.

azahar m orange/lemon blossom.

azar m unforeseen disaster; unexpected accident; fate; **por ~** by chance; **al ~** at random.

azaroso/sa adj unlucky, ominous; risky.

azogue m mercury.

azor m goshawk.

azorar vt to frighten, to terrify.

azotaina f drubbing, sound flogging.

azotar vt to whip, to lash.

azote m whip.

azotea f flat roof of a house.

azteca m/f Aztec.

azúcar m/f sugar.

azucarado/da adj sugared; sugary.

azucarar vt to sugar, to sweeten.

azucarero m sugar bowl.

azucena f white lily.

azufre m sulfur, brimstone.

azul adj blue; **~ celeste** sky blue.

azulado/da adj azure, bluish.

azulejo m tile.

azuzar vt to irritate, to stir up.

B

baba f dribble, spittle.

babear vi to dribble, to drool.

babel m bedlam.

babero m bib.

babia f: **estar en ~** to be absent-minded/ dreaming.

baboso/sa adj dribbling, drooling.

babucha f slipper.

baca f (auto) roof rack.

bacalao m cod.

bache m pothole.

bachillerato m baccalaureate; a sermon delivered to a graduating class.

báculo m stick.

bagaje m baggage.

bagatela f trinket, trifle.

bahía f bay.

bailador/ra m/f dancer.

bailar vi to dance.

bailarín/ina m/f dancer.

baile m dance, ball; **~ de disfraces** fancy-dress ball; **~ de gala** prom.

baja f fall; casualty.

bajada f descent; inclination; slope; ebb.

bajamar f low water, low tide.

bajar vt to lower, to let down; to lessen; to humble; to go/come down; to bend downward(s); * vi to descend; to go/come down; to grow less; **~se** vr to crouch; to lessen.

bajeza f meanness; lowliness.

bajío m shoal, sandbank; lowlands pl.

bajo/ja adj low; abject, despicable; common; dull (of colors); deep; humble; * prep under, underneath, below; * adv softly; quietly; * m (mus) bass; low place.

bajón m fall.

bakalao m (col) rave music.

bala f bullet; **lanzamiento de ~** Lat Am shot put.

balacear vt Lat Am to shoot.

balacera f Lat Am shootout.

baladronada f boast, brag; bravado.

balance m hesitation; balance sheet; balance; rocking chair; rolling (of a ship).

balancear vt, vi to balance; to roll; to waver; **~se** vr to swing.

balancín m balance beam; seesaw; balancing pole.

balanza f scale; balance.

balar vi to bleat.

balaustrada f balustrade, banister.

balazo m shot.

balbucear vt, vi to stutter.

balbuciente adj stammering, stuttering.

balcón m balcony.

baldar vt to cripple, to disable.

balde m bucket; **de ~** adv gratis, for nothing; **en ~** in vain.

baldío/día adj waste; uncultivated.

baldosa f floor; tile; paving stone, flagstone.

balear vt Lat Am to shoot.

baleo m Lat Am shootout.

balido m bleating, bleat.

balín m buckshot.

balística f ballistics pl.

ballena f whale; whalebone.

ballenato m calf of a whale.

ballenero m (mar) whaler.

ballesta f crossbow; **a tiro de ~** at a great distance.

ballestero m archer; crossbow-maker.

ballet m ballet.

balneario m spa; Lat Am seaside -resort.

balón m ball.

baloncesto m basketball.

balonmano m handball.

balonvolea m volleyball.

balsa[1] f balsa wood; raft, float.

balsa[2] f pool, pond.

bálsamo m balsam, balm.

baluarte m bastion; bulwark.

bamba f fat; (bot) swelling; flabbiness.

bambolear vi to reel; **~se** vr to sway.

bamboleo m reeling, staggering.

bambú m bamboo.

banana f banana; plantain.

banano m banana tree.

banasta f large basket.

banca f bench; banking; ~ **electrónica** electronic banking.

bancario/ria adj bank(ing) compd.

bancarrota f bankruptcy.

banco m bench; work bench; bank.

banda f band; sash; ribbon; troop; party; gang; touchline.

bandada f flock; shoal.

bandearse vr to move to and fro.

bandeja f tray, salver.

bandera f banner, standard; flag.

banderilla f small decorated dart used at a bullfight.

banderillear vt to plant banderillas in a bull's neck/shoulder.

banderillero m thrower of banderillas.

banderín m small flag, pennant.

bandido m bandit, outlaw.

bando m faction, party; edict.

bandolera f bandoleer.

bandolero m bandit.

bandurria f bandore (musical instrument resembling a lute).

banquero/ra m/f banker.

banqueta f three-legged stool; sidewalk.

banquete m banquet; formal dinner.

banquillo m dock; bench.

bañador m swimsuit.

bañar vt to bathe; to dip; to coat (with varnish); ~**se** vr to bathe; to swim; Lat Am to have a shower.

bañera f bath(tub).

bañero m lifeguard.

bañista m/f bather.

baño m bath; Lat Am shower; dip; bathtub; varnish; coating.

baptista m/f Baptist.

bar m bar.

baraja f pack of cards.

barajar vt to shuffle (cards); to jumble up.

baranda f rail.

barandilla f small balustrade, small railing.

baratijas fpl trifles pl, toys pl; trash, junk.

baratillo m secondhand goods pl; secondhand shop; bargain sale.

barato/ta adj cheap; de ~ gratis; * m cheapness; bargain sale; money extracted from winning gamblers.

baraúnda f noise, hurly-burly.

barba f chin; beard; ~ **a** ~ face to face; * m actor who impersonates old men.

barbacoa f barbecue.

barbaridad f barbarity, barbarism; outrage.

barbarie f barbarism; savagery.

barbarismo m barbarism (form of speech).

bárbaro/ra adj barbarous; cruel; rude; rough.

barbecho m first plowing, fallow land.

barbería f barber shop.

barbero m barber.

barbilampiño/ña adj clean-shaven; (fig) inexperienced.

barbilla f (tip of the) chin.

barbo m barbel.

barbudo/da adj bearded.

barca f boat.

barco m boat; ship.

barítono m (mus) baritone.

barman m barman.

barniz m varnish; glaze.

barnizar vt to varnish.

barómetro m barometer.

barón m baron.

baronesa f baroness.

barquero m boatman.

barquilla f (mar) log; basket (of an air balloon).

barquillo m wafer; cornet, cone.

barra f bar; rod; lever; French loaf; sandbank; **de ~ a ~** from place to place.

barrabasada f trick, plot.

barraca f hut.

barranco m gully, ravine; (fig) great difficulty.

barranquismo m (sport) canyoning.

barrena f drill, bit, auger.

barrenar vt to drill, to bore; (fig) to frustrate.

barrendero m sweeper.

barreno m large drill; borehole.

barreño m tub.

barrer vt to sweep; to overwhelm.

barrera f barrier; turnpike; claypit.

barriada f suburb, area of a city; Lat Am shanty town.

barricada f barricade.

barrido m sweep.

barriga f abdomen; belly.

barrigudo/da adj pot-bellied.

barril m barrel; cask.

barrio m area, district.

barrizal m claypit.

barro m clay, mud.

barroco/ca adj baroque.

barrote m ironwork (of doors, windows, tables); crosspiece.

barruntar vt to guess; to foresee; to conjecture.

barrunto m conjecture.

bártulos mpl gear, belongings pl.

barullo m uproar.

basamento m base.

basalto m basalt.

basar vt to base; ~**se** vr: ~ **en** to be based on.

basca f squeamishness, nausea.

báscula f scales pl.

base f base, basis.

básico/ca adj basic.

basílica f basilica.

basilisco m basilisk.

básquetbol m Lat Am basketball.

basquetbolista m/f Lat Am basketball player.

bastante adj sufficient, enough; * adv quite.

bastar vi to be sufficient, to be enough.

bastardo/da adj, m/f bastard.

bastidor m embroidery frame; ~**es** mpl scenery (on stage).

bastión *m* bastion.

basto/ta *adj* coarse, rude, unpolished.

bastón *m* cane, stick; truncheon; (*fig*) command.

bastonazo *m* beating.

bastos *mpl* clubs *pl* (in cards).

basura *f* garbage, trash, refuse; dung.

basurero *m* garbageman, refuse collector; dunghill.

bata *f* dressing gown; coveralls; laboratory coat.

batacazo *m* noise of a fall.

batalla *f* battle, combat; fight.

batallador/a *adj* battling.

batallar *vi* to battle, to fight; to fence with foils; to waver.

batallón *m* (*mil*) battalion.

batata *f* sweet potato.

bate *m* bat.

batería *m* battery; percussion.

bateristo/sta *m/f Lat Am* drummer.

batida *f* beating (of woodland/moorland); search; chase.

batido/da *adj* shot (of silk); well-trodden (of roads); * *m* batter; ~ **de leche** milk shake.

batidora *f* food mixer; whisk.

batir *vt* to beat; to whisk; to dash; to demolish; to defeat.

batista *f* fine cotton cloth, cambric.

batuta *f* baton.

baúl *m* trunk (of a car), trunk (luggage); (*col*) belly.

bautismal *adj* baptismal.

bautismo *m* baptism.

bautizar *vt* to baptize, to christen.

bautizo *m* baptism.

baya *f* berry.

bayeta *f* cloth.

bayo/ya *adj* bay (color of a horse).

bayoneta *f* bayonet.

bayonetazo *m* thrust with a bayonet.

baza *f* card trick.

bazar *m* bazaar.

bazo *m* spleen.

bazofia *f* refuse; hogwash.

be *m* baa (of sheep).

beatificación *f* beatification.

beatificar *vt* to beatify; to hallow, to sanctify, to make blessed.

beato/ta *adj* happy; blessed; devout; * *m* lay brother; *m/f* pious person; beatified person.

bebé *m/f* baby.

bebedero *m* drinking trough.

bebedizo *m* (love) potion.

bebedor/ra *m/f* (hard) drinker.

beber *vt* (*vi*) to drink.

bebida *f* drink, beverage.

beca *f* fellowship; grant, bursary, scholarship; sash; hood.

becada *f* woodcock.

becerro *m* yearling calf.

bedel *m* janitor; uniformed employee.

befa *f* jeer, taunt.

befarse *vr*: ~ **de** to mock, to ridicule.

beldad *f* beauty.

belén *m* nativity scene.

bélico/ca *adj* warlike, martial.

belicoso/sa *adj* warlike; aggressive.

beligerante *adj* belligerent.

bellaco/ca *adj* artful; cunning.

belladona *f* (*bot*) deadly nightshade.

belleza *f* beauty.

bello/lla *adj* beautiful; handsome; lovely; fine.

bellota *f* acorn; Adam's apple; pomander.

bemol *m* (*mus*) flat.

bencina *f* benzine.

bendecir *vt* to bless; to consecrate; to praise.

bendición *f* blessing, benediction.

bendito/ta *adj* saintly; blessed; simple; happy.

benedictino/na, benito/ta *adj*, *m/f* Benedictine.

beneficiado *m* incumbent; beneficiary.

beneficiar *vt* to benefit; to be of -benefit to.

beneficiario/ra *m/f* beneficiary.

beneficio *m* benefit, advantage; profit; benefit night.

beneficioso/sa *adj* beneficial.

benéfico/ca *adj* beneficent, kind.

benemérito/ta *adj* worthy, meritorious.

beneplácito *m* consent, approbation.

benevolencia *f* benevolence.

benévolo/la *adj* benevolent, kind-hearted.

benigno/na *adj* benign; kind; mild.

beodo/da *adj* drunk, drunken.

berberecho *m* cockle.

berenjena *f* eggplant.

bergantín *m* (*mar*) brig.

bermejo/ja *adj* red.

berrear *vi* to low, to bellow.

berrido *m* bellowing (of calf).

berrinche *m* anger, rage, tantrum (applied to children).

berro *m* watercress.

berza *f* cabbage.

besamanos *m invar* levee; royal audience.

besamel *f* white sauce.

besar *vt* to kiss; to graze; ~**se** *vr* to kiss.

beso *m* kiss; collision of persons/things.

bestia *f* beast, animal; idiot.

bestial *adj* bestial; (*col*) marvelous, great.

bestialidad *f* bestiality.

besugo *m* sea bream.

besuquear *vt* to cover with kisses.

besuqueo *m* repeated kisses *pl.*

betún *m* shoe polish.

bezo *m* thick lip; (*med*) swollen tissue in a wound.

biberón *m* feeding bottle.

Biblia *f* Bible.

bíblico/ca *adj* biblical.

bibliófilo/la *m/f* book-lover, bookworm.

bibliografía *f* bibliography.

bibliográfico/ca *adj* bibliographical.

bibliógrafo/fa *m/f* bibliographer.

biblioteca *f* library.

bibliotecario/ria *m/f* librarian.

bicarbonato *m* bicarbonate.

bicho *m* small animal; bug; **mal ~** villain.

bici *f* (*col*) bike.

bicicleta *f* bicycle; **~ de montaña** mountain bike.

bidé *m* bidet.

bielda *f* pitchfork.

bien *m* good, benefit; profit; **~es** *mpl* goods *pl*, property; wealth; **~es raíces** *mpl* real estate; * *adv* well, right; very; willingly; easily; **~ que** *conj* although; **está ~** he is well.

bienal *adj* biennial.

bienaventuranza *f* blessedness; bliss; happiness; prosperity; **~s** *fpl* the Beatitudes.

bienestar *m* wellbeing.

bienhablado/da *adj* well-spoken.

bienhecho/cha *adj* well-shaped.

bienhechor/ra *m/f* benefactor.

bienio *m* space of two years.

bienvenida *f* welcome.

bifurcación *f* fork.

bigamia *f* bigamy.

bígamo/ma *m/f* bigamist.

bigote *m* mustache; whiskers *pl*.

bigotudo/da *adj* with a big mustache.

bikini *m* bikini.

bilingüe *adj* bilingual.

bilioso/sa *adj* bilious.

bilis *f* bile.

billar *m* billiards *pl*.

billete *m* note, banknote, greenback; ticket; (*rail*) ticket; **~ sencillo** single ticket; **~ de ida y vuelta** return ticket.

billetero *m* billfold, wallet.

billón *m* trillion.

bimensual *adj* twice-monthly.

bimotor *m* twin-engined plane.

binario *m* binary.

binoculares *mpl* binoculars *pl*; opera glasses *pl*.

binóculos *mpl Lat Am* binoculars.

biodegradable *adj* biodegradable.

biodiversity *f* biodiversity.

biografía *f* biography.

biógrafo/fa *m/f* biographer.

biología *f* biology.

biológico/ca *adj* biological.

biólogo/ga *m/f* biologist.

biombo *m* screen.

biopsia *f* biopsy.

bípedo *m* biped.

birlar *vt* to knock down at one blow; (*col*) to pinch.

birreta *f* biretta.

bis *excl* encore.

bisabuela *f* great-grandmother.

bisabuelo *m* great-grandfather.

bisagra *f* hinge.

bisexual *adj* bisexual.

bisexualidad *f* bisexuality.

bisiesto *adj*: **año ~** leap year.

bisnieto/ta *m/f* great-grandson /daughter.

bisoño/na *adj* raw, inexperienced; novice.

bisonte *m* American bison, buffalo.

bistec *m* steak.

bisturí *m* scalpel.

bisutería *f* costume jewelry.

bizarro/rra *adj* brave, gallant; generous.

bizco/ca *adj* cross-eyed.

bizcocho *m* sponge cake; biscuit; ship's biscuit.

bizquear *vi* to squint.

blanco/ca *adj* white; blank; * *m* whiteness; White person; blank, blank space; target (to shoot at).

blancura *f* whiteness.

blandir *vt* to brandish a sword; **~se** *vr* to swing.

blando/da *adj* soft, smooth; mild, gentle; (*col*) cowardly.

blanducho/cha *adj* flabby.

blandura *f* softness; gentleness, mildness.

blanquear *vt* to bleach; to whitewash; to launder (money); * *vi* to show white.

blanquecino/na *adj* whitish.

blanqueo *m* laundering (of money).

blasfemador/ra *m/f* blasphemer.

blasfemar *vi* to blaspheme.

blasfemia *f* blasphemy; verbal insult.

blasfemo/ma *adj* blasphemous; * *m* blasphemer.

blasón *m* heraldry, honor, glory.

blasonar *vt* to emblazon; to praise highly.

bledo *m*: **me importa un ~** (*col*) I don't give a damn.

blindado/da *adj* armor-plated; bullet-proof.

bloc *m* writing pad.

bloque *m* block.

bloquear *vt* to block; to blockade.

bloqueo *m* blockade.

blusa *f* blouse.

boato *m* ostentation, pompous show.

bobada *f* folly, foolishness.

bobear *vt* to act/talk in a stupid manner.

bobería *f* silliness, foolishness.

bobina *f* bobbin.

bobo/ba *m/f* idiot, fool; clown, funny man; * *adj* stupid, silly.

boca *f* mouth; entrance, opening; mouth of a river; **~ en ~** *adv* by word of mouth; **a pedir de ~** to one's heart's content.

bocacalle *f* entrance to a street.

bocadillo *m* sandwich, roll.

bocado *m* mouthful.

bocal *m* pitcher; mouthpiece of a trumpet.

bocamanga *f* cuff, wristband.

bocanada *f* mouthful (of liquor); gust.

bocazas *m/f invar* loudmouth.

boceto *m* sketch.

bochinche *m Lat Am* (*col*) racket.

bochorno *m* sultry weather, scorching heat; blush.

bochornoso/sa *adj* sultry; shameful.

bocina *f* trumpet; megaphone; car horn.

bocón/ona *m/f Lat Am* (*col*) big mouth.

boda f wedding.

bodega f wine cellar; warehouse; bar.

bodegón m cheap restaurant, diner; still life (in art).

bodoque m pellet; lump; (col) idiot.

bodorrio m quiet wedding.

bofes mpl lungs; lights.

bofetada f slap (in the face).

bofetón m hard slap.

boga f fashion; (rail) bogie/bogy; rower; rowing; **estar en** ~ to be fashionable.

bogar vi to row, to paddle.

bohemio m/f Bohemian.

boicot m boycott.

boicotear vt to boycott.

boina f beret.

boj m box; boxwood; box tree.

bola f ball; marble; globe; slam (in cards); shoe polish; (col) lie, fib.

bolazo m blow with a ball.

bolchevique adj Bolshevik.

bolear vi to knock balls about (billiards); * vt to throw (a ball).

bolera f bowling alley.

bolero m bolero jacket; bolero dance.

boleta f entrance ticket; pass, permit.

boletería f Lat Am ticket office.

boletín m bulletin; journal, review.

boleto m Lat Am ticket.

boli m (col) (ballpoint) pen.

boliche m jack (at bowls); bowls, bowling alley; dragnet.

bolígrafo m (ballpoint) pen.

bolillo m bobbin.

bollo m bread roll; lump.

bolo m ninepin; (large) pill.

bolsa f purse, handbag; bag; pocket; sac; stock exchange; ~ **de dormir** Lat Am sleeping bag.

bolsillo m pocket; purse.

bolsista m/f stockbroker.

bolso m purse.

bomba f pump; bomb; surprise; **dar a la** ~ to pump; ~ **de gasolina** gas pump.

bombardear vt to bombard.

bombardeo m bombardment.

bombardero m bomber.

bombazo m explosion; bombshell.

bombero m firefighter, fireman.

bombilla f light bulb.

bombín m derby.

bombo m large drum.

bombón m candy; chocolate.

bonachón/ona adj good-natured.

bonanza f fair weather (at sea); prosperity; bonanza.

bondad f goodness, kindness; courtesy.

bondadoso/sa adj good, kind.

bonete m clerical hat; college cap.

bonito adj pretty, nice-looking; pretty good, passable; * m tuna (fish).

bono m bond (financial).

boñiga f cow pat.

bonsái m bonsai.

boqueada f act of opening the mouth; **la última** ~ the last gasp.

boquear vi to gape;, to gasp; to breathe one's last; * vt to pronounce, to utter (a word).

boquerón m anchovy; large hole.

boquete m gap, narrow entrance.

boquiabierto/ta adj open-mouthed; gaping.

boquilla f mouthpiece of a musical instrument; nozzle.

borbollón, borbotón m bubbling; **salir a borbollones** to gush forth.

borda f (mar) gunwale/gunnel; hut.

bordado m embroidery.

bordadora f embroiderer.

bordar vt to embroider; to do anything very well.

borde m border; margin; (mar) board.

bordear vi (mar) to tack; * vt to go along the edge of; to flank.

bordillo m curb.

bordo m (mar) board; **a** ~ on board (a ship).

boreal adj boreal, northern.

borgoña m burgundy wine.

borla f tassel; tuft.

borona f maize; corn; corn bread.

borrachera f drunkenness; hard drinking; spree.

borracho/cha adj drunk, intoxicated; blind with passion; * m/f drunk, drunkard.

borrador m first draft; scribbling pad; eraser.

borraja f (bot) borage.

borrar vt to erase, to rub out; to blur; to obscure.

borrasca f storm; violent squall of wind; hazard, danger.

borrascoso/sa adj stormy.

borrego/ga m/f yearling lamb; simpleton, blockhead.

borrico/ca m/f donkey, ass; blockhead.

borrón m blot, blur; rough draft of a writing; first sketch of a painting; stain, blemish.

borronear vt to sketch.

boscaje m grove, small wood; landscape (in painting).

bosque m forest; wood.

bosquejar vt to make a sketch of (a painting); to make a rough model of (a figure).

bosquejo m sketch (of a painting); unfinished work.

bostezar vi to yawn; to gape.

bostezo m yawn; yawning.

bota f leather wine-bag; boot.

botánica f botany.

botánico/ca adj botanic; * m/f botanist.

botanista m/f botanist.

botar vt to cast, to fling; to launch.

bote m bounce; thrust; tin, can; boat.

botella f bottle.

botica f drugstore.

boticario/ria m/f pharmacist.

botijo m earthenware jug.

botín m high boot, half-boot; gaiter; booty.

botiquín m medicine chest.

botón m button; knob (of a radio etc); (*bot*) bud.

botonadura f set of buttons.

botones m *invar* bellhop, bellboy.

bóveda f arch; vault, crypt.

box m *Lat Am* boxing.

boxeador m boxer.

boxeo m boxing.

boya f (*mar*) buoy.

boyante adj buoyant, floating; (*fig*) fortunate, successful.

bozal m muzzle.

bozo m down (on the upper lip/chin); headstall, head collar (of a horse).

braceada f violent movement of the arms.

bracear vi to swing the arms.

bracero m day-laborer; farmhand.

braga f sling, rope; diaper; **~s** fpl pants pl.

bragazas m *invar* henpecked husband.

braguero m truss.

bragueta f fly, flies pl (of trousers).

braille m Braille.

bramante m twine, string.

bramar vi to roar, to bellow; to storm, to bluster.

bramido m roar, bellow, howl.

brasa f live coal; **estar hecho una ~** to be very flushed.

brasero m brazier.

bravamente adv bravely, gallantly; fiercely; roughly; extremely well.

bravío/vía adj ferocious, savage, wild; coarse; * m fierceness, savageness.

bravo/va adj brave, valiant; bullying; savage, fierce; rough; sumptuous; excellent, fine; * excl well done!

bravura f ferocity; courage.

braza f fathom.

brazada f extension of the arms; armful.

brazado m armful.

brazal m armband; irrigation channel.

brazalete m bracelet.

brazo m arm; branch (of a tree); enterprise; courage; **luchar a ~ partido** to fight hand to hand.

brea f pitch; tar.

brear vt to pitch; to tar; to abuse, to ill-treat; to play a joke on.

brebaje m potion.

brecha f (*mil*) breach; gap, opening; **batir en ~** (*mil*) to make a breach.

bregar vi to struggle; to quarrel; to slog away.

breva f early fig; early large acorn.

breve m papal brief; * f (*mus*) breve; * adj brief, short; **en ~** shortly.

brevedad f brevity, shortness, conciseness.

breviario m breviary; (*fig*) daily reading.

brezo m (*bot*) heather.

bribón/ona adj dishonest, rascally.

bribonear vi to be idle; to play dirty tricks.

bricolaje m home improvement.

brida f bridle; clamp, flange.

bridge m bridge (card game).

brigada f brigade; squad, gang.

brigadier m brigadier.

brillante adj brilliant; bright, shining; * m diamond.

brillar vi to shine; to sparkle, to glisten; to shine, to be outstanding.

brillo m brilliance, brightness.

brincar vi to skip; to leap, to jump; to gambol; to fly into a passion.

brinco m leap, jump; bounce.

brindar vi: **~ a la salud de/~ por** to drink the health of, to toast; * vt to offer, to present.

brindis m *invar* toast.

brío m spirit, dash.

briosamente adv spiritedly, dashingly.

brioso/sa adj dashing, full of spirit; lively.

brisa f breeze.

brisca f card game.

broca f reel; drill; shoemaker's tack (nail).

brocado m gold/silver brocade; **~/da** adj embroidered; like brocade.

brocal m rim, mouth; curb.

brocha f large brush; **~ de afeitar** shaving brush.

brochada f brushstroke.

broche m clasp; brooch; cufflink.

broma f joke.

bromear vi to joke.

bromista m/f joker.

bronca f row.

bronce m bronze.

bronceado/da adj tanned; * m bronzing, suntan.

broncearse vr to get a suntan.

bronco/ca adj rough, coarse; rude; harsh.

bronquitis f bronchitis.

broquel m shield.

brotar vi (*bot*) to bud, to germinate; to gush, to rush out; (*med*) to break out.

brote m (*bot*) shoot; (*med*) outbreak.

bruces adv: **de ~** face downward(s).

bruja f witch.

brujería f witchcraft.

brujo m sorcerer, magician, wizard.

brújula f compass.

bruma f mist; (*mar*) sea mist.

brumoso/sa adj misty.

bruñido m polish.

bruñir vt to polish; to put rouge on.

brusco/ca adj rude; sudden; brusque.

brutal adj brutal, brutish.

brutalidad f brutality; brutal action.

bruto m brute, beast; **~/ta** adj stupid; gross; brutish.

buba f tumor.

bucal adj oral.

bucear vi to dive.

buceo m diving.

bucle m curl.

bucólica f pastoral poetry; (*col*) food.

buche m craw, maw; (*col*) guts pl; mouthful; crease (in clothes).

budismo *m* Buddhism.
buen *adj* (before **m** nouns) good.
buenamente *adv* easily; willingly.
buenaventura *f* fortune, good luck.
bueno/na *adj* good, perfect; fair; fit; proper; good-looking; **¡buenos días!** good morning!; **¡buenas tardes!** good afternoon; **¡buenas noches!** good night!; **¡~!** right!
buey *m* ox, bullock.
bufa *f* joke, mock.
búfalo *m* buffalo.
bufanda *f* scarf.
bufar *vi* to choke with anger; to snort.
bufete *m* desk, writing-table; lawyer's office.
bufido *m* snorting (of an animal).
bufo/fa *adj* comic; **ópera ~a** *f* comic opera.
bufón *m* buffoon; jester; **~/ona** *adj* funny, comical.
bufonada *f* buffoonery; joke.
buhardilla *f* attic.
búho *m* owl; unsociable person.
buhonero *m* hawker, peddler.
buitre *m* vulture.
bujía *f* candle; spark plug.
bula *f* papal bull.
bulbo *m* (*bot*) bulb.
bulboso/sa *adj* bulbous.
bulevar *m* boulevard.
bulla *f* confused noise, clatter; crowd; **meter ~** to make a noise.
bullicio *m* bustle; uproar.
bullicioso/sa *adj* lively, restless, noisy, busy; turbulent; boisterous.
bulto *m* bulk; tumor, swelling; bust; baggage.
buñuelo *m* donut/doughnut; fritter.
buque *m* vessel, ship, tonnage, capacity(of a ship); hull (of a ship).
burbuja *f* bubble.
burbujear *vi* to bubble.
burdel *m* brothel.
burdo/da *adj* coarse, rough.
burgués/esa *adj* bourgeois.
burguesía *f* bourgeoisie.
buril *m* engraver's chisel.
burla *f* trick; gibe; joke; **de ~s** in fun.
burlar *vt* to hoax; to defeat; to play tricks on, to deceive; to frustrate; **~se** *vr* to joke, to laugh at.
burlesco/ca *adj* burlesque; comical, funny.
burlón/ona *m/f* joker.
burocracia *f* bureaucracy.
burócrata *m/f* bureaucrat.
burrada *f* drove of asses; stupid action.
burro *m* ass, donkey; idiot; saw-horse.
bursátil *adj* stock exchange *compd*.
bus *m* bus.
busca *f* search, hunt; bleeper.
buscapiés *m invar* jumping jack (fireworks).
buscar *vt* to seek, to search for; to look for; to hunt after; * *vi* to look, to search, to seek
buscavidas *m* prying person, busybody.

buscón *m* petty thief, small-time crook.
búsqueda *f* search.
busto *m* bust.
butaca *f* armchair; seat.
butano *m* butane.
butifarra *f* Catalan sausage.
buzo *m* diver.
buzón *m* mailbox; conduit, canal; cover of a jar.

C

cabal *adj* just, exact; right; complete; accomplished.
cábalas *fpl* intrigue.
cabalgada *f* cavalcade; (*mil*) cavalry raid.
cabalgadura *f* mount, horse; beast of burden.
cabalgar *vi* to ride, to go riding.
cabalgata *f* procession.
cabalístico/ca *adj* cabalistic.
caballa *f* mackerel.
caballar *adj* equine.
caballería *f* mount, steed; cavalry; cavalry horse; chivalry; knighthood.
caballeriza *f* stable; stud; stablemen, stableboys *pl*.
caballerizo *m* groom.
caballero *m* knight; gentleman; -rider; horseman; horse soldier; **~ andante** knight errant.
caballerosidad *f* chivalry.
caballeroso/sa *adj* noble; gentlemanlike.
caballete *m* ridge of a roof; painter's easel; trestle; bridge (of the nose).
caballo *m* horse; **~ de carreras** racehorse; knight (at chess); queen (in cards); **a ~** on horseback.
cabaña *f* hut, cabin; hovel; livestock; balk (in billiards).
cabaré *m* cabaret.
cabecear *vi* to nod (with sleep); to shake one's head; (*mar*) to pitch.
cabeceo *m* nod; shaking (of the head).
cabecera *f* headboard; head; far end; pillow; headline; vignette.
cabecilla *m* ringleader.
cabellera *f* head of hair; wig; tail of a comet.
cabello *m* hair.
cabelludo/da *adj* hairy, shaggy.
caber *vi* to fit.
cabestrillo *m* sling.
cabestro *m* halter; leading/bell ox.
cabeza *f* head; chief, leader; main town, chief center.
cabezada *f* butt; nod/shake of the head.
cabezal *m* pillow; compress.
cabezón *m* collar (of a shirt); opening in a garment for the head.
cabezudo/da *adj* big-headed; pig-headed.
cabida *f* room, capacity; **tener ~ con una persona** to have influence with someone.

cabildo *m* chapter (of a church); meeting of a chapter; corporation of a town.

cabina *f* cabin; telephone booth.

cabizbajo/ja, cabizcaído/da *adj* crestfallen; pensive, thoughtful.

cable *m* cable, lead, wire.

cabo *m* end, extremity; cape, headland; (*mar*) cable, rope.

cabra *f* goat.

cabrero *m* goatherd.

cabrío/a *adj* goatish.

cabriola *f* caper; gambol.

cabritilla *f* kidskin.

cabrito *m* kid.

cabrón *m* cuckold; **¡~!** (*col*) bastard!

cacahuete *m* peanut.

cacao *m* (*bot*) cacao tree; cocoa.

cacarear *vi* to crow; to brag, to boast.

cacareo *m* crowing of a cock, cackling of a hen; boast, brag.

cacería *f* hunting-party.

cacerola *f* pan, saucepan; casserole.

cachalote *m* sperm whale.

cacharro *m* pot; piece of junk.

cachear *vt* to frisk.

cachemir *m* cashmere.

cacheo *m* frisking.

cachete *m* cheek; slap in the face.

cachimbo *m* *Lat Am* pipe.

cachiporra *f* club, truncheon.

cachivache *m* pot; piece of junk.

cacho *m* crumb, bit, small slice, piece; horn (of an animal).

cachondeo *m* (*col*) farce.

cachondo/da *adj* randy; funny.

cachorro/ra *m/f* puppy; cub (of any animal).

cacique *m* chief; local party boss.

caco *m* pickpocket; coward.

cacofonía *f* cacophony.

cacto/cactus *m* cactus.

cada *adj invar* each; every.

cadalso *m* scaffold.

cadáver *m* corpse, cadaver.

cadavérico/ca *adj* cadaverous.

cadena *f* chain; series, link; radio/TV network.

cadencia *f* cadence.

cadente *adj* harmonious.

cadera *f* hip.

cadete *m* (*mil*) cadet.

caducar *vi* to become senile; to expire, to lapse; to deteriorate.

caducidad *f* expiry.

caduco/ca *adj* worn out; decrepit; perishable; expired, lapsed.

caer *vi* to fall; to tumble down; to lapse; to happen; to die; **~se** *vr* to fall down.

café *m* coffee; coffee bar/shop.

cafetera *f* coffee pot.

cafetería *f* coffee shop/bar; small restaurant.

cafetero/ra *m/f* coffee merchant; coffee bar/shop owner.

cafre *adj* savage, inhuman; rude.

cagar *vi* (*col*) to have a shit.

caída *f* fall, falling; slope, descent.

caimán *m* cayman/caiman, alligator.

caja *f* box, case; casket; cashbox; cash desk; check-out, till; **~ de ahorros** savings bank; **~ de cambios** gearbox; **~ negra** black box.

cajero/ra *m/f* cashier, teller.

cajero automático *m* cash dispenser, cash machine, cash point, automated teller machine (ATM).

cajetilla *f* packet.

cajón *m* chest of drawers; locker.

cal *f* lime; **~ viva** quick lime.

cala *f* creek, small bay; small piece of melon etc; (*mar*) hold; dipstick.

calabacín *m* small marrow, courgette.

calabaza *f* pumpkin, squash.

calabozo *m* prison; cell.

calada *f* soaking; lowering of nets; puff, drag; swoop.

calado *m* openwork in metal/wood/linen.

calafatear *vt* (*mar*) to caulk.

calamar *m* squid.

calambre *m* cramp.

calamidad *f* calamity, disaster.

calamitoso/sa *adj* calamitous.

calaña *f* model; pattern.

calandria *f* lark.

calar *vt* to soak, to drench; to penetrate, to pierce; to see through; to lower; **~se** *vr* to stall (of a car).

calavera *f* skull; madcap.

calaverada *f* ridiculous/foolish action.

calcañar *m* heel.

calcar *vt* to trace, to copy.

calcáreo/rea *adj* chalky, calcareous.

calceta *f* (knee-length) stocking.

calcetín *m* sock.

calcio *m* calcium.

calco *m* tracing.

calcomanía *f* transfer.

calculable *adj* calculable.

calculadora *f* calculator.

calcular *vt* to calculate, to reckon; to compute.

cálculo *m* calculation, estimate; calculus; (*med*) gallstone.

caldear *vt* to weld; to warm, to heat up.

caldera *f* kettle, boiler; **las ~s de Pero Botero** (*col*) hell.

calderada *f* stew.

calderilla *f* holy-water vessel; small change.

caldero *m* small boiler.

caldo *m* stock; broth.

caldoso/sa *adj* having too much broth/gravy.

calefacción *f* heating.

calendario *m* calendar.

calentador *m* heater.

calentamiento global *m* global warming.

calentar *vt* to warm up, to heat up; **~se** *vr* to grow hot; to dispute.

calentura f fever.

calenturiento/ta adj feverish.

calesa f buggy, chaise.

calibre m caliber; (fig) caliber.

calidad f grade, quality, condition; kind.

cálido/da adj hot; (fig) warm.

caliente adj hot; fiery; **en ~** in the heat of the moment.

califa m caliph.

califato m caliphate.

calificación f qualification; grade.

calificar vt to qualify; to assess, to mark; **~se** vr to register as a voter.

caligrafía f calligraphy.

cáliz m chalice.

caliza f limestone.

calizo/za adj limy (of ground).

callado/da adj silent, quiet.

callandico adv softly, silently.

callar vi, **~se** vr to be silent, to keep quiet.

calle f street; road.

calleja f lane, narrow passage.

callejear vi to loiter about the streets.

callejero/ra adj loitering.

callejón m alley.

callejuela f lane, narrow passage; subterfuge.

callista m/f chiropodist, podiatrist.

callo m corn; callus; **~s** mpl tripe.

callosidad f hard patch, callosity.

calloso/sa adj callous; horny.

calma f calm, calmness.

calmante m (med) sedative.

calmar vt to calm, to quiet, to pacify; * vi to become calm.

calmoso/sa adj calm; tranquil.

calor m heat, warmth; ardor, passion.

caloría f calorie.

calumnia f calumny, slander.

calumniar vt to slander.

calumnioso/sa adj slanderous.

caluroso/sa adj warm; hot; lively.

calva f bald patch.

calvario m Calvary; (fig) debts pl.

calvicie f baldness.

calvinismo m Calvinism.

calvinista m/f Calvinist.

calvo/va adj bald; bare, barren.

calza f wedge.

calzado m footwear.

calzador m shoehorn.

calzar vt to put on (shoes); to wear (shoes); to stop (a wheel); **~se** vr to put on one's shoes.

calzón m shorts pl; pants pl; panties pl.

calzonazos m invar stupid guy; **es un ~** he is a weak-willed guy.

calzoncillos mpl underpants pl, shorts pl.

calzonudo m Lat Am stupid guy; **es un ~** he is a weak-willed guy.

cama f bed; **hacer la ~** to make the bed.

camada f litter (of animals); **~ de ladrones** gang of thieves.

camafeo m cameo.

camaleón m chameleon.

camalote m Lat Am water hyacinth.

camandulero/ra adj prudish; hypocritical; sly, tricky.

cámara f hall; chamber; room; camera; cine camera.

camarada m/f comrade, companion.

camarera f waitress; maid; Lat Am air stewardess.

camarero m waiter; Lat Am air steward.

camarilla f clique; lobby.

camarín m dressing room; elevator car.

camarón m shrimp, prawn.

camarote m berth, cabin.

cambalache m exchange, swap.

cambalachear vt to exchange, to swap.

cambiable adj changeable, variable; interchangeable.

cambiar vt to exchange; to change; * vi to change, to alter; **~se** vr to move house.

cambio m change, exchange; rate of exchange; bureau de change.

cambista m/f exchange broker.

camelar vt to flirt with.

camello m camel.

camilla f couch; cot; stretcher.

caminante m/f traveler; walker.

caminar vi to travel; to walk, to go.

caminata f long walk; hike.

camino m road; trail, way.

camión m truck.

camioneta f light truck, van.

camisa f shirt; chemise.

camiseta f T-shirt; undershirt.

camisón m nightgown.

camorra f quarrel, dispute.

camorrista m/f quarrelsome person.

campamento m (mil) encampment, camp.

campana f bell.

campaña f countryside; level country, plain; (mil) campaign.

campanada f peal of a bell; (fig) scandal.

campanario m belfry.

campaneo m bellringing, chime.

campanero m bell founder; bellringer.

campanilla f handbell; (med) uvula.

campante adj outstanding; smug.

campánula f bellflower.

campear vi to go out to pasture; to work in the fields.

campechano/na adj open.

campeón/ona m/f champion.

campeonato m championship.

campesino/na, **campestre** adj rural.

campiña f flat tract of cultivated farmland.

camping m camping, campsite.

campista m/f camper.

campo m country; countryside; field; camp; ground; pitch; scope, range; **~ de refugiados** refugee camp; **~ abierto** range, open countryside.

campus *m invar* campus.

camuflaje *m* camouflage.

caña *f* cane, reed; stalk; shinbone; glass of beer; ~ **dulce** sugar cane.

canal *m* channel; canal.

canalla *f* mob, rabble.

canalón *m* large gutter.

cáñamo *m* hemp.

cañamón *m* hemp seed.

canana *f* cartridge belt.

canapé *f* couch, sofa.

canario *m* canary.

canas *fpl* gray hair; **peinar** ~ to grow old.

canasta *f* basket, hamper.

canastilla *f* small basket.

canasto *m* large basket.

cañaveral *m* reedbed.

cancel *m* storm door.

cancelación *f* cancellation.

cancelar *vt* to cancel; to write off.

Cáncer *m* Cancer (zodiac sign).

cáncer *m* cancer.

canceriano/na *adj Lat Am* Cancerian.

cancerígeno/na *adj* carcinogenic.

canceroso/sa *adj* cancerous.

cancha *f* (*sport*) court, *Lat Am* course, *Lat Am* pitch.

canciller *m* chancellor; foreign minister.

canción *f* song.

cancionero *m* songbook.

candado *m* padlock.

candela *f* candle.

candelabro *m* candlestick.

candente *adj* red-hot.

candidato/ta *m/f* candidate.

cándido/da *adj* simple, naive; white, snowy.

candil *m* oil lamp.

candilejas *fpl* footlights *pl*.

candor *m* candor; innocence.

canela *f* cinnamon.

canelón *m* icicle.

cañería *f* water conduit, water pipe.

cangrejo *m* crab; crawfish.

canguro *m* kangaroo; * *f* baby-sitter.

caníbal *m/f* cannibal, man-eater.

canica *f* marble.

canícula *f* dog days *pl*.

canijo/ja *adj* weak, sickly.

canilla *f* shinbone; arm-bone; tap of a cask; spool.

canillera *f Lat Am* (*sport*) shin pad.

canino/na *adj* canine; **hambre** ~**a** *f* ravenous hunger.

canje *m* exchange.

canjear *vt* to exchange.

caño *m* tube, pipe; sewer.

cano/na *adj* gray-haired; white-haired.

canoa *f* canoe.

canon *m* canon; tax; royalty; rent.

cañón *m* tube, pipe; barrel; gun; canyon.

cañonazo *m* gunshot; (*fig*) bombshell.

cañonear *vt* to shell, to bombard.

cañoneo *m* shelling, gunfire.

cañonera *f* gunboat.

canónico/ca *adj* canonical.

canónigo *m* canon, prebendary.

canonización *f* canonization.

canonizar *vt* to canonize.

canoso/sa *adj* gray-haired; white-haired.

cansado/da *adj* weary, tired; tedious, tiresome.

cansancio *m* tiredness, fatigue.

cansar *vt* to tire, to tire out; to bore; ~**se** *vr* to get tired, to grow weary.

cantable *adj* suitable for singing.

cantante *m/f* singer.

cantar *m* song; * *vt* to sing; to chant; * *vi* to sing; to chirp.

cántara *f* large jug, pitcher.

cantarín/ina *m/f* someone who sings a lot.

cántaro *m* pitcher; jug; **llover a** ~**s** to rain heavily, to pour.

cantera *f* quarry.

cantero *m* quarryman.

cántico *m* canticle.

cantidad *f* quantity, amount; number.

cantimplora *f* water bottle; hip flask.

cantina *f* (*rail*) restaurant car; canteen; wine cellar.

cantinela *f* ballad, song.

canto *m* stone; singing; song; edge.

cantón *m* corner; canton.

cantonear *vi* to loaf around.

cantor/ra *m/f* singer.

canuto *m* (*col*) joint, marijuana cigarette.

caoba *f* mahogany.

caos *m* chaos; confusion.

capa *f* cloak; cape; layer, stratum; cover; pretext; ~ **de ozono** ozone layer.

capacho *m* hamper; big basket.

capacidad *f* capacity; extent; talent.

capar *vt* to geld; to castrate; (*fig*) to curtail.

caparazón *m* caparison.

capataz *m* foreman, overseer.

capaz *adj* capable; capacious, spacious, roomy.

capazo *m* large basket; carrycot.

capcionar *vt* to seize, to arrest.

capcioso/sa *adj* wily, deceitful.

capear *vt* to flourish (one's cloak in front of a bull); * *vi* (*mar*) to ride out/weather (a storm).

capellán *m* chaplain.

capeo *m* challenging of a bull with a cloak.

caperuza *f* hood.

capilar *adj* capillary.

capilla *f* hood, cowl; chapel.

capirote *m* hood.

capital *m* capital; capital sum; * *f* capital, capital city; * *adj* capital; principal.

capitalismo *m* capitalism.

capitalista *m/f* capitalist.

capitalizar *vt* to capitalize.

capitán *m* captain.

capitana *f* flagship; (*sport*) female captain.

capitanear *vt* to captain; to command.
capitanía *f* captaincy.
capitel *m* capital (of a column).
capitolio *m* capitol; imposing building.
capitulación *f* capitulation; agreement; **~ones** *fpl* marriage contract.
capitular *vi* to come to terms, to make an agreement.
capítulo *m* chapter (of a cathedral); chapter (of a book).
capó *m* (*auto*) hood.
capón *m* capon.
caporal *m* chief, ringleader.
capota *f* hat, bonnet; (*auto*) hood.
capote *m* greatcoat; bullfighter's cloak.
capricho *m* caprice, whim, fancy.
caprichoso/sa *adj* capricious, whimsical; obstinate.
capricorniano/na *adj Lat Am* Capricornean (zodiac sign).
Capricornio *m* Capricorn (zodiac sign).
cápsula *f* capsule.
captar *vt* to captivate; to understand; (*rad*) to tune in to, to receive.
captura *f* capture, arrest.
capturar *vt* to capture.
capucha *f* circumflex (accent); cap, cowl, hood of a cloak.
capuchino *m* Capuchin monk; (**café**) **~** cappuccino (coffee).
capullo *m* cocoon of a silkworm; rosebud; coarse cloth made of spun silk.
caqui *adj, m* khaki.
cara *f* face; appearance; **~ a ~** face to face.
carabina *f* carbine, rifle.
carabinero *m* carabineer.
caracol *m* snail; seashell; spiral.
caracola *f* shell.
caracolear *vi* to prance about (of a horse).
carácter *m* character; quality; condition; handwriting.
característico/ca *adj* characteristic.
caracterizar *vt* to characterize.
caradura *m/f*: **es un ~** he's got a nerve.
caramba *excl* well!
carámbano *m* icicle.
carambola *f* cannon (at billiards); trick.
caramelo *m* caramel (candy).
caramente *adv* dearly.
caramillo *m* small flute; piece of -gossip.
carantoña *f* hideous mask; dressed-up old woman; **~s** *fpl* caresses *pl*.
carátula *f* pasteboard mask; **la ~** the stage.
caravana *f* group of wagons/camels/pack mules etc traveling in single file ; tailback (of traffic); trailer.
caray *excl* well!
carbón *m* coal; carbon; carbon paper.
carbonada *f* grill; kind of pancake.
carboncillo *m* charcoal.
carbonera *f* coal tip; coal mine.

carbonería *f* coalyard.
carbonero *m* someone who sells coal; (*mar*) coal ship.
carbónico/ca *adj* carbonic.
carbonilla *f* coaldust.
carbonizar *vt* to carbonize.
carbono *m* (*chem*) carbon.
carbunclo, carbunco *m* carbuncle.
carburador *m* carburetor.
carcaj *m* quiver.
carcajada *f* (loud) laugh.
carcamal *m* nickname for an old person.
cárcel *f* prison; jail.
carcelero *m* warder, jailer.
carcoma *f* deathwatch beetle; woodworm; anxious concern.
carcomer *vt* to gnaw, to corrode; **~se** *vr* to get worm-eaten.
carcomido/da *adj* worm-eaten.
cardar *vt* to card (wool).
cardenal *m* cardinal; cardinal bird; (*med*) bruise, weal.
cardenalicio/cia *adj* belonging to a cardinal.
cárdeno/na *adj* purple; livid.
cardíaco/ca, cardiaco/ca *adj* cardiac; * heart *compd*.
cardinal *adj* cardinal, principal.
cardo *m* thistle.
carear *vt* to bring face to face; to compare; **~se** *vr* to come face to face.
carecer *vi*: **~ de** to want, to lack.
carencia *f* lack.
careo *m* confrontation.
carero/ra *adj* pricey.
carestía *f* scarcity, want; famine.
careta *f* pasteboard mask.
carga *f* load; freight, cargo; (*mil*) charge; duty, obligation; tax.
cargadero *m* loading place.
cargado/da *adj* loaded; live (electricity).
cargador *m* loader; carrier; longshoreman.
cargamento *m* cargo.
cargar *vt* to load, to burden; to charge; * *vi* to charge; to load (up); to lean.
cargo *m* burden, loading; employment, post; office; charge, care; obligation; accusation.
carguero *m* freighter.
cariarse *vr* to decay.
caricato *m Lat Am* caricature.
caricatura *f* caricature.
caricia *f* caress.
caridad *f* charity.
caries *f* (*med*) tooth decay, caries.
carilargo/ga *adj* long-faced.
carilla *f* side (of paper); beekeeper's mask.
cariño *m* fondness, tenderness; love.
cariñoso/sa *adj* affectionate; loving.
caritativo/va *adj* charitable.
cariz *m* look.
carmelita *adj, m/f* Carmelite.
carmesí *adj, m* crimson.

carmín *m* carmine; rouge; lipstick.

carnada *f* bait, lure.

carnal *adj* carnal, of the flesh; **primo ~** first cousin.

carnaval *m* carnival.

carn *f* flesh; meat; pulp (of fruit).

carné, carnet *m* driving license; **~ de identidad** identity card.

carnero *m* sheep; mutton.

carnicería *f* butcher's shop; carnage, slaughter.

carnicero/ra *m/f* butcher; * *adj* carnivorous.

carnívoro/ra *adj* carnivorous.

carnoso/sa, carnudo *adj* beefy, fat; fleshy.

caro/ra *adj* dear; affectionate; dear, expensive; * *adv* dearly.

carótida *f* carotid artery.

carpa *f* carp (fish); *Lat Am* tent.

carpeta *f* table cover; folder, file, portfolio.

carpintería *f* carpentry; carpenter's premises.

carpintero *m* carpenter.

carraca *f* carrack (ship); rattle.

carrasca *f* kermes oak tree.

carraspera *f* hoarseness.

carrera *f* career; course; race; run, running; route; journey; **a ~ abierta** at full speed.

carreta *f* long narrow cart.

carrete *m* reel, spool, bobbin.

carretera *f* road; **~ de circunvalación** belt, beltway, ring road.

carretero *m* carter, cartwright.

carretilla *f* carter; truck; trolley; go-cart; squib, cracker; wheelbarrow.

carretón *m* small cart.

carril *m* lane (of highway); furrow; **~ bus** bus lane.

carrillo *m* cheek; pulley.

carro *m* cart; car.

carrocería *f* bodywork, coachwork.

carromato *m* covered wagon, Gypsy caravan.

carroña *f* carrion.

carroza *f* state coach; (*mar*) awning.

carruaje *m* carriage; vehicle.

carrusel *m* merry-go-round.

carta *f* letter; map; document; playing card; menu; **~ blanca** carte blanche; **~ bomba** letter-bomb; **~ credencial/de creencia** credentials *pl*; **~ certificada** registered letter; **~ postal** *Lat Am* postcard; **~ verde** green card.

cartabón *m* square (tool).

cartapacio *m* notebook; folder.

cártel *m* cartel.

cartel *m* placard; poster; wall chart; cartel.

cartera *f* satchel; billfold; handbag; briefcase; postwoman.

carterista *m/f* pickpocket.

cartero *m* postman.

cartilaginoso/sa *adj* cartilaginous.

cartílago *m* cartilage.

cartilla *f* first reading book, primer.

cartón *m* cardboard, pasteboard; cartoon.

cartuchera *f* (*mil*) cartridge belt.

cartucho *m* (*mil*) cartridge.

cartuja *f* Carthusian order.

cartujo *m* Carthusian monk.

cartulina *f* card, pass; thin cardboard.

casa *f* house; home; firm, company; **~ de campo** country house; **~ de moneda** mint; **~ de huéspedes** boarding house.

casaca *f* coat.

casación *f* abrogation.

casadero/ra *adj* marriageable.

casado/da *adj* married.

casamentero/ra *m/f* marriage-maker, matchmaker.

casamiento *m* marriage, wedding.

casar *vt* to marry; to couple; to abrogate; to annul; **~se** *vr* to marry, to get married.

cascabel *m* small bell; rattlesnake.

cascada *f* cascade, waterfall.

cascanueces *m invar* nutcracker.

cascar *vt* to crack, to break into -pieces; (*col*) to beat; **~se** *vr* to be broken open.

cáscara *f* rind, peel; husk, shell; bark.

cascarón *m* eggshell.

casco *m* skull; helmet; fragment; shard; hulk (of a ship); crown (of a hat); hoof; empty bottle, returnable bottle; **~s azules** blue berets (soldiers of a UN peacekeeping force).

cascote *m* rubble, fragment of material used in building.

casera *f* landlady.

caserío *m* country house; small village.

casero *m* landlord; janitor; * **~/ra**, *adj* domestic; household *compd*; home-made.

cassette/casette *m* cassette; * *f* cassette-player.

casi *adv* almost, nearly; **~ nada** next to nothing; **~ nunca** hardly ever, almost never.

casilla *f* hut, cabin; box office; square (on a chess board); pigeonhole, compartment.

casillero *m* pigeonholes (set of) *pl*; baggage locker.

casino *m* club, social club.

caso *m* case; occurrence, event; happening; casualty; occasion; (*gr*) case; **en ese ~** in that case; **en todo ~** in any case; **~ que** in case.

casorio *m* unwise marriage.

caspa *f* dandruff.

casquete *m* helmet.

casquillo *m* bottle top; tip, cap; point.

casta *f* caste; race; lineage; breed; kind, quality.

castaña *f* chestnut; demijohn.

castañar *m* chestnut grove.

castañetear *vi* to play the castanets.

castaño *m* chestnut tree; **~/na** *adj* chestnut-colored, brown.

castañuela *f* castanet.

castellano *m* Castilian, Spanish.

castidad *f* chastity.

castigar *vt* to castigate, to punish; to afflict.

castigo *m* punishment; correction; penalty.

castillo *m* castle.

castizo/za *adj* pure, thoroughbred.

casto/ta *adj* pure, chaste.

castor *m* beaver.

castrar *vt* to geld, to castrate; to prune; to cut the honeycombs out of (beehives).

casual *adj* casual, accidental.

casualidad *f* chance, accident.

casucha *f* hovel; slum.

casulla *f* chasuble.

cata *f* tasting.

catacumbas *fpl* catacombs *pl*.

catador/ra *m/f* wine tester.

catadura *f* looks *pl*, face.

catalejo *m* telescope.

catalizador *m* catalyst; catalytic converter.

catálogo *m* catalog.

catamarán *m* catamaran.

cataplasma *f* poultice.

catapulta *f* catapult.

catar *vt* to taste; to inspect, to examine; to look at; to esteem.

catarata *f* (*med*) cataract; waterfall.

catarro *m* catarrh.

catarroso/sa *adj* catarrhal.

catástrofe *f* catastrophe.

catavino *m* small cup for tasting wine; ~s *m/f invar* wine-taster; tippler.

catecismo *m* catechism.

cátedra *f* professorship, chair (university).

catedral *f* cathedral.

catedrático/ca *m/f* professor (of a university).

categoría *f* category; rank.

categórico/ca *adj* categorical, decisive.

catequismo *m* catechism.

caterva *f* mob.

catolicismo *m* Catholicism.

católico/ca *adj*, *m/f* catholic.

catorce *adj*, *m* fourteen.

catre *m* cot.

cauce *m* riverbed; (*fig*) channel.

caucho *m* rubber; tire.

caución *f* caution; (*law*) security, bail.

caucionar *vt* to prevent, to guard against; (*law*) to bail.

caudal *m* volume, flow; property, wealth; plenty.

caudaloso/sa *adj* carrying much water (of rivers); wealthy, rich.

caudillo *m* leader.

causa *f* cause; motive, reason; lawsuit; a ~ de considering, because of.

causal *adj* causal.

causante *m/f* originator; * *adj* causing, originating.

causar *vt* to cause; to produce; to occasion.

cáustico *m* caustic; ~/ca *adj* caustic.

cautela *f* caution, cautiousness.

cauteloso/sa *adj* cautious, wary.

cauterizar *vt* (*med*) to cauterize; to apply a drastic remedy to.

cautivar *vt* to take prisoner in war; to captivate, to charm.

cautiverio *m* captivity.

cautividad *f* captivity.

cautivo/va *adj*, *m/f* captive.

cauto/ta *adj* cautious, wary.

cava *f* digging and earthing of vines; wine cellar; sparkling wine.

cavar *vt* to dig up, to excavate; * *vi* to dig, to delve; to think profoundly.

caverna *f* cavern, cave.

cavernoso/sa *adj* cavernous.

cavidad *f* cavity, hollow.

cavilación *f* deep thought.

cavilar *vt* to ponder, to consider carefully.

caviloso/sa *adj* obsessed; suspicious.

cayado/da *m/f* shepherd's crook.

caza *f* hunting; shooting; chase; game; * *m* fighter-plane.

cazador/ra *m/f* hunter; *m* huntsman; ~ furtivo poacher.

cazamoscas *m invar* flycatcher (bird).

cazar *vt* to chase, to hunt; to catch.

cazo *m* saucepan; ladle.

cazuela *f* casserole; pan.

cazurro/rra *adj* silent, taciturn.

cebada *f* barley.

cebar *vt* to feed (animals), to fatten.

cebo *m* feed, food; bait, lure; priming.

cebolla *f* onion; bulb.

cebolleta *f* spring onion, scallion.

cebollino *m* onion seed; chive.

cebón *m* fattened hog/pig.

cebra *f* zebra.

cecear *vt* to pronounce s the same as c; to lisp.

cecina *f* dried meat; salt beef.

cedazo *m* sieve, strainer.

ceder *vt* to hand over; to transfer, to make over; to yield, to give up; * *vi* to submit, to comply, to give in; to diminish, to grow less.

cederrón *m* CD-ROM.

cedro *m* cedar.

cédula *f* certificate; document; slip of paper; bill; ~ de cambio bill of exchange; ~ de identidad *Lat Am* identity card.

cegar *vi* to grow blind; * *vt* to blind; to block up.

cegato/ta *adj* short-sighted.

ceguera *f* blindness.

ceja *f* eyebrow; edging of clothes; (*mus*) bridge of a stringed instrument; brow of a hill.

cejar *vi* to go backward(s); to slacken, to give in.

celada *f* helmet; ambush; trick.

celador *m* guard, watchman; maintenance man; linesman.

celda *f* cell.

celdilla *f* cell; cavity.

celebración *f* celebration; praise.

celebrar *vt* to celebrate; to praise; ~ misa to say mass.

célebre *adj* famous, renowned; witty, funny.

celebridad *f* celebrity, fame.

celeridad *f* speed, velocity.

celeste *adj* heavenly; sky-blue.

celestial *adj* heavenly; delightful.

celibato *m* celibacy.

célibe *m/f* bachelor, spinster.

celo *m* zeal; rut (in animals); Sellotape™; **~s** *mpl* jealousy.

celofán *m* Cellophane™.

celosía *f* lattice (of a window).

celoso/sa *adj* zealous; jealous.

célula *f* cell.

celular *adj* cellular; * *m Lat Am* cellular phone, mobile phone.

celulitis *f* cellulitis.

celuloide *m* celluloid.

cementerio *m* graveyard.

cemento *m* cement; *Lat Am* glue.

cena *f* dinner, supper.

cenador *m* arbor.

cenagoso/sa *adj* miry, marshy.

cenagal *m* quagmire.

cenar *vt* to have for dinner; * *vi* to have supper, to have dinner.

cencerro *m* jangle, clatter.

cenicero *m* ashtray.

ceniciento/ta *adj* ash-colored.

ceñido/da *adj* tight-fitting; sparing, frugal.

ceñir *vt* to surround, to circle; to abbreviate, to abridge; to fit tightly.

cenit *m* zenith.

ceniza *f* ashes *pl*; **miércoles de ~** Ash Wednesday.

ceño *m* frown.

censo *m* census; tax; ground rent; **~ electoral** electoral roll.

censor/ra *m/f* censor; reviewer, -critic.

censura *f* censorship; review; censure, blame.

censurar *vt* to review, to criticize; to censure, to blame.

centella *f* lightning; spark.

centellear *vi* to sparkle.

centena *f* hundred.

centenadas *adv*: **a ~** by hundreds.

centenar *m* hundred.

centenario/ia *adj* centenary; * *m* centenary.

centeno *m* rye.

centésimo/ma *adj* hundredth; * *m* hundredth.

centígrado *m* centigrade.

centímetro *m* centimeter.

céntimo *m* cent.

centinela *f* sentry, guard; lookout.

central *adj* central; * *f* head office, headquarters; (telephone) exchange; **~ nuclear** nuclear power station.

centralización *m* centralization.

centralizar *vt* to centralize.

céntrico *adj* central.

centrífugo/ga *adj* centrifugal.

centrista *adj* centrist.

centro *m* center; **~ comercial** shopping center.

centuplicar *vt* to increase a hundredfold.

céntuplo/pla *adj* one hundredfold.

ceñudo/da *adj* frowning, grim.

cepa *f* stock (of a vine); origin (of a family).

cepillar *vt* to brush.

cepillo *m* brush; plane (tool).

cepo *m* branch, bough; trap; snare; poor box.

cera *f* wax; **~s** *fpl* honeycomb.

cerámica *f* pottery.

cerca *f* enclosure; fence; **~s** *mpl* objects *pl* in the foreground of a painting; * *adv* near, at hand, close by; **~ de** close, near.

cercanías *fpl* outskirts.

cercano/na *adj* near, close by; neighboring, adjoining.

cercar *vt* to enclose, to circle; to fence in.

cerciorar *vt* to assure, to ascertain, to affirm; **~se** *vr* to find out.

cerco *m* enclosure; *Lat Am* fence; (*mil*) siege.

cerdo *m* pig, hog.

cereal *m* cereal.

cerebelo *m* cerebellum.

cerebro *m* brain.

ceremonia *f* ceremony.

ceremonial *adj*, *m* ceremonial.

ceremonioso/sa *adj* ceremonious.

cereza *f* cherry; *Lat Am* coffee bean.

cerezo *m* cherry tree.

cerilla *f* wax taper; ear wax; match, safety match.

cerner *vt* to sift; * *vi* to bud, to blossom; to drizzle; **~se** *vr* to hover; to swagger.

cernido *m* sifting.

cero *m* nothing, zero.

cerquita *adv* close by.

cerrado/da *adj* closed, shut; locked; overcast, cloudy; broad (of accent).

cerradura *f* locking-up; lock.

cerrajería *f* trade of a locksmith; locksmith's (premises).

cerrajero *m* locksmith.

cerrar *vt* to close, to shut; to block up; to lock; **~ una cuenta** to close an account; **~se** *vr* to close; to heal; to cloud over; *vi* to close, to shut; to lock.

cerril *adj* mountainous; rough, wild, untamed.

cerro *m* hill; neck (of an animal); backbone; combed flax/hemp; **en ~** bareback.

cerrojo *m* bolt (of a door).

certamen *m* competition, contest.

certero *adj* accurate; well-aimed.

certeza, certidumbre *f* certainty.

certificación *f* certificate.

certificado *m* certificate; **~/da** *adj* registered (of a letter).

certificar *vt* to certify, to affirm.

cervato *m* fawn.

cervecería *f* bar; brewery.

cervecero *m* brewer.

cerveza *m* beer.

cerviz *f* nape of the neck; cervix.

cesación *f* cessation, stoppage.

cesar *vt* to cease, to stop; to fire (*col*); to remove from office; * *vi* to cease, to stop; to retire.

cese *m* suspension; dismissal; **~ del fuego** *Lat Am* ceasefire.

cesión *f* cession; transfer.

césped *m* grass; lawn.

cesta *f* basket, pannier.

cestería *f* shop that specializes in baskets; basketwork.

cesto *m* (large) basket.

cetrino/na *adj* greenish-yellow; sallow; jaundiced, melancholic.

cetro *m* scepter.

chabacano/na *adj* coarse, vulgar; shoddy.

chabola *f* shack.

cháchara *f* chitchat, chatter, idle talk.

chacolí *m* light white wine with a sharp taste.

chafar *vt* to crush; to ruin.

chal *m* shawl.

chalado/da *adj* crazy.

chale(t) *m* detached house.

chaleco *m* vest.

chalupa *f* (*mar*) boat, launch.

chamarra *f* sheepskin jacket.

champán *m* champagne.

champiñón *m* mushroom.

champú *m* shampoo.

chamuscar *vt* to singe, to scorch.

chamusquina *f* scorching; (*fig*) row, quarrel.

chance *m/f Lat Am* chance.

chancho *m Lat Am* pig, hog.

chanchullo *m* (*col*) fix, fiddle.

canciller *m* chancellor.

chancleta *f* slipper.

chanclo *m* clog; galosh.

chándal *m* tracksuit.

chanfaina *f* cheap stew.

chantaje *m* blackmail.

chanza *f* joke, jest; **~s** *fpl* fun.

chapa *f* metal plate; panel; (*auto*) license plate.

chaparrón *m* heavy rain shower.

chapotear *vt* to wet with a sponge; * *vi* to paddle (in water).

chapucear *vt* to botch, to bungle.

chapucero *m* bungler; **~/ra** *adj* clumsy, crude.

chapurrar *vt* to speak (a language) badly; to mix (drinks).

chapuza *f* badly done job.

chapuzarse *vr* to duck; to dive.

chaqueta *f* jacket, coat; **~ deportiva** sports coat, sports jacket.

charca *f* pool.

charco *m* pool, puddle.

charcutería *f* shop selling pork meat products.

charla *f* chat, talk.

charlar *vi* to chat.

charlatán/ana *m/f* chatterbox.

charlatanería *f* talkativeness.

charol *m* varnish; patent leather.

charrada *f* coarse thing; bad breeding; bad taste.

charretera *f* shoulder pad.

charro *m* coarse individual; **~/rra** *adj* coarse; gaudy.

charter *m* charter flight.

chasco *m* disappointment; joke, jest.

chasis *m invar* (*auto*) chassis.

chasquear *vt* to crack (a whip); to disappoint.

chasquido *m* crack; click.

chatarra *f* scrap.

chato/ta *adj* flat, flattish; snub-nosed.

chaval/la *m/f* lad/lass.

cheque *m* check.

chequeo *m* check-up; service.

chequera *f* checkbook.

chicano/na *adj* Chicano.

chicha *f* corn liquor.

chicharra *f* harvest fly.

chicharrón *m* pork crackling.

chichón *m* lump, bump.

chichonera *f* helmet.

chicle *m* chewing gum.

chico/ca *adj* little, small; * *m/f* boy/girl.

chicote *m Lat Am* whip.

chifla *f* whistle; hiss.

chiflado/da *adj* crazy.

chiflar *vt* to boo.

chile *m* chili pepper.

chillar *vi* to scream, to shriek; to howl; to creak.

chillido *m* squeak; shriek, howl.

chillón/ona *adj* loud, noisy; gaudy; * *m/f* whiner, moaner.

chimenea *f* chimney; fireplace.

china *f* pebble; porcelain, chinaware; China silk.

chinche *f* bug; *Lat Am* thumbtack; * *m* nuisance.

chincheta *f* thumbtack.

chinela *f* slipper.

chinita *f Lat Am* maid.

chino/na *adj*, *m/f* Chinese; * *m* Chinese language.

chiquero *m* pigpen.

chiripa *f* fluke.

chirla *f* mussel.

chirriar *vi* to hiss; to creak; to chirp.

chirrido *m* chirping (of birds); squeaking.

chis *excl* sh!

chisgarabís *m* (*col*) meddler.

chisme *m* tale, thing.

chismear *vi* to tell tales.

chismoso/sa *adj* gossiping; * *m/f* gossip.

chispa *f* spark; sparkle; wit; drop (of rain); drunkenness.

chispazo *m* spark.

chispeante *adj* sparkling.

chispear *vi* to sparkle; to drizzle.

chisporrotear *vi* to crackle; to sparkle; to hiss (of liquids).

chistar *vi* to speak.

chiste *m* funny story, joke.

chistoso/sa *adj* witty; amusing, -funny.

chivato *m* kid; child.

chivo/va *m/f* billy/nanny goat.

chocante *adj* startling; odd.

chocar *vi* to strike, to knock; to crash; * *vt* to shock.

chochear *vi* to dodder, to be senile; to dote.

chocho *adj* doddering; doting.

chocolate *m* chocolate.

chocolatero/ra *adj* fond of chocolate.

chófer *m* driver.

chollo *m* bargain.

chopo *m* black poplar tree.

choque *m* shock; crash, collision; clash, conflict.

chorizo *m* pork sausage.

chorlito *m* plover (bird).

chorrear *vi* to spout, to gush; to drip.

chorrera *f* channel; frill.

chorro *m* gush; jet; stream; **a ~s** abundantly.

choto *m* kid; calf.

choza *f* hut, shack.

chubasco *m* squall.

chuchería *f* trinket.

chucho *m* mongrel.

chufleta *f* joke; taunt, jeer.

chulada *f* funny speech/action.

chulear *vi* to brag.

chuleta *f* chop.

chulo *m* rascal; pimp.

chunga *f* fun, joke; **estar de ~** to be in good humor.

chunguearse *vr* to be in good humor.

chupado/da *adj* skinny; easy.

chupaflor *m Lat Am* hummingbird.

chupar *vt* to suck; to absorb.

chupete *m* pacifier.

chupetear *vi* to suck gently.

chupón/ona *m/f* (*col*) swindler, sponger.

churro *m* fritter.

churruscarse *vr* to scorch.

churrusco *m* burnt toast.

chusco/ca *adj* pleasant; funny.

chusma *f* rabble, mob.

chuzo *m* little spear/spike; **llover a ~s** to pour (with rain) heavily.

cianuro *m* cyanide.

ciática *f* sciatica.

ciático/ca *adj* sciatic.

cibercafé *m* Internet café.

ciberespacio *m* cyberspace.

cicatear *vi* to be mean.

cicatriz *f* scar.

cicatrizar *vt* to heal.

ciclismo *m* cycling.

ciclista *m/f* cyclist.

ciclo *m* cycle.

ciclón *m* cyclone.

cicloturismo *m* bicycle tourism.

cicuta *f* (*bot*) hemlock.

ciegamente *adv* blindly.

ciego/ga *adj* blind.

cielo *m* sky; heaven; atmosphere; -climate.

cien *adj*, *m* a hundred.

ciénaga *f* swamp.

ciencia *f* science.

cieno *m* mud; mire.

cienpiés *m invar* centipede.

científico/ca *adj* scientific.

ciento *adj*, *m* a hundred.

cierne *m*: **en ~** in blossom; **estar en ~** to be in its infancy.

cierre *m* zipper.

cierto/ta *adj* certain, sure; right, correct; **por ~** certainly.

cierva *f* hind.

ciervo *m* deer, stag; **~ volante** stag beetle.

cierzo *m* cold northerly wind.

cifra *f* number, numeral; quantity; -cipher; abbreviation.

cifrar *vt* to write in code; to abridge.

cigala *f* langoustine.

cigarra *f* cicada.

cigarrera *m* cigar case.

cigarrería *f Lat Am* tobacconist's (shop).

cigarrillo *m* cigarette.

cigarro *m* cigar; cigarette.

cigüeña *f* stork; crank, handle; winch.

cilicio *m* hair shirt; spiked belt.

cilíndrico/ca *adj* cylindrical.

cilindro *m* cylinder.

cima *f* summit; peak; top.

címbalo *m* cymbal.

cimbor(r)io *m* cupola, dome.

cimbr(e)ar *vt* to shake, to swish, to swing; **~ a uno** to give one a clout (with a stick); **~se** *vr* to sway.

cimbronazo *m Lat Am* shock wave.

cimentado *m* refinement of gold.

cimentar *vt* to lay the foundation of (a building); to found; to refine (metals); to strengthen, to cement.

cimiento *m* foundation, groundwork; basis, origin.

cinc *m* zinc.

cincel *m* chisel.

cincelar *vt* to chisel, to engrave.

cincha *f* girth.

cinchar *vt* to fasten a girth (on a horse).

cinco *adj*, *m* five.

cincuenta *adj*, *m* fifty.

cine *m* movie theater, movie house.

cineasta *m/f* film maker.

cinematográfico/ca *adj* cinematographic.

cínico/ca *adj* cynical.

cinismo *m* cynicism.

cinta *f* band, ribbon; reel.

cinto *m* belt.

cintura *f* waist.

cinturón *m* belt, girdle; (*fig*) zone; **~ de seguridad** seatbelt.

ciprés *m* cypress tree.

circo *m* circus.

circuito *m* circuit; circumference.

circulación *f* circulation; traffic.

circular *adj* circular; circulatory; * *vt* to circulate; * *vi* (*auto*) to drive.

círculo *m* circle; (*fig*) scope, compass.

circuncidar *vt* to circumcise.

circuncisión *f* circumcision.

circundar *vt* to surround, to encircle.
circunferencia *f* circumference.
circunflejo/ja *adj*: **acento ~** *m* circumflex.
circunscribir *vt* to circumscribe.
circunscripción *f* division; electoral district.
circunspección *f* circumspection.
circunspecto/ta *adj* circumspect, cautious.
circunstancia *f* circumstance.
circunstante *m/f* bystander.
circunvalación *f*: **carretera de ~** beltway, bypass.
cirio *m* wax candle.
ciruela *f* plum; **~ pasa** prune.
ciruelo *m* plum tree.
cirugía *f* surgery.
cirujano *m* surgeon.
cisco *m* coaldust.
cisma *m* schism; discord.
cismático/ca *adj* schismatic.
cisne *m* swan.
cisterna *f* cistern.
cisura *f* incision.
cita *f* quotation; appointment, meeting.
citación *f* quotation; (*law*) summons.
citar *vt* to make an appointment with; to quote; (*law*) to summon.
cítrico/ca *adj* citric; **~s** *mpl* citric fruits *pl*.
ciudad *f* city; town.
ciudadanía *f* citizenship.
ciudadano/na *m/f* citizen; * *adj* civic.
ciudadela *f* citadel.
cívico/ca *adj* civic.
civil *adj* civil; polite, courteous; * *m* Civil Guard; civilian.
civilización *f* civilization.
civilizar *vt* to civilize.
civismo *m* public spirit; patriotism.
cizaña *f* discord.
clamar *vt* to clamor for.
clamor *m* clamor, outcry; peal of bells.
clamoroso/sa *adj* noisy, loud.
clandestino/na *adj* clandestine, secret, concealed.
clara *f* egg-white.
claraboya *f* skylight.
clarear *vi* to dawn; **~se** *vr* to be transparent.
clarete *adj*, *m* claret.
claridad *f* brightness, clearness.
clarificar *vt* to brighten; to clarify.
clarín *m* bugle; bugler.
clarinete *m* clarinet; * *m/f* clarinetist.
claro/ra *adj* clear, bright; evident, manifest; * *m* opening; clearing (in a wood); skylight.
claroscuro *m* chiaroscuro (in painting).
clase *f* class; rank; order.
clásico/ca *adj* classical.
clasificación *f* classification.
clasificado *m* *Lat Am* classified ad/ advertisement.
clasificar *vt* to classify.
claudicar *vi* to limp; to act deceitfully; to back down.

claustro *m* cloister; faculty (of a university); womb, uterus.
cláusula *f* clause.
clausura *f* closure, closing.
clavado/da *adj* tight-fitting; nailed.
clavar *vt* to nail; to fasten in, to force in; to drive in; (*col*) to cheat, to deceive; **~se** *vr* to penetrate.
clave *f* key; (*mus*) clef; * *m* harpsichord.
clavel *m* (*bot*) carnation.
clavetear *vt* to decorate with studs.
clavicordio *m* clavichord.
clavícula *f* clavicle, collar bone.
clavija *f* pin, peg.
clavo *m* nail; corn (on the feet); clove.
claxon *m* horn.
clemencia *f* clemency.
clemente *adj* clement, merciful.
cleptómano/na *m/f* kleptomaniac.
clerecía *f* clergy.
clerical *adj* clerical.
clérigo *m* priest; clergyman.
clero *m* clergy.
clic, click *m* click.
cliché *m* cliché; negative (of a photo).
cliente *m/f* client.
clientela *f* clientele.
clima *m* climate.
climatizado/da *adj* air-conditioned.
clínica *f* clinic; private hospital.
clínico/ca *adj* clinical.
clip *m* paperclip.
cloaca *f* sewer.
cloquear *vi* to cluck.
clon *m* clone.
clonación *f* cloning.
clonar *vt* to clone.
clónico/ca *adj* cloned.
clóset *m* *Lat Am* fitted cupboard.
club *m* club.
clueca *f* broody hen.
coacción *f* coercion, compulsion.
coactivo/va *adj* coercive.
coadjutor/ra *m/f* coadjutor.
coagular *vt*, **~se** *vr* to coagulate; to curdle.
coágulo *m*: **~ sanguíneo** blood clot.
coalición *f* coalition.
coartada *f* (*law*) alibi.
coartar *vt* to limit, to restrict, to restrain.
cobalto *m* cobalt.
cobarde *adj* cowardly, timid.
cobardía *f* cowardice.
cobayo/ya *m/f* guinea pig.
cobertizo *m* small shed; shelter.
cobertura *f* cover; coverage; bedspread.
cobija *f* *Lat Am* blanket.
cobijar *vt* to cover; to shelter.
cobra *f* cobra.
cobrador/ra *m/f* conductor/conduc-tress; collector.
cobrar *vt* to recover; **~se** *vr* (*med*) to come to.

cobre *m* copper; kitchen utensils *pl*; (*mus*) brass.

cobrizo/za *adj* coppery.

cobro *m* payment; recovery.

cocaína *f* cocaine.

cocción *f* cooking.

cocear *vt* to kick; (*fig*) to resist.

cocer *vt* to boil; to bake (bricks); * *vi* to boil; to ferment; ~se *vr* to suffer intense pain.

cochambre *m* dirty, stinking object.

cochambroso/sa *adj* nasty; filthy, stinking.

coche *m* car; coach, carriage; baby carriage; ~ **bomba** car bomb; (*rail*) ~ **cama** sleeping car/carriage; (*rail*) ~ **restaurante** restaurant car/carriage.

cochera *f* garage, carport, depot.

cochero *m* coachman.

cochinilla *f* woodlouse; cochineal.

cochino/na *adj* dirty, filthy; nasty; * *m* hog, pig.

cochiquera *f* pigpen.

cocido/da *adj* boiled; (*fig*) skilled, experienced; * *m* stew.

cocina *f* kitchen; cooker; cookery.

cocinero/ra *m/f* cook.

coco *m* coconut; bogeyman.

cocodrilo *m* crocodile.

codazo *m* blow given with the elbow.

codear *vt*, *vi* to elbow; ~se *vr*: ~se con to rub shoulders with.

códice *m* codex, old manuscript.

codicia *m* covetousness, greediness.

codiciable *adj* covetable.

codiciar *vt* to covet, to desire.

codicilo *m* (*law*) codicil.

codicioso/sa *adj* greedy, covetous.

código *m* law; set of rules; code; ~ **postal** post code.

codillo *m* knee (animal); (*bot*) stump; (*tec*) elbow (joint), bend; angle iron.

codo *m* elbow.

codorniz *f* quail.

coerción *f* coercion; restraint.

coercitivo/va *adj* coercive.

coetáneo/nea *adj* contemporary.

coexistencia *f* coexistence.

coexistente *adj* coexistent.

coexistir *vi* to coexist.

cofia *f* (nurse's) cap.

cofrade *m* member (of a brotherhood).

cofradía *f* brotherhood, fraternity.

cofre *m* chest; case; trunk.

cogedor *m* shovel; dustpan.

coger *vt* to catch, to take hold of; to occupy, to take up; ~se *vr* to catch.

cognitivo/va *adj* cognitive.

cogollo *m* heart of a lettuce/cabbage; shoot of a plant.

cogote *m* back of the neck.

cohabitar *vi* to cohabit, to live together.

cohechar *vt* to bribe, to suborn.

cohecho *m* bribery.

coherencia *f* coherence.

coherente *adj* coherent.

cohete *m* rocket.

cohibido/da *adj* shy.

cohibir *vt* to prohibit; to restrain.

cohorte *m* cohort.

coincidencia *f* coincidence.

coincidente *adj* coincidental.

coincidir *vi* to coincide.

coito *m* intercourse, coitus.

cojear *vi* to limp, to hobble; (*fig*) to go astray.

cojera *f* lameness; limp.

cojín *m* cushion.

cojo/ja *adj* lame, crippled.

col *f* cabbage.

cola[1] *f* tail; queue; last place; *Lat Am* (*col*) bum.

cola[2] *f* glue.

colaborador/ra *m/f* collaborator; contributor.

colaborar *vi* to collaborate.

colación *f* comparison; light meal, snack; buffet meal.

colada *f* wash, washing; (*chem*) bleach; sheep run.

coladera *f Lat Am* colander, strainer.

coladero *m* colander, strainer.

colador *m* sieve.

colapso *m* collapse.

colar *vt* to strain, to filter; * *vi* to ooze; ~se *vr*: ~ **en** to get into without paying.

colateral *adj* collateral.

colcha *f* bedspread, counterpane.

colchón *m* mattress.

colchoneta *f* mattress.

coleada *f* wagging (of an animal's tail).

colear *vi* to wag the tail.

colección *f* collection.

coleccionar *vt* to collect.

coleccionista *m/f* collector.

colecta *f* collection (for charity).

colectar *vt* to collect (taxes).

colectivo/va *adj* collective.

colector *m* collector; sewer.

colega *m/f* colleague.

colegial *m* schoolboy.

colegiala *f* schoolgirl.

colegiata *f* collegiate church.

colegio *m* college; school.

colegir *vt* to collect; to deduce, to infer.

cólera *f* bile; anger; fury, rage.

coléricamente *adv* in a rage.

colérico/ca *adj* angry; furious; bad-tempered.

colesterol *m* cholesterol.

coleta *f* pigtail.

colgadero *m* hook, hanger, peg.

colgadura *f* tapestry; hangings *pl*, drapery.

colgajo *m* tatter, rag.

colgante *adj* hanging; * *m* pendant.

colgar *vt* to hang; to suspend; to decorate with tapestry; * *vi* to be suspended.

colibrí *m* hummingbird.

cólico *m* colic.

coliflor *m* cauliflower.
colilla *f* end/butt of a cigarette.
colina *f* hill.
colindante *adj* neighboring.
colindar *vi* to adjoin.
coliseo *m* coliseum; opera house; theater.
colisión *f* collision; friction.
collar *m* necklace; (dog) collar.
colmar *vt* to heap up; * *vi* to fulfill, to realize.
colmena *f* hive, beehive.
colmenar *m* apiary.
colmillo *m* eyetooth; tusk.
colmo *m* height, summit; extreme; **a ~**
plentifully.
colocación *f* employment; placing; situation.
colocar *vt* to arrange; to place; to provide with a
job; **~se** *vr* to get a job.
colon *m* (med) colon.
colonia *f* colony; silk ribbon.
colonial *adj* colonial.
colonización *f* colonization.
colonizador/a *m/f* settler; * *adj* colonizing.
colonizar *vt* to colonize.
colono *m* colonist; farmer.
coloquio *m* conversation; conference.
color *m* color, hue; dye; rouge; suit (in cards).
coloración *f* coloring, coloration.
colorado/da *adj* ruddy; red.
colorar *vt* to color; to dye.
colorear *vt* to color; to excuse.
colorete *m* rouge.
colorido *m* coloring.
colosal *adj* colossal.
columna *f* column.
columnata *f* colonnade.
columpiar *vt*, **~se** *vr* to swing to and fro.
columpio *m* swing, seesaw.
colusión *f* collusion.
colza *f* (bot) rape; rape seed.
coma *f* (gr) comma; * *m* (med) coma.
comadre *f* midwife; godmother; neighbor.
comadreja *f* weasel.
comadrón/ona *m/f* midwife.
comandancia *f* command.
comandante *m* commander.
comandar *vt* to command.
comarca *f* territory, district.
comba *f* curve; warp (of lumber); skipping rope.
combar *vt* to bend; **~se** *vr* to warp.
combate *m* combat, conflict; fighting.
combatiente *m* combatant.
combatir *vt* to combat, to fight; to attack; * *vi* to
fight.
combi *f* Lat Am minibus.
combinación *f* combination; (chem) compound;
cocktail; scheme.
combinar *vi* to combine.
combustible *adj* combustible; * *m* fuel.
combustión *f* combustion.
comedero *m* dining room; trough.
comedia *f* comedy; play, drama.

comediante *m/f* player, actor/actress.
comedido/da *adj* moderate, restrained.
comedirse *vr* to restrain oneself.
comedor/ra *m/f* glutton; * *m* dining room.
comendatorio/ria *adj* introductory (of letters).
comensal *m/f* fellow diner.
comentar *vt* to comment on, to expound.
comentario *m* comment, remark; commentary.
comentarista *m/f* commentator.
comenzar *vi* to commence, to begin.
comer *vt* to eat; to take (a piece at chess); * *vi*
to have lunch.
comercial *adj* commercial; * *m* Lat Am
commercial.
comerciante *m/f* trader, merchant, dealer.
comerciar *vi* to trade, to do business.
comercio *m* trade, commerce; business; **~**
electrónico e-commerce; **~ justo** fair trade.
comestible *adj* eatable;* *mpl* **~s** food, foodstuffs
pl.
cometa *m* comet; * *f* kite.
cometer *vt* to commit, to charge; to entrust.
cometido *m* task.
comezón *f* itch; itching.
comicios *mpl* elections *pl*.
cómico/ca *adj* comic, comical.
comida *f* food; eating; meal; lunch; **~ basura**
junk food.
comienzo *m* beginning.
comillas *fpl* quotation marks *pl*.
comilón/ona *m/f* great eater, glutton; * *f* blow-out.
comino *m* cumin (plant/seed).
comisaría *f* police station; commissariat.
comisario/-a *m/f* commissioner.
comisión *f* commission; committee.
comisionado/da *m/f* commissioner; committee
member.
comisionar *vt* to commission.
comité *m* committee.
comitiva *f* suite, retinue, followers *pl*.
como *adv* as; like; such as.
cómo *adv* how?; why? * *excl* what?
cómoda *f* chest of drawers.
comodidad *f* comfort; convenience; **~es** *fpl*
wealth, comforts *pl*.
comodín *m* joker.
cómodo/da *adj* convenient; comfortable; cozy.
compact disc *m* compact disc.
compacto/ta *adj* compact; close, dense.
compadecer *vt* to pity; **~se** *vr* to agree with each
other.
compadre *m* godfather; friend.
compaginar *vt* to arrange, to put in order; **~se**
vr to tally.
compañero/ra *m/f* companion, friend; comrade;
partner.
compañía *f* company.
comparación *f* comparison.
comparar *vt* to compare.
comparativo/va *adj* comparative.
comparecer *vi* to appear in court.

comparsa *m/f* extra (in the theater/movies).
compartimento *m* compartment.
compartir *vt* to divide into equal parts.
compás *m* compass; pair of compasses; (*mus*) measure, beat.
compasión *f* compassion, commiseration.
compasivo/va *adj* compassionate.
compatibilidad *f* compatibility.
compatible *adj*: ~ **con** compatible with, consistent with.
compatriota *m/f* countryman; countrywoman; fellow citizen.
compeler *vt* to compel, to constrain.
compendiar *vt* to abridge.
compendio *m* abridgment; summary.
compensación *f* compensation; recompense.
compensar *vt* to compensate; to recompense.
competencia *f* competition, rivalry; competence.
competente *adj* competent; adequate.
competer *vi* to be one's responsibility.
competición *f* competition.
competidor/ra *m/f* competitor, contestant; rival.
competir *vi* to vie; ~ **con** to compete with, to rival.
compilación *f* compilation.
compilador *m* compiler.
compilar *vt* to compile.
compinche *m* (*col*) pal, buddy.
complacencia *f* pleasure; indulgence.
complacer *vt* to please; ~**se** *vr* to be pleased with.
complaciente *adj* pleasing.
complejo *m* complex; ~**ja** *adj* complex.
complementario/ria *adj* complementary.
complemento *m* complement.
completar *vt* to complete.
completo/ta *adj* complete; perfect.
complexión *f* constitution, temperament; build.
complicado/da *adj* complicated.
complicar *vt* to complicate.
cómplice *m/f* accomplice.
complicidad *f* complicity.
complot *m* plot.
componer *vt* to compose; to constitute; to mend, to repair; to strengthen, to restore; to adorn; to adjust; to reconcile; to compose, to calm; ~**se** *vr*: ~ **de** to consist of.
comportamiento *m* behavior.
comportarse *vr* to behave.
composición *f* composition; composure, agreement; settlement.
compositor/ra *m/f* composer; compositor.
compostura *f* composition; composure, mending, repairing; discretion; modesty, demureness.
compota *f* sauce.
compra *f* purchase; ~ **a plazos** installment plan.
comprador/ra *m/f* buyer; customer, shopper.
comprar *vt* to buy, to purchase.
comprender *vt* to include, to contain; to comprehend, to understand.

comprensible *adj* comprehensible.
comprensión *f* comprehension, understanding.
comprensivo/va *adj* comprehensive.
compresa *f* sanitary napkin.
compresión *f* compression.
comprimido *m* pill.
comprimir *vt* to compress; to repress, to restrain.
comprobante *m* receipt; voucher.
comprobar *vt* to verify, to confirm; to prove.
comprometer *vt* to compromise; to embarrass; to implicate; to put in danger; ~**se** *vr* to compromise oneself.
compromiso *m* compromise.
compuerta *f* hatch; sluice.
compuesto *m* compound; ~/**ta** *adj* composed; made up of.
compulsar *vt* to collate, to compare; to make an authentic copy.
compulsivo/va *adj* compulsive.
compunción *f* compunction, regret.
compungirse *vr* to feel remorseful.
computación *f Lat Am* computing.
computador/dora *m/f* computer.
computar *vt* to calculate; to compute.
cómputo *m* computation; calculation.
comulgar *vt* to administer communion to; * *vi* to receive communion.
común *adj* common, usual, general; * *m* community; public; **en** ~ in common.
comunal *adj* communal.
comunicación *f* communication; report.
comunicado *m* announcement; communiqué.
comunicar *vt* to communicate; ~**se** *vr* to communicate (with each -other).
comunicativo/va *adj* communicative.
comunidad *f* community; **C~ Europea** European Community.
comunión *f* communion.
comunismo *m* communism.
comunista *adj, m/f* communist.
comunitario/ria *adj* of the European Union.
con *prep* with; by; ~ **que** so then, providing that.
coñac *m* brandy, cognac.
conato *m* endeavor; effort; attempt.
concavidad *f* concavity.
cóncavo/va *adj* concave.
concebir *vt* to conceive; * *vi* to become pregnant.
conceder *vt* to give; to grant; to concede, to allow.
concejal/la *m/f* member of a council.
concejo *m* council.
concentración *f* concentration.
concentrar *vt*, ~**se** *vr* to concentrate.
concéntrico/ca *adj* concentric.
concepción *f* conception; idea.
concepto *m* conceit, thought; judgement, opinion.
concerniente *adj*: ~ **a** concerning, relating to.
concernir *v imp* to regard, to concern.
concertar *vt* to coordinate; to settle; to adjust; to agree; to arrange, to fix up; * *vi* (*mus*) to harmonize, to be in tune.

concesión f concession.

concesionario m agent.

concha f shell; tortoiseshell.

conchabar vt to mix, to blend; **~se** vr to plot, to conspire.

conciencia f conscience.

concienciar vt to make aware; **~se** vr to become aware.

concientizar vt Lat Am to make aware; **~se** vr to become aware.

concierto m concert; agreement; concerto; **de ~** in agreement, in concert.

conciliación f conciliation, reconciliation.

conciliar vt to reconcile; * adj of a council.

conciliatorio/ra adj conciliatory.

concilio m council.

concisión f conciseness.

conciso/sa adj concise, brief.

conciudadanía f joint-citizenship.

conciudadano/na m/f fellow citizen.

cónclave m conclave.

concluir vt to conclude, to end, to complete; to infer, to deduce; **~se** vr to conclude.

conclusión f conclusion.

concluyente adj conclusive.

concordancia f concordance, concord; harmony.

concordar vt to reconcile, to make agree; * vi to agree, to correspond.

concordato m concordat.

concordia f conformity, agreement.

concretar vt to make concrete; to specify.

concreto/ta adj concrete; * m Lat Am concrete.

concubina f concubine.

concupiscencia f lust.

concurrencia f concurrence; coincidence; competition; crowd, gathering.

concurrido/da adj busy.

concurrir vi to meet; to contribute; to coincide; to compete.

concursante m/f competitor.

concurso m crowd; competition; help, cooperation.

concusión f concussion.

condado m county.

conde m earl, count.

condecoración f medal.

condecorar vt to adorn; (mil) to decorate.

condena f condemnation.

condenable adj culpable.

condenar vt to condemn; to find guilty; **~se** vr to blame oneself; to confess (one's guilt).

condenatorio/ria adj condemnatory.

condensación f condensation.

condensar vt to condense.

condesa f countess.

condescendencia f helpfulness, willingness; acquiescence; compliance.

condescender vi to acquiesce, to comply.

condición f condition, state; quality; status; rank; stipulation.

condicionado/da adj conditioned.

condicional adj conditional.

condimentar vt to flavor, to season.

condimento m condiment, seasoning.

condiscípulo/la m/f fellow pupil; fellow student.

condolerse vr to sympathize.

condón m condom.

condominio m Lat Am condominium.

condonar vt to condone; to forgive.

conducción f conveyance; management; (auto) driving.

conducente adj: **~ a** leading to.

conducir vt to convey, to conduct; to drive; to manage; * vi to drive; **~ (a)** to lead (to); **~se** vr to conduct oneself.

conducta f conduct, behavior; management.

conducto m conduit, pipe; drain; (fig) channel.

conductor/ra m/f conductor, guide; (rail) guard; driver.

conectado/da adj on-line.

conectar vt to connect.

conejera f warren, burrow.

conejo m rabbit.

conexión f connection; plug; relationship.

conexo/xa adj connected, related.

confabularse vr to conspire.

confección f preparation; clothing industry.

confeccionar vt to make up.

confederación f confederacy.

confederado/da adj confederate.

confederarse vr to confederate.

conferencia f conference; telephone call.

conferenciar vi to confer; to be in conference.

conferir vt to award; to compare.

confesar vt to confess; to admit.

confesión f confession.

confesionario m confessional.

confeso/sa adj (law) self-confessed.

confesonario m confessional.

confesor m confessor.

confeti m confetti.

confiable adj Lat Am reliable.

confiado/da adj trusting; confident; arrogant.

confianza f trust; confidence; conceit; familiarity; **en ~** confidential.

confiar vt to confide, to entrust; * vi to trust.

confidencia f confidence.

confidencial adj confidential.

confidente m/f confidant/e; informer.

configurar vt to shape, to form.

confín m limit, boundary.

confinar vt to confine; * vi: **~ con** to border upon.

confirmación f confirmation.

confirmar vt to confirm; to corroborate.

confiscación f confiscation.

confiscar vt to confiscate.

confite m candy.

confitería f , candy; candy store.

confitero/ra m/f confectioner.

confitura f preserve; jam.

conflagración f conflagration.

conflictivo/va adj controversial.

conflicto *m* conflict.

confluencia *f* confluence.

confluir *vi* to join (of rivers); to gather (of people).

conformar *vt* to shape; to adjust, to adapt; * *vi* to agree; **~se** *vr* to conform; to resign oneself.

conforme *adj* alike, similar; agreed; * *prep* according to.

conformidad *f* similarity; agreement; resignation.

conformista *m/f* conformist.

confortable *adj* comfortable.

confortar *vt* to comfort; to strengthen; to console.

confortativo/va *adj* comforting.

confraternidad *f* fraternity.

confrontación *f* confrontation.

confrontar *vt* to confront.

confundir *vt* to confound, to jumble; to confuse; **~se** *vr* to make a mistake.

confusamente *adv* confusedly.

confusión *f* confusion.

confuso/sa *adj* confused.

congelación *f* freezing.

congelado/da *adj* frozen; * *mpl:* **~s** frozen food.

congelador *m* freezer.

congelar *vt* to freeze; **~se** *vr* to congeal.

congeniar *vi* to get on well.

congestión *f* congestion.

congestionar *vt* to congest.

congoja *f* anguish, distress, grief.

congraciarse *vr* to ingratiate oneself.

congratulación *f* congratulation.

congratular *vt* to congratulate.

congregación *f* congregation, assembly.

congregar *vt*, **~se** *vr* to assemble, to meet, to collect.

congresista *m/f* delegate.

congreso *m* congress.

cónico/ca *adj* conical.

conjetura *f* conjecture, guess.

conjeturar *vt* to conjecture, to guess.

conjugación *f* (*gr*) conjugation.

conjugar *vt* (*gr*) to conjugate; to combine.

conjunción *f* conjunction.

conjuntamente *adv* together.

conjunto/ta *adj* united, joint; * *m* whole; (*mus*) ensemble, band; team.

conjuración *f* conspiracy, plot.

conjurado/da *m/f* conspirator.

conjurar *vt* to exorcise; * *vi* to conspire, to plot.

conjuro *m* incantation, exorcism.

conmemoración *f* commemoration.

conmemorar *vt* to commemorate.

conmigo *pn* with me.

conminación *f* threat.

conminar *vt* to threaten.

conminatorio/ria *adj* threatening.

conmiseración *f* commiseration, pity, sympathy.

conmoción *f* shock; upheaval; commotion; (*med*) concussion.

conmovedor/ra *adj* touching.

conmover *vt* to move; to disturb.

conmutación *f* commutation, exchange.

conmutador *m* switch; *Lat Am* switchboard.

conmutar *vt* (*law*) to commute; to exchange.

connotar *vt* to imply.

coño *excl* (*col*) hell!, damn!

cono *m* cone.

conocedor/ra *m/f* connoisseur.

conocer *vt* to know, to understand; **~se** *vr* to know one another.

conocido/da *m/f* acquaintance.

conocimiento *m* knowledge, understanding; (*med*) consciousness; acquaintance; (*mar*) bill of lading.

conque *m* condition.

conquista *f* conquest.

conquistador *m* conqueror; * *adj* **~/ra** *adj* conquering.

conquistar *vt* to conquer.

consabido/da *adj* well-known; above-mentioned.

consagración *f* consecration.

consagrar *vt* to consecrate.

consanguíneo/nea *adj* related by blood.

consanguinidad *f* blood relationship.

consecución *f* acquisition; attainment.

consecuencia *f* consequence; conclusion; consistency; **por ~** therefore.

consecuente *adj* consistent.

consecutivo/va *adj* consecutive.

conseguir *vt* to attain; to get, to obtain.

consejero/ra *m/f* adviser; councilor/councillor.

consejo *m* advice; council.

consenso *m* consensus.

consentido/da *adj* spoiled (of children).

consentimiento *m* consent.

consentir *vt* to consent to; to allow; to admit; to spoil (a child).

conserje *m/f* doorman, porter; janitor.

conservación *f* conservation.

conservante *m* preservative.

conservar *vt* to conserve; to keep; to preserve (fruit).

conservas *fpl* canned food.

conservatorio *m* (*mus*) conservatoire.

considerable *adj* considerable.

consideración *f* consideration; respect.

consideradamente *adv* considerately.

considerado/da *adj* respected; considerate.

considerar *vt* to consider.

consigna *f* (*mil*) watchword; order, instruction; (*rail*) checkroom.

consignación *f* consignment.

consignar *vt* to consign, to dispatch; to assign; to record, to register.

consignatario/ria *m/f* consignee.

consigo *pn* (*m*) with him; (*f*) with her; (*vd*) with you; (*reflexivo*) with oneself.

consiguiente *adj* consequent.

consistencia *f* consistence, consistency.

consistente adj consistent; firm, solid.

consistir vi: ~ **en** to consist of; to be due to.

consistorio m town council; town hall.

consocio/cia m/f fellow member; partner.

consola f control panel; console.

consolación f consolation.

consolador/ra adj consoling, comforting.

consolar vt to console, to comfort, to cheer.

consolidar vt to consolidate.

consomé m consommé.

consonancia f consonance.

consonante m rhyme; * f (gr) consonant; * adj consonant, harmonious.

consorcio m partnership.

consorte m/f consort, companion, partner; accomplice.

conspiración f conspiracy, plot.

conspirador/ra m/f conspirator, plotter.

conspirar vi to conspire, to plot.

constancia f constancy; steadiness.

constante adj constant; firm.

constar vi to be evident, to be certain; to be composed of, to consist of.

constatar vt to note; to check.

constelación f constellation.

consternación f consternation.

consternar vt to dismay; to shock.

constipado/da adj: estar ~ to have a cold.

constiparse vr to catch a cold.

constitución f constitution.

constitucional adj constitutional.

constituir vt to constitute; to establish; to appoint.

constitutivo/va adj constitutive; essential.

constituyente adj constituent.

constreñimiento m constraint.

constreñir vt to restrict; to force; (med) to constipate; to constrict.

constricción f constriction, contraction.

construcción f construction.

constructor/ra m/f builder.

construir vt to form; to build, to construct; to construe.

consuegro/gra m/f father-in-law/ mother-in-law of one's son/daughter.

consuelo m consolation, comfort.

cónsul m consul.

consulado m consulate.

consulta f consultation.

consultar vt to consult, to ask for advice.

consultivo/va adj consultative.

consultor/ra m/f adviser, consultant.

consultorio m (med) surgery.

consumación f consummation, finishing.

consumado/da adj consummate; complete; accomplished; perfect.

consumar vt to consummate, to finish; to carry out.

consumición f consumption; drink.

consumidor/ra m/f consumer.

consumir vt to consume; to burn, to use; to waste, to exhaust; ~**se** vr to waste away, to be consumed.

consumismo m consumerism.

consumo m consumption.

contabilidad f accounting; bookkeeping.

contable m/f accountant.

contacto m contact; (auto) ignition.

contado/da adj: ~**s** scarce, few; * m: **pagar al** ~ to pay (in) cash.

contador m meter; counter in a cafe; ~/a m/f Lat Am accountant.

contaduría f Lat Am accountancy; accountant's office.

contagiar vt to infect; ~**se** vr to get infected.

contagio m contagion.

contagioso/sa adj contagious.

contaminación f contamination; pollution.

contaminar vt to contaminate; to pollute; to corrupt.

contante m cash.

contar vt to count, to reckon; to tell; * vi to count; ~ **con** to rely upon.

contemplación f contemplation.

contemplar vt to look at; to contemplate, to consider; to meditate.

contemplativo/va adj contemplative.

contemporáneo/nea adj contemporary.

contemporizar vi to temporize.

contencioso/sa adj contentious; quarrelsome.

contender vi to contend, to compete.

contendiente m/f competitor.

contenedor m container.

contener vt to contain, to hold; to hold back; to repress; ~**se** vr to control oneself.

contenido/da adj moderate, restrained; * m contents pl.

contentar vt to content, to satisfy; to please; ~**se** vr to be pleased/satisfied.

contento/ta adj glad; pleased; content; * m contentment; (law) release.

contestación f answer, reply.

contestador m: ~ **automático** answering machine.

contestar vt to answer, to reply; to prove, to corroborate.

contexto m context.

contienda f contest, dispute.

contigo pn with you.

contigüidad f contiguity.

contiguo/gua adj contiguous, close.

continencia f continence, abstinence, moderation.

continental adj continental.

continente m continent, mainland; * adj continent.

contingencia f risk; contingency.

contingente adj contingent, accidental; * m contingent.

continuación f continuation; sequel.

continuar vt, vi to continue.

continuidad f continuity.

continuo/nua *adj* continuous.
contonearse *vr* to walk affectedly.
contoneo *m* affected manner of walking.
contorno *m* environs *pl*; contour, outline; **en ~** round about.
contorsión *f* contortion.
contra *prep* against; contrary to; opposite.
contraataque *m* counter-attack.
contrabajo *m* (*mus*) double bass; bass guitar; low bass.
contrabandista *m/f* smuggler.
contrabando *m* contraband; smuggling.
contracción *f* contraction.
contrachapado *m* plywood.
contradecir *vt* to contradict.
contradicción *f* contradiction.
contradictorio/ria *adj* contradictory.
contraer *vt* to contract, to shrink; to make (a bargain); **~se** *vr* to shrink, to contract.
contrafuerte *m* buttress; foothill; heel-pad.
contragolpe *m* backlash.
contrahecho/cha *adj* deformed; hunchbacked; counterfeit, fake, false.
contralto *m* (*mus*) contralto.
contramaestre *m* (*mar*) boatswain; foreman.
contrapartida *f* (*com*) balancing entry.
contrapaso *m* step backwards.
contrapelo *adv*: **a ~** against the grain.
contrapesar *vi* to counterbalance.
contrapeso *m* counterpoise; counterweight.
contraponer *vt* to compare, to oppose.
contraposición *f* comparison; contrast.
contraproducente *adj* counterproductive.
contraprogramación *f* competitive scheduling.
contrapunto *m* (*mus*) counterpoint.
contrariar *vt* to contradict, to oppose; to vex.
contrariedad *f* opposition; setback; annoyance.
contrario/ria *m/f* opponent; * *adj* contrary, opposite; **por el ~** on the contrary.
contrarreloj *f* time trial.
contrarrestar *vt* to return a ball; (*fig*) to counteract.
contrarrevolución *f* counterrevolu-tion.
contraseña *f* countersign; (*mil*) watchword.
contrasentido *m* contradiction.
contrastar *vt* to resist; to contradict; to assay (metals); to verify (measures and weights); * *vi* to contrast.
contraste *m* contrast.
contrata *f* contract.
contratación *f* signing-up, hiring.
contratar *vt* to contract; to hire, to engage.
contratiempo *m* setback; accident.
contratista *m* contractor.
contrato *m* contract, agreement.
contravención *f* contravention.
contraveneno *m* antidote.
contravenir *vi* to contravene, to transgress; to violate.
contraventana *f* shutter.
contribución *f* contribution; tax.

contribuir *vt, vi* to contribute.
contribuyente *m/f* contributor; taxpayer.
contrincante *m* competitor.
contrito/ta *adj* contrite, penitent.
controlador/ra *m/f* controller.
controlar *vt* to control; to check.
controversia *f* controversy, dispute.
contumacia *f* obstinacy, stubbornness; (*law*) contempt of court.
contumaz *adj* obstinate, stubborn; (*law*) guilty of contempt of court.
contundente *adj* overwhelming; blunt.
contusión *f* bruise.
convalecencia *f* convalescence.
convalecer *vi* to recover from sickness, to convalesce.
convaleciente *m/f, adj* convalescent.
convalidar *vt* to recognize.
convencer *vt* to convince.
convencimiento *m* conviction.
convención *f* convention, pact.
convencional *adj* conventional.
conveniencia *f* suitability; usefulness; agreement; **~s** *fpl* property.
conveniente *adj* useful; suitable.
convenio *m* convention, agreement, treaty.
convenir *vi* to agree, to suit.
convento *m* convent, nunnery; monastery.
conventual *adj* monastic.
convergencia *f* convergence.
converger *vi* to converge.
conversa *f Lat Am* conversation, talk.
conversación *f* conversation, talk; communication.
conversar *vi* to talk, to converse.
conversión *f* conversion, change.
converso/sa *m/f* convert.
convertir *vt*, **~se** *vr* to convert.
convexo/xa *adj* convex.
convicción *f* conviction.
convicto/ta *adj* convicted (found guilty).
convidado/da *m/f* guest.
convidar *vt* to invite.
convincente *adj* convincing.
convite *m* invitation; banquet.
convivencia *f* living together.
convocar *vt* to convoke, to assemble.
convocatoria *f* summons; notice of a meeting.
convoy *m* convoy.
convulsión *f* convulsion.
convulsivo/va *adj* convulsive.
conyugal *adj* conjugal, married.
cónyuge *m/f* spouse.
cooperar *vi* to cooperate.
cooperativa *f* cooperative.
cooperativo/va *adj* cooperative.
coordinadora *f* coordinating committee.
coordinar *vt* to arrange, to coordinate.
copa *f* cup; glass; top of a tree; crown of a hat; **~s** *fpl* hearts *pl* (in cards).
copete *m* quiff; pride.

copia *f* plenty, abundance; copy, duplicate.
copiador/ra *m/f* copyist; copier.
copiar *vt* to copy; to imitate.
copioso/sa *adj* copious, abundant, plentiful.
copla *f* verse; (*mus*) popular song, folk song.
copo *m* small bundle; flake of snow.
copropietario/ria *m/f* joint owner.
cópula *f* copulation; conjunction; (*gr*) copula.
copulativo/va *adj* copulative.
coqueta *f* coquette, flirt.
coquetear *vi* to flirt.
coquetería *f* coquetry, flirtation.
coraje *m* courage; anger, passion.
coral *m* coral; choir; * *adj* choral.
coraza *f* cuirass; armor-plating.
corazón *m* heart; core; **de ~** willingly.
corazonada *f* feeling; inspiration; quick decision; presentiment.
corbata *f* tie.
corbeta *f* corvette.
corcel *m* steed, charger.
corchea *f* (*mus*) quaver.
corchete *m* clasp; hook and eye.
corcho *m* cork; float (for fishing); cork bark.
cordel *m* cord, rope; (*mar*) line.
cordero *m* lamb; lambskin; meek/gentle person.
cordial *adj* cordial, affectionate; * *m* cordial.
cordialidad *f* cordiality.
cordillera *f* range of mountains.
cordón *m* cord, string; lace; cordon.
cordura *f* prudence, good sense, wisdom.
corista *m/f* chorister.
cornada *f* thrust with a bull's horn.
cornadura *f* horns *pl*.
cornamenta *f* horns *pl* of an animal.
córnea *f* cornea.
cornear *vt* to gore.
córneo/ea *adj* horny, corneous.
corneta *f* bugle.
cornisa *f* cornice.
cornudo/da *adj* horned.
coro *m* choir; chorus.
corona *f* crown; coronet; top of the head; crown (of a tooth); tonsure; halo.
coronación *f* coronation.
coronar *vt* to crown; to complete, to perfect.
coronario/ria *adj* coronary.
coronel *m* (*mil*) colonel.
coronilla *f* crown of the head.
corpiño *m* bodice.
corporación *f* corporation.
corporal *adj* corporal.
corpóreo/rea *adj* corporeal.
corpulencia *f* corpulence.
corpulento/ta *adj* corpulent, bulky.
Corpus *m* Corpus Christi.
corral *m* yard; farmyard; corral; playpen.
correa *f* leather strap, thong; flexibility.
correaje *m* leather straps *pl*.
corrección *f* correction; reprehension; amendment.

correccional *m* reformatory.
correctivo/va *adj* corrective.
correcto/ta *adj* exact, correct.
corrector/ra *m/f* proof-reader.
corredizo/za *adj* sliding; easy to be untied.
corredor/ra *adj* running; * *m/f* broker, runner; *m* corridor.
corregir *vt* to correct, to amend; to reprehend; **~se** *vr* to reform.
correlación *f* correlation.
correo *m* post, mail; courier; postman; **~ electrónico** e-mail; **a vuelta de ~** by return of post; **~s** *mpl* post office.
correoso/sa *adj* flexible, leathery.
correr *vt* to run; to flow; to travel over; to pull (a drape); * *vi* to run, to rush; to flow; to blow (applied to the wind); **~se** *vr* to be ashamed; to slide, to move; to run (of colors).
correría *f* incursion.
correspondencia *f* correspondence; communication; agreement.
corresponder *vi* to correspond; to answer; to be suitable; to belong; to concern; **~se** *vr* to love one another.
correspondiente *adj* corresponding, suitable.
corresponsal *m/f* correspondent.
corretear *vi* to rush around; to hang about the streets.
corrida *f* run, dash; bullfight.
corrido/da *adj* expert; knowing; ashamed.
corriente *f* current; course, progression; electric current; * *adj* current; common, ordinary, general; fluent; flowing, running.
corrillo *m* circle of persons; clique.
corro *m* circle of people.
corroborar *vt* to corroborate.
corroer *vt* to corrode, to erode.
corromper *vt* to corrupt; to rot; to turn bad; to seduce; to bribe; **~se** *vr* to rot; to become corrupted; * *vi* to stink.
corrosión *f* corrosion.
corrosivo/va *adj* corrosive.
corrupción *f* corruption; rot, decay.
corruptible *adj* corruptible.
corrupto/ta *adj* corrupted, corrupt.
corruptor/ra *m/f* corrupter, perverter.
corrusco *m* broken bread.
corsé *f* corset.
cortacésped *m* lawn mower.
cortada *f Lat Am* shortcut.
cortado *m* coffee with a little milk; **~/da** *adj* cut; sour; embarrassed.
cortadura *f* cut; cutting; incision; fissure; **~s** *fpl* shreds *pl*, cuttings *pl*, parings *pl*.
cortafuegos *m invar* fire lane, firebreak.
cortaplumas *m invar* penknife.
cortar *vt* to cut; to cut off, to curtail; to intersect; to carve; to chop; to cut (in cards); to interrupt; **~se** *vr* to be ashamed/embarrassed; to curdle.
cortauñas *m invar* nail clippers *pl*.

corte[1] *m* cutting; cut; section; length (of cloth); style.

corte[2] *f* (royal) court; capital city; *Lat Am law* court; **C~s** *fpl* Spanish Parliament.

cortedad *f* shortness, smallness; stupidity; bashfulness.

cortejar *vt* to court.

cortejo *m* entourage; courtship; procession; lover.

cortés/esa *adj* courteous, polite.

cortesana *f* courtesan.

cortesía *f* courtesy, good manners *pl*.

corteza *f* bark; peel; crust; (*fig*) outward appearance.

cortina *f* drape; **~s** drapes.

cortinaje *m* set of drapes.

corto/ta *adj* short; scanty, small; stupid; bashful; **a la ~a o a la larga** sooner or later.

corvo/va *adj* bent, crooked.

corzo/za *m/f* roe deer, fallow deer.

cosa *f* thing; matter, affair; **¡no hay tal ~!** nothing of the sort!

cosaco *m* Cossack.

cosecha *f* harvest; harvest time; **de su ~** of one's own invention.

cosechar *vt* to harvest, to reap.

coser *vt* to sew; to join.

cosido *m* stitching, sewing.

cosmético/a *adj*, *m* cosmetic.

cosmopolita *adj* cosmopolitan.

cosquillas *fpl* tickling; (*fig*) agitation.

costa *f* cost, price; charge, expense; coast, shore; **a toda ~** at all events.

costado *m* side; (*mil*) flank; side of a ship.

costal *m* sack, large bag.

costalada *f* heavy fall.

costar *vt* to cost; to need.

coste *m* cost, expense.

costear *vt* to pay for.

costera *f* side; slope; coast.

costero/ra *adj* coastal; (*mar*) coasting.

costilla *f* rib; (*fig*) wife; cutlet; **~s** *fpl* back, shoulders *pl*.

costillar *m* human ribs *pl*.

costo *m* cost, price; expense.

costoso/sa *adj* costly, dear, expensive.

costra *f* crust; (*med*) scab.

costumbre *f* custom, habit.

costura *f* sewing; seam; needlework.

costurera *f* seamstress.

costurero *m* sewing box.

cotejar *vt* to compare.

cotejo *m* comparison, collation.

cotidiano/na *adj* daily.

cotilla *m/f* gossip.

cotización *f* quotation.

cotizar *vt* to quote; **~se** *vr*: **~ a** to sell at; to be quoted at.

coto *m* enclosure; reserve; boundary stone.

cotorra *f* magpie; small parrot; (*col*) chatterbox.

covacha *f* small cave, grotto.

coyote *m* coyote.

coyuntura *f* joint, articulation; juncture.

coz *f* kick; recoil (of a gun); ebbing (of a flood); (*fig*) insult.

cráneo *m* skull.

cráter *m* crater.

creación *f* creation.

creador/ra *adj* creative; * *m/f* creator.

crear *vt* to create, to make; to establish.

crecer *vi* to grow, to increase; to rise.

creces *fpl* increase.

crecida *f* swell (of rivers).

crecido/da *adj* full-grown (of a person); large; (*fig*) vain.

creciente *f* crescent (moon); (*mar*) flood tide; * *adj* growing; crescent.

crecimiento *m* increase; growth.

credenciales *fpl* credentials *pl*.

credibilidad *f* credibility.

crédito *m* credit; belief, faith; reputation.

credo *m* creed.

credulidad *f* credulity.

crédulo/la *adj* credulous.

creencia *f* credence, belief.

creer *vt*, *vi* to believe; to think; to consider.

crema *f* cream; custard.

cremallera *f* zipper.

crepúsculo *m* twilight.

crespo/pa *adj* curled; angry, displeased.

crespón *m* crepe.

cresta *f* crest (of birds).

creyente *m/f* believer.

cría *f* breeding; young.

criada *f* servant, maid.

criadero *m* (*bot*) nursery; breeding place.

criadilla *f* testicle; small loaf; truffle.

criado/da *m/f* servant; *adj* reared, brought up, bred.

criador *m* creator; breeder.

crianza *f* breeding, rearing.

criar *vt* to create, to produce; to breed; to nurse; to breast-feed; to bring up, to raise.

criatura *f* creature; child.

criba *f* sieve.

cribar *vt* to sift.

crimen *m* crime.

criminal *adj*, *m/f* criminal.

criminalista *m/f* criminologist; criminal lawyer.

crin *f* mane; horsehair.

crío/a *m/f* (*col*) kid.

criollo/lla *adj*, *m/f* Creole.

cripta *f* crypt.

crisis *f invar* crisis.

crisma *f* holy oil, chrism.

crisol *m* crucible; melting pot.

crispar *vt* to set on edge; to tense up.

cristal *m* crystal; glass; pane; lens.

cristalino/na *adj* crystalline.

cristalización *f* crystallization.

cristalizar *vt* to crystallize.

cristiandad *f* Christianity.

cristianismo *m* Christianity.

cristiano/na *adj, m/f* Christian.

Cristo *m* Christ.

criterio *m* criterion.

crítica *m/f* criticism.

criticar *vt* to criticize.

crítico/ca *m/f* critic; * *adj* critical.

croar *vi* to croak.

cromo *m* chrome.

crónica *f* chronicle; news report; feature.

crónico/ca *adj* chronic.

cronista *m/f* chronicler; reporter, columnist.

cronología *f* chronology.

cronológico/ca *adj* chronological.

cronómetro *m* stopwatch.

cruce *m* crossing; crossroads.

crucero *m* cruiser; cruise; transept; crossing; Southern Cross (constellation).

crucificar *vt* to crucify; to torment.

crucifijo *m* crucifix.

crucigrama *m* crossword.

crudeza *f* unripeness; crudeness; undigested food (in the stomach).

crudo/da *adj* raw; green, unripe; crude; cruel; hard to digest.

cruel *adj* cruel.

crueldad *f* cruelty.

cruento/ta *adj* bloody; cruel.

crujido *m* crack; creak; clash; crackling.

crujiente *adj* crunchy.

crujir *vi* to crackle; to rustle.

crustáceo *m* crustacean.

cruz *f* cross; tails (of a coin).

cruzada *f* crusade.

cruzado *m* crusader; ~/da *adj* crossed.

cruzar *vt* to cross; (*mar*) to cruise ~se *vr* to cross; to pass each other.

cuaderna *f* fourth part; rib.

cuaderno *m* notebook; exercise book; logbook.

cuadra *f* block; stable.

cuadrado/da *adj, m* square.

cuadragenario/ria *adj* forty-year-old.

cuadragésimo/ma *adj, m* fortieth.

cuadrangular *adj* quadrangular, four-cornered; * *m Lat Am* home run.

cuadrángulo *m* quadrangle.

cuadrante *m* quadrant; dial.

cuadrar *vt, vi* to square; to fit, to suit, to correspond.

cuadricular *adj* squared.

cuadrilátero/ra *adj, m* quadrilateral.

cuadrilla *f* party, group; gang, crew.

cuadro *m* square; picture, painting; window frame; scene; chart; (*sport*) team; executive; *Lat Am* slaughterhouse.

cuadrúpedo/da *adj* quadruped.

cuádruple *adj* quadruple.

cuádruplo/pla *adj* quadruple, fourfold.

cuajada *f* curd.

cuajar *vt* to coagulate; to thicken; to adorn; to set; ~se *vr* to coagulate, to curdle; to set; to fill up.

cuál *pn* which (one).

cual *pn* which; who; whom; * *adv* as; like; * *adj* such as.

cualidad *f* quality.

cualquier *adj* any.

cualquiera *adj* anyone, anybody; someone, somebody; whoever; whichever.

cuándo *adv* when; ¿de ~ acá? since when?.

cuando *adv* when; if; even; * *conj* since; de ~ en ~ from time to time; ~ más/mucho at most/at best; ~ menos at least.

cuantía *f* quantity, amount; importance.

cuantioso/sa *adj* numerous; substantial.

cuantitativo/va *adj* quantitative, quantitive.

cuánto *adj* what a lot of; how much?; ¿~s? how many?; * *pn, adv* how; how much; how many.

cuanto/ta *adj* as many as; as much as; all; whatever; * *adv* en ~ as soon as; en ~ a as regards; ~ más moreover, the more as.

cuarenta *adj, m* forty.

cuarentena *f* space of forty days; Lent; quarantine.

cuaresma *f* Lent.

cuarta *f* fourth; span; (*mar*) point (of the compass).

cuartear *vt* to quarter, to divide up; ~se *vr* to split into pieces.

cuartel *m* quarter, district; barracks *pl*.

cuarteta *f* (*poet*) quatrain.

cuartilla *f* fourth part; sheet of paper.

cuarto *m* fourth part; quarter; room, apartment; span; ~s *mpl* cash, money; ~/ta *adj* fourth.

cuarzo *m* quartz.

cuatrero *m* horse thief.

cuatro *adj, m* four.

cuatrocientos/tas *adj* four hundred.

cuba *f* cask; tub; (*fig*) drunkard.

cubeta *f* small cask.

cúbico/ca *adj* cubic.

cubierta *f* cover; deck of a ship; (*auto*) hood; tire; pretext.

cubierto *m* cover; shelter; place at table; meal at a fixed charge; ~s *mpl* cutlery.

cubil *m* lair.

cubilete *m* tumbler; dice box.

cubo *m* cube; bucket.

cubo de la basura *m* ash can, trash can, garbage can.

cubrecama *m* bedspread.

cubrir *vt* to cover; to disguise; to protect; to roof a building; ~se *vr* to become overcast.

cucaña *f* (*col*) soft job; bargain; cinch.

cucaracha *f* cockroach.

cuchara *f* spoon.

cucharada *f* spoonful; ladleful.

cucharadita *f* teaspoonful.

cucharita *f* teaspoon.

cucharón *m* ladle; large spoon.

cuchichear *vi* to whisper.

cuchicheo *m* whispering.

cuchilla *f* large kitchen knife; chopping knife; blade.

cuchillada *f* cut; gash; **~s** *fpl* wrangles, quarrels.
cuchillo *m* knife.
cuchitril *m* pigpen.
cuclillas *adv*: **en ~** squatting.
cuclillo *m* cuckoo; (*fig*) cuckold.
cuco *m* cuckoo; **~/ca** *adj* sharp.
cucurucho *m* paper cornet.
cuello *m* neck; collar.
cuenca *m* bowl, deep valley; hollow; socket of the eye.
cuenco *m* earthenware bowl.
cuenta *f* calculation; account; check (in a restaurant); count, counting; bead; importance.
cuentakilómetros *m invar* odometer.
cuentapropista *m/f Lat Am* self-employed person.
cuentarrevoluciones *m invar* tachometer.
cuentista *m/f* storyteller.
cuento *m* tale, story, narrative.
cuerazo *m Lat Am* lash.
cuerda *f* rope; string; spring.
cuerdo/da *adj* sane; prudent, judicious, canny.
cuerear *vt Lat Am* to lash.
cuerno *m* horn.
cuero *m* hide, skin, leather; *Lat Am* whip.
cuerpo *m* body; cadaver, corpse.
cuervo *m* raven.
cuesta *f* slope, hill; incline; **ir ~ abajo** to go downhill; **~ arriba** uphill.
cuestión *f* question, matter; dispute; quarrel; problem.
cuestionable *adj* questionable, problematic.
cuestionar *vt* to question, to dispute.
cuete *m Lat Am* rocket.
cueva *f* cave; cellar.
cuidado *m* care, worry, concern; charge.
cuidadosamente *adv* observantly.
cuidadoso/sa *adj* careful; anxious.
cuidar *vt* to care for; to mind, to look after.
culata *f* butt, breech (of a gun); hindquarters *pl* (of an animal); rear of a horse.
culebra *f* snake.
culinario/ria *adj* culinary.
culminación *f* culmination.
culo *m* backside, bottom; (*col*) ass.
culpa *f* fault, blame; guilt.
culpabilidad *f* guilt.
culpable *adj* culpable; guilty; * *m/f* culprit.
culpar *vt* to accuse, to blame.
cultivación *f* cultivation, culture.
cultivar *vt* to cultivate.
cultivo *m* cultivation; crop.
culto/ta *adj* cultivated, cultured; refined, civilized; * *m* culture; worship.
cultura *f* culture.
cumbre *f* top, summit.
cumpleaños *m invar* birthday.
cumplido/da *adj* large, plentiful; complete, perfect, courteous; * *m* compliment.
cumplidor/ora *adj* reliable.

cumplimentar *vt* to compliment.
cumplimiento *m* fulfillment; accomplishment; completion.
cumplir *vt* to carry out, to fulfill; to serve (a prison sentence); to carry out (death penalty); to attain, to reach (a certain age); **~se** *vr* to be fulfilled; to expire, to be up.
cúmulo *m* heap, pile.
cuna *f* cradle.
cuña *f* wedge.
cuñado/da *m/f* brother/sister-in-law.
cundir *vi* to spread; to grow, to increase.
cuneta *f* ditch.
cuota *f* quota; fee; *Lat Am* installment.
cupé *m* (*auto*) coupé.
cupo *m* share.
cupón *m* coupon.
cúpula *f* cupola, dome.
cura *m* priest; * *f* cure; treatment.
curable *adj* curable.
curación *f* cure; curing; **primera ~** first aid.
curandero *m* quack (doctor).
curar *vt* to cure; to treat, to dress (a wound); to salt; to dress; to tan.
curativo/va *adj* curative, healing.
curia *f* ecclesiastical court.
curiosear *vt* to glance at; * *vi* to look round.
curiosidad *f* curiosity.
curioso/sa *adj* curious; * *m/f* bystander.
Curita™ *f Lat Am* Band-Aid™.
currante *m/f* (*col*) worker.
currar *vi* (*col*) to work.
currículum *m* curriculum vitae.
cursado/da *adj* skilled; versed.
cursar *vt* to frequent a place; to send, to dispatch; to study.
cursillo *m* short course of lectures (in a university).
cursivo/va *adj* italic (type).
curso *m* course, direction; year (at university); subject.
cursor *m* cursor.
curtidor *m* tanner.
curtidos *mpl* tanned leather.
curtir *vt* to tan leather; **~se** *vr* to become sunburned; to become inured.
curva *f* curve, bend.
curvatura *f* curvature.
curvilíneo/nea *adj* curvilinear.
curvo/va *adj* curved, bent.
cuscurro *m* little crust of bread.
cúspide *f* summit, peak; apex.
custodia *f* custody, safekeeping, care; monstrance.
custodio *m* guard, keeper; watchman.
cutáneo/nea *adj* cutaneous.
cutícula *f* cuticle.
cutis *m* skin.
cutre *adj* (*col*) unpleasant, nasty, mean; of poor quality.
cuyo/ya *pn* whose, of which, of whom.

D

dactilógrafo/fa *m/f* typist.

dádiva *f* gift, present; donation.

dadivoso/sa *adj* generous, open-handed.

dado *m* die; **~s** dice.

daga *f* dagger.

dale *excl* come on!

daltónico/ca *adj* color-blind.

dama *f* lady, gentlewoman; mistress; queen; actress who performs principal parts.

damasco *m* damask (fabric); damson (plum).

damasquino/na *adj* damask.

damnificar *vt* to hurt, to injure, to damage.

danza *f* dance.

danzar *vi* to dance; to meddle.

danzarín *m* fine dancer; meddler.

dañar *vt* to hurt, to injure, to damage.

dañino/na *adj* harmful; noxious; mischievous.

daño *m* harm, damage; prejudice; loss.

dar *vt* to give; to supply, to administer, to afford; to deliver; to bestow; to strike, to beat, to knock; to communicate; **~se** *vr* to conform (to the will of another); to give oneself up; **~se prisa** to hurry.

dardo *m* dart.

datar *vt* to date.

dátil *m* (*bot*) date.

dativo *m* (*gr*) dative.

dato *m* fact.

de *prep* of; from; for; by; on; to; with.

deambular *vi* to stroll.

deán *m* dean.

debajo *adv* under, underneath, below.

debate *m* debate, discussion; contest; altercation.

debatir *vt* to debate, to argue, to discuss.

debe *m* (*com*) debit; **~ y haber** debit and credit.

deber *m* obligation, duty; debt; * *vt* to owe; to be obliged to; * *vi*: **debe (de)** it must, it should.

debidamente *adv* justly, duly; exactly, perfectly.

débil *adj* feeble, weak; sickly; frail.

debilidad *f* dimness; weakness.

debilitar *vt* to debilitate, to weaken.

débito *m* debt; duty.

debutar *vi* to make one's debut.

década *f* decade.

decadencia *f* decay, decline.

decaer *vi* to decay, to molder; to decline, to fade.

decaimiento *m* decay, decline.

decálogo *m* Decalogue.

decano *m* senior; dean.

decantar *vt* to decant.

decapitación *f* decapitation, beheading.

decapitar *vt* to behead.

decena *f* ten.

decencia *f* decency.

decente *adj* decent; honest.

decepción *f* disappointment.

dechado *m*: **~ de virtudes** model of virtue and perfection.

decidir *vt* to decide, to determine.

decimal *adj* decimal.

décimo/ma *adj*, *m* tenth.

decir *vt* to say; to tell; to speak; to name.

decisión *f* decision; determination, resolution; sentence.

decisivo/va *adj* decisive; final.

declamación *f* declamation, discourse, oration.

declamar *vi* to declaim; to harangue.

declaración *f* declaration; explanation, interpretation; (*law*) deposition.

declarar *vt* to declare; to manifest; to expound; to explain; (*law*) to decide; **~se** *vr* to declare one's opinion; * *vi* to testify.

declinación *f* declination, descent; decline.

declinar *vi* to decline; to decay, to degenerate; * *vt* (*gr*) to decline.

declive *m* slope; decline.

decolaje *m* Lat Am take-off.

decolar *vi* Lat Am to take off.

decolorarse *vr* to become discolored.

decomiso *m* confiscation.

decoración *f* decoration.

decorado *m* scenery.

decorar *vt* to decorate, to adorn; to illustrate.

decorativo/va *adj* decorative.

decoro *m* honor, respect; circumspection; honesty; decency.

decoroso/sa *adj* decorous, decent.

decrecer *vi* to decrease.

decrépito/ta *adj* decrepit, worn out with age.

decrepitud *f* decrepitude.

decretar *vt* to decree, to determine.

decreto *m* decree; decision; judicial decree.

dedal *m* thimble; very small drinking glass.

dedicación *f* dedication; consecration.

dedicar *vt* to dedicate, to devote; to consecrate; **~se** *vr* to apply oneself to.

dedicatoria *f* dedication.

dedo *m* finger; toe; small bit; **~ meñique** little finger; **~ pulgar** thumb; **~ índice** index finger; **~ corazón** middle finger; **~ anular** ring finger.

deducción *f* deduction, inference; derivation.

deducir *vt* to deduce, to infer; to allege in pleading; to subtract.

defección *f* defection; apostasy.

defectivo/va *adj* defective.

defecto *m* defect; defectiveness.

defectuoso/sa *adj* defective, imperfect, faulty.

defender *vt* to defend, to protect; to justify, to assert, to maintain; to prohibit, to forbid; to resist, to oppose.

defensa *f* defense, justification, apology; guard, shelter, protection, fence.

defensiva *f* defensive.

defensivo *m* defense, safeguard; **~/va** *adj* defensive.

defensor/ra *m/f* defender, protector; lawyer, defense counsel.

deferente *adj* pliant, docile, yielding.
deferir *vi* to defer; to yield (to another's opinion);
* *vt* to communicate.
deficiencia *f* deficiency.
deficiente *adj* defective.
déficit *m* deficit.
definición *f* definition; decision.
definir *vt* to define, to describe, to explain; to
decide.
definitivo/va *adj* definitive; positive.
deformar *vt* to deform; ~**se** *vr* to become
deformed.
deforme *adj* deformed; ugly.
deformidad *f* deformity; ugliness; gross error.
defraudación *f* fraud; usurpation.
defraudar *vt* to defraud, to cheat; to usurp; to
disturb.
defunción *f* death; funeral.
degeneración *f* degeneration; degeneracy.
degenerar *vi* to degenerate.
degollación *f* beheading.
degollar *vt* to behead; to destroy, to ruin.
degradación *f* degradation.
degradar *vt* to degrade; ~**se** *vr* to degrade/
demean oneself.
degustar *vt* to taste.
dehesa *f* pasture, field.
deidad *f* deity, divinity; goddess.
dejadez *f* slovenliness, neglect.
dejado/da *adj* slovenly, idle, indolent; dejected.
dejar *vt* to leave, to quit; to omit; to let; to permit,
to allow; to leave, to forsake; to bequeath; to
pardon; ~ **de** to stop; to fail to; ~**se** *vr* to
abandon oneself.
dejo *m* accent; aftertaste, tang.
del *adj* of the (contraction of **de** and **el**).
delantal *m* apron.
delante *adv* in front; opposite; ahead; ~ **de** in
front of; before.
delantera *f* front, forepart (of something);
advantage; forward line.
delantero/ra *adj* front; * *m/f* forward.
delatar *vt* to accuse; to denounce.
delator *m* accuser; informer, denouncer.
delegación *f* delegation; substitution.
delegado/da *m/f* delegate; deputy.
delegar *vt* to delegate; to substitute.
deleitar *vt* to delight.
deletrear *vt* to spell; to examine; to conjecture.
delfín *m* dolphin; dauphin.
delgadez *f* thinness.
delgado/da *adj* thin; delicate, fine; light; slender,
lean; acute; ingenious; little, scanty.
deliberación *f* deliberation; resolution.
deliberadamente *adv* deliberately.
deliberar *vi* to consider, to deliberate; * *vt* to
debate; to consult.
delicadeza *f* tenderness, softness; delicacy,
daintiness; subtlety.
delicado/da *adj* delicate, tender; faint; exquisite;
delicious, dainty; slender, subtle.

delicia *f* delight, pleasure.
delicioso/sa *adj* delicious; delightful.
delincuencia *f* delinquency.
delincuente *m* delinquent.
delineante *m/f* draftsman/woman.
delinear *vt* to delineate, to sketch; to describe.
delinquir *vi* to offend.
delirante *adj* delirious.
delirar *vi* to rave; to talk nonsense.
delirio *m* delirium; dotage; nonsense.
delito *m* offense; crime.
demacrado/da *adj* pale and drawn.
demagogia *f* demagogy.
demagogo *m* demagog.
demanda *f* demand, claim; pretension,
complaint; challenge; request.
demandado/da *m/f* defendant.
demandante *m/f* claimant.
demandar *vt* to demand; to ask; to claim; to sue.
demarcación *f* demarcation; boundary line.
demarcar *vt* to mark out (limits).
demás *adj* other; remaining; * *pn* **los/las** ~ the
others, the rest; **estar** ~ to be over and above;
to be useless/superfluous; **por** ~ in vain, to
no purpose.
demasía *f* excess; arduous enterprise; rudeness;
want of respect; abundance, plenty; **en** ~
excessively.
demasiado/da *adj* too; excessive; * *adv* too, too
much.
demencia *f* madness.
demente *adj* mad, insane.
democracia *f* democracy.
demócrata *m/f* democrat.
democrático/ca *adj* democratic.
demoler *vt* to demolish; to destroy.
demolición *f* demolition.
demonio *m* demon.
demora *f* delay; demurrage.
demorar *vt* to delay; ~**se** *vr* to be delayed; * *vi*
to linger.
demostrable *adj* demonstrable.
demostración *f* demonstration; manifestation.
demostrar *vt* to prove, to demonstrate; to
manifest.
demostrativo/va *adj* demonstrative.
denegación *f* denial; refusal.
denegar *vt* to deny; to refuse.
dengue *m* prudery.
denigración *f* defamation; stigma, disgrace.
denigrar *vt* to blacken; to insult.
denominación *f* denomination.
denominar *vt* to name; to designate.
denotar *vt* to denote; to express.
densidad *f* density; obscurity.
denso/sa *adj* dense, thick; compact.
dentado/da *adj* jagged, toothed; perforated (of
stamps).
dentadura *f* set of teeth.
dentellada *f* gnashing of the teeth; nip; pinch
with the teeth; **a** ~**s** snappishly, peevishly.

dentera *f* (*fig*) the shivers *pl*.

dentición *f* dentition, teething.

dentífrico *m* toothpaste.

dentista *m/f* dentist.

dentro *adv* within; * *pn*: ~ **de** in, inside.

denuncia *f* denunciation; accusation; report.

denunciar *vt* to advise; to denounce; to report.

deparar *vt* to offer, to present.

departamento *m* department; (*rail*) compartment; apartment.

dependencia *f* dependency; relation, affinity; dependence; office; business, affair.

depender *vi*: ~ **de** to depend on, to be dependent on.

dependienta *f* saleswoman.

dependiente *m* shop/store assistant; * *adj* dependent.

depilar *vt* to depilate, remove hair from.

depilatorio *m* hair remover.

deplorable *adj* deplorable, lamentable.

deplorar *vt* to deplore.

deponer *vt* to depose; to declare; to displace; to deposit.

deportación *f* deportation.

deportar *vt* to deport.

deporte *m* sport.

deportista *m/f* sportsman/woman.

deportivo/va *adj* sports *compd*.

deposición *f* deposition; assertion, affirmation; (*law*) deposition upon oath.

depositar *vt* to deposit; to confide; to put away for safekeeping.

depósito *m* deposit; warehouse; tank.

depravación *f* depravity.

depravar *vt* to deprave, to corrupt.

depreciar *vt* to depreciate.

depredador/ra *adj* predatory; * *m* predator.

depresión *f* depression.

deprimido/da *adj* depressed.

deprimir *vt* to depress; ~**se** *vr* to become depressed.

deprisa *adv* quickly.

depuración *f* purification.

depuradora *f* purifier.

depurar *vt* to cleanse; to purify; to filter.

de quitapón *adj* detachable, removable.

derecha *f* right hand, right side; right.

derecho/cha *adj* right; straight; just; perfect; certain; * *m* right, justice; law; tax, duty; fee; * *adv* straight.

derivación *f* derivation; source; origin.

derivado/da *adj* derivative; * *m* derivative; by-product.

derivar *vt*, *vi* to derive; (*mar*) to drift.

dermatología *f* dermatology.

dermatólogo/ga *m/f* dermatologist.

derogar *vt* to derogate, to abolish; to reform.

derogatorio/ria *adj* derogatory.

derramamiento *m* effusion; waste; dispersion; ~ **de sangre** bloodshed.

derramar *vt* to drain off (water); to spread; to

spill, to scatter; to waste, to shed; ~**se** *vr* to pour out.

derrame *m* spelling; overflow; discharge; leakage.

derredor *m* circumference, circuit; **al/en** ~ around, about.

derrengado/da *adj* bent, crooked.

derrengar *vt* to sprain.

derretir *vt* to melt; to consume; to thaw; ~**se** *vr* to melt.

derribar *vt* to demolish; to flatten.

derribo *m* demolition; ruins of a demolished building *pl*.

derrocar *vt* to pull down, to demolish.

derrochador *m* spendthrift.

derrochar *vt* to dissipate; to squander.

derroche *m* waste.

derrota *f* ship's course; road, path; defeat.

derrotar *vt* to destroy; to defeat.

derrotero *m* collection of sea charts; ship's course; (*fig*) course, way.

derruir *vt* to demolish.

derrumbar *vt* to throw down; ~**se** *vr* to collapse.

desabastecer *vt* to cut off supplies from.

desabillé *m* deshabille/dishabille.

desabollar *vt* to take the bulges out of.

desabotonar *vt* to unbutton; ~**se** *vr* to come undone.

desabrido/da *adj* tasteless, insipid; rude; unpleasant.

desabrigado/da *adj* uncovered; unsheltered.

desabrigar *vt* to uncover; to deprive of clothes/shelter.

desabrochar *vt* to undo; ~**se** *vr* to come undone.

desacatar *vt* to treat in a disrespectful manner.

desacato *m* disrespect, incivility.

desacertado/da *adj* mistaken; unwise; inconsiderate.

desacierto *m* error, gross mistake, blunder.

desaconsejado/da *adj* inconsiderate; ill-advised.

desaconsejar *vt* to advise against.

desacorde *adj* discordant.

desacostumbrado/da *adj* unusual.

desacreditar *vt* to discredit.

desacuerdo *m* blunder; disagreement; forgetfulness.

desafiar *vt* to challenge; to defy.

desafilado/da *adj* blunt.

desafinado/da *adj* out of tune.

desafinar *vi* to be out of tune.

desafío *m* challenge; struggle; contest, combat.

desaforado/da *adj* huge; disorderly, lawless; impudent.

desafortunadamente *adv* unfortunately.

desafortunado/da *adj* unfortunate, unlucky.

desafuero *m* outrage; excess.

desagradable *adj* disagreeable, unpleasant.

desagradar *vt* to displease; to pester.

desagradecido/da *adj* ungrateful.

desagradecimiento *m* ingratitude.

desagrado *m* harshness; displeasure.

desagraviar *vt* to make amends for.

desagravio *m* amends *pl*; satisfaction.

desaguar *vt* to drain; * *vi* to drain off.

desagüe *m* channel, drain; drainpipe; drainage.

desaguisado *m* outrage.

desahogado/da *adj* comfortable; roomy.

desahogar *vt* to ease; to vent; ~**se** *vr* to recover; to relax; to let off steam.

desahogo *m* ease, relief; freedom.

desahuciar *vt* to cause to despair; to give up; to evict.

desahucio *m* eviction.

desairado/da *adj* disregarded; slighted.

desairar *vt* to disregard, to take no notice of.

desaire *m* disdain, disrespect; unattractiveness.

desajustar *vt* to make uneven; to unbalance; ~**se** *vr* to get out of order.

desajuste *m* disorder; imbalance.

desalentador/ra *adj* disheartening.

desalentar *vt* to make breathless; to discourage.

desaliento *m* dismay.

desaliño *m* slovenliness; carelessness.

desalinizadora *f* desalination plant.

desalinizar *vt* to desalinate.

desalmado/da *adj* cruel, inhuman.

desalojar *vt* to eject; to move out; * *vi* to move out.

desamarrar *vt* to cast off (a ship); to untie; to remove.

desamor *m* indifference.

desamparado/da *adj* helpless.

desamparar *vt* to forsake, to abandon; to relinquish.

desamparo *m* abandonment; helplessness; dereliction.

desamueblar *vt* to remove the furniture from.

desandar *vt* to retrace; to go back the same road.

desangrar *vt* to bleed; to drain (a pond); (*fig*) to exhaust (one's means); ~**se** *vr* to lose a lot of blood.

desanimado/da *adj* downhearted.

desanimar *vt* to discourage; ~**se** *vr* to lose heart.

desapacible *adj* disagreeable; unpleasant, harsh.

desaparecer *vi* to disappear.

desaparecido/da *adj* missing; * *mpl* ~**s** missing people.

desaparejar *vt* to unharness, unhitch (beasts); (*mar*) to unrig (a ship).

desaparición *f* disappearance.

desapego *m* coolness; lack of interest.

desapercibido/da *adj* unnoticed.

desaplicado/da *adj* lazy; careless, neglectful.

desapolillar *vt* to free from moths; ~**se** *vr* (*fig*) to get rid of the cobwebs.

desaprensivo/va *adj* unscrupulous.

desaprobación *f* disapproval.

desaprobar *vt* to disapprove; to condemn; to reject.

desaprovechado/da *adj* useless; unprofitable; backward; slack.

desaprovechar *vt* to waste, to turn to a bad use.

desarmar *vt* to disarm; to disband (troops); to dismantle; (*fig*) to -pacify.

desarme *m* disarmament.

desarraigar *vt* to uproot; to root out; to extirpate.

desarraigo *m* eradication.

desarrapado/da *adj* ragged.

desarreglado/da *adj* untidy.

desarreglar *vt* to disorder, to upset.

desarreglo *m* disorder; untidiness.

desarrollar *vt* to develop; to unroll; to unfold; ~**se** *vr* to develop; to be unfolded; to open.

desarrollo *m* development.

desarropar *vt* to undress.

desarticular *vt* to take apart.

desasir *vt* to loosen, to disentangle; ~**se** *vr* to extricate oneself.

desasosegar *vt* to disquiet, to disturb.

desasosiego *m* restlessness; anxiety.

desastrado/da *adj* wretched, miserable; ragged.

desastre *m* disaster; misfortune.

desastroso/sa *adj* disastrous.

desatado/da *adj* untied; wild.

desatar *vt* to untie; to loose; to separate; to solve; ~**se** *vr* to come undone; to break.

desatascar *vt* to unblock; to clear.

desatender *vt* to pay no attention to; to disregard.

desatinado/da *adj* foolish; extravagant; * *m* fool, madman.

desatinar *vi* to talk nonsense; to reel, to stagger.

desatino *m* blunder; nonsense.

desatornillar *vt* to unscrew.

desatrancar *vt* to unbar; to unblock.

desautorizado/da *adj* unauthorized.

desautorizar *vt* to deprive of authority; to deny.

desavenencia *f* discord, disagreement.

desavenido/da *adj* contrary, disagreeing.

desaventajado/da *adj* disadvantageous, unprofitable.

desayunar *vt* to have for breakfast; ~**se** *vr* to breakfast; * *vi* to have breakfast;

desayuno *m* breakfast.

desazón *f* disgust; uneasiness; annoyance.

desazonado/da *adj* ill-adapted; ill-humored.

desazonar *vt* to annoy; ~**se** *vr* to be annoyed; to be anxious.

desbancar *vt* to break (the bank in gambling); (*fig*) to supplant.

desbandarse *vr* to disband; to go off in all directions.

desbarajuste *m* confusion.

desbaratar *vt* to destroy.

desbarrar *vi* to talk rubbish.

desbastar *vt* to smooth; to polish; to waste.

desbloquear *vt* to unblock.

desbocado/da *adj* open-mouthed; wild (of a horse); foul-mouthed; indecent.

desbocarse *vr* to bolt (of a horse).

desbordar vt to exceed; **~se** vr to overflow.

descabalgar vi to dismount.

descabellado/da adj disheveled; disorderly; wild, unrestrained; disproportional; violent.

descabellar vt to ruffle.

descafeinado/da adj decaffeinated.

descalabrado/da adj wounded on the head; imprudent.

descalabrar vt to wound on the head; to smash.

descalabro m blow; misfortune; considerable loss.

descalificar vt to disqualify; to discredit.

descalzar vt, **~se** vr to take off one's shoes.

descalzo/za adj barefooted; (fig) destitute.

descambiar vt to exchange.

descaminado/da adj (fig) misguided.

descaminar vt to misguide, to lead astray.

descamisado/da adj shirtless.

descampado/da adj disengaged; free; open; * m open space, open country.

descansado/da adj rested, refreshed; quiet.

descansar vt to rest; * vi to rest; to lie down.

descansillo m landing.

descanso m rest, repose; break; interval.

descapotable m convertible.

descarado/da adj cheeky, barefaced.

descararse vr to behave insolently.

descarga f unloading; volley, discharge.

descargar vt to unload, to discharge; **~se** vr to unburden oneself.

descargo m discharge; evidence; receipt.

descarnado/da adj scrawny.

descarnar vt to strip the flesh from; to clean away the flesh from; to corrode; **~se** vr to grow thin.

descaro m nerve.

descarriar vt to lead astray; to misdirect; **~se** vr to lose one's way; to stray; to err.

descarrilamiento m (rail) derailment.

descarrilar vi (rail) to leave/run off the rails.

descarrío m losing of one's way.

descartar vt to discard; to dismiss; to rule out; **~se** vr to excuse oneself.

descascarillado/da adj peeling.

descastado adj degenerate; ungrateful.

descendencia f descent; offspring.

descendente adj descending; **tren ~** m (rail) down train.

descender vt to take down; * vi to descend, to walk down; to flow; to fall; **~ de** to be derived from.

descendiente adj descending; * m/f descendant.

descenso m descent; drop; relegation.

descerrajar vt to force the lock (of a door etc); to discharge firearms.

descifrar vt to decipher; to unravel.

desclavar vt to draw out nails (from).

descocado/da adj bold, impudent.

descodificador m decoder (for TV).

descolgar vt to take down; to pick up; **~se** vr to let oneself down.

descollar vi to excel.

descolorido/da adj pale, colorless.

descomedido/da adj impudent, insolent; huge.

descompaginar vt to disarrange.

descomponer vt to discompose, to set at odds; to disconcert; (chem) to decompose.

descomposición f disagreement; discomposure; decomposition.

descompuesto/ta adj decomposed; broken.

descomunal adj uncommon; huge.

desconcertado/da adj disconcerted; bewildered.

desconcertar vt to disturb; to confound; to disconcert; **~se** vr to be bewildered; to be upset.

desconchado/da adj peeling.

desconchar vt to peel off.

desconcierto m disorder, confusion; uncertainty.

desconectar vt to disconnect.

desconfiado/da adj mistrustful, distrustful.

desconfianza f distrust; jealousy.

desconfiar vi: **~ de** to mistrust, to suspect.

descongelar vt to defrost.

descongestionar vt to clear.

desconocer vt to disown, to disavow; to be totally ignorant of (a thing); not to know (a person); not to acknowledge (a favor received).

desconocido/da adj unknown; disguised; * m/f stranger.

desconocimiento m ignorance.

desconsiderado/da adj inconsiderate; imprudent.

desconsolado/da adj disconsolate; painful; sad.

desconsolar vt to distress.

desconsuelo m distress; trouble; despair.

descontado adj: **por ~** of course; **dar por ~** to take for granted.

descontar vt to discount; to deduct.

descontento m dissatisfaction; disgust.

descorazonar vt to dishearten, to discourage.

descorchar vt to uncork.

descorrer vt to draw.

descortés/esa adj impolite, rude.

descortesía f rudeness.

descoser vt to undo, take apart; to separate; **~se** vr to come apart at the seams.

descosido/da adj unstitched; disjointed.

descoyuntar vt to dislocate; to vex, to annoy.

descrédito m discredit.

descreído/da adj incredulous.

descremado/da adj skimmed.

describir vt to describe; to draw, to delineate.

descripción f description; delineation; inventory.

descriptivo/va adj descriptive.

descuartizar vt to quarter; to carve.

descubierto m deficit; overdraft; **~/ta** adj uncovered.

descubrimiento m discovery; revelation.

descubrir vt to discover, to disclose; to uncover; to reveal; to show; **~se** vr to reveal oneself; to take off one's hat; to confess.

descuento *m* discount; decrease.

descuida *excl* don't worry!

descuidado/da *adj* careless, negligent.

descuidar *vt* to neglect; * *vi*, **~se** *vr* to be careless.

descuido *m* carelessness, negligence; forgetfulness; incivility; improper action.

desde *prep* since; after; from; **~ luego** of course; **~ entonces** since then.

desdecirse *vr* to retract one's words.

desdén *m* disdain, scorn.

desdentado/da *adj* toothless.

desdentar *vt* to draw out (teeth).

desdeñable *adj* contemptible, despicable.

desdeñar *vt* to disdain, to scorn; **~se** *vr* to be disdainful.

desdeñoso/sa *adj* disdainful; contemptuous.

desdicha *f* misfortune, calamity; great poverty.

desdichado/da *adj* unfortunate; wretched, miserable.

desdoblar *vt* to unfold, to spread open.

desear *vt* to desire, to wish; to require, to demand.

desecación *f* desiccation.

desecar *vt* to dry up.

desechar *vt* to depreciate; to reject; to refuse; to throw away.

desecho *m* residue; **~s** *mpl* rubbish.

desembalar *vt* to unpack.

desembarazado/da *adj* free.

desembarazar *vt* to free; to clear; **~se** *vr*: **~ de** to get rid of.

desembarcadero *m* landing stage.

desembarcar *vt* to unload, to disembark; * *vi* to disembark, to land; *Lat Am* to get off.

desembarco *m* landing.

desembargo *m* (*law*) raising an embargo.

desembarque *m* landing.

desembocadura *f* mouth.

desembocar *vi*: **~ en** to flow into.

desembolsar *vt* to pay out.

desembolso *m* expenditure.

desembragar *vi* to declutch.

desembuchar *vt* to disgorge; to tell all.

desempaquetar *vt* to unpack.

desempatar *vi* (*sport*) to hold a play-off.

desempate *m* play-off.

desempeñar *vt* to redeem; to extricate from debt; to fulfill (any duty/promise); to acquit; **~se** *vr* to get out of debt.

desempeño *m* redeeming a pledge; occupation.

desempleado/da *adj* unemployed; * *m/f* unemployed person.

desempleo *m* unemployment.

desempolvorar *vt* to dust.

desencadenar *vt* to unchain; **~se** *vr* to break loose; to burst.

desencajar *vt* to disjoint; to dislocate; to disconnect.

desencallar *vt* to refloat.

desencanto *m* disenchantment.

desenchufar *vt* to unplug.

desenfadado/da *adj* free; unembarrassed.

desenfado *m* ease; facility; calmness, relaxation.

desenfocado/da *adj* out of focus.

desenfrenado/da *adj* outrageous; ungovernable.

desenfreno *m* wildness; lack of self-control.

desenganchar *vt* to unhook; to uncouple.

desengañado/da *adj* disillusioned.

desengañar *vt* to disillusion; **~se** *vr* to become disillusioned.

desengaño *m* disillusionment; disappointment.

desengrasar *vt* to take the grease off.

desenhebrar *vt* to unthread; to unravel.

desenlace *m* climax; outcome.

desenmarañar *vt* to disentangle; to unravel.

desenmascarar *vt* to unmask.

desenredar *vt* to disentangle.

desenrollar *vt* to unroll.

desenroscar *vt* to untwist; to unroll.

desentenderse *vr* to pretend not to understand; to pass by without noticing.

desenterrar *vt* to exhume; to dig up.

desentonar *vi* to be out of tune; to clash.

desentrañar *vt* to unravel.

desentumecer *vt* to stretch; to loosen up.

desenvainar *vt* to unsheathe; to show.

desenvoltura *f* sprightliness; cheerfulness; impudence, boldness.

desenvolver *vt* to unfold; to unroll; to decipher, to unravel; to develop; **~se** *vr* to develop; to cope.

desenvuelto/ta *adj* forward; natural.

deseo *m* desire, wish.

deseoso/sa *adj* anxious.

desequilibrado/da *adj* unbalanced.

deserción *f* desertion; defection.

desertar *vt* to desert; to abandon (a cause).

desertificación *f* desertification.

desertor *m* deserter; fugitive.

desesperación *f* despair, desperation; anger, fury.

desesperado/da *adj* desperate, hopeless.

desesperar *vi*, **~se** *vr* to despair; * *vt* to make desperate.

desestabilizar *vt* to destabilize.

desestatizar *vt Lat Am* to privatize.

desestatización *f Lat Am* privatization.

desestimar *vt* to disregard, to reject.

desfachatez *f* impudence.

desfalcar *vt* to embezzle.

desfalco *m* embezzlement.

desfallecer *vi* to get weak; to faint.

desfallecimiento *m* fainting.

desfasado/da *adj* old-fashioned.

desfase *m* gap.

desfavorable *adj* unfavorable.

desfigurar *vt* to disfigure, to deform; to disguise.

desfiladero *m* gorge.

desfilar *vi* (*mil*) to parade.

desfogarse *vr* to give vent to one's passion/anger.

desforestación *f* deforestation.

desgajar vt to tear off; to break in pieces; ~se vr to be separated; to be torn to pieces.

desgana f disgust; loss of appetite; aversion, reluctance.

desganado/da adj not hungry; half-hearted; **estar** ~ to lose all pleasure in doing a thing; to lose one's appetite.

desgano m Lat Am disgust; loss of appetite; aversion, reluctance.

desgañitarse vr to scream, to bawl.

desgarrador/a adj heartrending.

desgarrar vt to tear; to shatter.

desgarro m tear; grief; impudence.

desgarrón m large tear.

desgastar vt to waste; to corrode; ~se vr to get worn out.

desgaste m wear (and tear).

desglosar vt to break down.

desgracia f misfortune; disgrace; -accident setback.

desgraciado/da adj unfortunate; unhappy, miserable; out of favor; disagreeable.

desgreñado/da adj disheveled.

desgreñar vt to dishevel (the hair); to disorder.

desguarnecer vt to strip down; to dismantle.

deshabitado/da adj deserted, uninhabited; desolate.

deshacer vt to undo, to destroy; to cancel, to efface; to rout (an army); to solve; to melt; to break up, to divide; to dissolve in a liquid; to violate (a treaty); to diminish; to disband (troops); ~se vr to melt; to come apart.

desharrapado/da adj shabby; ragged, in tatters.

deshecho/cha adj undone, destroyed; wasted; melted; in pieces; * m Lat Am short cut.

deshelar vt to thaw; ~se vr to thaw, to melt.

desheredar vt to disinherit.

deshidratado/da adj dehydrated.

deshidratar vt to dehydrate.

deshielo m thaw.

deshilachar vt to unravel.

deshilar vt to fray.

deshinchar vt to deflate; ~se vr to go flat, to go down.

deshojar vt to strip the leaves off.

deshollinador m chimney sweep.

deshonesto/ta adj indecent.

deshonra f dishonor; shame.

deshonrar vt to affront, to insult, to defame; to dishonor.

deshonroso/sa adj dishonorable, indecent.

deshora f unseasonable time.

deshuesar vt to get rid of bones; to stone.

desidia f idleness, indolence.

desierto/ta adj deserted; solitary; * m desert; wilderness.

designación f designation.

designar vt to design; to intend; to appoint; to express, to name.

designio m design, purpose; road, course.

desigual adj unequal, unlike; uneven, craggy.

desigualdad f inequality, dissimilitude; inconstancy; roughness, unevenness.

desilusión f disappointment.

desilusionar vt to disappoint; ~se vr to become disillusioned.

desinfección f disinfection.

desinfectar vt to disinfect.

desinflar vt to deflate.

desintegración f disintegration.

desinterés m unselfishness; disinterestedness.

desinteresado/da adj disinterested; unselfish.

desistir vi to desist, to cease.

deslave m Lat Am landslide.

desleal adj disloyal; unfair.

deslealtad f disloyalty, breach of faith.

desleír vt to dilute; to dissolve.

deslenguado/da adj foul-mouthed.

desligar vt to separate; to loosen, to unbind; ~se vr to extricate oneself.

desliz m slip, sliding; lapse, weakness.

deslizadizo/za adj slippery, slippy; glib.

deslizar vt to slip, to slide; to let slip (a comment); ~se vr to slip; to skid; to flow softly; to creep in.

deslucido/da adj tarnished; dull; shabby.

deslucir vt to tarnish; to damage; to discredit.

deslumbramiento m glare; confusion.

deslumbrar vt to dazzle; to puzzle.

desmán m outrage; disaster; misconduct.

desmandarse vr to behave badly.

desmantelar vt to dismantle; to abandon, to forsake.

desmaquillador m make-up remover.

desmarañar vt to disentangle.

desmayado/da adj unconscious; dismayed; appalled; weak.

desmayar vi to be dispirited; to be faint-hearted; ~se vr to faint.

desmayo m unconsciousness; faint, swoon; dismay.

desmedido/da adj disproportionate.

desmejorar vt to impair; to weaken.

desmembrar vt to dismember; to separate.

desmemoriado/da adj forgetful.

desmentir vt to give the lie to; ~se vr to contradict oneself.

desmenuzar vt to crumble; to chip at; to fritter away; to examine minutely.

desmerecer vt to be unworthy of; * vi to deteriorate.

desmesurado/da adj excessive; huge; immeasurable.

desmontar vt to level; to remove (a heap of rubbish); to dismantle; * vi to dismount.

desmoralización f demoralization.

desmoralizar vt to demoralize.

desmoronar vt to destroy little by little; ~se vr to fall into disrepair.

desnatado/da adj skimmed.

desnatar vt to skim (milk); to take the choicest part of.

desnaturalizar *vt* to divest of naturalization rights; **~se** *vr* to forsake one's country.

desnivel *m* unevenness of the ground.

desnucar *vt* to break (one's neck).

desnudar *vt* to undress; to strip; to discover, to reveal; **~se** *vr* to undress.

desnudez *f* nakedness.

desnudo/da *adj* naked; bare, uncovered; ill-clothed; (*fig*) plain, evident.

desnutrición *f* malnutrition.

desnutrido/da *adj* undernourished.

desobedecer *vt, vi* to disobey.

desobediencia *f* disobedience; insubordination.

desobediente *adj* disobedient.

desocupado/da *adj* empty; at leisure.

desocupar *vt* to vacate; to empty; **~se** *vr* to retire from a business; to withdraw from an arrangement.

desodorante *m* deodorant.

desolación *f* destruction; affliction.

desolado/da *adj* desolate, disconsolate.

desolar *vt* to lay waste; to harass.

desollar *vt* to flay, to skin; (*fig*) to extort.

desorden *m* disorder, confusion.

desordenado/da *adj* disorderly; untidy.

desordenar *vt* to disorder; to untidy; **~se** *vr* to get out of order.

desorganización *f* disorganization.

desorganizar *vt* to disorganize.

desorientar *vt* to mislead; to confuse; **~se** *vr* to lose one's way.

desovar *vi* to spawn.

despabilado/da *adj* watchful, vigilant; wide-awake.

despabilar *vt* to snuff (a candle); (*fig*) to dispatch quickly; to sharpen; **~se** *vr* to wake up.

despacio *adv* slowly, leisurely; little by little; *Lat Am* quietly; **i~!** softly!, gently!

despachar *vt* to dispatch; to expedite; to sell; to send.

despacho *m* dispatch, expedition; cabinet; office; commission; warrant, patent; expedient; smart answer.

despachurrar *vt* to squash, to crush; to mangle.

desparejar *vt* to make unequal/uneven.

desparpajo *m* ease; savoir-faire.

desparramar *vt* to disseminate; to spread; to spill; to squander, to lavish; **~se** *vr* to be dissipated.

despavorido *adj* frightened.

despectivo/va *adj* pejorative, derogatory.

despecho *m* indignation; displeasure; spite; dismay, despair; deceit; derision, scorn; **a ~ de** in spite of.

despedazar *vt* to tear into pieces; to mangle.

despedida *f* farewell; sacking.

despedir *vt* to discharge; to dismiss (from office); to see off; **~se** *vr*: **~ de** to say goodbye to.

despegado/da *adj* cold; detached.

despegar *vt* to unglue; to take off; **~se** *vr* to come loose.

despego *m* detachment; coolness.

despegue *m* take-off.

despeinado/da *adj* disheveled.

despeinar *vt* to ruffle.

despejado/da *adj* sprightly, quick; clear.

despejar *vt* to clear away; **~se** *vr* to cheer up; to clear; * *vi* to clear.

despellejar *vt* to skin.

despensa *f* pantry, larder; provisions *pl*.

despeñadero *m* precipice.

despeñar *vt* to precipitate; **~se** *vr* to throw oneself headlong.

despepitarse *vr* to bawl.

desperdiciar *vt* to squander.

desperdicio *m* waste; **~s** *mpl* rubbish; waste.

desperdigar *vt* to separate; to scatter.

desperezarse *vr* to stretch oneself.

desperfecto *m* slight damage; flaw.

despertador *m* alarm clock.

despertar *vt* to wake up, to rouse from sleep; to excite; * *vi* to wake up; to grow lively/sprightly; **~se** *vr* to wake up.

despiadado/da *adj* heartless; merciless.

despido *m* dismissal.

despierto/ta *adj* awake; vigilant; fierce; brisk, sprightly.

despilfarrar *vt* to waste.

despilfarro *m* slovenliness; waste; mismanagement.

despintar *vt* to deface (a painting); to obscure (things); to mislead; **~se** to lose its color.

despistar *vt* to mislead; to throw off the track; **~se** *vr* to take the wrong way; to become confused.

desplante *m* bold statement; wrong stance; insolence.

desplazamiento *m* displacement.

desplazar *vt* to move; to scroll; **~se** *vr* to travel.

desplegar *vt* to unfold, to display; to explain, to elucidate; (*mar*) to unfurl; **~se** *vr* to open out; to travel.

despliegue *m* display.

desplomarse *vr* to fall to the ground; to collapse.

desplumar *vt* to fleece; to pluck.

despoblado/da *adj* desert.

despoblar *vt* to depopulate; to desolate; **~se** *vr* to become depopulated.

despojar *vt*: **~ (de)** to strip (of); to deprive (of); **~se** *vr* to undress.

despojo *m* plunder; loot; **~s** *mpl* giblets *pl*; remains *pl*; offal.

desposado/da *adj* newlywed.

desposar *vt* to marry, to betroth; **~se** *vr* to be betrothed/married.

desposeer *vt* to dispossess.

desposeimiento *m* dispossession.

déspota *m* despot.

despótico/ca *adj* despotic.

despotismo *m* despotism.

despreciable *adj* contemptible, despicable.

despreciar *vt* to offend; to despise.

desprecio *m* scorn, contempt.

desprender *vt* to unfasten, to loosen; to separate; **~se** *vr* to give way; to fall down; to extricate oneself.

desprendimiento *m* alienation, disinterestedness.

despreocupado/da *adj* careless; unworried.

despreocuparse *vr* to be carefree.

desprestigiar *vt* to run down.

desprevenido/da *adj* unawares, unprepared.

desproporción *f* disproportion.

desproporcionado/da *adj* disproportionate.

desproporcionar *vt* to disproportion.

despropósito *m* absurdity.

desprovisto/ta *adj* unprovided.

después *adv* after, afterwards; next.

despuntar *vt* to blunt; * *vi* to sprout; to dawn; **al ~ del día** at break of day.

desquiciar *vt* to upset; to discompose; to disorder.

desquitar *vt* to retrieve (a loss); **~se** *vr* to win one's money back again; to return by giving like for like; to take revenge.

desquite *m* recovery of a loss; revenge, retaliation.

desrizar *vt* to uncurl.

destacamento *m* (*mil*) detachment; **~ de policía** *Lat Am* police station.

destacar *vt* to emphasize; (*mil*) to detach (a body of troops); **~se** *vr* to stand out.

destajo *m* piecework; **trabajar a ~** to do piecework.

destapar *vt* to uncover; to open; **~se** *vr* to be uncovered.

destartalado/da *adj* untidy.

destello *m* signal light; sparkle.

destemplado/da *adj* out of tune; badly blended (of paint); intemperate.

desteñir *vt* to discolor; **~se** *vr* to fade.

desternillarse *vr:* **~ de risa** to roar with laughter.

desterrar *vt* to banish; to expel, to drive away.

destetar *vt* to wean.

destete *m* weaning.

destierro *m* exile, banishment.

destilación *f* distillation.

destilar *vt, vi* to distill.

destinar *vt* to assign to; to destine for, to intend for.

destinatario/a *m/f* addressee.

destino *m* destiny; fate, doom; destination; office.

destitución *f* destitution, abandonment.

destituir *vt* to dismiss.

destornillador *m* screwdriver.

destornillar *vt* to unscrew.

destreza *f* dexterity, cleverness, cunning, expertness, skill.

destripar *vt* to disembowel; to trample.

destronar *vt* to dethrone.

destrozar *vt* to destroy, to break into pieces; (*mil*) to defeat.

destrozo *m* destruction; (*mil*) defeat, massacre.

destrucción *f* destruction, ruin.

destructivo/va *adj* destructive.

destruir *vt* to destroy.

desunir *vt* to separate, to disunite; to cause discord between.

desuso *m* disuse.

desvaído/da *adj* tall and graceless.

desvalido/da *adj* helpless; destitute.

desvalijar *vt* to rob; to burgle.

desván *m* garret.

desvanecer *vt* to dispel; **~se** *vr* to grow vapid, to become insipid; to vanish; to be affected with giddiness; to faint.

desvanecimiento *m* pride, haughtiness; giddiness; fainting fit.

desvariar *vi* to be delirious.

desvarío *m* delirium; giddiness; inconstancy, caprice; extravagance.

desvelar *vt* to keep awake; **~se** *vr* to stay awake.

desvelo *m* want of sleep; watchfulness.

desvencijado/da *adj* broken-down, rickety.

desvencijar *vt* to disunite; to divide; to weaken; **~se** *vr* to be ruptured; to come apart.

desventaja *f* disadvantage; damage.

desventura *f* misfortune; calamity.

desventurado/da *adj* unfortunate; calamitous.

desvergonzado/da *adj* impudent, shameless.

desvergonzarse *vr* to behave in an impudent manner.

desvergüenza *f* impudence; shamelessness.

desvestir *vt*, **~se** *vr* to undress.

desviar *vt* to divert; to dissuade; to parry (at fencing); **~se** *vr* to go off course.

desvío *m* turning away, going astray; aversion; disdain; indifference.

desvivirse *vr:* **~ por** to long for.

detallar *vt* to detail, to relate minutely.

detalle *m* detail.

detallista *m* retailer.

detención *f* detention; delay.

detener *vt* to stop, to detain; to arrest; to keep back; to reserve; to withhold; **~se** *vr* to stop; to stay.

detenidamente *adv* carefully.

detenido/da *adj* detailed; sparing, niggardly; slow, inactive.

detergente *m* detergent.

deterioración *f* deterioration; damage.

deteriorar *vt* to damage.

deterioro *m* deterioration.

determinación *f* determination, resolution; boldness.

determinado/da *adj* determined; resolute.

determinar *vt* to determine; **~se** *vr* to decide.

detestable *adj* detestable.

detestar *vt* to detest, to abhor.

detonación *f* detonation.

detonar *vi* to detonate.

detractar *vt* to denigrate, to defame, to slander.

detrás *adv* behind; at the back, in the back.

detrimento *m* detriment; damage; loss.

deuda *f* debt; fault; offense.

deudor/ra *m/f* debtor.

devaluación *f* devaluation.

devanar *vt* to reel; to wrap up.

devastación *f* devastation, desolation.

devastador/ra *adj* devastating.

devastar *vt* to devastate.

devengar *vt* to accrue.

devoción *f* devotion, piety; strong affection; ardent love.

devolución *f* return; (*law*) devolution.

devolutivo/va *adj* (*law*) transferable.

devolver *vt* to return; to send back; to refund; to throw up; * *vi* to be sick.

devorar *vt* to devour, to swallow up.

devoto/ta *adj* devout, pious; devotional; strongly attached.

día *m* day.

diablo *m* devil.

diablura *f* prank.

diabólico/ca *adj* diabolical; devilish.

diácono *m* deacon.

diadema *m/f* diadem; halo.

diafragma *m* diaphragm; midriff.

diagnosis *f invar* diagnosis.

diagnóstico *m* diagnosis.

diagonal *adj* diagonal.

diagrama *m* diagram.

dialecto *m* dialect.

diálisis *f invar* dialysis.

diálogo *m* dialog.

diamante *m* diamond.

diámetro *m* diameter.

diana *f* (*mil*) reveille; bull's-eye.

diapasón *m* (*mus*) diapason, octave.

diapositiva *f* transparency, slide.

diario *m* journal, diary; daily newspaper; daily expenses *pl*; ~/ria *adj* daily.

diarrea *f* diarrhea.

dibujar *vt* to draw, to design.

dibujo *m* drawing; sketch, draft; description.

dicción *f* diction; style; expression.

diccionario *m* dictionary.

diciembre *m* December.

dictado *m* dictation.

dictador *m* dictator.

dictadura *f* dictatorship.

dictamen *m* opinion, notion, suggestion, insinuation; judgement.

dictar *vt* to dictate; *Lat Am* to teach.

dicha *f* happiness, good fortune; **por ~** by chance.

dicho *m* saying; sentence; declaration; promise of marriage; ~/cha *adj* said.

dichoso/sa *adj* happy, prosperous.

diecinueve *adj, m* nineteen.

dieciocho *adj, m* eighteen.

dieciséis *adj, m* sixteen.

diecisiete *adj, m* seventeen.

diente *m* tooth; fang; tusk.

diestro/tra *adj* right; dexterous, skillful, clever; sagacious, prudent; sly, cunning; * *m* skillful fencer; halter; bridle.

diesel, diésel *adj* diesel *compd*.

dieta *f* diet, regimen; diet, assembly.

dietista *m/f Lat Am* dietician.

diez *adj, m* ten.

diezmar *vt* to decimate.

diezmo *m* tithe.

difamación *f* defamation.

difamar *vt* to defame, to libel.

difamatorio/ria *adj* defamatory, calumnious.

diferencia *f* difference.

diferencial *adj* differential.

diferenciar *vt* to differentiate, to distinguish; ~se *vr* to differ, to distinguish oneself.

diferente *adj* different, unlike.

diferido/da *adj* recorded.

diferir *vt* to defer, to put off; to differ.

difícil *adj* difficult.

dificultad *f* difficulty.

dificultar *vt* to put difficulties in the way of; to render difficult.

dificultoso/sa *adj* difficult; painful.

difundir *vt* to diffuse, to spread; to divulge; ~se *vr* to spread (out).

difunto/ta *adj* dead, deceased; late.

difusión *f* diffusion.

difuso/sa *adj* diffusive, copious; large; long-winded; circumstantial.

digerir *vt* to digest; to bear with patience; to adjust, to arrange; (*chem*) to digest.

digestión *f* digestion; concoction.

digestivo/va *adj* digestive.

digitador/a *m/f Lat Am* (*comput*) someone who keys in text by means of a keyboard.

digital *adj* digital.

digitalizar *vt* to digitize.

digitar *vt Lat Am* (*comput*) to key in.

dignarse *vr* to condescend, to deign.

dignidad *f* dignity, rank.

digno/na *adj* worthy; suitable.

dije *m* relic; trinket.

dilapidar *vt* to squander, to waste.

dilatación *f* dilation, extension; greatness of mind; calmness.

dilatado/da *adj* large; numerous; prolix; spacious, extensive.

dilatar *vt* to dilate, to expand; to spread out; to defer, to protract.

dilatorio/ria *adj* dilatory.

dilema *m* dilemma.

diligencia *f* diligence; affair, business; call of nature; stage coach.

diligente *adj* diligent, assiduous, prompt, swift.

dilucidar *vt* to elucidate, to explain.

diluir *vt* to dilute.

diluviar *vi* to rain in torrents.

diluvio *m* flood, deluge, inundation; abundance.

dimensión f dimension; extent; capacity, bulk.

diminutivo/va adj diminutive.

diminuto/ta adj defective, faulty; minute, small.

dimisión f resignation.

dimitir vt to give up, to abdicate; * vi to resign.

dinámica f dynamics.

dinámico/ca adj dynamic.

dinamita f dynamite.

dínamo, dinamo f dynamo.

dínamo, dinamo m Lat Am dynamo.

dinastía f dynasty.

dineral m large sum of money.

dinero m money.

diocesano/na adj diocesan.

diócesis f diocese.

Dios m God.

diosa f goddess.

diploma m diploma, patent.

diplomacia, diplomática f diplomacy.

diplomado/da adj qualified.

diplomático/ca adj diplomatic; * m/f diplomat.

diptongo m diphthong.

diputación f deputation.

diputado m deputy.

diputar vt to depute.

dique m dike, dam.

dirección f direction, guidance; administration; steering.

directivo/va adj governing.

directo/ta adj direct, straight; apparent, evident; live.

director/ra m/f director; conductor; president; manager; headmaster (of a private school).

dirigir vt to direct; to conduct; to regulate, to govern; ~se vr to go toward(s); to address oneself to.

discernimiento m discernment.

discernir vt to discern, to distinguish.

disciplina f discipline.

discípulo m disciple; scholar.

disco m disc; record; discus; light; face (of the sun/moon); lens (of a telescope); ~ compacto compact disc.

díscolo/la adj ungovernable; peevish.

disconforme adj differing.

discordancia f disagreement, discord.

discordante adj dissonant, discordant.

discordar vi to clash, to disagree.

discorde adj discordant; (mus) dissonant.

discordia f discord, disagreement.

discoteca m discotheque, disco.

discreción f discretion; acuteness of mind.

discrecional adj discretionary.

discrepancia f discrepancy.

discrepar vi to differ.

discreto/ta adj discreet; ingenious; witty, eloquent.

discriminación f discrimination.

disculpa f apology; excuse.

disculpar vt to exculpate; to excuse; to acquit, to absolve; ~se vr to apologize; to excuse oneself.

discurrir vi to ramble about; to run to and fro; to discourse (upon a subject); * vt to invent, to contrive; to meditate.

discurso m speech; conversation; dissertation; space of time.

discusión f discussion.

discutir vt, vi to discuss.

disecar vt to dissect; to stuff.

disección f dissection.

diseminar vt to scatter; to disseminate, to propagate.

disentería f dysentery.

disentir vi to dissent, to disagree.

diseñador/ra m/f designer.

diseñar vt to draw; to design.

diseño m design; draft; description; picture.

disfraz m disguise; mask.

disfrazar vt to disguise, to conceal; to cloak, to dissemble; ~se vr to disguise oneself as.

disfrutar vt to enjoy; ~se vr to enjoy oneself.

disgustar vt to disgust; to offend; ~se vr to be displeased; to fall out.

disgusto m disgust, aversion; quarrel; annoyance; grief, sorrow.

disidente adj dissident; * m/f dissident, dissenter.

disimular vt to hide; to tolerate.

disimulo m dissimulation; tolerance.

disipado/da adj prodigal, lavish.

disipar vt to dissipate, to disperse, to scatter; to lavish.

dislocación f dislocation.

dislocarse vr to be dislocated/out of joint.

disminución f diminution.

disminuir vt to diminish; to decrease.

disolución f dissolution; liquidation.

disolver vt to loosen, to untie; to dissolve; to disunite; to melt, to liquefy; to interrupt.

disonancia f dissonance; disagreement, discord.

disparada f Lat Am flight; stampede.

disparar vt to shoot, to discharge, to fire; to let off; to throw with violence; * vi to shoot, to fire.

disparatado/da adj inconsistent; absurd, extravagant.

disparate m nonsense, absurdity, extravagance.

disparo m shot; discharge; explosion.

dispensar vt to dispense; to excuse; to dispense with; to distribute.

displicencia f displeasure; dislike.

disponer vt to arrange, to prepare; to dispose.

disponible adj available; disposable.

disposición f disposition, order; resolution; command; power, authority.

dispositivo m device.

dispuesto/ta adj disposed; fit, ready.

disputa f dispute, controversy.

disputar vt to dispute, to controvert, to question; * vi to debate, to argue.

disquera f Lat Am record company.

disquete m floppy disk.

distancia f distance; interval; difference.

distanciarse vr to become estranged.

distante adj distant, far off.

distinción f distinction; difference; prerogative.

distinguido/da adj distinguished, conspicuous.

distinguir vt to distinguish; to discern; ~**se** vr to distinguish oneself.

distintivo m distinctive mark; particular attribute.

distinto/ta adj distinct, different; clear.

distracción f distraction, want of attention.

distraer vt to distract; ~**se** vr to be absent-minded, to be inattentive.

distraído/da adj absent-minded, inattentive.

distribución f distribution; division, separation; arrangement.

distribuidor m distributor.

distribuir vt to distribute.

distrito m district; territory.

disturbar vt to disturb, to interrupt.

disturbio m riot; disturbance, interruption.

disuadir vt to dissuade.

disuasión f dissuasion.

diurno/na adj daily.

diva f prima donna.

divagar vt to digress.

diván m divan.

divergencia f divergence.

divergente adj divergent.

diversidad f diversity; variety of things.

diversificar vt to diversify; to vary.

diversión f diversion; sport; amusement; (mil) diversion.

diverso/sa adj diverse, different; several, sundry.

divertido/da adj amused; amusing.

divertir vt to divert (the attention); to amuse, entertain; (mil) to draw off; ~**se** vr to amuse oneself.

dividir vt to divide; to disunite; to separate; to share out.

divieso m (med) boil.

divinidad f divinity.

divino/na adj divine, heavenly; excellent.

divisa f emblem.

divisar vt to perceive.

divisible adj divisible.

división f division; partition; separation; difference.

divorciar vt to divorce; to separate; ~**se** vr to get divorced.

divorcio m divorce; separation, disunion.

divulgación f publication; dissemination.

divulgar vt to publish, to divulge.

dobladillo m hem; cuff.

dobladura f fold.

doblar vt to double; to fold; to bend; * vi to turn; to toll (bell); ~**se** vr to bend, to bow, to submit.

doble adj double; dual; deceitful; **al ~** doubly; * m double.

doblegar vt to bend; ~**se** vr to yield.

doblez m crease; fold; turn-up; * f duplicity.

doce adj, m twelve.

docena f dozen.

docente adj teaching.

dócil adj docile, tractable.

docilidad f docility, gentleness; compliance.

doctor/ra m/f doctor.

doctorado m doctorate.

doctrina f doctrine, instruction; science.

doctrinal m catechism; * adj doctrinal.

documentación f documentation.

documento m document; record.

dogma m dogma.

dólar m dollar.

dolencia f disease; affliction.

doler vi to feel pain; to ache; ~**se** vr to feel for the sufferings of others; to complain.

dolor m pain; aching, ache; affliction.

doloroso/sa adj painful.

domador/ra m/f trainer; tamer.

domar vt to tame; to subdue, to master.

domesticar vt to domesticate.

domiciliarse vr to establish oneself in a residence.

domicilio m domicile; home, abode.

dominación f domination; dominion; authority, power.

dominante adj dominant; domineering.

dominar vt to dominate; to be fluent in; ~**se** vr to moderate one's passions.

domingo m Sunday; (Christian) Sabbath.

dominguero/ra adj done/worn on Sunday; * m/f Sunday driver.

dominical adj Sunday.

dominio m dominion; domination; power, authority; domain.

donación f donation; gift.

donar vt to donate; to bestow.

donativo m contribution.

doncella f virgin, maiden; lady's maid.

donde adv where.

dónde adv where; ¿de ~? from where?; ¿por ~? where?

dondequiera adv anywhere.

dorado/da adj gilt compd; golden; * m gilding.

dorar vt to gild; (fig) to palliate.

dormilón/ona m/f dull, sleepy person.

dormir vi to sleep; ~**se** vr to fall asleep.

dormitorio m dormitory.

dorsal adj dorsal.

dos adj, m two.

dosaje m Lat Am dose.

doscientos/tas adj pl two hundred.

dosis f invar dose.

dotado/da adj gifted.

dotar vt to endow.

dote f dowry; ~**s** fpl gifts of nature pl; endowments pl.

dragón m dragon; (mil) dragoon.

drama m drama.

dramático/ca adj dramatic.

dramatizar vt to dramatize.

dramaturgo/ga *m/f* dramatist.
droga *f* drug; stratagem; artifice, deceit.
drogadicción *f* drug addiction.
drogadicto/ta *m/f* drug addict.
droguería *f* hardware store.
dromedario *m* dromedary.
dubitativo/va *adj* doubtful, dubious; uncertain.
ducado *m* duchy; ducat.
ducha *f* shower; (*med*) douche.
ducharse *vr* to have a shower.
ducho/cha *adj* skilled, experienced.
duda *f* doubt; suspense; hesitation.
dudar *vt* to doubt.
dudoso/sa *adj* doubtful, dubious.
duelo *m* grief, affliction; mourning.
duende *m* elf, hobgoblin.
dueño/ña *m/f* owner; landlord/lady; employer.
dulce *adj* sweet; mild, gentle, meek; soft; * *m* candy.
dulcificar *vt* to sweeten.
dulzura *f* sweetness; gentleness; softness.
dúo *m* (*mus*) duo, duet.
duodécimo/ma *adj* twelfth.
duplicación *f* duplication.
duplicado *m* duplicate.
duplicar *vt* to duplicate, to double; to repeat.
duplicidad *f* duplicity; falseness.
duplo *m* double.
duque *m* duke.
duquesa *f* duchess.
duración *f* duration.
duradero/ra *adj* lasting, durable.
durante *adv* during.
durar *vi* to last, to continue.
duraznero *m Lat Am* peach tree.
durazno *m Lat Am* peach; peach tree.
dureza *f* hardness; harshness; ~ **de oído** hardness of hearing.
durmiente *adj* sleeping; * *m* (*rail*) sleeping car.
duro/ra *adj* hard; cruel; harsh, rough; * *m* five peseta coin; * *adv* hard.
duunviro *m* magistrate in ancient Rome.

E

e *conj* and (before words starting with **i** and **hi**).
ea *interj* hey!, come on!; **¡~ pues!** well then!, let's see!
ebanista *m* cabinet-maker, carpenter.
ébano *m* ebony.
ebrio/ia *adj* drunk.
ebullición *f* boiling.
eccema *m* eczema.
echar *vt* to throw; to add; to fire; to pour out; to mail; to give off; to bud; **~se** *vr* to lie down; to rest; to stretch out.
eclesiástico/ca *adj* ecclesiastical.
eclipsar *vt* to eclipse; to outshine.
eclipse *m* eclipse.
eco *m* echo.
ecografía *f* ultrasound scan.

ecología *f* ecology.
ecologismo *m* green movement.
ecologista *m/f* ecologist, environmentalist.
economato *m* cut-rate store.
economía *f* economy.
económico/ca *adj* economic; cheap; thrifty; financial; avaricious.
economista *m/f* economist.
ecosistema *m* ecosystem.
ecotasa *f* ecotax.
ecoturismo *m* ecotourism.
ecuación *f* equation.
ecuador *m* equator.
ecuánime *adj* level-headed.
ecuestre *adj* equestrian.
ecuménico/ca *adj* ecumenical; universal.
edad *f* age.
edecán *m* (*mil*) aide-de-camp.
edición *f* edition; publication.
edicto *m* edict.
edificación *f* construction.
edificante *adj* edifying, instructive.
edificar *vt* to build, to construct; to edify.
edificio *m* building; structure.
editar *vt* to edit; to publish.
editor/ra *m/f* editor; publisher.
educación *f* education; upbringing; (good) manners *pl*.
educador/ra *m/f* teacher, educator.
educando/da *m/f* pupil.
educar *vt* to educate, to instruct; to bring up.
efectivamente *adv* exactly; really; in fact.
efectivo/va *adj* effective; true; certain.
efecto *m* effect; consequence; purpose; ~ **invernadero** greenhouse effect ~**s** *mpl* effects *pl*, goods *pl*; **en ~** in fact, really.
efectuar *vt* to effect, to carry out.
efeméride *f* event (remembered on its anniversary).
efervescencia *f* effervescence, fizziness.
eficacia *f* effectiveness, efficacy.
eficaz *adj* efficient; effective.
eficiente *adj* efficient.
efigie *f* effigy, image.
efímero/ra *adj* ephemeral.
efluvio *m* outflow.
efusión *f* effusion.
efusivo/va *adj* effusive.
égloga *f* (*poet*) eclogue.
egoísmo *m* selfishness.
egoísta *m/f* self-seeker; * *adj* selfish.
egregio/gia *adj* eminent, remarkable.
egresado/da *m/f Lat Am* graduate.
egresar *vi Lat Am* to graduate.
egreso *m Lat Am* graduation.
eje *m* axle; axis.
ejecución *f* execution.
ejecutar *vt* to execute, to carry out, to perform; to put to death; (*law*) to attach, to seize.
ejecutivo/va *adj* executive; * *m/f* executive.
ejecutor/ra *m/f* executor.

ejecutoria *f (law)* writ of execution.
ejecutorio/ria *adj (law)* executory.
ejemplar *m* specimen; copy; example; * *adj* exemplary.
ejemplificar *vt* to exemplify.
ejemplo *m* example; **por ~** for example, for instance.
ejercer *vt* to exercise.
ejercicio *m* exercise.
ejercitación *f* exercise, practice.
ejercitar *vt* to exercise; **~se** *vr* to train.
ejército *m* army.
ejote *m* green bean.
el *art*, *m* the.
él *pn* he, it.
elaboración *f* elaboration.
elaborado/da *adj* elaborate.
elaborar *vt* to elaborate.
elasticidad *f* elasticity.
elástico/ca *adj* elastic.
elección *f* election; choice.
eleccionario/a *adj Lat Am* electoral.
elector/ra *m/f* elector.
electorado *m* electorate.
electoral *adj* electoral.
electricidad *f* electricity.
electricista *m/f* electrician.
eléctrico/ca *adj* electric, electrical.
electrización *f* electrification.
electrizar *vt* to electrify.
electrocardiograma *m* electrocardiogram.
electrocutar *vt* to electrocute.
electrodoméstico *m* (electrical) domestic appliance.
electrónico/ca *adj* electronic.
electrotecnia *f* electrical engineering.
elefante *m* elephant.
elegancia *f* elegance.
elegante *adj* elegant, fine.
elegía *f* elegy.
elegir *vt* to choose, to elect.
elemental *adj* elemental; elementary.
elemento *m* element; **~s** *mpl* elements *pl*, rudiments *pl*, first principles *pl*.
elevación *f* elevation; highness; rise; haughtiness, pride; height; altitude.
elevar *vt* to raise; to elevate; **~se** *vr* to rise; to be enraptured; to be conceited.
eliminar *vt* to eliminate, to remove.
eliminatoria *f* preliminary (round).
elipse *f (geom)* ellipse.
elipsis *f (gr)* ellipsis.
elite, élite *f* elite.
elixir *m* elixir.
ella *pn* she; it.
ello *pn* it.
elocución *f* elocution.
elocuencia *f* eloquence.
elocuente *adj* eloquent.
elogiar *vt* to praise, to eulogize.
elogio *m* eulogy, praise.

elote *m* corn on the cob.
elucidación *f* elucidation, explanation.
eludir *vt* to elude, to escape.
emanación *f* emanation.
emanar *vi* to emanate.
emancipación *f* emancipation.
emancipar *vt* to emancipate, to set free.
embadurnar *vt* to smear, to bedaub.
embajada *f* embassy.
embajador/ra *m/f* ambassador.
embalaje *m* packing, package.
embalar *vt* to bale, to pack in bales.
embaldosar *vt* to pave with tiles.
embalsamador *m* embalmer.
embalsamar *vt* to embalm.
embalse *m* reservoir.
embarazada *f* pregnant woman; * *adj* pregnant.
embarazar *vt* to embarrass; to make pregnant; **~se** *vr* to become intricate.
embarazo *m* pregnancy; embarrassment; obstacle.
embarazoso/sa *adj* difficult; intricate, entangled.
embarcación *f* embarkation; any vessel/ship.
embarcadero *m* quay, wharf; port; harbor.
embarcar *vt* to embark; **~se** *vr* to go on board; *(fig)* to get involved (in a matter).
embargar *vt* to lay on an embargo; to impede, to restrain.
embargo *m* embargo; **sin ~** still, however.
embarque *m* embarkation.
embastar *vt* to stitch, to tack.
embate *m* breakers *pl*, surf, surge; sudden attack.
embaucador/ra *m/f* swindler; impostor.
embaucar *vt* to deceive; to trick.
embebecer *vt* to fascinate; **~se** *vr* to be fascinated.
embebecimiento *m* amazement, astonishment; fascination.
embeber *vt* to soak; to saturate; * *vi* to shrink; **~se** *vr* to be enraptured; to be absorbed.
embelesamiento *m* rapture.
embelesar *vt* to amaze, to astonish.
embeleso *m* amazement, enchantment.
embellecer *vt* to embellish, to beautify.
emberrincharse *vr* to have a tantrum.
embestida *f* assault, violent attack.
embestir *vt* to assault, to attack.
emblanquecer *vt* to whiten; **~se** *vr* to grow white; to bleach.
emblema *m* emblem.
embobado/da *adj* amazed; fascinated.
embobamiento *m* astonishment; fascination.
embobar *vt* to amaze; to fascinate; **~se** *vr* to be amazed; to stand gaping.
embobecer *vt* to make silly; **~se** *vr* to get silly.
embobecimiento *m* silliness.
émbolo *m* plunger; piston.
embolsar *vt* to put money into (a purse); to pocket.

emborrachar vt to intoxicate, to inebriate; ~**se** vr to get drunk.

emboscada f (mil) ambush.

emboscarse vr (mil) to lie in ambush.

embotar vt to blunt; ~**se** vr to go numb.

embotellamiento m traffic jam.

embotellar vt to bottle (wine).

embozado/da adj covered; covert.

embozar vt to muffle up (the face); (fig) to cloak, to conceal.

embozo m part of a cloak, veil, anything with which the face is muffled; covering of one's face.

embrague m clutch.

embrear vt to cover with tar/pitch.

embriagar vt to intoxicate, to inebriate; to transport, to enrapture.

embriaguez f intoxication, drunkenness; rapture, delight.

embrión m embryo.

embrollador/ra m/f troublemaker.

embrollar vt to muddle; to entangle, to embroil.

embrollo m muddle.

embromar vt to tease; to cajole, to wheedle.

embrujar vt to bewitch.

embrutecer vt to brutalize; ~**se** vr to become depraved.

embudo m funnel.

embuste m fraud; lie, fib, story (col).

embustero/ra m/f impostor, cheat; liar; * adj deceitful.

embutido m sausage; inlay.

embutir vt to insert; to stuff; to inlay; to cram.

emergencia f emergency.

emerger vi to emerge, to appear.

emético/ca adj emetic.

emigración f emigration; migration.

emigrado/da adj emigrated; * m/f emigrant.

emigrante m/f emigrant.

emigrar vi to emigrate.

eminencia f eminence.

eminente adj eminent, high; excellent, conspicuous.

emisario m emissary.

emisión f emission; broadcasting; program; issue.

emisora f broadcasting station.

emitir vt to emit, to send forth; to issue; to broadcast.

emoción f emotion; feeling; excitement.

emocionante adj exciting.

emocionar vt to excite; to move, to touch.

emoliente adj emollient, softening.

emolumento m emolument.

emotivo/va adj emotional.

empacar vt to pack; to crate.

empachar vt to give indigestion; ~**se** vr to have indigestion.

empacho m (med) indigestion.

empachoso/sa adj indigestible.

empadronamiento m register; census.

empadronarse vr to register.

empalagar vt to sicken; to disgust.

empalago m disgust; boredom.

empalagoso/sa adj cloying; tiresome.

empalizada f (mil) palisade.

empalmadura f join; weld; splice.

empalmar vt to join.

empalme m (rail) junction; connection.

empanada f (meat) pie.

empanar vt to cover with breadcrumbs.

empantanarse vr to get swamped; to get bogged down.

empañar vt to wrap up (baby); to mist; to steam up; ~**se** vr to steam up; to tarnish one's reputation.

empapar vt to soak; to soak up; ~**se** vr to soak.

empapelar vt to paper.

empaquetar vt to pack, to parcel up.

emparedado m sandwich.

emparejar vt to level; to match, to fit; to equalize.

emparentar vi to be related by marriage.

emparrado m vine arbor.

empastar vt to paste; to fill (a tooth).

empaste m filling (of a tooth).

empatar vi to draw, tie, have a dead heat.

empate m draw, dead heat.

empedernido/da adj inveterate; heartless.

empedernir vt to harden; ~**se** to be inflexible.

empedrado m paving.

empedrador m paver.

empedrar vt to pave.

empeine m instep.

empellón m push; heavy blow.

empeñado/da adj determined; pawned.

empeñar vt to pawn, to pledge; ~**se** vr to pledge oneself to pay debts; to get into debt; ~**se en algo** to insist on something.

empeño m obligation; determination; perseverance.

empeorar vt to make worse; * vi, ~**se** vr to grow worse.

empequeñecer vt to dwarf; (fig) to belittle.

emperador m emperor.

emperatriz f empress.

emperifollarse vt to dress oneself up.

empero conj yet, however.

emperrarse vr to get stubborn; to be obstinate.

empezar vt to begin, to start.

empinado/da adj high; proud.

empinar vt to raise; to exalt; * vi to drink heavily; ~**se** vr to stand on tiptoe; to soar.

empírico/ca adj empirical.

empirismo m empiricism.

empizarrado m slate roofing.

empizarrar vt to slate, to roof with slate.

emplasto m plaster.

emplazamiento m summons; location.

emplazar vt to summon; to locate.

empleado/da m/f official; employee.

emplear vt to employ; to occupy; to commission.

empleo *m* employ, employment, occupation.

empobrecer *vt* to reduce to poverty; * *vi* to become poor.

empobrecimiento *m* impoverishment.

empollar *vt* to incubate; to hatch; (*col*) to cram.

empolvar *vt* to powder; to sprinkle powder upon.

emponzoñador/ra *m/f* poisoner.

emponzoñamiento *m* poisoning.

emponzoñar *vt* to poison; to taint, to corrupt.

emporio *m* emporium.

empotrado/da *adj* built-in.

empotrar *vt* to embed; to build in.

emprendedor/ra *m/f* entrepreneur.

emprender *vt* to embark on; to tackle; to undertake.

empresa *f* (*com*) company; enterprise, undertaking.

empresario/ria *m/f* manager.

empréstito *m* loan.

empujar *vt* to push; to press forward.

empuje *m* thrust; pressure; (*fig*) drive.

empujón *m* push; impulse; **a ~ones** in fits and starts.

empuñadura *f* hilt (of a sword).

empuñar *vt* to clench, to grip with the fist; to clutch.

emulación *f* emulation.

emular *vt* to emulate, to rival.

emulsión *f* emulsion.

en *prep* in; for; on, upon.

enaguas *fpl* petticoat.

enajenación *f* alienation; absent-mindedness.

enajenamiento *m* alienation; absent-mindedness.

enajenar *vt* to alienate; **~se** *vr* to fall out.

enamoradamente *adv* lovingly.

enamoradizo/za *adj* inclined to fall in love.

enamorado/da *adj* in love, lovesick.

enamoramiento *m* falling in love.

enamorar *vt* to inspire love in; **~se** *vr* to fall in love.

enano/na *adj* dwarfish; * *m* dwarf.

enarbolar *vt* to hoist, to raise high.

enardecer *vt* to fire with passion, to inflame.

enarenar *vt* to fill with sand.

encabezamiento *m* heading; foreword.

encabezar *vt* to head; to put a heading to; to lead.

encabritarse *vr* to rear (of horses).

encadenamiento *m* linking together, chaining.

encadenar *vt* to chain, to link together; to connect, to unite.

encajadura *f* insertion; socket; groove.

encajar *vt* to insert; to drive in; to encase; to intrude; **~se** *vr* to squeeze; to gatecrash; * *vi* to fit (well).

encaje *m* encasing; joining; socket; groove; inlaid work.

encajera *f* lacemaker.

encajonamiento *m* packing into boxes etc.

encajonar *vt* to pack up in a box.

encalabrinar *vt* to make confused; **~se** *vr* to become obstinate.

encaladura *f* whitening, whitewash.

encalar *vt* to whitewash.

encallar *vi* (*mar*) to run aground.

encallecer *vi* to get corns.

encamarse *vr* to take to one's bed.

encaminar *vt* to guide, to show the way; **~se** *vr*: **~ a** to take the road to.

encandilar *vt* to dazzle.

encanecer *vi* to grow gray; to grow old.

encantado/da *adj* bewitched; delighted; pleased.

encantador/ra *adj* charming; *m/f* magician.

encantamiento *m* enchantment.

encantar *vt* to enchant, to charm; (*fig*) to delight.

encanto *m* enchantment; spell, charm.

encañonar *vt* to hold up; to point a gun at; * *vi* to grow feathers.

encapotar *vt* to cover with a cloak; **~se** *vr* to be cloudy.

encapricharse *vr* to become stubborn.

encapuchar *vt* to cover with a hood.

encaramar *vt* to raise; to extoll; *Lat Am* to make blush.

encararse *vr*: **~ a** to come face to face with.

encarcelación *f* incarceration.

encarcelar *vt* to imprison.

encarecer *vt* to raise the price of; **~se** *vr* to get dearer.

encarecimiento *m* price increase; **con ~** insistently.

encargado/da *adj* in charge; * *m/f* representative; person in charge.

encargar *vt* to charge; to commission.

encargo *m* charge; commission; job; order.

encariñarse *vr*: **~ con** to grow fond of.

encarnación *f* incarnation, embodiment.

encarnado/da *adj* incarnate; flesh-colored; * *m* flesh color.

encarnar *vt* to embody, to personify.

encarnizado/da *adj* bloodshot, inflamed; bloody, fierce.

encarrilar *vt* to put back on the rails; to put on the right track.

encasillar *vt* to pigeonhole; to typecast.

encasquetar *vt* to pull on (a hat).

encastillarse *vr* to refuse to yield.

encauzar *vt* to channel.

encebollado *m* casserole of beef/lamb and onions, seasoned with spice.

encenagado/da *adj* muddy, mud-stained.

encenagamiento *m* wallowing in mud.

encenagarse *vr* to wallow in mud.

encendedor *m* lighter, cigarette lighter.

encender *vt* to kindle, to light, to set on fire; to inflame, to incite; to switch on, to turn on; **~se** *vr* to catch fire; to flare up.

encendido/da *adj* inflamed; high-colored; * *m* ignition (of car).

encerado *m* chalkboard; adhesive tape.

encerar *vt* to wax; to polish.

encerrar *vt* to shut up, to confine; to contain; ~**se** *vr* to withdraw from the world.

encespedar *vt* to turf.

enchapar *vt* to veneer.

encharcarse *vr* to be flooded.

enchufar *vt* to plug in; to connect.

enchufe *m* plug; socket; connection; (*col*) contact, connection.

encía *f* gum (of the teeth).

encíclica *f* encyclical.

enciclopedia *f* encyclopedia.

enciclopédico/ca *adj* encyclopedic.

encierro *m* confinement; enclosure; prison; bullpen; penning (of bulls).

encima *adv* above; over; at the top; besides; ~ **de** *prep* above; over; at the top of; besides.

encina *f* holm oak, evergreen oak.

encinar *m* holm oak wood/grove.

encinta *adj* pregnant.

enclaustrado,da *adj* cloistered; hidden away.

enclenque *adj* weak, sickly; * *m* weakling.

encoger *vt* to contract, to shorten; to shrink; to discourage; ~**se** *vr* to shrink; (*fig*) to cringe.

encogidamente *adv* shyly, timidly, bashfully.

encogido/da *adj* shy, timid, bashful.

encogimiento *m* contraction; shrinkage; shyness; timidness; bashfulness.

encoladura *f* gluing.

encolar *vt* to glue.

encolerizar *vt* to provoke, to irritate; ~**se** *vr* to get angry.

encomendar *vt* to recommend; to entrust; ~**se** *vr*: ~ **a** to entrust oneself to; to put one's trust in.

encomiar *vt* to praise.

encomienda *m* commission, charge; message; (*mil*) command; patronage, protection; *Lat Am* parcel post.

encomio *m* eulogy, praise; commendation.

enconar *vt* to inflame; to irritate.

encono *m* ill-feeling, rancor.

enconoso/sa *adj* hurtful, prejudicial; malevolent.

encontrado/da *adj* conflicting; hostile.

encontrar *vt* to meet, to encounter; ~**se** *vr*: ~**se con** to run into; * *vi* to assemble, to come together.

encopetado/da *adj* presumptuous, boastful.

encorvadura *f* curvature; crookedness.

encorvar *vt* to bend, to curve.

encrespar *vt* to curl, to frizzle (hair); (*fig*) to anger; ~**se** *vr* to get rough (of the sea); (*fig*) to get cross.

encrucijada *f* crossroads; junction.

encuadernación *f* binding.

encuadernador/ra *m/f* bookbinder.

encuadernar *vt* to bind (books).

encubiertamente *adv* secretly; deceitfully.

encubierto/ta *adj* hidden, concealed.

encubridor/ra *m/f* concealer, harborer; receiver of stolen goods.

encubrimiento *m* concealment, hiding; receiving of stolen goods.

encubrir *vt* to hide, to conceal.

encuentro *m* meeting; collision, crash; match, game.

encuesta *f* inquiry; opinion poll.

encumbrado/da *adj* high; elevated.

encumbramiento *m* elevation; height.

encumbrar *vt* to raise, to elevate; ~**se** *vr* to be raised; (*fig*) to become conceited.

encurtir *vt* to pickle.

endeble *adj* feeble, weak.

endecasílabo/ba *adj* consisting of eleven syllables.

endecha *f* dirge, lament.

endemoniado/da *adj* possessed with the devil; devilish.

enderezamiento *m* guidance, direction.

enderezar *vt* to straighten out; to set right; ~**se** *vr* to stand upright.

endeudarse *vr* to get into debt.

endiablado/da *adj* devilish, diabolical; ugly.

endiosar *vt* to deify; ~**se** *vr* to be high and mighty.

endosar *vt* to endorse.

endoso *m* endorsement.

endrina *f* sloe, fruit of the blackthorn.

endrino *m* blackthorn, sloe.

endulzar *vt* to sweeten; to soften.

endurecer *vt* to harden, to toughen; ~**se** *vr* to become cruel; to grow hard.

endurecidamente *adv* cruelly.

endurecimiento *m* hardness; obstinacy; hard-heartedness.

enebro *m* (*bot*) juniper.

enemigo/ga *adj* hostile; * *m* enemy.

enemistad *f* enmity.

enemistar *vt* to make an enemy; ~**se** *vr* to become enemies; to fall out.

energía *f* energy, power, drive; strength of will; ~ **nuclear** nuclear power; ~ **solar** solar energy; ~ **renovables** renewable forms of energy.

enérgico/ca *adj* energetic; forceful.

energúmeno/na *m/f* (*col*) madman/woman.

enero *m* January.

enervar *vt* to enervate.

enfadadizo/za *adj* irritable, crotchety.

enfadar *vt* to anger, to irritate; to trouble; ~**se** *vr* to become angry.

enfado *m* irritation; anger.

enfadoso/sa *adj* annoying, troublesome.

énfasis *m* emphasis.

enfático/ca *adj* emphatic.

enfermar *vi* to fall ill; * *vt* to make sick; to weaken.

enfermedad *f* illness.

enfermería *f* infirmary; sick bay.

enfermero/ra *m/f* nurse.

enfermizo/za *adj* infirm, sickly.

enfermo/ma *adj* sick, ill; * *m/f* invalid, sick person; patient.

enfervorizar *vt* to arouse; to inflame, to incite.

enflaquecer *vt* to weaken; to make thin.

enflaquecimiento *m* loss of weight; (*fig*) weakening.

enfocar *vt* to focus; to consider (a problem).

enfoque *m* focus.

enfrascarse *vr* to be deeply embroiled.

enfrentar *vt* to confront; to put face to face; ~se *vr* to face each other; to meet (two teams).

enfrente *adv* over against, opposite; in front.

enfriamiento *m* refrigeration; (*med*) cold, chill.

enfriar *vt* to cool; to refrigerate; ~se *vr* to cool down; (*med*) to catch a cold/chill.

enfurecer *vt* to madden, to enrage; ~se *vr* to get rough (of the wind and sea); to become furious/enraged.

enfurruñarse *vr* to get sulky; to frown.

engalanar *vt* to adorn, to deck.

engallarse *vr* to be arrogant.

engañabobos *m invar* trickster; trick, trap.

engañadizo/za *adj* gullible, easily deceived.

engañador/ra *adj* cheating; deceptive; * *m/f* cheat, impostor, deceiver.

engañar *vt* to deceive, to cheat; ~se *vr* to be deceived; to make a mistake.

enganchar *vt* to hook, to hang up; to hitch up; to couple, to connect; to recruit into military service; ~se *vr* (*mil*) to enlist.

engañifa *f* deceit, trick.

engaño *m* mistake; misunderstanding; deceit, fraud.

engañoso/sa *adj* deceitful, artful, false.

engarzar *vt* to thread; to link; to curl.

engastar *vt* to set, to mount.

engaste *m* setting, mount.

engatusamiento *m* deception, coaxing.

engatusar *vt* to coax.

engendrar *vt* to beget, to engender; to produce.

engendro *m* fetus, embryo; (*fig*) monstrosity; brainchild.

englobar *vt* to include.

engolfarse *vr* (*mar*) to sail out to sea; ~ en to be deeply involved in.

engolosinar *vt* to entice; ~se *vr* to find delight in.

engomadura *f* gluing.

engomar *vt* to glue.

engordar *vt* to fatten; * *vi* to grow fat; to put on weight.

engorro *m* nuisance, bother.

engorroso/sa *adj* troublesome, cumbersome.

engranaje *m* gear; gears, gearing.

engrandecer *vt* to augment; to magnify; to speak highly of; to exaggerate.

engrandecimiento *m* increase; aggrandizement; exaggeration.

engrapadora *f Lat Am* stapler.

engrapar *vt Lat Am* to staple.

engrasar *vt* to grease, to lubricate.

engreído/da *adj* conceited, vain.

engreimiento *m* presumption, vanity.

engreír *vt* to make proud; ~se *vr* to grow proud.

engrosar *vt* to enlarge; to increase.

engrudo *m* paste.

engullidor/ra *m/f* devourer; guzzler.

engullir *vt* to swallow; to gobble, to devour.

enharinar *vt* to cover/sprinkle with flour.

enhebrar *vt* to thread.

enhilar *vt* to thread.

enhorabuena *f* congratulations *pl*; * *interj* congratulations!

enhoramala *interj* good riddance.

enigma *m* enigma, riddle.

enigmático/ca *adj* enigmatic; dark, obscure.

enjabonar *vt* to soap; (*col*) to soft soap.

enjaezar *vt* to harness (a horse).

enjalbegar *vt* to whitewash.

enjambre *m* swarm (of bees); crowd, multitude.

enjaular *vt* to shut up in a cage; to imprison.

enjoyar *vt* to adorn with jewels.

enjuagar *vt* to rinse out; to wash out.

enjuague *m* (*med*) mouthwash; rinsing, rinse.

enjugar *vt* to dry (the tears); to wipe off.

enjuiciar *vt* to prosecute, to try; to pass judgement on, to judge.

enjuto/ta *adj* dried up; (*fig*) lean.

enlace *m* connection, link; relationship.

enladrillado *m* brick paving.

enladrillador *m* bricklayer.

enladrillar *vt* to pave with bricks.

enlazable *adj* able to be fastened together.

enlazar *vt* to join, to unite; to tie.

enlodar *vt* to cover in mud; (*fig*) to stain.

enloquecer *vt* to madden, to drive crazy; * *vi* to go mad.

enloquecimiento *m* madness.

enlosar *vt* to pave with flagstones.

enlutar *vt* to put into mourning; ~se *vr* to go into mourning.

enmaderar *vt* to roof with lumber.

enmarañar *vt* to entangle; to complicate; to confuse; ~se *vr* to become entangled; to get confused.

enmascarar *vt* to mask; ~se *vr* to go in disguise, to masquerade.

enmendar *vt* to correct; to reform; to repair, to compensate for; to amend; ~se *vr* to mend one's ways.

enmienda *f* correction, amendment.

enmohecer *vt* to make moldy; to rust; ~se *vr* to grow moldy/musty; to rust.

enmohecido/da *adj* moldy.

enmudecer *vt* to silence; ~se *vr* to grow dumb; to be silent.

ennegrecer *vt* to blacken; to darken; to obscure.

ennoblecer *vt* to ennoble.

ennoblecimiento *m* ennoblement.

enojadizo/za *adj* peevish; short-tempered, irritable.

enojar *vt* to irritate, to make angry; to annoy; to upset; to offend; ~se *vr* to get angry.

enojo *m* anger, annoyance.

enojoso/sa *adj* offensive, annoying.

enorgullecerse *vr*: ~ **(de)** to be proud (of).

enorme *adj* enormous, vast, huge; horrible.

enormidad *f* enormity; monstrousness.

enramar *vt* to cover with the branches of trees.

enranciarse *vr* to grow rancid.

enrarecer *vt* to thin, to rarefy.

enredadera *f* climbing plant; bindweed.

enredador/ra *m/f* gossip; troublemaker; busybody.

enredar *vt* to entangle, to ensnare, to confound, to perplex; to puzzle; to sow discord among; ~**se** *vr* to get entangled; to get complicated; to get embroiled.

enredo *m* entanglement; mischievous lie; plot of a play.

enredoso/sa *adj* complicated.

enrejado *m* trelliswork.

enrejar *vt* to fix a grating to (a window); to grate, to lattice.

enrevesado/da *adj* complicated.

enriquecer *vt* to enrich; to adorn; ~**se** *vr* to grow rich.

enristrar *vt* to string (garlic, onions); to straighten out; to go straight to.

enrobustecer *vt* to strengthen.

enrojecer *vt* to redden; * *vi* to blush.

enrolar *vt* to recruit; ~**se** *vr* (*mil*) to join up.

enrollar *vt* to roll (up).

enronquecer *vt* to make hoarse; * *vi* to grow hoarse.

enroscadura *f* twist.

enroscar *vt* to twist; ~**se** *vr* to curl/roll up.

ensalada *f* salad.

ensaladera *f* salad bowl.

ensaladilla (rusa) *f* Russian salad.

ensalmar *vt* to set (dislocated bones); to heal by spells.

ensalmo *m* enchantment, spell.

ensalzar *vt* to exalt, to aggrandize; to exaggerate.

ensamblador/ra *m/f* joiner.

ensamblar *vt* to assemble.

ensanchar *vt* to widen; to extend; to enlarge; ~**se** *vr* to expand; to assume an air of importance.

ensanche *m* dilation, augmentation; widening; expansion.

ensangrentar *vt* to stain with blood.

ensañar *vt* to irritate, to enrage; ~**se con** *vr* to treat brutally.

ensartar *vt* to string (beads etc).

ensayar *vt* to test; to rehearse.

ensayo *m* test, trial; rehearsal of a play; essay.

ensenada *f* creek.

enseña *f* colors *pl*, standard.

enseñanza *f* teaching, instruction; education.

enseñar *vt* to teach, to instruct; to show.

enseres *mpl* belongings *pl*.

ensillar *vt* to saddle.

ensimismarse *vr* to be/become lost in thought.

ensoberbecer *vt* to make proud; ~**se** *vr* to become proud; (*mar*) to get rough.

ensordecer *vt* to deafen; * *vi* to grow deaf.

ensordecimiento *m* deafness.

ensortijar *vt* to fix a ring in (the nose); to curl the hair.

ensuciar *vt* to stain, to soil; to defile; ~**se** *vr* to wet oneself; to dirty oneself.

ensueño *m* fantasy; daydream; illusion.

entablar *vt* to board (up); to strike up (conversation); * *vi Lat Am* to draw.

entablillar *vt* (*med*) to put in a splint.

entallar *vt* to tailor (a suit); * *vi* to fit.

ente *m* organization; entity, being; (*col*) odd character.

entendederas *fpl* understanding; brains *pl*.

entender *vt, vi* to understand, to comprehend; to remark, to take notice (of); to reason, to think; **a mi** ~ in my opinion; ~**se** *vr* to understand each other.

entendido/da *adj* understood; wise; learned, knowing.

entendimiento *m* understanding; knowledge; judgement.

enteramente *adv* entirely, completely.

enterar *vt* to inform; to instruct; ~**se** *vr* to find out.

entereza *f* entireness, integrity; firmness of mind.

enternecer *vt* to soften; to move (to pity); ~**se** *vr* to be moved.

enternecimiento *m* compassion, pity.

entero/ra *adj* entire, complete; perfect; honest; resolute; **por** ~ entirely, completely.

enterrador *m* gravedigger.

enterrar *vt* to inter, to bury.

entibiar *vt* to cool.

entidad *f* entity; company; body; society.

entierro *m* burial; funeral.

entoldar *vt* to cover with an awning.

entomología *f* entomology.

entonación *f* intonation; modulation; (*fig*) presumption, pride.

entonar *vt* to tune, to intone; to tone; * *vi* to be in tune; ~**se** *vr* to give oneself airs.

entonces *adv* then, at that time.

entontecer *vt* to fool; * *vi*, ~**se** *vr* to get silly.

entontecimiento *m* silliness.

entornar *vt* to half close.

entorpecer *vt* to dull; to make lethargic; to hinder; to delay.

entorpecimiento *m* numbness; lethargy.

entrada *f* entrance, entry; (*com*) receipts *pl*; entree; ticket (for movies, theater etc).

entrambos/bas *pn, pl* both.

entrampar *vt* to trap, to snare; to mess up; to burden with debts; ~**se** *vr* get into debt.

entrañable *adj* intimate; affectionate.

entrañas *fpl* entrails *pl*, intestines *pl*.

entrante *adj* coming, next.

entrar *vi* to enter, to go in; to commence.

entre *prep* between; among(st); in; ~ **manos** in hand.

entreabrir *vt* to half open (a door), to leave ajar.

entrecano/na *adj* gray-black, grayish.

entrecejo *m* space between the eyebrows; frown.

entrecortado/da *adj* faltering; difficult.

entredicho *m* (*law*) injunction; **estar en** ~ to be banned; **poner en** ~ to cast doubt on.

entrega *f* delivery; installment.

entregar *vt* to deliver; to hand over; ~**se** *vr* to surrender; to devote oneself.

entrelazar *vt* to interlace.

entremedias *adv* in the meantime.

entremeses *mpl* hors d'oeuvres *pl*.

entremeter *vt* to put (one thing) between (others); ~**se** *vr* to interfere, to meddle.

entremetido/da *m/f* meddler; * *adj* meddling.

entremetimiento *m* insertion; meddling.

entrenador/ra *m/f* trainer, coach.

entrenar *vt* to train; ~**se** *vr* to train.

entreoír *vt* to half hear.

entrepaño *m* panel.

entrepierna *f* crotch.

entresaca *f* thinning out (of trees).

entresacar *vt* to thin out; to sift, to separate.

entresuelo *m* mezzanine floor, entresol.

entretanto *adv* meanwhile.

entretejer *vt* to interweave.

entretela *f* interfacing, stiffening, interlining.

entretener *vt* to amuse; to entertain, to divert; to hold up; to maintain; ~**se** *vr* to amuse oneself; to linger.

entretenido/da *adj* pleasant; amusing; entertaining.

entretenimiento *m* amusement, entertainment.

entrever *vt* to have a glimpse of.

entreverado/da *adj* patchy; streaky.

entrevista *f* interview.

entrevistar *vt* to interview; ~**se** *vr* to have an interview.

entristecer *vt* to sadden.

entrometer *vt* to put (one thing) between (others); ~**se** *vr* to interfere, to meddle.

entrometido/da *m/f* meddler; * *adj* meddling.

entroncar *vi* to be related/connected.

entronización *f* enthronement.

entronizar *vt* to enthrone.

entumecer *vt* to swell; to numb; ~**se** *vr* to become numb.

entumecido/da *adj* numb, stiff.

entumecimiento *m* numbness.

enturbiar *vt* to make cloudy; to obscure, to confound; ~**se** *vr* to become cloudy; (*fig*) to get confused.

entusiasmar *vt* to excite, to fill with enthusiasm; to delight.

entusiasmo *m* enthusiasm.

entusiasta *m/f* enthusiast.

enumeración *f* enumeration.

enumerar *vt* to enumerate.

enunciación *f*, **enunciado** *m* enunciation, declaration.

enunciar *vt* to enunciate, to declare.

envainar *vt* to sheath(e).

envalentonar *vt* to give courage to; ~**se** *vr* to boast.

envanecer *vt* to make vain; to swell with pride; ~**se** *vr* to become proud.

envaramiento *m* stiffness; numbness.

envarar *vt* to numb.

envasar *vt* to pack; to bottle; to can.

envase *m* packing; bottling; canning; container; package; bottle; can.

envejecer *vt* to make old; * *vi*, ~**se** *vr* to grow old.

envenenador/ra *m/f* poisoner.

envenenar *vt* to poison; to embitter.

envenenamiento *m* poisoning.

envergadura *f* (*fig*) scope.

envés *m* wrong side (of material).

enviado/da *m/f* envoy, messenger.

enviar *vt* to send, to transmit, to convey, to dispatch.

enviciar *vt* to vitiate, to corrupt; ~**se** *vr* to get corrupted.

envidia *f* envy; jealousy.

envidiable *adj* enviable.

envidiar *vt* to envy; to grudge; to be jealous of.

envidioso/sa *adj* envious; jealous.

envilecer *vt* to vilify, to debase; ~**se** *vr* to degrade oneself.

envío *m* (*com*) dispatch, remittance of goods; consignment.

enviudar *vi* to become a widower/widow.

envoltorio *m* bundle of clothes.

envoltura *f* cover; wrapping.

envolver *vt* to involve; to wrap up.

enyesar *vt* to plaster; (*med*) to put in a plaster cast.

enzarzarse *vr* to get involved in a dispute; to get oneself into trouble.

épico/ca *adj* epic.

epicúreo/rea *adj* Epicurean.

epidemia *f* epidemic.

epidémico/ca *adj* epidemic.

epidermis *f* epidermis; cuticle.

Epifanía *f* Epiphany.

epígrafe *f* epigraph, inscription; motto; headline.

epigrama *m* epigram.

epilepsia *f* epilepsy.

epílogo *m* epilog.

episcopado *m* episcopacy; bishopric.

episcopal *adj* Episcopal.

episódico/ca *adj* episodic.

episodio *m* episode, installment.

epístola *f* epistle, letter.

epistolar *adj* epistolary.

epistolario *m* collected letters *pl*.

epitafio *m* epitaph.

epíteto *m* epithet.

epítome *m* epitome; compendium.

época f epoch; period, time.

epopeya f epic.

equidad f equity, honesty; impartiality, justice.

equidistar vi to be equidistant.

equilátero/ra adj equilateral.

equilibrar vt to balance; to poise.

equilibrio m balance, equilibrium.

equinoccial adj equinoctial.

equinoccio m equinox.

equipaje m baggage; fixings; equipment.

equipar vt to fit out, to equip, to furnish.

equipararse vr: ~ con to be on a level with.

equipo m equipment; team; shift.

equitación f horsemanship; riding.

equitativo/va adj equitable; just.

equivalencia f equivalence.

equivalente adj equivalent.

equivaler vi to be of equal value.

equivocación f mistake, error; misunderstanding.

equivocado/da adj mistaken, wrong.

equivocar vt to mistake; ~se vr to make a mistake, to be wrong.

equívoco/ca adj equivocal, ambiguous; * m equivocation; quibble.

era f era, age; threshing floor.

erario m treasury; public funds pl.

erección f foundation, establishment; erection, elevation.

erguir vt to erect, to raise up straight; ~se vr to straighten up.

erial m fallow land.

erigir vt to erect, to raise, to build; to establish.

erizamiento m standing on end (of hair etc).

erizarse vr to bristle; to stand on end.

erizo m hedgehog; ~ de mar sea urchin.

ermita f hermitage.

ermitaño m hermit.

erosionar vt to erode.

erótico/ca adj erotic.

erotismo m eroticism.

errante adj errant; stray; roving.

errar vi to be mistaken; to wander.

errata f misprint.

erre: ~ que ~ adv obstinately.

erróneo/nea adj erroneous.

error m error, mistake, fault.

eructar vi to belch, to burp.

eructo m belch, burp.

erudición f erudition, learning.

erudito/ta adj learned, erudite.

erupción f eruption, outbreak.

esa f of **ese**.

ésa f of **ése**.

esbelto/ta adj slim, slender.

esbirro m bailiff; henchman; killer.

esbozo m outline.

escabechar vt to marinate; to pickle.

escabeche m pickle; pickled fish.

escabel m footstool.

escabrosidad f unevenness, roughness; harshness.

escabroso/sa adj rough, uneven; craggy; rude, risqué.

escabullirse vr to escape, to evade; to slip through one's fingers.

escafandra f diving suit; space suit.

escala f ladder; (mus) scale; port of call; stopover.

escalador/ra m/f climber.

escalar vt to climb.

escaldado/da adj cautious, suspicious, wary.

escaldar vt to scald.

escalera f staircase; ladder.

escalfar vt to poach (eggs).

escalofríos mpl shivers pl.

escalofriante adj chilling.

escalón m step of a stair; rung.

escama f (fish) scale.

escamado/da adj wary, cautious.

escamar vt to scale, to take off the scales; ~se vr to flake off; to become suspicious.

escamoso/sa adj scaly.

escamotear vt to swipe; to make disappear.

escampar vi to stop raining.

escanciador m wine waiter; cupbearer.

escanciar vt to pour (wine).

escandalizar vt to scandalize; ~se vr to be shocked.

escándalo m scandal; uproar.

escandaloso/sa adj scandalous; shocking.

escanear vt to scan.

escáner m scanner.

escaño m bench with a back.

escapada f escape, flight.

escapar vi to escape; ~se vr to get away; to leak (water etc).

escaparate m shop/store front, shop/store window; wardrobe.

escapatoria f escape, flight; excuse.

escape m escape, flight; leak; exhaust (of motor); a todo ~ at full speed.

escapulario m scapulary.

escarabajo m beetle.

escaramuza f skirmish; dispute, quarrel.

escaramuzar vt to skirmish.

escarbadura f act and effect of scratching.

escarbar vt to scratch (the earth as hens do); to inquire into.

escarcha f white frost.

escarchar vi to be frosty.

escardador m weeding hoe.

escardillo m small weeding hoe.

escarlata adj scarlet.

escarlatina f scarlet fever.

escarmentar vi to learn one's lesson; * vt to punish severely.

escarmiento m warning, caution; punishment.

escarnecer vt to mock, to ridicule.

escarnio m gibe, ridicule.

escarola f (bot) endive.

escarpa f slope; escarpment.

escarpado/da adj sloped; craggy.

escarpín *m* sock; pump (shoe).
escasear *vi* to be scarce.
escasez *f* shortage; poverty.
escaso/sa *adj* small, short, little; sparing; scarce; scanty.
escatimar *vt* to curtail, to lessen; to be scanty with.
escena *f* stage; scene.
escenario *m* stage; set.
escepticismo *m* skepticism.
escéptico/ca *adj* skeptical.
esclarecer *vt* to lighten; to illuminate; to illustrate; to shed light on (problem etc).
esclarecido/da *adj* illustrious, noble.
esclarecimiento *m* clarification; enlightenment.
esclavina *f* short cloak/cape.
esclavitud *f* slavery, servitude.
esclavizar *vt* to enslave.
esclavo/va *m/f* slave; captive.
esclusa *f* sluice, floodgate.
escoba *f* broom, brush.
escobazo *m* blow given with a broom.
escobilla *f* brush, small broom; blade.
escobillar *vt Lat Am* to brush.
escocer *vt* to sting; to burn; **~se** *vr* to chafe.
escoger *vt* to choose, to select.
escolar *m/f* schoolboy/girl; * *adj* scholastic.
escolástico/ca *adj* scholastic; * *m* scholar.
escollo *m* reef, rock.
escolta *f* escort.
escoltar *vt* to escort.
escombros *mpl* rubbish; debris.
esconder *vt* to hide, to conceal; **~se** *vr* to be hidden.
escondidas: a ~ *adv* in a secret manner.
escondite *m* hiding place; **juego del ~** hide-and-seek.
escondrijo *m* hiding place.
escopeta *f* shotgun; **a tiro de ~** within gunshot.
escopetazo *m* gunshot; gunshot wound.
escopetero *m* gunsmith.
escoplo *m* chisel.
escorbuto *m* scurvy.
escoria *f* dross; scum; dregs *pl*.
Escorpio *m* Scorpio (zodiac sign).
escorpión *m* scorpion.
escotado/da *adj* low-cut.
escotadura *f* low neck(line).
escotar *vt* to cut low in front.
escote *m* low neck (of a dress).
escotilla *f* (*mar*) hatchway.
escozor *m* smart; burning pain; sting(ing).
escriba *m* scribe (of the Hebrews).
escribanía *f* clerk's office; writing desk.
escribano *m* court clerk; lawyer's clerk.
escribiente *m* transcriber; copyist; clerk.
escribir *vt* to write; to spell; * *vi* to write.
escrito *m* document; manuscript, text.
escritor/ra *m/f* writer, author.
escritorio *m* writing desk; office, study.
escritura *f* writing; deed.

escrúpulo *m* doubt, scruple, scrupulousness.
escrupulosidad *f* scrupulousness.
escrupuloso/sa *adj* scrupulous; exact.
escrutar *vt* to examine; to count (ballot papers).
escrutinio *m* scrutiny, inquiry.
escrutiñador *m* scrutinizer, inquirer.
escuadra *f* square; squadron; squad.
escuadrar *vt* to square.
escuadrón *m* squadron.
escuálido/da *adj* skinny; squalid.
escucha *f* listening(-in); * *m* scout.
escuchar *vt* to listen to, to heed.
escudar *vt* to shield; to guard from danger; **~se** *vr* to protect oneself.
escudero *m* squire; page.
escudilla *f* bowl.
escudo *m* shield.
escudriñamiento *m* investigation, scrutiny.
escudriñar *vt* to search, to examine; to pry into.
escuela *f* school; **~ primaria** grade school; **~ secundaria** secondary/high school.
escueto/ta *adj* plain; simple.
esculpir *vt* to sculpt.
escultor/ra *m/f* sculptor.
escultura *f* sculpture.
escupidera *f* cuspidor.
escupidura *f* spit.
escupir *vt* to spit.
escurreplatos *m invar* plate rack.
escurridizo/za *adj* slippery.
escurrir *vt* to drain; to drip; **~se** *vr* to slip away; to slip, to slide; * *vi* to wring out.
ese/esa *adj* that; **esos/as** *pl* those.
ése/ésa *pn* that (one); **ésos/as** *pl* those (ones).
esencia *f* essence.
esencial *adj* essential; principal.
esfera *f* sphere; globe.
esférico/ca *adj* spherical.
esferoide *f* spheroid.
esfinge *m* sphinx.
esforzado/da *adj* strong, vigorous; valiant.
esforzarse *vr* to exert oneself, to make an effort.
esfuerzo *m* effort.
esfumarse *vr* to fade away.
esgrima *f* fencing.
esgrimidor *m* fencer.
esgrimir *vi* to fence.
esguince *m* (*med*) sprain.
eslabón *m* link of a chain; steel; shackle.
eslabonar *vt* to link; to unite.
esmaltador *m* enameler.
esmaltar *vt* to enamel.
esmalte *m* enamel.
esmerado/da *adj* careful, neat.
esmeralda *f* emerald.
esmerar *vt* to polish; **~se** *vr* to take great care; to work hard.
esmeril *m* emery.
esmerilar *vt* to polish with emery.
esmero *m* careful attention, great care.
esnob *adj* snobbish; * *m/f* snob.

eso *pn* that.

esófago *m* esophagus; throat.

esos, ésos *pl* of **ese, ése**.

espabilar *vt* to wake up; **~se** *vr* to wake up; (*fig*) to get a move on.

espacial *adj* space *compd*.

espaciar *vt* to spread out; to space (out).

espacio *m* space; (*rad/TV*) program.

espaciosidad *f* spaciousness, capacity.

espacioso/sa *adj* spacious, roomy.

espada *f* sword; ace of spades.

espadachín *m* bully.

espadaña *f* (*bot*) bulrush.

espadín *m* small short sword.

espaguetis *mpl* spaghetti.

espalda *f* back, back-part; **~s** *fpl* shoulders *pl*.

espaldilla *f* shoulder blade.

espantadizo/za *adj* timid, easily frightened.

espantajo *m* scarecrow; bogeyman.

espantapájaros *m invar* scarecrow.

espantar *vt* to frighten; to chase/drive away.

espanto *m* fright; menace, threat; astonishment; *Lat Am* ghost.

espantoso/sa *adj* frightful, dreadful; amazing.

español/la *adj* Spanish; * *m/f* Spaniard; * *m* Spanish (language).

esparadrapo *m* adhesive tape.

esparcir *vt* to scatter; to divulge; **~se** *vr* to amuse oneself.

espárrago *m* asparagus.

esparto *m* (*bot*) esparto.

espasmo *m* spasm.

espátula *f* spatula.

especia *f* spice.

especial *adj* special; particular; **en ~** especially.

especialidad *f* specialty.

especie *f* species; kind, sort; matter.

especificación *f* specification.

especificar *vt* to specify.

específico/ca *adj* specific.

espectáculo *m* spectacle; show.

espectador/ra *m/f* spectator.

espectro *m* specter, phantom, ghost, apparition.

especulación *f* speculation; contemplation; venture.

especulador/ra *m/f* speculator.

especular *vt* to speculate.

especulativo/va *adj* speculative; thoughtful.

espejismo *m* mirage.

espejo *m* mirror.

espeluznante *adj* horrifying.

espera *f* stay, waiting; (*law*) respite, adjournment, delay.

esperanza *f* hope.

esperanzar *vt* to give hope to.

esperar *vt* to hope; to expect, to wait for.

esperma *f* sperm.

espesar *vt* to thicken; to condense; **~se** *vr* to grow thick; to solidify.

espeso/sa *adj* thick, dense.

espesor *m* thickness.

espesura *f* thickness; density, solidity.

espía *m/f* spy.

espiar *vt* to spy.

espiga *f* ear (of corn).

espigón *m* ear of corn; sting; (*mar*) breakwater.

espina *f* thorn; fishbone.

espinaca *f* (*bot*) spinach.

espinazo *m* spine, backbone.

espinilla *f* shinbone.

espino *m* hawthorn.

espinoso/sa *adj* thorny; dangerous.

espionaje *m* spying, espionage.

espiral *adj, f* spiral.

espirar *vt* to exhale.

espíritu *m* spirit, soul; mind; intelligence; **el E~ Santo** the Holy Ghost; **~s** *pl* demons *pl*, hobgoblins *pl*.

espiritual *adj* spiritual; ghostly.

espiritualidad *f* spirituality.

espiritualizar *vt* to spiritualize.

esplendidez *f* splendor.

espléndido/da *adj* splendid.

esplendor *m* splendor.

espliego *m* (*bot*) lavender.

espolear *vt* to spur, to instigate, to incite.

espolón *m* spur (of a cock); spur (of a mountain range); sea wall; jetty; (*mar*) buttress.

espolvorear *vt* to sprinkle.

espondeo *m* (*poet*) spondee.

esponja *f* sponge.

esponjar *vt* to sponge; **~se** *vr* to be puffed up with pride.

esponjoso/sa *adj* spongy.

esponsales *mpl* betrothal.

espontaneidad *f* spontaneity.

espontáneo/nea *adj* spontaneous.

esposa *f* wife.

esposar *vt* to handcuff.

esposas *fpl* handcuffs *pl*.

esposo *m* husband.

espuela *f* spur; stimulus; (*bot*) larkspur.

espuerta *f* pannier, basket.

espulgar *vt* to delouse; to examine closely.

espuma *f* froth, foam.

espumadera *f* skimmer.

espumajear *vi* to foam at the mouth.

espumar *vt* to skim, to take the scum off.

espumarajo *m* foam, froth (from the mouth).

espumoso/sa *adj* frothy, foamy; sparkling (wine).

espurio/ria *adj* spurious; adulterated; illegitimate.

esputo *m* spit, saliva.

esqueje *m* cutting (of plant).

esquela *f* note, slip of paper.

esqueleto *m* skeleton.

esquema *m* scheme; diagram; plan.

esquí *m* ski; skiing.

esquiar *vi* to ski.

esquife *m* skiff, small boat.

esquilador *m* sheep-shearer.

esquilar vt to shear sheep.
esquina f corner, angle.
esquinado/da adj cornered, angled.
esquinar vt to form a corner with.
esquirol m blackleg.
esquivar vt to shun, to avoid, to evade.
esquivez f disdain; shyness.
esquivo/va adj scornful; shy, reserved.
esta f of **este**.
ésta f of **éste**.
estabilidad f stability.
estable adj stable.
establecer vt to establish.
establecimiento m establishment.
establo m stable.
estaca f stake; stick; post.
estacada f fence; fencing; stockade.
estacazo m blow with a stick.
estación f season (of the year); station; railroad station, terminus; ~ **de autobuses** bus station; ~ **de servicio** service station.
estacional adj seasonal.
estacionamiento m parking; parking lot; (mil) stationing.
estacionar vt to park; (mil) to station.
estacionario/ria adj stationary.
estadía f Lat Am stay.
estadio m phase; stadium.
estadista m statesman; statistician.
estadística f statistics pl.
estadístico/ca adj statistical.
estado m state, condition.
Estados Unidos mpl United States (of America).
estafa f trick, fraud.
estafador/ra m/f swindler, racketeer.
estafar vt to deceive, to defraud.
estafeta f post office.
estallar vi to crack; to burst; to break out.
estallido m explosion; (fig) outbreak.
estambre m stamen.
estamento m estate; body; layer; class.
estameña f serge.
estampa f print; engraving; appearance.
estampado/da adj printed; * m printing; print; stamping.
estampar vt to print.
estampida f stampede.
estampido m report (of a gun); crack.
estampilla f seal; Lat Am stamp.
estancar vt to check (a current); to monopolize; to prohibit, to suspend; ~**se** vr to stagnate.
estancia f stay; bedroom; ranch; (poet) stanza.
estanco m tobacconist's (shop); ~/**ca** adj watertight.
estándar adj, m standard.
estandarizar vt to standardize.
estandarte m banner, standard.
estanque m pond, pool; reservoir.
estanquero/ra m/f tobacconist.
estante m shelf (for books).
estantería f shelves pl, shelving.

estaño m tin.
estar vi to be; to be (in a place).
estatal adj state compd.
estática f statics pl.
estático/ca adj static.
estatua f statue.
estatura f stature.
estatuto m statute, law.
este[1] m east;
este/ta[2] adj this; **estos/tas** pl these.
éste pn m this (one); **éstos/tas** pl these (ones).
estera f mat.
estercolar vt to manure.
estercolero m dunghill.
estéreo adj invar, m stereo.
estereotipar vt to stereotype.
estereotipo m stereotype.
estéril adj sterile, infertile.
esterilidad f sterility, infertility.
esterilla f mat; Lat Am canework.
esterlina adj: **libra** ~ pound sterling.
estético/ca adj esthetic; * f esthetics.
estiércol m dung; manure.
estilar vi, ~**se** vr to be in fashion; to be used.
estilo m style; fashion; stroke (in swimming).
estima f esteem.
estimable adj estimable, worthy of esteem.
estimación f estimation, valuation.
estimar vt to estimate, to value; to esteem; to judge; to think.
estimulante adj stimulating; * m stimulant.
estimular vt to stimulate, to excite; to goad.
estímulo m stimulus.
estío m summer.
estipendiario m stipendiary.
estipulación f stipulation.
estipular vt to stipulate.
estirado/da adj stretched tight; (fig) pompous.
estirar vt to stretch out.
estirón m pulling; tugging; **dar un** ~ to grow rapidly.
estirpe f race, origin, stock.
estival adj summer compd.
esto pn this.
estocada f stab.
estofa f: **de baja** ~ poor quality.
estofado m stew.
estola f stole.
estolidez f stupidity.
estólido/da adj stupid.
estomacal adj stomach compd.
estómago m stomach.
estopa f tow.
estoque m rapier, sword.
estorbar vt to hinder; (fig) to bother; * vi to be in the way.
estorbo m obstacle, hindrance, impediment.
estornudar vi to sneeze.
estornudo m sneeze.
estos, éstos pl of **este, éste**.
estrada f highway; expressway.

estrado *m* drawing room; stage, platform; **~ de los testigos** witness stand.

estrafalario/ria *adj* slovenly; eccentric.

estrago *m* ruin, destruction; havoc.

estrambótico/ca *adj* eccentric, odd.

estrangulador/ra *m/f* strangler.

estrangulamiento *m* bottleneck.

estrangular *vt* to strangle; (*med*) to strangulate.

estraperlo *m* black market.

estratagema *f* stratagem, trick.

estrategia *f* strategy.

estratégico/ca *adj* strategic.

estrato *m* stratum, layer.

estraza *f* rag; **papel de ~** brown -paper.

estrechar *vt* to tighten; to contract, to constrain; to compress; **~ la mano** to shake hands; **~se** *vr* to grow narrow; to embrace.

estrechez *f* strictness, narrowness; shortage of money.

estrecho *m* straits *pl*; **~/cha** *adj* narrow, close; tight; intimate; rigid, austere; short (of money).

estrella *f* star.

estrellado/da *adj* starry; **huevos ~s** fried eggs.

estrellar *vt* to dash to pieces; **~se** *vr* to smash; to crash; to fail.

estremecer *vt* to shake, to make tremble; **~se** *vr* to shake, to tremble.

estremecimiento *m* trembling, shaking.

estrenar *vt* to wear for the first time; to move into (a house); to show (a film) for the first time; **~se** *vr* to make one's debut.

estreñido/da *adj* constipated.

estreñimiento *m* constipation.

estrépito *m* noise, racket; fuss.

estrepitoso/sa *adj* noisy.

estribar *vi*: **~ en** to be supported by; to be based on.

estribillo *m* chorus.

estribo *m* buttress; stirrup; bracket; brace; **perder los ~s** to fly off the handle (*col*).

estribor *m* (*mar*) starboard.

estrictez *f Lat Am* strictness.

estricto/ta *adj* strict; severe.

estrofa *f* (*poet*) verse, strophe.

estropajo *m* scourer.

estropajoso/sa *adj* tough, leathery; despicable; mean; stammering.

estropear *vt* to spoil; to damage; **~se** *vr* to get damaged.

estructura *f* structure.

estruendo *m* clamor, noise; confusion, uproar; pomp, ostentation.

estrujar *vt* to press, to squeeze.

estrujón *m* pressing, squeezing.

estuario *m* estuary.

estuche *m* case (for scissors etc); sheath.

estudiante *m/f* student.

estudiantil *adj* student *compd*.

estudiar *vt* to study.

estudio *m* study; studio; **~s** *mpl* studies *pl*; learning.

estudioso/sa *adj* studious.

estufa *f* heater, fire.

estufilla *f* muff; small stove.

estupefacción *f* stupefaction.

estupefaciente *m* narcotic.

estupefacto/a *adj* speechless; thunderstruck.

estupendo/da *adj* terrific, marvelous.

estupidez *f* stupidity.

estúpido/da *adj* stupid.

estupor *m* stupor; astonishment.

estupro *m* rape.

etapa *f* stage; stopping place; (*fig*) phase.

etcétera *adv* etcetera, and so on.

éter *m* ether.

etéreo/rea *adj* ethereal.

eternidad *f* eternity.

eternizar *vt* to eternalize, to perpetuate.

eterno/na *adj* eternal.

ética *f* ethics.

ético/ca *adj* ethical, moral.

etimología *f* etymology.

etimológico/ca *adj* etymological.

etiqueta *f* etiquette; label, tag.

Eucaristía *f* Eucharist.

eufemismo *m* euphemism.

euforia *f* euphoria.

euro *m* euro.

eurocámara *f* European Parliament.

eurodiputado/da *m/f* Euro-MP.

euroescéptico/ca *m/f* Euroskeptic.

Europa *f* Europe.

eurotúnel *m* Eurotunnel, Channel tunnel.

evacuación *f* evacuation.

evacuar *vt* to evacuate, to empty.

evadir *vt* to evade, to escape.

evaluar *vt* to evaluate.

evangélico/ca *adj* evangelical.

evangelio *m* gospel.

evangelista *m* evangelist.

evangelizar *vt* to evangelize.

evaporar *vt* to evaporate; **~se** *vr* to vanish.

evasión *f* evasion, escape.

evasivo/va *adj* evasive; ***** *f* excuse.

eventual *adj* possible; temporary, casual (worker).

evidencia *f* evidence, proof.

evidente *adj* evident, clear.

evitable *adj* avoidable.

evitar *vt* to avoid.

evocación *f* evocation; invocation.

evocar *vt* to call out; to invoke.

evolución *f* evolution, development; change; (*mil*) maneuver.

evolucionar *vi* to evolve.

ex *adj* ex.

exacción *f* exaction; extortion.

exacerbar *vt* to exacerbate; to irritate.

exactamente *adv* exactly.

exactitud *f* exactness.

exacto/ta *adj* exact; punctual; accurate.

exageración *f* exaggeration.

exagerar *vt* to exaggerate.
exaltación *f* exaltation, elation.
exaltar *vt* to exalt, to elevate; to praise, to extoll;
~**se** *vr* to get excited.
examen *m* exam, examination, test; inquiry.
examinador *m* examiner.
examinar *vt* to examine.
exánime *adj* lifeless, weak.
exasperación *f* exasperation.
exasperar *vt* to exasperate, to irritate.
excavación *f* excavation.
excavadora *f* excavator.
excavar *vt* to excavate, to dig out.
excedente *adj* excessive.
exceder *vt* to exceed, to surpass, to excel, to
outdo.
excelencia *f* excellence.
Excelencia *f* Excellency (title).
excelente *adj* excellent.
excelso/sa *adj* elevated, sublime, lofty.
excentricidad *f* eccentricity.
excéntrico/ca *adj* eccentric.
excepción *f* exception.
excepto *adv* excepting, except (for).
exceptuar *vt* to except, to exempt.
excesivo/va *adj* excessive.
exceso *m* excess.
excitación *f* excitement; excitation.
excitar *vt* to excite; ~**se** *vr* to get excited.
exclamación *f* exclamation.
exclamar *vt* to exclaim, to cry out.
excluir *vt* to exclude.
exclusión *f* exclusion.
exclusiva *f* exclusive; (*com*) sole right.
exclusivamente, exclusive *adv* exclusively.
exclusivo/va *adj* exclusive.
excomulgar *vt* to excommunicate.
excomunión *f* excommunication.
excremento *m* excrement.
excursión *f* excursion, trip.
excusa *f* excuse, apology.
excusable *adj* excusable.
excusado *m* bathroom, lavatory.
excusar *vt* to excuse; to avoid; ~ **de** to exempt
from; ~**se** *vr* to apologize.
execrable *adj* execrable, abhorrent.
execrar *vt* to execrate, to curse.
exención *f* exemption; immunity, privilege.
exento/ta *adj* exempt, free.
exequias *fpl* funeral rites *pl*, obsequies *pl*.
exhalación *f* exhalation; fumes *pl*, vapor.
exhalar *vt* to exhale; to give off; to heave (a
sigh).
exhausto/ta *adj* exhausted.
exhibición *f* exhibition, display.
exhibir *vt* to exhibit.
exhortación *f* exhortation.
exhortar *vt* to exhort.
exhumación *f* exhumation.
exhumar *vt* to disinter, to exhume.
exigencia *f* demand, requirement.

exigir *vt* to demand, to require.
exiguo/gua *adj* meager, small.
exiliado/da *adj* exiled; * *m/f* exile.
exilio *m* exile.
eximir *vt* to exempt, to free; to excuse.
existencia *f* existence, being.
existente *adj* existing, in existence.
existir *vi* to exist, to be.
éxito *m* outcome; success; (*mus*) hit; **tener ~ to**
be successful.
exoneración *f* exoneration.
exonerar *vt* to exonerate.
exorbitante *adj* exorbitant, excessive.
exorcismo *m* exorcism.
exorcista *m* exorcist.
exorcizar *vt* to exorcise.
exótico/ca *adj* exotic.
expandir *vt* to expand.
expansión *f* expansion; extension.
expansivo/va *adj* expansive.
expatriarse *vr* to emigrate; to go into exile.
expectativa *f* expectation; prospect.
expectoración *f* expectoration.
expectorar *vt* to expectorate.
expedición *f* expedition.
expedicionario/ria *adj* expeditionary.
expediente *m* expedient; means; (*law*)
proceedings *pl*; dossier, file.
expedir *vt* to send, to forward, to dispatch.
expeditivo/va *adj* expeditious.
expedito/ta *adj* speedy; clear, free.
expeler *vt* to expel.
expendio *m* *Lat Am* shop.
expensas *fpl*: **a** ~ **de** at the expense of.
experiencia *f* experience; trial.
experimentado/da *adj* experienced; expert.
experimental *adj* experimental.
experimentar *vt* to experience; * *vi*: ~ **con** to
experiment with.
experimento *m* experiment, trial.
experto/ta *adj* expert; experienced.
expiación *f* expiation; purification.
expiar *vt* to atone for; to purify.
expiatorio/ria *adj* expiatory.
expirar *vi* to expire.
explanada *f* esplanade.
explayarse *vr* to speak at length.
explicación *f* explanation.
explicar *vt* to explain, to expound; ~**se** *vr* to
explain oneself.
explícito/ta *adj* explicit.
exploración *f* exploration.
explorador/ra *m/f* explorer.
explorar *vt* to explore.
explosión *f* explosion.
explotación *f* exploitation; running.
explotar *vt* to exploit; to run; * *vi* to explode.
exponente *m* (*math*) exponent.
exponer *vt* to expose; to explain.
exportación *f* export; exports *pl*.
exportar *vt* to export.

exposición f exposure; exhibition; explanation; account.

expresar vt to express.

expresión f expression.

expresivo/va adj expressive; energetic.

expreso/sa adj express, clear, specific; fast (train).

express m (rail) express train.

exprimidor m squeezer.

exprimir vt to squeeze out.

ex profeso adv on purpose.

expropiar vt to expropriate.

expuesto/ta adj exposed; on display.

expulsar vt to expel, to drive out.

expulsión f expulsion.

exquisito/ta adj exquisite; excellent.

éxtasis m ecstasy, enthusiasm.

extático/ca adj ecstatic.

extender vt to extend, to stretch out; **~se** vr to extend; to spread.

extensión f extension; extent.

extensivo/va adj extensive.

extenso/sa adj extensive.

extenuación f emaciation; debility, exhaustion.

extenuar vt to exhaust, to debilitate.

exterior adj exterior, external; * m exterior, outward appearance.

exteriormente adv externally.

exterminador m exterminator.

exterminar vt to exterminate.

exterminio m extermination.

externo/na adj external, outer; * m/f day pupil/ student.

extinción f extinction.

extinguidor m Lat Am (fire) extinguisher.

extinguir vt to wipe out; to extinguish.

extintor m (fire) extinguisher.

extirpación f extirpation, extermination.

extirpar vt to extirpate, to root out.

extorsión f extortion.

extra adj invar extra; good quality; * m/f extra; * m bonus.

extracción f extraction.

extracto m extract.

extradición f extradition.

extraditar vt to extradite.

extraer vt to extract.

extranjero/ra m/f stranger; foreigner; * adj foreign, alien.

extrañar vt to find strange; to miss; **~se** vr to be surprised; to grow apart.

extrañeza f strangeness; surprise.

extraño/ña adj foreign; rare; singular, strange, odd.

extraordinario/ria adj extraordinary, uncommon, odd.

extravagancia f extravagance.

extravagante adj extravagant.

extraviado/da adj lost, missing.

extraviar vt to mislead; **~se** vr to lose one's way.

extravío m deviation; loss.

extremado/da adj extreme; accomplished.

extremaunción f extreme unction.

extremidad f extremity; brim; tip; **~es** fpl extremities pl.

extremo/ma adj extreme, last; * m extreme, highest degree; **en ~** extremely.

extrínseco/ca adj extrinsic, external.

extrovertido/da adj, m/f extrovert.

exuberancia f exuberance; luxuriance.

F

fábrica f factory.

fabricación f manufacture, production.

fabricante m/f producer, manufacturer.

fabricar vt to build, to construct; to manufacture; (fig) to fabricate.

fabril adj manufacturing compd, industrial.

fábula f fable; fiction; rumor, common talk.

fabulista m/f writer of fables.

fabuloso/sa adj fabulous, fictitious.

facción f (political) faction; feature.

faccioso/sa adj factious, turbulent.

facha f appearance, look; face.

fachada f facade, face, front.

fácil adj facile, easy.

facilidad f facility, easiness; **con ~** adv cozily, easily.

facilitar vt to facilitate.

fácilmente adv easily.

facineroso adj wicked, criminal.

facsímil m facsimile, fax.

factible adj feasible, practicable.

factor m (math) factor; (com) factor, agent.

factoría f agency; factory.

factura f invoice.

facultad f faculty; Lat Am college.

facultativo/va adj optional; * m/f doctor, practitioner.

faena f task, job; hard work.

faisán m pheasant.

faja f band, sash; strip (of land); corset.

fajo m bundle; wad.

falacia f fallacy; fraud.

falange f phalanx.

falaz adj deceitful, fraudulent; fallacious.

falda f skirt; lap; flap; train; slope, hillside.

faldero/ra adj: **hombre ~** ladies' man; **perrito ~** lap-dog.

faldón m coat-tails pl; skirt.

falencia f Lat Am bankruptcy.

falible adj fallible.

falla f Lat Am mistake.

fallar vt (law) to pronounce sentence on, to judge; * vi to fail.

fallecer vi to die.

fallecimiento m decease, death.

fallido/da adj unsuccessful, frustrated.

fallo m judgement, sentence; failure.

falsamente adv falsely.

falsario/ria *adj* falsifying, forging.
falsear *vt* to falsify, to counterfeit.
falsedad *f* falsehood; untruth, lie; hypocrisy.
falsete *m* (*tec*) plug; bung; (*mus*) falsetto.
falsificación *f* falsification.
falsificador/ora *m/f* forger, counterfeiter.
falsificar *vt* to falsify, to forge, to counterfeit.
falso/sa *adj* false, untrue; deceitful; fake.
falta *f* fault, defect; want; flaw, mistake; (*sport*) foul.
faltante *m Lat Am* deficit.
faltar *vi* to be wanting; to fail; not to fulfill one's promise; to need; to be missing.
falto/ta *adj* wanting, deficient, lacking; miserable, wretched.
faltriquera *f* pocket.
fama *f* fame; reputation, name.
famélico/ca *adj* starving.
familia *f* family.
familiar *adj* familiar; homely, domestic; * *m/f* relative, relation.
familiaridad *f* familiarity.
familiarizarse *vr*: ~ **con** to familiarize oneself with.
famoso/sa *adj* famous.
fan *m/f* fan.
fanático/ca *adj* fanatical; enthusiastic; * *m/f* fanatic; fan.
fandango *m* fandango.
fanfarrón/ona *m/f* bully, braggart.
fanfarronada *f* boast, brag.
fanfarronear *vi* to bully, to brag.
fanfarronería *f* boast, brag.
fango *m* mire, mud.
fangoso/sa *adj* muddy, miry.
fantasía *f* fancy; fantasy; caprice; presumption.
fantasma *f* phantom, ghost.
fantástico/ca *adj* fantastic, whimsical; presumptuous.
fardo *m* bale, parcel.
farfullar *vi* to talk with a stammer.
farisaico/ca *adj* pharisaical; hypocritical.
fariseo *m* Pharisee; hypocrite.
farmacéutico/ca *adj* pharmaceutical; * *m/f* druggist.
farmacia *f* drugstore.
faro *m* (*mar*) lighthouse; (*auto*) headlamp/light; floodlight.
farol *m* lantern.
farola *f* street light.
farsa *f* farce.
farsante *m/f* fraud, fake.
fascículo *m* part, installment.
fascinación *f* fascination.
fascinar *vt* to fascinate; to enchant.
fascismo *m* fascism.
fascista *adj*, *m/f* fascist.
fase *f* phase.
fastidiar *vt* to annoy; to offend; to spoil.
fastidio *m* annoyance; boredom; disgust.
fastidioso/sa *adj* annoying; tedious.

fatal *adj* fatal; mortal; awful.
fatalidad *f* fatality; mischance, ill-luck.
fatalismo *m* fatalism.
fatalista *m/f* fatalist.
fatiga *f* weariness, fatigue.
fatigar *vt* to fatigue, to tire; to harass.
fatigoso/sa *adj* tiresome, troublesome.
fatuidad *f* fatuity, foolishness, silliness.
fatuo/tua *adj* fatuous, stupid, foolish; conceited.
fauces *fpl* jaws *pl*; gullet.
fausto/ta *adj* happy, fortunate; * *m* splendor, pomp.
favor *m* favor; protection; good turn.
favorable *adj* favorable.
favorecer *vt* to favor, to protect.
favorecido/da *m/f Lat Am* prizewinner.
favorito/ta *adj* favorite.
fax *m* fax.
faz *f* face.
fe *f* faith, belief.
fealdad *f* ugliness.
febrero *m* February.
febril *adj* feverish.
fecha *f* date (of a letter etc).
fechar *vt* to date.
fechoría *f* misdeed; exploit.
fecundar *vt* to fertilize.
fecundidad *f* fecundity, fertility.
fecundo/da *adj* fruitful, fertile.
federación *f* federation.
felicidad *f* happiness.
felicitaciones *interj Lat Am* congratulations!
felicitar *vt* to congratulate.
feligrés/esa *m/f* parishioner.
feliz *adj* happy, fortunate.
felpa *f* plush; toweling.
felpudo *m* doormat.
femenil *adj* feminine, womanly.
femenino/na *adj* feminine; female.
feminismo *m* feminism.
feminista *adj*, *m/f* feminist.
fenómeno *m* phenomenon; (*fig*) freak, accident; * *adj* (*col*) great, marvelous.
feo/ea *adj* ugly; bad, nasty.
feracidad *f* productivity, fertility.
feraz *adj* fertile, fruitful.
féretro *m* bier, casket.
feria *f* fair, rest day; village market.
feriado *m Lat Am* public holiday.
fermentación *f* fermentation.
fermentar *vi* to ferment.
fermento *m* ferment; leaven.
ferocidad *f* ferocity, wildness; cruelty.
feroz *adj* ferocious, savage; cruel.
ferretería *f* hardware store.
ferrocarril *m* railroad.
ferroviario/ria *adj* rail *compd*.
ferry *m* ferry.
fértil *adj* fertile, fruitful.
fertilidad *f* fertility, fruitfulness.
fertilización *f* fertilization.

fertilizar vt to fertilize.

férula f ferule; (med) splint.

ferviente adj fervent; ardent.

fervor m fervor, zeal; ardor.

fervoroso/sa adj fervent, ardent, passionate.

festejar vt to feast; to court, to woo.

festejo m courtship; feast.

festín m feast.

festividad f festivity.

festivo/va adj festive, merry; witty; **día** ~ holiday.

festón m garland; festoon.

festonear vt to decorate with garlands.

fétido/da adj fetid, stinking.

feto m fetus.

feudal adj feudal.

fiable adj trustworthy; reliable.

fiador/ra m/f guarantor; (com) backer.

fiambre m cold meat.

fiambrera f dinner pail; lunch basket.

fianza f (law) surety.

fiar vt to entrust, to confide; to bail; to sell on credit; to buy on credit; * vi to trust.

fibra f fiber.

fibroso/sa adj fibrous.

ficción f fiction.

ficha f token, counter (at games); (index) card.

ficticio/cia adj fictitious.

fidedigno/na adj reliable, trustworthy.

fideicomisario/ria m/f trustee.

fideicomiso f trust.

fidelidad f fidelity; loyalty.

fideos mpl vermicelli pl.

fiebre f fever.

fiel adj faithful, loyal; * mpl **los** ~**es** the faithful pl.

fieltro m felt.

fiera f wild beast.

fiereza f fierceness, ferocity; cruelty.

fiero/ra adj fierce, ferocious; cruel; rough, harsh.

fierrero/ra m/f Lat Am weightlifter.

fierro m Lat Am iron.

fiesta f party; festivity; ~**s** f pl feast days; holidays pl.

figura f figure, shape.

figurado/da adj figurative.

figurar vt to figure; ~**se** vr to fancy, to imagine.

figurilla f ridiculous little figure.

fijador m fixative; gel (for the hair).

fijar vt to fix, to fasten; ~**se** vr to become fixed; to establish oneself; ~**se en** to notice.

fijo/ja adj fixed, firm; settled, permanent.

fila f row, line; (mil) rank; **en** ~ in a line, in a row.

filamento m filament.

filantropía f philanthropy.

filántropo/pa m/f philanthropist.

fildeador/ra m/f Lat Am fielder.

fildear vi Lat Am to field.

fildeo m Lat Am fielding.

filete m fillet; fillet steak.

filiación f lineage; personal description, personal particulars pl.

filial adj filial; * f (com) subsidiary.

filibustero m pirate.

filigrana f filigree.

filmar vt to film.

filo m edge, blade.

filología f philology.

filológico/ca adj philological.

filólogo/ga m/f philologist.

filoso/sa adj Lat Am sharp.

filosofar vt to philosophize.

filosofía f philosophy.

filosófico/ca adj philosophical.

filósofo/fa m/f philosopher.

filtración f filtration.

filtrar vt to filter, to strain.

filtro m filter.

fin m end; termination, conclusion; aim, purpose; **al** ~ at last; **en** ~ (fig) well then; **por** ~ finally, lastly.

final adj final; * m end; termination, conclusion; * f (sport) final.

finalizar vt to finish, to conclude; * vi to be finished.

finalmente adv finally, at last.

financiar vt to finance.

financista m/f Lat Am financier.

finca f land, property, real estate; country house; farm; Lat Am plantation.

fineza f fineness, perfection; eleg-ance; courtesy; small gift.

fingido/da adj feigned, fake, sham.

fingimiento m simulation, pretense.

fingir vt to feign, to fake; to invent; to imitate; ~**se** vr to pretend to be; * vi to pretend.

finito/ta adj finite.

fino/na adj fine, pure; slender; polite; acute; dry (of sherry).

finura f fineness.

firma f signature; (com) company.

firmamento m firmament, sky, -heaven.

firmar vt to sign.

firme adj firm, stable, strong, secure; constant; resolute; * m road surface.

firmeza f firmness, stability, constancy.

fiscal adj fiscal; * m/f district attor-ney.

fiscalía f office and business of the district attorney.

fiscalizar vt to inspect; to criticize.

fisco m treasury.

fisgar vt to pry into.

fisgón/ona m/f prying person, -snooper.

física f physics.

físico/ca adj physical; * m/f physicist; * m physique.

fisonomía f physiognomy.

fisonomista m/f: **ser buen** ~ to have a good memory for faces.

flaco/ca adj lean, skinny; feeble.

flagelación f flagellation.

flagrante adj flagrant.

flamante adj flaming, bright; brand-new.

flan *m* crème caramel.

flanco *m* flank.

flanquear *vt* (*mil*) to flank.

flaquear *vi* to flag; to weaken.

flaqueza *f* thinness, leanness; feebleness, weakness.

flash *m* flash.

flato *m* (*med*) flatulence; depression.

flatulento/ta *adj* flatulent.

flauta *f* (*mus*) flute.

flautista *m/f* flute player, flautist.

flecha *f* arrow.

fleco *m* hair cut straight across the forehead, fringe.

flema *f* phlegm.

flemático/ca *adj* phlegmatic.

flemón *m* ulcer in the gums.

flequillo *m* hair cut straight across the forehead, fringe.

fletar *vt* to freight (a ship).

flete *m* (*mar*) freight; charter.

flexibilidad *f* flexibility.

flexible *adj* flexible; compliant; -docile.

flojedad *f* feebleness; laxity, laziness; negligence.

flojera *f*: me da ~ I can't be bothered.

flojo/ja *adj* loose; flexible; lax, slack; lazy.

flor *f* flower.

florecer *vi* to blossom.

florero *m* vase.

floresta *f* wood, grove; beauty spot.

florete *m* fencing foil.

florido/da *adj* full of flowers; in bloom; choice.

florista *m/f* florist.

flota *f* fleet.

flotador *m* float.

flotante *adj* floating.

flotar *vi* to float.

flote *m*: a ~ afloat.

flotilla *f* small fleet, flotilla.

fluctuación *f* fluctuation; uncertainty.

fluctuar *vi* to fluctuate; to waver.

fluidez *f* fluidity; fluency.

fluido/da *adj* fluid; (*fig*) fluent; * *m* fluid.

fluir *vi* to flow.

flujo *m* flux; flow; ~ de sangre (*med*) loss of blood.

fluvial *adj* fluvial, river *compd*.

foca *f* seal.

foco *m* focus; center; source; floodlight; (light) bulb; *Lat Am* street light; *Lat Am* car headlight.

fofo/fa *adj* spongy; soft; bland.

fogata *f* blaze; bonfire.

fogón *m* stove; hearth.

fogonazo *m* flash; explosion.

fogosidad *f* dash, verve; fieriness.

fogoso/sa *adj* fiery; ardent, fervent; impetuous, boisterous.

folk *m* folk music.

follaje *m* foliage.

folletista *m/f* pamphleteer.

folleto *m* pamphlet; folder, brochure.

follón *m* (*col*) mess; fuss.

fomentar *vt* to encourage; to promote.

fomento *m* promotion.

fonda *f* hotel; inn; boarding house.

fondeadero *m* anchorage.

fondeado/da *adj Lat Am* wealthy.

fondear *vi* to drop anchor.

fondista *m/f* innkeeper.

fondo *m* bottom; back; background; space; ~s *mpl* stock, funds *pl*, capital; a ~ perfectly, completely.

fontanería *f* plumbing.

fontanero/ra *m/f* plumber.

footing *m* jogging.

forajido *m* outlaw.

foral *adj* belonging to the statute law of a country.

forastero/ra *adj* strange, exotic; * *m/f* stranger.

forcejear *vi* to struggle.

forense *adj* forensic; * *m/f* forensic scientist.

forjador/ra *m/f* framer; forger.

forjadura *f* forging.

forjar *vt* to forge; to frame; to invent.

forma *f* form, shape; pattern; (*med*) fitness; (*sport*) form; means, method; de ~ que in such a manner that.

formación *f* formation; form, figure; education; training.

formal *adj* formal; proper, genuine; serious, grave.

formalidad *f* formality; gravity.

formalizar *vt* (*law*) to formalize; to regularize; ~se *vr* to be regularized.

formar *vt* to form, to shape.

formidable *adj* formidable, dreadful; (*col*) terrific.

fórmula *f* formula.

formulario *m* formulary.

fornicación *f* fornication.

fornicador *m* fornicator.

fornicar *vi* to commit fornication, to fornicate.

fornido/da *adj* well-built.

foro *m* court of justice; forum.

forraje *m* forage.

forrajear *vt* to forage.

forrar *vt* to line; to face; to cover.

forro *m* lining; book jacket.

fortalecer *vt* to fortify, to strengthen.

fortaleza *f* courage; strength, vigor; (*mil*) fortress, stronghold.

fortificación *f* fortification.

fortificar *vt* to strengthen; to fortify (a place).

fortín *m* (*mil*) small fort.

fortuito/ta *adj* fortuitous.

fortuna *f* fortune; wealth.

forzar *vt* to force.

forzoso/sa *adj* indispensable, necessary.

forzudo/da *adj* strong, vigorous.

fosa *f* grave; pit.

fósforo *m* phosphorus; ~s *mpl* matches *pl*.

fósil *adj*, *m* fossil.

foso *vt* pit; moat, ditch, fosse.

foto f photo.
fotocopia f photocopy.
fotocopiar vt to photocopy.
fotografía f photography; photograph.
fotógrafo/fa m/f photographer.
frac m tails, dress coat.
fracasar vi to fail.
fracaso m failure.
fracción f fraction.
fractura f fracture.
fracturar vt to break (a bone).
fragancia f fragrance, sweetness of smell; odor.
fragante adj fragrant, scented.
fragata f (mar) frigate.
frágil adj fragile, frail.
fragilidad f fragility, brittleness; -frailty.
fragmento m fragment.
fragosidad f roughness; denseness.
fragoso/sa adj craggy, rough, uneven.
fragua f forge.
fraguar vt to forge; to contrive; * vi to solidify, to harden.
fraile m friar, monk.
frambuesa f raspberry.
francés/sa adj French; * m French (language); * m/f Frenchman/woman.
franco/ca adj frank; candid; free, gratis.
franela f flannel; undershirt.
franja f strip, band, fringe.
franquear vt to clear; to overcome; to stamp (letters); **~se** to unbosom oneself.
franqueo m postage.
franqueza f frankness.
franquicia f immunity from taxes.
frasco m flask.
frase f phrase.
fraternal adj fraternal, brotherly.
fraternidad f fraternity, brotherhood.
fratricida m/f fratricide (person).
fratricidio m fratricide (act).
fraude m fraud, deceit; cheat.
fraudulento/ta adj fraudulent, deceitful.
frazada f Lat Am blanket.
frecuencia f frequency.
frecuentar vt to frequent.
frecuente adj frequent.
freezer m Lat Am freezer.
fregadero m (kitchen) sink.
fregado m scouring, scrubbing; (fig) intrigue; underhand work.
fregar vt to scrub; to wash up.
fregona f kitchen maid, someone who washes dishes.
freír vt to fry.
frenar vt to brake; (fig) to check.
frenesí m frenzy.
frenético/ca adj frantic; frenzied, wild.
frenillo m speech impediment.
freno m bit (horse's); brake; (fig) check.
frente m front; (mil) front; face; **~ a ~** face to face; **en ~** opposite; * m forehead.

fresa f strawberry.
fresal m strawberry plant; ground bearing strawberry plants.
fresco/ca adj fresh; cool; new; ruddy; * m fresh air; * m/f (col) shameless/impudent person.
frescura f freshness; frankness; cheek, nerve.
fresno m ash tree.
frialdad f coldness; indifference.
fricción f friction.
friega f rubbing; nuisance.
frígido/da adj frigid.
frigorífico m refrigerator.
frijol m bean.
frío/fría adj cold; indifferent; * m cold; indifference.
friolento/ta adj Lat Am chilly.
friolera f trifle.
friso m frieze; wainscot.
fritada f dish of fried meat/fish.
fritar vt Lat Am to fry.
frito/ta adj fried.
frivolidad f frivolity.
frívolo/la adj frivolous.
frondosidad f foliage.
frondoso/sa adj leafy.
frontera f frontier.
fronterizo/za adj frontier compd; bordering.
frontón m (sport) pelota court; -pelota.
frotación, frotadura f friction, rubbing.
frotar vt to rub.
fructífero/ra adj fruit-bearing, fruitful.
fructificar vi to bear fruit; to come to fruition.
fructuoso/sa adj fruitful.
frugal adj frugal, sparing.
frugalidad f frugality, parsimony.
fruncir vt to pleat; to knit; to contract; **~ las cejas** to knit the eyebrows.
frustrar vt to frustrate.
fruta f fruit; **~ del tiempo** seasonal fruit.
frutal m fruit tree.
frutera f fruit dish.
frutería f fruit shop.
frutero/ra m/f fruiterer, fruit seller; * m fruit basket.
frutilla f strawberry.
fruto m fruit; benefit, profit.
fuego m fire.
fuelle m bellows pl.
fuente f fountain; spring; source; large dish.
fuera adv out(side); away; **~ de** prep outside; **¡~!** out of the way!
fueraborda m outboard motor.
fuero m statute law of a country; jurisdiction.
fuerte m (mil) fortification, fort; forte; * adj vigorous, tough; strong; loud; heavy; * adv strongly; hard.
fuerza f force, strength; (electric) power; violence; **a ~ de** by dint of; **~s** mpl troops pl.
fuga f flight, escape; leak (of gas).
fugarse vr to escape, to flee.
fugaz adj fleeting.

fugitivo/va *adj, m/f* fugitive.

fulano/na *m/f* so-and-so, what's-his-name/ what's-her-name.

fulgurar *vi* to flash.

fullería *f* cheating.

fullero *m* cardsharp, cheat.

fulminar *vt* to fulminate; ** vi* to explode.

fumador/ra *m/f* smoker.

fumar *vt, vi* to smoke.

fumigación *f* fumigation.

funambulista *m/f* tightrope walker.

función *f* function; duties *pl*; show, performance.

funcionar *vi* to function; to work (of a machine).

funcionario/ria *m/f* official; civil servant.

funda *f* case, sheath; ~ **de almohada** pillowcase.

fundación *f* foundation.

fundador/ra *m/f* founder.

fundamental *adj* fundamental.

fundamentalismo *m* fundamentalism.

fundamentalista *adj, m/f* fundamentalist.

fundamento *m* foundation; groundwork; reason, cause.

fundar *vt* to found; to establish; to ground.

fundición *f* fusion; foundry.

fundir *vt* to fuse; to melt; to smelt; ~**se** *vr* (*com*) to merge; to bankrupt; to blow (of a fuse).

fúnebre *adj* mournful, sad; funereal.

funeral *m* funeral; ~**es** *mpl* funeral, funeral rites *pl*, obsequies *pl*.

funerario/ria *adj* funeral *compd*, funereal.

funesto/ta *adj* ill-fated, unfortunate; fatal.

furgón *m* wagon.

furgoneta *f* pick-up truck; station wagon.

furia *f* fury, rage.

furibundo/da *adj* furious; frenzied.

furioso/sa *adj* furious.

furor *m* fury, rage.

furtivamente *adv* furtively.

furtivo/va *adj* furtive.

furúnculo *m* (*med*) boil.

fusible *m* fuse.

fusil *m* rifle.

fusilar *vt* to shoot.

fusilero *m* rifleman.

fusión *f* fusion; (*com*) merger.

fusta *f* riding crop.

fútbol *m* football; ~ **americano** American football.

futbolista *m/f* football player, footballer.

fútil *adj* futile; trifling.

futilidad *f* futility.

futuro/ra *adj, m* future.

G

gabán *m* overcoat.

gabardina *f* raincoat.

gabarra *f* (*mar*) lighter.

gabinete *m* cabinet (in politics), study; office (of lawyers etc).

gaceta *f* gazette.

gachas *fpl* any soft/semi-liquid food; porridge.

gacho/cha *adj* curved, bent downward.

gafas *fpl* glasses *pl*, spectacles *pl*.

gafe *m* jinx.

gaita *f* bagpipe; flageolet.

gaitero/ra *m/f* bagpiper, bagpipe player.

gaje *m*: ~**s del oficio** occupational hazards *pl*.

gajo *m* segment (of orange).

gala *f* full dress; (*fig*) cream, flower; ~**s** *fpl* finery; **hacer** ~ **de** to display, to show off.

galán *m* lover; handsome young man; (*theat*) male lead.

galante *adj* gallant.

galanteador *m* lover, suitor.

galantear *vt* to court, to woo.

galanteo *m* gallantry, courtship.

galantería *f* gallantry; politeness; compliment.

galápago *m* tortoise.

galardón *m* reward, prize.

galardonar *vt* to reward, to recompense.

galaxia *f* galaxy.

galbana *f* laziness, idleness.

galeón *m* (*mar*) galleon.

galera *f* (*mar*) galley; wagon.

galería *f* gallery.

galgo *m* greyhound.

gallardete *m* (*mar*) pennant, -streamer.

gallardía *f* fineness, elegance, gracefulness; dash.

gallardo/da *adj* graceful, elegant; brave, daring.

gallería *f Lat Am* cockpit.

galleta *f* cookie.

gallina *f* hen; ** m/f* (*fig*) coward; ~ **ciega** blindman's buff.

gallinazo *m Lat Am* turkey vulture/buzzard.

gallinero *m* henhouse, coop; poulterer; (*theat*) top gallery; hubbub.

gallineta *f Lat Am* woodcock (bird).

gallo *m* cock.

galón *m* (*mil*) stripe; braid; galloon.

galopar *vi* to gallop.

galope *m* gallop.

galvánico/ca *adj* galvanic.

galvanismo *m* galvanism.

gama[1] *f* (*mus*) scale; (*fig*) range, -gamut.

gama[2] *f* doe (of the fallow deer).

gamba *f* shrimp; prawn.

gamberro/rra *m/f* hooligan.

gamo *m* buck (of the fallow deer).

gamuza *f* chamois (goat antelope); chamois leather.

gana *f* desire, wish; appetite; will, longing; **de buena** ~ with pleasure, voluntarily; **de mala** ~ unwillingly, with reluctance.

ganadería *f* cattle raising; cattle; livestock.

ganadero *m* rancher; cattle dealer.

ganado *m* livestock, cattle *pl*; ~ **mayor** horses and mules *pl*; ~ **menor** sheep, goats and pigs *pl*.

ganancia *f* gain, profit; increase.

ganancial *adj* lucrative.

ganar *vt* to gain; to win; to earn; * *vi* to win.

gancho *m* hook; crook.

gandul *adj*, *m*/*f* layabout, lazy person.

ganga *f* bargain.

gangoso/sa *adj* nasal.

gangrena *f* gangrene.

gangrenarse *vr* to become gangrenous.

gangrenoso/sa *adj* gangrenous.

ganso/sa *m*/*f* gander; goose; (*col*) -idiot.

garabatear *vi*, *vt* to scrawl, to scribble.

garabatos *mpl* scrawling letters/characters *pl*.

garaje *m* garage.

garage *m Lat Am* garage.

garante *m*/*f* guarantor; * *adj* responsible.

garantía *f* warranty, guarantee.

garañón *m* jackass, male donkey.

garapatear *vi*, *vt* to scrawl, to scribble.

garapiñar *vt* to freeze; to ice.

garbanzo *m* chickpea.

garbo *m* gracefulness, elegance; stylishness; generosity.

garboso/sa *adj* graceful; elegant, stylish; generous.

garduña *f* marten (animal).

gargajo *m* phlegm, spit.

garganta *f* throat, gullet; instep; neck (of a bottle); narrow pass between mountains; river gorge.

gargantilla *f* necklace.

gárgara *f* noise made by gargling.

gargarismo *m* gargling, gargle.

gargarizar *vi* to gargle.

garita *f* (*mil*) sentry box; (*rail*) signal box.

garra *f* claw; talon; paw.

garrafa *f* carafe; (gas) cylinder.

garrafal *adj* great, vast, huge.

garrapata *f* tick (insect).

garrocha *f Lat Am* vaulting pole.

garrotazo *m* blow with a stick/club.

garrote *m* stick, club, cudgel; (*med*) tourniquet; (*law*) garrote.

garrotillo *m* (*med*) croup.

garrucha *f* pulley.

garza *f* heron.

garzo/za *adj* blue-eyed.

gas *m* gas; petrol, gas.

gasa *f* gauze.

gaseoso/sa *adj* fizzy; * *f* lemonade.

gasfitero/ra *m*/*f* plumber.

gasoil *m* diesel (oil).

gasolina *f* gasoline.

gasolinera *f* service station.

gasómetro *m* gasometer.

gastador/ra *m*/*f* spendthrift.

gastar *vt* to spend; to expend; to waste; to wear away; to use up; **-se** *vr* to wear out; to waste.

gasto *m* expense, expenditure; use.

gastronomía *f* gastronomy.

gata *f* she-cat; **a -s** on all fours.

gatear *vi* to go on all fours.

gatera *f* catlover; (*mar*) cat hole.

gatillazo *m* click of the trigger in firing.

gatillo *m* trigger of a gun; (*med*) dental forceps.

gato *m* tomcat; jack, clamp, vice.

gatuno/na *adj* catlike, feline.

gaveta *f* drawer of a desk, locker.

gavilán *m* sparrow hawk.

gavilla *f* sheaf of corn.

gaviota *f* seagull.

gay *adj invar*, *m* (*col*) gay; homosexual.

gazapo *m* young rabbit; liar; lie.

gazmoñada, **gazmoñería** *f* prudery; hypocrisy.

gazmoñero/ra, **gazmoño/ña** *adj* hypocritical.

gaznate *m* gullet, wind pipe.

gazpacho *m* Spanish cold tomato soup.

gazuza *f* ravenous hunger.

gelatina *f* jelly; gelatin.

gemelo/la *m*/*f* twin.

gemido *m* groan, moan, howl.

geminiano/na *adj Lat Am* Geminian (zodiac sign).

Géminis *m* Gemini (zodiac sign).

gemir *vi* to groan, to moan.

genciana *f* (*bot*) gentian.

gendarme *m* policeman.

gendarmería *f* police.

genealogía *f* genealogy.

genealógico/ca *adj* genealogical.

generación *f* generation; progeny, race.

general *m* general; * *adj* general; **en ~** generally, in general.

generalidad *f* generality.

generalizar *vt* to generalize.

generalmente *adv* generally.

genérico/ca *adj* generic.

género *m* genus; kind, type; gender; (*com*) cloth, material; **~s** goods *pl*, commodities *pl*.

generosidad *f* generosity.

generoso/sa *adj* noble, generous.

Génesis *f* Genesis.

genial *adj* inspired, brilliant; genial.

genio *m* nature, character; genius.

genital *adj* genital; * *mpl* **~es** genitals *pl*.

genitivo *m* (*gr*) genitive case.

gente *f* people; nation; family.

gentil *m*/*f* pagan, heathen; * *adj* elegant; graceful; charming.

gentileza *f* grace; charm; politeness.

gentilhombre *m* gentleman.

gentío *m* crowd, throng.

genuflexión *f* genuflection.

genuino/na *adj* genuine; pure.

geografía *f* geography.

geográfico/ca *adj* geographical.

geógrafo/fa *m*/*f* geographer.

geología *f* geology.

geólogo/ga *m*/*f* geologist.

geometría *f* geometry.

geométrico/ca *adj* geometrical, geometric.

geranio *m* (*bot*) geranium.

gerenciar *vt Lat Am* to manage.

gerente *m/f* manager; director.

geriatría *f (med)* geriatrics.

germen *m* germ, bud; source, origin.

germinar *vi* to germinate, to bud.

gerundio *m (gr)* gerund.

gesticular *vi* to gesticulate.

gestión *f* management; negotiation.

gesto *m* face; grimace; gesture.

giganta *f* giantess.

gigante *m* giant; * *adj* gigantic.

gigantesco/ca *adj* gigantic, giant.

gilipollas *adj invar* (col) stupid; * *m/f invar* wimp.

gimnasia *f* gymnastics.

gimnasio *m* gymnasium.

gimnasta *m/f* gymnast.

gimnástico/ca *adj* gymnastic.

ginebra *f* gin.

ginecólogo/ga *m/f* gynecologist.

gira *f* trip, tour.

girar *vt* to turn around; to swivel; (com) to draw, to issue; * *vi* to go round, to revolve; (com) to do business; to draw.

giratorio/ria *adj* revolving.

girasol *m* sunflower.

giro *m* turning round; tendency; change; (com) draft.

gitano/na *m/f* Gypsy.

glacial *adj* icy.

glaciar *m* glacier.

glándula *f* gland.

glandular *adj* glandular.

globalización *f* globalization.

globo *m* globe; sphere; orb; balloon; ~ aerostático air balloon.

glóbulo *m* globule; corpuscle.

gloria *f* glory.

gloriarse *vr*: ~ **en** to glory in, to take pride in; to take delight in.

glorieta *f* bower, arbor; traffic circle.

glorificación *f* glorification; praise.

glorificar *vt* to glorify.

glorioso/sa *adj* glorious.

glosa *f* gloss; comment.

glosar *vt* to gloss; to comment on.

glotón/ona *m/f* glutton.

glotonería *f* gluttony.

gobernación *f* government.

gobernador/ra *m/f* governor.

gobernar *vt* to govern; to regulate; to direct.

gobierno *m* government.

goce *m* enjoyment.

gol *m* goal.

goleta *f* schooner.

golf *m* golf.

golfa *f* (col) slut.

golfito *m* Lat Am mini-golf.

golfo[1] *m* gulf, bay.

golfo[2] *(col)* urchin; lout.

golondrina *f* swallow.

golosina *f* delicacy, tidbit; bauble, trifle; sweet tooth.

goloso/sa *adj* sweet-toothed.

golpe *m* blow, stroke, hit; knock; clash; coup; **de ~** suddenly.

golpear *vt* to beat, to knock; to punch.

golpiza *f* Lat Am beating.

goma *f* gum; rubber; elastic.

gomosidad *f* stickiness, viscosity.

gomoso/sa *adj* gummy, viscous.

góndola *f* gondola; (rail) freight car.

gondolero *m* gondolier.

gordinflón/ona *m/f* very fat person.

gordo/da *adj* fat, plump, big-bellied; first, main; (col) enormous.

gordura *f* grease; fatness, corpulence, obesity.

gorgojo *m* grub, weevil.

gorgorito *m* trill, warble.

gorila *m* gorilla.

gorjear *vi* to twitter, to chirp.

gorjeo *m* chirping.

gorra *f* cap; bonnet; (mil) bearskin.

gorrión *m* sparrow.

gorro *m* cap; bonnet.

gorrón/ona *m/f* scrounger.

gota *f* drop; (med) gout.

gotear *vt* to drip; to drizzle.

gotera *f* leak.

gótico/ca *adj* Gothic.

gotoso/sa *adj* gouty.

gozar *vt* to enjoy, to have, to possess; ~**se** *vr* to enjoy oneself, to rejoice.

gozne *m* hinge.

gozo *m* joy, pleasure.

gozoso/sa *adj* joyful, cheerful; content, glad, pleased.

grabación *f* recording.

grabado *m* engraving.

grabador *m* engraver.

grabadora *f* tape recorder.

grabar *vt* to engrave; to record.

gracejo *m* wit; charm; gracefulness.

gracia *f* grace, gracefulness; wit; **¡(muchas) ~s!** thanks (very much); **tener ~** to be funny.

gracioso/sa *adj* graceful; beautiful; funny; pleasing; * *m* comic character.

grada *f* step of a staircase; tier, row; ~**s** *fpl* seats *pl* of a stadium/theater.

gradería *f* (flight of) steps *pl*; row of seats; Lat Am terraces.

grado *m* step; degree; **de buen ~** willingly.

graduación *f* graduation; (mil) rank.

gradual *adj* gradual.

graduar *vt* to graduate.

gráfico/ca *adj* graphic; * *m* diagram; * *f* graph.

grajo/ja *m/f* rook.

grama *f* grass; Lat Am lawn.

gramática *f* grammar.

gramatical *adj* grammatical.

gramático/ca *m/f* grammarian.

gramo *m* gram.

gran *adj* = **grande**.

grana *f* grain; scarlet.

granada f (*mil*) grenade; pomegranate.

granadero m (*mil*) grenadier.

granadilla f passionflower; passion fruit.

granado m pomegranate tree.

granate m garnet (precious stone).

grande *adj* great; big; tall; grand; * *m/f* adult.

grandeza f greatness; grandeur; size.

grandiosidad f greatness; grandeur, magnificence.

grandioso/sa *adj* grand, magnificent.

granel *adv*: **a** ~ in bulk.

granero m granary.

granito m granite.

granizada f hail; hailstorm; shower, volley.

granizado m iced drink.

granizar *vi* to hail (weather).

granizo m hail (weather).

granja f farm.

granjero/ra m/f farmer.

grano m grain.

granuja m rogue; urchin.

grapa f staple; clamp.

grasa f suet, fat; grease.

grasiento/ta *adj* greasy; rusty; filthy.

grasoso/sa *adj Lat Am* greasy; rusty; filthy.

gratificación f gratification; recompense.

gratificar *vt* to gratify; to reward, to recompense.

gratis *adj* free; *adv* freely.

gratitud f gratitude, gratefulness.

grato/ta *adj* pleasant, agreeable.

gratuito/ta *adj* gratuitous; free.

gravamen m charge, obligation; nuisance; tax.

gravar *vt* to burden; (*com*) to tax.

grave *adj* weighty, heavy; grave, important; serious.

gravedad f gravity; graveness.

gravemente *adv* gravely, seriously.

gravilla f gravel.

gravitación f gravitation.

gravitar *vt* to gravitate; to weigh down on.

gravoso/sa *adj* onerous, burdensome; costly.

graznar *vi* to croak; to cackle; to quack.

graznido m croak; cackle; quack.

greda f clay.

gremial f *Lat Am* (labor) union.

gremialista m/f *Lat Am* union member.

gremio m union, guild; society; company; corporation.

greña f tangle; shock of hair.

greñudo/da *adj* disheveled.

gresca f clatter; outcry; confusion; wrangle, quarrel.

grieta f crevice, crack, chink.

grifo m faucet; gas station.

grilletes *mpl* shackles *pl*; fetters *pl*.

grillo m cricket; bud, shoot; ~s *mpl* fetters *pl*, irons *pl*.

grima f disgust; annoyance.

gripe f flu, influenza.

gris *adj* gray.

gritar *vi* to cry out, to shout, to yell.

gritería f shouting, clamor, uproar.

grito m shout, cry, scream.

grosella f redcurrant; ~ **negra** blackcurrant.

grosellero m currant bush.

grosería f coarseness, rudeness; vulgar comment.

grosero/ra *adj* coarse; rude, bad-mannered.

grosor m thickness.

grotesco/ca *adj* grotesque.

grúa f crane (machine); derrick.

grueso/sa *adj* thick; bulky; large; coarse; * *m* bulk.

grulla f crane (bird).

grumo m clot; curd.

grumoso/sa *adj* clotted.

gruñido m grunt; growl.

gruñidor/ra m/f grunter, mumbler; (*fig*) grumbler.

gruñir *vi* to grunt; to grumble; to creak (of hinges etc).

grupa f rump.

grupo m group.

gruta f grotto.

guachimán m *Lat Am* night watchman.

guadaña f scythe.

guagua f trifle, small thing.

gualdrapa f trappings *pl* (of a horse); tatter, rag.

guantada f slap.

guante m glove.

guapo/pa *adj* good-looking; handsome; smart.

guarda m/f guard, keeper; * f custody, keeping.

guardaagujas m *invar* (*rail*) switchman.

guardabosque m ranger, gamekeeper, forester.

guardacostas m *invar* coastguard vessel.

guardaespaldas m/f *invar* bodyguard.

guardafuegos m *invar* firescreen.

guardameta m/f goalkeeper.

guardapolvo m dust cover; coveralls *pl*.

guardar *vt* to keep, to preserve; to save (money); to guard; ~**se** *vr* to be on one's guard; ~**se de** to avoid, to abstain from.

guardarropa m wardrobe; cloakroom.

guardavallas m/f *invar Lat Am* goalkeeper.

guardia f guard; (*mar*) watch; care, custody; * m/f guard; policeman/woman; * m (*mil*) guardsman.

guardián/ana m/f keeper; guardian.

guardilla f garret, attic.

guarecer *vt* to protect; to shelter; ~**se** *vr* to take refuge.

guarida f den, lair; shelter; hiding place.

guarismo m figure, numeral.

guarnecer *vt* to provide, to equip; to reinforce; to garnish, to set (in gold etc); to adorn.

guarnición f trimming; gold setting; sword guard; garnish; (*mil*) garrison.

guasa f joke.

guasón/ona m/f joker, jester.

gubernativo/va *adj* governmental.

guedeja f lock of hair.

guerra f war; hostility.

guerrear *vi* to fight, to wage war.

guerrero/ra m/f warrior; * *adj* martial, warlike.

guerrilla f guerrilla warfare; guerrilla group.
gueto m ghetto.
guía m/f guide; * f guidebook.
guiar vt to guide; (auto) to steer.
guijarral m stony place.
guijarro m pebble.
guillotina f guillotine.
guillotinar vt to guillotine.
guinda f cherry.
guindal m cherry tree.
guindilla f chili pepper.
guiñapo m tatter, rag; rogue.
guiñar vt to wink.
guión m hyphen (in writing); script (of film).
guirigay m gibberish, confused language.
guirnalda f garland, wreath.
güiro m Lat Am gourd.
guisado m stew.
guisante m (bot) pea.
guisar vt to cook.
guiso m cooked dish; stew; seasoning.
guisote m hash; (col) grub.
guitarra f guitar.
guitarrista m/f guitar player.
gula f gluttony.
gusano m maggot, worm.
gustar vt to taste; to sample; * vi to please, to be pleasing; **me gusta…** I like… .
gusto m taste; pleasure, delight; liking.
gustosamente adv gladly, with pleasure.
gustoso/sa adj pleasant; tasty.
gutural adj guttural.

H

haba f broad bean.
haber vt to get, to lay hands on; to occur; * v imp: **hay** there is, there are; * v aux to have; **~se con uno vr: habérselas con uno** to have it out with somebody; * m income, salary; assets pl; (com) credit.
habichuela f bean.
hábil adj able, clever, skillful, dexterous, apt.
habilidad f ability, ableness, dexterity, aptitude.
habilitación f entitlement, qualification.
habilitar vt to qualify, to enable; to finance.
habitable adj habitable.
habitación f habitation, abode, lodging, dwelling, residence; room.
habitante m/f inhabitant, occupant.
habitar vt to inhabit, to live in.
hábito m dress; habit, custom.
habitual adj habitual, customary.
habituar vt to accustom; **~se** vr to become accustomed to.
habla f speech; language; dialect.
hablador/ra m/f talkative person.
habladuría f rumor; **~s** fpl gossip.
hablante adj speaking; * m/f speaker.
hablar vt (vi) to speak; to talk.

hacedor/ra m/f maker; author.
hacendado m property owner; landowner; rancher.
hacendoso/sa adj industrious.
hacer vt to make; to do; to put into practice; to perform; to effect; to prepare; to imagine; to force; (math) to amount to, to make; * vi to act, to behave; **~se** vr to become.
hacha f torch; ax, hatchet.
hachazo m blow with an ax.
hacia adv toward(s); about; **~ arriba/abajo** up(wards)/down(wards).
hacienda f property; large farm; ranch; **H~** Treasury.
hacinar vt to stack/pile up; to hoard.
hada f fairy.
hado m fate, destiny.
halagar vt to cajole, to flatter.
halago m cajolery; pleasure.
halagüeño adj attractive, flattering.
halcón m falcon.
halconero m falconer.
hálito m breath; gentle breeze.
hall m hall; (theat) foyer.
hallar vt to find; to meet with; to discover; **~se** vr to find oneself; to be.
hallazgo m finding, discovery.
hamaca f hammock.
hambre f hunger; famine; longing.
hambreado/da adj Lat Am hungry; starved.
hambriento/ta adj hungry; starved.
hamburguesa f hamburger.
haragán/ana m/f idler, good-for-nothing.
haraganear vi to idle, to loiter.
haraganería f idleness, laziness.
harapo m rag, tatter.
haraposo adj ragged.
hardware m (comput) hardware.
harina f flour; **~ de maíz** cornstarch.
harinoso/sa adj floury.
hartar vt to satiate; to glut; to tire, to sicken; **~se** vr to gorge oneself (with food); to get fed up.
harto/ta adj full; fed up; * adv enough.
hartura f surfeit; plenty, abundance.
hasta prep up to; down to; until, as far as; * adv even.
hastío m loathing; disgust; boredom.
hatajo m lot, collection.
hato m clothes pl; herd of cattle, flock of sheep; provisions pl; crowd, gang, collection.
haya f beech tree.
haz m bunch, bundle; beam (of light).
hazaña f exploit, achievement.
hazmerreír m invar ridiculous person, laughing stock.
hebilla f buckle.
hebra f thread; vein of minerals/metals; grain of wood.
hebraico/ca adj belonging to the Hebrews.
hebreo/ea m/f Hebrew; Israeli; * m Hebrew language; * adj Hebrew; Israeli.

hechicería f witchcraft; charm.

hechicero/ra adj charming, bewitching; * m/f sorcerer/ sorceress.

hechizar vt to bewitch, to enchant; to charm.

hechizo m bewitchment, enchantment.

hecho/cha adj made; done; mature; ready-to-wear; cooked; * m action; act; fact; matter; event.

hechura f form, shape; fashion; making; workmanship; creature.

hectárea f hectare.

heder vi to stink, to smell bad.

hediondez f strong stench.

hediondo/da adj fetid, stinking.

hedor m stench, stink.

helada f frost; freeze-up.

helado/da adj frozen; glacial; icy; astonished; astounded; * m ice cream.

helar vt to freeze; to congeal; to astonish, to amaze; ~se vr to be frozen; to turn into ice; to congeal; * vi to freeze; to congeal.

helecho m fern.

hélice f spiral, helix; propeller.

helicóptero m helicopter.

hembra f female.

hemisferio m hemisphere.

hemorragia f hemorrhage.

hemorroides fpl hemorrhoids pl, piles pl.

henchir vt to fill up; ~se vr to fill/stuff oneself.

hendedura f fissure, chink, crevice.

hender vt to crack, to split; to go through; to open a passage.

hendidura f = hendedura.

heno m hay.

heraldo m herald.

herborizar vi to pick herbs; to collect plants.

heredad f inherited property; country estate, ranch, large farm.

heredar vt to inherit.

heredera f heiress.

heredero m heir.

hereditario/ria adj hereditary.

hereje m/f heretic.

herejía f heresy.

herencia f inheritance, heritage, heredity.

herida f wound, injury.

herido/da adj wounded, hurt.

herir vt to wound, to hurt; to beat, to strike; to affect, to touch, to move; to offend.

hermafrodita m hermaphrodite.

hermana f sister.

hermanar vt to match, to suit, to harmonize.

hermanastra f step-sister, half-sister.

hermanastro m step-brother, half-brother.

hermandad f fraternity; brotherhood.

hermano m brother; ~/na adj matched; resembling.

hermético/ca adj hermetic, watertight.

hermoso/sa adj beautiful, handsome, lovely; large, robust.

hermosura f beauty.

hernia f hernia, rupture.

héroe m hero.

heroicidad f heroism; heroic deed.

heroico/ca adj heroic.

heroína[1] f heroine.

heroína[2] f heroin (drug).

heroísmo m heroism.

herpes m herpes; * fpl (med) shingles.

herrador m farrier, blacksmith.

herradura f horseshoe.

herramienta f tool.

herrar vt to shoe (horses).

herrería f ironworks; forge.

herrero m smith, blacksmith.

hervidero m boiling; unrest; swarm.

hervir vt to boil; to cook; * vi to boil; to bubble; to seethe.

hervor m boiling; fervor, passion.

heterogeneidad f heterogeneousness.

heterogéneo/nea adj heterogeneous.

heterosexual adj, m/f heterosexual.

heterosexualidad f heterosexuality.

hexámetro m hexameter.

hez f sediment, dregs pl.

hidalgo m nobleman.

hidalguía f nobility.

hidra f hydra.

hidráulica f hydraulics.

hidráulico/ca adj hydraulic.

hidroavión m hydroplane, seaplane.

hidrofobia f hydrophobia.

hidrógeno m (chem) hydrogen.

hidromasaje m whirlpool bath.

hidrovía f Lat Am waterway.

hiedra f ivy.

hiel f gall, bile.

hielo m frost; ice.

hiena f hyena.

hierba f grass; herb.

hierro m iron.

hígado m liver; (fig) courage, pluck.

higiene f hygiene.

higiénico/ca adj hygienic.

higo m fig.

higuera f fig tree.

hijastro/tra m/f stepson/step-daughter.

hijo/ja m/f son/daughter; child; offspring.

hilandero/ra m/f spinner.

hilar vt to spin.

hilera f row, line, file.

hilo m thread; wire.

hilván m tacking.

hilvanar vt to tack; to perform in a hurry.

himno m hymn.

hincada f Lat Am genuflection.

hincapié m: hacer ~ en to emphasize.

hincar vt to thrust in, to drive in.

hincha m/f (col) fan, supporter.

hinchado/da adj swollen; vain, arrogant.

hinchar vt to swell; to inflate; (fig) to exaggerate; ~se vr to swell; to become vain.

hinchazón f swelling, lump.
hinojo m (bot) fennel.
hipar vi to hiccup.
hipérbola f hyperbola, section of a cone.
hipérbole f hyperbole, exaggeration.
hiperbólico/ca adj hyperbolic, hyperbolical.
hipermercado, híper m hypermarket, superstore.
hípica f horseracing; showjumping.
hipnotismo m hypnotism.
hipo m hiccups pl.
hipocondria f hypochondria.
hipocondríaco/ca adj hypochondriac.
hipocresía f hypocrisy.
hipócrita adj hypocritical; * m/f hypocrite.
hipódromo m racetrack.
hipopótamo m hippopotamus.
hipoteca f mortgage.
hipotecar vt to mortgage.
hipotecario/ria adj belonging to a mortgage.
hipótesis f hypothesis.
hipotético/ca adj hypothetical.
hisopo m (bot) hyssop; water sprinkler; paintbrush.
hispano/na adj Hispanic.
Hispanoamérica f Spanish America.
hispanoamericano/na adj,m/f Spanish American.
histeria f hysteria.
histérico/ca adj hysterical.
historia f history; tale, story.
historiador/ra m/f historian.
histórico/ca adj historical; historic.
historieta f short story; short novel; comic strip.
hito m landmark; boundary post; target.
hocico m snout; **meter el ~ en todo** to meddle in everything.
hogar m hearth, fireplace; (fig) house, home; family life.
hogaza f large loaf of bread.
hoguera f bonfire; blaze.
hoja f leaf; petal; sheet of paper; blade.
hojalata f tin plate.
hojaldre f puff pastry.
hojarasca f dead leaves pl; rubbish.
hojear vt to turn the pages of.
hola excl hello!
holgado/da adj loose, wide, baggy; at leisure; idle, unoccupied, well-to-do; well-off.
holgar vi to rest; to be out of work; to be superfluous.
holgazán/ana m/f idler, loafer.
holgazanear vt to idle, to loaf around, to lounge around.
holgazanería f idleness, laziness.
holgura f looseness, bagginess; leisure; comfort; enjoyment.
hollín m soot.
holocausto m holocaust.
hombre m man; human being.
hombrera f shoulder pad.

hombro m shoulder.
hombruno/na adj manlike; virile, manly.
homenaje m homage.
homicida m/f murderer; * adj murderous, homicidal.
homicidio m murder.
homilía f homily.
homogeneidad f homogeneity.
homogéneo/nea adj homogeneous.
homólogo/ga adj homologous; synonymous.
homosexual adj, m/f homosexual.
honda f sling, catapult.
hondazo m throw with a sling.
hondo/da adj deep; profound; intense.
hondonada f dale, hollow; ravine.
hondura f depth, profundity.
honestidad f honesty; modesty; decency.
honesto/ta adj honest; modest.
hongo m mushroom; fungus; derby (hat).
honor m honor.
honorable adj honorable.
honorario/ria adj honorary; ~s mpl fees pl.
honorífico/ca adj creditable, honorable.
honra f honor, reverence; self-esteem; reputation; integrity; ~s funebres pl funeral honors pl.
honradez f honesty, integrity.
honrado/da adj honest; honorable; reputable.
honrar vt to honor.
honroso/sa adj honorable; respectable; honest.
hora f hour; time.
horadar vt to drill, to bore.
horario/ria adj hourly, hour compd; * m timetable.
horca f gallows; pitchfork; string (of garlic/ onions etc).
horcajadas adv: **a ~** astride.
horchata f a drink made from almonds/barley and orange flower water.
horero m Lat Am hour hand.
horizontal adj horizontal.
horizonte m horizon.
horma f mold, form.
hormiga f ant.
hormigón m concrete.
hormiguear vi to itch; to swarm, to team.
hormiguero m anthill; place swarming with people.
hormona f hormone.
hornada f batch.
horno m oven; furnace.
horóscopo m horoscope.
horqueta f Lat Am fork.
horquilla f pitchfork; hairpin.
horrendo/da adj horrible; frightful.
hórreo m granary.
horrible adj horrid, horrible.
horripilante adj hair-raising.
horror m horror, fright; atrocity.
horrorizar vt to horrify; ~se vr to be terrified.
horroroso/sa adj horrid, hideous, frightful.

hortaliza *f* vegetable.
hortelano/na *m/f* gardener; truck farmer.
hortera *m* shop/store assistant; (*fig*) coarse person.
hosco/ca *adj* sullen, gloomy.
hospedaje *m* board and lodging.
hospedar *vt* to put up, to lodge; to entertain.
hospedería *f* inn; guest room; hospice.
hospedero/ra *m/f* landlord/lady; host/hostess.
hospicio *m* orphanage; hospice.
hospital *m* hospital.
hospitalario/ria *adj* hospitable.
hospitalidad *f* hospitality.
hostal *m* small hotel.
hostelería *f* hotel business/trade.
hostería *f* inn, tavern, hostelry.
hostia *f* host; wafer; (*col*) whack, punch.
hostigar *vt* to lash, to whip; to trouble, to pester, to bore.
hostil *adj* hostile; adverse.
hostilidad *f* hostility.
hostilizar *vt* (*mil*) to harry, to harass.
hotel *m* hotel.
hoy *adv* today; now, nowadays; **de ~ en adelante** as from today.
hoya *f* hole, pit; *Lat Am* river basin.
hoyito *m Lat Am* dimple.
hoyo *m* hole, pit; excavation.
hoz *f* sickle; gorge.
hozar *vi* to grub (of pigs).
hucha *f* money-box.
hueco/ca *adj* hollow, concave; empty; vain, ostentatious; * *m* interval; gap, hole; vacancy.
huelga *f* strike.
huella *f* track, footstep.
huérfano/na *adj*, *m/f* orphan.
huero/ra *adj* empty; addled.
huerta *f* truck farm; irrigated region.
huerto *m* orchard; kitchen garden; ~ **de hortalizas** truck farm.
hueso *m* bone; stone, core.
huésped/da *m/f* guest, lodger; innkeeper.
hueste *f* army; crowd.
huesudo/da *adj* bony.
huevera *f* eggcup.
huevo *m* egg.
huida *f* flight, escape.
huir *vi* to flee, to escape.
hule *m* oilcloth.
humanidad *f* humanity; corpulence; **~es** *fpl* humanities *pl*.
humano/na *adj* human; humane, kind.
humareda *f* cloud of smoke.
humeante *adj* smoking; steaming.
humear *vi* to smoke; * *vt Lat Am* to fumigate.
humedad *f* humidity, moisture; wetness.
humedecer *vt* to moisten; to wet; to soak.
húmedo/da *adj* humid; wet; moist, damp.
humildad *f* humility, humbleness; submission.
humilde *adj* humble.
humillación *f* humiliation, submission.

humillar *vt* to humble; to subdue; **~se** *vr* to humble oneself.
humo *m* smoke; fumes *pl*.
humor *m* mood, temper; humor.
hundir *vt* to submerge; to sink; to ruin; **~se** *vr* to sink, to go to the bottom; to collapse; to be ruined.
huracán *m* hurricane.
huraño/ña *adj* shy; unsociable.
hurgar *vt* to stir; to poke.
hurón *m* ferret; (*fig*) shy person; busybody.
huronear *vt* to ferret out.
hurtadillas *adv*: **a ~** by stealth.
hurtar *vt* to steal, to rob.
hurto *m* theft, robbery.
húsar *m* hussar.
husmear *vt* to scent; to pry into.
huso *m* spindle.

I

ictericia *f* jaundice.
ida *f* departure, going; (**viaje de**) **~** outward journey; **~ y vuelta** round trip; **~s y venidas** comings and goings *pl*.
idea *f* idea; scheme.
ideal *adj* ideal.
idealmente *adv* ideally.
idear *vt* to conceive; to think, to contrive.
ídem *pn* ditto.
idéntico/ca *adj* identical.
identidad *f* identity.
identificar *vt* to identify.
ideología *f* ideology.
idilio *m* idyll.
idioma *m* language.
idiosincrasia *f* idiosyncrasy.
idiota *m/f* idiot.
idiotez *f* idiocy.
idólatra *m/f* idolater.
idolatrar *vt* to idolize; to worship.
idolatría *f* idolatry.
ídolo *m* idol.
idoneidad *f* aptitude, fitness.
idóneo/nea *adj* suitable, fit.
iglesia *f* church.
ignominia *f* ignominy; infamy.
ignominioso/sa *adj* ignominious.
ignorancia *f* ignorance.
ignorante *adj* ignorant, uninformed.
ignorar *vt* to be ignorant of, not to know.
igual *adj* equal; similar; the same; **al ~** equally.
igualar *vt* to equalize, to equal; to match; to level off; **~se** *vr* to be equal; to agree.
igualdad *f* equality.
igualmente *adv* equally.
ijar *m* flank.
ilegal *adj* illegal, unlawful.
ilegalidad *f* illegality.
ilegitimidad *f* illegitimacy.

ilegítimo/ma *adj* illegal; illegitimate.
ileso/sa *adj* unhurt.
ilícito/ta *adj* illicit, unlawful; * *m Lat Am* crime.
ilimitado/da *adj* unlimited.
ilustrar *vt* to illustrate; to instruct.
iluminación *f* illumination.
iluminar *vt* to illumine, to illuminate, to enlighten.
ilusión *f* illusion; hope; **hacerse ~ones** to build up one's hopes.
ilusionista *m/f* conjurer.
iluso/sa *adj* easily deceived.
ilusorio/ria *adj* illusory.
ilustración *f* illustration; enlightenment.
ilustre *adj* illustrious, famous.
imagen *f* image.
imaginable *adj* imaginable.
imaginación *f* imagination; fancy.
imaginar *vt* to imagine; to think up; * *vi,* **~se** *vr* to imagine.
imán *m* magnet.
imbécil *m/f* imbecile, idiot.
imbecilidad *f* imbecility.
imbuir *vt* to imbue; to infuse.
imitable *adj* imitable.
imitación *f* imitation; **a ~ de** in imitation of.
imitador/ra *m/f* imitator.
imitar *vt* to imitate, to copy; to counterfeit.
impaciencia *f* impatience.
impacientar *vt* to make impatient; to irritate.
impaciente *adj* impatient.
impacto *m* impact.
impago/ga *adj Lat Am* unpaid.
impar *adj* odd.
imparcial *adj* impartial.
imparcialidad *f* impartiality.
impasibilidad *f* impassivity.
impasible *adj* impassive.
impavidez *f* intrepidity; cheek(iness).
impávido/da *adj* dauntless, intrepid; cheeky.
impecable *adj* impeccable.
impedimento *f* impediment, obstacle.
impedir *vt* to impede, to hinder; to prevent.
impeler *vt* to drive, to propel; to impel; to incite, to stimulate.
impenetrable *adj* impenetrable, impervious; incomprehensible.
impenitente *adj* impenitent.
impensado/da *adj* impenitent.
imperativo/va *adj, m* imperative.
imperceptible *adj* imperceptible.
imperdible *m* safety pin.
imperdonable *adj* unforgivable.
imperfección *f* imperfection.
imperfecto/ta *adj* imperfect.
imperial *adj* imperial.
impericia *f* lack of experience.
imperio *m* empire.
imperioso/sa *adj* imperious; arrogant, haughty; urgent.
impermeable *adj* waterproof; * *m* raincoat.

impermutable *adj* immutable.
impersonal *adj* impersonal.
impertérrito/ta *adj* intrepid, fearless.
impertinencia *f* impertinence; irrelevance.
impertinente *adj* not pertinent; touchy; impertinent.
imperturbable *adj* imperturbable; unruffled.
ímpetu *m* impetus; impetuosity.
impetuoso/sa *adj* impetuous.
implacable *adj* implacable, inexorable.
implicación *f* implication.
implicar *vt* to implicate, to involve.
implícito/ta *adj* implicit.
implorar *vt* to beg, to implore.
imponderable *adj* imponderable; (*fig*) priceless.
imponer *vt* to impose; to command; **~se** *vr* to assert oneself; to prevail.
impopular *adj* unpopular.
importación *f* importing; imports *pl.*
importancia *f* importance; significance, weight; size.
importante *adj* important, considerable.
importar *vi* to be important, to matter; * *vt* to import; to be worth.
importe *m* amount, cost.
importunar *vt* to bother, to pester.
importunidad *f* pestering; annoyance.
importuno/na *adj* annoying; unreasonable.
imposibilidad *f* impossibility.
imposibilitar *vt* to make impossible.
imposible *adj* impossible; extremely difficult; slovenly.
imposición *f* imposition; tax; deposit.
impostor/ra *m/f* impostor, fraud.
impostura *f* imposture, deceit, cheat.
impotencia *f* impotence.
impotente *adj* impotent.
impracticable *adj* impracticable, unworkable.
imprecación *f* curse.
imprecar *vt* to curse.
imprecatorio/ria *adj* containing curses, full of evil wishes.
impreciso/sa *adj* imprecise, vague.
impregnarse *vr* to be impregnated.
imprenta *f* printing; press; printing office.
imprescindible *adj* essential.
impresión *f* impression; stamp; print; edition.
impresionante *adj* impressive; marvelous; tremendous.
impresionar *vt* to move; to impress; **~se** *vr* to be impressed; to be moved.
impreso *m* printed paper; printed book.
impresor *m* printer.
impresora *f* printer; **~ láser** laser printer.
imprevisto/ta *adj* unforeseen, unexpected.
imprimir *vt* to print; to imprint; to stamp.
improbable *adj* improbable, unlikely.
improperio *m* insult, taunt.
impropio/pia *adj* improper; unfit; unbecoming.
improvisar *vt* to extemporize; to improvize.
improviso/sa *adj:* **de ~** unexpectedly.

imprudencia *f* imprudence; indiscretion; carelessness.

imprudente *adj* imprudent; indiscreet; unwise.

impudencia *f* shamelessness.

impudente *adj* shameless.

impúdico/ca *adj* shameless; lecherous.

impuesto/ta *adj* imposed; * *m* tax, duty.

impugnación *f* opposition, contradiction.

impugnar *vt* to oppose; challenge; impugn.

impulsivo/va *adj* impulsive.

impulso *m* impulse; thrust; (*fig*) impulse.

impune *adj* unpunished.

impunidad *f* impunity.

impureza *f* impurity.

impuro/ra *adj* impure;, foul.

imputable *adj* attributable, chargeable.

imputar *vt* to impute, to attribute.

inaccesible *adj* inaccessible.

inacción *f* inaction, inactivity.

inadmisible *adj* inadmissible.

inadvertencia *f* carelessness, inadvertence.

inadvertido/da *adj* unnoticed.

inagotable *adj* inexhaustible.

inaguantable *adj* unbearable, intolerable.

inalterable *adj* unalterable.

inapelable *adj* without appeal.

inapreciable *adj* imperceptible; invaluable.

inaudito/ta *adj* unheard-of.

inauguración *f* inauguration, opening.

inaugurar *vt* to inaugurate.

incalculable *adj* incalculable.

incandescente *adj* incandescent.

incansable *adj* untiring, tireless.

incapacidad *f* incapacity, inability.

incapaz *adj* incapable, unable.

incauto/ta *adj* incautious, unwary.

incendiar *vt* to kindle, to set on fire.

incendiario/ria *adj* incendiary; * *m/f* arsonist.

incendio *m* fire.

incentivo *m* incentive.

incertidumbre *f* doubt, uncertainty.

incesante *adj* incessant, continual.

incesto *m* incest.

incestuoso/sa *adj* incestuous.

incidencia *f* incidence; incident.

incidente *m* incident.

incidir *vi*: ~ **en** to fall upon; to influence, to affect.

incienso *m* incense.

incierto/ta *adj* uncertain, doubtful.

incineración *f* incineration; cremation.

incipiente *adj* incipient.

incisión *f* incision, cut.

incisivo/va *adj* incisive.

inciso *m* (*gr*) comma.

incitación *f* incitement.

incitar *vt* to incite; to excite.

incivil *adj* uncivil, rude.

inclemencia *f* inclemency, severity; inclemency (of the weather).

inclinación *f* inclination.

inclinar *vt* to incline; to nod, to bow (the head); ~**se** *vr* to bow; to stoop.

incluir *vt* to include, to comprise; to incorporate; to enclose.

inclusión *f* inclusion.

inclusive *adv* inclusive.

incluso/sa *adj* included; * *adv* inclusively; even.

incógnito/ta *adj* unknown; **de** ~ incognito.

incoherencia *f* incoherence.

incoherente *adj* incoherent.

incombustible *adj* incombustible, fireproof.

incomodar *vt* to inconvenience; to bother, to annoy.

incomodidad *f* inconvenience; annoyance; discomfort.

incómodo/da *adj* uncomfortable; annoying; inconvenient.

incomparable *adj* incomparable, matchless.

incompatibilidad *f* incompatibility.

incompatible *adj* incompatible.

incompetencia *f* incompetence.

incompetente *adj* incompetent.

incompleto/ta *adj* incomplete.

incomprehensible *adj* incomprehensible.

incomunicación *f* isolation; lack of communication.

incomunicado/da *adj* isolated, cut off; in solitary confinement.

inconcebible *adj* inconceivable.

incondicional *adj* unconditional; wholehearted; staunch.

inconexo/xa *adj* unconnected, disconnected.

inconfundible *adj* unmistakable.

incongruencia *f* incongruity, incongruence.

incongruo/grua *adj* incongruous.

inconmensurable *adj* immeasurable.

inconsciencia *f* unconsciousness; thoughtlessness.

inconsciente *adj* unconscious; thoughtless.

inconsecuencia *f* inconsequence.

inconsiderado/da *adj* inconsiderate, thoughtless.

inconsolable *adj* inconsolable.

inconstancia *f* inconstancy, unsteadiness.

inconstante *adj* inconstant, variable, fickle.

incontestable *adj* indisputable, incontrovertible, undeniable.

incontinencia *f* incontinence.

incontinente *adj* incontinent.

inconveniencia *f* inconvenience; impoliteness; unsuitability.

inconveniente *adj* inconvenient, unsuitable; impolite.

incorporación *f* incorporation, involvement.

incorporar *vt* to incorporate; ~**se** *vr* to sit up; to join (an organization), to become incorporated.

incorrecto/ta *adj* incorrect.

incorregible *adj* incorrigible.

incorruptible *adj* incorruptible.

incredulidad *f* incredulity.

incrédulo/la *adj* incredulous.

increíble *adj* incredible.

incremento *m* increment, increase; growth; rise.

increpar *vt* to reprehend, to reprimand.

incruento/ta *adj* bloodless.

inculcar *vt* to inculcate.

inculpar *vt* to accuse, to blame.

inculto/ta *adj* uncultivated; uneducated; uncouth.

incumbencia *f* obligation; duty.

incumbir *vi*: ~ **a uno** to be incumbent upon one.

incurable *adj* incurable; irremediable.

incurrir *vt*: ~ **en** to incur; to commit (a crime).

incursión *f* incursion, raid.

indagación *f* search, inquiry.

indagar *vt* to inquire into.

indebido/da *adj* undue; illegal, unlawful.

indecencia *f* indecency.

indecente *adj* indecent.

indecible *adj* unspeakable, unutterable.

indecisión *f* hesitation; indecision.

indeciso/sa *adj* hesitant; undecided.

indecoroso/sa *adj* unseemly, unbecoming.

indefectible *adj* infallible.

indefenso/sa *adj* defenseless.

indefinible *adj* indefinable.

indefinido/da *adj* indefinite.

indeleble *adj* indelible.

indemnización *f* indemnification, compensation.

indemnizar *vt* to indemnify, to compensate.

independencia *f* independence.

independiente *adj* independent.

indestructible *adj* indestructible.

indeterminado/da *adj* indeterminate; indefinite.

indicación *f* indication.

indicador *m* indicator; gage.

indicar *vt* to indicate.

indicativo/va *adj, m* indicative.

índice *m* ratio, rate; hand (of a watch/clock); index, table of contents; catalog; forefinger, index finger.

indicio *m* indication, mark; sign, token; clue.

indiferencia *f* indifference, apathy.

indiferente *adj* indifferent.

indígena *adj* indigenous, native; * *m/f* native.

indigencia *f* indigence, poverty, need.

indigente *adj* indigent, poor, destitute.

indigestión *f* indigestion.

indigesto/ta *adj* undigested; indigestible.

indignación *f* indignation, anger.

indignar *vt* to irritate;.to provoke, to tease; ~**se** *vr*: ~ **por** to get indignant about.

indigno/na *adj* unworthy, contemptible, low.

indirecta *f* innuendo, hint.

indirecto/ta *adj* indirect.

indisciplinado/da *adj* undisciplined.

indiscreción *f* indiscretion, tactlessness; gaffe.

indiscreto/ta *adj* indiscreet, tactless.

indisoluble *adj* indissoluble.

indispensable *adj* indispensable.

indisponer *vt* to spoil, to upset; to make ill; ~**se** *vr* to fall ill.

indisposición *f* indisposition, slight illness.

indispuesto/ta *adj* indisposed.

indisputable *adj* indisputable, incontrovertible.

indistinto/ta *adj* indistinct.

individual *adj* individual; single (of a room); * *m* (*sport*) singles.

individualidad *f* individuality.

individualizar *vt* to specify individually.

individuo *m* individual.

indivisible *adj* indivisible.

indocilidad *f* disobedience.

índole *f* disposition, nature, character; class, kind.

indolencia *f* indolence, laziness.

indolente *adj* indolent, lazy.

indómito/ta *adj* untamed, ungoverned.

inducción *f* induction, persuasion.

inducir *vt* to induce, to persuade.

inductivo/va *adj* inductive.

indudable *adj* undoubted; unquestionable.

indulgencia *f* indulgence.

indulgente *adj* indulgent.

indultar *vt* to pardon; to exempt.

indulto *m* pardon; exemption.

industria *f* industry; skill.

industrial *adj* industrial.

industrialización *f* industrialization.

inédito/ta *adj* unpublished; (*fig*) new.

inefable *adj* ineffable, indescribable.

ineficacia *f* inefficacy.

ineficaz *adj* ineffective; inefficient.

ineptitud *f* inability; unfitness, ineptitude.

inepto/ta *adj* inept, unfit, useless.

inercia *f* inertia, inactivity.

inerme *adj* unarmed; defenseless.

inerte *adj* inert; dull; sluggish, motionless.

inescrutable *adj* inscrutable.

inesperado/da *adj* unexpected, unforeseen.

inestable *adj* unstable.

inestimable *adj* inestimable.

inevitable *adj* unavoidable.

inexactitud *f* inaccuracy.

inexacto/ta *adj* inaccurate, untrue.

inexorable *adj* inexorable.

inexperto/ta *adj* inexperienced.

infalibilidad *f* infallibility.

infalible *adj* infallible.

infame *adj* infamous.

infancia *f* infancy, childhood.

infanta *f* infanta, princess.

infante *m* infante, prince; (*mil*) infantryman.

infantería *f* infantry.

infanticida *m/f* infanticide (person).

infanticidio *m* infanticide (act).

infantil *adj* infantile; childlike; children's.

infarto *m* heart attack; ~ **de miocardio** heart attack.

infatigable *adj* tireless, untiring.

infección *f* infection.

infectar *vt* to infect.

infeliz *adj* unhappy, unfortunate.

inferior *adj* inferior.

inferioridad *f* inferiority.

inferir *vt* to infer.

infernal *adj* infernal, hellish.

infestar *vt* to harass; to infest.

infidelidad *f* infidelity, unfaithfulness.

infiel *adj* unfaithful; disloyal; inaccurate.

infierno *m* hell.

infiltración *f* infiltration.

infiltrarse *vr* to infiltrate.

ínfimo/ma *adj* lowest; of very poor quality.

infinidad *f* infinity; immensity.

infinitivo *m* (*gr*) infinitive.

infinito/ta *adj* infinite; immense.

inflación *f* inflation.

inflamable *adj* flammable.

inflamación *f* ignition; inflammation.

inflamar *vt* to inflame; to excite, to arouse; **~se** *vr* to catch fire.

inflamatorio/ria *adj* inflammatory.

inflar *vt* to inflate, to blow up; (*fig*) to exaggerate.

inflexibilidad *f* inflexibility.

inflexible *adj* inflexible.

influencia *f* influence.

influir *vt* to influence.

influjo *m* influence.

infografía *f* computer graphics.

información *f* information; news; (*mil*) intelligence; investigation, judicial inquiry.

informal *adj* irregular, incorrect; untrustworthy; informal.

informalidad *f* irregularity; untrustworthiness; informality.

informar *vt* to inform; to reveal, to make known; **~se** *vr* to find out; * *vi* to report; (*law*) to plead; to inform.

informática *f* computer science, information technology.

informe *m* report, statement; piece of information, account; * *adj* shapeless, formless.

infortunio *m* misfortune, ill luck.

infracción *f* infraction; breach, infringement.

infraccionar *vt* *Lat Am* to fine.

infractor/ra *m/f* offender.

infructuoso/sa *adj* fruitless, unproductive, unprofitable.

infundado/da *adj* groundless.

infundir *vt* to infuse, to instil.

infusión *f* infusion.

infuso/sa *adj* infused; introduced.

ingeniar *vt* to devise; **~se** *vr*: **~ para** to manage to.

ingeniería *f* engineering; **~ genética** genetic engineering.

ingeniero/ra *m/f* engineer.

ingenio *m* talent; wit; ingenuity; engine; **~ de azúcar** sugar mill.

ingenioso/sa *adj* ingenious, clever; witty.

ingenuidad *f* ingenuousness; candor, frankness.

ingenuo/nua *adj* ingenuous.

ingerir *vt* to ingest; to swallow; to consume.

ingle *f* groin.

inglés/esa *adj* English; * *m* English (language); * *m/f* Englishman/woman.

ingratitud *f* ingratitude, unthankfulness.

ingrato/ta *adj* ungrateful, thankless; disagreeable.

ingrediente *m* ingredient.

ingresar *vt* to deposit; * *vi* to come in.

ingreso *m* entry; admission; **~s** *mpl* income; takings *pl*.

inhabilitar *vt* to disqualify, to disable.

inhabitable *adj* uninhabitable.

inherente *adj* inherent.

inhibición *f* inhibition.

inhibir *vt* to inhibit; to restrain.

inhumano/na *adj* inhuman.

inicial *adj, f* initial.

iniciar *vt* to initiate; to begin.

iniciativa *f* initiative.

inimaginable *adj* unimaginable, inconceivable.

inimitable *adj* inimitable.

ininteligible *adj* unintelligible.

iniquidad *f* iniquity, injustice.

injertar *vt* to graft.

injerto *m* graft.

injuria *f* offense; insult.

injuriar *vt* to insult, to wrong.

injurioso/sa *adj* insulting; offensive.

injusticia *f* injustice.

injusto/ta *adj* unjust.

inmaculado/da *adj* immaculate.

inmadurez *f* immaturity.

inmediaciones *fpl* neighborhood; surrounding area.

inmediatamente *adv* immediately, at once.

inmediato/ta *adj* immediate.

inmemorial *adj* immemorial.

inmensidad *f* immensity.

inmenso/sa *adj* immense.

inmensurable *adj* immeasurable.

inmigración *f* immigration.

inmigrante *m/f* immigrant.

inmigrar *vi* to immigrate.

inminente *adj* imminent.

inmobiliario/ria *adj* real-estate *compd*; * *f* estate agency.

inmoral *adj* immoral.

inmortal *adj* immortal.

inmortalidad *f* immortality.

inmortalizar *vt* to immortalize.

inmóvil *adj* immovable.

inmovilidad *f* immobility.

inmueble *m* property; * *adj*: **bienes ~s** real estate.

inmundicia *f* nastiness, filth.

inmundo/da *adj* filthy, dirty; nasty.

inmune *adj* (*med*) immune; free, exempt.

inmunidad *f* immunity; exemption.

inmutabilidad *f* immutability.

inmutable *adj* immutable.

inmutarse *vr* to turn pale.

innato/ta *adj* inborn, innate.

innecesario/ria *adj* unnecessary.

innegable *adj* undeniable.

innovación f innovation.

innovador/ra m/f innovator.

innovar vt to innovate.

innumerable adj innumerable, countless.

inocencia f innocence.

inocentada f practical joke.

inocente adj innocent.

inoculación f inoculation.

inocular vt to inoculate.

inodoro m lavatory.

inofensivo/va adj harmless.

inolvidable adj unforgettable.

inopinado/da adj unexpected.

inoxidable adj: **acero ~** stainless steel.

inquietar vt to worry, to disturb; **~se** vr to worry, to get worried.

inquieto/ta adj anxious, worried.

inquietud f uneasiness, anxiety.

inquilino/na m/f tenant; lodger.

inquirir vt to inquire into, to investigate.

insaciable adj insatiable.

insalubre adj unhealthy.

insalubridad f unhealthiness.

insano/na adj insane, mad.

inscribir vt to inscribe; to list, to register.

inscripción f inscription; enrollment, registration.

insecticida m insecticide.

insecto m insect.

inseguridad f insecurity.

inseminación f insemination; **~ artificial** artificial insemination.

insensatez f stupidity, folly.

insensato/ta adj senseless, stupid; mad.

insensibilidad f insensitivity; callousness.

insensible adj insensitive; imperceptible; numb.

insensiblemente adv insensitively; imperceptibly.

inseparable adj inseparable.

inserción f insertion.

insertar vt to insert.

inservible adj useless.

insidioso/sa adj insidious.

insigne adj notable.

insignificante adj insignificant.

insignia f badge; **~s** fpl insignia pl.

insinuación f insinuation.

insinuar vt to insinuate; **~se** vr: to make advances; **~ en** to worm one's way into.

insipidez f insipidness.

insípido/da adj insipid.

insistencia f persistence; insistence.

insistir vi to insist.

insolación f (med) sunstroke.

insolencia f insolence, rudeness, effrontery.

insolente adj insolent, rude.

insólito/ta adj unusual.

insolvencia f insolvency.

insolvente adj insolvent.

insomnio m insomnia.

insondable adj unfathomable; inscrutable.

insoportable adj unbearable.

inspección f inspection, survey; check.

inspeccionar vt to inspect; to supervise.

inspector/ra m/f inspector; superintendent.

inspiración f inspiration.

inspirar vt to inspire; (med) to inhale.

instalación f installation.

instalar vt to install; Lat Am to set up.

instancia f instance.

instantáneo/nea adj instantaneous; * f snap(shot); **café ~** instant coffee.

instante m instant; **al ~** immediately, instantly.

instar vt to press, to urge.

instigación f instigation.

instigar vt to instigate.

instinto m instinct.

institución f institution.

instituir vt to institute.

instituto m institute.

institutriz f governess.

instrucción f instruction.

instructivo/va adj instructive; educational.

instructor/ra m/f instructor, teacher.

instruir vt to instruct, to teach.

instrumento m instrument; tool, implement.

insuficiencia f lack, inadequacy.

insuficiente adj insufficient, inadequate.

insufrible adj insufferable, insupportable.

insulina f insulin.

insulso/sa adj insipid; dull.

insultar vt to insult.

insulto m insult.

insumos mpl Lat Am supplies pl; raw materials pl.

insuperable adj insuperable, insurmountable.

insurgente m/f insurgent.

insurrección f insurrection.

intacto/ta adj untouched; entire; intact.

integral adj integral, whole; **pan ~** wholewheat bread.

integrar vt to make up; to integrate.

integridad f integrity; completeness.

íntegro/gra adj integral, entire.

intelectual adj, m/f intellectual.

inteligencia f intelligence; understanding.

inteligente adj intelligent.

inteligible adj intelligible.

intemperie f: **a la ~** out in the open.

intempestivo/va adj untimely.

intención f intention, purpose; plan.

intencionado/da adj meaningful; deliberate.

intendencia f administration, management.

intendente m manager.

intensidad f intensity; strength.

intenso/sa adj intense, strong; deep.

intentar vt to try, to attempt.

intento m intent, purpose; attempt.

intercalación f insertion.

intercalar vt to insert.

intercambio m exchange, swap.

interceder vi to intercede.

interceptar vt to intercept.

intercesión *f* intercession, mediation.

intercesor/ra *m/f* intercessor, mediator.

interés *m* interest; share, part; concern, advantage; profit.

interesado/da *adj* interested; prejudiced; mercenary.

interesante *adj* interesting; useful, convenient.

interesar *vt* to be of interest to, to interest; ~**se** *vr*: ~**se en/por** to take an interest in; * *vi* to be of interest.

interfaz, **interface** *f* interface.

interferir *vt* to interfere with; to jam (a telephone); * *vi* to interfere.

interfono *m* intercom.

interinato *m Lat Am* temporary post.

interinidad *f* temporary holding of office.

interino/na *adj* provisional, temporary; * *m/f* temporary holder of a post; stand-in.

interior *adj* interior, internal; * *m* interior, inside.

interioridad *f* inwardness.

interiorismo *m* interior design.

interiorista *m/f* interior designer.

interjección *f* (*gr*) interjection.

interlocutor/ra *m/f* speaker.

intermediar *vt* to interpose.

intermedio/dia *adj* intermediate; * *m* interval.

interminable *adj* interminable, endless.

intermitente *adj* intermittent; *m* (*auto*) indicator.

internacional *adj* international.

internado *m* boarding school.

internar *vt* to intern; to commit; ~**se** *vr* to penetrate.

interno/na *adj* interior, internal; * *m/f* boarder.

interpelación *f* interpellation, appeal, plea.

interpelar *vt* to appeal to.

interpolar *vt* to interpolate; to interrupt.

interponer *vt* to interpose, to put in.

interposición *f* insertion; interjection.

interpretación *f* interpretation.

interpretar *vt* to interpret, to explain; (*theat*) to perform; to translate.

intérprete *m/f* interpreter; translator; (*theat*) performer.

interracial *adj* interracial.

interrogación *f* interrogation; question mark.

interrogante *adj* questioning.

interrogar *vt* to interrogate.

interrogatorio *m* questioning; (*law*) examination; questionnaire.

interrumpir *vt* to interrupt.

interrupción *f* interruption.

interruptor *m* switch.

intertanto *adv Lat Am* meanwhile.

intervalo *m* interval.

intervención *f* supervision, control; (*com*) auditing; (*med*) operation; intervention.

intervenir *vt* to control, to supervise; (*com*) to audit; (*med*) to operate on; * *vi* to participate; to intervene.

interventor/ra *m/f* inspector; (*com*) auditor; *Lat Am* administrator.

interviú *f* interview.

intestino/na *adj* internal, interior; * *m* intestine.

intimar *vt* to intimate; * *vi* to become friendly.

intimidad *f* intimacy; private life.

intimidar *vt* intimidate.

íntimo/ma *adj* internal, innermost; intimate, private.

intolerable *adj* intolerable, insufferable.

intolerancia *f* intolerance.

intolerante *adj* intolerant.

intranquilizarse *vr* to get anxious/worried.

intranquilo/la *adj* worried.

intransigente *adj* intransigent.

intransitable *adj* impassable.

intransitivo/va *adj* (*gr*) intransitive.

intratable *adj* intractable, difficult.

intrepidez *f* intrepidity; fearlessness.

intrépido/da *adj* intrepid, daring.

intriga *f* intrigue.

intrigante *m/f* intriguer.

intrigar *vt*, *vi* to intrigue.

intrínseco/ca *adj* intrinsic.

introducción *f* introduction.

introducir *vt* to introduce; to insert.

introductor *m* introducer.

introvertido/da *adj*, *m/f* introvert.

intrusión *f* intrusion.

intruso/sa *adj* intrusive; * *m/f* intruder.

intuición *f* intuition.

intuitivo/va *adj* intuitive.

inundación *f* inundation, flood(ing).

inundar *vt* to inundate, to overflow; to flood.

inusitado/da *adj* unusual.

inútil *adj* useless.

inutilidad *f* uselessness.

inutilizar *vt* to render useless.

invadir *vt* (*mil*) to invade; to overrun.

invalidar *vt* to invalidate, to render null and void.

inválido/da *adj* invalid, null and void; * *m/f* invalid.

invariable *adj* invariable.

invasión *f* invasion.

invasor/ra *adj* invading; * *m/f* invader.

invencible *adj* invincible.

invención *f* invention.

inventar *vt* to invent.

inventario *m* inventory.

invento *m* invention.

inventor/ra *m/f* inventor.

invernadero *m* greenhouse.

invernar *vi* to pass the winter.

inverosímil *adj* unlikely, improbable.

inverosimilitud *f* unlikeliness, improbability.

inversión *f* (*com*) investment; inversion.

inverso/sa *adj* inverse; inverted; contrary.

invertir *vt* (*com*) to invest; to invert.

investidura *f* investiture.

investigación *f* investigation, research.

investigar *vt* to investigate; to do research into.

investir *vt* to confer.

invicto/ta *adj* unconquerable.

invierno *m* winter.
inviolabilidad *f* inviolability.
inviolable *adj* inviolable.
invisible *adj* invisible.
invitado/da *m/f* guest.
invitar *vt* to invite; to entice; to pay for.
invocación *f* invocation.
invocar *vt* to invoke.
involucrar *vt Lat Am* to involve.
involuntario/ria *adj* involuntary.
invulnerable *adj* invulnerable.
inyección *f* injection.
ir *vi* to go; to walk; to travel; **~se** *vr* to go away, to depart.
ira *f* anger, wrath.
iracundo/da *adj* irate; irascible.
iris *m* iris (eye); **arco ~** rainbow.
ironía *f* irony.
irónico/ca *adj* ironic(al).
irracional *adj* irrational.
irradiación *f* irradiation.
irrazonable *adj* unreasonable.
irreal *adj* unreal.
irreconciliable *adj* irreconcilable.
irreflexión *f* rashness, thoughtlessness.
irregular *adj* irregular; abnormal.
irregularidad *f* irregularity; abnormality.
irremediable *adj* irremediable; incurable.
irremisible *adj* irretrievable; unpardonable.
irreparable *adj* irreparable.
irresistible *adj* irresistible.
irresoluto/ta *adj* irresolute; hesitant.
irreverencia *f* irreverence; disrespect.
irreverente *adj* irreverent; disrespectful.
irrevocable *adj* irrevocable.
irrisorio/ria *adj* derisory, ridiculous.
irritación *f* irritation.
irritar *vt* to irritate, to exasperate; to stir up; to inflame.
irrupción *f* irruption; invasion.
isla *f* island, isle.
islam *m* Islam.
islámico/ca *adj* Islamic.
islote *m* small island.
istmo *m* isthmus.
italiano/na *adj* Italian; * *m* Italian (language); * *m/f* Italian man/woman.
ítem *m* item.
itemizar *vt Lat Am* to itemize.
itinerario *m* itinerary.
izar *vt* (*mar*) to hoist.
izquierda *f* left; left-hand side.
izquierdo/da *adj* left; left-handed.

J

jabalí *m* wild boar.
jabalina *f* wild sow; (*sport*) javelin.
jabón *m* soap.
jabonar *vt* to soap.

jaca *f* pony; *Lat Am* fighting cock.
jacinto *m* hyacinth.
jacuzzi *m* jacuzzi.
jactancia *f* boasting.
jactancioso/sa *adj* boastful.
jactarse *vr* to boast.
jadear *vi* to pant.
jaguar *m* jaguar.
jalea *f* jelly.
jaleo *m* racket, uproar.
jalón *m* pull, tug.
jamás *adv* never; **para siempre ~** for ever and ever.
jamón *m* ham; **~ de York** (cooked) ham; **~ serrano** cured ham.
jaque *m* check (at game of chess); **~ mate** checkmate.
jaqueca *f* migraine.
jarabe *m* syrup.
jarcia *f* (*mar*) ropes *pl*, rigging.
jardín *m* garden.
jardinería *f* gardening.
jardinero/ra *m/f* gardener; *Lat Am* outfielder.
jarra *f* jug, jar, pitcher; **en ~s, de ~s** with arms akimbo; with hands to the sides.
jarro *m* jug.
jarrón *m* vase.
jaspe *m* jasper.
jaspear *vt* to marble; to speckle.
jaula *f* cage; cell for mad people.
jauría *f* pack of hounds.
jazmín *m* jasmin.
jazz *m* jazz.
jean *m Lat Am* jeans.
jefatura *f:* **~ de policía** police headquarters.
jefe *m* chief, head, leader; (*rail*) **~ de tren** guard, conductor.
jején *m Lat Am* gnat.
jengibre *m* ginger.
jerarquía *f* hierarchy.
jerárquico/ca *adj* hierarchical.
jerga *f* coarse cloth; jargon.
jergón *m* coarse mattress.
jerigonza *f* jargon, gibberish.
jeringa *f* syringe.
jeroglífico/ca *adj* hieroglyphic; * *m* hieroglyph, hieroglyphic.
jersey *m* sweater, pullover.
Jesucristo *m* Jesus Christ.
jesuita *m* Jesuit.
jesuítico/ca *adj* Jesuitical.
jibia *f* cuttlefish.
jícara *f* small cup (for chocolate).
jilguero *m* goldfinch.
jinete/ta *m/f* horseman/woman, rider.
jipijapa *m* straw hat.
jirafa *f* giraffe.
jirón *m* rag, shred.
jocosidad *f* humor, jocularity.
jocoso/sa *adj* good-humored.
jol *m Lat Am* hall.

jonrón *m Lat Am* home run.
jonronear *vi Lat Am* to hit a home run.
jornada *f* journey; day's journey; working day.
jornal *m* day's wage.
jornalero *m* (day) laborer.
joroba *f* hump; * *m/f* hunchback.
jorobado/da *adj* hunchbacked.
jorobar *vt* to pester, to annoy.
jota *f* jot, iota; Spanish dance.
joven *adj* young; * *m/f* youth; young woman.
jovial *adj* jovial, cheerful.
jovialidad *f* joviality, cheerfulness.
joya *f* jewel; ~**s** *fpl* jewelry.
joyería *f* jewelry; jeweler's place of business.
joyero/ra *m/f* jeweler.
juanete *m* (*med*) bunion.
jubilación *f* retirement.
jubilado/da *adj* retired; * *m/f* senior citizen.
jubilar *vt* to pension off; to superannuate; to discard; ~**se** *vr* to retire.
jubileo *m* jubilee.
júbilo *m* joy, rejoicing.
judaico/ca *adj* Judaic, Jewish.
judaísmo *m* Judaism.
judía *f* bean; ~ **verde** green bean, French bean.
judicatura *f* judicature; office of a judge.
judicial *adj* judicial.
judío/día *adj* Jewish; * *m/f* Jewish man/woman.
juego *m* play; amusement; sport; game; *Lat Am* match; gambling; ~**s Olímpicos** Olympic Games.
juerga *f* binge; party.
jueves *m invar* Thursday.
juez *m/f* judge.
jugada *f* playing of a card; stroke, shot.
jugador/ra *m/f* player; gambler.
jugar *vt, vi* to play, to sport, to gamble.
jugarreta *f* bad play, unskillful play.
jugo *m* sap, juice.
jugoso/sa *adj* juicy, succulent.
juguete *m* toy, plaything.
juguetear *vi* to play.
juguetón/ona *adj* playful.
juicio *m* judgement, reason; sanity; opinion.
juicioso/sa *adj* judicious, prudent.
julio *m* July.
junco *m* (*bot*) rush; junk (small Chinese ship).
jungla *f* jungle.
junio *m* June.
junta *f* meeting; assembly; congress; council.
juntamente *adv* jointly; at the same time.
juntar *vt* to join; to unite; ~**se** *vr* to meet, to assemble; to draw closer.
junto/ta *adj* joined; united; near; adjacent; ~**s** together; * *adv*: **todo** ~ all at once.
juntura *f* junction; joint.
Júpiter *m* Jupiter (planet).
jurado *m* jury; juror; member of a panel.
juramento *m* oath; curse.
jurar *vt, vi* to swear.
jurídico/ca *adj* lawful, legal; juridical.

jurisdicción *f* jurisdiction; district.
jurisprudencia *f* jurisprudence.
jurista *m/f* jurist.
justa *f* joust, tournament.
justamente *adv* justly; just.
justicia *f* justice; equity.
justificación *f* justification.
justificante *m* voucher; receipt.
justificar *vt* to justify.
justo/ta *adj* just; fair, right; exact, correct; tight; * *adv* exactly, precisely; just in time.
juvenil *adj* youthful.
juventud *f* youthfulness, youth; young people *pl*.
juzgado *m* tribunal; court.
juzgar *vt, vi* to judge.

K

karaoke *m* karaoke.
ketchup *m* ketchup.
kilogramo *m* kilogram.
kilometraje *m* distance in kilometers.
kilómetro *m* kilometer.
kilovatio *m* kilowatt.
kiosco *m* kiosk.

L

la *art f* the; * *pn* her; you; it.
laberinto *m* labyrinth.
labia *f* fluency; (*col*) the gift of the gab.
labio *m* lip; edge.
labor *f* labor, task; needlework; farmwork; plowing.
laboratorio *m* laboratory.
laboriosidad *f* laboriousness.
laborioso/sa *adj* laborious; hard-working.
labrado/da *adj* worked; carved; wrought; * *m* cultivated land.
labrador/ra *m/f* farmer; peasant.
labranza *f* farming; cultivation; farmland.
labrar *vt* to work; to carve; to farm; (*fig*) to bring about.
labriego/ga *m/f* peasant.
laca *f* lacquer; hairspray.
lacayo *m* lackey, footman.
lacerar *vt* to tear to pieces, to lacerate.
lacio/cia *adj* faded, withered; languid; lank (hair).
lacónico/ca *adj* laconic.
laconismo *m* laconic style, terseness.
lacra *f* scar; blot, blemish; *Lat Am* scab.
lacrar *vt* to seal (with sealing wax).
lacre *m* sealing wax.
lactancia *f* lactation; breast-feeding.
lácteo/tea *adj*: **productos** ~**s** dairy products.
ladear *vt* to move to one side; to incline; ~**se** *vr* to lean; to tilt.
ladera *f* slope.

ladino/na *adj* cunning, crafty.

lado *m* side; faction, party; favor, protection; (*mil*) flank; **al ~ de** beside; **poner a un ~** to put aside; **por todos ~s** on all sides.

ladrar *vt* to bark.

ladrido *m* bark, barking.

ladrillo *m* brick.

ladrón/ona *m/f* thief, robber, burglar.

lagar *m* wine press.

lagartija *f* (small) lizard.

lagarto *m* lizard.

lago *m* lake.

lágrima *f* tear.

lagrimal *m* corner of the eye.

lagrimoso/sa *adj* weeping, shedding tears.

laguna *f* lake; lagoon; gap.

laico/ca *adj* lay; * *m* layman.

lama *f Lat Am* slime; moss.

lamedura *f* licking.

lamentable *adj* lamentable, deplorable; pitiable.

lamentación *f* lamentation.

lamentar *vt* to be sorry about; to lament, to regret; * *vi*, **~se** *vr* to lament, to complain; to mourn.

lamento *m* lament.

lamer *vt* to lick, to lap.

lámina *f* plate, sheet of metal; engraving.

lámpara *f* lamp.

lamparilla *f* nightlight.

lamparón *m* grease spot.

lampiño/na *adj* beardless.

lamprea *f* lamprey (fish).

lana *f* wool.

lance *m* cast, throw; move, play (in a game); event, incident.

lancero *m* (*mil*) lancer.

lancha *f* barge, lighter; launch.

langosta *f* locust; lobster.

langostino *m* king prawn.

languidez *f* languor.

lánguido/da *adj* languid, faint, weak.

lanudo/da *adj* wooly, fleecy.

lanza *f* lance, spear.

lanzada *f* stroke with a lance.

lanzadera *f* shuttle.

lanzamiento *m* throwing; (*mar*, *com*) launch, launching.

lanzar *vt* to throw; (*sport*) to bowl, to pitch; to launch, to fling; (*law*) to evict.

lapicero *m* pencil, ballpoint pen; *Lat Am* propelling pencil.

lápida *f* flat stone, tablet.

lapidario/ria *adj*, *m* lapidary.

lápiz *m* pencil; propelling pencil.

lapso *m* interval; error.

lapsus *m* error, mistake.

largamente *adv* for a long time.

largar *vt* to loosen, to slacken; to let go; to launch; to throw out; **~se** *vr* (*col*) to beat it.

largo/ga *adj* long; lengthy, generous; copious; **a la ~a** in the end, eventually.

largueza *f* liberality, generosity.

largura *f* length.

laringe *f* larynx.

laringitis *f* laryngitis.

las *art fpl* the; * *pn* them; you.

lascivia *f* lasciviousness; lewdness.

lascivo/va *adj* lascivious; lewd.

láser *m* laser.

lasitud *f* lassitude, weariness.

lástima *f* compassion, pity; shame.

lastimadura *f Lat Am* graze.

lastimar *vt* to hurt; to wound; to feel pity for; **~se** *vr* to hurt oneself.

lastimero/ra *adj* pitiful, pathetic.

lastimoso/sa *adj* pathetic, mournful.

lastrar *vt* to ballast (a ship).

lastre *m* ballast; good sense.

lata *f* tin; can; (*col*) nuisance.

lateral *adj* lateral.

latero/ra *m/f Lat Am* tinsmith.

latido *m* (heart)beat.

latifundio *m* large estate.

latigazo *m* lash, crack (of a whip).

látigo *m* whip.

latín *m* Latin.

latinizar *vt* to Latinize.

latino/na *adj* Latin.

Latinoamérica *f* Latin America.

latinoamericano/na *adj*, *m/f* Latin American.

latir *vi* to beat, to palpitate.

latitud *f* latitude.

latón *m* brass.

latoso/sa *adj* annoying; boring.

latrocinio *m* theft, robbery.

laúd *f* lute (musical instrument).

laudable *adj* laudable, praiseworthy.

láudano *m* laudanum.

laureado/da *adj* honored; * *m* laureate.

laurel *m* (*bot*) laurel; reward.

lava *f* lava.

lavabo *m* washbasin; washroom.

lavadero *m* washing place; laundry.

lavado *m* washing; laundry.

lavadora *f* washing machine.

lavanda *f* lavender.

lavandera *f* laundress.

lavandería *f* laundry; **~ automática** Laundromat™.

lavaparabrisas *m invar* windshield washer.

lavaplatos *m invar* dishwasher.

lavar *vt* to wash; to wipe away; **~se** *vr* to wash oneself.

lavativa *f* (*med*) enema; (*fig*) nuisance.

laxante *m* (*med*) laxative.

laxitud *f* laxity, slackness, laxness.

laxo/xa *adj* lax, slack.

lazada *f* bow, knot.

lazarillo *m*: **perro ~** guide dog.

lazo *m* knot; bow; snare, trap; tie; bond.

le *pn* him; you; (*dative*) to him; to her; to it; to you.

leal *adj* loyal; faithful.

lealtad *f* loyalty.

lebrel *m* greyhound.

lebrillo *m* glazed earthenware dish.

lección *f* reading; lesson; lecture; class.

leche *f* milk.

lechera *f* milkmaid, dairymaid; milk can, milk churn.

lechería *f* dairy.

lecho *m* bed; layer.

lechón *m* sucking pig.

lechuga *f* lettuce.

lechuza *f* owl.

lector/ra *m/f* reader.

lectura *f* reading.

leer *vt, vi* to read.

legado *m* bequest, legacy; legate.

legajo *m* file.

legal *adj* legal; trustworthy.

legalidad *f* legality.

legalización *f* legalization.

legalizar *vt* to legalize.

legaña *f* sleep (in eyes).

legar *vt* to leave, to bequeath.

legible *adj* legible.

legión *f* legion.

legionario/ria *m/f* legionary.

legislación *f* legislation.

legislador/ra *m/f* legislator, lawmaker.

legislar *vt* to legislate.

legislativo/va *adj* legislative.

legislatura *f* legislature.

legitimar *vt* to legitimize.

legitimidad *f* legitimacy.

legítimo/ma *adj* legitimate, lawful; authentic.

legua *f* league.

legumbres *fpl* pulses *pl*.

leído/da *adj* well-read.

lejano/na *adj* distant, remote; far.

lejía *f* bleach.

lejos *adv* at a great distance, far off.

lelo/la *adj* stupid, ignorant; * *m/f* -idiot.

lema *m* motto; slogan.

lencería *f* linen, drapery.

lengua *f* tongue; language.

lenguado *m* sole.

lenguaje *m* language.

lente *m/f* lens; ~ **de contacto** contact lense; ~**s** *mpl Lat Am* glasses.

lenteja *f* lentil.

lentilla *f* contact lens.

lentitud *f* slowness.

lento/ta *adj* slow.

leña *f* wood, lumber.

leñador *m* woodsman, woodcutter.

leño *m* block, log; trunk of a tree.

leñoso/sa *adj* woody.

Leo *m* Leo (zodiac sign).

león *m* lion; *Lat Am* puma.

leona *f* lioness.

leonado/da *adj* lion-colored, tawny.

leonino/na *adj Lat Am* Leonian (zodiac sign).

leopardo *m* leopard.

leotardos *mpl* tights.

lepra *f* leprosy.

leproso/sa *adj* leprous; * *m/f* leper.

lerdo/da *adj* slow, heavy, dull; slow-witted.

les *pn* them; you; *(dativo)* to them; to you.

lesbiana *adj*, *f* lesbian.

lesión *f* wound; injury; damage.

letal *adj* mortal, deadly.

letanía *f* litany.

letárgico/ca *adj* lethargic.

letargo *m* lethargy.

letra *f* letter; handwriting; printing type; draft of a song; draft; ~**s** *fpl* letters *pl*, learning.

letrado/da *adj* learned, lettered; * *m/f* lawyer; counsel.

letrero *m* sign; label.

letrina *f* latrine.

leucemia *f* leukemia.

leva *m* (*mar*) weighing anchor; (*mil*) levy.

levadizo/za *adj* that can be lifted/raised; **puente** ~ drawbridge.

levadura *f* yeast; brewer's yeast.

levantamiento *m* raising; insurrection.

levantar *vt* to raise, to lift up; to build; to elevate; to hearten, to cheer up; ~**se** *vr* to get up; to stand up.

levante *m* Levant; east; east wind.

leve *adj* light; trivial.

levita *f* a heavy overcoat; greatcoat, frock coat.

léxico *m* vocabulary.

ley *f* law; standard (for metal).

leyenda *f* legend.

liar *vt* to tie, to bind; to confuse.

libelo *m* petition; satire, lampoon.

libélula *f* dragonfly.

liberación *f* liberation; release.

liberal *adj* liberal, generous; * *m/f* liberal.

liberalidad *f* liberality, generosity.

libertad *f* liberty, freedom.

libertador/ra *m/f* liberator.

libertar *vt* to free, to set at liberty; to exempt, to clear from an obligation/debt.

libertinaje *m* licentiousness.

libertino/na *m/f* permissive person.

libra *f* pound; ~ **esterlina** pound sterling.

Libra *f* Libra (zodiac sign).

librano/na *adj Lat Am* Libran (zodiac sign).

librar *vt* to free, to deliver; (*com*) to draw; to make out (a check); (*law*) to exempt; to fight (a battle); ~**se** *vr* to escape.

libre *adj* free; exempt; vacant.

libremente *adv* freely.

librería *f* bookshop.

librero/ra *m/f* bookseller.

libreta *f* notebook; ~ **de ahorros** savings book.

libretista *m/f Lat Am* screenwriter.

libreto *m Lat Am* script.

libro *m* book.

licencia *f* license; licentiousness; *Lat Am* leave.

licenciado/da *adj* licensed; * *m/f* graduate.
licenciar *vt* to permit, to allow; to license; to discharge; to confer a degree upon; **~se** *vr* to graduate.
licencioso/sa *adj* licentious, dissolute.
liceo *m* lyceum; secondary school.
lícitamente *adv* lawfully.
lícito/ta *adj* lawful, fair; permissible.
licor *m* liquor.
licuadora *f* blender, liquidizer.
lid *m* contest, fight; dispute.
líder *m/f* leader.
liderazgo *m* leadership.
liebre *f* hare.
lienzo *m* linen; canvas; face/front of a building.
liga *f* garter; birdlime; league; coalition; alloy.
ligadura *f* (*med*, *mus*) ligature; binding; bond, tie.
ligamento *m* ligament; tie; bond.
ligar *vt* to tie, to bind, to fasten; **~se** *vr* to commit oneself; * *vi* to mix, blend; (*col*) to pick up.
ligazón *f* union, connection.
ligereza *f* lightness; swiftness; agility; superficiality.
ligero/ra *adj* light, swift; agile; superficial.
liguero *m* garter belt.
lija *f* dogfish; sandpaper.
lijar *vt* to smooth, to sandpaper.
lila *f* lilac.
lima *f* file.
limadura *f* filing.
limar *vt* to file; to polish.
limitación *f* limitation, restriction.
limitado/da *adj* limited.
limitar *vt* to limit; to restrict; to cut down.
límite *m* limit, boundary.
limítrofe *adj* neighboring, bordering.
limón *m* lemon.
limonada *f* lemonade.
limonar *m* plantation/orchard of lemon trees.
limosna *f* alms *pl*, charity.
limpiabotas *m/f invar* shoeshine boy/girl.
limpiaparabrisas *m invar* windshield wiper.
limpiar *vt* to clean; to cleanse; to purify; to polish; (*fig*) to clean up.
limpieza *f* cleanliness; cleaning; cleansing; polishing; purity.
limpio/pia *adj* clean; neat; pure.
linaje *m* lineage, family, descent.
linaza *f* linseed.
lince *m* lynx.
linchar *vt* to lynch.
lindar *vi* to be adjacent.
linde *m* boundary.
lindero *m* edge; boundary.
lindo/da *adj* pretty; lovely.
lindura *f Lat Am* prettiness.
línea *f* line; cable; outline.
lineal *adj* linear.
lingote *m* ingot.

lingüista *m/f* linguist.
lino *m* flax.
linterna *f* flashlight; lantern, lamp; torch.
lío *m* bundle, parcel; (*col*) muddle, mess.
liposucción *f* liposuction.
liquidación *f* liquidation.
liquidar *vt* to liquidate; to settle (accounts).
líquido/da *adj* liquid.
lira *f* (*mus*) lyre.
lirio *m* (*bot*) iris.
lirón *m* dormouse; (*fig*) sleepyhead.
lisiado/da *adj* injured; * *m/f* physically disabled person.
lisiar *vt* to injure; to hurt.
liso/sa *adj* plain, even, flat, smooth.
lisonja *f* adulation, flattery.
lisonjear *vt* to flatter.
lisonjero/ra *m/f* flatterer; * *adj* flattering; pleasing.
lista *f* list; school register; catalog; menu.
lista de correos *f* general delivery.
listo/ta *adj* ready; smart, clever.
listón *m* ribbon; strip (of wood/metal).
litera *f* berth; bunk, bunk bed.
literal *adj* literal.
literario/ria *adj* literary.
literato/ta *adj* literary; * *m/f* writer, literary person; **~s** *mpl* literati *pl*.
literatura *f* literature.
litigar *vt* to fight; * *vi* (*law*) to go to law; (*fig*) to dispute.
litigio *m* lawsuit.
litografía *f* lithography.
litográfico/ca *adj* lithographic.
litoral *adj* coastal; * *m* coast.
litro *m* liter.
liturgia *f* liturgy.
litúrgico/ca *adj* liturgical.
liviandad *f* fickleness; triviality; lightness.
liviano/na *adj* light; fickle; trivial.
lívido/da *adj* livid.
llaga *f* wound; sore.
llama *f* flame; llama (animal).
llamada *f* call.
llamado *m Lat Am* call.
llamador *m* door-knocker.
llamamiento *m* call.
llamar *vt* to call; to name; to summon; to ring up, to telephone; * *vi* to knock at the door; to ring up, to telephone; **~se** *vr* to be named.
llamarada *f* blaze; outburst.
llamativo/va *adj* showy; loud (color).
llano/na *adj* plain; even, level, smooth; clear, evident; * *m* plain.
llanta *f* (wheel) rim; tire; inner (tube); *Lat Am* tire.
llanto *m* flood of tears, crying.
llanura *f* evenness, flatness; plain, prairie.
llave *f* faucet; key; **~ maestra** master key.
llavero *m* key ring.
llegada *f* arrival, coming.

llegar *vi* to arrive; ~ **a** to reach; ~**se** *vr* to come near, to approach.

llenar *vt* to fill; to cover; to fill out (a form); to satisfy, to fulfill; ~**se** *vr* to gorge oneself.

lleno/na *adj* full, full up; complete.

llevadero/ra *adj* tolerable.

llevar *vt* to take; to wear; to carry; to convey, to transport; to drive; to lead; to bear; ~**se** *vr* to carry off, to take away.

llorar *vt, vi* to weep, to cry.

lloriquear *vt* to whine.

lloro *m* weeping, crying.

llorón/ona *m/f* tearful person; crybaby.

lloroso/sa *adj* mournful, full of tears.

llover *vi* to rain.

lloviznar *vi* to drizzle.

lluvia *f* rain; ~ **ácida** acid rain.

lluvioso/sa *adj* rainy.

lo *pn* it; him; you; * *art* the.

loable *adj* laudable.

loar *vt* to praise.

lobato *m* young wolf.

lobo *m* wolf.

lóbrego/ga *adj* murky, dark, gloomy.

lóbulo *m* lobe.

local *adj* local; * *m* place, site.

localidad *f* locality; location.

localizar *vt* to localize.

loción *f* lotion.

loco/ca *adj* mad; * *m/f* mad person.

locomoción *f Lat Am* public transport.

locomotora *f* locomotive.

locuacidad *f* loquacity.

locuaz *adj* loquacious, talkative.

locución *f* expression.

locura *f* madness, folly.

locutor/ra *m/f* (*rad*) announcer; (*TV*) newsreader.

locutorio *m* telephone booth.

lodazal *m* muddy place.

lodo *m* mud, mire.

logaritmo *m* logarithm.

lógica *f* logic.

lógico/ca *adj* logical.

lograr *vt* to achieve; to gain, to obtain.

logro *m* achievement; success.

loma *f* small hill, hillock.

lombarda *f* red cabbage.

lombriz *f* worm.

lomo *m* loin; back (of an animal); spine (of a book); **llevar/traer a** ~ to carry on the back.

lona *f* canvas.

loncha *f* slice; rasher.

longaniza *f* pork sausage.

longitud *f* length; longitude.

lonja¹ *f* slice; rasher.

lonja² *f* market, exchange; ~ **de pescado** fish market.

loro *m* parrot.

los *art mpl* the; * *pn* them; you.

losa *f* flagstone.

lote *m* lot; portion; *Lat Am* plot of land.

lotería *f* lottery.

loza *f* crockery.

lozanía *f* luxuriance, lushness; vigor; self-assurance.

lozano/na *adj* luxuriant, lush; sprightly.

lubricante *m* lubricant.

lucero *m* bright star; ~ **del alba** morning star.

lucha *f* struggle, fight.

luchador/ra *m/f* fighter; * *m* wrestler.

luchar *vi* to struggle; to wrestle.

lúcido/da *adj* lucid.

luciérnaga *f* glowworm.

lucimiento *m* splendor, luster; brightness.

lución *m* slowworm.

lucir *vt* to light (up); to show off; * *vi* to shine; *Lat Am* to look; ~**se** *vr* to make a fool of oneself.

lucrativo/va *adj* lucrative.

lucro *m* gain, profit.

luego *adv* next; afterward(s); **desde** ~ of course.

lugar *m* place, spot; village; reason; **en** ~ **de** instead of, in lieu of.

lugareño/ña *adj* belonging to a village; * *m/f* inhabitant of a village.

lugarteniente *m* deputy.

lúgubre *adj* lugubrious; sad, gloomy.

lujo *m* luxury; abundance.

lujoso/sa *adj* luxurious; showy; profuse, lavish.

lujuria *f* lust.

lujurioso/sa *adj* lustful, lewd.

lumbre *f* fire; light.

lumbrera *f* luminary; skylight.

luminaria *f* illumination.

luminoso/sa *adj* luminous, shining.

luna *f* moon; glass plate for mirrors; lens.

lunar *m* mole, spot; * *adj* lunar.

lunático/ca *adj, m/f* lunatic.

lunes *m invar* Monday.

lupa *f* magnifying glass, magnifier.

lupanar *m* brothel.

lustre *m* gloss, luster; splendor.

lustro *m* lustrum, space of five years.

lustroso/sa *adj* bright, brilliant.

luteranismo *m* Lutheranism.

luterano/na *adj, m/f* Lutheran.

luto *m* mourning (dress); grief.

luz *f* light.

M

macarrones *mpl* macaroni.

macedonia *f*: ~ **de frutas** fruit salad.

macerar *vt* to macerate, to soften.

maceta *f* flowerpot.

machacar *vt* to pound, to crush; * *vi* to insist, to go on.

machacón/ona *adj* wearisome, tedious.

machete *m* machete, cutlass.

machista adj, m sexist.
macho adj male; (fig) virile; * m male; (fig) he-man.
machucar vt to pound, to bruise.
macilento/ta adj lean; haggard, withered.
macizo/za adj massive; solid; * m mass, chunk.
madeja f skein of thread; mop of hair.
madera f lumber, timber, wood.
madero m lumber beam, timber beam.
madrastra f stepmother.
madraza f loving mother.
madre f mother; womb.
madreperla f mother-of-pearl.
madreselva f honeysuckle.
madrigal m madrigal.
madriguera f burrow; den.
madrina f godmother.
madroño m strawberry plant.
madrugada f dawn; **de ~** at day break.
madrugador/ra m/f early riser.
madrugar vi to get up early; to get ahead.
madurar vt to ripen; * vi to ripen, to grow ripe; to mature.
madurez f maturity; ripeness; wisdom.
maduro/ra adj ripe, mature.
maestra f mistress; schoolmistress; teacher.
maestría f mastery, skill; Lat Am master's degree.
maestro m master; teacher; ~/tra adj masterly, skilled; principal.
magia f magic.
mágico/ca adj magical.
magisterio m teaching; teaching profession; teachers pl.
magistrado/da m/f magistrate.
magistral adj magisterial; masterly.
magistratura f magistracy.
magnanimidad f magnanimity.
magnánimo/ma adj magnanimous.
magnate m magnate.
magnético/ca adj magnetic.
magnetismo m magnetism.
magnetizar vt to magnetize.
magnetofón, magnetófono m tape recorder.
magnetofónico/ca adj: **cinta magnetofónica** recording tape.
magnificencia f magnificence, splendor.
magnífico/ca adj magnificent, splendid.
magnitud f magnitude.
mago/ga m/f magician.
magro/gra adj thin, lean; meager.
magulladura f bruise.
magullar vt to bruise; to damage; (col) to bash.
magullón m Lat Am bruise.
mahometano/na m/f, adj Muslim.
mahometanismo m Islam.
mahonesa f mayonnaise.
maíz m corn; maize.
maizal m corn field.
majada f sheepfold.
majadería f absurdity; silliness.

majadero/ra adj dull; silly, stupid; * m idiot.
majestad f majesty.
majestuoso/sa adj majestic.
majo/ja adj nice; attractive; smart.
majuelo m vine (newly planted); hawthorn.
mal m evil; hurt; harm, damage; misfortune; illness; * adj (before masculine nouns) bad.
malamente adv badly.
malaria f malaria.
malcriado/da adj rude, ill-behaved; naughty; spoiled.
maldad f wickedness.
maldecir vt to curse.
maldición f curse.
maldito/ta adj wicked; damned, cursed.
malear vt to damage; to corrupt.
malecón m pier.
maledicencia f slander; scandal.
maleducado/da adj bad-mannered, rude.
maleficio m curse; spell; witchcraft.
maléfico/ca adj harmful, damaging, evil.
malestar m discomfort; (fig) uneasiness; unrest.
maleta f suitcase; (auto) trunk.
maletero f (auto) trunk.
malevolencia f malevolence.
malévolo/la adj malevolent.
maleza f weeds pl; thicket.
malgastar vt to waste, to ruin.
malhablado/da adj foul-mouthed.
malhechor/ra m/f malefactor; criminal.
malhumorado/da adj cross, bad-tempered.
malicia f malice, wickedness; suspicion; cunning.
malicioso/sa adj malicious, wicked, evil; sly, crafty; spiteful.
malignidad f (med) malignancy; evil nature; malice.
maligno/na adj malignant; malicious.
malinformar vt Lat Am to misinform.
malla f mesh, network; ~s fpl leotard.
malo/la adj bad; ill; wicked; * m/f villain.
malograr vt to spoil; to upset (a plan); to waste; ~se vr to fail; to die early.
malparado/da adj: **salir ~** to come off badly.
malparida f woman who has had a miscarriage.
malparir vi to miscarry, to have a miscarriage.
malsano/na adj unhealthy.
malteada f Lat Am milk shake.
maltratamiento m ill-treatment.
maltratar vt to ill-treat, to abuse, to mistreat.
malva f (bot) mallow.
malvado/da adj wicked, villainous.
malversación f embezzlement.
malversador/ra m/f embezzler.
malversar vt to embezzle.
mama f teat; breast.
mamá f (col) mom, mommy.
mamar vt, vi to suck.
mamarrachada f ridiculous sight.
mamarracho m mess, botch-up.
mamífero m mammal.

mamita f (col) Lat Am mom, mommy.

mamón/ona m/f small baby; -scrounger.

mampara f partition; screen.

mampostería f masonry; stonemasonry.

maná m manna.

manada f flock, herd; pack; crowd.

manantial m source, spring; origin.

manar vt to run with, to flow; * vi to spring from; to flow; to abound.

mancha f stain, spot.

manchado/da adj spotted.

manchar vt to stain, to soil.

mancilla f spot, blemish.

manco/ca adj one-armed; one-handed; maimed; faulty.

mancomunar vt to associate, to unite; to make jointly responsible.

mancomunidad f union, fellowship; community; (law) joint responsibility.

mandado m command; errand, message.

mandamiento m order, command; commandment.

mandar vt to command, to order; to bequeath; to send.

mandarín m mandarin.

mandarina f tangerine; mandarin orange.

mandatario/ria m/f agent; leader.

mandato m mandate, order; term of office.

mandíbula f jaw.

mandil m apron.

mando m command, authority, -power; term of office; ~ a distancia remote control.

mandón/ona adj bossy, domineering.

manecilla f small hand (of a watch/meter); book-clasp.

manejable adj manageable.

manejar vt to manage; to operate; to handle; Lat Am (auto) to drive; ~se vr to manage; to behave; Lat Am to drive.

manejo m management; handling; Lat Am driving; confidence.

manera f manner, way; fashion; kind.

manga f sleeve; hose, hosepipe.

mango[1] m handle.

mango[2] m mango.

mangonear vi to interfere; * vt to boss about.

manguera f hose; hosepipe.

manguito m muff.

maní m peanut.

manía f mania; craze; dislike; spite.

maniatar vt to tie the hands of; to handcuff.

maniático/ca adj maniac, mad, frantic; * m/f maniac.

manicomio m mental home, lunatic asylum.

manicura f manicure.

manifestación f manifestation; show; demonstration; mass meeting.

manifestar vt to manifest, to declare.

manifiesto/ta adj manifest, open, clear; * m manifesto.

manija f Lat Am handle.

maniobra f maneuvering; handling; (mil) maneuver.

maniobrar vt to maneuver; to -handle.

manipulación f manipulation.

manipular vt to manipulate.

maniquí m dummy; * m/f model.

manirroto/ta adj lavish, extravagant.

manivela f crank.

manjar m (tasty) dish.

mano f hand; hand (of a clock or watch); foot, paw (of an animal); coat (of paint); lot, series; hand (at game); Lat Am bunch (of bananas); a ~ by hand; a ~s llenas liberally, generously.

manojo m handful, bunch.

manopla f gauntlet; glove; washcloth.

manosear vt to handle; to finger, to mess up.

manoseo m handling; fingering.

manotazo m slap, smack.

manoteo m gesticulation.

mansalva f: a ~ adv indiscriminately.

mansedumbre f meekness, gentleness.

mansión f mansion.

manso/sa adj tame; gentle, soft.

manta f blanket.

manteca f fat; ~ de cerdo lard.

mantecado m cake eaten at Christmas; ice cream.

mantecoso/sa adj greasy.

mantel m tablecloth.

mantelería f table linen.

mantener vt to maintain, to support; to nourish; to keep; ~se vr to hold one's ground; to support oneself.

mantenimiento m maintenance; subsistence.

mantequilla f butter.

mantilla f mantilla (head covering for women); ~s fpl baby clothes pl.

manto m mantle; cloak, robe.

mantón m shawl.

manual adj manual; * m manual, handbook.

manubrio m Lat Am handlebars pl.

manufactura f manufacture.

manufacturar vt to manufacture.

manuscrito m manuscript; * adj handwritten.

manutención f support, maintenance.

manzana f apple.

manzanilla f chamomile; chamomile tea; manzanilla sherry.

manzano m apple tree.

maña f handiness, dexterity, cleverness, cunning; habit, custom; trick.

mañana f morning; * adv tomorrow.

mañoso/sa adj skillful, handy; cunning.

mapa m map.

mapamundi f map of the world.

maquillaje m make-up; making up.

maquillar vt to make up; ~se vr to put on make-up.

máquina f machine; (rail) engine; camera; (fig) machinery; plan, project.

maquinación f machination.

maquinador/ra *m/f* schemer, plotter.

maquinalmente *adv* mechanically.

maquinar *vt, vi* to machinate; to conspire.

maquinaria *f* machinery; mechanism.

maquinilla *f*: ~ **de afeitar** razor.

maquinista *m* (*rail*) train driver; operator; (*mar*) engineer.

mar *m/f* sea.

maraña *f* shrub, thicket; tangle.

maravilla *f* wonder.

maravillar *vt* to astonish, to amaze; ~**se** *vr* to be amazed, to be astonished.

maravilloso/sa *adj* wonderful, marvelous.

marca *f* mark; stamp; (*com*) make, brand.

marcado/da *adj* strong, marked.

marcador *m* scoreboard; scorer; *Lat Am* felt-tip pen.

marcar *vt* to mark; to dial; to score; to record; to set (hair); * *vi* to score; to dial.

marcha *f* march; running; gear; speed; (*fig*) progress.

marchar *vi* to go; to work; ~**se** *vr* to go away.

marchitar *vt* to wither; to fade.

marchito/ta *adj* faded; withered.

marcial *adj* martial, warlike.

marciano/na *adj* Martian.

marco *m* frame; framework; (*sport*) goalposts *pl*.

marea *f* tide; ~ **negra** oil slick.

marear *vt* (*mar*) to sail, to navigate; to annoy, to upset; ~**se** *vr* to feel sick; to feel faint; to feel dizzy.

marejada *f* swell, heavy sea, surge.

mareo *m* sick feeling; dizziness; nuisance.

marfil *m* ivory.

margarina *f* margarine.

margarita *f* daisy.

margen *m* margin; border; * *f* bank (of river).

marginal *adj* marginal.

marginar *vt* to exclude; to leave margins on (a page); to make notes in the margin of.

marica *m* (*col*) sissy.

maricón *m* (*col*) queer.

marido *m* husband.

mariguana, marihuana *f* cannabis.

marimacho *f* (*col*) mannish woman.

marina *f* navy.

marinero/ra *adj* sea *compd*; seaworthy; * *m* sailor.

marino/na *adj* marine; * *m* sailor, seaman.

marioneta *f* puppet.

mariposa *f* butterfly.

mariquita *f* ladybug.

mariscal *m* marshal.

marisco *m* shellfish.

marital *adj* marital.

maritimo/ma *adj* maritime, marine.

marmita *f* pot.

mármol *m* marble.

marmóreo/rea *adj* marbled, marble *compd*.

marmota *f* marmot.

maroma *f* rope.

marqués *m* marquis.

marquesa *f* marchioness.

marrano *m* hog, boar; pig.

marrón *adj* brown.

marrullería *f* plausibility; plausible excuse; ~**s** *fpl* cajolery.

marrullero/ra *adj* crafty, cunning.

marta *f* marten, sable.

Marte *m* Mars (planet).

martes *m invar* Tuesday.

martillar *vt* to hammer.

martillo *m* hammer.

mártir *m/f* martyr.

martirio *m* martyrdom.

martirizar *vt* to martyr.

marxismo *m* Marxism.

marxista *adj*, *m/f* Marxist.

marzo *m* March.

mas *adv* but, yet.

más *adv* more; most; besides, moreover; **a ~ tardar** at latest; **sin ~ ni ~** without more ado.

masa *f* dough, paste; mortar; mass.

masacre *m* massacre.

masaje *m* massage.

mascar *vt* to chew.

máscara *m/f* masked person; * *f* mask.

mascarada *f* masquerade.

mascarilla *f* (*med*) mask.

masculino/na *adj* masculine, male.

mascullar *vt* to mumble, to mutter.

masivo/va *adj* massive, en masse.

masoquista *m/f* masochist.

masticación *f* mastication.

masticar *vt* to masticate, to chew.

mástil *m* (*mar*) mast.

mastín *m* mastiff.

masturbación *f* masturbation.

masturbarse *vr* to masturbate.

mata *f* shrub; sprig, blade; grove, group of trees; mop of hair.

matadero *m* slaughterhouse.

matador/ra *adj* killing; * *m/f* killer; * *m* bullfighter.

matanza *f* slaughtering; massacre.

matar *vt* to kill; to execute; to murder; ~**se** *vr* to kill oneself, to commit suicide.

matasanos *m invar* quack (doctor).

matasellos *m invar* postmark.

mate¹ *m* checkmate.

mate² *adj* matte.

matemáticas *fpl* mathematics; math.

matemático/ca *adj* mathematical; * *m/f* mathematician.

materia *m* matter, materials *pl*; subject.

material *adj* material, physical; * *m* equipment, materials *pl*.

materialidad *f* outward appearance.

materialismo *m* materialism.

materialista *m/f* materialist.

maternal *adj* maternal, motherly.

maternidad *f* motherhood.

materno/na *adj* maternal.

matinal *adj* morning *compd*.

matiz *m* shade of color; shading.

matizar *vt* to mix colors; to tinge, to tint.

matón *m* bully.

matorral *m* shrub, thicket.

matraca *f* rattle.

matricida *m/f* matricide (person).

matricidio *m* matricide (act).

matrícula *f* register, list; (*auto*) registration number; license plate.

matricular *vt* to register, to enroll.

matrimonial *adj* matrimonial.

matrimonio *m* marriage, matrimony.

matriz *f* matrix; womb; mold, form.

matrona *f* matron.

matutino/na *adj* morning.

maullar *vi* to mew.

maullido *m* mew (of a cat).

mausoleo *m* mausoleum.

máxima *f* maxim.

máxime *adv* principally.

máximo/ma *adj* maximum; top; highest.

mayo *m* May.

mayonesa *f* mayonnaise.

mayor *adj* main, chief; (*mus*) major; biggest; eldest; greater, larger; elderly; * *m* chief, boss; adult; **al por ~** wholesale; **~es** *mpl* forefathers.

mayoral *m* foreman.

mayordomo *m* steward.

mayoreo *m* Lat Am wholesale.

mayoría *f* majority, greater part; **~ de edad** coming of age.

mayorista *m/f* wholesaler.

mayormente *adv* principally, chiefly.

mayúsculo/la *adj* (*fig*) tremendous; * *f* capital letter.

maza *f* club; mace.

mazada *f* blow with a club.

mazapán *m* marzipan.

mazmorra *f* dungeon.

mazo *m* bunch, handful; club, mallet; bat.

mazorca *f* cob; corncob; ear.

me *pn* me; to me.

mear *vi* (*col*) to pee, to piss.

mecánica *f* mechanics.

mecánico/ca *adj* mechanical; * *m/f* mechanic.

mecanismo *m* mechanism.

mecanografía *f* typing.

mecanógrafo/fa *m/f* typist.

mecate *m* rope.

mecedora *f* rocking chair.

mecer *vt* to rock; to dandle (a child).

mecha *f* wick; fuse.

mechar *vt* to lard; to stuff.

mechero *m* (cigarette) lighter.

mechón *m* lock of hair; large bundle of threads/ fibers.

medalla *f* medal.

medallón *m* medallion.

media *f* stocking; sock; average.

mediación *f* mediation, intervention.

mediado/da *adj* half-full; half-complete; **a ~s de** in the middle of.

mediador/ra *m/f* mediator; go-between.

medialuna *f* Lat Am croissant.

mediana *f* median strip.

medianero/ra *adj* dividing; adjacent.

mediano/na *adj* medium; middling; mediocre.

medianoche *f* midnight.

mediante *prep* by means of.

mediar *vi* to intervene; to mediate.

medias *fpl* pantyhose *pl*.

medicación *f* medication.

medicamento *m* medicine.

medicina *f* medicine.

medicinal *adj* medicinal.

médico/ca *adj* medical; * *m/f* doctor.

medida *f* measure.

medidor *m* Lat Am meter.

medio/dia *adj* half; **a medias** partly; * *m* middle; average; way, means; medium.

mediocre *adj* middling; moderate; mediocre.

mediocridad *f* mediocrity.

mediodía *m* noon, midday.

medir *vt* to measure; **~se** *vr* to be moderate.

meditación *f* meditation.

meditar *vt* to meditate.

mediterráneo/nea *adj* Mediterranean; * *m*: **el M~** the Mediterranean.

medrar *vi* to grow, to thrive, to prosper; to improve.

medroso/sa *adj* fearful, timid.

médula *f* marrow; essence, substance; pith.

medusa *f* jellyfish.

megafonía *f* public-address system.

megáfono *m* megaphone.

mejilla *f* cheek.

mejillón *m* mussel.

mejor *adj*, *adv* better; best.

mejora *f* improvement.

mejorar *vt* to improve, to ameliorate; to enhance; * *vi* to improve; (*med*) to recover, to get better; **~se** *vr* to improve, to get better.

mejoría *f* improvement; recovery.

melancolía *f* melancholy.

melancólico/ca *adj* melancholy, sad, gloomy.

melena *f* long hair, loose hair; mane.

melenudo/da *adj* long-haired.

melindroso/sa *adj* prudish, finicky.

mella *f* notch in edged tools; gap.

mellado/da *adj* jagged; gap-toothed.

mellar *vt* to notch.

mellizo/za *adj*, *m/f* twin.

melocotón *m* peach.

melodía *f* melody.

melodioso/sa *adj* melodious.

melodrama *f* melodrama.

melón *m* melon.

melosidad *f* sweetness.

meloso/sa *adj* honeyed; mellow.

membrana *f* membrane.

membranoso/sa *adj* membranous.

membresía *f Lat Am* membership.

membrete *m* letterhead.

membrillo *m* quince; quince tree.

membrudo/da *adj* strong, robust; burly.

memorable *adj* memorable.

memorándum *m* notebook; memorandum.

memoria *f* memory; report; record; ~**s** *fpl* memoirs *pl*.

memorial *m* memorial; petition.

mención *f* mention.

mencionar *vt* to mention.

mendigar *vt* to beg.

mendigo/ga *m/f* beggar.

mendrugo *m* crust.

menear *vt* to move from place to place; (*fig*) to handle; ~**se** *vr* to move; to shake; to sway.

meneo *m* movement; shake; swaying.

menester *m* necessity; need; want; ~**es** *mpl* duties *pl*.

menesteroso/sa *adj* needy.

menestra *f* vegetable soup/stew.

menguante *f* decreasing.

menguar *vi* to diminish; to discredit.

menopausia *f* menopause.

menor *m/f* young person, juvenile; * *adj* less; smaller; minor; **al por ~** retail.

menoría *f*: **a ~** retail.

menos *adv* less; least; **a lo ~/por lo ~** at least; * *prep* except; minus.

menoscabar *vt* to damage; to harm; to lessen; to discredit.

menoscabo *m* damage; harm; loss.

menospreciar *vt* to undervalue; to despise, to scorn.

menosprecio *m* contempt, scorn; undervaluation.

mensaje *m* message.

mensajero/ra *m/f* messenger; courier.

menstruación *f* menstruation.

mensual *adj* monthly.

menta *f* mint.

mental *adj* mental; intellectual.

mentar *vt* to mention.

mente *f* mind; understanding.

mentecato/ta *adj* silly, stupid; * *m/f* idiot.

mentir *vt* to feign; to pretend; * *vi* to lie.

mentira *f* lie, falsehood.

mentiroso/sa *adj* lying; * *m/f* liar.

menú *m* menu; set meal.

menudencia *f* trifle, small thing; minuteness; ~**s** *fpl* odds and ends *pl*.

menudillos *mpl* giblets *pl*.

menudo/da *adj* small; minute; petty, insignificant; **a ~** frequently, often.

meñique *m* little finger.

meollo *m* marrow; (*fig*) core.

mequetrefe *m* good-for-nothing; busybody.

meramente *adv* merely, solely.

mercader *m* dealer, trader.

mercadería *f* commodity; trade; ~**s** *fpl Lat Am* merchandise.

mercado *m* market; marketplace.

mercancía *f* commodity; ~**s** *fpl* goods *pl*, merchandise.

mercantil *adj* commercial, mercantile.

mercenario/ria *adj* mercenary; * *m* mercenary; laborer.

mercería *f* dry goods store.

mercurio *m* mercury.

Mercurio *m* Mercury (planet).

merecedor/ra *adj* deserving.

merecer *vt* to deserve, to merit.

merecido/da *adj* deserved.

merendar *vi* to have tea; to have a picnic.

merengue *m* meringue.

meridiano *m* meridian.

meridional *adj* southern.

merienda *f* (light) tea; afternoon snack; picnic.

mérito *m* merit; worth, value.

meritorio/ria *adj* meritorious.

merluza *f* hake.

merma *f* waste, leakage.

mermar *vi* to waste, to diminish.

mermelada *f* jelly, jam.

mero *m* pollack (fish); ~/**ra** *adj* mere, pure.

merodeador *m* (*mil*) marauder.

merodear *vi* to pillage, to go marauding.

mes *m* month.

mesa *f* table; desk; plateau; ~ **redonda** round table.

mesada *f Lat Am* monthly installment.

meseta *f* meseta, tableland, plateau.

mesón *m* inn.

mestizo/za *adj* of mixed race; crossbred; * *m/f* half-caste.

mesura *f* gravity; politeness; moderation.

mesurado/da *adj* moderate; dignified; courteous.

meta *f* goal; finish.

metabolismo *m* metabolism.

metafísica *f* metaphysics.

metafísico/ca *adj* metaphysical.

metáfora *f* metaphor.

metafórico/ca *adj* metaphorical.

metal *m* metal; (*mus*) brass; timbre/timber (of the voice).

metálico/ca *adj* metallic.

metalurgia *f* metallurgy.

metamorfosis *f invar* metamorphosis; transformation.

meteoro *m* meteor.

meteorología *f* meteorology.

meter *vt* to place, to put; to insert, to put in; to involve; to make, to cause; ~**se** *vr* to meddle, to interfere.

metódico/ca *adj* methodical.

método *m* method.

metralla *f* (*mil*) shrapnel.

metralleta *f* submachine-gun.

métrico/ca *adj* metric.

metro[1] *m* meter.

metro[2] *m* subway.

metrópoli *f* metropolis; mother country.

mezcla *f* mixture; medley.

mezclar *vt* to mix; ~**se** *vr* to mix; to mingle.

mezquindad *f* meanness; pettiness; wretchedness.

mezquino/na *adj* mean; small-minded, petty; wretched.

mezquita *f* mosque.

mi *adj* my.

mí *pn* me; myself.

microbio *m* microbe.

microbús *m* minibus.

microchip *m* microchip.

micrófono *m* microphone.

microondas *m inv* microwave oven.

microplaqueta *f* microchip.

microscópico/ca *adj* microscopic.

microscopio *m* microscope.

miedo *m* fear, dread.

miel *f* honey.

miembro *m* member.

mientras *adv* meanwhile; * *conj* while; as long as.

miércoles *m invar* Wednesday.

mierda *f* (*col*) shit.

mies *f* harvest.

miga *f* crumb; ~**s** *fpl* fried breadcrumbs *pl*.

migaja *f* scrap, crumb.

migración *f* migration.

mijo *m* (*bot*) millet.

mil *m* one thousand.

milagro *m* miracle, wonder.

milagroso/sa *adj* miraculous.

milano *m* kite (bird).

milésimo/ma *adj*, *m* thousandth.

mili *f*: **hacer la ~** (*col*) to do one's military service.

milicia *f* militia; military service.

miliciano *m* militiaman.

milímetro *m* millimeter.

militante *adj* militant.

militar *adj* military; * *m* soldier; * *vi* to serve in the army; (*fig*) to be a member of a party.

milla *f* mile.

millar *m* thousand.

millón *m* million.

millonario/ria *m/f* millionaire.

mimar *vt* to spoil, pamper.

mimbre *m* wicker.

mímica *f* sign language; mimicry.

mimo *m* caress; spoiling; mime.

mimoso/sa *adj* spoilt, pampered; delicate.

mina *f* mine; underground passage.

minar *vt* to undermine; to mine.

mineral *m* mineral; * *adj* mineral.

mineralogía *f* mineralogy.

minero/ra *m/f* miner.

miniatura *f* miniature.

minicadena *f* midi system.

minifalda *f* miniskirt.

mínimo/ma *adj* minimum.

ministerio *m* ministry.

ministro/ra *m/f* minister.

minoría *f* minority.

minucioso/sa *adj* meticulous; very detailed.

minúsculo/la *adj* minute; * *f* small letter.

minusválido/da *adj* (physically) handicapped; * *m/f* (physically) handicapped person.

minuta *f* minute, first draft; menu.

minutero *m* minute hand (of a watch/clock).

minuto *m* minute.

mío/mía *adj* mine.

miope *adj* short-sighted.

mira *f* sight of a gun; (*fig*) aim.

mirada *f* glance; gaze.

mirador *m* viewpoint, vantage point.

miramiento *m* consideration; circumspection.

mirar *vt* to look at; to observe; to consider; * *vi* to look; ~**se** *vr* to look at oneself; to look at one another.

mirilla *f* peephole.

mirlo *m* blackbird.

mirón/ona *m/f* spectator, onlooker, bystander; voyeur.

misa *f* mass; ~ **del gallo** midnight mass.

misal *m* missal.

misantropía *f* misanthropy.

misántropo/pa *m/f* misanthropist.

miserable *adj* miserable; mean; squalid (place); (*col*) despicable; * *m/f* rotter.

miseria *f* misery; poverty; meanness; squalor.

misericordia *f* mercy.

misil *m* missile.

misión *f* mission.

misionero/ra *m/f* missionary.

mismo/ma *adj* same; very.

misterio *m* mystery.

misterioso/sa *adj* mysterious.

mística *f* mysticism.

místico/ca *adj* mystic(al); * *m/f* mystic.

mitad *f* half; middle.

mitigación *f* mitigation.

mitigar *vt* to mitigate.

mitin *m* (political) rally.

mito *m* myth.

mitología *f* mythology.

mitológico/ca *adj* mythological.

mitones *mpl* mittens *pl*.

mixto/ta *adj* mixed.

mobiliario *m* furniture.

mochila *f* backpack.

mochuelo *m* red owl.

moción *f* motion.

moco *m* mucus; (*col*) snot.

moda *f* fashion, style.

modales *mpl* manners *pl*.

modalidad *f* kind, variety.

modelaje *m Lat Am* modeling.

modelar *vt* to model, to form.

modelo *m* model, pattern.

módem *m* modem.

moderación *f* moderation.

moderado/da *adj* moderate.

moderar *vt* to moderate.

moderno/na *adj* modern.

modestia *f* modesty, decency.

modesto,ta *adj* modest.

módico/ca *adj* moderate.

modificación *f* modification.

modificar *vt* to modify.

modisto/ta *m/f* dressmaker.

modo *m* mode, method, manner.

modorra *f* drowsiness.

modulación *f* modulation.

modular *vt* to modulate.

mofa *f* mockery.

mofarse *vr:* ~ **de** to mock, to scoff at.

moflete *m* fat cheek.

moho *m* rust; mold, mildew.

mohoso/sa *adj* moldy, musty.

mojar *vt* to wet, to moisten; ~**se** *vr* to get wet.

mojigato *adj* hypocritical.

mojón *m* landmark.

molde *m* mold; *Lat Am* pattern; model.

moldura *f* molding.

mole *f* bulk; pile.

molécula *f* molecule.

moler *vt* to grind, to pound; to tire out; to annoy, to bore.

molestar *vt* to annoy, to bother; to trouble; * *vi* to be a nuisance.

molestia *f* trouble; inconvenience; (*med*) discomfort.

molesto/ta *adj* annoying; inconvenient; uncomfortable; annoyed.

molinero *m* miller.

molinillo *m:* ~ **de café** coffee grinder.

molino *m* mill.

molusco *m* mollusk.

momentáneo/nea *adj* momentary.

momento *m* moment.

momia *f* mummy (as in Egyptian).

monacal *adj* monastic.

monaguillo *m* acolyte.

monarca *m/f* monarch.

monarquía *f* monarchy.

monárquico/ca *adj* monarchical; * *m/f* royalist, monarchist.

monasterio *m* monastery, convent.

monástico/ca *adj* monastic.

mondadientes *m invar* toothpick.

mondar *vt* to clean; to cleanse; to peel; ~**se** *vr:* ~ **de risa** (*col*) to split one's sides laughing.

mondo/da *adj* clean; pure; ~ **y lirondo** bare, plain; pure and simple.

moneda *f* money; currency; coin.

monedero *m* purse; *Lat Am* phone booth.

monería *f* funny face; mimicry; prank; trifle.

monetario/ria *adj* monetary, financial.

monitor *m* monitor.

monja *f* nun.

monje *f* monk.

mono[1] *m* monkey; ape.

mono[2] *m* coveralls *pl*, overalls *pl*.

mono/na[3] *adj* lovely; pretty; nice.

monólogo *m* monolog.

monopolio *m* monopoly.

monopolista *m* monopolist.

monosílabo/ba *adj* monosyllabic.

monotonía *f* monotony.

monótono/na *adj* monotonous.

monovolumen *m* people mover.

monstruo *m* monster.

monstruosidad *f* monstrosity.

monstruoso/sa *adj* monstrous.

monta *f* amount, sum total.

montaje *m* assembly; decor (of theater); montage.

montaña *f* mountain.

montañes/esa *adj* mountain *compd*; * *m/f* highlander.

montañoso/sa *adj* mountainous.

montar *vt* to mount, to get on (a bicycle, horse etc); to assemble, to put together; to overlap; to set up (a business); to beat, to whip (in cooking); * *vi* to mount; to ride; ~ **a** to amount to.

montaraz *adj* mountainous; wild, untamed.

monte *m* mountain; woodland; ~ **alto** forest; ~ **bajo** scrub.

montería *f* hunting, chase.

montés/esa *adj* wild, untamed.

montón *m* heap, pile; mass; **a ~ones**, abundantly, by the score.

montura *f* mount; saddle.

monumento *m* monument.

monzón *m* monsoon.

moño *m* bun; *Lat Am* bow.

moquillo *m* distemper (disease in dogs).

mora *f* blackberry.

morada *f* home, abode, residence.

morado/da *adj* violet, purple.

morador/ra *m/f* inhabitant.

moral[1] *m* mulberry tree.

moral[2] *f* morals *pl*, ethics *pl*; * *adj* moral.

moraleja *f* moral.

moralidad *f* morality.

moralista *m/f* moralist.

moralizar *vi* to moralize.

moralmente *adv* morally.

morar *vi* to inhabit, to dwell.

moratoria *f* moratorium.

mórbido/da *adj* morbid, diseased.

morboso/sa *adj* diseased, morbid.

morcilla *f* blood sausage, black pudding.

mordacidad *f* sharpness, pungency.

mordaz *adj* biting, scathing; pungent.

mordaza *f* gag; clamp.

mordedura *f* bite.

morder *vt* to bite; to nibble; to corrode; to eat away.

mordisco *m* bite.

moreno/na *adj* brown; swarthy; dark-skinned.

moribundo/da *adj* dying.

morigeración f temperance.

morir vi to die; to expire; to die down; **~se** vr to die; (fig) to be dying.

morisco/ca adj Moorish.

moro/ra adj Moorish.

morosidad f slowness, sluggishness.

moroso/sa adj slow, sluggish; (com) slow to pay up.

morral m haversack.

morriña f depression; sadness.

morro m snout; nose (of plane etc).

morsa f walrus.

mortaja f shroud; cigarette paper.

mortal adj mortal; fatal, deadly.

mortalidad f mortality.

mortandad f death toll.

mortero m mortar (cannon).

mortífero/ra adj deadly, fatal.

mortificación f mortification.

mortificar vt to mortify.

mortuorio m mortuary.

moruno/na adj Moorish.

mosca f fly.

moscardón m botfly, hornet; (col) pest, bore.

moscatel adj, m muscatel.

moscón m (col) pest, bore.

mosquearse vr (col) to get cross; (col) to take offense.

mosquetero m musketeer.

mosquitero m mosquito net.

mosquito m gnat, mosquito.

mostaza f mustard.

mosto m must, new wine.

mostrador m counter, bar.

mostrar vt to show, to exhibit; to explain; **~se** vr to appear, to show oneself.

mota f speck, tiny piece; dot; defect, fault.

mote m nickname.

motejar vt to nickname.

motín m revolt; mutiny.

motivar vt to motivate; to explain, to justify.

motivo m motive, cause, reason.

moto f (col) motor scooter, motorbike.

motocicleta f motorcycle.

motor m engine, motor.

movedizo/za adj movable; variable, changeable; fickle.

mover vt to move; to shake; to drive; (fig) to cause; **~se** vr to move; (fig) to get a move on.

móvil adj mobile, movable; moving; * m motive; cellular phone.

movilidad f mobility.

movimiento m movement, motion.

mozo/za adj young; * m/f youth, young man/girl; waiter/waitress.

muchacho/a m/f boy/girl; * f maid(servant).

muchedumbre f crowd.

mucho/cha adj a lot of, much; * adv much, a lot; long.

muda f change of clothes.

mudable adj changeable, variable; mutable.

mudanza f change; move.

mudar vt to change; to shed, to molt; **~se** vr to change one's clothes; to change house; * vi to change;

mudo/da adj dumb; silent, mute.

mueble m piece of furniture; **~s** mpl furniture.

mueca f grimace, funny face.

muela f tooth, molar.

muelle m spring; regulator; quay, wharf.

muérdago m (bot) mistletoe.

muerte f death.

muerto m corpse; **~/ta** adj dead.

muesca f notch, groove.

muestra f pattern; indication; demonstration; proof; sample; token; model.

mugido m lowing (of cattle).

mugir vi to low, to bellow.

mugre m dirt, filth.

mugriento/ta adj greasy; dirty, filthy.

mujer f woman.

mulato/ta adj mulatto.

muleta f crutch.

mullido/da adj soft; springy.

mulo/la m/f mule.

multa f fine, penalty.

multar vt to fine.

multimedia adj multimedia.

múltiple adj multiple; **~s** many, numerous.

multiplicación f multiplication.

multiplicado m (math) multiplicand.

multiplicar vt to multiply.

multiplicidad f multiplicity.

multitud f multitude.

mundano/na adj worldly; mundane.

mundial adj worldwide; world compd.

mundo m world.

munición f ammunition.

municipio m town council; municipality.

municipal adj municipal.

muñeca f wrist; child's doll.

muñeco m scarecrow, puppet.

muñón m stump.

muralla f rampart, wall.

murciélago m bat (animal).

murmullo m murmur, mutter.

murmuración f backbiting, gossip.

murmurador/ra m/f detractor, backbiter.

murmurar vi to murmur; to gossip, to backbite.

muro m wall.

muscular adj muscular.

músculo m muscle.

muselina f muslin.

museo m museum.

musgo m moss.

música f music.

musical adj musical.

músico/ca m/f musician; * adj musical.

muslo m thigh.

mustio/tia adj parched, withered; sad, sorrowful.

musulmán/ana adj, m/f Muslim.

mutabilidad f mutability.

mutación *f* mutation, change.
mutilación *f* mutilation.
mutilar *vt* to mutilate, to maim.
mutuo/tua *adj* mutual, reciprocal.
mutuamente *adv* mutually.
muy *adv* very; too; greatly; ~ **ilustre** most illustrious.

N

nabo *m* turnip.
nácar *m* mother-of-pearl, nacre.
nacarado/da *adj* mother-of-pearl *compd*; pearl-colored.
nacer *vi* to be born; to bud, to shoot (of plants); to rise; to grow.
nacido/da *adj* born; **recién** ~ newborn.
nacimiento *m* birth; nativity.
nación *f* nation.
nacional *adj* national.
nacionalidad *f* nationality.
nacionalizar *vt* to nationalize; ~**se** to become naturalized.
nada *f* nothing; * *adv* no way, not at all, by no means.
nadador/ra *m/f* swimmer.
nadar *vi* to swim.
nadie *pn* nobody, no one.
nado *adv*: **a** ~ afloat.
naipe *m* (playing) card.
nalgas *fpl* buttocks *pl*.
naranja *f* orange.
naranjada *f* orangeade.
naranjal *m* orange grove.
naranjo *m* orange tree.
narciso *m* (*bot*) daffodil; narcissus (flower); fop.
narcótico/ca *adj* narcotic; * *m* drug, narcotic.
narcotraficante *m/f* drug trafficker.
nardo *m* (*bot*) spikenard, nard.
narigón/ona, narigudo/da *adj* big-nosed.
nariz *f* nose; sense of smell.
narración *f* narration.
narrar *vt* to narrate, to tell.
narrativa *f* narrative; story.
nata *f* cream.
natación *f* swimming.
natal *adj* natal, native.
natalicio *m* birthday.
natillas *fpl* custard.
natividad *f* nativity.
nativo/va *adj, m/f* native.
natural *m* temperament, natural disposition; native; inhabitant; * *adj* natural; native; common, usual; **al** ~ unaffectedly.
naturaleza *f* nature.
naturalidad *f* naturalness.
naturalista *m* naturalist.
naturalizar *vi* to naturalize; ~**se** *vr* to become naturalized; to become acclimatized.
naturalmente *adv* in a natural way; **¡~!** of course!

naturópata *m/f* naturopath.
naufragar *vi* to be shipwrecked; to suffer ruin in one's affairs.
naufragio *m* shipwreck.
náufrago/ga *adj* shipwrecked.
nauseabundo/da *adj* nauseating.
náuseas *fpl* nauseousness, nausea.
náutica *f* navigation.
navaja *f* pocketknife, penknife; razor.
naval *adj* naval.
nave *f* ship; nave.
navegable *adj* navigable.
navegación *f* navigation; sea journey.
navegador *m* (*comput*) browser.
navegante *m* navigator.
navegar *vt, vi* to navigate; to sail; to fly.
navidad *f* Christmas.
navideño/ña *adj* Christmas *compd*.
navío *m* ship.
nazi *adj, m/f* Nazi.
neblina *f* mist; fine rain, drizzle.
nebuloso/sa *adj* misty; cloudy; nebulous; foggy; hazy; drizzling; * *f* nebula.
necedad *f* gross ignorance, stupidity; imprudence.
necesario/ria *adj* necessary.
neceser *m* toilet bag; carryall.
necesidad *f* necessity, need, want.
necesitado/da *adj* necessitous, very needy.
necesitar *vt* to need; * *vi* to want, to need.
necio/cia *adj* ignorant; stupid, foolish; imprudent; *Lat Am* stubborn.
necrología *f* obituary.
nectarina *f* nectarine.
néctar *m* nectar.
nefando/da *adj* base, nefarious, abominable.
nefasto/ta *adj* unlucky.
negación *f* negation; denial.
negado/da *adj* incapable, unfit.
negar *vt* to deny; to refuse; ~**se** *vr*: ~ **a hacer** to refuse to do.
negativo/va *adj, m* negative; * *f* negative; refusal.
negligencia *f* negligence.
negligente *adj* negligent; careless, heedless.
negociación *f* negotiation; commerce.
negociante *m/f* trader, dealer.
negociar *vt, vi* to negotiate.
negocio *m* business, affair; transaction; firm; place of business.
negro/gra *adj* black; dark; * *m* black; * *m/f* Black person, Negro/Negress.
negrura *f* blackness.
negruzco/ca *adj* blackish.
nene *m*, **nena** *f* baby.
nenúfar *m* water lily.
neófito *m* neophyte.
Neptuno *m* Neptune (planet).
nervio *m* nerve.
nervioso/sa *adj* nervous.
neto/ta *adj* neat, pure; net.
neumático/ca *adj* pneumatic; * *m* tire.

neurona f neuron.
neutral adj neutral; neuter.
neutralidad f neutrality.
neutralizar vt to neutralize; to counteract.
neutro/tra adj neutral; neuter; * m Lat Am neutral.
neutrón m neutron.
nevada f heavy fall of snow.
nevar vi to snow.
nevera f icebox.
nevería f ice-cream parlor.
nexo m link.
ni conj neither, nor.
nica m/f Lat Am (col) Nicaraguan.
nicho m niche.
nido m nest; hiding place.
niebla f fog; mist.
nieta f granddaughter.
nieto m grandson.
nieve f snow.
nigromancia f necromancy.
nimiedad f small-mindedness; triviality.
nimio/mia adj trivial.
ninfa f nymph.
ningún, ninguno/na adj no; * pn nobody; none; not one; neither.
niña f little girl; pupil (of eye).
niñera f nursemaid.
niñería f childishness; childish act.
niñero/ra adj fond of children.
niñez f childhood.
niño/ña adj childish; * m/f child;infant; **desde ~** from infancy, from a child; * m boy.
níspero m medlar.
nitidez f clarity; brightness; sharpness.
nitrato m (chem) nitrate.
nitrógeno m nitrogen.
nivel m level; standard; height; **a ~** perfectly level.
niveladora f bulldozer.
nivelar vt to level; to even up; to balance.
no adv no; not; * excl no!
noble adj noble, illustrious; generous.
nobleza f nobleness, nobility.
nocaut m Lat Am knockout.
noción f notion, idea.
nocivo/va adj harmful.
nocturno/na adj nocturnal, nightly; * m nocturne.
noche f night; evening; darkness; **¡buenas ~s!** good night!
Nochebuena f Christmas Eve.
Nochevieja f New Year's Eve.
nodriza f nurse.
nogal m walnut tree.
nómada adj nomadic; * m/f nomad.
nomás adv Lat Am just.
nombramiento m nomination; appointment.
nombrar vt to name; to nominate; to appoint.
nombre m name; title; reputation.
nomenclatura f nomenclature.

nómina f list; (com) payroll.
nominador m nominator.
nominal adj nominal.
nominativo m (gr) nominative.
non adj odd, uneven; * m odd number.
nonagenario/ria adj ninety-year-old; * m/f nonagenarian.
no obstante adv nevertheless, notwithstanding.
noquear vt Lat Am to thrash.
nor(d)este adj northeast, northeastern; * m northeast.
nórdico/ca adj northern; Nordic.
noria f water wheel; big wheel.
normal adj normal; usual.
normalizar vt to normalize; to standardize; **~se** vr to return to normal.
normar vt Lat Am to regulate.
noroeste adj northwest, northwestern; * m northwest.
norte adj north, northern; * m north; (fig) rule, guide.
nos pn us; to us; for us; from us; to ourselves.
nosocomio m Lat Am hospital.
nosotros/tras pn we; us.
nostalgia f homesickness.
nota f note; notice, remark; mark.
notable adj notable, remarkable.
notar vt to note; to mark; to remark; **~se** vr to be obvious.
notaría f notary profession; notary's office.
notario m notary.
noticia f notice; knowledge, information; note; **~s** fpl news.
noticiario m newsreel; news bulletin.
noticiero m news bulletin.
notificación f notification.
notificar vt to notify, to inform.
notoriedad f notoriety.
notorio/ria adj notorious.
novato/ta adj inexperienced; * m/f beginner; freshman.
novecientos/tas adj nine hundred.
novedad f novelty; modernness; newness; piece of news; change.
novela f novel.
novelero/ra adj highly imaginative.
novelesco/ca adj fictional; romantic; fantastic.
noveno/na adj ninth.
noventa adj, m ninety.
novia f bride; girlfriend; fiancée.
noviazgo m engagement.
novicio/na m novice.
noviembre m November.
novilla f heifer.
novillada f drove of young bulls; bullfight with young bulls and novice bullfighters.
novillo m young bull/ox.
novio m bridegroom; boyfriend; fiancé.
nubarrón m large cloud.
nube f cloud.
nublado/da adj cloudy; * m storm cloud.

nublarse *vr* to grow dark.

nublazón *m Lat Am* storm cloud.

nuca *f* nape (of the neck); scruff of the neck.

nuclear *adj* nuclear; * *vt Lat Am* to bring together.

núcleo *m* core; nucleus.

nudillo *m* knuckle.

nudo *m* knot.

nuera *f* daughter-in-law.

nuestro/tra *adj* our; * *pn* ours.

nuevamente *adv* again; anew.

nueve *adj, m* nine.

nuevo/va *adj* new; modern; fresh; * *f* piece of news; ¿qué hay de ~? is there any news?, what's new?

nuez *f* nut; walnut; Adam's apple; ~ **moscada** nutmeg.

nulidad *f* incompetence; (*law*) nullity; nonentity.

nulo/la *adj* useless; drawn; null.

numeración *f* numeration.

numerador *m* numerator.

numeral *m* numeral.

numerar *vt* to number.

numérico/ca *adj* numerical.

número *m* number; cipher.

numeroso/sa *adj* numerous.

nunca *adv* never.

nuncio *m* nuncio.

nupcial *adj* nuptial.

nupcias *fpl* nuptials *pl*, wedding.

nutria *f* otter.

nutrición *f* nutrition.

nutrir *vt* to nourish; to feed.

nutritivo/va *adj* nutritious, nourishing.

nylon *m* nylon.

ñato/ta *adj* snub-nosed.

ñoñería *f* insipidness.

ñoño/ña *adj* insipid; spineless; silly.

O

o *conj* or; either.

oasis *m invar* oasis.

obcecación *f* obduracy.

obcecar *vt* to blind; to darken.

obedecer *vt* to obey.

obediencia *f* obedience.

obediente *adj* obedient.

obelisco *m* obelisk.

obertura *f* (*mus*) overture.

obesidad *f* obesity.

obeso/sa *adj* obese, fat.

obispado *m* bishopric, episcopate.

obispo *m* bishop.

objeción *f* objection, opposition, exception.

objetar *vi* to object.

objetor *m* ~ **de conciencia** conscientious objector.

objetivo/va *adj, m* objective.

objeto *m* object; aim.

oblea *f* wafer.

oblicuo/cua *adj* oblique.

obligación *f* obligation; (*com*) bond.

obligar *vt* to force; ~**se** *vr* to bind oneself.

obligatorio/ria *adj* obligatory.

oblongo/ga *adj* oblong.

oboe *m* oboe.

obra *f* work; building, construction; play; **por ~ de** thanks to.

obrar *vt* to work, to operate; to put into practice; * *vi* to behave, to act; to have an effect.

obrero/ra *adj* working; labor *compd*; * *m/f* workman; laborer.

obscenidad *f* obscenity.

obsceno/na *adj* obscene.

obsequiar *vt* to lavish attention on; ~ **con** to present with.

obsequio *m* gift; courtesy.

obsequioso/sa *adj* obsequious, compliant; officious.

observación *f* observation; remark.

observador/ra *m/f* observer.

observancia *f* observance.

observar *vt* to observe; to notice.

observatorio *m* observatory.

obsesión *f* obsession.

obsesionar *vt* to obsess.

obstáculo *m* obstacle, impediment, hindrance.

obstar *vi*: ~ **a**, ~ **para** to oppose, to obstruct, to hinder.

obstetricia *f* obstetrics.

obstinación *f* obstinacy, stubbornness.

obstinado/da *adj* obstinate.

obstinarse *vr* to be obstinate; ~ **en** to persist in.

obstrucción *f* obstruction.

obstruir *vt* to obstruct; ~**se** *vr* to be blocked up, to be obstructed.

obtener *vt* to obtain; to gain.

obtuso/sa *adj* obtuse, blunt.

obús *m* (*mil*) shell.

obviar *vt* to obviate, to remove.

obvio/via *adj* obvious, evident.

ocasión *f* occasion, opportunity.

ocasional *adj* occasional.

ocasionar *vt* to cause, to occasion.

ocaso *m* (*fig*) decline.

occidental *adj* occidental, western.

occidente *m* occident, west.

océano *m* ocean.

ochenta *adj, m* eighty.

ocho *adj, m* eight.

ochocientos *m, adj* eight hundred.

ocio *m* leisure; pastime.

ociosidad *f* idleness, leisure.

ocioso/sa *adj* idle; useless.

ocre *m* ocher.

octavilla *f* pamphlet.

octavo/va *adj* eighth.

octogenario/ria *adj, m/f* octogenarian.

octubre *m* October.

ocular *adj* ocular; eye *compd*.
oculista *m/f* oculist.
ocultar *vt* to hide, to conceal.
oculto/ta *adj* hidden, concealed; secret.-
ocupación *f* occupation; business; employment.
ocupado/da *adj* busy; occupied; engaged.
ocupar *vt* to occupy; to hold (an office); **~se** *vr*: **~ de/~ en** to concern oneself with; to look after.
ocurrencia *f* event; bright idea.
ocurrir *vi* to occur, to happen.
oda *f* ode.
odiar *vt* to hate;**~se** *vr* to hate one another.
odio *m* hatred.
odioso/sa *adj* odious, hateful.
odontólogo/ga *m/f* dentist.
odorífero/ra *adj* odoriferous, odorous.
oeste *adj* west, western; * *m* west.
ofender *vt* to offend; to injure **~se** *vr* to be vexed; to take offense.
ofensa *f* offense; injury.
ofensivo/va *adj* offensive, injurious.
ofensor *m* offender.
oferta *f* offer; offering.
oficial *adj* official; * *m* officer; official.
oficialismo *m Lat Am*: **el ~** the Government.
oficialista *adj Lat Am* pro-government.
oficiar *vi* to officiate, to minister (of clergymen etc).
oficina *f* office.
oficio *m* office; employment, occupation; ministry; function; trade, business; **~s** *mpl* divine service.
oficiosidad *f* diligence; officiousness; importunity.
oficioso/sa *adj* officious; diligent; unofficial, informal.
ofrecer *vt* to offer; to present; to exhibit; **~se** *vr* to offer oneself; to occur, to present itself.
ofrecimiento *m* offer, promise.
ofrenda *f* offering, oblation.
ofrendar *vt* to offer, to contribute.
oftalmólogo/ga *m/f* ophthalmologist.
ofuscación *f* dimness of sight; obfuscation.
ofuscar *vt* to darken, to render obscure; to bewilder.
oídas *fpl*: **de ~** by hearsay.
oído *m* hearing; ear.
oír *vt*, *vi* to hear; to listen (to).
ojal *m* buttonhole.
¡ojalá! *conj* if only!, would that!
ojeada *f* glance.
ojear *vt* to eye, to view; to glance.
ojera *f* bag under the eyes.
ojeriza *f* spite, grudge, ill-will.
okey *interj Lat Am* OK.
okupa *m/f* (col) squatter.
ojo *m* eye; sight; eye of a needle; arch of a bridge.
ola *f* wave.
oleada *f* surge; violent emotion.
oleaje *m* succession of waves, sea swell.
óleo *m* oil.

oler *vt* to smell, to scent; * *vi* to smell; **~ a** to smack of.
olfatear *vt* to smell; (*fig*) to sniff out.
olfato *m* sense of smell.
oligarquía *f* oligarchy.
oligárquico/ca *adj* oligarchical.
olimpíada *f* Olympiad; **las O~s** the Olympics.
olímpico/ca *adj* Olympic.
oliva *f* olive.
olivar *m* olive grove.
olivo *m* olive tree.
olla *f* pan; stew; **~ podrida** dish composed of different boiled meats and vegetables; **~ exprés/~ a presión** pressure cooker.
olmo *m* elm tree.
olor *m* smell, odor; scent.
oloroso/sa *adj* fragrant; odorous.
olvidadizo/za *adj* forgetful.
olvidar *vt* to forget.
olvido *m* forgetfulness.
ombligo *m* navel.
omelet *f Lat Am* omelet.
omisión *f* omission.
omitir *vt* to omit.
omnipotencia *f* omnipotence.
omnipotente *adj* omnipotent, almighty.
once *adj*, *m* eleven.
onda *f* wave.
ondear *vi* to undulate; to fluctuate.
ondulado/da *adj* wavy.
oneroso/sa *adj* burdensome.
onomástico *m Lat Am* birthday.
opa *f* takeover bid.
opacidad *f* opacity; gloom, darkness.
opaco/ca *adj* opaque; dark.
opción *f* option, choice.
ópera *f* opera.
operación *f* operation; **~ de cesárea** *f* cesarean section/operation.
operador/ra *m/f* operator; projectionist; cameraman/woman.
operar *vi* to operate; to act.
operativo *m Lat Am* operation.
opinar *vi* to think; * *vi* to give one's opinion.
opinión *f* opinion.
opio *m* opium.
oponente *m/f* opponent.
oponer *vt* to oppose; **~se** *vr* to be opposed, **~ a** to oppose.
oportunidad *f* opportunity.
oportunismo *m* opportunism.
oportuno/na *adj* seasonable, opportune.
oposición *f* opposition; **~ones** *fpl* public examinations *pl*.
opositor/ra *m/f* opponent; candidate (in public examination).
opresión *f* oppression.
opresivo/va *adj* oppressive.
opresor *m* oppressor.
oprimir *vt* to oppress; to crush; to press; to squeeze.

optar *vt* to choose, to elect.
optativo/va *adj* optional.
óptica *f* optics.
óptico/ca *adj* optical; * *m/f* optician.
optimista *m/f* optimist.
óptimo/ma *adj* best.
opuesto/ta *adj* opposite; contrary; adverse.
opulencia *f* wealth, riches *pl*.
opulento/ta *adj* opulent, wealthy.
oración *f* oration, speech; prayer.
orador,ra *m/f* orator.
oral *adj* oral.
orangután *m* orang-utan.
orar *vi* to pray.
oratoria *f* oratory, rhetorical skill.
órbita *f* orbit.
orden *m/f* order; ~ **del día** order of the day.
ordenación *f* arrangement; ordination; edict, ordinance.
ordenado/da *adj* methodical; orderly.
ordenador *m* computer.
ordenanza *f* order; statute, ordinance; ordination.
ordenar *vt* to arrange; to order; to ordain; ~**se** *vr* to take holy orders.
ordeña *f Lat Am* milking.
ordeñar *vt* to milk.
órdenes sagradas *fpl* holy orders *pl*.
ordinal *adj* ordinal.
ordinario/ria *adj* ordinary, common; **de ~** regularly, commonly, ordinarily.
orégano *m* oregano.
oreja *f* ear.
orejera *f* earflap.
orfanato *m* orphanage.
orfandad *f* orphanhood.
orgánico/ca *adj* organic; harmonious.
organigrama *m* flowchart.
organismo *m* organism; organization.
organista *m/f* organist.
organización *f* organization; arrange-ment.
organizar *vt* to organize.
órgano *m* organ.
orgasmo *m* orgasm.
orgía *f* orgy.
orgullo *m* pride, haughtiness.
orgulloso/sa *adj* proud, haughty.
orientación *f* position; direction.
oriental *adj* oriental, eastern; *Lat Am* Uruguayan.
orientar *vt* to orient; to point; to direct; to guide; ~**se** *vr* to get one's bearings; to decide on a course of action.
oriente *m* orient.
orificio *m* orifice; mouth; aperture.
origen *m* origin, source; native country; family, extraction.
original *adj* original, primitive; * *m* original, first copy.
originalidad *f* originality.
originar *vt, vi* to originate.

originario/ria *adj* original.
orilla *f* limit, border, margin; edge (of cloth); shore.
orín *m* rust.
orina *f* urine.
orinal *m* chamber pot.
orinar *vi* to pass water, urinate.
oriundo/da *adj*: ~ **de** native of.
ornamento *m* ornament, embellishment.
ornitología *f* ornithology.
oro *m* gold.
oros *mpl* diamonds *pl* (in cards).
orquesta *f* orchestra.
orquídea *f* orchid.
ortiga *f* (*bot*) nettle.
ortodoxia *f* orthodoxy.
ortodoxo/xa *adj* orthodox.
ortografía *f* orthography.
ortográfico/ca *adj* orthographic(al).
oruga *f* (*bot*) caterpillar.
orza *f* jar.
orzuelo *m* (*med*) stye,sty.
os *pn* you; to you.
osa *f* she-bear; **O~ Mayor/Menor** Great/Little Bear.
osadamente *adv* boldly, daringly.
osadía *f* boldness, intrepidity; zeal, fervor.
osamenta *f* skeleton.
osar *vi* to dare, to venture.
óscar *m* Oscar.
oscilación *f* oscillation.
oscilar *vi* to oscillate.
oscurecer *vt* to obscure; to darken; * *vi* to grow dark; ~**se** *vr* to disappear.
oscuridad *f* obscurity; darkness.
oscuro/ra *adj* obscure; dark.
osificarse *vr* to ossify.
oso *m* bear; ~ **blanco** polar bear.
ostensible *adj* ostensible, apparent.
ostentación *f* ostentation, ambitious display, show.
ostentar *vt* to show; * *vi* to boast, to brag.
ostentoso/sa *adj* sumptuous, ostentatious.
ostra *f* oyster.
otitis *f* earache.
otoñal *adj* fall.
otoño *m* fall.
otorgamiento *m* granting; execution.
otorgar *vt* to concede; to grant.
otorrino/na, otorrinolaringólogo/ga *m/f* ear, nose and throat specialist.
otro/tra *adj* another; other.
ovación *f* ovation.
ovalado/da *adj* oval.
óvalo *m* oval.
ovario *m* ovary.
oveja *f* sheep.
overol *m Lat Am* coveralls *pl*.
ovillo *m* ball of wool.
ovíparo/ra *adj* oviparous, egg-bearing.
ovulación *f* ovulation.

óvulo m ovum.
oxidación f rusting.
oxidar vt to rust; **~se** vr to go rusty.
óxido f (chem) oxide.
oxígeno m (chem) oxygen.
oyente m/f listener, hearer.

P

pabellón m pavilion; summer house; block, section.
pábilo m wick.
pacer vt to pasture, to graze.
paciencia f patience.
paciente adj, m/f patient.
pacificación f pacification.
pacificar vt to pacify, to appease.
pacífico/ca adj pacific, peaceful; * m: **el P~** the Pacific.
pacotilla f: **de ~** third-rate; cheap.
pactar vt to covenant; to contract; to stipulate.
pacto m contract, pact.
padecer vt to suffer; to sustain (an injury); to put up with.
padecimiento m suffering, sufferance.
padrastro m stepfather.
padrazo m loving, over-indulgent father.
padre m father; **~s** mpl parents pl.
padrino m godfather.
padrón m census; register; pattern; model.
paella f paella (dish of rice with shellfish, meat etc).
paga f payment, fee.
pagadero/ra adj payable.
paganismo m paganism, heathenism.
pagano/na adj, m/f heathen, pagan.
pagar vt to pay; to pay for; (fig) to repay; * vi to pay.
pagaré m bond, note of hand, promissory note, IOU (I owe you).
página f page.
pago m payment; reward.
país m country; region.
paisaje m landscape.
paisano/na adj of the same country; * m/f fellow countryman/woman.
paja f straw; (fig) trash.
pajar m straw loft.
pajarita f bow tie.
pájaro m bird; sly, acute fellow.
pajarraco m large bird; cunning fellow.
paje m page.
pajita f (drinking) straw.
pajizo/za adj straw-colored.
pala f spade, shovel.
palabra f word; **de ~** by word of mouth.
palabrota f swearword.
palaciego/ga adj pertaining/relating to the palace; * m courtier.
palacio m palace.

paladar m palate; taste, relish.
paladear vt to taste.
palanca f lever; **tener ~** Lat Am to have connections.
palanca de cambios f gear shift.
palangana f basin; Lat Am wooden platter.
palco m box (in a theater).
paleta f bat; palette; trowel.
paleto/ta m/f rustic.
paliar vt to mitigate.
paliativo/va adj, m palliative.
palidecer vi to turn pale.
palidez f paleness, wanness.
pálido/da adj pallid, pale.
palillo m small stick; toothpick; **~s** mpl chopsticks pl.
paliza f beating, thrashing.
palma f palm tree; palm of the hand; palm leaf.
palmada f slap, clap; **~s** fpl clapping of hands, applause.
palmatoria f candlestick; cane.
palmear vi to slap; to clap.
palmera f palm tree.
palmeta f cane.
palmo m palm; small amount.
palmotear vi to slap; to applaud.
palmoteo m clapping of hands.
palo m stick; cudgel; blow given with a stick; post; mast; bat; suit (in cards); Lat Am tree.
paloma f pigeon, dove; **~ torcaz** ring dove/wood pigeon; **~ mensajera** carrier pigeon, homing pigeon.
palomar m pigeon house/loft.
palomilla f moth; wing nut; angle iron.
palomino m young pigeon.
palomitas fpl popcorn.
palpable adj palpable, evident.
palpar vt to feel, to touch.
palpitación f palpitation; panting.
palpitante adj palpitating; (fig) burning.
palta f avocado (pear).
paludismo m malaria.
palpitar vi to palpitate.
palurdo/da adj rustic, clownish, rude.
pampa f pampa(s), prairie.
pámpano m vine branch.
pamplina f trifle.
pan m bread; loaf.
pana f corduroy.
panacea f panacea, universal medicine.
panadería f baker's (shop).
panadero/ra m/f baker.
panal m honeycomb; sweet rusk.
pancarta f placard.
pancito m Lat Am bread roll.
panda m panda (bear).
pandereta f tambourine.
pandilla f group; gang; clique.
panecito m Lat Am bread roll.
panegírico/ca adj panegyrical; * m eulogy.
panel m panel.

panfleto *m* pamphlet.

pánico *m* panic.

panorama *m* panorama.

panqueque *m Lat Am* pancake.

pantalla *f* screen; lampshade.

pantalón *m*, **pantalones** *mpl* pants *pl*, women's slacks *pl*.

pantano *m* swamp; marsh; reservoir; obstacle, difficulty.

pantanoso/sa *adj* swampy, marshy.

panteísta *f* pantheist.

panteón *m*: ~ **familiar** family tomb.

pantera *f* panther.

pantomima *f* pantomime.

pantorrilla *f* calf (of the leg).

pantufla *m* slipper.

panza *f* belly, paunch.

panzada *f* bellyful of food.

panzón/ona *adj Lat Am* big-bellied.

panzudo/da *adj* big-bellied.

pañal *m* diaper; ~ **desechable** disposable diaper.

paño *m* cloth; piece of cloth; duster, rag.

pañuelo *m* handkerchief.

papa *f* potato; * *m*: **el P~** the Pope.

papá *m* (*col*) pop, dad.

papada *f* double chin.

papagayo *m* parrot.

papal *adj* papal.

papanatas *m invar* (*col*) simpleton.

Papanicolau *m Lat Am* smear test.

paparrucha *f* piece of nonsense.

papaya *f* papaya, pawpaw.

papel *m* paper; writing; part, role (acted in a play); ~ **de estraza** brown paper; ~ **sellado** stamped paper.

papeleo *m* red tape.

papelera *f* writing desk; wastepaper basket.

papelería *f* stationer's (shop).

papeleta *f* slip of paper; ballot paper; report.

paperas *fpl* mumps.

papilla *f* baby food.

papista *m* papist.

paquete *m* packet; parcel; package tour.

par *adj* equal; alike; even; * *m* pair; couple; peer; **sin** ~ matchless.

para *prep* for; to, in order to; toward(s).

parabién *m* congratulations *pl*; felicitations *pl*.

parábola *f* parable; parabola.

parabólico/ca *adj* parabolic(al).

parabrisas *m invar* windshield.

paracaídas *m invar* parachute.

paracaidista *m/f* parachutist; (*mil*) paratrooper.

parachoques *m invar* fender; shock absorber.

parada *f* halt; suspension; pause; stop; shutdown; stopping place; ~ **a petición** flag stop; ~ **de autobús** bus stop.

paradero *m* halting place; term, end.

parado/da *adj* motionless; at a standstill; stopped; *Lat Am* standing (up); unemployed; * *m/f* unemployed person.

paradoja *f* paradox.

parador *m* parador, state-owned hotel.

parafrasear *vt* to paraphrase.

paráfrasis *f invar* paraphrase.

parágrafo *m Lat Am* paragraph.

paraguas *m invar* umbrella.

paraíso *m* paradise.

paraje *m* place, spot.

paralelo/la *adj*, *m* parallel.

paralítico/ca *adj* paralytic, palsied.

paralizar *vt* to paralyze; ~**se** *vr* to become paralyzed; (*fig*) to come to a standstill.

páramo *m* desert; wilderness.

parangón *m* paragon, model; comparison.

paranoico/ca *m/f* paranoiac.

parapente *m* paragliding.

parapeto *m* parapet.

parar *vi* to stop, to halt; * *vt* to stop, to detain; *Lat Am* to raise; **sin** ~ instantly, without delay; ~**se** *vr* to stop, to halt; *Lat Am* to stand up.

pararrayos *m invar* lightning conductor/rod.

parásito *m* parasite; (*fig*) sponger.

parasol *m* parasol.

parcela *f* piece of ground.

parche *m* patch.

parcial *adj* partial.

parcialidad *f* prejudice; bias.

parco/ca *adj* sober, moderate.

pardo/da *adj* gray.

parear *vt* to match, to pair, to couple.

parecer *m* opinion, advice, counsel; countenance, air, mien; * *vi* to appear; to seem; ~**se** *vr*: ~ **a** to resemble.

parecido/da *adj* resembling, like.

pared *f* wall; (*law*) ~ **medianera** party-wall.

pareja *f* pair, couple; a lumber/timber beam that serves as a support, brace.

parejo/ja *adj* equal; even.

parentela *f* parentage, kindred.

parentesco *m* relationship.

paréntesis *m invar* parenthesis.

parida *f* woman who has recently given birth.

paridad *f* parity, equality.

pariente/ta *m/f* relative, relation.

parir *vt* to give birth to; * *vi* to give birth.

parking *m* parking lot.

parlamentar *vi* to parley.

parlamentario/ria *m/f* member of parliament; * *adj* parliamentary.

parlamento *m* parliament.

parlanchín/ina *adj*, *m/f* chatterer, jabberer.

parlante *m Lat Am* speaker.

parlotear *vi* to prattle, to chatter, to gossip.

paro *m* unemployment; *Lat Am* strike.

parodia *f* parody.

parpadear *vi* to blink; to flicker.

párpado *m* eyelid.

parque *m* park; ~ **eólico** wind farm.

parque de bomberos *m* fire station, fire house.

parquímetro *m* parking meter.

parra *f* vine raised on stakes/nailed to a wall.

párrafo *m* paragraph.

parricida *m/f* parricide (person).

parricidio *m* parricide (act).

parrilla *f* grill; grille; *Lat Am* roof rack.

párroco *m* parish priest.

parroquia *f* parish; customers *pl*.

parroquial *adj* parochial.

parroquiano *m* parishioner; customer; **~/na** *adj* parochial.

parsimonia *f* parsimony.

parte *m* message; report; * *f* part; side; party; **de ocho días a esta ~** within these last eight days; **de ~ a ~** from side to side, through and through.

partera *f* midwife.

partición *f* partition, division.

participación *f* participation.

participante *m/f* participant.

participar *vi* to participate, to partake.

partícipe *m/f* participant.

participio *m* participle.

partícula *f* particle.

particular *adj* particular, special; * *m* private individual; particular matter/subject.

particularidad *f* particularity.

particularizar(se) *vt* (*vr*) to particularize; to distinguish; to specify.

partida *f* departure; party; item in an account; parcel; game.

partidario/ria *adj* partisan; * *m/f* supporter.

partido *m* party; match; team.

Partido Democrático *m* Democratic Party.

Partido Republicano *m* Republican Party.

partidor *m* apportioner, divider.

partir *vt* to part; to divide, to separate; to cut; to break; * *vi* to depart; **~se** *vr* to break (in two etc).

parto *m* birth.

parvulario *m* kindergarten.

pasa *f* raisin.

pasada *f* passage, passing; **de ~** on the way, in passing.

pasadizo *m* narrow passage; narrow, covered way.

pasado/da *adj* past; bad; overdone; out of date; **~ mañana** the day after tomorrow; **la semana pasada** last week; * *m* past.

pasador *m* bolt; hair slide; grip.

pasaje *m* passage; fare; passengers *pl*.

pasajero/ra *adj* transient; transitory; fugitive; * *m/f* traveler; passenger.

pasamanos *m invar* (hand)rail; banister.

pasamontañas *m invar* balaclava helmet.

pasaporte *m* passport.

pasar *vt* to pass; to surpass; to suffer; to strain; to dissemble; * *vi* to pass; to happen; **~se** *vr* to go over (to another party); to go bad/off.

pasarela *f* footbridge; gangway.

pasatiempo *m* pastime, amusement.

Pascua *f* Passover; Easter.

pase *m* pass; showing; permit.

paseante *m* walker.

pasear *vt* to walk; *vi*, **~se** *vr* to walk; to walk about.

paseo *m* walk; *Lat Am* trip; shopping mall.

pasillo *m* passage.

pasión *f* passion.

pasionaria *f* passionflower, granadilla.

pasivo/va *adj* passive.

pasmar *vt* to amaze; to numb; to chill; **~se** *vr* to be astonished.

pasmo *m* astonishment, amazement.

pasmoso/sa *adj* marvelous, wonderful.

paso *m* pace, step; passage; manner of walking; flight of steps; accident; (*rail*) **~ a nivel** grade crossing; **al ~** on the way, in passing.

paso de peatones *m* crosswalk.

pasota *adj*, *m/f* (*col*) dropout; **ser un ~** not to care about anything.

pasta *f* paste; dough; pastry; (*col*) dough, money; **~s** *fpl* pastries *pl*; pasta; **~ de dientes** toothpaste.

pastar *vt* to pasture, to graze.

pastel *m* cake; pie; pastel drawing; crayon.

pastelería *f* shop that sells cakes and pastries.

pasteurizado/da *adj* pasteurized.

pastilla *f* bar (of soap); tablet, pill.

pasto *m* pasture; *Lat Am* lawn, grass; **a ~** abundantly.

pastor *m* shepherd; pastor.

pastoso/sa *adj* mellow,pleasant (voice); soft, doughy.

pata *f* leg (of animal/furniture); foot; **a la ~ coja** hopscotch (children's game); **a ~** (*col*) on foot; **meter la ~** to put one's foot in it.

patada *f* kick; *Lat Am* electric shock.

patalear *vi* to kick violently.

pataleo *m* act of stamping one's foot.

pataleta *f* fit, convulsion; swoon.

patán *m* clown; churl, surly person.

patata *f* potato.

patatús *m* dizzy spell, fainting fit.

paté *m* pâté.

patear *vt* to kick; to stamp on.

patente *adj* patent, manifest, evident; * *f* patent; warrant.

paternal *adj* paternal, fatherly.

paternidad *f* paternity, fatherhood.

paterno/na *adj* paternal, fatherly.

patético/ca *adj* pathetic.

patíbulo *m* scaffold; gallows.

patillas *fpl* sideburns *pl*.

patín *m* skate; runner.

patinaje *m* skating.

patinar *vi* to skate; to skid; (*col*) to blunder.

patinete *m* scooter (child's).

patio *m* courtyard; playground (in schools).

patizambo/ba *adj* knock-kneed.

pato *m* duck.

patochada *f* blunder, folly; nonsense.

patología *f* pathology.

patológico/ca *adj* pathological.

patón/ona *adj Lat Am* (*col*) clumsy.
patoso/sa *adj* (*col*) clumsy.
patraña *f* lie.
patria *f* native country.
patriarca *m* patriarch.
patriarcado *m* patriarchy.
patriarcal *adj* patriarchal.
patrimonial *adj* patrimonial.
patrimonio *m* patrimony.
patrio/tria *adj* native; paternal.
patriota *m/f* patriot.
patriótico/ca *adj* patriotic.
patriotismo *m* patriotism.
patrocinar *vt* to sponsor; to back, to support.
patrocinio *m* sponsorship; backing, support.
patrón/ona *m/f* boss, master/mistress; landlord/
lady; patron saint; * *m* pattern.
patronal *adj*: **la clase ~** management.
patronato *m* patronage, sponsorship; trust,
foundation.
patronímico *m* patronymic.
patrulla *f* patrol.
patrullar *vi* to patrol.
patudo/da *adj Lat Am* (*col*) clumsy.
paulatino/na *adj* gradual, slow.
pausa *f* pause; repose.
pausado/da *adj* slow, deliberate; calm, quiet.
pausar *vi* to pause.
pauta *f* guideline.
pavesa *f* embers *pl*, hot cinders *pl*.
pavimento *m* sidewalk; paving.
pavo *m* turkey; **~ real** peacock.
pavonearse *vr* to strut, to walk with affected
dignity.
pavor *m* dread, terror.
pavoroso/sa *adj* awful, formidable.
payaso/sa *m/f* clown.
payo/ya *m/f* non-Gypsy (for a Gypsy).
paz *f* peace; tranquility, ease.
peaje *m* toll.
peal *m Lat Am* lasso.
peana *f* pedestal; footstool.
peatón *m* pedestrian.
peca *f* freckle; spot.
pecado *m* sin.
pecador/ra *m/f* sinner.
pecaminoso/sa *adj* sinful.
pecar *vi* to sin.
pecho *m* chest; breast(s) (*pl*); teat; bosom; *Lat
Am* breaststroke; (*fig*) courage, valor; **dar el
~ a** to breast-feed; **tomar a ~** to take to heart.
pechuga *f* breast (of a fowl); (*col*) bosom.
pecoso/sa *adj* freckled.
peculiar *adj* peculiar; special.
pecuniario/ria *adj* pecuniary.
pedagogía *f* pedagogy.
pedagógico/ca *adj* pedagogic.
pedagogo/ga *m/f* pedagog.
pedal *m* pedal.
pedalear *vi* to pedal.
pedante *adj* pedantic; * *m/f* pedant.

pedantería *f* pedantry.
pedazo *m* piece, tidbit.
pedernal *m* flint.
pedestal *m* pedestal, foot.
pediatra *m/f* pediatrician.
pediatría *f*. pediatrics *pl*.
pedicurista *m/f Lat Am* podiatrist.
pedicuro/ra *m/f* podiatrist, chiropodist.
pedido *m* (*com*) order; *Lat Am* request.
pedir *vt* to ask for; to petition; to beg; to order;
to need; to solicit; * *vi* to ask.
pedo *m* (*col*) fart; **tirarse un ~** to fart.
pedrada *f* throw (of a stone).
pedregal *m* stony place.
pedregoso/sa *adj* stony.
pedrería *f* (collection of) precious stones *pl*.
pedrisco *m* hailstone.
pedrusco *m* rough piece of stone.
pegadizo/za *adj* clammy, sticky; catchy;
contagious.
pegajoso/sa *adj* sticky, viscous; contagious;
attractive.
pegamento *m* glue.
pegar *vt* to cement; to join, to unite; to beat; **~
fuego a** to set fire to; * *vi* to stick; to match;
~se *vr* to intrude; to steal in.
pegatina *f* sticker.
pegote *m* adhesive tape, sticking plaster;
intruder; hanger-on, (*col*) sponger.
peinado *m* hairstyle.
peinador/ra *m/f Lat Am* hairdresser.
peinar *vt* to comb; to style.
peine *m* comb.
peineta *f* convex comb for women.
peladilla *f* sugared almond, burnt almond; small
pebble.
pelado/da *adj* peeled; shorn; bare; broke; * *m*
(*col*) haircut.
peladura *f* peeling; plucking.
pelaje *m* fur coat; (*fig*) appearance.
pelapapas *m inv Lat Am* potato peeler.
pelar *vt* to cut (hair); to pluck (feathers); to peel;
~se *vr* to peel off; to have one's hair cut.
peldaño *m* step (of a flight of stairs).
pelea *f* battle, fight; quarrel.
pelear *vt* to fight, to combat; **~se** *vr* to scuffle.
pelele *m* dummy; man of straw.
peletería *f* fur shop.
peletero *m* furrier.
peliagudo/da *adj* tricky; arduous, difficult.
pelícano *m* pelican.
película *f* film; pellicle.
peligrar *vi* to be in danger; **~ de** to risk.
peligro *m* danger, peril; risk.
peligroso/sa *adj* dangerous, perilous.
pelirrojo/ja *m/f* redhead; * *adj* red-haired.
pellejo *m* skin; hide, pelt; peel; wine skin, leather
bag for wine; oilskin; drunkard.
pelliza *f* fur jacket.
pellizcar *vt* to pinch.
pellizco *m* pinch; nip; small bit; (*fig*) remorse.

pelmo/ma, pelmazo/za m/f (col) pain (in the neck).

pelo m hair; pile; flaw (in precious stones).

pelón/ona adj hairless, bald.

pelota f ball.

pelotazo m blow with a ball.

pelotera f quarrel.

pelotero/ra m/f Lat Am baseball player.

pelotón m large ball; crowd; posse; (mil) platoon.

peluca f wig.

peluche m: **muñeco de ~** soft toy.

peludo/da adj hairy.

peluquería f hairdresser's (premises); barber shop.

peluquero/ra m/f hairdresser; barber.

pelusa f bloom (on fruit); fluff.

pena f punishment, pain; **a duras ~s** with great difficulty/trouble.

penacho m tuft on the heads of some birds; crest.

penal adj penal; * m Lat Am penalty (kick).

penalidad f suffering, trouble; hardship; penalty.

penar vi to suffer pain; * vt to chastise.

pendencia f quarrel, dispute.

pendenciero/ra adj quarrelsome.

pender vi to hang; to be pending; to depend.

pendiente f slope, declivity; * m earring; * adj pending; unsettled.

pendón m standard; banner.

péndulo m pendulum.

pene m penis.

penetración f penetration; perception.

penetrante adj deep; sharp; piercing; searching; biting.

penetrar vt to penetrate.

penicilina f penicillin.

península f peninsula.

penique m penny.

penitencia f penitence; penalty, fine.

penitenciaría f penitentiary.

penitente adj penitent, repentant; * m penitent.

penoso/sa adj painful.

pensador/ra m/f thinker.

pensamiento m thought, thinking.

pensar vi to think.

pensativo/va adj pensive, thoughtful.

pensión f pension; guest-house; worry; regret.

pensionista m/f pensioner; lodger.

Pentecostés m Pentecost, Whitsuntide.

penúltimo/ma adj penultimate, last but one.

penumbra f half-light.

penuria f penury, poverty, neediness, extreme want.

peña f rock, large stone.

peñasco m large rock.

peñón m rocky mountain.

peón m (day)laborer; foot soldier; pawn (at chess).

peonía f (bot) peony.

peonza f spinning top.

peor adj, adv worse; **cada vez ~** worse and worse.

pepinillo m gherkin.

pepino m cucumber.

pepita f kernel; pip.

pepitoria f fricassee.

pequeñez f smallness; childhood, infancy; triviality.

pequeño/ña adj little, small; young.

pera f pear.

peral m pear tree.

percance m perquisite (perk); bad luck, setback.

percatarse vr: **~ de** to notice.

percepción f perception; notion.

perceptible adj perceptible, perceivable.

percha f coat hook; coat hanger; perch.

percibir vt to receive; to perceive, to comprehend.

percusión f percussion.

perder vt to lose; to waste; to miss; **~se** vr to go astray; to be lost; to be spoiled.

perdición f loss, losing; perdition, ruin.

pérdida f loss, damage; lost object.

perdido/da adj lost; stray.

perdigón m young partridge; **~ones** mpl buckshot, pellets.

perdiz f partridge.

perdón m pardon; mercy; **¡~!** sorry!; excuse me!

perdonable adj pardonable.

perdonar vt to pardon, to forgive; to excuse.

perdurable adj perpetual, everlasting.

perdurar vi to last; to still exist.

perecedero/ra adj perishable.

perecer vi to perish, to die; to shatter (an object).

peregrinación f pilgrimage.

peregrinar vi to go on a pilgrimage.

peregrino/na adj (fig) strange; * m/f pilgrim.

perejil m parsley.

perenne adj perennial; perpetual.

perentorio/ria adj peremptory; urgent.

pereza f laziness, idleness.

perezoso/sa adj lazy, idle.

perfección f perfection.

perfeccionar vt to perfect; to complete, to finish.

perfecto/ta adj perfect; complete.

perfidia f perfidy.

pérfido/da adj perfidious.

perfil m profile.

perfilado/da adj well-formed, delicate (of features).

perfilar vt to outline; **~se** vr: **~ en** to show up against.

perforar vt to perforate; to drill; to punch a hole in; * vi to drill.

performance m Lat Am performance.

perfumador m perfumer.

perfumar vt to perfume.

perfume m perfume.

perfumería f perfumery.

pergamino m parchment.

pericia f skill, knowledge; expertise.

periferia f periphery; outskirts pl.

periférico m beltway, bypass, ring road.

perífrasis *f invar* periphrasis, circumlocution.

perímetro *m* perimeter; circumference.

periódico/ca *adj* periodical; * *m* newspaper.

periodista *m/f* journalist.

período/periodo *m* period; sentence; (*med*) menstrual period.

peripecia *f* vicissitude; sudden change.

peripuesto/ta *adj* dressed up, very spruce.

periquito *m* budgie, budgerigar.

perito/ta *adj* skillful, experienced; * *m/f* expert; skilled worker; technician.

perjudicar *vt* to prejudice, to damage; to injure, to hurt.

perjudicial *adj* prejudicial, damaging.

perjuicio *m* damage, harm.

perjurar *vi* to perjure, to swear falsely; to swear.

perjurio *m* perjury; false oath.

perjuro/ra *adj* perjured; * *m/f* perjurer.

perla *f* pearl; **de ~s** fine.

permanecer *vi* to stay; to continue to be.

permanencia *f* permanence; stay.

permanente *adj* permanent.

permiso *m* permission, leave, license.

permitir *vt* to permit, to allow.

permuta *f* permutation, exchange.

permutar *vt* to exchange, to permute.

pernera *f* trouser leg.

pernicioso/sa *adj* pernicious, destructive; wicked.

pernio *m* hinge.

perno *m* bolt.

pernoctar *vi* to spend the night.

pero *m* kind of apple; * *conj* but, yet.

perogrullada *f* truism, platitude.

perol *m* large metal pan.

perorata *f* harangue, speech.

perpendicular *adj* perpendicular.

perpetrar *vt* to perpetrate, to commit (a crime).

perpetuar *vt* to perpetuate.

perpetuidad *f* perpetuity.

perpetuo/tua *adj* perpetual.

perplejidad *f* perplexity.

perplejo/ja *adj* perplexed.

perra *f* bitch; (*col*) money.

perrera *f* kennel.

perro *m* dog.

persecución *f* persecution; toil, trouble; fatigue.

perseguidor *m* persecutor.

perseguir *vt* to pursue; to persecute; to chase after.

perseverancia *f* perseverance, constancy.

perseverante *adj* persistent.

perseverar *vi* to persevere, to persist.

persiana *f* (Venetian) blind.

persignarse *vr* to make the sign of the cross.

persistencia *f* persistence; steadiness.

persistir *vi* to persist.

persona *f* person; **de ~ a ~** from person to person.

personaje *m* celebrity; character.

personal *adj* personal; single; * *m* personnel.

personalidad *f* personality.

personarse *vr* to appear in person.

personero/ra *m/f Lat Am* spokesperson.

personificar *vt* to personify.

perspectiva *f* perspective; view; outlook.

perspicacia *f* perspicacity, clear-sightedness.

perspicaz *adj* perspicacious, clear-sighted.

persuadir *vt* to persuade; **~se** *vr* to be persuaded.

persuasión *f* persuasion.

persuasivo/va *adj* persuasive.

pertenecer *vi:* **~ a** to belong to; to appertain, to concern.

pertenencia *f* ownership; **~s** *fpl* possessions *pl.*

perteneciente *adj:* **~ a** belonging to.

pértiga *f* long pole/rod.

pertinacia *f* pertinacity; obstinacy, stubbornness.

pertinaz *adj* pertinacious; obstinate.

pertinente *adj* relevant; appropriate.

pertrechar *vt* to supply with ammunition and other warlike stores; to dispose; to arrange, to prepare; **~se** *vr* to be provided with the necessary defensive stores and arms.

pertrechos *mpl* tools *pl*, instruments *pl*; ammunition, fixings *pl.*

perturbación *f* perturbation; disturbance.

perturbado/da *adj* mentally unbalanced.

perturbador *m* disturber (of the peace).

perturbar *vt* to perturb, to disturb.

perversidad *f* perversity.

perversión *f* perversion; depravation, corruption.

perverso/sa *adj* perverse; extremely wicked.

pervertido/da *adj* perverted; * *m/f* pervert.

pervertir *vt* to pervert; to corrupt.

pesa *f* weight.

pesadez *f* heaviness, weight; gravity; slowness; peevishness, fretfulness; trouble; fatigue.

pesadilla *f* nightmare.

pesado/da *adj* peevish; troublesome; cumbersome; tedious; heavy, weighty.

pesadumbre *f* weightiness; gravity; quarrel, dispute; grief; trouble.

pésame *m* message of condolence.

pesar *m* sorrow, grief; repentance; **a ~ de** in spite of, notwithstanding; * *vi* to weigh; to repent; * *vt* to weigh.

pesario *m* pessary.

pesaroso/sa *adj* sorrowful, full of repentance; restless, uneasy.

pesca *f* fishing.

pescadería *f* fish market; shop that sells only fish.

pescado *m* fish (in general).

pescador *m* fisher, fisherman.

pescar *vt* to fish for, to catch (fish); * *vi* to fish.

pescuezo *m* neck.

pesebre *m* crib, manger.

peseta *f* peseta.

pesimista *m* pessimist.

pésimo/ma *adj* very bad.

peso *m* weight, heaviness; balance scales *pl*.

pespunte *m* back-stitching.

pesquero/ra *adj* fishing *compd*.

pesquisa *f* inquiry, examination.

pestaña *f* eyelash.

pestañear *vi* to blink.

pestañeo *m* blink.

peste *f* pest, plague, pestilence.

pesticida *m* pesticide.

pestífero/ra *adj* pestilential.

pestilencia *f* pestilence.

pestillo *m* bolt.

petaca *f* covered hamper; tobacco pouch.

pétalo *m* petal.

petardo *m* petard; cheat, fraud; imposition.

petate *m* straw bed; sleeping mat of the Indians; (*mar*) sailors' bedding on board ship; (*mar*) passengers' baggage; poor fellow.

petición *f* petition, demand.

peticionante *m/f Lat Am* petitioner.

peticionar *vt Lat Am* to petition.

peto *m* breastplate; bodice.

petrificar(se) *vt, vr* to petrify.

petróleo *m* oil, petroleum.

petrolero/ra *adj* petroleum *compd*; * *m* (oil) tanker; (*com*) oil man.

petulancia *f* petulance; insolence.

petulante *adj* petulant; insolent.

peyorativo/va *adj* pejorative.

pez *m* fish; * *f* pitch.

pezón *m* nipple.

pezuña *f* hoof.

piadoso/sa *adj* pious; mild; merciful; moderate.

pial *m Lat Am* lasso.

pianista *m/f* pianist.

piano *m* piano.

piar *vi* to squeak; to chirp.

piara *f* herd (of cattle); flock (of sheep).

pibe/ba *m/f* boy/girl.

pica *f* pike.

picacho *m* sharp point.

picadero *m* riding school.

picadillo *m* minced meat.

picado/da *adj* pricked; minced, chopped; bad (tooth); cross.

picador *m* riding master; picador.

picadura *f* prick; puncture.

picaflor *m Lat Am* hummingbird.

picana *f Lat Am* goad.

picanear *vt Lat Am* to goad.

picante *adj* hot, spicy; racy.

picapedrero *m* stonecutter.

picaporte *m* door handle; latch.

picar *vt* to prick; to sting; to mince; to nibble; * *vi* to prick; to sting; to itch; ~**se** *vr* to be piqued; to take offense; to be moth-eaten; to begin to rot.

picardía *f* roguery; deceit; malice; lewdness.

picaresco/ca *adj* roguish; picaresque.

pícaro/ra *adj* roguish; mischievous, malicious, sly; * *m/f* rogue, knave.

picazón *f* itching; stinging; displeasure.

pichón *m* young pigeon.

pico *m* beak; bill, nib; peak; pick-ax.

picotazo *m* peck (of a bird).

picotear *vt* to peck (of birds).

picudo/da *adj* with a beak; sharp-pointed.

pie *m* foot; leg; basis; trunk (tree); foundation; occasion; **a ~** on foot.

piedad *f* piety; mercy, pity.

piedra *f* stone.

piel *f* skin; hide; peel.

pienso *m* fodder.

pierna *f* leg.

pieza *f* piece; room.

pigmeo/mea *m/f, adj* pigmy.

pijama *m* pajamas *pl*.

pila *f* battery; trough; font; sink; pile, heap; **nombre de ~** first name.

pilar[1] *m* basin.

pilar[2] *m* pillar, column; mainstay.

píldora *f* pill.

pileta *f* basin; swimming pool.

pillaje *m* pillage, plunder.

pillar *vt* to pillage, to plunder, to foray, to seize; to catch onto; to catch.

pillo/lla *adj, m* rascal, scoundrel.

pilotaje *m* pilotage.

piloto *m/f* pilot.

piltrafa *f* piece of meat that is nearly all skin.

pimentón *m* paprika.

pimienta *f* allspice; pepper, pimento.

pimiento *m* sweet pepper, pimiento.

pinacoteca *f* art gallery.

pináculo *m* pinnacle.

pinar *m* grove of pine trees.

pincel *m* paintbrush.

pincelada *f* dash with a paintbrush.

pinchar *vt* to prick; to puncture.

pinchazo *m* prick; puncture; (*fig*) prod.

pinchito *m* small snack.

pincho *m* thorn; snack.

pingajo *m* rag, tatter.

ping-pong *m* table tennis.

pingüe *adj* fat, greasy; fertile.

pingüino *m* penguin.

pino *m* pine tree.

pinta *f* spot, blemish; scar; mark (on playing cards); pint.

pintado/da *adj* painted, mottled; **venir ~** to fit exactly.

pintar *vt* to paint; to picture; to describe; to exaggerate; * *vi* to paint; (*col*) to count, to be important; ~**se** *vr* to put on make-up.

pintarrajear *vt* to daub.

pintarrajo *m* daub.

pintor/-ra *m/f* painter.

pintoresco/ca *adj* picturesque.

pintura *f* painting.

pinza *f* claw; clothes peg; pincers *pl*; ~**s** *fpl* tweezers *pl*.

piña *f* pineapple; fir cone; group.

piñal *m Lat Am* pineapple plantation.

piñón *m* pine nut; pinion.

pío/pía *adj* pious, devout; merciful.

piojo *m* louse; troublesome hanger-on.

piojoso/sa *adj* lousy; miserable, stingy.

piola *f Lat Am* cord.

pionero/ra *adj* pioneering; * *m/f* pioneer.

pipa *f* pipe (for smoking); seed; sunflower seed.

pipí *m* (*col*) **hacer** ~ to have to go (to urinate).

pique *m* pique, offense taken; rivalry; **echar a** ~ to sink a ship; **a** ~ in danger; **a** ~ **de** on the point of.

piquete *m* slight prick/sting; picket.

pira *f* funeral pyre.

piragua *f* canoe.

piragüismo *m* canoeing.

piramidal *adj* pyramidal.

pirámide *f* pyramid.

pirata *m* pirate.

piropo *m* compliment; flattery.

pirotecnia *f* fireworks *pl*.

pirueta *f* pirouette.

pisada *f* footstep; footprint.

pisar *vt* to tread, to trample; to stamp on (the ground); to hammer down; * *vi* to tread, to walk.

pisciano/na *adj Lat Am* Piscean (zodiac sign).

piscina *f* swimming pool; ~ **para niños** paddling pool.

Piscis *m* Pisces (zodiac sign).

piso *m* flat, apartment; tread, trampling; floor, pavement; floor, story.

pisotear *vt* to trample, to tread under foot.

pista *f* trace, footprint; clue.

pisto *m* thick soup/broth.

pistola *f* pistol.

pistolera *f* pistol holster.

pistolero/ra *m/f* gunman/woman, gangster.

pistoletazo *m* pistol shot.

pistón *m* piston; (musical) key.

pita *f* (*bot*) any plant of the family *Agavaceae*, with tall flowers and thick, fleshy leaves.

pitada *f Lat Am* (*col*) puff.

pitar *vt* to blow; to whistle at; * *vi* to whistle; to toot one's horn; to smoke.

pitillo *m* cigarette.

pito *m* whistle; horn.

pitón *m* python.

pitonisa *f* sorceress, enchantress.

pitorreo *m* joke; **estar de** ~ to be joking.

piyama *m/f Lat Am* pajamas.

pizarra *f* slate.

pizarral *m* slate quarry, slate pit.

pizarrón *m Lat Am* chalkboard.

pizca *f* mite; pinch.

placa *f* plate; badge; ~ **de matrícula** license plate.

placentero/ra *adj* joyful, merry.

placer *m* pleasure; delight; * *vt* to please.

plácido/da *adj* placid.

plaga *f* plague.

plagar *vt* to plague, to torment.

plagio *m* plagiarism.

plan *m* plan; design; plot.

plana *f* trowel; page (of a book); level; ~ **mayor** (*mil*) staff.

plancha *f* plate; iron; gangway; press-up.

planchar *vt* to iron.

planchuela *n* doorplate *f*.

planeador *m* glider.

planear *vt* to plan; * *vi* to glide.

planeta *m* planet.

planetario/ria *adj* planetary.

planicie *f* plain.

planificación *f* planning; ~ **familiar** family planning, birth control.

planilla *f Lat Am* form.

plano/na *adj* plain, level, flat; * *m* plan; ground plot; ~ **inclinado** (*rail*) dead level.

planta *f* plant; plantation.

plantación *f* plantation.

plantar *vt* to plant; to fix upright; to strike/hit (a blow); to found; to establish; ~**se** *vr* to stand upright.

plantear *vt* to plan; to implant.

plantel *m Lat Am* team.

plantilla *f* personnel; insole of a shoe.

plantón *m* long wait; (*mil*) sentry.

plañir *vi* to lament, to grieve, to bewail.

plasmar *vt* to mold; to represent.

plasta *f* paste, soft clay; mess.

plástico/ca *adj* plastic; * *m* plastic; * *f* sculpture (the art of).

plata *f* silver; plate (wrought silver); cash; *Lat Am* money; **en** ~ briefly.

plataforma *f* platform; ~ **giratoria** (*rail*) turntable.

plátano *m* banana tree; plane tree.

plateado/da *adj* silvered; silver-plated.

platería *f* silversmith's (premises); trade of silversmithing.

plática *f* discourse, conversation.

platicar *vi* to converse.

platillo *m* saucer; ~**s** *mpl* cymbals *pl*; ~ **volador/** ~ **volante** flying saucer.

platino *m* platinum; ~**s** *mpl* contact points *pl*.

plato *m* dish; plate.

platónico/ca *adj* platonic.

plausible *adj* plausible.

playa *f* beach.

playera *f* T-shirt; ~**s** *fpl* sneakers *pl*, tennis shoes *pl*.

plaza *f* square; place; office, employment; room; seat.

plazo *m* term; installment; expiry date.

pleamar *f* (*mar*) high water.

plebe *f* common people *pl*, populace.

plebeyo/ya *adj* plebeian; * *m* commoner.

plebiscito *m* plebiscite.

plegable *adj* pliable; folding.

plegar *vt* to fold; to plait.

plegaria *f* prayer.

pleitear *vi* to plead, to litigate.

pleito *m* contract, bargain; dispute, controversy, *Lat Am* debate; lawsuit.

plenamente *adv* fully; completely.

plenario/ria *adj* complete; full.

plenilunio *m* full moon.

plenipotenciario *m* plenipotentiary.

plenitud *f* fullness; abundance.

pleno/na *adj* full; complete; * *m* plenum.

pliego *m* sheet of paper.

pliegue *m* fold; plait.

plisado/da *adj* pleated; * *m* pleating.

plomero *m* plumber.

plomizo/za *adj* leaden.

plomo *m* lead; **a ~** perpendicularly.

pluma *f* feather, plume.

plumaje *m* plumage; plume.

plumero *m* bunch of feathers; feather duster.

plumón *m* felt-tip pen; marker; down (feathers).

plural *adj* (*gr*) plural.

pluralidad *f* plurality.

Plutón *m* Pluto (planet).

población *f* population; town.

poblado *m* town; village; inhabited place.

poblador/ra *m*/*f* populator, founder.

poblar *vt* to populate, to people; to fill, to occupy.

pobre *adj* poor.

pobreza *f* poverty, poorness.

pocilga *f* pigpen.

pocillo *m* coffee cup.

pócima, poción *f* potion.

poco/ca *adj* little, scanty; few *pl*; * *adv* little; **a ~** gently; little by little; * *m* small part; little.

poda *f* pruning (of trees).

podadera *f* pruning knife.

podadora *f Lat Am* pruning knife.

podar *vt* to prune.

podenco *m* hound.

poder *m* power, authority; command; force; * *vi* to be able to; to possess the power of doing/performing.

poderío *m* power, authority; wealth, riches *pl*.

poderoso/sa *adj* powerful; eminent, excellent.

podiatra *m*/*f Lat Am* podiatrist.

podredumbre *f* putrid matter; grief.

podrido/da *adj* rotten, bad; (*fig*) -rotten.

podrir *vt* to rot, to putrefy; **~se** *vr* to rot, to decay.

poema *m* poem.

poesía *f* poetry.

poeta *m* poet.

poético/ca *adj* poetical.

poetisa *f* poetess.

poetizar *vt* to poetize.

polar *adj* polar.

polea *f* pulley; (*mar*) tackle-block.

polémica *f* polemic.

polémico/ca *adj* polemical.

polen *m* pollen.

policía *f* police; * *m*/*f* police officer.

polideportivo *m* sports center.

poligamia *f* polygamy.

polígamo *m* polygamist.

polígono *m* polygon.

polilla *f* moth.

polio *f* polio.

pólipo *m* polypus.

politécnico/ca *adj* polytechnic.

política *f* politics; policy.

político/ca *adj* political; * *m*/*f* politician.

póliza *f* written order; policy.

polizón *m* stowaway.

pollera *f* skirt.

pollería *f* poulterer's (shop).

pollo *m* chicken.

polo *m* pole; Popsicle™; polo; polo neck.

polución *f* pollution.

polvareda *f* cloud of dust.

polvera *f* powder compact.

polvo *m* powder, dust.

pólvora *f* gunpowder.

polvoriento/ta *adj* dusty.

polvorín *m* powder reduced to the finest dust; powder flask.

pomada *f* cream, ointment.

pomelo *m* grapefruit.

pómez *f*: **piedra ~** pumice stone.

pompa *f* pomp; bubble.

pomposo/sa *adj* pompous.

pómulo *m* cheekbone.

ponchar *vt Lat Am* to strike out.

ponche *m* punch.

poncho/cha *adj* soft, mild; * *m* -poncho.

ponderación *f* pondering, considering; exaggeration.

ponderar *vt* to ponder, to weigh; to exaggerate.

ponedero/ra *adj* egg-laying; capable of being laid/placed; * *m* nest; nest egg.

poner *vt* to put, to place; to put on; to impose; to lay (eggs); **~se** *vr* to oppose; to set (of stars); to become.

poniente *m* west; west wind.

pontificado *m* pontificate.

pontífice *m* Pope, pontiff.

pontificio/cia *adj* pontifical.

pontón *m* pontoon.

ponzoña *f* poison.

ponzoñoso/sa *adj* poisonous.

popa *f* (*mar*) poop, stern.

populacho *m* populace, mob.

popular *adj* popular.

popularidad *f* popularity.

popularizarse *vr* to become popular.

populoso/sa *adj* populous.

poquedad *f* paucity, smallness; cowardice.

por *prep* for; by; about; by means of; through; on account of.

porcelana *f* porcelain, china.

porcentaje *m* percentage.

porción *f* part, portion; lot.

porcuno/na *adj* hoggish, piggish; porcine.

pordiosero/ra *m*/*f* beggar.

porfiar *vt* to dispute obstinately; to persist in a pursuit.

pormenor f detail.
pornografía f pornography.
poro m pore.
porosidad f porosity.
poroso/sa adj porous.
porque conj because; since; so that.
porqué m cause, reason.
porquería f nastiness, foulness; brutishness, rudeness; trifle; dirty action.
porqueriza f pigpen.
porra f cudgel.
porrillo: a ~ adv copiously, abundantly.
porrón m spouted wine jar.
portada f portal, porch; frontispiece.
portador/ra m/f carrier, porter.
portaequipajes m invar trunk (in car); baggage rack.
portal m porch; portal.
portaligas m inv Lat Am garter belt.
portamonedas m invar purse.
portarse vr to behave.
portátil adj portable; * m laptop.
portaaviones m invar aircraft carrier.
portavoz m/f spokesman/woman.
portazo m bang of a door; the act of banging a door in someone's face.
porte m transportation charges pl; deportment, demeanor, conduct.
portento m prodigy, portent.
portentoso/sa adj prodigious, marvelous, strange.
portería f porter's office; goal (sport).
portero/ra m/f porter; janitor; gatekeeper; goalkeeper.
portezuela f little door.
pórtico m portico, porch, lobby.
portilla f, **portillo** m aperture in a wall; gate; gap, breach.
portón m main door (of a house).
porvenir m future.
pos prep: **en ~ de** after, behind; in pursuit of.
posada f shelter; inn, hotel.
posaderas fpl buttocks pl.
posadero m innkeeper.
posar vi to sit, to pose; * vt to lay down (a burden); **~se** vr to settle; to perch; to land.
posdata f postscript.
pose f pose.
poseedor/ra m/f owner, possessor; holder.
poseer vt to hold, to possess.
poseído/da adj possessed by the devil.
posesión f possession.
posesivo/va adj possessive.
posesor/ra m/f possessor.
posibilidad f possibility.
posibilitar vt to make possible; to make feasible.
posible adj possible.
posición f position; posture; situation.
positivo/va adj positive.
poso m sediment, dregs pl.
posponer vt to postpone.

posta f: **a ~** on purpose.
postal adj postal; * f postal card, postcard.
poste m pole, post, pillar.
póster m poster.
postergación f missing out, passing over; putting over.
postergar vt to leave behind; to postpone.
posteridad f posterity.
posterior adj posterior.
posterioridad f: **con ~** subsequently, later.
postigo m postern; small door; shutter (of a window).
postizo/za adj artificial (not natural); * m wig.
postor m bidder at a public sale; -better.
postración f prostration.
postrar vt to humble, to humiliate; **~se** vr to prostrate oneself.
postre m dessert.
postrer(o)/ra adj last, hindmost.
postrimerías fpl dying moments; final stages.
póstumo/ma adj posthumous.
postulante m/f Lat Am candidate.
postura f posture, position; attitude; bet, wager; agreement, convention.
potable adj drinkable.
potaje m pottage; drink made up of several ingredients; medley of various useless things.
pote m pot, jar; flower pot.
potencia f power; mightiness.
potencial m potential.
potentado m potentate; prince.
potente adj potent, powerful, mighty.
potestad f power; dominion; jurisdiction.
potrero m Lat Am pasture.
potro/ra m/f colt; foal.
poyo m stone seat/bench.
pozo m well.
práctica f practice.
practicable adj practicable, feasible.
practicante adj practicing; * m/f practitioner.
practicar vt to practice.
práctico/ca adj practical; skillful, experienced.
pradera f meadow.
prado m lawn; meadow.
pragmático/ca adj pragmatic.
preámbulo m preamble; circumlocution.
prebenda f prebend.
precampaña f run-up to an election campaign.
precario/ria adj precarious.
precaución f precaution.
precaver vt to prevent; to guard against.
precedencia f precedence; preference; superiority.
precedente adj preceding, foregoing.
preceder vt to precede, to go before.
precepto m precept, order.
preceptor/ra m/f master, teacher, preceptor.
preciado/da adj esteemed, valued.
preciarse vr to boast; **~ de** to take pride in.
precinto m seal.
precio m price; value.

preciosidad *f* excellence; preciousness.

precioso/sa *adj* precious; (*col*) beautiful.

precipicio *m* precipice; violent, sudden fall; ruin, destruction.

precipitación *f* precipitation, rush.

precipitado/da *adj* precipitate, headlong, hasty.

precipitar *vt* to precipitate; ~**se** *vr* to act hastily; to rush.

precisamente *adv* precisely; exactly.

precisar *vt* to compel, to oblige; to need.

precisión *f* necessity, compulsion; preciseness.

preciso/sa *adj* necessary, requisite; precise, exact; abstracted.

precocidad *f* precocity.

preconizar *vt* to proclaim; to recommend.

precoz *adj* precocious.

precursor/ra *m/f* harbinger, forerunner.

predecesor/ra *m/f* predecessor.

predecir *vt* to foretell.

predestinación *f* predestination.

predestinar *vt* to predestine.

predicación *f* preaching; sermon.

predicado *m* predicate.

predicador *m* preacher.

predicar *vt* to preach.

predicción *f* prediction.

predilección *f* predilection.

predilecto/ta *adj* darling, favorite.

predio *m Lat Am* building.

predisponer *vt* to predispose; to prejudice.

predisposición *f* inclination; prejudice.

predominar *vi* to predominate, to prevail.

predominio *m* predominant power, superiority.

preeminencia *f* pre-eminence; superiority.

preeminente *adj* pre-eminent; superior.

preescolar *adj* pre-school.

preestreno *m* prevue.

preexistencia *f* pre-existence.

preexistente *adj* pre-existent.

preexistir *vt* to pre-exist, to exist before.

prefabricado/da *adj* prefabricated.

prefacio *m* preface.

prefecto *m* prefect.

prefectura *f* prefecture.

preferencia *f* preference.

preferible *adj* preferable.

preferir *vt* to prefer.

prefijar *vt* (*gr*) to prefix; to fix beforehand.

prefijo *m* dial code.

pregón *m* proclamation; hue and cry.

pregonar *vt* to proclaim.

pregonero *m* town crier.

pregunta *f* question; inquiry.

preguntar *vt* to ask; to question; to demand; to inquire.

preguntón/ona *m/f* inquisitive person.

prehistórico/ca *adj* prehistoric.

prejuicio *m* prejudgement; preconception; prejudice.

prelado *m* prelate.

preliminar *adj, m* preliminary.

preludio *m* prelude.

prematuro/ra *adj* premature.

premeditación *f* premeditation, forethought.

premeditar *vt* to premeditate, to think out.

premiar *vt* to reward, to remunerate.

premio *m* reward, recompense; premium.

premisa *f* premise.

premura *f* pressure, haste, hurry.

prenatal *adj* pre-natal.

prenda *f* pledge; garment; sweetheart; person/thing dearly loved; ~**s** *fpl* accomplishments *pl*, talents *pl*.

prendar *vt* to enchant; ~**se** *vr*: ~ **de** to fall in love with.

prendedor *m* brooch.

prender *vt* to seize, to catch, to lay hold of; to imprison; *Lat Am* to switch on; ~**se** *vr* to catch fire; * *vi* to take root.

prendimiento *m* seizure; capture.

prensa *f* press.

prensar *vt* to press.

preñado/da *adj* pregnant.

preñez *f* pregnancy.

preocupación *f* worry, preoccupation.

preocupado/da *adj* worried, anxious.

preocupar(se) *vt* (*vr*) to worry.

preparación *f* preparation.

preparador/ra *m/f* trainer.

preparar *vt* to prepare; ~**se** *vr* to be prepared.

preparativo/va *adj* preparatory; preliminary; qualifying; * *m* preparation.

preparatorio/ria *adj* preparatory.

preponderancia *f* preponderance.

preponderar *vt* to preponderate, to prevail.

preposición *f* (*gr*) preposition.

prepucio *m* foreskin.

prerrogativa *f* prerogative, privilege.

presa *f* capture, seizure; dike, dam.

presagiar *vt* to presage, to forebode.

presagio *m* omen.

presbítero *m* priest, clergyman.

presciencia *f* prescience, foreknowledge.

prescindir *vi*: ~ **de** to do without; to dispense with.

prescribir *vt* to prescribe.

prescripción *f* prescription.

presencia *f* presence.

presenciar *vt* to attend; to be present at; to witness.

presentación *f* presentation.

presentador/ra *m/f* (*rad, TV*) presenter; compere.

presentar *vt* to present; to introduce; to offer; to show; ~**se** *vr* to present oneself; to appear; to run (as candidate); to apply.

presente *m* present, gift; * *adj* present.

presentemente *adv* presently, now.

presentimiento *m* presentiment.

presentir *vt* to have a premonition of.

preservación *f* preservation.

preservar *vt* to preserve; to defend.

preservativo *m* condom, sheath; *Lat Am* preservative.

presidencia *f* presidency.

presidente/ta *m/f* president.

presidiario/ria *m/f* convict.

presidio *m* penitentiary, prison.

presidir *vt* to preside at.

presilla *f* clip; loop (in clothes).

presión *f* pressure, pressing; ~ **de los neumáticos** tire pressure.

presionar *vt* to press; (*fig*) to put pressure on.

preso/sa *m/f* prisoner.

prestado/da *adj* on loan; **pedir** ~ to borrow.

prestamista *m* borrower, lender.

préstamo *m* loan.

prestar *vt* to lend.

presteza *f* quickness; haste, speed.

prestigio *m* prestige.

presto/ta *adj* quick; prompt; ready; * *adv* soon; quickly.

presumible *adj* presumable.

presumido/da *adj* presumptuous, arrogant.

presumir *vt* to presume, to conjecture; * *vi* to be conceited.

presunción *f* presumption, conjecture; conceit.

presunto/ta *adj* supposed; so-called.

presuntuoso/sa *adj* presumptuous.

presuponer *vt* to presuppose.

presupuesto *m* estimate; budget.

presuroso/sa *adj* hasty, quick; prompt; nimble.

pretencioso/sa *adj* pretentious.

pretender *vt* to pretend, to claim; to try, to attempt.

pretendiente *m* pretender; suitor.

pretensión *f* pretension.

pretérito/ta *adj* past.

pretextar *vt* to plead, use as an excuse.

pretexto *m* pretext; pretense; plea, excuse.

prevalecer *vi* to prevail; to triumph; to take root.

prevención *f* disposition, preparation; supply of provisions; foresight; prevention; (*mil*) guardroom, guardhouse.

prevenido/da *adj* prepared; careful, cautious; foreseeing.

prevenir *vt* to prepare; to foresee, to know in advance; to prevent; to warn; ~**se** *vr* to be prepared; to be predisposed.

preventivo/va *adj* preventive.

prever *vt* to foresee, to forecast.

previo/via *adj* previous.

previsión *f* foresight, prevision; forecast.

previsor/ra *adj* far-sighted.

previsivo/va *adj Lat Am* far-sighted.

prima *f* bonus; (female) cousin.

primacía *f* priority; primacy.

primado *m* primate.

primario/ria *adj* primary.

primavera *f* spring (the season).

primeramente *adv* in the first place, mainly.

primer(o)/ra *adj* first; prior; former; * *adv* first; rather, sooner.

primicias *fpl* first fruits *pl*.

primitivo/va *adj* primitive; original.

primo/ma *m* cousin.

primogénito/ta *adj*, *m/f* first-born.

primogenitura *f* primogeniture.

primor *m* beauty; dexterity, ability.

primordial *adj* basic, fundamental.

primoroso/sa *adj* neat, elegant; fine, excellent; handsome.

princesa *f* princess.

principal *adj*, *m* principal, chief.

príncipe *m* prince.

principiante *m* beginner, learner.

principiar *vt*, *vi* to commence, to begin.

principio *m* beginning, commencement; principle.

pringoso/sa *adj* greasy; sticky.

pringue *m/f* grease; lard, fat.

prioridad *f* priority.

prisa *f* speed; hurry; urgency; promptness.

prisión *f* prison; imprisonment.

prisionero *m* prisoner.

prisma *m* prism.

prismáticos *mpl* binoculars *pl*.

privación *f* deprivation, want.

privado/da *adj* private; particular.

privar *vt* to deprive; to prohibit; ~**se** *vr* to deprive oneself.

privativo/va *adj* private, one's own; particular, peculiar.

privilegiado/da *adj* privileged; very good.

privilegiar *vt* to privilege.

privilegio *m* privilege.

pro *m/f* profit; benefit; advantage.

proa *f* (*mar*) prow.

probabilidad *f* probability, likelihood.

probable *adj* probable, likely.

probado/da *adj* proved, tried.

probador *m* fitting room.

probar *vt* to try; to prove; to taste; * *vi* to try.

probeta *f* test tube.

problema *m* problem.

problemático/ca *adj* problematic.

procedencia *m* derivation.

procedente *adj* reasonable; proper; ~ **de** coming from.

proceder *m* procedure; * *vi* to proceed, to go on; to act.

procedimiento *m* proceeding; legal procedure.

procesado/da *m/f* accused.

procesador *m*: ~ **de textos** word processor.

procesar *vt* to put on trial.

procesión *f* procession.

proceso *m* process; lawsuit.

proclama *f* proclamation, publication.

proclamación *f* proclamation; acclamation.

proclamar *vt* to proclaim.

procreación *f* procreation, generation.

procrear *vt* to procreate, to generate.

procura *f Lat Am* search.

procurador/ra *m/f* procurer; attorney; solicitor.

procurar vt to try; to obtain; to produce.
prodigalidad f plenty, abundance.
prodigar vt to waste, to lavish.
prodigio m prodigy; monster.
prodigioso/sa adj prodigious, monstrous; exquisite; excellent.
pródigo/ga adj prodigal.
producción f production.
producir vt to produce; (law) to produce as evidence; ~se vr to come about; to arise; to be made; to break out.
productividad f productivity.
productivo/va adj productive.
producto m product.
productor/ra adj productive; * m/f producer.
proeza f prowess, valor, bravery.
profanación f desecration.
profanar vt to profane, to desecrate.
profano/na adj profane.
profecía f prophecy.
profesar vt to profess, to practice.
profesión f profession.
profesional adj, m/f professional.
profeso/sa adj professed.
profesor/ra m/f teacher; lecturer.
profesorado m teaching profession.
profeta m prophet.
profético/ca adj prophetic.
profetizar vt to prophesy.
prófugo/ga m/f fugitive.
profundidad f profundity, profoundness; depth; grandeur.
profundizar vt to go deeply into; to deepen; to penetrate.
profundo/da adj profound.
profusamente adv profusely.
profusión f profusion; prodigality.
progenie f progeny, offspring; race; generation.
progenitor m progenitor, ancestor, forefather.
programa m program.
programación f computer programing.
programador/ra m/f programer.
programar vt to program.
progresar vi to progress.
progresión f progression.
progresista adj, m/f progressive.
progreso m progress.
progresivo/va adj progressive.
prohibición f prohibition, ban.
prohibir vt to prohibit, to forbid; to hinder.
prójimo m fellow creature; neighbor.
prole f offspring, progeny; race.
proletariado m proletariat.
proletario/ria adj proletarian.
proliferación f proliferation.
proliferar vi to proliferate.
prolífico/ca adj prolific.
prolijidad f prolixity; minute attention to detail.
prolijo/ja adj long-winded; tedious.
prólogo m prolog.
prolongación f prolongation.

prolongar vt to prolong.
promedio m average; middle.
promesa f promise.
prometer vt to promise; to assure; ~se vr to become engaged.
prometido/da adj promised; engaged; * m/f fiancé/fiancée.
prominencia f protuberance.
prominente adj prominent, jutting out.
promiscuo/cua adj promiscuous; confusedly mingled; ambiguous.
promoción f promotion.
promontorio m promontory, cape.
promotor m promoter.
promover vt to promote, to advance; to stir up.
promulgación f promulgation.
promulgar vt to promulgate, to publish.
pronombre m (gr) pronoun.
pronosticar vt to predict, to foretell; to conjecture.
pronóstico m prediction; forecast.
prontitud f promptness.
pronto/ta adj prompt; ready; * adv promptly.
pronunciación f pronunciation.
pronunciamiento m (law) publication; insurrection, sedition.
pronunciar vt to pronounce; to deliver; ~se vr to rebel.
propagación f propagation; extension.
propagador/ra m/f propagator.
propaganda f propaganda; advertising.
propagar vt to propagate.
propasar vt to go beyond, to exceed.
propender vi to incline.
propensión f propensity, inclination.
propenso/sa adj prone, inclined.
propiamente adv properly; really.
propiciar vt to favor; to cause.
propiciatorio/ria adj propitiatory.
propicio/cia adj propitious.
propiedad f property, possessions pl; right of property; propriety.
propietario/ria adj proprietary; * m/f proprietor.
propina f tip.
propinar vt to hit; to give.
propio/pia adj proper; own; typical; very.
proponer vt to propose.
proporción f proportion; symmetry.
proporcionado/da adj proportionate; fit; bien ~ well-proportioned.
proporcional adj proportional.
proporcionar vt to provide; to adjust, to adapt.
proposición f proposition.
propósito m aim, purpose; a ~ on purpose.
propuesta f proposal, offer; representation.
propulsar vt to propel; (fig) to promote.
prórroga f prolongation; extension; extra time.
prorrogable adj extendable.
prorrogar vt to extend; to postpone.
prorrumpir vi to break forth, to burst forth.
prosa f prose.

prosaico/ca *adj* prosaic.
proscribir *vt* to proscribe, to outlaw.
proscripción *f* proscription.
proscrito/ta *adj* banned.
prosecución *f* continuation.
proseguir *vt* to continue; * *vi* to continue, to go on.
prospección *f* exploration; prospecting.
prospecto *m* prospectus.
prosperar *vi* to prosper, to thrive.
prosperidad *f* prosperity.
próspero/ra *adj* prosperous.
prostíbulo *m* brothel.
prostitución *f* prostitution.
prostituir *vt* to prostitute.
prostituta *f* prostitute.
protagonista *m/f* protagonist.
protagonizar *vt* to take the chief role in.
protección *f* protection.
protector *m* to protect.
proteger *vt* protector.
proteína *f* protein.
protesta *f* protest.
protestante *m/f* Protestant.
protestar *vt* to protest; to make a public declaration (of faith); * *vi* to protest.
protocolo *m* protocol.
prototipo *m* prototype.
provecho *m* profit; advantage.
provechoso/sa *adj* profitable; advantageous.
proveedor/ra *m/f* purveyor.
proveer *vt* to provide; to provision; to decree.
provenir *vi* to arise, to originate; to issue.
proverbial *adj* proverbial.
proverbio *m* proverb; **~s** *mpl* Book of Proverbs.
providencia *f* providence; foresight; divine providence.
providencial *adj* providential.
provincia *f* province.
provincial *adj*, *m* provincial.
provinciano/na *adj* provincial; country *compd*.
provisión *f* provision; store.
provisional *adj* provisional.
provisionalmente *adv* provisionally.
provisorio/ria *adj Lat Am* provisional.
provocación *f* provocation.
provocador/ra *adj* provocative.
provocar *vt* to provoke; to lead to; to excite.
provocativo/va *adj* provocative.
próximamente *adv* soon.
proximidad *f* proximity, closeness.
próximo/ma *adj* next; neighboring; close, nearby.
proyección *f* projection; showing; influence.
proyectar *vt* to throw; to cast; to screen; to plan.
proyectil *m* projectile, missile.
proyecto *m* plan; project.
proyector *m* projector.
prudencia *f* prudence, wisdom.
prudente *adj* prudent.
prueba *f* proof; reason; argument; token; experiment; essay; attempt; relish, taste.

prurito *m* itching.
psicoanálisis *m* psychoanalysis.
psicoanalista *m/f* psychoanalyst.
psicología *f* psychology.
psicólogo/ga *m/f* psychologist.
psiquiatra *m/f* psychiatrist.
psiquiátrico/ca *adj* psychiatric.
psíquico/ca *adj* psychic(al).
púa *f* sharp point, prickle; shoot; pick.
pubertad *f* puberty.
publicación *f* publication.
publicar *vt* to publish; to make public.
publicidad *f* publicity.
público/ca *adj* public; * *m* public; audience; crowd.
puchero *m* pot; stew.
púdico/ca *adj* chaste, pure.
pudiente *adj* rich, opulent.
pudor *m* bashfulness.
pudrir *vt* to rot, to putrefy; **~se** *vr* to decay, to rot.
pueblo *m* people *pl*; town, village; population; populace.
puente *m* bridge.
puenting *m* bungee-jumping.
puerco/ca *adj* nasty; filthy, dirty; rude, coarse; * *m* hog, pig; **~ espín** porcupine.
pueril *adj* childish; puerile.
puerilidad *f* puerility.
puerro *m* leek.
puerta *f* door; doorway; gateway; **~ trasera** back door.
puerto *m* port, harbor; haven; pass; narrow pass.
pues *adv* then; therefore; well; **i~!** well, then!
puesto *m* place; particular spot; post, employment; barracks *pl*; stand.
púgil *m* boxer.
pugilato *m* boxing.
pugna *f* combat, battle.
pugnar *vi* to fight, to combat; to struggle.
pujante *adj* powerful, strong; robust; stout, strapping.
pujanza *f* power, strength.
pujar *vt* to outbid; to strain.
pulcritud *f* beauty.
pulcro/cra *adj* beautiful; affected.
pulga *f* flea; **tener malas ~s** to be easily piqued; to be ill-tempered.
pulgada *f* inch.
pulgar *m* thumb.
pulir *vt* to polish; to put the last touches to.
pulla *f* smart repartee; obscene expression.
pulmón *m* lung.
pulmonía *f* pneumonia.
pulpa *f* pulp; soft part (of fruit).
pulpería *f* small grocery shop.
púlpito *m* pulpit.
pulpo *m* octopus.
pulsación *f* pulsation.
pulsador *m* push button.
pulsar *vt* to touch; to play; to press.

pulsera f bracelet.
pulso m pulse; wrist; firmness/steadiness of the hand.
pulular vi to swarm.
pulverización f pulverization.
pulverizador m spray gun.
pulverizar vt to pulverize.
puna f (med) mountain sickness.
pungir vt to punch, to prick.
punición f punishment, chastisement.
punitivo/va adj punitive.
punta f point; end; trace.
puntada f stitch.
puntaje m Lat Am grade.
puntal m prop, stay; buttress.
puntapié m kick.
puntear vt to tick; to pluck (the guitar); to stitch.
puntería f aiming.
puntero m pointer; ~/ra adj leading.
puntiagudo/da adj sharp-pointed.
puntilla f narrow lace edging; de ~s on tiptoe.
punto m point; end; spot; stitch.
puntuación f punctuation.
puntual adj punctual; exact; reliable.
puntualidad f punctuality.
puntualizar vt to fix; to specify.
puntuar vt to punctuate; to evaluate.
punzada f prick; sting; pain; compunction.
punzante adj sharp.
punzar vt to punch; to prick; to sting.
punzón m punch.
puñado m handful.
puñal m dagger.
puñalada f stab.
puñetazo m punch.
puño m fist; handful; wrist-band; cuff; handle.
pupila f pupil (of eye).
pupitre m desk.
puré m puree; (thick) soup; ~ de patatas mashed potatoes pl.
pureza f purity, chastity.
purga f purge.
purgante m purgative.
purgar vt to purge; to purify; to atone, to expiate.
purgativo/va adj purgative, purging.
purgatorio m purgatory.
purificación f purification.
purificador/ra m/f purifier; * adj purifying.
purificar vt to purify.
purismo m purism.
purista m purist.
puritano/na adj puritanical; * m/f Puritan.
puro/ra adj pure; mere; clear; genuine.
púrpura f purple.
purpúreo/rea adj purple.
purulento/ta adj purulent.
pus m pus.
pusilánime adj pusillanimous, fainthearted.
pusilanimidad f pusillanimity.
pústula f pustule, pimple.
puta f whore.

putrefacción f putrefaction.
pútrido/da adj putrid, rotten.

Q

que pn that; who; which; what; * conj that; than.
qué adj what; which; * pn what; which.
quebrada f broken, uneven ground; Lat Am stream.
quebradero m breaker; ~ de cabeza worry.
quebradizo/za adj brittle; flexible.
quebrado m (math) fraction.
quebradura f fracture; rupture, hernia.
quebrantamiento m fracture; rupture; breaking; weariness, fatigue; violation (of the law).
quebrantar vt to break; to crack; to burst; to pound, to grind; to violate; to fatigue; to weaken.
quebranto m weakness; great loss, severe damage.
quebrar vt to break; to transgress; to violate (a law); * vi to go bankrupt; ~se vr to break into pieces; to be ruptured.
queda f resting time; (mil) tattoo.
quedar vi to stay; ~se vr to remain.
quedo/da adj quiet, still; * adv softly, gently.
quehacer m task.
queja f complaint.
quejarse vr to complain of.
quejido m complaint.
quejoso/sa adj complaining, querulous.
quejumbroso/sa adj complaining, plaintive.
quema f burning, combustion; fire.
quemador m burner.
quemadura f burn.
quemar vt to burn; to kindle; ~se vr to be parched with heat; to burn oneself; * vi to be too hot.
quemarropa f: a ~ adv point-blank.
quemazón f burn; itch.
querella f charge; dispute; complaint.
querellarse vr to complain; to file a complaint.
querendón/ona adj Lat Am affectionate.
querer vt to want; to desire; to will; to love; * m will, desire.
querido/da adj dear, beloved; * m/f darling; lover; ~do mío/~da mía my dear, my love, my darling.
querosén m Lat Am kerosene/kerosine.
queroseno m kerosene/kerosine.
querubín m cherub.
quesería f shop that specializes in cheese.
queso m cheese.
quicio m hook, hinge (of a door).
quiebra f break, fracture; bankruptcy; slump.
quien pn who; whom.
quién pn who; whom.
quienquiera adj whoever.
quieto/ta adj still, peaceable.
quietud f quietness, peace, tranquility, calmness.
quijada f jaw; jawbone.

quijotada f quixotic action.
quijote m quixotic person.
quijotesco/ca adj quixotic.
quilate m carat.
quilla f keel.
quimera f chimera.
quimérico/ca adj chimerical, fantastic.
química f chemistry.
químico/ca m/f chemist; * adj chemical.
quimioterapia f chemotherapy.
quina f Peruvian bark, quinine.
quincalla f hardware.
quince adj, m fifteen; fifteenth.
quincena f fortnight.
quinientos/tas adj five hundred.
quinina f quinine.
quinquenal adj quinquennial.
quinquenio m space of five years.
quinqui m delinquent.
quinta f country house; levy, drafting of soldiers.
quintaesencia f quintessence.
quintilla f (poet) metrical composition of five verses.
quinto adj fifth; * m fifth; drafted soldier.
quíntuplo/pla adj quintuple, fivefold.
quiosco m bandstand; newsstand.
quirófano m operating theater.
quiromancia f palmistry.
quirúrgico/ca adj surgical.
quisquilloso/sa adj difficult, touchy; peevish, irritable.
quiste m cyst.
quitaesmalte m nail-polish remover.
quitamanchas m invar stain remover.
quitanieves m invar snowplow.
quitar vt to take away, to remove; to take off; to relieve; to annul; ~se vr to take off (clothes etc); to withdraw.
quitasol m parasol.
quizá, quizás adv perhaps.

R

rabadilla f coccyx; rump, croup (of a horse/other four-legged animal).
rábano m radish.
rabí m rabbi.
rabia f rage, fury.
rabiar vi to be furious, to rage.
rabieta f touchiness, petulance; fit of bad temper.
rabino m rabbi.
rabioso/sa adj rabid; furious.
rabo m tail.
racha f gust of wind; **buena/mala** ~ spell of good/bad luck.
racial adj racial, race compd.
racimo m bunch of grapes.
raciocinio m reasoning; argument.
ración f ration.
racional adj rational; reasonable.

racionalidad f rationality.
racionar vt to ration (out).
racismo m racialism.
racista adj, m/f racist.
radar m radar.
radiación f radiation.
radiactivo/va, radioactivo/va adj radioactive.
radiador m radiator.
radiante adj radiant.
radiar vt to radiate.
radicación f taking root; becoming rooted (of a habit).
radical adj radical.
radicar vt to take root; ~se vr to establish oneself.
radio f radio; radio (set); * m radius; ray.
radiografía f radiography; X-ray.
radioso/sa adj Lat Am radiant.
radioterapia f radiotherapy.
raer vt to scrape; to grate; to erase.
ráfaga f gust; flash; burst.
rafting m rafting.
raído/da adj scraped; worn-out; impudent.
raíz f root; base, basis; origin.
raja f splinter, chip (of wood); chink, fissure.
rajar vt to split; to chop, to cleave.
rajatabla: **a** ~ adv strictly.
ralea f race; breed, species.
rallador m grater.
rallar vt to grate.
ralo/la adj thin, rare.
rama f branch (of a tree, of a family).
ramadán m Ramadan.
ramaje m branches pl.
rambla f avenue.
ramera f whore, prostitute.
ramificación f ramification.
ramificarse vr to ramify.
ramillete m bunch.
ramo m branch (of a tree).
rampa f ramp.
rampante adj rampant.
rana f frog.
ranchera f station wagon.
ranchero m rancher; farmer.
rancho m grub; ranch; farm; settlement, camp.
rancio/cia adj rank; rancid.
rango m rank, standing.
ranúnculo m (bot) buttercup.
ranura f groove; slot.
rapacidad f rapacity.
rapadura f shaving; baldness.
rapar vt to shave; to plunder.
rapaz/za adj rapacious; * m/f young boy/girl.
rape m quick shave; monkfish.
rapé m snuff.
rapidez f speed, rapidity.
rápido/da adj quick, rapid, swift.
rapiña f robbery.
rappel m abseiling.
raptar vt to kidnap.

rapto m kidnaping; (fig) ecstasy, rapture.

raqueta f racket.

raquítico/ca adj stunted; (fig) inadequate.

rareza f rarity, rareness.

raro/ra adj rare, scarce; extraordinary.

ras m: **a ~ de** level with; **a ~ de tierra** at ground level.

rasar vt to level.

rascacielos m invar skyscraper.

rascar vt to scratch, to scrape.

rasgar vt to tear, to rip.

rasgo m dash, stroke; grand/magnanimous action; **~s** mpl features pl.

rasguear vi to form bold strokes with a pen; (mus) to strum.

rasguñar vt to scratch, to scrape.

rasguño m scratch.

rasguñón m Lat Am scratch.

raso/sa adj plain; flat; * m satin; **al raso** in the open air.

raspa f beard (of an ear of corn); backbone (of fish); stalk (of grapes); rasp.

raspadura f filing, scraping; filings pl.

raspar vt to scrape, to rasp.

rastra f rake; **a ~s** by dragging.

rastreador m tracker.

rastrear vt to trace; to inquire into; * vi to skim along close to the ground (of birds).

rastrero/ra adj creeping; low, humble, cringing.

rastrillar vt to rake.

rastrillo m rake.

rastro m track; rake; trace.

rastrojera f stubble field.

rastrojo m stubble.

rasurador/ra m/f electric shaver.

rasurarse vr to shave.

rata f rat.

ratería f larceny, petty theft.

ratero/ra adj creeping, mean, vile; * m/f pickpocket; burglar.

ratificación f ratification.

ratificar vt to ratify; to approve of.

rato m moment; **a ~s perdidos** in leisure time.

ratón m mouse.

ratonera f mousetrap.

raudal m torrent.

raya f stroke; line; part; frontier; ray (fish); roach (fish).

rayado/da adj ruled; crossed; striped.

rayar vt to draw lines on; to cross out; to underline; to cross; to rifle.

rayo m ray, beam (of light).

rayón m rayon.

raza f race, lineage; quality.

razón f reason; right; reasonableness; account; calculation.

razonable adj reasonable.

razonado/da adj rational; prudent.

razonamiento m reasoning; discourse.

razonar vi to reason; to discourse, to talk.

reacción f reaction.

reaccionar vi to react.

reaccionario/ria adj reactionary.

reacio/cia adj stubborn.

reactor m reactor.

reajuste m readjustment.

real adj real, actual; royal; * m (mil) camp.

realce m embossment; flash; luster, splendor.

realidad f reality; sincerity.

realista m realist; royalist.

realizador/ra m/f producer (in TV etc).

realizar vt to realize; to achieve; to undertake.

realmente adv really, actually.

realzar vt to raise, to elevate; to emboss; to heighten.

reanimar vt to cheer, to encourage; to reanimate.

reanudar vt to renew; to resume.

reaparición f reappearance.

reasumir vt to retake, to resume.

reata f collar, leash; string (of horses).

rebaja f abatement; deduction; **~s** fpl sale.

rebajar vt to abate, to lessen, to diminish; to lower.

rebanada f slice.

rebaño m flock (of sheep), herd (of cattle).

rebasar vt to exceed.

rebatir vt to resist; to parry, to ward off; to refute; to repress.

rebeca f cardigan.

rebelarse vr to revolt; to rebel; to resist.

rebelde m/f rebel; * adj rebellious.

rebeldía f rebelliousness, disobedience; (law) contumacy; **en ~** by default.

rebelión f rebellion, revolt.

rebosar vi to run over, to overflow; to abound.

rebotar vt to bounce; to clinch; to repel; * vi to rebound.

rebote m rebound; **de ~** on the rebound.

rebozado/da adj fried in batter/breadcrumbs.

rebozar vt to wrap up; to fry in batter/breadcrumbs.

rebozo m Lat Am shawl.

rebullir vi to stir, to begin to move.

rebuscado/da adj affected; recherché; far-fetched.

rebuznar vi to bray.

rebuzno m braying (of an ass).

recabar vt to obtain by entreaty.

recado m message; gift.

recaer vi to fall back.

recaída f relapse.

recalcar vt to stress, to emphasize.

recalcitrante adj recalcitrant.

recalentamiento m overheating.

recalentar vt to heat again; to overheat.

recámara f bedroom.

recambio m spare; refill.

recapacitar vt to reflect.

recapitulación f recapitulation.

recapitular vt to recapitulate.

recargado/da adj overloaded.

recargar vt to overload; to recharge; to charge again.

recargo *m* extra load; new charge/accusation.

recatado/da *adj* prudent; circumspect; modest.

recato *m* prudence; circumspection; modesty; bashfulness.

recaudación *f* take, income; recovery of debts; tax collector's office.

recaudador *m* tax collector.

recaudar *vt* to gather; to obtain; to recover.

recelar *vt* to fear; to suspect, to doubt.

recelo *m* dread; suspicion, mistrust.

receloso/sa *adj* mistrustful; shy.

recepción *f* reception.

recepcionar *vt Lat Am* to receive.

recepcionista *m/f* receptionist.

receptáculo *m* receptacle.

receptor *m* receiver; investigating official.

recesión *f* (com) recession.

receta *f* recipe; prescription.

recetar *vt* to prescribe.

rechazar *vt* to refuse; to repulse; to contradict.

rechazo *m* rebound; denial; recoil.

rechifla *f* booing; (*fig*) derision.

rechiflar *vt* to boo.

rechinar *vi* to gnash (teeth).

rechistar *vi*: **sin ~** without a murmur.

rechoncho/cha *adj* chubby.

recibidor *m* entrance hall.

recibimiento *m* reception.

recibir *vt* to receive, to accept; to let in; to go to meet; **~se** *vr*: **~ de** *Lat Am* to qualify as.

recibo *m* receipt.

reciclado/da *adj* recycled.

reciclar *vt* to recycle.

recién *adv* recently, lately; *Lat Am* only.

reciente *adj* recent; new, fresh; modern.

recinto *m* district, precinct.

recio/cia *adj* stout; strong, robust; coarse, thick; rude; arduous, rigid; * *adv* strongly, stoutly; **hablar ~** to talk loud.

recipiente *m* container.

reciprocidad *f* reciprocity.

recíproco/ca *adj* reciprocal, mutual.

recitación *f* recitation.

recital *m* recital; reading.

recitar *vt* to recite.

recitativo/va *adj* recitative.

reclamación *f* claim; reclamation; protest.

reclamar *vt* to claim.

reclame *m Lat Am* advertisement.

reclamo *m* claim; advertisement; attraction; decoy bird; catchword (in printing); *Lat Am* complaint.

reclinar *vt* to recline; **~se** *vr* to lean back.

recluir *vt* to shut up.

reclusión *f* seclusion; prison.

recluta *f* recruitment; * *m/f* recruit.

reclutador *m* recruitment officer.

reclutar *vt* to recruit.

recobrar *vt* to recover; **~se** *vr* to recover (from sickness).

recodo *m* corner/angle jutting out.

recogedor *m* scraper (instrument).

recoger *vt* to collect; to retake, to take back; to get; to gather; to shelter; to compile; **~se** *vr* to take shelter/refuge; to retire; to withdraw from the world.

recogido/da *adj* retired, secluded; quiet.

recogimiento *m* collection; retreat; shelter; abstraction from all worldly concerns.

recolección *f* summary; recollection.

recomendación *f* recommendation.

recomendado/da *adj Lat Am* registered.

recomendar *vt* to recommend.

recompensa *f* compensation; recompense, reward.

recompensar *vt* to recompense, to reward.

recomponer *vt* to recompose; to mend.

reconcentrar *vt* to concentrate on.

reconciliación *f* reconciliation.

reconciliar *vt* to reconcile; **~se** *vr* to make one's peace.

recóndito/ta *adj* recondite, secret, concealed.

reconfortar *vt* to comfort.

reconocer *vt* to recognize; to examine closely; to acknowledge; to consider; (*mil*) to reconnoiter.

reconocido/da *adj* recognized; grateful.

reconocimiento *m* recognition; acknowledgement; gratitude; confession; search; submission; inquiry; (*mil*) reconnaissance.

reconquista *f* reconquest.

reconquistar *vt* to reconquer.

reconstituyente *m* tonic.

reconstruir *vt* to reconstruct.

reconvenir *vt* to return the accusations of.

reconversión *f*: **~ industrial** industrial rationalization.

recopilación *f* summary, abridgement.

recopilador *m* compiler.

recopilar *vt* to compile.

récord *adj invar* record; * *m* record.

recordar *vt* to remember; to remind; * *vi* to remember.

recorrer *vt* to run over, to peruse; to cover.

recorrida *f Lat Am* journey.

recortar *vt* to cut out.

recorte *m* cutting; trimming.

recostar *vt* to lean, to recline; **~se** *vr* to lie down.

recoveco *m* cubbyhole; bend.

recrear *vt* to amuse, to entertain; to delight.

recreativo/va *adj* recreational.

recreo *m* recreation; playtime (at school).

recriminación *f* recrimination.

recriminar *vt* to recriminate.

recrudecer *vt*, *vi*, **~se** *vr* to worsen.

recrudecimiento *m* upsurge.

recta *f* straight line.

rectángulo/la *adj* rectangular; * *m* rectangle.

rectificación *f* rectification.

rectificar *vt* to rectify.

rectilíneo/nea *adj* rectilinear.

rectitud *f* straightness; rectitude; justness, honesty; exactitude.

recto/ta *adj* straight; right; just, honest; * *m* rectum.

rector/ra *m/f* superior of a community or establishment; vice-chancellor (of a university); presiding judge; curate, rector; * *adj* governing.

rectorado *m* rectorship; vice-chancellorship.

rectoría *f* rectory; rectorship.

recua *f* train (of mules, pack animals).

recuadro *m* box; inset.

recuento *m* inventory.

recuerdo *m* souvenir; memory.

recular *vi* to fall back, to recoil.

recuperable *adj* recoverable.

recuperación *f* recovery.

recuperar *vt* to recover; ~**se** *vr* to recover (from sickness).

recurrir *vi*: ~ **a** to resort to.

recurso *m* recourse.

recusación *f* refusal.

recusar *vt* to refuse; to refuse to admit.

red *f* net; network; snare.

redacción *f* editing; editor's office.

redactar *vt* to draft; to edit.

redactor/ra *m/f* editor.

redada *f*: ~ **policial** police raid.

redecilla *f* hairnet.

rededor *m* environs *pl*; **al** ~ round about.

redención *f* redemption.

redentor/ra *m/f* redeemer.

redescubrir *vt* to rediscover.

redicho/cha *adj* affected.

redil *m* enclosure for sheep.

redimible *adj* redeemable.

redimir *vt* to redeem; to ransom.

rédito *m* revenue, rent.

redoblado/da *adj* redoubled; stout and thick; reinforced.

redoblar *vt* to redouble; to rivet.

redoble *m* doubling, repetition; (*mil*) roll of a drum.

redomado/da *adj* sly; out-and-out.

redondear *vt* to round.

redondel *m* circle; traffic circle.

redondez *f* roundness, circular form.

redondo/da *adj* round; complete.

reducción *f* reduction.

reducible *adj* reducible; convertible.

reducido/da *adj* reduced; limited; small.

reducir *adj* to reduce; to limit; ~**se** *vr* to diminish.

reducto *m* (*mil*) redoubt.

redundancia *f* superfluity, redundancy, excess.

redundar *vi* to contribute.

reelegir *vt* to re-elect, to elect again.

reembolsar *vt* to refund; to reimburse.

reembolso *m* reimbursement; refund; **contra** ~ C.O.D.

reemplazar *vt* to replace; to restore.

reemplazo *m* replacement; reserve.

reenganchar *vt* (*mil*) to re-enlist; ~**se** *vr* to enlist again.

referencia *f* reference.

referéndum *m* referendum.

referí *m Lat Am* referee.

referir *vt* to refer, to relate, to report; ~**se** *vr* to refer/relate to.

refilón *m*: **de** ~ *adv* obliquely.

refinado/da *adj* refined; subtle, artful.

refinar *vt* to refine.

refinería *f* refinery.

reflejar *vt* to reflect.

reflejo *m* reflex; reflection.

reflexión *f* meditation, reflection.

reflexionar *vt* to reflect on; * *vi* to reflect, to meditate.

reflexivo/va *adj* reflexive; thoughtful.

reflujo *m* reflux, ebb; **flujo** ~ the tides *pl*.

reforma *f* reform; correction; repair.

reformar *vt* to reform; to correct; to restore; ~**se** *vr* to mend.

reformatorio *m* reformatory.

reforzar *vt* to strengthen, to fortify; to encourage.

refracción *f* refraction.

refractario/ria *adj* refractory.

refrán *m* proverb.

refregar *vt* to scrub.

refrenar *vt* to refrain; to check.

refrendar *vt* to countersign; to approve.

refrescante *adj* refreshing.

refrescar *vt* to refresh; ~**se** *vr* to get cooler; to go out for a breath of fresh air; * *vi* to cool down.

refresco *m* refreshment.

refriega *f* affray, skirmish, fray.

refrigerador/ra *m/f* refrigerator, fridge.

refrigerar *vt* to cool; to refresh; to refrigerate; to comfort.

refrigerio *m* refrigeration; refreshment; consolation, comfort.

refuerzo *m* reinforcement.

refugiado/da *m/f* refugee.

refugiar *vt* to shelter; ~**se** *vr* to take refuge.

refugio *m* refuge, asylum.

refulgir *vi* to shine.

refunfuñar *vi* to snarl; to growl; to grumble.

refutación *f* refutation.

refutar *vt* to refute.

regadera *f* watering can.

regadío *m* irrigated land.

regalar *vt* to give (as present); to give away; to pamper; to caress.

regalía *f* regalia; bonus; royalty; privilege.

regaliz *m* licorice.

regalo *m* present, gift; pleasure; comfort.

regañadientes: **a** ~ *adv* reluctantly.

regañar *vt* to scold; * *vi* to growl; to grumble; to quarrel.

regañón/ona *adj* snarling, growling; grumbling; troublesome.

regar vt to water, to irrigate.

regata f irrigation ditch; regatta.

regatear vt (com) to bargain over; to be mean with; * vi to haggle; to dribble (in sport).

regateo m haggling; bartering; dribbling.

regazo m lap.

regencia f regency.

regeneración f regeneration.

regenerar vt to regenerate.

regentar vt to rule; to govern.

regente m regent; manager.

régimen m regime, management; diet; (gr) rules of verbs pl.

regimiento m regime; (mil) regiment.

regio/gia adj royal, regal.

región f region.

regir vt to rule, to govern; to direct; * vi to apply.

registrador/ra m/f registrar; controller.

registradora f Lat Am cash register.

registrar vt to survey; to inspect, to examine; to record, to enter in a register; ~se vr to register; to happen.

registro m examining; enrolling office; register; registration.

regla f rule, ruler; period.

reglamentar vt to regulate.

reglamentario/ria adj statutory.

reglamento m regulation; bylaw/bye-law.

regocijar vt to gladden; ~se vr to rejoice.

regocijo m joy, pleasure; merriment, rejoicing.

regodearse vr to be delighted; to trifle, to play the fool; to joke, to jest.

regodeo m joy, merriment.

regordete adj chubby, plump.

regresar vi to return, to go back.

regreso m return, regression.

reguero m small rivulet; trickle of spilt liquid; drain, gutter.

regulación f regulation.

regulador/ra m/f regulator; knob, control.

regular vt to regulate, to adjust; * adj regular; ordinary.

regularidad f regularity.

regularizar vt to regularize.

rehabilitación f rehabilitation.

rehabilitar vt to rehabilitate.

rehacer vt to repair, to make again; to redo; ~se vr to recover; (mil) to rally.

rehén m hostage.

rehuir vt to avoid.

rehusar vt to refuse, to decline.

reimpresión f reprint.

reimprimir vt to reprint.

reina f queen.

reinado m reign.

reinante adj (fig) prevailing.

reinar vi to reign; to govern.

reincidencia f relapse.

reincidir vi: ~ en to relapse into, to fall back into.

reino m kingdom, reign.

reintegración f reintegration, restoration.

reintegrar vt to reintegrate, to restore; ~se vr to be reinstated/restored.

reintegro m reintegration.

reír(se) vi (vr) to laugh.

reiteración f repetition, reiteration.

reiterar vt to reiterate, to repeat.

reivindicación f claim; vindication.

reivindicar vt to claim.

reja f plowshare; lattice, grating.

rejilla f grating, grille; vent; rack (for baggage).

rejoneador m mounted bullfighter.

rejonear vt to spear (bulls).

rejuvenecer vt, vi to rejuvenate.

relación f relation; relationship; report; account.

relacionar vt to relate.

relajación f relaxation; remission; laxity.

relajar vt to relax, to slacken; ~se vr to relax.

relajo m Lat Am (col) mess; racket.

relamerse vr to lick one's lips; to relish.

relamido/da adj affected; overdressed.

relámpago m flash of lightning.

relampaguear vi to flash.

relatar vt to relate, to tell.

relativo/va adj relative.

relato m story; recital.

relax m relaxation.

releer vt to reread.

relegación f relegation; exile.

relegar vt to relegate; to banish, to exile.

relente m evening dew.

relevante adj excellent, great; eminent.

relevar vt to emboss, to work in relief; to exonerate; to relieve; to assist.

relevo m (mil) relief.

relicario m reliquary.

relieve m relief; (fig) prominence.

religión f religion.

religiosidad f religiousness.

religioso/sa adj religious.

relinchar vi to neigh.

relincho m neigh, neighing.

reliquia f residue, remains pl; (saintly) relic.

rellano m landing (of stairs).

rellenar vt to fill up; to stuff.

relleno/na adj satiated, full up; stuffed; * m stuffing.

reloj m clock; watch.

relojero m watchmaker.

relucir vi to shine, to glitter; to excel, to be brilliant.

relumbrar vi to sparkle, to shine.

remachar vt to rivet; (fig) to drive home.

remanente m remainder; (com) balance; surplus.

remangar vt to roll up.

remansarse vr to form a pool.

remanso m stagnant water; quiet place.

remar vi to row.

rematadamente adv entirely, totally.

rematado/da adj utter, complete.

rematar vt to terminate, to finish; to sell off cheaply; * vi to end.

remate *m* end, conclusion; shot; tip; last/best bid.

remedar *vt* to copy, to imitate; to mimic.

remediable *adj* remediable.

remediar *vt* to remedy; to assist, to help; to free from danger; to avoid.

remedio *m* amendment, correction; recourse; refuge.

remedo *m* imitation, copy.

remendar *vt* to patch, to mend; to correct.

remero *m* rower, oarsman.

remesa *f* shipment; remittance.

remiendo *m* patch; mend.

remilgado/da *adj* prim; affected.

remilgo *m* primness, affectation.

reminiscencia *f* reminiscence, recollection.

remiso/sa *adj* remiss, careless; indolent.

remitente *m* sender.

remitir *vt* to remit, to send; to pardon (a fault); to suspend, to put off; * *vi*, ~**se** *vr* to slacken.

remo *m* oar; rowing.

remojar *vt* to steep; to dunk.

remojo *m* steeping, soaking.

remolacha *f* beet (crop).

remolcar *vt* to tow.

remolino *m* whirlwind; whirlpool; crowd.

remolón/ona *adj* stubborn; lazy.

remolque *m* tow, towing; tow rope.

remontar *vt* to mend; ~**se** *vr* to tower, to soar.

remorder *vt* to disturb.

remordimiento *m* remorse.

remoto/ta *adj* remote, distant; far.

remover *vt* to stir; to move around; *Lat Am* to dismiss.

remozar *vt* to rejuvenate; to renovate.

remuneración *f* remuneration, recompense.

remunerador/ra *m/f* remunerator.

remunerar *vt* to reward, to remunerate.

renacer *vi* to be born again; to revive.

renacimiento *m* regeneration; rebirth.

renacuajo *m* tadpole.

renal *adj* renal, kidney *compd*.

rencilla *f* quarrel.

rencor *m* rancor, grudge.

rencoroso/sa *adj* rancorous.

rendición *f* surrender; profit.

rendido/da *adj* submissive; exhausted.

rendija *f* crevice, crack, cleft.

rendimiento *m* output; efficiency.

rendir *vt* to subject, to subdue; ~**se** *vr* to yield; to surrender; to be tired out.

renegado *m* apostate; wicked person.

renegar *vt* to deny; to disown; to detest, to abhor; * *vi* to apostatize; to blaspheme, to curse.

renglón *m* line; item.

reno *m* caribou, reindeer.

renombrado/da *adj* renowned.

renombre *m* renown.

renovación *f* renovation; renewal.

renovar *vt* to renew; to renovate; to reform.

renquear *vi* to limp.

renta *f* income; rent; profit.

renuncia *f* renunciation; resignation.

renunciar *vt* to renounce; * *vi* to resign.

reñido/da *adj* at variance, at odds; hard-fought.

reñir *vt*, *vi* to wrangle, to quarrel, to scold, to chide.

reo *m* offender, criminal.

reojo *m*: **mirar de ~** to look at furtively.

reparación *f* repair; reparation.

reparar *vt* to repair; to consider, to observe; to parry; * *vi*: ~ **en** to notice; to pass (in cards).

reparo *m* repair, reparation; consideration; difficulty.

repartición *f* distribution.

repartidor *m/f* distributor; assessor of taxes.

repartir *vt* to distribute; to deliver.

reparto *m* distribution; delivery; cost; property development.

repasar *vt* to pass again; to revise; to check; to mend.

repaso *m* revision; check-up.

repatriar *vt* to repatriate.

repecho *m* slope.

repelente *adj* repellent, repulsive.

repeler *vt* to repel; to refute, to reject.

repente: **de ~** *adv* suddenly.

repentino/na *adj* sudden, unforeseen.

repercusión *f* reverberation.

repercutir *vi* to reverberate; to rebound.

repertorio *m* repertory; list.

repetición *f* repetition; (*mus*) encore.

repetidor/ra *m/f* repeater.

repetir *vt*, *vi* to repeat.

repicar *vt* to ring.

repique *m* chime.

repiquetear *vt* to ring merrily.

repisa *f* pedestal, stand; shelf; windowsill.

replegar *vt* to redouble; to fold over; ~**se** *vr* (*mil*) to fall back.

repleto/ta *adj* replete, very full.

réplica *f* reply, answer; repartee.

replicar *vi* to reply.

repoblación *f* repopulation; restocking; ~ **forestal** reforestation.

repoblar *vt* to repopulate; to reforest.

repollo *m* cabbage.

reponer *vt* to replace; to restore; ~**se** *vr* to recover lost health/property.

reportaje *m* report, article; *Lat Am* interview.

reportero/ra *m/f* reporter.

reposado/da *adj* quiet, peaceful; settled (wine).

reposar *vi* to rest, to repose.

reposición *f* replacement; remake.

reposo *m* rest, repose.

repostería *f* confectioner's (shop).

repostero *m* confectioner.

reprender *vt* to reprimand.

represa *f* dam; lake.

represalia *f* reprisal.

representación *f* representation; authority.

representante *m/f* representative; understudy (theater).

representar *vt* to represent; to play on the stage; to look (age).

representativo/va *adj* representative.

represión *f* repression.

reprimenda *f* reprimand.

reprimir *vt* to repress; to check; to contain.

reprobable *adj* reprehensible.

reprobación *f* reprobation, reproof.

reprobar *vt* to reject; to condemn, to upbraid; *Lat Am* to fail.

réprobo *m* reprobate.

reprochar *vt* to reproach.

reproche *m* reproach.

reproducción *f* reproduction.

reproducir *vt* to reproduce.

reptil *m* reptile.

república *f* republic.

republicano/na *adj, m/f* republican.

repudiar *vt* to repudiate.

repudio *m* repudiation.

repuesto *m* supply; spare part.

repugnancia *f* reluctance; repugnance.

repugnante *adj* repugnant.

repugnar *vt* to disgust.

repulsa *f* refusal.

repulsar *vt* to reject; to decline, to refuse.

repulsión *f* repulsion.

repulsivo/va *adj* repulsive.

repuntar *vi Lat Am* to improve.

reputación *f* reputation, renown.

reputar to consider.

requebrar *vt* to woo, to court.

requerimiento *m* request; requisition; intimation; summons.

requerir *vt* to intimate, to notify; to request; to require, to need; to summon.

requesón *m* cottage cheese.

requiebro *m* endearing expression.

réquiem *m* requiem.

requisa *f* inspection; (*mil*) requisition.

requisito *m* requisite.

res *f* animal; head of cattle; **-es** *Lat Am* cattle.

resabio *m* (unpleasant) aftertaste; vicious habit, bad custom.

resaca *f* surge, surf; (*fig*) backlash; (*col*) hangover.

resaltar *vi* to rebound; to jut out; to be evident; to stand out.

resarcimiento *m* compensation, reparation.

resarcir *vt* to compensate, to make amends for.

resbalada *f Lat Am* slip, slide.

resbaladizo/za *adj* slippery.

resbalar(se) *vi* (*vr*) to slip, to slide.

resbalón *m* slip, slide.

rescatar *vt* to ransom, to redeem.

rescate *m* ransom.

rescindir *vt* to rescind, to annul.

rescisión *f* rescindment, revocation.

rescoldo *m* embers *pl*, cinders *pl*.

resecarse *vr* to dry up.

reseco/ca *adj* very dry.

resentido/da *adj* resentful.

resentimiento *m* resentment.

resentirse *vr*: **~ de** to suffer; **~ con** to resent.

reseña *f* review; account.

reseñar *vt* to describe; to review.

reserva *f* reserve; reservation.

reservado/da *adj* reserved, cautious, circumspect.

reservar *vt* to keep; to reserve; **~se** *vr* to preserve oneself; to keep to oneself.

resfriado *m* cold.

resfriarse *vr* to catch cold.

resguardar *vt* to preserve, to defend; **~se** *vr* to be on one's guard.

resguardo *m* guard; security, safety; voucher; receipt.

residencia *f* residence.

residente *adj* residing, resident; * *m/f* resident.

residir *vi* to reside, to dwell.

residuo *m* residue, remainder.

resignación *f* resignation.

resignadamente *adv* resignedly.

resignarse *vr* to resign oneself.

resina *f* resin.

resinoso/sa *adj* resinous.

resistencia *f* resistance, opposition.

resistente *adj* strong; resistant.

resistir *vt* to resist, to oppose; to put up with; * *vi* to resist; to hold out.

resma *f* ream (of paper).

resol *m* glare (of the sun).

resollar *vi* to wheeze; to breath with difficulty.

resolución *f* resolution, boldness; decision.

resolver *vt* to resolve, to decide; to analyze; **~se** *vr* to resolve, to determine.

resonar *vi* to resound.

resoplar *vi* to snore; to snort.

resoplido *m* heavy breathing.

resorte *m* spring.

respaldar *vt* to endorse; **~se** *vr* to lean back.

respaldo *m* backing; endorsement; back of a seat.

respectivo/va *adj* respective.

respecto *m* respect; relation; **al ~** on this matter.

respetable *adj* respectable.

respetar *vt* to respect; to revere.

respeto *m* respect, regard, consideration; homage.

respetuoso/sa *adj* respectful.

respingar *vi* to shy.

respingo *m* start; jump.

respiración *f* respiration, breathing.

respiradero *m* vent, breathing hole; rest, repose.

respirar *vi* to breathe.

respiratorio/ria *adj* respiratory.

respiro *m* breathing; (*fig*) respite.

resplandecer *vi* to shine; to glisten.

resplandeciente *adj* resplendent.

resplandor *m* splendor, brilliance.

responder *vt* to answer; * *vi* to answer; to correspond; **~ de** to be responsible for.

respondón/ona adj ever ready to reply; cheeky.
responsable adj responsible; accountable, answerable.
responsabilidad f responsibility.
responsabilizarse vr to take charge.
responso m prayer for the dead.
respuesta f answer, reply.
resquemor m resentment.
resquicio m crack, cleft; (fig) chance.
restablecer vt to re-establish; ~**se** vr to recover.
restablecimiento m re-establishment.
restallar vi to crack; to click.
restante adj remaining.
restar vt to subtract, to take away; * vi to be left.
restauración f restoration.
restaurant m Lat Am diner.
restaurante m diner.
restaurar vt to restore.
restitución f restitution.
restituir vt to restore; to return.
resto m remainder, rest.
restregar vt to scrub, to rub.
restricción f restriction, limitation.
restringir vt to restrict, to limit; to restrain.
resucitar vt to resuscitate, to revive; to renew.
resuello m breath, breathing.
resuelto/ta adj resolute, determined; prompt.
resultado m result, consequence.
resultar vi to be; to turn out; to amount to.
resumen m summary.
resumidamente adv summarily.
resumir vt to abridge; to sum up; to summarize.
resurrección f resurrection, revival.
retablo m picture drawn on a board; splendid altarpiece.
retaguardia f rearguard.
retahíla f range, series.
retal m remnant.
retar vt to challenge.
retardar vt to retard; to delay.
retardo m delay.
retazo m remnant; cutting.
retén m Lat Am reformatory.
retención f retention.
retener vt to retain, to keep back.
retentiva f memory.
reticencia f reticence.
retina f retina.
retintín m tinkling sound; affected tone of voice.
retirada f (mil) retreat, withdrawal; recall.
retirar vt to withdraw, to retire; to remove; ~**se** vr to retire, to retreat; to go to bed.
retiro m retreat, retirement; pension.
reto m challenge; threat, menace.
retocar vt to retouch; to mend; to -finish off (work).
retoñar vi to sprout.
retoño m shoot; offspring.
retoque m finishing stroke; retouching.
retorcer vt to twist; to wring.
retorcimiento m twisting, contortion.

retórica f rhetoric.
retórico/ca adj rhetorical; * f rhetoric; affectedness.
retornar vt, vi to return.
retorno m return; barter, exchange.
retortero: andar al ~ to bustle about.
retortijón m twisting; ~ **de tripas** stomach cramp.
retozar vi to frisk, to skip.
retozo m romp.
retozón/ona adj wanton; romping.
retracción f retraction.
retractar vt to retract.
retraer vt to draw back; to dissuade; ~**se** vr to take refuge; to flee.
retraído/da adj shy.
retransmisión f broadcast.
retransmitir vt to broadcast; to relay; to retransmit.
retrasado/da adj late; (med) mentally handicapped; backward.
retraso m delay; slowness; backwardness; lateness; (rail): **el tren ha tenido** ~ the train is overdue/late.
retratar vt to portray; to photograph; to describe.
retrato m portrait, effigy.
retreta f (mil) retreat.
retrete m bathroom, lavatory.
retribución f retribution.
retribuir vt to repay.
retroacción f retroaction.
retroactivo/va adj retroactive.
retroceder vi to go backward(s), to fly back; to back down.
retrógrado/da adj retrograde; reactionary.
retrospectivo/va adj retrospective.
retrovisor m rear-view mirror.
retumbar vi to resound, to jingle.
reuma f rheumatism.
reumático/ca adj rheumatic.
reumatismo m rheumatism.
reunión f reunion, meeting.
reunir vt to reunite; to unite; ~**se** vr to gather, to meet.
revalidación f confirmation, ratification.
revalidar vt to ratify, to confirm.
revancha f revenge.
revelación f revelation.
revelado m developing.
revelar vt to reveal; to develop (photographs).
reventar vi to burst, to explode; to toil, to overwork.
reventón m (auto) blow-out.
reverberación f reverberation.
reverberar vi to reverberate.
reverdecer vi to grow green again; to revive.
reverencia f reverence, veneration; respect.
reverenciar vt to venerate, to revere.
reverendo/da adj reverend.
reverente adj respectful, reverent.
reverso m reverse.

revés *m* back; wrong side; disappointment, setback.

revestir *vt* to put on; to coat, to cover.

revisar *vt* to revise, to review; *Lat Am* to search.

revisión *f* revision.

revisor/ra *m/f* inspector; ticket collector.

revista *f* magazine; review, revision.

revivir *vi* to revive.

revocación *f* revocation.

revocar *vt* to revoke.

revolcarse *vr* to wallow.

revolotear *vi* to flutter.

revoloteo *m* fluttering.

revoltijo *m* confusion, disorder.

revoltoso/sa *adj* rebellious, unruly.

revolución *f* revolution.

revolucionario/ria *adj*, *m/f* revolutionary.

revolver *vt* to move about; to turn around; to mess up; to revolve; **~se** *vr* to turn round; to change (of the weather).

revólver *m* revolver.

revuelo *m* fluttering; (*fig*) commotion.

revuelta *f* turn; disturbance, revolt.

rey *m* king; king (in cards/chess).

reyerta *f* quarrel, brawl.

rezagar *vt* to leave behind; to defer; **~se** *vr* to remain behind.

rezar *vi* to pray, to say one's prayers.

rezo *m* prayer.

rezongar *vi* to grumble.

rezumar *vt* to ooze, to leak.

ría *f* estuary.

riada *f* flood.

ribera *f* shore, bank.

ribereño/ña *adj* coastal; riverside.

ribete *m* trimming; seam, border.

ribetear *vt* to hem, to border.

ricino *m*: **aceite de ~** castor oil.

rico/ca *adj* rich; delicious; lovely; cute.

ridiculez *f* absurdity.

ridiculizar *vt* to ridicule.

ridículo/la *adj* ridiculous.

riego *m* irrigation.

riel *m* (*rail*) rail.

rienda *f* rein of a bridle; **dar ~ suelta** to give free rein to.

riesgo *m* risk, danger.

riesgoso/sa *adj Lat Am* risky.

rifa *f* raffle, lottery.

rifar *vt* to raffle.

rifle *m* rifle.

rigidez *f* rigidity.

rígido/da *adj* rigid, inflexible; severe.

rigor *m* rigor.

riguroso/sa *adj* rigorous.

rima *f* rhyme.

rimar *vi* to rhyme.

rimbombante *adj* pompous.

rímel, rimmel *m* mascara.

rincón *m* (inside) corner.

rinoceronte *m* rhinoceros.

riña *f* quarrel, dispute.

riñón *m* kidney.

río *m* river, stream.

rioja *m* rioja (wine).

riqueza *f* riches *pl*, wealth.

risa *f* laugh, laughter.

risco *m* steep rock.

risible *adj* risible, laughable.

risotada *f* loud laugh.

ristra *f* string.

risueño/na *adj* smiling.

rítmico/ca *adj* rhythmic.

ritmo *m* rhythm.

rito *m* rite, ceremony.

ritual *adj*, *m* ritual.

rival *adj*, *m/f* rival.

rivalidad *f* rivalry.

rivalizar *vi*: **~ con** to rival, to vie with.

rizado/da *adj* curly.

rizar *vt* to curl (hair).

rizo *m* curl; ripple (on water).

robar *vt* to rob; to steal; to break into.

roble *m* oak tree.

robledal *m* oakwood.

robo *m* robbery; theft.

robot *m* robot.

robustez *f* robustness.

robusto/ta *adj* robust, strong.

roca *f* rock.

rocalla *f* pebbles *pl*.

roce *m* rub; brush; friction.

rociada *f* sprinkling; spray, shower.

rociar *vt* to sprinkle; to spray.

rocín *m* nag; hack; stupid person.

rocío *m* dew.

rocoso/sa *adj* rocky.

rodada *f* rut, track of a wheel.

rodador *m Lat Am* gnat.

rodadura *f* act of rolling.

rodaja *f* slice.

rodaje *m* filming; **en ~** (*auto*) running in.

rodar *vi* to roll.

rodear *vi* to make a detour; * *vt* to surround, to enclose; *Lat Am* to round up.

rodeo *m* detour; subterfuge; evasion; rodeo.

rodilla *f* knee; **de ~s** on one's knees.

rodillo *m* roller.

roedor/ra *adj* gnawing; * *m* rodent.

roedura *f* gnawing.

roer *vt* to gnaw; to corrode.

rogar *vt*, *vi* to ask for; to beg, to entreat; to pray.

rogativa *f* supplication, prayer.

rojez *f* redness.

rojizo/za *adj* reddish.

rojo/ja *adj* red; ruddy.

rol *m* list, roll, catalog; role.

rollizo/za *adj* round; plump, chubby.

rollo *m* roll; coil.

romance *m* Romance language; romance.

romancero *m* collection of romances/ballads.

romanticismo *m* romanticism.

romántico/ca *adj* romantic.
rombo *m* rhombus.
romboide *m* rhomboid.
romería *f* pilgrimage.
romero *m* (*bot*) rosemary.
romo/ma *adj* blunt; snub-nosed.
rompecabezas *m invar* riddle; jigsaw.
romper *vt* to break; to tear up; to wear out; to break up (land); * *vi* to break (of waves); to break through.
rompimiento *m Lat Am* tearing, breaking; crack.
ron *m* rum.
roncar *vi* to snore; to roar.
roncha *f* weal, bruise.
ronco/ca *adj* hoarse; husky; raucous.
ronda *f* night patrol; round (of drinks, cards etc).
rondar *vt, vi* to patrol; to prowl around.
ronquera *f* hoarseness.
ronquido *m* snore; roar.
ronzal *m* halter.
ronronear *vi* to purr.
roña *f* scab, mange; grime; rust.
roñoso/sa *adj* filthy; mean.
ropa *f* clothes *pl*; clothing; dress.
ropaje *m* gown, robes *pl*; drapery.
ropero *m* linen cupboard; closet.
rosa *f* rose; birthmark.
rosado/da *adj* pink; rosy.
rosal *m* rosebush.
rosario *m* rosary.
rosca *f* thread (of a screw); coil, spiral.
rosedal *m Lat Am* rose garden.
rosetón *m* rosette; rose window, wheel window.
rosquilla *f* doughnut, donut.
rostro *m* face.
rotación *f* rotation.
roto/ta *adj* broken, destroyed; debauched.
rótula *f* kneecap; ball-and-socket joint.
rotulador *m* felt-tip pen, fiber-tip pen.
rotular *vt* to inscribe, to label.
rótulo *m* inscription; label, ticket; placard, poster.
rotundo/da *adj* round; emphatic.
rotura *f* breaking; crack; tear.
roturar *vt* to plow.
rozadura *f* graze, scratch.
rozar *vt* to rub; to chafe; to nibble (the grass); to scrape; to touch lightly.
rubí *m* ruby.
rubicundo/da *adj* reddish.
rubio/bia *adj* fair-haired, blond/blonde; * *m/f* blond/blonde.
rubor *m* blush; bashfulness.
rúbrica *f* red mark; flourish at the end of a signature; title, heading, rubric.
rubricar *vt* to sign with a flourish; to sign and seal.
rubro *m Lat Am* heading; item.
rudeza *f* roughness, rudeness; stupidity.
rudimento *m* principle; beginning; ~**s** *mpl* rudiments *pl*.
rudo/da *adj* rough, coarse; plain, simple; stupid.

rueca *f* distaff.
rueda *f* wheel; circle; slice, round.
ruedo *m* rotation; border, selvage; arena, bullring.
ruego *m* request, entreaty.
rufián *m* pimp, pander; lout.
rugby *m* rugby.
rugido *m* roar.
rugir *vi* to roar, to bellow.
rugoso/sa *adj* wrinkled.
ruibarbo *m* rhubarb.
ruido *m* noise, sound; din, row; fuss.
ruidoso/sa *adj* noisy, loud.
ruin *adj* mean, despicable; mean, stingy.
ruina *f* ruin, collapse; downfall, destruction; ~**s** *fpl* ruins *pl*.
ruindad *f* meanness, lowness; mean act.
ruinoso/sa *adj* ruinous, disastrous.
ruiseñor *m* nightingale.
ruleta *f* roulette.
rulo *m* rolling pin; hair curler.
rumba *f* rumba.
rumbo *m* (*mar*) course, bearing; road, route, way; course of events, pomp, ostentation.
rumboso/sa *adj* generous, lavish.
rumiante *m* ruminant.
rumiar *vt* to chew; * *vi* to ruminate.
rumor *m* rumor; murmur.
runrún *m* rumor; sound of voices, whirr.
ruptura *f* rupture.
rural *adj* rural.
rusticidad *f* rusticity; coarseness.
rústico/ca *adj* rustic; * *m/f* peasant.
ruta *f* route, itinerary.
rutina *f* routine; habit.

S

sábado *m* Saturday; (Jewish) Sabbath.
sábana *f* sheet; altar cloth.
sabandija *f* bug, insect.
sabañón *m* chilblain.
sabelotodo *m/f invar* know-all.
saber *vt* to know; to be able to; to find out, to learn; to experience; * *vi*: ~ **a** to taste of; * *m* learning, knowledge.
sabiduría *f* learning, knowledge; wisdom.
sabiendas *adv*: **a ~** knowingly.
sabihondo/da *adj* know-all; pedantic.
sabio/bia *adj* sage, wise; * *m/f* sage, wise person.
sablazo *m* sword wound; (*col*) sponging, scrounging.
sable *m* saber, cutlass.
sabor *m* taste, savor, flavor.
saborear *vt* to savor, to taste; to enjoy.
sabotaje *m* sabotage.
saboteador/ora *m/f* saboteur.
sabotear *vt* to sabotage.
sabroso/sa *adj* tasty, delicious; pleasant; salted.
sabueso *m* bloodhound.

sacacorchos m invar corkscrew.

sacapuntas m invar pencil sharpener.

sacar vt to take out, to extract; to get out; to bring out (a book etc); to take off (clothes); to receive, to get; (sport) to serve.

sacarina f saccharin.

sacerdotal adj priestly.

sacerdote m priest.

sacerdotisa f priestess.

saciar vt to satiate.

saciedad f satiety.

saco m bag, sack; Lat Am jacket; Lat Am coat; ~ de dormir sleeping bag.

sacramental adj sacramental.

sacramento m sacrament.

sacrificar vt to sacrifice.

sacrificio m sacrifice.

sacrilegio m sacrilege.

sacrílego/ga adj sacrilegious.

sacristán m sacristan, sexton.

sacristía f sacristy, vestry.

sacro/cra adj holy, sacred.

sacrosanto/ta adj sacrosanct.

sacudida f shake, jerk.

sacudir vt to shake, to jerk; to beat, to hit.

sacudón m Lat Am shake, jerk.

sádico/ca adj sadistic; * m/f sadist.

sadismo m sadism.

saeta f arrow, dart.

sagacidad f shrewdness, cleverness, sagacity.

sagaz adj shrewd, clever, sagacious.

sagitariano/na adj Lat Am Sagittarian (zodiac sign).

Sagitario m Sagittarius (zodiac sign).

sagrado/da adj sacred, holy.

sagrario m shrine; tabernacle.

sainete m (theat) farce; flavor, relish; seasoning.

saíno m Lat Am peccary.

sal f salt.

sala f large room; (theat) house, auditorium; public hall; (law) court; (med) ward.

salado/da adj salted; witty, amusing.

salamandra f salamander.

salar vt to salt.

salarial adj wage compd, salary compd.

salario m salary.

salazón f salting.

salchicha f sausage.

salchichón m salami-type sausage.

saldar vt to pay; to sell off; (fig) to settle.

saldo m settlement; balance; remainder; ~s mpl sale.

saledizo/za adj projecting, salient.

salero m salt cellar.

saleroso adj witty, amusing.

salida f exit, way out; leaving, departure; production, output; (com) sale; sales outlet.

saliente adj projecting; rising; (fig) outstanding.

salina f saltworks, salt mine.

salino/na adj saline.

salir vi to go out, to leave; to depart, to set out; to appear; to turn out, to prove; ~se vr to escape, to leak.

salitre m saltpeter.

saliva f saliva.

salmo m psalm.

salmón m salmon.

salmonete m red mullet.

salmuera f brine.

salobre adj brackish, salty.

salón m living room, lounge; public hall.

salpicadero m dashboard.

salpicar vt to sprinkle, to splash, to spatter.

salpimentar vt to season with pepper and salt.

salsa f sauce.

salsera f sauce boat; gravy boat.

saltamontes m invar grasshopper.

saltar vt to jump, to leap; to skip, to miss out; * vi to leap, to jump; to bounce; (fig) to explode, to blow up.

salteador m highwayman.

saltear vt to rob in a stick-up; to assault; to sauté (in cooking).

saltimbanqui m/f acrobat.

salto m leap, jump.

saltón/ona adj bulging; protruding.

salubre adj healthy.

salubridad f healthiness.

salud f health.

saludable adj healthy.

saludar vt to greet; (mil) to salute.

saludo m greeting.

salutación f salutation, greeting.

salva f (mil) salute, salvo.

salvación f salvation; rescue.

salvado m bran.

salvaguardar vt to safeguard.

salvaguardia m safeguard.

salvaje adj savage.

salvajismo m savagery.

salvar vt to save; to rescue; to overcome; to cross, to jump across; to cover, to travel; to exclude; ~se vr to escape from danger.

salvavidas adj invar: bote ~ lifeboat; chaleco ~ life preserver.

salvia f (bot) sage.

salvo/va adj safe; * adv save, except (for).

salvoconducto m safe-conduct.

san adj saint (as title).

sanamente adv healthily.

sanar vt, vi to heal.

sanatorio m sanitarium; nursing home.

sanción f sanction.

sancionar vt to sanction.

sandalia f sandal.

sándalo m sandal, sandalwood.

sandez f folly, stupidity.

sandía f watermelon.

sánduche m Lat Am sandwich.

sandwich m sandwich.

saneamiento m sanitation.

sanear vt to drain.

sangrar *vt, vi* to bleed.

sangre *f* blood; **a ~ fría** in cold blood; **a ~ y fuego** without mercy.

sangría *f* sangria (drink); bleeding.

sangriento/ta *adj* bloody, blood-stained, gory; cruel.

sanguijuela *f* leech.

sanguinario/ria *adj* bloodthirsty, -cruel.

sanguíneo/nea *adj* blood *compd*.

sanidad *f* sanitation; health.

sanitario/ria *adj* sanitary; health; **~s** *mpl* bathroom facilities *pl*.

sano/na *adj* healthy, fit; intact, sound.

santiamén *m*: **en un ~** in no time at all.

santidad *f* sanctity.

santificar *vt* to sanctify; to make holy.

santiguarse *vr* to make the sign of the cross.

santo/ta *adj* holy; sacred; * *m/f* saint; **~ y seña** password, watchword.

santuario *m* sanctuary.

saña *f* anger, passion.

sañudo/da *adj* furious, enraged.

sapo *m* toad.

saque *m* (*sport*) serve, service, throw-in.

saqueador/ra *m/f* ransacker, looter.

saquear *vt* to ransack, to plunder.

saqueo *m* looting, sacking.

sarampión *m* measles.

sarao *m* evening party, soiree.

sarcasmo *m* sarcasm.

sarcástico/ca *adj* sarcastic.

sarcófago *m* sarcophagus.

sardina *f* sardine.

sardónico/ca *adj* sardonic; ironic(al).

sargento *m* sergeant.

sarmiento *m* vine shoot.

sarna *f* itch; mange; (*med*) scabies.

sarnoso/sa *adj* itchy, scabby, mangy.

sarpullido *m* (*med*) rash.

sarro *m* (*med*) tartar.

sarta *f* string of beads etc; string, row.

sartén *f* frying pan.

sastre *m* tailor.

sastrería *f* tailor's premises.

Satanás *m* Satan.

satélite *m* satellite.

sátira *f* satire.

satírico/ca *adj* satirical.

satirizar *vt* to satirize.

sátiro *m* satyr.

satisfacción *f* satisfaction; apology.

satisfacer *vt* to satisfy; to pay (a debt); **~se** *vr* to satisfy oneself; to take revenge.

satisfactorio/ria *adj* satisfactory.

satisfecho/cha *adj* satisfied.

saturación *f* (*chem*) saturation.

Saturno *m* Saturn (planet).

sauce *m* willow tree.

saúco *m* elder tree.

sauna *f* sauna.

savia *f* sap.

saxofón *m* saxophone.

sazonado/da *adj* flavored, seasoned.

sazonar *vt* to ripen; to season.

se *pn reflexivo*: himself; herself; itself; yourself; themselves; yourselves; each other; one another; oneself.

sebo *m* fat, grease.

seboso/sa *adj* fat, greasy.

secador *m*: **~ de pelo** hairdryer.

secadora *f* tumble dryer.

secamente *adv* drily/dryly, curtly.

secano *m* dry, arable land which is not irrigated.

secar *vt* to dry; **~se** *vr* to dry up; to dry oneself.

sección *f* section.

seco/ca *adj* dry; dried up; skinny; cold (of character); brusque, sharp; bare.

secreción *f* secretion.

secretaría *f* secretariat.

secretario/ria *m/f* secretary.

secreto/ta *adj* secret; hidden; * *m* -secret; secrecy.

secta *f* sect.

sectario/ria *adj, m/f* sectarian.

sector *m* sector.

secuela *f* sequel; consequence.

secuencia *f* sequence.

secuestrador/ra *m/f* kidnaper.

secuestrar *vt* to kidnap; to confiscate.

secuestro *m* kidnaping; confiscation.

secular *adj* secular.

secularización *f* secularization.

secularizar *vt* to secularize.

secundar *vt* to second.

secundario/ria *adj* secondary.

sed *f* thirst; **tener ~** to be thirsty.

seda *f* silk.

sedal *m* fishing line.

sedante *m* sedative.

sede *f* see; seat; headquarters.

sedentario/ria *adj* sedentary.

sedición *f* sedition.

sedicioso/sa *adj* seditious, mutinous.

sediento/ta *adj* thirsty; eager.

sedoso/sa *adj* silky.

seducción *f* seduction.

seducir *vt* to seduce; to bribe; to charm; to attract.

seductor/ra *adj* seductive; charming; attractive; * *m/f* seducer.

segador/ra *m/f* reaper, harvester.

segadora-trilladora *f* combine (harvester).

segar *vt* to reap, to harvest; to mow.

seglar *adj* secular, lay.

segmento *m* segment.

segregación *f* segregation, separation.

segregar *vt* to segregate, to separate.

seguido/da *adj* continuous; successive; long-lasting; * *adv* straight (on); after; *Lat Am* often.

seguidor/ra *m/f* follower; supporter.

seguimiento *m* pursuit; continuation.

seguir *vt* to follow, to pursue; to continue; * *vi*

to follow; to carry on; **~se** *vr* to follow, to ensue.

según *prep* according to.

segundo/da *adj* second; * *m* second (of time).

seguramente *adv* surely; for sure.

seguridad *f* security; certainty; safety; confidence; stability.

seguro/ra *adj* safe, secure; sure, certain; firm, constant; * *adv* for sure; * *m* safety device; insurance; safety, certainty.

seis *adj*, *m* six; sixth.

seiscientos/tas *adj* six hundred.

seísmo *m* earthquake.

selección *f* selection, choice.

seleccionar *vt* to select, to choose.

selecto/ta *adj* select, choice.

sellar *vt* to seal; to stamp (a document).

sello *m* seal; stamp.

selva *f* forest.

semáforo *m* traffic lights *pl*; signal.

semana *f* week.

semanada *f Lat Am* weekly pocket money.

semanal *adj* weekly.

semanario/ria *m* weekly (magazine).

semblante *m* face; (*fig*) look; appearance.

sembrado *m* sown field.

sembrar *vt* to sow; to sprinkle, to scatter.

semejante *adj* similar, like; * *m* fellow man.

semejanza *f* resemblance, likeness.

semejar *vi* to resemble; **~se** *vr* to look alike.

semen *m* semen.

semental *m* stud.

sementera *f* sowing time; land sown with seed.

semestral *adj* half-yearly.

semicircular *adj* semicircular.

semicírculo *m* semicircle.

semifinal *f* semifinal.

semilla *f* seed, bean.

semilla de soja *f* soybean.

semillero *m* seed plot.

seminario *m* seedbed; seminary.

seminarista *m* seminarist.

semitono *m* (*mus*) half step, semitone.

sémola *f* semolina.

sempiterno/na *adj* everlasting.

senado *m* senate.

senador/ra *m/f* senator.

sencillez *f* plainness; simplicity; naturalness.

sencillo/lla *adj* simple; natural; unaffected; single.

senda *f m* path, footpath.

senderismo *m* hillwalking.

senderista *m/f* hillwalker.

sendero *m* path, footpath.

senil *adj* senile.

seno *m* bosom; lap; womb; hole, cavity; sinus; **~s** *mpl* breasts *pl*.

sensación *f* sensation, feeling; sense.

sensacional *adj* sensational.

sensato/ta *adj* sensible.

sensibilidad *f* sensibility, sensitivity.

sensible *adj* sensitive; perceptible, appreciable; regrettable.

sensitivo/va *adj* sense *compd*, sensitive.

sensorial *adj* sensorial, sensory.

sensual *adj* sensuous, sensual.

sensualidad *f* sensuousness; sensuality; sexiness.

sentado/da *adj* sitting, seated; sedate; settled.

sentar *vt* to seat; (*fig*) to establish; * *vi* to suit; **~se** *vr* to sit down.

sentencia *f* (*law*) sentence; opinion; saying.

sentenciar *vt* (*law*) to sentence, to pass judgement on; * *vi* to give one's opinion.

sentencioso/sa *adj* sententious.

sentido *m* sense; feeling; meaning; **~/da** *adj* regrettable; sensitive.

sentimental *adj* sentimental.

sentimiento *m* feeling, emotion, sentiment; sympathy; regret, grief.

sentir *vt* to feel; to hear; to perceive; to sense; to suffer from; to regret, to be sorry for; **~se** *vr* to feel; to feel pain; to crack (of walls etc); * *m* opinion, judgement.

seña *f* sign, mark, token; signal; (*mil*) password; **~s** *fpl* address.

señal *f* sign, token; symptom; signal; landmark; (*com*) deposit.

señalado/da *adj* distinct; special; distinguished, notable.

señalar *vt* to stamp, to mark; to signpost; to point out; to fix, to settle; **~se** *vr* to distinguish oneself, to excel.

señor *m* man; gentleman; master; Mr; sir.

señora *f* lady; Mrs; madam; wife.

señorita *f* Miss; young lady.

señorito *m* Master; young gentleman; rich kid.

señuelo *m* decoy; bait, lure.

separable *adj* separable.

separación *f* separation.

separar *vt* to separate; **~se** *vr* to separate; to come away, to come apart; to withdraw.

septentrional *adj* north, northern.

séptico *adj* septic.

septiembre *m* September.

séptimo/ma *adj* seventh.

sepulcral *adj* sepulchral.

sepulcro *m* sepulcher, grave, tomb.

sepultar *vt* to bury, to inter.

sepultura *f* burial, interment; grave, tomb.

sepulturero *m* gravedigger, sexton.

sequedad *f* dryness; brusqueness.

sequía *f* dryness; thirst; drought.

séquito *m* retinue, suite; group of supporters; aftermath.

ser *vi* to be; to exist; **~ de** to come from; to be made of; to belong to; * *m* being.

serenarse *vr* to calm down.

serenata *f* (*mus*) serenade.

serenidad *f* serenity.

sereno *m* night watchman; **~/na** *adj* serene, calm, quiet.

serial *m* serial.

serie *f* series; sequence.

seriedad *f* seriousness, gravity; reliability; sincerity.

serio/ria *adj* serious; grave; reliable.

sermón *m* sermon.

sermonear *vt* to lecture; * *vi* to sermonize.

seronegativo/va *adj* HIV-negative.

seropositivo/va *adj* HIV-positive.

serpentear *vi* to wriggle; to wind, to snake.

serpentina *f* streamer.

serpiente *f* snake.

serranía *f* range of mountains; mountainous country.

serrano/na *m/f* highlander.

serrar *vt* to saw.

serrín *m* sawdust.

serruchar *vt Lat Am* to saw up.

serrucho *m* handsaw.

servible *adj* serviceable.

servicial *adj* helpful, obliging.

servicio *m* service; service charge; service, set of dishes; **~s** *mpl* bathroom facilities *pl*.

servidor/ra *m/f* servant.

servidumbre *f* servitude; servants *pl*, staff.

servil *adj* servile.

servilleta *f* napkin, serviette.

servir *vt* to serve; to wait on; * *vi* to serve; to be of use; to be in service; **~se** *vr* to serve oneself, to help oneself; to deign, to please; to make use of.

sesenta *adj, m* sixty; sixtieth.

sesentón/ona *m/f* person of about sixty years of age.

sesgar *vt* to slope, to slant.

sesgo *m* slope.

sesión *f* session; sitting; performance; showing.

seso *m* brain.

sestear *vi* to take a nap.

sesudo/da *adj* sensible, prudent.

seta *f* mushroom.

setecientos/tas *adj* seven hundred.

setenta *adj, m* seventy.

setiembre *m* September.

seto *m* fence; enclosure; hedge.

seudo- *pref* pseudo-.

seudónimo *m* pseudonym.

severidad *f* severity.

severo/ra *adj* severe, strict; grave, serious.

sexagenario/ria *adj* sixty years old.

sexagésimo/ma *adj* sixtieth.

sexenio *m* space of six years.

sexo *m* sex.

sexto/ta *adj, m* sixth.

sexual *adj* sexual.

short *m Lat Am* shorts.

si *conj* whether; if.

sí *adv* yes; certainly; indeed; * *pn* oneself; himself; herself; itself; yourself; themselves; yourselves; each other; one another.

siderúrgico/ca *adj* iron and steel *compd*.

sidra *f* cider.

siega *f* harvest, mowing.

siembra *f* sowing time.

siempre *adv* always; all the time; ever; *Lat Am* still; **~ jamás** for ever and ever.

sien *f* temple (of the head).

sierra *f* saw; range of mountains.

siervo/va *m/f* slave.

siesta *f* siesta, afternoon nap.

siete *adj, m* seven.

sietemesino/na *adj* born seven months after conception; premature; (*fig*) half-witted.

sífilis *f* syphilis.

sifón *m* siphon; soda.

sigilo *m* secrecy.

sigiloso/sa *adj* reserved; silent.

sigla *f* acronym; abbreviation.

siglo *m* century.

significación *f* significance, meaning.

significado *m* significance, meaning.

significar *vt* to signify, to mean; to make known, to express.

significativo/va *adj* significant.

signo *m* sign, mark.

siguiente *adj* following, successive, next.

sílaba *f* syllable.

silbar *vt, vi* to hiss; to whistle.

silbato *m* whistle.

silbido/silbo *m* hiss; whistling.

silencio *m* silence; **¡~!** silence!, quiet!

silencioso/sa *adj* silent.

silla *f* chair; saddle; seat; **~ de ruedas** wheelchair.

sillón *m* armchair, easy chair; rocking chair.

silo *m* silo.

silogismo *m* syllogism.

silueta *f* silhouette; outline; figure.

silvestre *adj* wild, uncultivated; rustic.

sima *f* abyss; pothole, cavern.

simbólico/ca *adj* symbolic.

simbolizar *vt* to symbolize.

símbolo *m* symbol.

simetría *f* symmetry.

simétrico/ca *adj* symmetrical.

simiente *f* seed.

similar *adj* similar.

similitud *f* similarity, similitude.

simio *m* ape.

simpatía *f* liking; kindness; solidarity; affection.

simpático/ca *adj* pleasant; kind.

simpatizante *m/f* sympathizer.

simpatizar *vi*: **~ con** to get on well with.

simple *adj* single; simple, easy; mere; sheer; silly; * *m/f* simpleton.

simpleza *f* simpleness, gullibility; silliness.

simplicidad *f* simplicity.

simplificar *vt* to simplify.

simulación *f* simulation.

simulacro *m* simulacrum, idol.

simuladamente *adv* deceptively, hypocritically.

simular *vt* to simulate.

simultaneidad f simultaneousness.

simultáneo/nea adj simultaneous.

sin prep without.

sinagoga f synagogue.

sinceridad f sincerity.

sincero/ra adj sincere.

síncope f (med) syncope, fainting fit.

sincronizar vt to synchronize.

sindical adj union compd.

sindicato m labor union; syndicate.

sinfín m: un ~ de a great many.

sinfonía f symphony.

singular adj singular; exceptional; peculiar, odd.

singularidad f singularity.

singularizar vt to distinguish; to singularize; ~se vr to distinguish oneself; to stand out.

siniestro/tra adj left; (fig) sinister; * m accident.

sinnúmero m = **sinfín**.

sino conj but; except; save; only; * m fate.

sinónimo/ma adj synonymous; * m synonym.

sinsabor m unpleasantness; disgust.

sintaxis f syntax.

síntesis f synthesis.

sintético/ca adj synthetic.

sintetizar vt synthesize.

síntoma m symptom.

sinuosidad f sinuosity; curve, wave.

sinuoso/sa adj sinuous; wavy.

sinvergüenza m/f rogue.

siquiera conj even if, even though; * adv at least.

sirena f siren; mermaid; car horn.

sirviente/ta m/f servant.

sisa f petty theft; cut, percentage.

sisear vt, vi to hiss.

sistema m system.

sistemático/ca adj systematic.

sitiar vt to besiege.

sitio m place; spot; site, location; room, space; job, post; (mil) siege, blockade.

situación f situation, position; standing.

situar vt to place, to situate; to invest; ~se vr to be established in place/business.

slip m underpants pl, briefs pl.

smoking m tuxedo.

sobaco m armpit, armhole.

sobar vt to handle, to soften; to knead; to massage, to rub hard; to rumple (clothes); to fondle.

soberanía f sovereignty.

soberano/na adj, m/f sovereign.

soberbia f pride, haughtiness; magnificence.

soberbio/bia adj proud, haughty; magnificent.

sobornar vt to suborn, to bribe.

soborno m subornation, bribery; bribe.

sobra f surplus, excess; de ~ spare, surplus, extra.

sobradamente adv too; amply.

sobrante adj remaining; * m surplus, remainder.

sobrar vt to exceed, to surpass; * vi to be more than enough; to remain, to be left.

sobrasada f pork sausage spread.

sobre prep on; on top of; above, over; more than; besides; * m envelope; Lat Am purse, handbag.

sobreabundancia f superabundance.

sobreabundar vi to superabound.

sobrecarga f extra load; (com) surcharge.

sobrecargar vt to overload; (com) to surcharge.

sobrecoger vt to surprise.

sobredosis f invar overdose.

sobreentender vt to deduce; ~se vr: se sobreentiende que . . . it is implied that . . . .

sobrehumano/na adj superhuman.

sobrellevar vt to carry; to tolerate.

sobremanera adv excessively.

sobremesa f: de ~ immediately after dinner.

sobrenatural adj supernatural.

sobrenaturalmente adv supernaturally.

sobrenombre m nickname.

sobrepasar vt to surpass.

sobreponer vt to put (something) over/on top of; ~se vr to pull through.

sobresaliente adj projecting; (fig) outstanding.

sobresalir vi to project; (fig) to stand out.

sobresaltar vt to frighten.

sobresalto m start, scare; sudden shock.

sobreseer vt: ~ una causa (law) to stay a case; * vi: ~ de to desist from.

sobreseimiento m dismissal, suspension.

sobrevenir vi to happen, to come unexpectedly; to supervene.

sobrevida f Lat Am survival.

sobreviviente adj surviving; * m/f survivor.

sobrevivir vi to survive.

sobrevolar vt to fly over.

sobriedad f sobriety.

sobrino/na m/f nephew/niece.

sobrio/ria adj sober, frugal.

socarrón/ona adj sarcastic; ironic(al).

socarronería f sarcasm; irony.

socavar vt to undermine.

socavón m hole.

sociabilidad f sociability.

sociable adj sociable.

social adj social.

socialdemócrata adj, m/f social democrat.

socialista adj, m/f socialist.

sociedad f society.

socio/cia m/f associate, member.

sociología f sociology.

sociólogo/ga m/f sociologist.

socorrer vt to help.

socorrido/da adj well-stocked/supplied.

socorrista m/f first aider; lifeguard.

socorro m help, aid, assistance, relief.

soda f soda; soda water.

sodomía f sodomy.

sodomita m sodomite.

soez adj dirty, obscene.

sofá m sofa.

sofisma m sophism.

sofista m/f sophist.

sofisticación f sophistication.
sofocar vt to suffocate.
software m (comput) software.
soga f rope.
sojuzgar vt to conquer, to subdue.
sol m sun; sunshine, sunlight.
solamente adv only, solely.
solapa f lapel.
solapado/da adj cunning, crafty, artful.
solar m building site; piece of land; ancestral home of a family; * adj solar.
solariego/ga adj belonging to the ancestral home of a family.
solaz m recreation, relaxation; solace, consolation.
solazar vt to provide relaxation for; to comfort.
soldada f wages pl.
soldadesca f military profession.
soldado m/f soldier; ~ raso private.
soldador m welder; soldering iron.
soldadura f soldering; solder.
soldar vt to solder; to weld; to unite.
soleado/da adj sunny.
soledad f solitude; loneliness.
solemne adj solemn; impressive, grand.
solemnidad f solemnity.
solemnizar vt to solemnize; to praise.
soler vi to be accustomed to, to be in the habit of.
solfeo m (mus) solfa.
solicitar vt to ask for, to seek; to apply for (a job); to canvass for; to chase after, to pursue.
solícito/ta adj diligent; solicitous.
solicitud f care, solicitude; request, petition.
solidaridad f solidarity.
solidario/ria adj joint; mutually binding.
solidez f solidity.
sólido/da adj solid.
soliloquio m soliloquy, monolog.
solista m/f soloist.
solitario/ria adj lonesome, solitary; * m solitaire; * m/f hermit.
sollozar vi to sob.
sollozo m sob.
solo m (mus) solo; ~/la adj alone, single; **a solas** alone, unaided.
sólo adv only.
solomillo m sirloin.
solsticio m solstice.
soltar vt to untie, to loosen; to set free, to let out; ~se vr to get loose; to come undone.
soltero/ra m/f bachelor/single woman; * adj single, unmarried.
soltura f looseness, slackness; agility, activity; fluency.
soluble adj soluble; solvable.
solución f solution; denouement.
solucionar vt to solve; to resolve.
solvente adj, m solvent.
sombra f shade; shadow.
sombrear vt to shade.

sombrero m hat.
sombrilla f parasol.
sombrío/bría adj shady, gloomy; sad.
somero/ra adj superficial.
someter vt to conquer (a country); to subject to one's will; to submit; to subdue; ~se vr to give in, to submit.
sometimiento m submission.
somnífero m sleeping pill.
somnolencia f sleepiness, drowsiness.
son m sound; rumor.
sonado/da adj celebrated; famous; generally reported.
sonaja f (mus) timbrel.
sonajero m (mus) small timbrel.
sonámbulo/la m/f sleepwalker; somnambulist.
sonar vt to ring; * vi to sound; to make a noise; to be pronounced; to be talked of; to sound familiar; ~se vr to blow one's nose.
sonata f (mus) sonata.
sonda f sounding; (med) probe.
sondear vt (mar) to sound; to probe; to bore.
sondeo m sounding; boring; (fig) poll.
soneto m sonnet.
sónico/ca adj sonic.
sonido m sound.
sonoro/ra adj sonorous.
sonreír(se) vi (vr) to smile.
sonrisa f smile.
sonrojarse vr to blush.
sonrojo m blush.
sonsacar vt to wheedle, cajole; to obtain by cunning.
sonsear vi Lat Am to fool around.
sonsera f Lat Am nonsense.
sonso/sa m/f Lat Am fool.
sonsonete m tapping noise; monotonous voice.
soñador/ra m/f dreamer.
soñar vt, vi to dream.
soñoliento/ta adj sleepy, drowsy.
sopa f soup; sop.
sopapo m punch, thump.
sopera f soup dish.
sopero m soup plate.
sopetón m: de ~ suddenly.
soplar vt to blow away, to blow off; to blow up, to inflate; * vi to blow, to puff.
soplete m blowlamp.
soplo m blowing; puff of wind; (col) tip-off.
soplón/ona m/f telltale.
sopor m drowsiness, sleepiness.
soporífero/ra adj soporific; * m sleeping pill.
soportable adj tolerable, bearable.
soportal m portico.
soportar vt to suffer, to tolerate; to support.
sorber vt to sip; to inhale; to swallow; to absorb.
sorbete m sherbet; sorbet.
sorbo m sip; gulp, swallow.
sordera f deafness.
sordidez f sordidness; dirtiness; meanness.
sórdido/da adj sordid; dirty; mean.

sorda/da *adj* deaf; silent, quiet; * *m/f* deaf person.

sordomudo/da *adj* deaf and dumb.

sorna *f* slyness; sarcasm; slowness.

soroche *m* mountain sickness.

sorprender *vt* to surprise.

sorpresa *f* surprise.

sortear *vt* to draw/cast (lots); to raffle; to avoid.

sorteo *m* draw; raffle.

sortija *f* ring; ringlet, curl.

sortilegio *m* sorcery.

sosegado/da *adj* quiet, peaceful.

sosegar *vt* to appease, to calm; * *vi* to rest.

sosería *f* insipidness; dullness.

sosiego *m* tranquility, calmness.

soslayar *vt* to do/place (something) obliquely.

soslayo *adv*: **al/de ~** obliquely, sideways.

soso/sa *adj* insipid, tasteless; dull.

sospecha *f* suspicion.

sospechar *vt* to suspect.

sospechoso/sa *adj* suspicious; suspect; * *m/f* suspect.

sostén *m* support; bra; sustenance.

sostener *vt* to sustain, to maintain; **~se** *vr* to support/maintain oneself; to contrive, to remain.

sostenimiento *m* support; maintenance; sustenance.

sota *f* jack, knave (in cards).

sotana *f* cassock.

sótano *m* basement, cellar.

sotavento *m* (*mar*) leeward, lee.

soto *m* grove, thicket.

squash *m* squash.

status *m* *invar* status.

su *pn* his, her, its, one's; their; your.

suave *adj* smooth, soft; delicate; gentle; mild, meek.

suavidad *f* softness, sweetness; suavity.

suavizar *vt* to soften.

subalterno/na *adj* secondary; auxiliary.

subasta *f* auction.

subastar *vt* to sell by auction.

subcampeón/ona *m/f* runner-up.

subconsciente *adj*, *m* subconscious.

subdesarrollado/da *adj* underdeveloped.

subdesarrollo *m* underdevelopment.

subdirector/ora *m/f* assistant director.

súbdito/ta *adj*, *m/f* subject.

subdividir *vt* to subdivide.

subdivisión *f* subdivision.

subestimar *vt* to underestimate.

subida *f* climb, ascent, rise in value/price.

subido/da *adj* deep-colored; high (price).

subir *vt*, *vi* to raise, to lift up; to go up; to climb, to ascend; to increase, to swell; to get in, to get on, to board; to rise (in price).

súbito/ta *adj* sudden, hasty; unforeseen.

subjetivo/va *adj* subjective.

subjuntivo *m* (*gr*) subjunctive.

sublevación *f* sedition, revolt.

sublevar *vt* to excite (a rebellion); to incite (a revolt); **~se** *vr* to revolt.

sublime *adj* sublime.

sublimidad *f* sublimity.

submarino/na *adj* underwater; * *m* submarine.

subnormal *adj* subnormal; * *m/f* person of low intelligence.

subordinación *f* subordination.

subrayar *vt* to underline.

subrepticio/cia *adj* surreptitious.

subsanar *vt* to excuse; to mend, to repair; to overcome.

subsidio *m* subsidy, aid; benefit, allowance.

subsistencia *f* subsistence.

subsistir *vi* to subsist.

su(b)stancia *f* substance.

su(b)stancial *adj* substantial.

su(b)stancioso/sa *adj* substantial; nutritious.

su(b)stracción *f* removal; (*math*) subtraction.

su(b)straer *vt* to remove; (*math*) to subtract; **~se** *vr* to avoid; to withdraw.

subterfugio *f* subterfuge.

subterráneo/nea *adj* subterranean, underground; * *m* underground passage; (*rail*) subway.

suburbio *m* slum quarter; suburbs *pl*.

subvencionar *vt* to subsidize.

subversión *f* subversion, overthrow.

subversivo/va *adj* subversive.

subvertir *vt* to subvert, to overthrow.

subyugar *vt* to subdue, to subjugate.

sucedáneo/nea *adj* substitute; * *m* substitute (food).

suceder *vt* to succeed, to inherit; * *vi* to happen.

sucesión *f* succession; issue, offspring; inheritance.

sucesivamente *adv*: **y así ~** and so on.

sucesivo/va *adj* successive.

suceso *m* event; incident.

sucesor/ra *m/f* successor; heir.

suciedad *f* dirtiness, filthiness; dirt.

sucinto/ta *adj* succinct, concise.

sucio/cia *adj* dirty, filthy; obscene; dishonest.

suculento/ta *adj* succulent, juicy.

sucumbir *vt* to succumb.

sucursal *f* branch (office).

sudar *vt*, *vi* to sweat.

sudeste *adj* southeast, southeastern; * *m* southeast.

sudoeste *adj* southwest, southwestern; * *m* southwest.

sudor *m* sweat.

sudorífico/ca *adj* sweaty.

suegra *f* mother-in-law.

suegro *m* father-in-law.

suela *f* sole (shoe).

sueldo *m* wages *pl*, salary.

suelo *m* ground; floor; soil, surface.

suelto/ta *adj* loose; free; detached; swift; * *m* loose change.

sueño *m* sleep; dream.

suero *m* (*med*) serum; whey.

suerte *f* fate, destiny, chance, lot, fortune, good luck; kind, sort.

suéter *m* sweater.

suficiencia *f* sufficiency, competence, fitness.

suficiente *adj* enough, sufficient; fit, capable.

sufragar *vt* to aid, to assist; * *vi Lat Am* to vote.

sufragio *m* vote, suffrage; aid, assistance.

sufrible *adj* bearable.

sufrido/da *adj* long-suffering, patient; hard-wearing.

sufrimiento *m* suffering; patience.

sufrir *vt* to suffer; to bear, to put up with; to support.

sugerencia *f* suggestion.

sugerir *vt* to suggest.

sugestión *f* suggestion.

suicida *adj* suicidal; * *m/f* suicide; suicidal person.

suicidio *m* suicide.

sujeción *f* subjection.

sujetacorbata *m Lat Am* tie-pin.

sujetador *m* fastener; bra.

sujetar *vt* to fasten, to hold down; to subdue; to subject; **~se** *vr* to subject oneself.

sujeto/ta *adj* fastened, secure; subject, liable; * *m* subject; individual.

sulfúrico *adj* sulfuric.

sultán *m* sultan.

sultana *f* sultana.

suma *f* total, sum; adding up; summary.

sumamente *adv* extremely.

sumar *vt* to add, to add up; to collect, to gather; * *vi* to add up.

sumario/ria *adj* brief, concise; * *m* summary.

sumergir *vt* to submerge, to sink; to immerse.

sumidero *m* sewer, drain.

suministrador/ra *m/f* provider, supplier.

suministrar *vt* to supply, to furnish.

sumir *vt* to sink, to submerge; (*fig*) to plunge.

sumisión *f* submission.

sumiso/sa *adj* submissive, docile.

sumo/ma *adj* great, extreme; highest, greatest; **a lo ~** at most.

suntuosidad *f* sumptuousness.

suntuoso/sa *adj* sumptuous.

súper *f* four-star (gas).

superable *adj* surmountable.

superabundancia *f* superabundance.

superabundar *vi* to superabound.

superar *vt* to surpass; to overcome; to exceed, to go beyond.

superficial *adj* superficial; shallow.

superficie *f* surface; area.

superfluo/lua *adj* superfluous.

superintendencia *f* supervision.

superintendente *m/f* superintendent, supervisor; floorwalker.

superior *adj* superior; upper; higher; better; * *m/f* superior.

superioridad *f* superiority.

superlativo/va *adj*, *m* (*gr*) superlative.

supermercado *m* supermarket.

superstición *f* superstition.

supersticioso/sa *adj* superstitious.

supervisor/ra *m/f* supervisor.

supervivencia *f* survival.

superviviente *m/f* survivor; * *adj* surviving.

suplantación *f* supplanting.

suplantar *vt* to supplant.

suplemento *m* supplement.

suplente *m/f* substitute.

supletorio/ria *adj* supplementary.

súplica *f* petition, request; supplication.

suplicante *adj*, *m/f* applicant; supplicant.

suplicar *vt* to beg (for), to plead (for); to beg; to plead with.

suplicio *m* torture.

suplir *vt* to supply; to make good, to make up for; to replace.

suponer *vt* to suppose; * *vi* to have authority.

suposición *f* supposition; authority.

supremo/ma *adj* supreme.

supresión *f* suppression; abolition; removal.

suprimir *vt* to suppress; to abolish; to remove; to delete.

supuesto *m* assumption; **~/ta** *adj* supposed; **~ que** *conj* since, granted that.

supuración *f* suppuration.

supurar *vt* to suppurate.

sur *adj* south, southern; * *m* south; south wind.

surcar *vt* to furrow; to cut, to score.

surco *m* furrow; groove.

surgir *vi* to emerge; to crop up.

surtido *m* assortment, supply.

surtir *vt* to supply, to furnish, to provide; * *vi* to spout, to spurt.

susceptible *adj* susceptible; impressionable.

suscitar *vt* to excite, to stir up.

suscribir *vt* to sign; to subscribe to.

suscripción *f* subscription.

suscriptor/ra *m/f* subscriber.

susodicho/cha *adj* above-mentioned.

suspender *vt* to suspend, to hang up; to stop; to fail (an exam etc).

suspensión *f* suspension; stoppage.

suspenso/sa *adj* hanging; suspended; failed; * *m Lat Am* suspense.

suspicacia *f* suspicion, mistrust.

suspicaz *adj* suspicious, mistrustful.

suspirar *vi* to sigh.

suspiro *m* sigh.

sustancia *f* = **substancia**.

sustancial *adj* = **substancial**.

sustancioso *adj* = **substancioso**.

sustantivo/va *adj*, *m* (*gr*) substantive, noun.

sustentar *vt* to sustain; to support, to nourish.

sustento *m* food, sustenance; support.

sustitución *f* substitution.

sustituir *vt* to substitute.

sustituto/ta *adj*, *m/f* substitute.

susto *m* fright, scare.

sustracción *f* subtraction.

sustraer *vt* to take away; to subtract.

susurrar *vi* to whisper; to murmur; to rustle; **~se** *vr* to be whispered about.

susurro *m* whisper; murmur.

sutil *adj* subtle; thin; delicate; very soft; keen, observant.

sutileza *f* subtlety; thinness; keenness.

suyo/ya *adj* his; hers; theirs; one's; his; her; its own; one's own; their own; **de ~** per se; **los ~s** *mpl* his own, near friends, relations, family, supporters.

T

tabaco *m* tobacco; (*col*) cigarettes *pl*.

tábano *m* horsefly.

tabaquería *f Lat Am* cigar store.

taberna *f* bar, tavern.

tabernero/ra *m/f* barman/barmaid, bartender.

tabicar *vt* to wall up.

tabique *m* thin wall; partition wall.

tabla *f* board; shelf; plank; slab; index of a book; bed of earth in a garden.

tablado *m* scaffold; platform; stage.

tablero *m* plank, board; chessboard; checkerboard; (*auto*) dashboard; bulletin board; gambling den.

tableta *f* tablet; (chocolate) bar.

tablilla *f* small board; (*med*) splint.

tablón *m* plank; beam; **~ de anuncios** bulletin board.

tabú *m* taboo.

taburete *m* stool.

tacañería *f* meanness; craftiness.

tacaño/ña *adj* mean, stingy; crafty.

tacha *f* fault, defect; small nail.

tachar *vt* to find fault with; to cross out, to erase.

tachuela *f* tack, nail.

tácito/ta *adj* tacit, silent; implied.

taciturno/na *adj* tacit, silent; sulky.

taco *m* stopper, plug; heel (of a shoe); wad; book of coupons; billiard cue.

tacón *m* heel.

taconear *vi* to stamp with one's heels; to walk on one's heels.

taconeo *m* stamping of the heels in dancing.

táctica *f* tactics *pl*.

tacto *m* touch, feeling; tact.

tafetán *m* taffeta.

tafilete *m* morocco leather.

tahona *f* bakery.

tahúr *m* gambler; cheat.

taimado/da *adj* sly, cunning, crafty.

tajada *f* slice; (*med*) hoarseness.

tajante *adj* sharp.

tajar *vt* to cut; to chop; to slice.

tajo *m* cut, incision; cleft, sheer drop; working area; chopping block.

tal *adj* such; **con ~ que** provided that; **no hay ~** no such thing.

tala *f* felling of trees.

taladrar *vt* to bore; to pierce.

taladro *m* drill; borer.

talante *m* mood; appearance; aspect; will.

talar *vt* to fell (trees); to desolate.

talco *m* talc.

talego/ga *m/f* bag; bagful.

talento *m* talent.

talismán *m* talisman.

talla *f* raised work; sculpture; stature, size; measure (of anything); hand, draw, turn (in cards).

tallado/da *adj* cut; carved; engraved.

tallador *m* engraver.

tallar *vt* to cut, to chop; to carve in wood; to engrave; to measure.

tallarines *mpl* noodles.

talle *m* shape; size; proportion; waist.

taller *m* workshop, laboratory.

tallo *m* shoot, sprout.

talón *m* heel; receipt; check.

talonario *m* check book; receipt book.

talonear *vt Lat Am* to spur.

talvez *adv Lat Am* perhaps.

tamaño *m* size, shape, bulk.

tamarindo *m* tamarind tree.

tambalearse *vr* to stagger, to waver.

tambaleo *m* staggering, reeling.

también *adv* also, as well; likewise; besides.

tambor *m* drum; drummer; eardrum.

tamborilear *vi* to drum.

tamborilero *m* drummer.

tamiz *m* fine sieve.

tampoco *adv* neither, nor.

tampón *m* tampon.

tan *adv* so.

tanda *f* turn; rotation; task; gang; number of persons employed in a workforce.

tangente *f* tangent.

tangible *adj* tangible.

tanque *m* tank; tanker.

tantear *vt* to reckon (up); to measure, to proportion; to consider; to examine.

tanteo *m* computation, calculation; valuation; test; scoring.

tanto *m* certain sum/quantity; point; goal; **~/ta** *adj* so much, as much; very great; * *adv* so much, as much; so long, as long.

tañido *m* tune; sound; clink.

tapa *f* lid, cover; snack; (*col*) **~ de los sesos** skull.

tapadera *f* lid (of a pot), cover.

tapar *vt* to stop up, to cover; to conceal, to hide.

taparrabo *m* loincloth.

tapete *m* tablecloth; *Lat Am* carpet.

tapia *f* wall.

tapiar *vt* to brick up; to stop up (a passage).

tapicería *f* tapestry; upholstery; upholsterer's place of business.

tapicero *m* tapestry-maker; upholsterer.

tapiz *m* tapestry; carpet.

tapizar vt to upholster.

tapón m cork, plug, bung; *Lat Am* fuse.

taquigrafía f stenography; shorthand.

taquígrafo/fa m/f stenographer.

taquilla f booking office; takings pl.

taquillero/ra m/f ticket clerk.

tara f (com) tare.

tarántula f tarantula.

tardanza f slowness, delay.

tardar vi to delay; to take a long time; to be late.

tarde f afternoon; evening; * adv late.

tardío/día adj late; slow, tardy.

tardo/da adj sluggish, tardy.

tarea f task.

tarifa f tariff; price list.

tarima f platform; step.

tarjeta f card; visiting card; ~ **postal** postcard; ~ **de crédito** credit card.

tarro m pot.

tarta f tart; cake.

tartamudear vi to stutter, to stammer.

tartamudo/da adj stammering.

tarugo m wooden peg/pin.

tasa f rate; measure, rule; valuation; ~**s de aeropuerto** airport tax.

tasación f valuation, appraisal.

tasador m appraiser.

tasar vt to appraise, to value.

tasca f (col) joint, barroom, saloon.

tata m *Lat Am* (col) pop, dad.

tatarabuelo/la m/f great-great-grandfather/mother.

tataranieto/ta m/f great-great-grandson/daughter.

tatuaje m tattoo; tattooing.

tatuar vt to tattoo.

taurino/na adj bullfighting compd; *Lat Am* Taurean (zodiac sign).

Tauro m Taurus (zodiac sign).

taxi m taxi.

taxista m/f taxi driver.

taza f cup; basin of a fountain.

té m (bot) tea.

te pn you.

tea f torch.

teatral adj theatrical.

teatro m theater, playhouse.

tebeo m comic.

techo m roof; ceiling.

techumbre f upper roof, ceiling.

tecla f key (of an organ, piano etc).

teclado m keyboard.

técnico/ca adj technical.

tecnología f technology.

tedio m boredom; dislike, abhorrence.

teja f tile.

tejado m roof covered with tiles.

tejanos mpl jeans pl.

tejar vt to tile.

tejedor m weaver.

tejemaneje m artfulness, cleverness; restlessness.

tejer vt to weave.

tejido m texture; web.

tejo m quoit (a ring of iron, plastic etc used in the game of quoits); hopscotch; yew tree.

tejón m badger.

tela f cloth; material.

telar m loom.

telaraña f cobweb.

telebanca f telephone banking.

telecomedia f sitcom.

telediario m television news.

telefax m invar fax; fax (machine).

telefonear vt to telephone.

telefonema m *Lat Am* telephone call.

telefónico/ca adj telephone compd.

teléfono m (tele)phone.

teléfono público m payphone.

telegráfico/ca adj telegraphic.

telégrafo m telegraph.

telegrama m telegram.

telescopio m telescope.

teletienda f home shopping program.

teletrabajador/ra m/f teleworker.

teletrabajo m teleworking.

televidente m/f viewer.

televisar vt to televise.

televisión f television; ~ **por cable** cable television.

televisor m television set.

télex m telex.

telón m drape.

tema m theme.

temblar vi to tremble.

temblón/ona adj trembling.

temblor m trembling; earthquake.

temer vt to fear, to doubt; * vi to be afraid.

temerario/ria adj rash.

temeridad f temerity, imprudence.

temeroso/sa adj timid; frightful.

temible adj dreadful, terrible.

temor m dread, fear.

témpano m ice-floe.

temperamento m temperament.

temperatura f temperature.

tempested f tempest, storm; violent commotion.

tempestuoso/sa adj tempestuous, stormy.

templado/da adj temperate, tempered.

templanza f temperance, moderation.

templar vt to temper, to moderate, to cool; to tune; ~**se** vr to be moderate.

temple m temperature; tempera; temperament; tuning; **al** ~ painted in distemper.

templo m temple.

temporada f time, season; epoch, -period.

temporal adj temporary, temporal; * m tempest, storm.

temporariamente adv *Lat Am* temporarily.

temporario/ria adj *Lat Am* temporary.

temprano/na adj early, anticipated; * adv early; very early, prematurely.

tenacidad f tenacity; obstinacy.

tenacillas fpl small tongs pl.

tenaz adj tenacious; stubborn.

tenaza(s) f(pl) tongs pl, pincers pl.

tenazmente adv tenaciously; obstinately.

tendedero m clothes line.

tendencia f tendency.

tender vt to stretch out; to expand; to extend; to hang out; to lay; Lat Am to lay, to set; ~**se** vr to stretch oneself out.

tenderete m stall; display of goods.

tendero/ra m/f shopkeeper.

tendido/da adj lying down; hanging; * m row of seats for the spectators at a bullfight.

tendón m tendon, sinew.

tenebroso/sa adj dark, obscure.

tenedor m holder, keeper, tenant; fork.

tenencia f possession; tenancy; tenure.

tener vt to have; to take; to hold; to possess; ~**se** vr to stand upright; to stop, to halt; to resist; to adhere.

tenia f tapeworm.

teniente m lieutenant.

tenis m tennis.

tenista m/f tennis player.

tenor m meaning; (mus) tenor.

tensar vt to tauten; to draw.

tensión f tension.

tenso/sa adj tense.

tentación f temptation.

tentador/ra m/f tempter.

tentar vt to touch; to try; to tempt; to attempt.

tentativa f attempt.

tentempié m (col) snack.

tenue adj thin; tenuous, slender.

tenuidad f slenderness; weakness; trifle.

teñir vt to tinge, to dye.

teología f theology, divinity.

teológico/ca adj theological.

teólogo m theologian, divine.

teorema f theorem.

teoría, teórica f theory.

teórico/ca adj theoretical.

terapéutico/ca adj therapeutic.

terapia f therapy.

tercermundista adj Third World compd.

tercer(o)/ra adj third; * m (law) third party.

tercerización f Lat Am outsourcing.

tercerizar vt Lat Am to outsource.

terceto m (mus) trio.

terciar vt to put on sideways; to divide into three parts; * vi to mediate; to take part.

terciarización f Lat Am outsourcing.

terciarizar vt Lat Am to outsource.

tercio/cia adj third; * m third part.

terciopelo m velvet.

terco/ca adj obstinate.

tergiversación f distortion; evasion.

tergiversar vt to distort.

termal adj thermal.

termas fpl thermal waters pl.

terminación f termination; conclusion; last syllable of a word.

terminal adj, m/f terminal.

terminante adj decisive; categorical.

terminar vt to finish; to end; to terminate; * vi to end; to stop.

término m term; end; boundary; limit; terminus.

terminología f terminology.

termodinámico/ca adj thermodynamic.

termómetro m thermometer.

termo m flask.

termostato m thermostat.

ternero/ra m/f calf; veal; heifer.

ternilla f gristle.

ternilloso/sa adj gristly.

terno m three-piece suit.

ternura f tenderness.

terquedad f stubbornness, obstinacy.

terrado m terrace.

terraplén m terrace; platform.

terrateniente m/f landowner.

terraza f balcony; (flat) roof; terrace (in fields).

terremoto m earthquake.

terrenal adj terrestrial, earthly.

terreno/na adj earthly, terrestrial; * m land, ground, field.

terrestre adj terrestrial.

terrible adj terrible, dreadful; ferocious.

territorial adj territorial.

territorio m territory.

terrón m clod of earth; lump; ~**ones** mpl real estate.

terror m terror, dread.

terrorismo m terrorism.

terrorista m/f terrorist.

terso/sa adj smooth, glossy.

tersura f smoothness; shine.

tertulia f club, assembly, circle.

tesis f invar thesis.

tesón m tenacity, firmness.

tesorero m treasurer.

tesoro m treasure; exchequer.

testamentaría f testamentary execution.

testamentario m executor of a will; ~**/ria** adj testamentary.

testamento m will, testament.

testar vt, vi to make one's will.

testarudo/da adj obstinate.

testículo m testicle.

testificación f attestation.

testificar vt to attest, to witness.

testigo m witness, deponent.

testimoniar vt to attest, to bear witness to.

testimonio m testimony.

teta f teat.

tétanos m tetanus.

tetera f teapot.

tetilla f nipple; teat (of a bottle).

tétrico/ca adj gloomy, sullen, surly.

textil adj textile compd.

texto m text.

textual adj textual.

textura f texture.

tez f complexion, hue.

ti *pn* you; yourself.

tía *f* aunt; (*col*) dame.

tiara *f* tiara.

tibieza *f* lukewarmness.

tibio/bia *adj* lukewarm.

tiburón *m* shark.

tico/ca *m/f Lat Am* (*col*) Costa -Rican.

tiempo *m* time; term; weather; (*gr*) tense; occasion, opportunity; season.

tienda *f* tent; awning; tilt; store.

tiento *m* touch; circumspection; **a ~/a tientas** gropingly.

tierno/na *adj* tender; * *m Lat Am* baby.

tierra *f* earth; land, ground; native country.

tieso/sa *adj* stiff, hard, firm; robust; valiant; stubborn.

tiesto *m* large earthenware pot.

tifón *m* typhoon.

tifus *m* typhus.

tigre *m* tiger; *Lat Am* jaguar.

tijeras *fpl* scissors *pl*.

tijeretada *f* cut (with scissors), clip.

tijereta *f* earwig.

tijeretear *vt* to cut (with scissors).

tildar *vt* to brand, to stigmatize.

tilde *f* tilde (ñ).

tilo *m* lime tree.

timar *vt* to steal; to swindle.

timbrar *vt* to stamp.

timbre *m* stamp; bell; timbre; stamp duty.

timidez *f* timidity.

tímido/da *adj* timid; cowardly.

timo *m* swindle.

timón *m* helm, rudder.

tímpano *m* eardrum; small drum.

tina *f* tub; bath (tub).

tinaja *f* large earthenware jar.

tinglado *m* shed; trick; intrigue.

tinieblas *fpl* darkness; shadows *pl*.

tino *m* skill; judgement, prudence.

tinta *f* ink; tint, dye; color.

tinte *m* tint, dye; dry cleaner's (premises).

tintero *m* inkwell.

tinto/ta *adj* dyed; * *m* red wine.

tintorería *f* dry cleaner's (place of business).

tintura *f* tincture; dyeing.

tiña *f* scab.

tiñoso/sa *adj* scabby, scurvy; niggardly.

tío *m* uncle; (*col*) guy.

tiovivo *m* merry-go-round.

tipear *vt Lat Am* to type.

típico/ca *adj* typical.

tiple *m* (*mus*) treble; * *f* soprano.

tipo *m* type; norm; pattern; guy.

tipografía *f* typography.

tipográfico/ca *adj* typographical.

tipógrafo *m* printer, typographer.

tiquet *m* ticket; cash slip.

tiquismiquis *m invar* fussy person.

tira *f* abundance; strip.

tirabuzón *m* curl.

tirachinas *m invar* catapult.

tirado/da *adj* dirt-cheap; (*col*) very easy; * *f* cast; distance; series; edition.

tirador *m* handle.

tiraje *m Lat Am* print run.

tiranía *f* tyranny.

tiránico/ca *adj* tyrannical.

tiranizar *vt* to tyrannize.

tirano/na *m/f* tyrant.

tirante *m* joist; stay; strap; brace; * *adj* taut, extended, drawn.

tirantez *f* tension; tautness.

tirar *vt* to throw; to pull; to draw; to drop; to tend, to aim at; * *vi* to shoot; to pull; to go; to tend to.

Tirita™ *f* Band-Aid™, adhesive tape, sticking plaster.

tiritar *vi* to shiver.

tiritona *f* shiver; shaking with cold.

tiro *m* throw, shot; prank; set of coach horses; **errar el ~** to miss (at shooting).

tirón *m* pull, haul, tug.

tirotear *vt* to shoot at.

tiroteo *m* shooting; sharpshooting.

tirria *f* antipathy.

tísico/ca *adj* consumptive.

tisis *f* tuberculosis.

títere *m* puppet; ridiculous little fellow.

titiritero/ra *m/f* puppeteer.

titubear *vi* to stammer; to stagger; to hesitate.

titubeo *m* staggering; hesitation.

titular *adj* titular; * *m/f* occupant; * *m* headline; * *vt* to title; **~se** *vr* to obtain a title.

título *m* title; name; **a ~** on pretense, under pretext.

tiza *f* chalk.

tiznar *vt* to stain; to tarnish.

tizne *m* soot; smut.

tiznón *m* spot, stain.

tizón *m* half-burnt wood.

toalla *f* towel; **~ higiénica** *Lat Am* sanitary napkin.

tobillo *m* ankle.

tobogán *m* toboggan, sled; roller-coaster; slide.

toca *f* headdress.

tocadiscos *m invar* record player.

tocado *m* headdress, headgear.

tocador *m* dressing table; dressing room.

tocante *prep*: **~ a** concerning, relating to.

tocar *vt* to touch; to strike; (*mus*) to play; to ring (a bell); * *vi* to belong; to concern; to knock; to call; to be a duty/obligation.

tocayo/ya *m/f* namesake.

tocino *m* bacon.

todavía *adv* even; yet, still.

todo/da *adj* all, entire; every; * *pn* everything, all; * *m* whole.

todopoderoso/sa *adj* almighty.

todoterreno *m* all-terrain vehicle.

toga *f* toga; gown.

toldo *m* awning; parasol.

tolerable *adj* tolerable.

tolerancia *f* tolerance, indulgence.

tolerante *adj* tolerant.

tolerar *vt* to tolerate, to suffer.

toma *f* taking (as in the taking of vows); (*med*) dose; plug, socket.

tomacorriente *f Lat Am* socket.

tomar *vt* to take; to seize, to grasp; to understand; to interpret, to perceive; to drink; to acquire; * *vi Lat Am* to drink; to take.

tomate *m* tomato.

tomillo *m* thyme.

tomo *m* bulk; tome; volume.

ton *m*: **sin ~ ni son** without rhyme or reason.

tonada *f* tune, melody.

tonadilla *f* interlude of music; short tune.

tonalidad *f* tone.

tonel *m* cask, barrel.

tonelada *f* ton; (*mar*) tonnage duty.

tónico/ca *adj* tonic, strengthening; * *m* tonic; * *f* tonic (water); (*mus*) tonic; (*fig*) keynote.

tonificar *vt* to tone up.

tono *m* tone.

tono de marcar *m* dial tone.

tontada *f* nonsense.

tontear *vi* to talk nonsense; to act foolishly.

tontera *f Lat Am* foolery, nonsense.

tontería *f* foolery, nonsense.

tonto/ta *adj* stupid, foolish.

topacio *m* topaz.

topar *vt* to run into; to find.

tope *m* butt; scuffle; **~s** *mpl* (*rail*) buffers *pl*.

topera *f* molehill.

tópico/ca *adj* topical.

topo *m* mole; stumbler.

topografía *f* topography.

topográfico/ca *adj* topographical.

toque *m* touch; bell-ringing; crisis.

toquilla *f* headscarf; shawl.

tórax *m* thorax.

torbellino *m* whirlwind.

torcedura *f* twisting.

torcer *vt* to twist, to curve; to turn; to sprain; **~se** *vr* to bend; to go wrong; * *vi* to turn off.

torcido/da *adj* oblique; crooked.

torcimiento *m* bending; deflection; circumlocution.

tordo *m* thrush; **~/da** *adj* speckled black and white.

torear *vt* to avoid; to tease; * *vi* to fight bulls.

toreo *m* bullfighting.

torero *m* bullfighter.

toril *m* bull pen (at bullfight).

tormenta *f* storm, tempest.

tormento *m* torment, pain, anguish; torture.

tornar *vt* to return; to restore; **~se** *vr* to become; * *vi* to return; **~ a hacer** to do again.

tornasolado *adj* iridescent; shimmering.

torneo *m* tournament.

tornillo *m* screw.

torniquete *m* turnstile; (*med*) tourniquet.

torno *m* winch; revolution.

toro *m* bull.

toronja *f* grapefruit.

torpe *adj* dull, heavy; stupid.

torpedo *m* torpedo.

torpeza *f* heaviness, dullness; torpor; stupidity.

torre *f* tower; turret; steeple of a church.

torrefacto/ta *adj* roasted.

torreja *f Lat Am* French toast.

torrente *m* torrent.

tórrido/da *adj* torrid, parched, hot.

torrija *f* French toast.

torso *m* torso.

torta *f* cake; (*col*) slap.

tortícolis *f invar* stiff neck.

tortilla *f* omelet; pancake; *Lat Am* tortilla.

tórtola *f* turtledove.

tortuga *f* tortoise.

tortuoso/sa *adj* tortuous, circuitous.

tortura *f* torture.

torvo/va *adj* stern, grim.

tos *f* cough.

toscamente *adv* coarsely, grossly.

tosco/ca *adj* coarse, ill-bred, clumsy.

toser *vi* to cough.

tostada *f* slice of toast.

tostado/da *adj* parched; sunburnt; light-yellow; light-brown.

tostador *m* toaster.

tostar *vt* to toast, to roast.

total *m* whole, totality; * *adj* total, entire; * *adv* in short.

totalidad *f* totality.

totalitario/ria *adj* totalitarian.

totuma *f Lat Am* calabash.

tóxico/ca *adj* toxic; * *m* poison.

toxicómano/na *m/f* drug addict.

tozudo/da *adj* obstinate.

traba *f* obstacle, impediment; trammel, fetter.

trabajador/ra *adj* working; * *m/f* worker.

trabajar *vt* to work, to labor; to persuade; to push; * *vi* to strive.

trabajo *m* work, labor, toil; difficulty; **~s** *mpl* troubles *pl*.

trabajoso/sa *adj* laborious; painful.

trabalenguas *m invar* tongue twister.

trabar *vt* to join, to unite; to take hold of; to fetter, to shackle.

trabucarse *vr* to mistake.

tracción *f* traction; **~ delantera/trasera** front-wheel/rear-wheel drive.

tractor *m* tractor.

tradición *f* tradition.

traducción *f* translation.

traducir *vt* to translate.

traductor,ra *m/f* translator.

traer *vt* to bring, to carry; to attract; to persuade; to wear; to cause.

traficante *m* merchant, dealer.

traficar *vi* to trade, to do business, to deal.

tráfico *m* traffic, trade.

tragaldabas *m/f invar* glutton.

tragaluz *m* skylight.

tragamonedas *f invar Lat Am* slot machine.

tragaperras *f invar* slot machine.

tragar *vt* to swallow; to swallow up.

tragedia *f* tragedy.

trágico/ca *adj* tragic.

trago *m* drink; gulp; adversity, misfortune.

tragón/ona *adj* gluttonous.

traición *f* treason.

traicionar *vt* to betray.

traicionero/ra *adj* treacherous.

traidor/ra *m/f* traitor; * *adj* treacherous.

traje *m* dress, costume; suit.

trajín *m* haulage; (*col*) bustle.

trajinar *vt* to carry; * *vi* to bustle about; to travel around.

trama *f* weft, woof; (*fig*) plot; intrigue.

tramar *vt* to weave; to plot.

tramitar *vt* to transact; to negotiate; to handle.

trámite *m* path; (*law*) procedure.

tramo *m* section; piece of ground; flight of stairs.

tramoya *f* scene, theatrical decoration; trick.

tramoyista *m* scene-painter; swindler.

trampa *f* trap, snare; trapdoor; fraud.

trampear *vt* to swindle, to deceive; * *vi* to cheat.

trampolín *m* trampoline; diving board.

tramposo/sa *adj* deceitful, swindling.

tranca *f* bar, crossbeam.

trance *m* danger; last stage of life; trance.

tranco *m* long step/stride.

tranquilidad *f* tranquility; repose, heart's ease.

tranquilizar *vt* to calm; to reassure.

tranquilo/la *adj* tranquil, calm, quiet.

transacción *f* transaction.

transbordador *m* ferry.

transbordar *vt* to transfer.

transbordo *m* transfer; **hacer ~** to change (trains).

transcribir *vt* to transcribe; to copy.

transcurrir *vi* to pass; to turn out.

transcurso *m*: **~ del tiempo** course of time.

transeúnte *adj* transitory; * *m* passerby.

transferencia *f* transference; (*com*) transfer.

transferir *vt* to transfer; to defer.

transfiguración *f* transformation, transfiguration.

transformación *f* transformation.

transformador *m* transformer.

transformar *vt* to transform; **~se** *vr* to change one's sentiments/manners.

tránsfuga, **tránsfugo** *mp* deserter; fugitive; defector.

transfusión *f* transfusion.

transgresión *f* transgression.

transgresor *m* transgressor.

transición *f* transition.

transido/da *adj* worn out with anguish, overcome.

transigir *vi* to compromise.

transistor *m* transistor.

transitar *vi* to travel, to pass through a place.

transitivo/va *adj* transitive.

tránsito *m* passage; transition; road, way; change; removal; death of holy/virtuous persons.

transitorio/ria *adj* transitory.

transmisión *f* transmission; transfer; broadcast.

transmitir *vt* to transmit; to broadcast.

transmutación *f* transmutation.

transmutar *vt* to transmute.

transparencia *f* transparency; clearness; slide.

transparentarse *vr* to be transparent; to shine through.

transparente *adj* transparent.

transpiración *f* perspiration; transpiration.

transpirar *vt* to perspire; to transpire.

transportar *vt* to transport, to convey.

transporte *m* transportation.

transposición *f* transposition, transposal.

transversal *adj* transverse; collateral.

tranvía *m* streetcar, trolley car.

trapacería *f* fraud, deceit.

trapacero/ra *adj* deceitful.

trapecio *m* trapeze.

trapecista *m/f* trapeze artist.

trapero/ra *m/f* ragpicker; dealer in rags.

trapicheo *m* (*col*) fiddle.

trapo *m* rag, tatter.

tráquea *f* windpipe.

traqueteo *m* rattling.

tras *prep* after, behind.

trascendencia *f* transcendency; penetration.

trascendental *adj* transcendental.

trascender *vi* to smell; to come out; **~ de** to go beyond.

trasegar *vt* to move about; to decant.

trasero/ra *adj* back; * *m* bottom.

trasfondo *m* background.

trasgredir *vt* to contravene.

trashumante *adj* migrating.

trasiego *m* removal; decanting (of drinks).

trasladar *vt* to transport; to transfer; to postpone; to transcribe, to copy; **~se** *vr* to move.

traslado *m* move; removal.

traslucirse *vr* to be transparent; to conjecture.

trasluz *m* reflected light.

trasnochar *vi* to watch, to sit up the whole night.

traspaperlarse *vr* to get mislaid among other papers.

traspasar *vt* to remove, to transport; to transfix, to pierce; to return; to exceed (the proper bounds); to transfer.

traspaso *m* transfer, sale.

traspié *m* trip; slip, stumble.

trasplantar *vt* to transplant.

trasplante *m* transplant.

trasquilar *vt* to shear (sheep); to clip.

trasquilón *m* cut (of the shears); badly cut hair.

traste *m* fret (of a guitar); **dar al ~ con algo** to ruin something.

trastear *vt* to move (furniture).

trastera f lumber.

trastero m lumber room.

trastienda f back room behind a shop/store.

trasto m piece of junk; useless person.

trastornado/da adj crazy.

trastornar vt to overthrow, to overturn; to confuse; **~se** vr to go crazy.

trastorno m overturning; confusion.

trastrocar vt to invert (the order of things).

tratable adj friendly.

tratado m treaty, convention; treatise.

tratamiento m treatment; style of address.

tratante m dealer.

tratar vt to traffic, to trade; to use; to treat; to handle; to address; **~se** vr to treat each other.

trato m treatment; manner, address; trade, traffic; conversation; (com) agreement.

trauma m trauma.

través m (fig) reverse; **de/al ~** across, crossways; **a ~ de** prep across; over; through.

travesaño m crossbeam; transom.

travesía f crossing; crossroad; side street; trajectory; (mar) crosswind.

travesura f wit; wickedness.

travieso/sa adj restless, uneasy, fidgety; turbulent; lively; naughty.

trayecto m road; journey, stretch; course.

trayectoria f trajectory; path.

traza f first sketch; trace, outline; project; manner; means; appearance.

trazar vt to plan out; to project; to trace.

trazo m sketch, plan, design.

trébedes fpl trivet, tripod.

trébol m trefoil, clover.

trece adj m thirteen; thirteenth.

trecho m space, distance of time/place; **a ~s** at intervals.

tregua f truce, cessation of hostilities.

treinta adj, m thirty.

tremendo/da adj terrible, formidable; awful, grand.

tremolar vt to hoist (the colors); to wave.

trémulo/la adj tremulous, trembling.

tren m train, retinue; baggage; (rail) train; **~ de alta velocidad** high-speed train; **~ de mercancías** freight train.

trenza f plait (in hair); braid.

trenzar vt to braid, to plait.

trepar vi to climb; to crawl.

tres adj, m three.

tresillo m three-piece suite; (mus) triplet.

treta f thrust (fencing); trick.

triangular adj triangular.

triángulo m triangle.

tribu f tribe.

tribulación f tribulation, affliction.

tribuna f tribune.

tribunal m tribunal, court of justice.

tributar vt to pay; to contribute to; to pay (homage, respect).

tributario/ria adj tributary.

tributo m tribute.

tricolor adj tricolored.

tricotar vi to knit.

tridente m trident.

trienal adj triennial.

trienio m period of three years.

trigal m wheat field.

trigésimo/ma adj thirtieth.

trigo m wheat.

trigueño/ña adj corn-colored; olive-skinned.

trillado/da adj beaten; trite, stale, hackneyed; **camino ~** common routine.

trilladora f threshing machine.

trillar vt to thresh.

trimestral adj quarterly, three-monthly.

trimestre m period of three months.

trinar vi to trill, to quaver; to be angry.

trincar vt to tie up; to pinion.

trinchante m carver; carving knife.

trinchar vt to carve, to cut up (meat).

trinchera f trench, entrenchment.

trineo m sled, sleigh.

Trinidad f Trinity.

trino m trill.

trío m (mus) trio.

tripa f gut, intestine; **~s** fpl guts; tripe.

triple adj triple, treble.

triplicar vt to treble.

trípode m tripod, trivet.

tripulación f crew.

tripulante m/f crewman/woman.

tripular vt to man; to drive.

triquiñuela f trick.

triquitraque m clack, clatter; clashing.

tris m invar: **estar en un ~ de** to be on the point of.

triste adj sad, mournful, melancholy.

tristeza f sadness, mourning.

trituración f pulverization.

triturar vt to reduce to powder; to grind, to pound.

triunfal adj triumphal.

triunfar vi to triumph; to trump (in cards).

triunfo m triumph; trump (in cards).

trivial adj trivial.

trivialidad f triviality.

triza f: **hacer ~s** to smash to bits; to tear to shreds.

trocar vt to exchange.

trocha f short cut.

troche: **a ~ y moche** adv helter-skelter.

trofeo m trophy.

tromba f whirlwind.

trombón m trombone.

trombosis f invar thrombosis.

trompa f trumpet; proboscis; spinning top.

trompazo m heavy blow; accident; Lat Am punch.

trompear vt Lat Am to punch.

trompeta f trumpet; * m trumpeter.

trompetilla f small trumpet; speaking-trumpet.

trompicón *m* stumble.

trompo *m* spinning top.

tronar *vi* to thunder; to rage.

troncar *vt* to truncate, to mutilate.

troncha *f Lat Am* chunk.

tronchar *vt* to cut off; to shatter; to tire out.

troncho *m* sprig, stem/stalk.

tronco *m* trunk (of the body, tree); log; stock.

tronera *f* loophole; small window; pocket (of a billiard table).

trono *m* throne.

tropa *f* troop.

tropel *m* confused noise; hurry; bustle, confusion; heap of things; crowd; **en ~** in a tumultuous and confused manner.

tropelía *f* outrage.

tropezar *vi* to stumble; * *vt* to meet accidentally.

tropezón/ona *adj* stumbling; * *m* trip; **a ~ones** by fits and starts.

tropical *adj* tropical.

trópico *m* tropic.

tropiezo *m* stumble, trip; obstacle; slip, fault; quarrel; dispute.

trotamundos *m invar* globetrotter.

trotar *vi* to trot.

trote *m* trot; traveling.

trovador/ra *m/f* troubadour.

trozar *vt Lat Am* to cut up.

trozo *m* piece.

trucha *f* trout.

truco *m* knack; trick.

trueno *m* thunderclap.

trueque *m* exchange.

trufa *f* truffle.

truhán *adj* rogue.

truncado/da *adj* truncated.

truncamiento *m* truncation.

truncar *vt* to truncate, to maim.

trunco/ca *adj Lat Am* incomplete.

tu *adj* your.

tú *pn* you.

tubérculo *m* tuber.

tuberculosis *f* tuberculosis.

tubería *f* pipe; pipeline.

tubo *m* tube.

tuerca *f* screw.

tuerto/ta *adj* one-eyed; squint-eyed; * *m/f* one-eyed person.

tuétano *m* marrow.

tufarada *f* strong scent/smell.

tufo *m* warm vapor arising from the earth; offensive smell.

tugurio *m* slum.

tul *m* tulle.

tulipán *m* tulip.

tullido/da *adj* disabled, maimed.

tumba *f* tomb.

tumbar *vt* to knock down; * *vi* to tumble (to fall down); **~se** *vr* to lie down to sleep.

tumbo *m* fall; jolt.

tumbona *f* easy chair; beach chair.

tumor *m* tumor, growth.

túmulo *m* tomb; sepulchral monument.

tumulto *m* tumult, uproar.

tumultuoso/sa *adj* tumultuous.

tuna *f* student music group; *Lat Am* prickly pear.

tunda *f* beating.

túnel *m* tunnel.

túnica *f* tunic.

tuno *m* rogue.

tupé *m* toupee, wig/hairpiece.

tupido/da *adj* dense.

tupir *vt* to press close; **~se** *vr* to stuff oneself.

turbación *f* perturbation, confusion; trouble, disorder.

turbado/da *adj* disturbed.

turbante *m* turban.

turbar *vt* to disturb, to trouble; **~se** *vr* to be disturbed.

turbina *f* turbine.

turbio/bia *adj* muddy; troubled.

turbulencia *f* turbulence; disturbance.

turbulento/ta *adj* muddy; turbulent.

turismo *m* tourism; **~ rural** rural tourism.

turista *m/f* tourist, vacationer.

turístico/ca *adj* tourist *compd*.

turnar *vi* to alternate.

turno *m* turn; shift; opportunity.

turquesa *f* turquoise.

turrón *m* nougat (almond cake).

tutear *vt* to address as **tu**.

tutela *f* guardianship, tutelage.

tutelar *adj* tutelar, tutelary.

tutor *m* guardian, tutor.

tutora *f* tutoress.

tutoría *f* tutelage.

tuyo/ya *adj* yours; **~s** *pl* friends and relations of the party addressed.

U

u *conj* o (instead of **o** before **o** and **ho**).

ubicar *vt* to place; *Lat Am* to locate; *Lat Am* to find; **~se** *vr* to be located.

ubre *f* udder.

ufanarse *vr* to boast.

ufano/na *adj* haughty, arrogant.

ujier *m* usher.

úlcera *f* ulcer.

ulcerar *vi* to ulcerate.

ulterior *adj* ulterior; farther, further.

últimamente *adv* lately.

ultimar *vt* to finalize; to finish; *Lat Am* to kill.

ultimátum *m* ultimatum.

último/ma *adj* last; latest; bottom; top.

ultrajar *vt* to outrage; to despise; to abuse.

ultraje *m* outrage.

ultramar *adj, m* overseas.

ultramarinos *mpl* foodstuffs, groceries.

ultrasónico/ca *adj* ultrasonic.

umbilical *adj* umbilical.

umbral *m* threshold.
un/una *art* a, an; * *adj, m* one (for **uno**).
unánime *adj* unanimous.
unanimidad *f* unanimity.
unción *f* unction; extreme/last unction.
ungir *vt* to anoint.
ungüento *m* ointment.
únicamente *adv* only, simply.
único/ca *adj* only; singular, unique.
unicornio *m* unicorn.
unidad *f* unity; unit; conformity; union.
unificar *vt* to unite.
uniformar *vt* to make uniform.
uniforme *adj* uniform; * *m* (*mil*) uniform,
   regimentals *pl*.
uniformidad *f* uniformity.
unilateral *adj* unilateral.
unión *f* union; **U~ Europea** European Union.
unir *vt* to join, to unite; to mingle; to bind, to
   tie; **~se** *vr* to associate.
unísono/na *adj* unison.
universal *adj* universal.
universalidad *f* universality.
universidad *f* university.
universitario/ria *adj* university *compd*; * *m/f*
   student.
universo *m* universe.
uno *m* one; **~/una** *adj* one; sole, only; **~ a otro** one
   another; **~ a ~** one by one; **a una** jointly together.
untar *vt* to anoint; to grease; (*col*) to bribe.
uña *f* nail; hoof; claw, talon.
¡upa! up! up!
urbanidad *f* urbanity, politeness.
uranio *m* uranium.
Urano *m* Uranus (planet).
urbanismo *m* town planning.
urbanización *f* urban development.
urbano/na *adj* urban; urbane, polite.
urdimbre *f* warp; intrigue.
urdir *vt* to warp; to contrive.
urgencia *f* urgency; emergency; need, necessity.
urgente *adj* urgent.
urgentemente *adv* urgently.
urgir *vi* to be urgent.
urinario/ria *adj* urinary; * *m* urinal.
urna *f* urn; ballot box.
urraca *f* magpie.
usado/da *adj* used; experienced; worn.
usanza *f* usage, use, custom.
usar *vt* to use, to make use of; to wear; **~se** *vr*
   to be used.
uso *m* use, service; custom; mode.
usted *pn* you.
usuario *m* user.
usufructo *m* (*law*) usufruct, use.
usura *f* usury.
usurario/ria *adj* usurious.
usurero *m* usurer.
usurpación *f* usurpation.
usurpar *vt* to usurp.
utensilio *m* utensil.

uterino/na *adj* uterine.
útero *m* uterus, womb.
útil *adj* useful, profitable; * *m* utility.
utilidad *f* utility; **~es** *Lat Am* profits *pl*.
utilizar *vt* to use; to make useful.
utopía *f* Utopia.
utópico/ca *adj* Utopian.
uva *f* grape.

V

vaca *f* cow; beef.
vacaciones *fpl* vacation; holidays *pl*.
vacante *adj* vacant; * *f* vacancy.
vaciar *vt* to empty, to clear; to mold; * *vi* to fall,
   to decrease (of waters); **~se** *vr* to empty.
vacilación *f* hesitation; irresolution.
vacilar *vi* to hesitate; to falter; to fail.
vacío/cía *adj* void, empty; unoccupied; concave;
   vain; presumptuous; * *m* vacuum; emptiness.
vacuna *f* vaccine.
vacunar *vt* to vaccinate.
vacuno/na *adj* bovine, cow *compd*.
vadear *vt* to wade, to ford.
vagabundo/da *adj* wandering; * *m* vagrant, hobo.
vagancia *f* vagrancy.
vagar *vi* to rove/loiter about; to wander.
vagido *m* cry of a child; convulsive sob.
vagina *f* vagina.
vago/ga *adj* vagrant; restless; vague.
vagón *m* (*rail*) wagon; car, carriage; **~ de
   mercancías** goods wagon.
vaguear *vi* to rove, to loiter; to wander.
vahído *m* vertigo, giddiness.
vaho *m* steam, vapor.
vaina *f* scabbard (of a sword); pod, husk.
vainilla *f* (*bot*) vanilla; *Lat Am* hemstitch.
vaivén *m* fluctuation, instability; giddiness.
vajilla *f* crockery.
vale *m* farewell; promissory note, IOU.
valedero/ra *adj* valid; efficacious; binding.
valentía *f* valor, courage.
valentón *m* braggart.
valentonada *f* brag, boast.
valer *vi* to be valuable; to be deserving; to cost;
   to be valid; to be worth; to produce; to be
   current; * *vt* to protect, to favor; to be worth;
   to be equivalent to; **~se** *vr* to employ, to make
   use of; to have recourse to.
valeroso/sa *adj* valiant, brave; strong, powerful.
valía *f* valuation; worth.
validar *vt* to validate.
validez *f* validity; stability.
válido/da *adj* valid.
valiente *adj* robust, vigorous; valiant; brave;
   boasting.
valija *f* suitcase.
valioso/sa *adj* valuable.
valla *f* fence; hurdle; barricade.
vallar *vt* to fence in.

valle m valley.

valor m value; price; validity; force; power; courage, valor.

valoración f valuation.

valorar vt to value; to evaluate.

valuación f valuation.

vals m invar waltz.

válvula f valve.

vampiro m vampire.

vanagloriarse vr to boast.

vandalismo m vandalism.

vándalo/la adj, m vandal.

vanguardia f vanguard.

vanidad f vanity; ostentation.

vanidoso/sa adj vain, showy; haughty; conceited.

vano/na adj vain; useless; frivolous; arrogant; futile; **en ~** in vain.

vapor m vapor, steam; breath; steamer, steamboat, steamship.

vaporizador m atomizer.

vaporizar vt to vaporize.

vaporoso/sa adj vaporous.

vapular vt to whip, to flog.

vaquerizo/za adj cattle compd; * m cowboy, cowhand; cowman.

vaquero m cowboy, cowhand; cowman; **~/ra** adj belonging to a cowboy/cowgirl; **~s** mpl jeans pl.

vara f rod; pole, staff; stick.

varejón m Lat Am thin pole.

variable adj variable, changeable.

variación f variation.

variado/da adj varied; variegated.

variar vt to vary; to modify; to change; * vi to vary.

várice f Lat Am varicose vein.

varices fpl varicose veins pl.

variedad f variety; inconstancy.

varilla f small rod; curtain rod; spindle, pivot.

vario/ria adj varied, different; vague; variegated; **~s** pl some; several.

varón m man, male.

varonil adj male, masculine; manly.

vasco/ca adj, m/f Basque.

vascuence m Basque.

Vaselina™ f Vaseline™.

vasija f vessel.

vaso m glass; vessel; vase.

vástago m bud, shoot; offspring.

vasto/ta adj vast, huge.

vaticinar vt to divine, to foretell.

vaticinio m prophecy.

vatio m watt.

vecindad f inhabitants of a place; neighborhood.

vecindario m number of inhabitants of a place; neighborhood.

vecino/na adj neighboring; near; * m neighbor, inhabitant.

veda f prohibition.

vedar vt to prohibit, to forbid; to impede.

vegetación f vegetation.

vegetal adj vegetable.

vegetar vi to vegetate.

vegetariano/na adj, m/f vegetarian.

vehemencia f vehemence, force.

vehemente adj vehement, violent.

vehículo m vehicle.

veinte adj, m twenty.

veintena f twentieth part; score.

vejación f vexation; embarrassment.

vejar vt to vex; to humiliate.

vejestorio m old man.

vejez f old age.

vejiga f bladder.

vela f wakefulness; vigil; night work; candle; sail; **hacerse a la ~** to set sail.

velado/da adj veiled; blurred; * f soiree.

velador m night watchman, guard; observer; candlestick; pedestal table.

velar vi to stay awake; to be attentive; * vt to guard, to watch.

veleidad f feeble will; inconstancy.

velero/ra adj swift-sailing.

veleta f weather cock, weather vane.

vello m down; gossamer; short downy hair.

vellón m fleece.

velludo/da adj shaggy, woolly.

velo m veil; pretext.

velocidad f speed; velocity.

velocímetro m speedometer.

veloz(mente) adj (adv) swift(ly), fast.

vena f vein.

venado m deer; venison.

vencedor/ra m/f conqueror, victor, winner.

vencer vt to defeat; to conquer, to vanquish; * vi to win; to expire.

vencido/da adj defeated; due.

vencimiento m victory; maturity.

vendaje m bandage, dressing for wounds.

vendal f bandage.

vendar vt to bandage; to hoodwink.

vendaval m gale.

vendedor/ra m/f seller; **~ de periódicos** newsdealer; **~ ambulante** peddler.

vender vt to sell.

vendimia f grape harvest; vintage.

vendimiador/ra m/f grape harvester, vintager.

vendimiar vt to harvest; to pick (grapes); (col) to make a killing with.

veneno m poison, venom.

venenoso/sa adj venomous, poisonous.

venerable adj venerable.

veneración f veneration, worship.

venerar vt to venerate, to worship.

venéreo/rea adj venereal.

venganza f revenge, vengeance.

vengar vt to revenge, to avenge; **~se** vr to take revenge.

vengativo/va adj revengeful.

venia f pardon; leave, permission; bow.

venial adj venial.

venida f arrival; return; overflow of a river.

venidero/ra adj future; **~s** mpl posterity.

venir *vi* to come, to arrive; to follow, to succeed; to happen; to spring from; **~se** *vr* to ferment.

venta *f* sale.

ventaja *f* advantage.

ventajoso/sa *adj* advantageous.

ventana *f* window; window shutter; nostril.

ventanilla *f* window.

venta por correo *f* mail order.

ventarrón *m* violent wind.

ventilación *f* ventilation; draft.

ventilar *vt* to ventilate; to fan; to discuss.

ventisco/sca *m/f* snowstorm.

ventiscar *vi* to drift, to lie in drifts (snow).

ventisquero *m* snowdrift; **~s** *mpl* glaciers *pl*.

ventolera *f* gust; pride, loftiness.

ventosidad *f* flatulence.

ventoso/sa *adj* windy; flatulent.

ventrículo *m* ventricle.

ventrílocuo *m* ventriloquist.

ventura *f* happiness; luck, chance, fortune; **por ~** by chance.

venturoso/sa *adj* lucky, fortunate, happy.

Venus *f* Venus (planet).

ver *vt* to see, to look at; to observe; to visit; * *vi* to understand; to see; **~se** *vr* to be seen; to be conspicuous; to find oneself; **~se con uno** to have a bone to pick with someone; * *m* sense of sight; appearance.

vera *f* edge; bank.

veracidad *f* truth; veracity.

veranear *vi* to spend the holiday, to vacation.

veraneo *m* summer vacation.

veraniego/ga *adj* summer.

verano *m* summer.

veras *fpl* truth, sincerity; **de ~** in truth, really.

veraz *adj* truthful.

verbal *adj* verbal.

verbena *f* fair; dance.

verbo *m* word, term; (*gr*) verb.

verbosidad *f* verbosity.

verdad *f* truth, veracity; reality; reliability.

verdaderamente *adv* truly, in fact.

verdadero/ra *adj* true; real; sincere.

verde *adj*, *m* green.

verdear, verdecer *vi* to turn green.

verdín *m* bright green; verdure.

verdor *m* greenness; verdure; youth.

verdoso/sa *adj* greenish, greeny.

verdugo *m* hangman; very cruel person.

verdulero/ra *m/f* produce dealer.

verdura *f* verdure; vegetables *pl*, greens *pl*.

vereda *f* path; sidewalk.

veredicto *m* verdict.

vergel *m* orchard.

vergonzoso/sa *adj* bashful; shamefaced.

vergüenza *f* shame; bashfulness; confusion.

verídico/ca *adj* truthful.

verificación *f* verification.

verificar *vt* to check, to verify; **~se** *vr* to happen.

verisímil *adj* probable.

verja *f* grate, lattice.

vermut *m* vermouth.

verosímil *adj* likely; credible.

verosimilitud *f* likeliness; credibility.

verraco *m* boar.

verruga *f* wart, pimple.

versado/da *adj* versed.

versátil *adj* versatile.

versículo *m* versicle; short verse.

versificar *vt* to versify.

versión *f* translation, version.

verso *m* verse.

vértebra *f* vertebra.

vertedero *m* sewer, drain; tip.

verter *vt* to pour; to spill; to empty; * *vi* to flow.

vertical *adj* vertical.

vértice *m* vertex, zenith; crown of the head.

vertiente *f* slope; waterfall, cascade.

vertiginoso/sa *adj* giddy.

vértigo *m* giddiness, vertigo.

vesícula *f* blister.

vespertino/na *adj* evening *compd*.

vestíbulo *m* vestibule, lobby; foyer.

vestido *m* dress; clothes *pl*.

vestidura *f* dress; clothing.

vestigio *m* vestige; footstep; trace.

vestimenta *f* clothing.

vestir *vt* to put on; to wear; to dress; to cloak, to disguise; * *vi* to dress; **~se** *vr* to get dressed.

vestuario *m* clothes *pl*; uniform; vestry; changing room.

veta *f* vein (in mines, wood etc); streak; grain.

vetado/da *adj* striped, veined.

vetar *vt* to veto.

veterano/na *adj* experienced, practiced; * *m* veteran, old soldier.

veterinario/ria *adj* veterinary; * *m/f* veterinarian; * *f* veterinary science.

veto *m* veto.

vez *f* time; turn; return; **cada ~** each time; **una ~** once; **a veces** sometimes, by turns.

vía *f* way; road, route; mode, manner, method; (*rail*) railway line.

viajante *m* sales representative.

viajar *vi* to travel.

viaje *m* journey; voyage; travel.

viajero/ra *m/f* traveler.

vial *adj* road *compd*.

viático *m* viaticum; travel allowance.

víbora *f* viper.

vibración *f* vibration.

vibrador *m* vibrator.

vibrante *adj* vibrant.

vibrar *vt*, *vi* to vibrate.

vicaría *f* vicarship; vicarage.

vice- *pref* vice- (deputy etc).

vicealmirante *m* vice-admiral.

viceconsulado *m* vice-consulate.

vicepresidente/ta *m/f* vice-president.

viciar *vt* to vitiate, to corrupt; to invalidate.

vicio *m* vice.

vicioso/sa *adj* vicious; depraved.

vicisitud *f* vicissitude.

víctima *f* victim; sacrifice.

victimar *vt Lat Am* to kill.

victimario/ria *m/f Lat Am* killer.

victoria *f* victory.

victorioso/sa *adj* victorious.

vicuña *m* vicuna.

vid *f* (*bot*) vine.

vida *f* life.

vidriado *m* glazed earthenware, crockery.

video *m Lat Am* video.

vídeo *m* video.

videocámara *f* video camera, camcorder.

videocasete *m* video cassette.

videoclip *m* pop video.

videojuego *m* video game.

vidriar *vt* to glaze.

vidriera *f* stained-glass window; *Lat Am* shop/store window.

vidriero *m* glazier.

vidrio *m* glass; *Lat Am* window; *Lat Am* lense.

vidrioso/sa *adj* glassy; brittle; slippery; very delicate.

vieira *f* scallop.

viejo/ja *adj* old; ancient, antiquated.

viento *m* wind; air.

vientre *m* belly.

viernes *m invar* Friday; **V~ Santo** Good Friday.

viga *f* beam; girder.

vigencia *f* validity.

vigente *adj* in force.

vigésimo/ma *adj, m* twentieth.

vigía *f* (*mar*) lookout; * *m* watchman, guard.

vigilancia *f* vigilance, watchfulness.

vigilante *adj* watchful, vigilant.

vigilar *vt* to watch over; * *vi* to keep watch.

vigilia *f* vigil; watch.

vigor *m* vigor, strength.

vigoroso/sa *adj* vigorous.

vil *adj* mean, sordid, low; worthless; infamous; ungrateful.

vileza *f* meanness, lowness; abjectness.

vilipendiar *vt* to despise, to revile.

villa *f* villa; small town.

villancico *m* Christmas carol.

villano/na *adj* rustic, clownish; villainous; * *m* villain; rustic.

villorio *m* one-horse town; (*col*) dump; shanty town.

vilo: en ~ *adv* in the air; in suspense.

vinagre *m* vinegar.

vinagrera *f* vinegar bottle; ~s cruet set/stand; *Lat Am* heartburn.

vinagreta *f* vinaigrette sauce/dressing.

vinculación *f* link; linking.

vincular *vt* to link.

vínculo *m* tie, link, chain; entail.

vindicación *f* revenge.

vindicar *vt* to avenge.

vindicativo/va *adj* vindictive.

vinicultura *f* wine growing.

vino *m* wine; ~ **tinto** red wine.

viña *f* vineyard.

viñedo *m* vineyard.

viñeta *f* vignette.

viola[1] *f* (*bot*) viola.

viola[2] *f* (*mus*) viola.

violación *f* violation; rape.

violado/da *adj* violet-colored; violated.

violador/ra *m/f* rapist; violator; profaner.

violar *vt* to rape; to violate; to profane.

violencia *f* violence.

violentar *vt* to force.

violento/ta *adj* violent; forced; absurd; embarrassing.

violeta *f* violet.

violín *m* violin, fiddle.

violinista *m* violinist.

violón *m* double bass.

violoncelo, violonchelo *m* violoncello, cello.

vip *m/f* VIP.

viperino/na *adj* viperish.

viraje *m* turn; bend.

virar *vi* to swerve.

virgen *m/f* virgin.

virgiano/na *adj Lat Am* Virgoan (zodiac sign).

virginidad *f* virginity.

Virgo *f* Virgo (zodiac sign).

viril *adj* virile, manly.

virilidad *f* virility, manhood.

virrey *m* viceroy.

virtual *adj* virtual.

virtud *f* virtue.

virtuoso/sa *adj* virtuous.

viruela *f* smallpox.

virulencia *f* virulence.

virulento/ta *adj* virulent.

virus *m invar* virus.

visa *f*, visado *m* visa.

viscosidad *f* viscosity.

viscoso/sa *adj* viscous, glutinous.

visera *f* visor.

visibilidad *f* visibility.

visible *adj* visible; apparent.

visillos *mpl* lace curtains *pl*.

visión *f* sight, vision; fantasy.

visionario/ria *adj* visionary.

visita *f* visit; visitor.

visitar *vt* to visit.

vislumbrar *vt* to catch a glimpse of; to perceive indistinctly.

visón *m* mink.

víspera *f* eve; evening before; ~s *pl* vespers.

vista *f* sight, view; vision; eyesight; appearance; looks *pl*; prospect; intention; (*law*) trial; * *m* customs officer.

vistazo *m* glance.

visto: ~ que *conj* considering that.

vistoso/sa *adj* colorful, attractive, lively.

visual *adj* visual.

vital *adj* life *compd*; vital.

vitalicio/cia *adj* for life.

vitalidad *f* vitality.

vitamina *f* vitamin.
viticultor/ra *m/f* wine grower.
viticultura *f* wine growing.
vitorear *vt* to shout, to applaud.
vítreo/trea *adj* vitreous.
vitriolo *m* vitriol.
vitrina *f* showcase; *Lat Am* shop/store window.
vituperación *f* condemnation, censure.
vituperar *vt* to condemn, to censure.
vituperio *m* condemnation, censure; insult.
viuda *f* widow.
viudedad *f* widowhood; widow's pension.
viudez *f* widowhood.
viudo *m* widower.
vivacidad *f* vivacity, liveliness.
vivamente *adv* in lively fashion.
vivaracho/cha *adj* lively, sprightly; bright.
vivaz *adj* lively.
víveres *mpl* provisions.
vivero *m* plant nursery; fish farm.
viveza *f* liveliness; sharpness.
vividor/ra *adj* (*perj*) sharp, clever; unscrupulous.
vivienda *f* housing; apartment.
viviente *adj* living.
vivificar *vt* to vivify, to enliven.
vivíparo/ra *adj* viviparous.
vivir *vt* to live through; to go through; * *vi* to
　live; to last.
vivo/va *adj* living; lively; **al ~** to the life; very
　realistically.
vizconde *m* viscount.
vocablo *m* word, term.
vocabulario *m* vocabulary.
vocación *f* vocation.
vocacional *adj* vocational.
vocal *f* vowel; * *m/f* member (of a committee);
　* *adj* vocal, oral.
vocativo *m* (*gr*) vocative.
vocear *vt* to cry; to shout; to cheer; to shriek; *
　vi to yell.
vocerío/ría *m/f* shouting.
vocero/ra *m/f Lat Am* spokesperson.
vociferar *vt* to shout; to proclaim in a loud voice;
　* *vi* to yell.
vodka *m/f* vodka.
volador/ra *adj* flying; fast.
volandas: en ~ *adv* in the air; (*fig*) swiftly.
volante *adj* flying; * *m* (*auto*) steering wheel;
　note; pamphlet; shuttlecock.
volar *vi* to fly; to pass swiftly (of time); to rush,
　to hurry; * *vt* to blow up, to explode.
volatería *f* falconry; fowling; birds *pl*.
volátil *adj* volatile; changeable.
volatilizar *vt* to volatilize, to vaporize.
volcán *m* volcano.
volcánico *adj* volcanic.
volcar *vt* to upset, to overturn; to make giddy;
　to empty out; to exasperate; **~se** *vr* to tip over.
voleibol *m* volleyball.
vóleibol *m Lat Am* volleyball.
voleo *m* volley.

volquete *m* tipper truck; dump truck.
voltaje *m* voltage.
voltear *vt* to turn over; to overturn; *Lat Am* to
　knock over; * *vi* to roll over, to tumble.
voltereta *f* tumble; somersault.
voltio *m* volt.
voluble *adj* unpredictable; fickle.
volumen *m* volume; size.
voluminoso/sa *adj* voluminous.
voluntad *f* will, willpower; wish, desire.
voluntario/ria *adj* voluntary; * *m/f* volunteer.
voluptuoso/sa *adj* voluptuous.
volver *vt* to turn (over); to turn upside down; to
　turn inside out; * *vi* to return, to go back; **~se**
　vr to turn around.
vomitar *vt, vi* to vomit.
vómito *m* vomiting; vomit.
vomitona *f* violent vomiting.
voracidad *f* voracity.
voraz(**mente**) *adj*, (*adv*) voracious(ly).
vórtice *m* whirlpool.
vos *pn Lat Am* you.
vosotros/tras *pn pl* you.
votación *f* voting; vote.
votar *vi* to vow; to vote.
voto *m* vow; vote; opinion, advice; swearword;
　curse; **~s** *mpl* good wishes *pl*.
voz *f* voice; shout; rumor; word, term.
vuelco *m* overturning.
vuelo *m* flight; wing; projection of a building;
　ruffle, frill; **cazar al ~** to catch in flight; **~
　chárter** charter flight.
vuelta *f* turn; circuit; return; row of stitches; cuff;
　change; bend, curve; reverse, other side;
　return journey.
vuelto *m Lat Am* change.
vuestro/tra *adj* your; * *pn* yours.
vulgar *adj* vulgar, common.
vulgaridad *f* vulgarity, commonness.
vulgo *m* common people *pl*.
vulnerable *adj* vulnerable.

W

wáter *m* toilet.
whisky *m* whisky.
windsurf *m* windsurfing.
windsurfista *m/f* windsurfer.

X

xenofobia *f* xenophobia.
xilófono *m* xylophone.
xilógrafo *m* xylographer; wood engraver.

Y

y *conj* and.

160

ya *adv* already; now; immediately; at once; soon; *
  conj: ~ **que** since, seeing that; ¡~! of course!, sure!
yacer *vi* to lie, to lie down.
yacimiento *m* deposit.
yagüré *m Lat Am* skunk.
yanqui *m/f* Yankee.
yate *m* yacht, sailing boat.
yedra *f* ivy.
yegua *f* mare.
yema *f* bud; leaf; egg yolk; ~ **del dedo** tip of the
  finger.
yermo *m* wasteland, wilderness; ~/**ma** *adj* waste;
  (*fig*) barren.
yerno *m* son-in-law.
yerro *m* error, mistake, fault.
yerto/ta *adj* stiff, inflexible; rigid.
yesca *f* tinder.
yeso *m* gypsum; plaster; ~ **mate** plaster of Paris.
yo *pn* I; ~ **mismo** I myself.
yodo *m* iodine.
yogur *m* yogurt.
yugo *m* yoke.
yugular *adj* jugular.
yunque *m* anvil.
yunta *f* yoke; ~**s** *fpl* couple, pair.
yute *m* jute.
yuxtaponer *vt* to juxtapose.
yuxtaposición *f* juxtaposition.

Z

zafado/da *adj Lat Am* crazy, mad.
zafar *vt* to loosen, to untie; to lighten (a ship);
  ~**se** *vr* to escape; ~**se de** to avoid; to free
  oneself from (trouble).
zafio/fia *adj* uncouth, coarse.
zafiro *m* sapphire.
zafra *f Lat Am* sugar cane harvest.
zaga *f* rear; **a la** ~ behind.
zagal/la *m/f* boy/girl.
zaguán *m* porch, entrance hall.
zaherir *vt* to criticize; to upbraid.
zahorí *m* clairvoyant.
zalamería *f* flattery.
zalamero/ra *adj* flattering; * *m/f* wheedler,
  flatterer.
zamarra *f* sheepskin; sheepskin jacket.
zambo/ba *adj* knock-kneed.
zambomba *f* rural drum.
zambullida *f* plunge, dive; dipping, submersion.
zambullirse *vr* to plunge/dive into water.
zampar *vt* to gobble down; to put away hurriedly;
  ~**se** *vr* to thrust oneself suddenly into any
  place; to crash, to hurtle.
zanahoria *f* carrot.
zancada *f* stride.
zancadilla *f* trip; trick.
zanco *m* stilt.
zancudo/da *adj* long-legged; * *m Lat Am* mosquito.
zángano *m* drone; idler, slacker.

zanja *f* ditch, trench.
zanjar *vt* to dig (ditches); (*fig*) to surmount; to
  resolve.
zapador *m* (*mil*) sapper.
zapata *f* boot; ~ **de freno** (*auto*) brake shoe.
zapatazo *m* stamp (dancing).
zapatear *vt* to tap with the shoe; to beat time
  with the sole of the shoe.
zapatería *f* shoemaking; shoe shop; shoe factory.
zapatero/ra *m/f* shoemaker; ~ **de viejo** cobbler.
zapatilla *f* slipper; pump (shoe); (*sport*) ~**s de
  lona** *fpl* sneakers *pl*.
zapato *m* shoe.
zapping *m* channel-hopping.
zar *m* czar.
zarandear *vt* to shake vigorously.
zarcillo *m* earring; tendril.
zarpa *f* mud splash, dirt on clothes; claw, paw.
zarpar *vi* to weigh anchor.
zarpazo *m* thud.
zarrapastroso/sa *adj* shabby, rough-looking.
zarza *f* bramble.
zarzal *m* bramble patch.
zarzamora *f* blackberry.
zigzag *adj* zigzag.
zigzaguear *vi* to zigzag.
zinc *m* zinc.
zócalo *m* plinth, base; base-board.
zocato/ta *adj Lat Am* stale.
zodiaco *m* zodiac.
zona *f* zone; area, belt.
zoncear *vi Lat Am* to fool around.
zoncera *f Lat Am* nonsense.
zonzo/sa *m/f Lat Am* fool.
zoo *m* zoo.
zoología *f* zoology.
zoológico/ca *adj* zoological; * *m* zoo.
zoólogo/ga *m/f* zoologist.
zopenco/ca *adj* dull, very stupid.
zoquete *m* block; crust of bread; (*col*) blockhead.
zorra *f* fox; vixen; (*col*) whore, tart.
zorro *m* male fox; cunning person.
zozobra *f* (*mar*) capsizing; uneasiness, anxiety.
zozobrar *vi* (*mar*) to founder, to capsize; (*fig*)
  to fail; to be anxious.
zueco *m* wooden shoe; clog.
zumba *f* banter, teasing; beating.
zumbar *vt* to hit; ~**se** *vr* to hit each other; * *vi*
  to buzz.
zumbido *m* humming, buzzing sound.
zumbón/ona *adj* waggish, funny, teasing.
zumo *m* juice.
zurcir *vt* to darn; (*fig*) to join, to unite; to hatch
  (lies).
zurdo/da *adj* left; left-handed.
zurra *f* flogging; drudgery.
zurrar *vt* (*col*) to flog, to lay into; (*fig*) to criticize
  harshly.
zurrón *m* pouch.
zutano/na *m/f* so-and-so; ~ **y fulano** such and
  such a one, so-and-so.

English–Spanish

A

a *art* un, uno, una; * *prep* a, al, en.

aback *adv* detrás, atrás; **to be taken ~** *vi* quedar consternado/da.

abacus *n* ábaco *m*.

abandon *vt* abandonar, dejar.

abandonment *n* abandono *m*; desamparo *m*.

abase *vt* abatir, humillar.

abasement *n* abatimiento *m*; humillación *f*.

abash *vt* avergonzar, causar confusión.

abate *vt* disminuir, rebajar; * *vi* disminuirse.

abatement *n* rebaja, disminución *f*.

abbess *n* abadesa *f*.

abbey *n* abadía *f*.

abbot *n* abad *m*.

abbreviate *vt* abreviar, acortar.

abbreviation *n* abreviatura *f*.

abdicate *vt* abdicar; renunciar.

abdication *n* abdicación *f*; renuncia *f*.

abdomen *n* abdomen *m*.

abdominal *adj* abdominal.

abduct *vt* secuestrar.

abductor *n* músculo abductor *m*.

abed *adv* en (la) cama.

aberrant *adj* anormal.

aberration *n* error *m*; aberración *f*.

abet *vt*: **to aid and ~** ser cómplice de.

abeyance *n* desuso *m*.

abhor *vt* aborrecer, detestar.

abhorrence *n* aborrecimiento, odio *m*.

abhorrent *adj* repugnante.

abide *vt* soportar, sufrir.

ability *n* habilidad, capacidad, aptitud *f*; **~ ies** *pl* talento *m*.

abject *adj* vil, despreciable, bajo/ja; **~ly** *adv* vilmente, bajamente.

abjure *vt* abjurar; renunciar.

ablative *n* (*gr*) ablativo *m*.

ablaze *adj* en llamas.

able *adj* capaz, hábil; **to be ~** poder.

able-bodied *adj* robusto/ta, vigoroso/sa.

ablution *n* ablución *f*.

ably *adv* con habilidad.

abnegation *n* abnegación, resignación *f*.

abnormal *adj* anormal.

abnormality *n* anormalidad *f*.

aboard *adv* a bordo.

abode *n* domicilio *m*.

abolish *vt* abolir, anular, revocar.

abolition *n* abolición, anulación *f*.

abominable *adj* abominable, detestable; **~bly** *adv* abominablemente.

abomination *n* abominación *f*.

aboriginal *adj* aborigen.

aborigines *npl* aborígenes *mpl*.

abort *vi* abortar.

abortion *n* aborto *m*.

abortive *adj* fracasado/da.

abound *vi* abundar; **to ~ with** abundar en.

about *prep* acerca de, acerca; **I carry no money ~ me** no traigo dinero; * *adv* aquí y allá; **to be ~ to** estar a punto de; **to go ~** andar acá y acullá; **to go ~ a thing** emprender alguna cosa; **all ~** en todo lugar.

above *prep* encima; * *adv* arriba, *Lat Am* arriba de; **~ all** sobre todo, principalmente; **~ mentioned** ya mencionado.

aboveboard *adj* legítimo/ma.

abrasion *n* abrasión *f*.

abrasive *adj* abrasivo/va.

abreast *adv* de costado.

abridge *vt* abreviar, compendiar; acortar.

abridgement *n* compendio *m*, recopilación *f*.

abroad *adv* en el extranjero; **to go ~** salir del país.

abrogate *vt* abrogar, anular.

abrogation *n* abrogación, anulación *f*.

abrupt *adj* brusco/ca; **~ly** *adv* precipitadamente; bruscamente.

abscess *n* absceso *m*.

abscond *vi* esconderse; huir.

abseiling *n* rappel *m*.

absence *n* ausencia *f*.

absent *adj* ausente; * *vi* ausentarse.

absentee *n* ausente *m*.

absenteeism *n* absentismo *m*.

absent-minded *adj* distraído/da.

absolute *adj* absoluto/ta; categórico/ca; **~ly** *adv* totalmente.

absolution *n* absolución *f*.

absolutism *n* absolutismo *m*.

absolve *vt* absolver.

absorb *vt* absorber.

absorbent *adj* absorbente.

absorbent cotton *n* algodón hidrófilo *m*.

absorption *n* absorción *f*.

abstain *vi* abstenerse, privarse.

abstemious *adj* abstemio/mia, sobrio/ria; **~ly** *adv* moderadamente.

abstemiousness *n* sobriedad, abstinencia *f*.

abstinence *n* abstinencia *f*; templanza *f*.

abstinent *adj* abstinente, sobrio/ria.

abstract *adj* abstracto/ta; * *n* extracto *m*; sumario *m*; **in the ~** de modo abstracto.

abstraction *n* abstracción *f*.

abstractly *adv* en abstracto.

abstruse *adj* oscuro/ra; **~ly** *adv* oscuramente.

absurd *adj* absurdo/da; ~ly *adv* absurdamente.

absurdity *n* absurdidad *f*.

abundance *n* abundancia *f*.

abundant *adj* abundante; ~ly *adv* abundantemente.

abuse *vt* abusar; maltratar; * *n* abuso *m*; injurias *fpl*.

abusive *adj* abusivo/va, ofensivo/va; ~ly *adv* abusivamente.

abut *vi* confinar.

abysmal *adj* abismal; insondable.

abyss *n* abismo *m*.

acacia *n* acacia *f*.

academic *adj* académico/ca.

academician *n* académico *m*.

academy *n* academia *f*.

accede *vi* acceder.

accelerate *vt* acelerar.

accelerator *n* acelerador *m*.

acceleration *n* aceleración *f*.

accent *n* acento *m*; tono *m*; * *vt* acentuar.

accentuate *vt* acentuar.

accentuation *n* acentuación *f*.

accept *vt* aceptar; admitir.

acceptable *adj* aceptable.

acceptability *n* aceptabilidad *f*.

acceptance *n* aceptación *f*.

access *n* acceso *m*; entrada *f*.

accessible *adj* accesible.

accession *n* acceso *m*.

accessory *n* accesorio *m*; (*law*) cómplice *m*.

accident *n* accidente *m*; casualidad *f*.

accidental *adj* casual; ~ly *adv* por casualidad.

acclaim *vt* aclamar, aplaudir.

acclamation *n* aclamación *f*; aplauso *m*.

acclimatize *vt* aclimatar.

accommodate *vt* alojar; complacer.

accommodating *adj* servicial.

accommodations *npl* alojamiento *m*.

accompaniment *n* (*mus*) acompañamiento *m*.

accompanist *n* (*mus*) acompañante *m*.

accompany *vt* acompañar.

accomplice *n* cómplice *m*.

accomplish *vt* efectuar, completar.

accomplished *adj* elegante, consu-mado/da.

accomplishment *n* cumplimiento *m*; ~s *pl* talentos, conocimientos *mpl*.

accord *n* acuerdo, convenio *m*; with one ~ unánimemente; of one's own ~ espontáneamente.

accordance *n*: in ~ with de acuerdo con.

according *prep* según, conforme; ~ to según; ~ly *adv* por consiguiente.

accordion *n* (*mus*) acordeón *m*.

accost *vt* trabar conversación con.

account *n* cuenta *f*; on no ~ de ninguna manera; bajo ningún concepto; on ~ of por motivo de; to call to ~ pedir cuenta; to turn to ~ hacer provechoso; * *vt* to ~ for explicar.

accountability *n* responsabilidad *f*.

accountable *adj* responsable.

accountancy *n* contabilidad *f*, *Lat Am* contaduría *f*.

accountant *n* contable *m*, *Lat Am* contador *m*.

account book *n* libro *m* de cuentas.

account number *n* número *m* de cuenta.

accrue *vi* resultar, provenir.

accumulate *vt* acumular; amontonar; * *vi* crecer.

accumulation *n* acumulación *f*; amontonamiento *m*.

accuracy *n* exactitud *f*.

accurate *adj* exacto/ta; ~ly *adv* exactamente.

accursed *adj* maldito/ta.

accusation *n* acusación *f*.

accusative *n* (*gr*) acusativo *m*.

accusatory *adj* acusatorio/ria.

accuse *vt* acusar; culpar.

accused *n* acusado *m*.

accuser *n* acusador/a *m/f*.

accustom *vt* acostumbrar.

accustomed *adj* acostumbrado/da, habitual.

ace *n* as *m*; within an ~ of... casi, por poco no....

acerbic *adj* mordaz.

acetate *n* (*chem*) acetato *m*.

ache *n* dolor *m*; * *vi* doler.

achieve *vt* realizar; obtener.

achievement *n* realización *f*; hazaña *f*.

acid *adj* ácido/da; agrio/ria; * *n* ácido *m*.

acid rain *n* lluvia ácida *f*.

acidity *n* acidez *f*.

acknowledge *vt* reconocer, confesar.

acknowledgement *n* reconocimiento *m*; gratitud *f*.

acme *n* apogeo *m*.

acne *n* acne *m*.

acorn *n* bellota *f*.

acoustics *n* acústica *f*.

acquaint *vt* informar, avisar.

acquaintance *n* conocimiento *m*; conocido *m*.

acquiesce *vi* someterse, consentir, asentir.

acquiescence *n* consentimiento *m*.

acquiescent *adj* deferente.

acquire *vt* adquirir.

acquisition *n* adquisición, obtención *f*.

acquit *vt* absolver.

acquittal *n* absolución *f*.

acre *n* acre *m*.

acrid *adj* acre.

acrimonious *adj* mordaz.

acrimony *n* acrimonia, acritud *f*.

across *adv* de una parte a otra; * *prep* a través de; to come ~ toparse con.

act *vt* representar; * *vi* hacer; * *n* acto, hecho *m*; acción *f*; ~s of the apostles Hechos *mpl* de los Apóstoles.

acting *adj* interino/na.

action *n* acción *f*; batalla *f*.

action replay *n* repetición *f*.

activate *vt* activar.

active *adj* activo/va; ~ly *adv* activamente.

activity *n* actividad *f*.

actor *n* actor *m*.

actress *n* actriz *f.*

actual *adj* real; efectivo/va; **~ly** *adv* en efecto, realmente.

actuary *n* actuario *m* de seguros.

acumen *n* agudeza, perspicacia *f.*

acupuncture *n* acupuntura *f.*

acute *adj* agudo/da; ingenioso/sa; **~ accent** *n* acento agudo *m;* **~ angle** *n* ángulo agudo *m;* **~ly** *adv* con agudeza.

acuteness *n* perspicacia, sagacidad *f.*

adage *n* proverbio *m.*

adamant *adj* inflexible.

adapt *vt* adaptar, acomodar; ajustar.

adaptability *n* facilidad de adaptarse *f.*

adaptable *adj* adaptable.

adaptation *n* adaptación *f.*

adapter *n* adaptador *m.*

add *vt* añadir, agregar; **to ~ up** sumar.

addendum *n* suplemento *m.*

adder *n* culebra *f;* víbora *f.*

addict *n* drogadicto *m.*

addiction *n* dependencia *f.*

addictive *adj* que crea dependencia.

addition *n* adición *f.*

additional *adj* adicional; **~ly** *adv* en/por adición.

additive *n* aditivo *m.*

address *vt* dirigir; * *n* dirección *f;* discurso *m.*

adduce *vt* alegar, aducir.

adenoids *npl* vegetaciones adenoideas *fpl.*

adept *adj* hábil.

adequacy *n* suficiencia *f.*

adequate *adj* adecuado/da; suficiente; **~ly** *adv* adecuadamente.

adhere *vi* adherir.

adherence *n* adherencia *f.*

adherent *n* adherente, partidario *m.*

adhesion *n* adhesión *f.*

adhesive *adj* pegajoso/sa.

adhesiveness *n* adhesividad *f.*

adhesive tape *n* esparadrapo *m.*

adieu *adv* adiós; * *n* despedida *f.*

adipose *adj* adiposo/sa.

adjacent *adj* adyacente, contiguo/gua.

adjectival *adj* adjetivado/da; **~ly** *adv* como adjetivo.

adjective *n* adjetivo *m.*

adjoin *vi* estar contiguo/gua.

adjoining *adj* contiguo/gua.

adjourn *vt* aplazar.

adjournment *n* prórroga *f.*

adjudicate *vt* adjudicar.

adjunct *n* adjunto *m.*

adjust *vt* ajustar, acomodar.

adjustable *adj* ajustable.

adjustment *n* ajustamiento, arreglo *m.*

adjutant *n.* (*mil*) ayudante *m.*

ad lib *vt* improvisar.

administer *vt* administrar; gobernar; **to ~ an oath** prestar juramento.

administration *n* administración *f;* gobierno *m.*

administrative *adj* administrativo/va.

administrator *n* administrador/a *m/f.*

admirable *adj* admirable; **~bly** *adv* admirablemente.

admiral *n* almirante *m.*

admiralship *n* almirante *f.*

admiralty *n* almirantazgo *m.*

admiration *n* admiración *f.*

admire *vt* admirar.

admirer *n* admira/a *m/f.*

admiringly *adv* con admiración.

admissible *adj* admisible.

admission *adj* entrada *f.*

admit *vt* admitir; **to ~ to** confesarse culpable de.

admittance *n* entrada *f.*

admittedly *adj* de acuerdo que.

admixture *n* mixtura, mezcla *f.*

admonish *vt* amonestar, reprender.

admonition *n* amonestación *f;* consejo, aviso *m.*

admonitory *adj* exhortatorio/ria.

ad nauseam *adv* hasta el cansancio.

adolescence *n* adolescencia *f.*

adopt *vt* adoptar.

adopted *adj* adoptivo/va.

adoption *n* adopción *f.*

adoptive *adj* adoptivo/va.

adorable *adj* adorable.

adorably *adv* de modo adorable.

adoration *n* adoración *f.*

adore *vt* adorar.

adorn *vt* adornar.

adornment *n* adorno *m.*

adrift *adv* a la deriva.

adroit *adj* diestro/tra, hábil.

adroitness *n* destreza *f.*

adulation *n* adulación, zalamería *f.*

adulatory *adj* lisonjero/ra.

adult *adj* adulto/ta; * *n* adulto *m;* adulta *f.*

adulterate *vt* adulterar, corromper; * *adj* adulterado/da, falsificado/da.

adulteration *n* adulteración, corrupción *f.*

adulterer *n* adúltero *m.*

adulteress *n* adúltera *f.*

adulterous *adj* adúltero/ra.

adultery *n* adulterio *m.*

advance *vt* avanzar; promover; pagar por adelantado; * *vi* hacer progresos; **to make ~s** insinuarse; * *n* avance *m;* paga adelantada *f.*

advanced *adj* avanzado/da.

advancement *n* adelantamiento *m;* progreso *m;* promoción *f.*

advantage *n* ventaja *f;* **to take ~ of** sacar provecho de.

advantageous *adj* ventajoso/sa; **~ly** *adv* ventajosamente.

advantageousness *n* ventaja, utilidad *f.*

advent *n* venida *f.*

Advent *n* Adviento *m.*

adventitious *adj* adventicio/cia.

adventure *n* aventura *f.*

adventurer *n* aventurero *m.*

adventurous *adj* intrépido/da; vale-roso/sa; **~ly** *adv* arriesgadamente.

adverb *n* adverbio *m*.

adverbial *adj* adverbial; **~ly** *adv* como adverbio.

adversary *n* adversario, enemigo *m*.

adverse *adj* adverso/sa, contrario/ria.

adversity *n* calamidad *f*; infortunio *m*.

advertise/advertize *vt* anunciar.

advertisement/advertizement *n* anuncio *m*; *Lat Am* aviso *m*, *Lat Am* reclame *m*.

advertising *n* publicidad *f*.

advice *n* consejo *m*; aviso *m*.

advisability *n* prudencia, conveniencia *f*.

advisable *adj* prudente, conveniente.

advise *vt* aconsejar; avisar.

advisedly *adv* prudentemente, avisadamente.

advisory *adj* consultivo/va.

advocacy *n* defensa *f*.

advocate *n* abogado *m*; protector *m*; * *vt* abogar por.

advocateship *n* abogacía *f*.

aerial *n* antena *f*.

aerobics *npl* aerobic *m*, *Lat Am* aerobismo *m*.

aerometer *n* areómetro *m*.

aerosol *n* aerosol *m*.

aerostat *n* globo aerostático *m*.

afar *adv* lejos, distante; **from ~** desde lejos.

affability *n* afabilidad, urbanidad *f*.

affable *adj* afable, complaciente; **~bly** *adv* afablemente.

affair *n* asunto *m*; negocio *m*.

affect *vt* conmover; afectar.

affectation *n* afectación *f*.

affected *adj* afectado/da, lleno/na de afectación; **~ly** *adv* con afectación.

affectingly *adv* con afecto.

affection *n* cariño *m*.

affectionate *adj* afectuoso/sa, *Lat Am* querendón/ona; **~ly** *adv* cariñosamente.

affidavit *n* declaración jurada *f*.

affiliate *vt* afiliar.

affiliation *n* afiliación *f*.

affinity *n* afinidad *f*.

affirm *vt* afirmar, declarar.

affirmation *n* afirmación *f*.

affirmative *adj* afirmativo/va; **~ly** *adv* afirmativamente.

affix *vt* pegar; * *n* (*gr*) afijo *m*.

afflict *vt* afligir.

affliction *n* aflicción *f*; dolor *m*.

affluence *n* abundancia *f*.

affluent *adj* opulento/ta.

afflux *n* confluencia, afluencia *f*.

afford *vt* dar; proveer.

affray *n* asalto *m*; tumulto *m*.

affront *n* afrenta, injuria *f*; * *vt* afrentar, insultar, ultrajar.

aflame *adv* en llamas.

afloat *adv* flotante, a flote.

afraid *adj* espantado/da, tímido/da; **I am ~** temo.

afresh *adv* de nuevo, otra vez.

African-American *adj*, *n* afroameri-cano/na *m/ f*.

aft *adv* (*mar*) a popa.

after *prep* después; detrás; según; * *adv* después; **~ all** después de todo.

afterbirth *n* secundinas *fpl*.

after-effects *npl* consecuencias *fpl*.

afterlife *n* vida venidera *f*.

aftermath *n* consecuencias *fpl*.

afternoon *n* tarde *f*.

aftershave *n* aftershave *m*.

aftertaste *n* resabio *m*.

afterwards *adv* después.

again *adv* otra vez; **~ and ~** muchas veces; **as much ~** otra vez tanto.

against *prep* contra; **~ the grain** a contrapelo, de mala gana.

agate *n* ágata *f*.

age *n* edad *f*; **under ~** menor; * *vt* envejecer.

aged *adj* viejo/ja, anciano/na.

agency *n* agencia *f*.

agenda *n* orden del día *m*.

agent *n* agente *m*.

agglomerate *vt* aglomerar.

agglomeration *n* aglomeración *f*.

aggrandizement *n* engrandecimiento *m*.

aggravate *vt* agravar, exagerar.

aggravation *n* agravación *f*.

aggregate *n* agregado *m*.

aggregation *n* agregación *f*.

aggression *n* agresión *f*.

aggressive *adj* ofensivo/va.

aggressor *n* agresor *m*.

aggrieved *adj* ofendido/da.

aghast *adj* horrorizado/da.

agile *adj* ágil; diestro/tra.

agility *n* agilidad *f*; destreza *f*.

agitate *vt* agitar.

agitation *n* agitación *f*; perturbación *f*.

agitator *n* agitador, incitador *m*.

ago *adv* pasado, largo tiempo; después; **how long ~?** ¿cuánto hace?

agog *adj* emocionado/da.

agonizing *adj* atroz.

agony *n* agonía *f*.

agree *vt* convenir; * *vi* estar de acuerdo/da.

agreeable *adj* agradable; amable; **~bly** *adv* agradablemente; **~ with** según, conforme a.

agreeableness *n* amabilidad, gracia *f*.

agreed *adj* establecido/da, conveni-do/da; **~!** *adv* ¡de acuerdo!

agreement *n* acuerdo *m*.

agricultural *adj* agrario/ria.

agriculture *n* agricultura *f*.

agriculturist *n* agricultor *m*.

agronomy *n* agronomía *f*.

aground *adv* (*mar*) encallado.

ah! *excl* ¡ah!, ¡ay!

ahead *adv* más allá, delante de otro; (*mar*) por la proa.

ahoy! *excl* (*mar*) ¡ohe!

aid vt ayudar, socorrer; **to ~ and abet** ser cómplice de; * n ayuda f; auxilio, socorro m.
aide-de-camp n (mil) ayudante de campo m.
AIDS n SIDA m.
ail vt afligir, molestar.
ailing adj doliente.
ailment n dolencia, indisposición f.
aim vt apuntar aspirar a; intentar; * n designio m; puntería f.
aimless adj sin designio, sin objeto; **~ly** a la deriva.
air n aire m; * vt airear; ventilar.
airbag n airbag m.
air balloon n globo aerostático m.
airborne adj aerotransportado/da.
air-conditioned adj climatizado/da.
air conditioning n aire acondicionado m.
aircraft n avión m.
air cushion n cojinete rellenado de aire m.
air force n fuerzas aéreas fpl.
air freshener n ambientador m.
air gun n escopeta de aire comprimido f.
air hole n respiradero m.
airless adj falto de ventilación, sofocado/da.
airlift n puente aéreo m.
airline n línea aérea f.
airmail n: **by ~** por avión.
airplane n avión m.
airport n aeropuerto m.
airport tax n tasas de aeropuerto f.
air pump n bomba de aire f.
airsick adj mareado/da.
airstrip n pista de aterrizaje f.
air terminal n terminal f.
airtight adj herméticamente cerrado/da.
airy adj bien ventilado/da.
aisle n nave de una iglesia f.
ajar adj entreabierto/ta.
akimbo adj corvo/va.
akin adj parecido/da.
alabaster n alabastro m; * adj alabastrino/na.
alacrity n presteza f.
alarm n alarma f; * vt alarmar; inquietar.
alarm bell n timbre de alarma m.
alarmist n alarmista m.
alas adv desgraciadamente.
albeit conj aunque.
album n álbum m.
alchemist n alquimista m.
alchemy n alquimia f.
alcohol n alcohol m.
alcoholic adj alcohólico/ca; * n alcoholizado/m.
alcove n nicho m.
alder n aliso m.
ale n cerveza f.
alert adj vigilante; alerto/ta; * n alerta f.
alertness n cuidado m; vigilancia f.
algae npl alga f.
algebra n álgebra f.
algebraic adj algebraico/ca.
alias adj alias.

alibi n (law) coartada f.
alien adj ajeno/na; * n forastero m.
alienate vt enajenar.
alienation n enajenación f.
alight vi apearse; * adj encendido/da.
align vt alinear.
alike adj semejante, igual; * adv igualmente.
alimentation n alimentación f.
alimony n alimentos mpl.
alive adj vivo/va, viviente; activo/va.
alkali n álcali m.
alkaline adj alcalino/na.
all adj todo/da; * adv totalmente; **~ at once**, **~ of a sudden** de repente; **~ the same** sin embargo; **~ the better** tanto mejor; **not at ~!** ino hay de qué!; **once for ~** una vez por todas; * n todo m.
allay vt aliviar.
all clear n luz verde f.
allegation n alegación f.
allege vt alegar; declarar.
allegiance n lealtad, fidelidad f.
allegorical adj alegórico/ca; **~ly** adv alegóricamente.
allegory n alegoría f.
allegro n (mus) alegro m.
allergy n alergia f.
alleviate vt aliviar, aligerar.
alleviation n alivio m; mitigación f.
alley n callejuela f.
alliance n alianza f.
allied adj aliado/da.
alligator n caimán m.
alliteration n aliteración f.
all-night adj abierto/ta toda la noche.
allocate vt repartir.
allocation n cuota f.
allot vt asignar.
allow vt conceder; permitir; dar, pagar; **to ~ for** tener en cuenta.
allowable adj admisible, permitido/da.
allowance n concesión f.
alloy n liga, mezcla, aleación f.
all right adv bien.
all-round adj completo/ta.
allspice n pimienta de Jamaica f.
allude vt aludir.
allure n fascinación f.
alluring adj seductor/a; **~ly** adv seductoramente.
allurement n aliciente, atractivo m.
allusion n alusión f.
allusive adj alusivo/va; **~ly** adv de modo alusivo.
alluvial adj aluvial.
ally n aliado m; * vt aliar.
almanac n almanaque m.
almighty adj omnipotente, todopo-deroso/sa.
almond n almendra f.
almond tree n almendro m.
almost adv casi; cerca de.
alms n limosna f.

aloft *prep* arriba.

alone *adj* solo; * *adv* solamente, sólo; **to leave ~** dejar en paz.

along *adv* a lo largo; **~ side** al lado.

aloof *adv* lejos.

aloud *adj* en voz alta.

alphabet *n* alfabeto *m*.

alphabetical *adj* alfabético/ca; **~ly** *adv* por orden alfabético.

alpine *adj* alpino/na.

already *adv* ya.

also *adv* también, además.

altar *n* altar *m*.

altarpiece *n* retablo *m*.

alter *vt* modificar.

alteration *n* alteración *f*.

altercation *n* altercado *m*.

alternate *adj* alterno/na; * *vt* alternar, variar; **~ly** *adv* alternativamente.

alternating *adj* alterno/na.

alternation *n* alternación *f*.

alternator *n* alternador *m*.

alternative *n* alternativa *f*; * *adj* alternative; **~ly** *adv* si no.

although *conj* aunque, no obstante.

altitude *n* altitud, altura *f*.

altogether *adv* del todo.

alum *n* alumbre *m*.

aluminous *adj* aluminoso/sa.

aluminum *n* aluminio *m*.

always *adv* siempre, constantemente.

a.m. *adv* de la mañana.

amalgam *n* amalgama *f*.

amalgamate *vt,vi* amalgamar(se).

amalgamation *n* amalgamación *f*.

amanuensis *n* amanuense, secretario *m*.

amaryllis *n* (*bot*) amarillas *f*.

amass *vt* acumular, amontonar.

amateur *n* aficionado *m*, amateur *m/f*.

amateurish *adj* torpe.

amatory *adj* amatorio/ria; erótico/ca.

amaze *vt* asombrar.

amazement *n* asombro *m*.

amazing *adj* pasmoso/sa; **~ly** *adv* extraordinariamente.

amazon *n* amazona *f*.

ambassador *n* embajador *m*.

ambassadress *n* embajadora *f*.

amber *n* ámbar *m*; * *adj* ambarino/na.

ambidextrous *adj* ambidextro/tra, ambidiestro/tra.

ambient *adj* ambiente.

ambiguity *n* ambigüedad, duda *f*.

ambiguous *adj* ambiguo; **~ly** *adv* ambiguamente.

ambition *n* ambición *f*.

ambitious *adj* ambicioso/sa; **~ly** *adv* ambiciosamente.

amble *vi* andar sin prisa.

ambulance *n* ambulancia *f*.

ambush *n* emboscada *f*; **to lie in ~** estar emboscado/da; * *vt* tender una emboscada a.

ameliorate *vt* mejorar.

amelioration *n* mejoramiento *m*.

amenable *adj* sensible.

amend *vt* enmendar.

amendable *adj* reparable, corregible.

amendment *n* enmienda *f*.

amends *npl* compensación *f*.

amenities *npl* comodidades *fpl*.

America *n* América *f*.

American *adj* americano/na.

amethyst *n* amatista *f*.

amiability *n* amabilidad *f*.

amiable *adj* amable.

amiableness *n* amabilidad *f*.

amiably *adv* amablemente.

amicable *adj* amigable, amistoso/sa; **~bly** *adv* amistosamente.

amid(st) *prep* entre, en medio de.

amiss *adv*: **something's ~** algo pasa.

ammonia *n* amoniaco *m*.

ammunition *n* municiones *fpl*.

amnesia *n* amnesia *f*.

amnesty *n* amnistía *f*.

among(st) *prep* entre, en medio de.

amoral *adj* amoral.

amorous *adj* amoroso/sa; **~ly** *adv* amorosamente.

amorphous *adj* informe.

amount *n* importe *m*; cantidad *f*; * *vi* sumar.

amp(ere) *n* amperio *m*.

amphibian *n* anfibio *m*.

amphibious *adj* anfibio/bia.

amphitheater *n* anfiteatro *m*.

ample *adj* amplio/lia.

ampleness *n* amplitud, abundancia *f*.

amplification *n* amplificación *f*; extensión *f*.

amplifier *n* amplificador *m*.

amplify *vt* ampliar, extender.

amplitude *n* amplitud, extensión *f*.

amply *adv* ampliamente.

amputate *vt* amputar.

amputation *n* amputación *f*.

amulet *n* amuleto *m*.

amuse *vt* entretener, divertir.

amusement *n* diversión *f*, pasatiempo, entretenimiento *m*.

amusing *adj* divertido/da; **~ly** *adv* entretenidamente.

an *art* un, uno, una.

anachronism *n* anacronismo *m*.

analog *adj* (*comput*) analógico/ca.

analogous *adj* análogo.

analogy *n* analogía *f*.

analyze *vt* analizar.

analysis *n* análisis *m invar*.

analyst *n* analizador/a *m/f*.

analytical *adj* analítico/ca; **~ly** *adv* analíticamente.

anarchic *adj* anárquico/ca.

anarchist *adj* anarquista.

anarchy *n* anarquía *f*.

anatomical *adj* anatómico/ca; ~**ly** *adv* anatómicamente.

anatomize *vt* anatomizar.

anatomy *n* anatomía *f*.

ancestor *n*: ~**s** *pl* antepasados *mpl*.

ancestral *adj* hereditario/ria.

ancestry *n* raza, alcurnia *f*.

anchor *n* ancla *f*; * *vi* anclar; **to weigh** ~ zarpar.

anchorage *n* fondeadero *m*.

anchovy *n* anchoa *f*.

ancient *adj* antiguo.

ancillary *adj* auxiliar.

and *conj* y, e.

anecdotal *adj* anecdótico/ca.

anecdote *n* anécdota *f*

anemia *n* anemia *f*.

anemic *adj* (*med*) anémico/ca.

anemone *n* (*bot*) anémona *f*

anesthetic *n* anestesia *f*.

anew *adv* de nuevo, nuevamente.

angel *n* ángel *m*

angelic *adj* angélico/ca.

anger *n* cólera *f*; * *vt* enojar, irritar.

angle *n* ángulo *m*; * *vt* pescar con caña.

angled *adj* anguloso/sa.

angler *n* pescador/a de caña *m/f*.

Anglicanism *n* anglicismo *m*.

angling *n* pesca con caña *f*

angrily *adv* enojado.

angry *adj* enojado/da.

anguish *n* ansia, angustia *f*

angular *adj* angular.

angularity *n* forma angular *f*.

animal *n adj* animal *m*.

animate *vt* animar; * *adj* viviente.

animated *adj* vivo/va.

animation *n* animación *f*

animosity *n* rencor *m*.

animus *n* odio *m*

anise *n* anís *m*

aniseed *n* anís *m*

ankle *n* tobillo *m*; ~ **bone** hueso del tobillo *m*

annals *n* anales *mpl*.

annex *vt* anejar; * *n* anejo *m*.

annexation *n* anexión *f*.

annihilate *vt* aniquilar.

annihilation *n* aniquilación *f*.

anniversary *n* aniversario *m*.

annotate *vi* anotar.

annotation *n* anotación *f*.

announce *vt* anunciar, publicar.

announcement *n* anuncio *m*.

announcer *n* locutor/a *m/f*.

annoy *vt* molestar.

annoyance *n* molestia *f*.

annoying *adj* molesto/ta; fastidioso/sa.

annual *adj* anual; ~**ly** *adv* anualmente, cada año.

annuity *n* renta vitalicia *f*.

annul *vt* anular.

annulment *n* anulación *f*.

annunciation *n* anunciación *f*

anodyne *adj* anodino/na.

anoint *vt* untar, ungir.

anomalous *adj* anómalo.

anomaly *n* anomalía, irregularidad *f*.

anon *adv* más tarde.

anonymity *n* anonimato *m*.

anonymous *adj* anónimo/ma; ~**ly** *adj* anónimamente.

anorexia *n* anorexia *f*.

another *adj* otro/tra, diferente; **one** ~ uno a otro.

answer *vt* responder, replicar; corresponder; **to** ~ **for** responder de/por; **to** ~ **to** corresponder a; * *n* respuesta, réplica *f*.

answerable *adj* responsable.

answering machine *n* contestador automático *m*.

ant *n* hormiga *f*.

antagonism *n* antagonismo *m*; rivalidad *f*.

antagonist *n* antagonista *m*.

antagonize *vt* provocar.

Antarctic *adj* antártico/ca.

anteater *n* oso hormiguero *m*

antecedent *n*: ~**s** *pl* antecedentes *mpl*.

antechamber *n* antecámara *f*

antedate *vt* antedatar.

antelope *n* antílope *m*.

antenna *npl* antena *f*.

anterior *adj* anterior, precedente.

anthem *n* himno *m*.

ant hill *n* hormiguero *m*.

anthology *n* antología *f*.

anthracite *n* antracita *f*.

anthropologist *n* antropólogo/ga *m/f*.

anthropology *n* antropología *f*

anti-aircraft *adj* antiaéreo/rea.

antibiotic *n* antibiótico *m*.

antibody *n* anticuerpo *m*.

Antichrist *n* Anticristo *m*.

anticipate *vt* anticipar, prevenir.

anticipation *n* anticipación *f*.

anticlockwise *adv* en sentido contrario al de las agujas del reloj.

antidote *n* antídoto *m*.

antifreeze *n* anticongelante *m*.

antimony *n* antimonio *m*.

antipathy *n* antipatía *f*.

antipodes *npl* antípodas *fpl*

antiquarian *n* anticuario *m*.

antiquated *adj* antiguo/gua; * *n* antigüedad *f*.

antiquity *n* antigüedad *f*.

antiseptic *adj* antiséptico/ca.

antisocial *adj* antisocial.

antithesis *n* antítesis *f*.

antler *n* cuerna *f*.

anvil *n* yunque *m*.

anxiety *n* ansiedad *f*, ansia *f*; afán *m*, zozobra *f*.

anxious *adj* ansioso/sa; ~**ly** *adv* ansiosamente; **to be** ~ *vi* zozobrar.

any *adj pn* cualquier, cualquiera; alguno, alguna; todo; ~**body** alguien, nadie, cualquiera; ~**how** de cualquier manera; ~**more** más; ~**place** en ninguna parte; ~**thing** algo, nada, cualquier cosa.

apace *adv* rápidamente.

apart *adv* aparte, separadamente.

apartment *n* apartamento, departamento *m*.

apartment house *n* casa de apartamentos *f*.

apathetic *adj* apático/ca.

apathy *n* apatía *f*.

ape *n* mono *m*; * *vt* remedar.

aperture *n* abertura *f*.

apex *n* ápice *m*.

aphorism *n* aforismo *m*; máxima *f*.

apiary *n* colmenar *m*, *Lat Am* apiario *m*.

apiece *adv* por cabeza, por persona.

aplomb *n* aplomo *m*.

Apocalypse *n* Apocalipsis *m*.

apocrypha *npl* libros apócrifos *mpl*.

apocryphal *adj* apócrifo/fa, no canónico/ca.

apologetic *adj* de disculpa.

apologist *n* apologista *m*.

apologize *vt* disculpar.

apology *n* apología, defensa *f*.

apoplexy *n* apoplejía *f*

apostle *n* apóstol *m*.

apostolic *adj* apostólico/ca.

apostrophe *n* apóstrofe *m*.

apotheosis *n* apoteosis *f*.

appall *vt* espantar, aterrar.

appalling *adj* espantoso/sa.

apparatus *n* aparato *m*.

apparel *n* traje, vestido *m*.

apparent *adj* evidente, aparente; ~**ly** *adv* por lo visto.

apparition *n* aparición, visión *f*.

appeal *vi* apelar, recurrir a un tribunal superior; * *n* (*law*) apelación *f*.

appealing *adj* atractivo/va.

appear *vi* aparecer.

appearance *n* apariencia *f*.

appease *vt* aplacar.

appellant *n* (*law*) apelante *m*.

append *vt* anejar.

appendage *n* cosa accesoria *f*.

appendicitis *n* apendicitis *f*.

appendix *n* apéndice *m*.

appertain *vi* tocar a.

appetite *n* apetito *m*.

appetizing *adj* apetitivo/va.

applaud *vi* aplaudir.

applause *n* aplausos *mpl*

apple *n* manzana *f*.

apple pie *n* pastelillo de manzanas *m*; **in ~ order** en sumo orden.

apple tree *n* manzano *m*.

appliance *n* aparato *m*.

applicability *n* aplicabilidad *f*.

applicable *adj* aplicable.

applicant *n* aspirante, candidato *m*.

application *n* aplicación *f*; solicitud *f*.

applied *adj* aplicado/da.

apply *vt* aplicar; * *vi* dirigirse a, recurrir a.

appoint *vt* nombrar.

appointee *n* persona nombrada *f*.

appointment *n* cita *f*; nombramiento *m*.

apportion *vt* repartir.

apportionment *n* repartición *f*.

apposite *adj* adaptado/da.

apposition *n* aposición *f*.

appraisal *n* estimación *f*.

appraise *vt* tasar; estimar.

appreciable *adj* sensible.

appreciably *adv* sensiblemente.

appreciate *vt* apreciar; agradecer.

appreciation *n* aprecio *m*.

appreciative *adj* agradecido/da.

apprehend *vt* arrestar.

apprehension *n* aprensión *f*.

apprehensive *adj* aprensivo/va, tímido/da.

apprentice *n* aprendiz *m*; * *vt* poner de aprendiz.

apprenticeship *n* aprendizaje *m*.

apprise *vt* informar.

approach *vt* (*vi*) aproximar(se); * *n* acceso *m*.

approachable *adj* accesible.

approbation *n* aprobación *f*.

appropriate *vt* apropiarse de; * *adj* apropiado/da.

approval *n* aprobación *f*.

approve (of) *vt* aprobar.

approximate *vi* acercarse; * *adj* aproximativo/va; ~**ly** *adv* aproximadamente.

approximation *n* aproximación *f*.

apricot *n* damasco, albaricoque *m*.

April *n* abril *m*.

apron *n* delantal *m*.

apse *n* ábside *m*.

apt *adj* apto/ta, idóneo/nea; ~**ly** *adv* oportunamente.

aptitude *n* aptitud *f*.

aqualung *n* escafandra autónoma *f*.

aquarium *n* acuario *m*.

Aquarius *n* Acuario *m*.

aquatic *adj* acuático/ca.

aqueduct *n* acueducto *m*.

aquiline *adj* aguileño/ña.

arabesque *n* arabesco *m*.

arable *adj* labrantío/tía.

arbiter *n* árbitro *m*.

arbitrariness *n* arbitrariedad *f*.

arbitrary *adj* arbitrario/ria.

arbitrate *vt* arbitrar, juzgar como árbitro.

arbitration *n* arbitrio *m*.

arbitrator *n* árbitro *m*.

arbor *n* emparrado *m*; enramada *f*.

arcade *n* galería *f*.

arch *n* arco *m*; * *adj* malicioso/sa.

archaic *adj* arcaico/ca.

archangel *n* arcángel *m*.

archbishop *n* arzobispo *m*.

archbishopric *n* arzobispado *m*.

archeological *adj* arqueológico/ca.

archeologist *n* arqueólogo/ga *m/f*.

archeology *n* arqueología *f*.

archer n arquero m.

archery n tiro con arco m.

architect n arquitecto/ta m/f.

architectural adj arquitectónico/ca.

architecture n arquitectura f.

archives npl archivos mpl.

archivist n archivero/ra m/f.

archly adv maliciosamente.

archway n arcada, bóveda f.

arctic adj ártico/ca.

ardent adj apasionado/da; ~ly adv con pasión.

ardor n ardor m; vehemencia f; pasión f.

arduous adj arduo, difícil.

area n área f; espacio m, zona f.

arena n arena f.

arguably adv posiblemente.

argue vi discutir; * vt sostener.

argument n argumento m, controversia f.

argumentation n argumentación f.

argumentative adj discutidor/a.

aria n (mus) aria f.

arid adj árido/da, estéril.

aridity n sequedad f.

Aries n Aries m.

aright adv bien; **to set** ~ rectificar.

arise vi levantarse; nacer.

aristocracy n aristocracia f.

aristocrat n aristócrata m/f.

aristocratic adj aristocrático/ca; ~ally adv aristocráticamente.

arithmetic n aritmética f.

arithmetical adj aritmético/ca; ~ly adv aritméticamente.

ark n arca f.

arm n brazo m; arma f; * vt (vi) armar(se).

armament n armamento m.

armchair n sillón m.

armed adj armado/da.

armful n brazada f.

armhole n sobaco m.

armistice n armisticio m.

armor n armadura f.

armored car n carro blindado m.

armory n arsenal m.

armpit n sobaco m.

armrest n apoyabrazos m invar.

army n ejército m; tropas fpl.

aroma n aroma m.

aromatherapy n aromaterapia f.

aromatic adj aromático/ca.

around prep alrededor de; * adv alrededor.

arouse vt despertar; excitar.

arraign vt acusar.

arraignment n acusación f; proceso criminal m.

arrange vt organizar.

arrangement n colocación f; arreglo m.

arrant adj consumado/da.

array n serie f.

arrears npl resto de una deuda m; atraso m.

arrest n arresto m; * vt detener, arrestar.

arrival n llegada f.

arrive vi llegar.

arrogance n arrogancia, presunción f.

arrogant adj arrogante, presuntuoso/sa; ~ly adv arrogantemente.

arrogate vt arrogarse.

arrogation n arrogación f.

arrow n flecha f.

arsenal n (mil) arsenal m; (mar) atarazana, armería f.

arsenic n arsénico m.

arson n fuego incendiario m.

art n arte m.

arterial adj arterial.

artesian well n pozo artesiano m.

artery n arteria f.

artful adj ingenioso/sa.

artfulness n astucia, habilidad f.

art gallery n pinacoteca f.

arthritis n artritis f.

artichoke n alcachofa f.

article n artículo m.

articulate vt articular, pronunciar distintamente.

articulated adj articulado/da.

articulation n articulación f.

artifice n artificio, fraude m.

artificial adj artificial; artificioso/sa; ~ly adv artificialmente; artificiosamente.

artificial insemination n inseminación artificial f.

artificiality n artificialidad f.

artillery n artillería f.

artisan n artesano/na m/f.

artist n artista m.

artistic adj artístico/ca.

artistry n habilidad f.

artless adj sencillo, simple; ~ly adv sencillamente, naturalmente.

artlessness n sencillez f.

as conj como; mientras; también; visto que; puesto que; ~ for, ~ to en cuanto a.

asbestos n asbesto, amianto m.

ascend vi ascender, subir.

ascendancy n dominio m.

ascension n ascensión f.

ascent n subida f.

ascertain vt establecer.

ascetic adj ascético/ca; * n asceta m.

ascribe vt atribuir.

ash n (bot) fresno m; ceniza f

ashcan n cubo de la basura m.

ashamed adj avergonzado/da.

ashore adv en tierra, a tierra; **to go** ~ desembarcar.

ashtray n cenicero m.

Ash Wednesday n miércoles de ceniza m.

aside adv a un lado.

ask vt pedir, rogar; **to** ~ **after** preguntar por; **to** ~ **for** pedir; **to** ~ **out** invitar.

askance adv desconfiado/da.

askew adv de lado.

asleep adj dormido/da; **to fall** ~ dormirse.

asparagus n espárrago m.

aspect n aspecto m.

aspen n álamo temblón m.

aspersion n calumnia f.

asphalt n asfalto m.

asphyxia n (med) asfixia f.

asphyxiate vt asfixiar.

asphyxiation n asfixia f.

aspirant n aspirante m.

aspirate vt aspirar, pronunciar con aspiración; * n sonido aspirado m.

aspiration n aspiración f.

aspire vi aspirar, desear.

aspirin n aspirina f.

ass n asno m; **she ~** burra f.

assail vt asaltar, atacar.

assailant n asaltante m/f, agresor/a m/f.

assassin n asesino/na m/f.

assassinate vt asesinar.

assassination n asesinato m.

assault n asalto m; * vt acometer, asaltar.

assemblage n multitud f.

assemble vt reunir, convocar; * vi juntarse.

assembly n asamblea, junta f; congreso m.

assembly line n cadena de montaje f.

assent n asentimiento m; * vi asentir.

assert vt sostener, mantener; afirmar.

assertion n aserción f.

assertive adj perentorio/ria.

assess vt valorar.

assessment n valoración f.

assessor n asesor/a m/f.

assets npl bienes mpl.

assiduous adj diligente, aplicado/da; **~ly** adv diligentemente.

assign vt asignar.

assignation n cita f.

assignment n asignación f; tarea f.

assimilate vt asimilar.

assimilation n asimilación f.

assist vt asistir, ayudar, socorrer.

assistance n asistencia f; socorro m.

assistant n asistente, ayudante m.

associate vt asociar; * adj asociado/da; * n socio m.

association n asociación, sociedad f.

assonance n asonancia f.

assorted adj surtido/da.

assortment n surtido m.

assuage vt mitigar, suavizar.

assume vt asumir; suponer.

assumption n supuesto m.

Assumption n Asunción f.

assurance n seguro m.

assure vt asegurar.

assuredly adv sin duda.

asterisk n asterisco m.

astern adv (mar) a popa.

asthma n asma f.

asthmatic adj asmático/ca.

astonish vt pasmar, sorprender.

astonishing adj asombroso/sa; **~ly** adv asombrosamente.

astonishment n asombro m.

astound vt pasmar.

astray adv: **to go ~** extraviarse; **to lead ~** llevar por mal camino.

astride adv a horcajadas.

astringent adj astringente.

astrologer n astrólogo/ga m/f.

astrological adj astrológico/ca.

astrology n astrología f.

astronaut n astronauta m/f.

astronomer n astrónomo m.

astronomical adj astronómico/ca.

astronomy n astronomía f.

astute adj astuto/ta.

asylum n asilo, refugio m.

at prep a; en; **~ once** en seguida; ya; **~ all** en absoluto; **~ all events** en todo caso; **~ first** al principio; **~ last** por fin.

atheism n ateísmo m.

atheist n ateo m, atea f.

athlete n atleta m/f.

athletic adj atlético/ca.

atlas n atlas m invar.

atmosphere n atmósfera f.

atmospheric adj atmosférico/ca.

atom n átomo m.

atom bomb n bomba atómica f.

atomic adj atómico/ca.

atone vt expiar.

atonement n expiación f.

atop adv encima.

atrocious adj atroz; **~ly** adv atrozmente.

atrocity n atrocidad, enormidad f.

atrophy n (med) atrofia f.

attach vt adjuntar.

attaché n agregado m.

attachment n afecto m.

attack vt atacar; acometer; * n ataque m.

attacker n asaltante m.

attain vt conseguir, obtener.

attainable adj asequible.

attempt vt intentar; probar, experimentar; * n intento m, tentativa f.

attend vt servir; asistir; **to ~ to** ocuparse de; * vi prestar atención.

attendance n presencia f.

attendant n sirviente m.

attention n atención f; cuidado m.

attentive adj atento/ta; cuidadoso/sa; **~ly** adv con atención.

attenuate vt atenuar, disminuir.

attest vt atestiguar.

attic n desván m; guardilla f.

attire n atavío m.

attitude n actitud, postura f.

attorney-at-law n abogado/da m/f.

attract vt atraer.

attraction n atracción f; atractivo m.

attractive adj atractivo/va.

attribute *vt* atribuir; * *n* atributo *m*.
attrition *n* agotamiento *m*.
auburn *adj* moreno/na, castaño/ña.
auction *n* subasta *f*.
auctioneer *n* subastador/a, remata-dor/a *m/f*.
audacious *adj* audaz, temerario/ria; ~ly *adv* atrevidamente.
audacity *n* audacia, osadía *f*.
audible *adj* perceptible al oído; ~ly *adv* de manera audible.
audience *n* audiencia *f*; auditorio *m*.
audit *n* auditoría *f*; * *vt* auditar.
auditor *n* censor/a de cuentas *m/f*.
auditory *adj* auditivo/va.
augment *vt* aumentar, acrecentar; * *vi* crecer.
augmentation *n* aumentación *f*; aumento *m*.
August *n* agosto *m*.
august *adj* majestuoso/sa.
aunt *n* tía *f*.
au pair *n* au pair *f*.
aura *n* aura *f*.
auspices *npl* auspicios *mpl*.
auspicious *adj* propicio/cia; ~ly *adv* favorablemente.
austere *adj* austero/ra, severo/ra; ~ly *adv* austeramente.
austerity *n* austeridad *f*.
authentic *adj* auténtico/ca; ~ly *adv* auténticamente.
authenticate *vt* autenticar.
authenticity *n* autenticidad *f*.
author *n* autor/a *m/f*; escritor/a *m/f*.
authoress *n* autora; escritora *f*.
authoritarian *adj* autoritario/ria.
authoritative *adj* autoritativo/va; ~ly *adv* autoritativamente, con autoridad.
authority *n* autoridad *f*.
authorization *n* autorización *f*.
authorize *vt* autorizar.
authorship *n* autoría *f*.
auto, automobile *n* carro, coche, auto *m*.
autocrat *n* autócrata *m*.
autocratic *adj* autocrático/ca.
autograph *n* autógrafo *m*.
automated *adj* automatizado/da.
automatic *adj* automático/ca.
automaton *n* autómata *m*.
autonomy *n* autonomía *f*.
autopsy *n* autopsia *f*.
autumn *n* otoño *m*.
autumnal *adj* otoñal.
auxiliary *adj* auxiliar, asistente.
avail *vt*: to ~ **oneself of** aprovecharse de; * *n*: **to no ~** en vano.
available *adj* disponible.
avalanche *n* alud *m*.
avarice *n* avaricia *f*.
avaricious *adj* avaro/ra.
avenge *vt* vengarse, castigar.
avenue *n* avenida *f*.
aver *vt* afirmar, declarar.

average *vt* tomar un término medio; * *n* término medio *m*.
aversion *n* aversión *f*, disgusto *m*.
avert *vt* desviar, apartar.
aviary *n* pajarera *f*.
avoid *vt* evitar, escapar, huir; * *vr* zafarse de.
avoidable *adj* evitable.
await *vt* aguardar.
awake *vt* despertar; * *vi* despertarse; * *adj* despierto/ta.
awakening *n* despertar.
award *vt* otorgar; *Lat Am* acordar; * *n* premio *m*; sentencia, decisión *f*.
aware *adj* consciente; vigilante.
awareness *n* conciencia *f*.
away *adv* ausente, fuera; ~! ¡fuera! , ¡quita de ahí!, ¡marcha! **far and ~** de mucho, con mucho.
away game *n* partido fuera de casa *m*.
awe *n* miedo, temor *m*.
awe-inspiring, awesome *adj* imponente.
awful *adj* tremendo/da; horroroso/sa; ~ly *adv* terriblemente.
awhile *adv* un rato, algún tiempo.
awkward *adj* torpe, rudo/da, poco diestro/tra; ~ly *adv* groseramente, toscamente.
awkwardness *n* tosquedad, grosería, poca habilidad *f*.
awl *n* lezna *f*.
awning *n* (*mar*) toldo *m*.
awry *adv* oblicuamente, torcidamente, al través.
ax *n* hacha *f*; * *vt* despedir; cortar.
axiom *n* axioma *m*.
axis *n* eje *m*.
axle *n* eje *m*.
ay(e) *excl* sí.

B

baa *n* balido *m*; * *vi* balar.
babble *vi* charlar, parlotear; ~ , **babbling** *n* charla, cháchara *f*.
babbler *n* charlador/a, charlatán/ana *m/f*.
babe, baby *n* niño/a, pequeño/a, nene/a, *Lat Am* tierno/na *m/f*; **small** ~ mamón/ona *m/f*.
baboon *n* babuino *m*.
babyhood *n* niñez *f*.
babyish *adj* niñero/ra; pueril.
baby carriage *n* cochecito *m*.
baby linen *n* ropita de niño *f*.
bachelor *n* soltero *m*; bachiller *m*.
bachelorship *n* soltería *f*; bachillerato *m*.
back *n* dorso *m*; revés de la mano *m*; * *adv* atrás, detrás; **a few years ~** hace algunos años; * *vt* sostener, apoyar, favorecer.
backbite *vt* hablar mal del que está ausente; difamar.
backbiter *n* detractor/a *m/f*.
backbone *n* hueso dorsal, espinazo *m*.
backdate *vt* antedatar.

backdoor n puerta trasera f.

backer n partidario/ria m/f.

backgammon n backgammon m.

background n fondo m.

backlash n reacción f.

backlog n trabajo acumulado m.

back number n número atrasado m.

backpack n mochila f.

back payment n paga atrasada f.

backside n trasero m.

back-up lights npl (auto) luces de marcha atrás fpl.

backward adj tardo/da, lento/ta; * adv hacia atrás.

bacon n tocino m.

bad adj mal/malo; perverso/sa; infeliz; dañoso/sa; indispuesto/ta; **~ly** adv malamente.

badge n señal f; símbolo m; divisa f.

badger n tejón m; * vt fatigar; cansar, atormentar.

badminton n bádminton m.

badness n maldad, mala calidad f.

baffle vt confundir, hundir; acosar.

bag n saco m; bolsa f.

baggage n bagaje, equipaje m.

bagpipe n gaita f.

bail n fianza, caución (juratoria) f; fiador m; * vt caucionar, fiar.

bailiff n alguacil m; mayordomo m.

bait vt cebar; atraer; * n cebo m; anzuelo m.

baize n bayeta f.

bake vt cocer en horno.

bakery n panadería f.

baker n hornero/ra, panadero/ra m/f; **~'s dozen** trece piezas.

baking n cocción f.

baking powder n levadura f.

balance n balanza f; equilibrio m; saldo de una cuenta m; **to lose one's ~** caerse, dar en tierra; * vt pesar en balanza; contrapesar; saldar; considerar, examinar.

balance sheet n balance m.

balcony n balcón m.

bald adj calvo/va.

baldness n calvicie f.

bale n bala f; * vt embalar; tirar el agua del bote.

baleful adj triste, funesto/ta; **~ly** adv tristemente; míseramente.

ball n bola f; pelota f; baile m, balón m.

ballad n balada f.

ballast n lastre, m * vt lastrar.

ballerina n bailarina f.

ballet n ballet m.

ballistic adj balístico/ca.

balloon n globo m.

ballot n voto m; escrutinio m; * vi votar.

ballpoint (pen) n bolígrafo m.

ballroom n salón de baile m.

balm, balsam n bálsamo m; * vt untar con bálsamo.

balmy adj balsámico/ca; fragante.

balustrade n balaustrada f.

bamboo n bambú m.

bamboozle vt (col) engañar.

ban n prohibición f; * vt prohibir.

banal adj vulgar.

banana n plátano m.

band n faja f; cuadrilla f; banda (de soldados) f; orquesta f.

bandage n venda f, vendaje m; * vt vendar.

Band-Aid™ n Tirita™ f, Lat Am Curita™ f.

bandit n bandido/da m/f.

bandstand n quiosco m.

bandy vt pelotear; discutir.

bandy-legged adj patizambo/ba.

bang n golpe m; * vt golpear; cerrar con violencia.

bangle n brazalete m.

bangs npl flequillo m.

banish vt desterrar, echar fuera, proscribir, expatriar.

banishment n destierro m.

banister(s) n(pl) pasamanos m.

banjo n banjo m.

bank n orilla (de río) f; montón de tierra m; banco m; dique m; escollo m; * vt poner dinero en un banco; **to ~ on** contar con.

bank account n cuenta de banco f.

bank card n tarjeta bancaria f.

banker n banquero/ra m/f.

banking n banca f; **electronic ~** banca electrónica.

banknote n billete de banco m.

bankrupt adj insolvente; * n fallido/da, quebrado/da m.

bankruptcy n bancarrota, quiebra f, Lat Am valencia f.

bank statement n detalle de cuenta m.

banner n bandera f; estandarte m.

banquet n banquete m.

banter n zumba f.

baptism n bautismo m.

baptismal adj bautismal.

baptistery n bautisterio m.

baptize vt bautizar.

bar n bar m; barra f; tranca f; obstáculo m; (law) abogacía f; * vt impedir; prohibir; excluir.

barbarian n bárbaro/ra m/f; * adj bárbaro/ra, cruel.

barbaric adj bárbaro/ra.

barbarism n (gr) barbarismo m; crueldad f.

barbarity n barbaridad, inhumanidad f.

barbarous adj bárbaro/ra, cruel.

barbecue n barbacoa f.

barber n peluquero/ra.

barber shop n peluquería f.

bar code n código de barras m.

bard n bardo m; poeta m.

bare adj desnudo/da, descubierto/ta; simple; puro/ra; * vt desnudar, descubrir.

barefaced adj desvergonzado/da, impudente.

barefoot(ed) adj descalzo, sin zapatos.

bareheaded *adj* descubierto/ta.

barelegged *adj* con las piernas desnudas.

barely *adv* apenas, solamente.

bareness *n* desnudez *f*.

bargain *n* ganga *f*; contrato, pacto *m*; * *vi* pactar; negociar; **to ~ for** esperar.

barge *n* barcaza *f*.

baritone *n* (*mus*) barítono *m*.

bark *n* corteza *f*; ladrido *m* (del perro); * *vi* ladrar.

barley *n* cebada *f*.

barmaid *n* camarera *f*.

barman *n* barman *m*.

barn *n* granero, pajar *m*.

barnacles *npl* percebe *m*.

barometer *n* barómetro *m*.

baron *n* barón *m*.

baroness *n* baronesa *f*.

baronial *adj* de barón.

barracks *npl* cuartel *m*.

barrage *n* descarga *f*; (*fig*) lluvia *f*.

barrel *n* barril *m*; cañón de escopeta *m*.

barrel organ *n* organillo de cilindro *m*.

barren *adj* estéril, infructuoso/sa; (*fig*) yermo/ma.

barricade *n* barricada *f*; estacada *f*; barrera *f*; * *vt* cerrar con barreras, empalizar.

barrier *n* barrera *f*; obstáculo *m*.

barring *adv* excepto, fuera de.

barrow *n* carretilla *f*.

bartender *n* barman *m*.

barter *vi* baratar; * *vt* cambiar, trocar.

base *n* fondo *m*; base *f*; basa *f*; pedestal *m*; zócalo *m*; * *vt* apoyar; * *adj* bajo/ja, vil.

baseball *n* béisbol *m*.

base-board *n* zócalo *m*.

baseless *adj* sin fondo/base.

basement *n* sótano *m*.

baseness *n* bajeza, vileza *f*.

bash *vt* golpear.

bashful *adj* vergonzoso/sa, modesto/ta, tímido/da; **~ly** *adv* vergonzosamente.

basic *adj* básico/ca; **~ally** *adv* básicamente.

basilisk *n* basilisco *m*.

basin *n* jofaina, bacía *f*.

basis *n* base *f*; fundamento *m*.

bask *vi* ponerse a tomar el sol.

basket *n* cesta, canasta *f*.

basketball *n* baloncesto *m*, *Lat Am* básquetbol *m*.

bass *n* (*mus*) contrabajo *m*.

bassoon *n* bajón *m*.

bass viol *n* viola *f*.

bass voice *n* bajo cantante *m*.

bastard *n, adj* bastardo/da *m/f*.

bastardy *n* bastardía *f*.

baste *vt* pringar; hilvanar.

basting *n* hilván *m*; apaleamiento *m*; paliza *f*.

bastion *n* (*mil*) bastión *m*.

bat *n* murciélago *m*.

batch *n* serie *f*.

bath *n* baño *m*.

bathe *vt* (*vt*) bañar(se).

bathing suit *n* traje de baño *m*.

bathos *n* estilo bajo en la poesía *m*.

bathroom *n* (cuarto de) baño *m*.

baths *npl* piscina *f*.

bathtub *n* baño *m*, bañera *f*.

baton *n* batuta *f*.

battalion *n* (*mil*) batallón *m*.

batter *vt* apalear; batir, cañonear; * *n* batido *m*.

battering ram *n* (*mil*) ariete *m*.

battery *n* batería *f*.

battle *n* combate *m*; batalla *f*; * *vi* batallar, combatir.

battle array *n* orden de batalla *f*.

battlefield *n* campo de batalla *m*.

battlement *n* muralla almenada *f*.

battleship *n* acorazado *m*.

bawdy *adj* indecente.

bawl *vi* gritar, vocear.

bay *n* bahía *f*; laurel, lauro *m*; * *vi* balar; * *adj* bayo.

bayonet *n* bayoneta *f*.

bay window *n* ventana salediza *f*.

bazaar *n* bazar *m*.

be *vi* ser; estar.

beach *n* playa, orilla *f*.

beacon *n* almenara *f*.

bead *n* cuenta *f*; **~s** *npl* rosario *m*.

beagle *n* sabueso *m*.

beak *n* pico *m*.

beaker *n* taza con pico *f*.

beam *n* rayo de luz *m*; travesaño *m*; pareja *f*; * *vi* brillar.

bean *n* alubia *f*, frijol *m*, judía *f*; **green ~, French ~** judía verde *f*.

beansprouts *npl* brotes de soja *mpl*.

bear *vt* llevar; sostener; soportar; producir; parir; * *vi* sufrir (algún dolor).

bear *n* oso *m*; **she ~** osa *f*.

bearable *adj* soportable.

beard *n* barba *f*.

bearded *adj* barbado/da.

bearer *n* portador/a *m/f*; árbol fructífero *m*.

bearing *n* relación *f*.

beast *n* bestia *f*; hombre brutal *m*; **~ of burden** acémila *f*.

beastliness *n* bestialidad, brutalidad *f*.

beastly *adj* bestial, brutal; * *adv* brutalmente.

beat *vt* golpear; tocar (un tambor); **to ~ time** (with the sole of the shoe) zapatear; * *vi* pulsar, palpitar; * *n* golpe *m*; pulsación *f*.

beatific *adj* beatífico/ca.

beatify *vt* beatificar, santificar.

beating *n* paliza, zurra *f*, *Lat Am* golpiza *f*; pulsación *f*, zumba *f*.

beatitude *n* beatitud, felicidad *f*.

beautiful *adj* hermoso/sa, bello; **~ly** *adv* con belleza/perfección.

beautify *vt* hermosear; embellecer; adornar.

beauty *n* hermosura, belleza *f*; **~ salon** *n* salón de belleza *m*; **~ spot** *n* lunar *m*.

beaver n castor m.

because conj porque, a causa de.

beckon vi hacer seña con la cabeza/la mano.

become vt convenir; estar bien; * vi hacerse, convertirse, venir a parar.

becoming adj decente, conveniente.

bed n cama f.

bedclothes npl cobertores npl, mantas/colchas fpl.

bedding n ropa de cama f.

bedecked adj adornado/da.

bedlam n manicomio m.

bedpost n pilar de cama m.

bedridden adj postrado/da en cama, encamado/da.

bedroom n dormitorio m.

bedspread n colcha f.

bedtime n hora de irse a la cama f.

bee n abeja f.

beech n haya f.

beef n carne de vaca f.

beefburger n hamburguesa f.

beefsteak n bistec m.

beehive n colmena f.

beeline n línea recta f.

beer n cerveza f.

beeswax n cera f.

beet n remolacha f.

beetle n escarabajo m.

befall vi suceder, acontecer, sobrevenir.

befit vt convenir, acomodarse a.

before adv, prep antes de; delante, enfrente; ante.

beforehand adv de antemano, anticipadamente.

befriend vt proteger, amparar.

beg vt mendigar, rogar; suplicar; suponer; * vi vivir de limosna.

beget vt engendrar.

beggar n mendigo/ga m/f.

begin vt, vi comenzar, empezar.

beginner n principiante m; novicio/cia m/f.

beginning n principio, origen m.

begrudge vt envidiar.

behalf n on ~ of de parte de.

behave vi comportarse, portarse, conducirse.

behavior n conducta f; modo de portarse m.

behead vt decapitar, cortar la cabeza.

behind prep detrás; atrás; a la, en zaga; * adv atrasadamente.

behold vt ver, contemplar, observar.

behoove vi importar, ser útil; incumbir.

beige adj color beige.

being n existencia f; estado m; ser m.

belated adj atrasado/da.

belch vi eructar, vomitar; * n eructo m.

belfry n campanario m.

belie vt desmentir, calumniar.

belief n fe, creencia f; opinión f; -credo m.

believable adj creíble.

believe vt creer; * vi pensar, imaginar.

believer n creyente, fiel, cristiano/na m/f.

belittle vt minimizar.

bell n campana f.

bellicose adj belicoso/sa.

belligerent adj beligerante.

bellow vi bramar; rugir; vociferar; * n bramido m.

bellows npl fuelle m.

belly n vientre m; panza f.

bellyful n panzada f; hartura f.

belong vi pertenecer.

belongings npl pertenencias fpl.

beloved adj querido/da, amado/da.

below adv, prep debajo, inferior; abajo.

belt n cinturón, cinto m; zona f.

beltway n periférico m; carretera de circunvalación f.

bemoan vt deplorar, lamentar.

bemused adj confundido/da.

bench n banco m, banquillo m.

bend vt encorvar, inclinar, plegar; hacer una reverencia; * vi encorvarse, inclinarse; * n curva f.

beneath adv, prep debajo, abajo.

benediction n bendición f.

benefactor n bienhechor m.

benefice n beneficio m; beneficio eclesiástico m.

beneficent adj benéfico/ca.

beneficial adj beneficioso/sa, provechoso/sa, útil.

beneficiary n beneficiario/ria m.

benefit n beneficio m; utilidad f; provecho m; * vt beneficiar; * vi utilizarse; prevalerse.

benefit night n representación dramática a beneficio de un actor/de una actriz f.

benevolence n benevolencia f; donativo gratuito m.

benevolent adj benévolo/la.

benign adj benigno/na; afable; liberal.

bent n inclinación f.

benzene n (chem) bencina f.

bequeath vt legar en testamento.

bequest n legado m.

bereave vt privar.

bereavement n pérdida f.

beret n boina f.

berm n arcén m.

berry n baya f.

berserk adj loco/ca.

berth n (mar) amarradero m, camarote m.

beseech vt suplicar, implorar, conjurar, rogar.

beset vt acosar.

beside(s) prep al lado de; excepto; sobre; fuera de; * adv por otra parte.

besiege vt sitiar, bloquear.

best adj mejor; * adv (lo) mejor; * n lo mejor m.

bestial adj bestial, brutal; ~ly adv bestialmente.

bestiality n bestialidad, brutalidad f.

bestow vt dar, conferir; otorgar.

bestseller n bestseller m.

bet n apuesta f; * vt apostar.

betray *vt* traicionar; divulgar algún secreto.

betrayal *n* traición *f*.

betroth *vt* contraer esponsales.

betrothal *n* esponsales *mpl*.

better *adj*, *adv* mejor; **so much the ~** tanto mejor; * *vt* mejorar, reformar.

betting *n* juego *m*.

between *prep* entre, en medio de.

bevel *n* cartabón *m*.

beverage *n* bebida *f*; trago *m*.

bevy *n* bandada (de aves) *f*.

beware *vi* guardarse.

bewilder *vt* pasmar.

bewilderment *n* perplejidad *f*.

bewitch *vt* encantar, hechizar.

beyond *prep* más allá, más adelante, fuera de.

bias *n* propensión, inclinación *f*; sesgo *m*; prejuicio *m*.

bib *n* babador *m*.

Bible *n* Biblia *f*.

biblical *adj* bíblico/ca.

bibliography *n* bibliografía *f*.

bicarbonate of soda *n* bicarbonato de soda *m*.

bicker *vi* escaramucear, reñir, disputar.

bicycle *n* bicicleta *f*.

bid *vt* mandar, ordenar; ofrecer; * *n* oferta *f*; tentativa *f*.

bidding *n* orden *f*; mandato *m*; ofrecimiento *m*.

bide *vt* sufrir, aguantar.

biennial *adj* bienal.

bifocals *npl* gafas bifocales *fpl*.

bifurcated *adj* bifurcado/da.

big *adj* grande, lleno/na; inflado/da.

bigamist *n* bígamo/ma *m/f*.

bigamy *n* bigamia *f*.

big dipper *n* montaña rusa *f*.

bigheaded *adj* engreído/da.

bigness *n* grandeza *f*.

bigot *n* fanático/ca *m/f*.

bigoted *adj* fanático/ca.

bike *n* bici *f*; bicicleta *f*; **mountain ~** bicicleta de montaña.

bikini *n* bikini *m*.

bilberry *n* arándano *m*.

bile *n* bilis *f*.

bilingual *adj* bilingüe.

bilious *adj* bilioso/sa.

bill *n* pico de ave *m*; billete *m*; cuenta *f*.

billboard *n* cartelera *f*.

billet *n* alojamiento *m*.

billfold *n* cartera *f*.

billiards *npl* billar *m*.

billiard-table *n* mesa de billar *f*.

billion *n* mil millones *mpl*, millardo *m*.

billy *n* porra *f*.

bin *n* cubo de la basura *m*.

bind *vt* atar; unir; encuadernar.

binder *n* encuadernador/a *m/f*.

binding *n* venda, faja *f*.

binge *n* juerga *f*.

bingo *n* bingo *m*.

biochemistry *n* bioquímica *f*.

biodegradable *adj* biodegradable.

biodiversity *n* biodiversity *f*.

binoculars *npl* prismáticos *mpl*, *Lat Am* binóculos *mpl*.

biographer *n* biógrafo/fa *m/f*.

biographical *adj* biográfico/ca.

biography *n* biografía *f*.

biological *adj* biológico/ca.

biology *n* biología *f*.

biped *n* bípedo *m*.

birch *n* abedul *m*.

bird *n* ave *f*; pájaro *m*.

bird's-eye view *n* vista de pájaro *f*.

bird-watcher *n* ornitólogo/ga *m/f*.

birth *n* nacimiento *m*; origen *m*; parto *m*.

birth certificate *n* partida de nacimiento *f*.

birth control *n* control de natalidad *m*.

birthday *n* cumpleaños *m invar*, *Lat Am* onomástica *f*.

birthplace *n* lugar de nacimiento *m*.

birthright *n* derechos de nacimiento *mpl*; primogenitura *f*.

biscuit *n* bizcocho *m*.

bisect *vt* bisecar.

bishop *n* obispo *m*.

bison *n* bisonte *m*.

bit *n* bocado *m*; pedacito *m*.

bitch *n* perra *f*; (*fig*) zorra *f*.

bite *vt* morder; picar; **~ the dust** (*col*) morder la tierra, morir; * *n* mordedura *f*.

bitter *adj* amargo/ga, áspero/ra; mordaz, satírico/ca; penoso/sa; **~ly** *adv* amargamente; con pena; severamente.

bitterness *n* amargor *m*; rencor *m*; pena *f*; dolor *m*.

bitumen *n* betún *m*.

bizarre *adj* raro/ra, extravagante.

blab *vi* chismear.

black *adj* negro/gra, oscuro/ra; funesto/ta; * *n* color negro *m*.

blackberry *n* zarzamora *f*.

blackbird *n* mirlo *m*.

black box *n* caja negra *f*.

blacken *vt* teñir de negro; ennegrecer.

black ice *n* hielo invisible *m*.

blackjack *n* veintiuna *f*.

blackleg *n* esquirol *m*.

blacklist *n* lista negra *f*.

blackmail *n* chantaje *m*; * *vt* chantajear.

black market *n* mercado negro *m*.

blackness *n* negrura *f*.

black pudding *n* morcilla *f*.

black sheep *n* oveja negra *f*.

blacksmith *n* herrero *m*.

blackthorn *n* endrino *m*.

bladder *n* vejiga *f*.

blade *n* hoja *f*; filo *m*; escobilla *f*.

blame *vt* culpar; * *n* culpa *f*.

blameless *adj* inocente, irreprensible, puro/ra; **~ly** *adv* inocentemente.

blanch *vt* blanquear.

bland *adj* blando/da, suave, dulce, apacible.

blank *adj* blanco/ca; pálido/da; * *n* blanco *m*.

blank check *n* cheque en blanco *m*.

blanket *n* manta *f*, *Lat Am* cobija *f*, *Lat Am* frazada *f*.

blare *vi* resonar.

blasé *adj* indiferente.

blaspheme *vt* blasfemar, jurar, decir blasfemias.

blasphemous *adj* blasfemo/ma.

blasphemy *n* blasfemia *f*.

blast *n* soplo de aire *m*; carga explosiva *f*; * *vt* volar.

blast-off *n* lanzamiento *m*.

blatant *adj* obvio.

blaze *n* llama *f*; * *vi* encenderse en llamas; brillar, resplandecer.

bleach *vt* blanquear al sol; * *vi* blanquear; * *n* lejía *f*.

bleached *adj* teñido/da de rubio; descolorido/da.

bleachers *npl* gradas al sol *fpl*.

bleak *adj* pálido/da, descolorido/da; frío, helado/da.

bleakness *n* frialdad *f*; palidez *f*.

bleary(-eyed) *adj* legañoso/sa.

bleat *n* balido *m*; * *vi* balar.

bleed *vi, vt* sangrar.

bleeding *n* sangría *f*.

bleeper *n* busca *m*.

blemish *vt* manchar, ensuciar; infamar; * *n* tacha *f*; deshonra, infamia *f*.

blend *vt* mezclar.

bless *vt* bendecir.

blessing *n* bendición *f*; beneficio *m*; ventaja *f*.

blight *vt* arruinar.

blind *adj* ciego/ga; ~ **alley** *n* callejón sin salida *m*; * *vt* cegar; deslumbrar; * *n* velo *m*; (**Venetian**) ~ persiana *f*.

blinders *npl* anteojeras *fpl*.

blindfold *vt* vendar los ojos; ~**ed** *adj* con los ojos vendados.

blindly *adv* ciegamente, a ciegas.

blindness *n* ceguera *f*.

blind side *n* punto ciego *m*.

blind spot *n* punto ciego *m*.

blink *vi* parpadear.

blinkers *npl* anteojeras *fpl*.

bliss *n* felicidad (eterna) *f*.

blissful *adj* feliz en sumo grado; beato/ta, bienaventurado/da; ~**ly** *adv* felizmente.

blissfulness *n* suprema felicidad *f*.

blister *n* ampolla *f*; * *vi* ampollarse.

blitz *n* bombardeo aéreo *m*.

blizzard *n* ventisca *f*.

bloated *adj* hinchado/da.

blob *n* gota *f*.

bloc *n* bloque *m*.

block *n* bloque *m*; obstáculo *m*; zoquete *m*; manzana *f*, *Lat Am* cuadra *f*; ~ (**up**) *vt* bloquear.

blockade *n* bloqueo *m*; * *vt* bloquear.

blockage *n* obstrucción *f*.

blockbuster *n* éxito de público *m*.

blockhead *n* bruto, necio, zopenco *m*; (*col*) zoquete *m*.

blond *adj* rubio/bia; * *n* rubio/bia *m/f*.

blood *n* sangre *f*.

blood donor *n* donante de sangre *m/f*.

blood group *n* grupo sanguíneo *m*.

bloodhound *n* sabueso *m*.

bloodily *adv* sangrientamente, inhumanamente.

bloodiness *n* (*fig*) crueldad *f*.

bloodless *adj* exangüe; sin efusión de sangre.

blood poisoning *n* septicemia *f*.

blood pressure *n* presión sanguínea *f*.

blood sausage *n* morcilla *f*.

bloodshed *n* efusión de sangre *f*; matanza *f*, derramamiento de sangre *m*.

bloodshot *adj* ensangrentado/da.

bloodstream *n* corriente sanguínea *f*.

bloodsucker *n* sanguijuela *f*; (*fig*) desollador/a *m/f*.

blood test *n* análisis de sangre *m invar*.

bloodthirsty *adj* sanguinario/ria.

blood transfusion *n* transfusión sanguínea *f*.

blood vessel *n* vena *f*; vaso sanguíneo *m*.

bloody *adj* sangriento/ta, ensangren-tado/da; cruel; ~ **minded** *adj* sanguinario/ria.

bloom *n* flor *f*; (*also fig*); * *vi* florecer.

blossom *n* flor *f*.

blot *vt* manchar (lo escrito); cancelar; denigrar; * *n* mancha *f*.

blotchy *adj* muy manchado/da.

blotting paper *n* papel secante *m*.

blouse *n* blusa *f*.

blow *vi* soplar; sonar; * *vt* soplar; inflar; **to ~ up** volar; * *n* golpe *m*.

blowout *n* pinchazo *m*.

blowpipe *n* soplete *m*.

blubber *n* grasa de ballena *f*; * *vi* lloriquear.

bludgeon *n* cachiporra *f*; palocorto *m*.

blue *adj* azul.

bluebell, harebell *n* (*bot*) campanilla *f*.

blue berets *npl* cascos azules *mpl*.

bluebottle *n* moscarda *f*.

blueness *n* color azul *m*.

blueprint *n* (*fig*) anteproyecto *m*.

bluff *n* farol *m*; * *vt* farolear.

bluish *adj* azulado/da.

blunder *n* metedura de pata *f*; error craso *m*; * *vi* meter la pata.

blunt *adj* obtuso/sa; grosero/ra; * *vt* embotar.

bluntly *adv* sin artificio; claramente; obtusamente.

bluntness *n* embotadura, franqueza *f*.

blur *n* contorno borroso *m*; * *vt* hacer borroso.

blurt out *vt* descolgarse con.

blush *n* rubor *m*; sonrojo *m*; * *vi* ponerse colorado/da, sonrojarse.

blustery *adj* tempestuoso/sa.

boa n boa f (serpiente).

boar n verraco m; **wild ~** jabalí m.

board n tabla f; mesa f; consejo m; * vt embarcarse en; subir a.

boarder n pensionista m/f.

boarding card n tarjeta de embarque f.

boarding house n pensión f, casa de huéspedes f.

boarding school n internado m.

boast vi jactarse; * n jactancia f; ostentación f.

boastful adj jactancioso/sa.

boat n barco m; bote m; barca f.

boating n canotaje m; paseo en barquilla m; regata f.

bobsleigh n bob m.

bode vt presagiar, pronosticar.

bodice n corsé m.

bodily adj, adv corpóreo/rea; corporalmente.

body n cuerpo m; individuo m; gremio m; **any ~** cualquier; **every ~** cada uno.

body-building n culturismo m.

bodyguard n guardaespaldas m/f invar.

bodywork n (auto) carrocería f.

bog n pantano m.

boggy adj pantanoso/sa, palustre.

bogus adj postizo.

boil vi hervir; bullir; hervirle a uno la sangre; * vt cocer; * n furúnculo m.

boiled egg n huevo duro m, huevo pasado por agua m.

boiled potatoes npl patatas hervidas fpl.

boiler n marmita f; caldero m.

boiling point n punto de ebullición m.

boisterous adj borrascoso/sa, tem-pes-tuoso/sa; violento/ta; **~ly** adv tumultuosamente, furiosamente.

bold adj ardiente, valiente; audaz; temerario/ria; impudente; **~ly** adv descaradamente.

boldness n intrepidez f; valentía f; osadía f.

bolster n travesero m; cabezal m; * vt reforzar.

bolt n cerrojo m; * vt cerrar con cerrojo.

bomb n bomba f; **~ disposal** desactivación de explosivos f.

bombard vt bombardear.

bombardier n bombardero m.

bombardment n bombardeo m.

bombshell n (fig) bomba f.

bond n ligadura f; vínculo m; vale m; obligación f.

bondage n esclavitud, servidumbre f.

bond holder n titular de bonos m/f.

bone n hueso m; * vt desosar.

boneless adj sin huesos; desosado/da.

bonfire n hoguera f.

bonnet n gorra f; bonete m.

bonny adj bonito/ta.

bonsai n bonsái m.

bonus n cuota, prima f.

bony adj osudo/da.

boo vt abuchear.

booby trap n trampa explosiva f.

book n libro m; **to bring to ~** vt pedir cuentas a alguien.

bookbinder n encuadernador/a m/f.

bookcase n estantería f.

bookkeeper n tenedor/a de libros m/f.

bookkeeping n teneduría de libros f.

bookmaker n corredor de apuestas m.

bookmarker n registro de un libro m.

bookseller n librero/ra m/f.

bookstore n librería f.

bookworm n polilla f; ratón de biblioteca m.

boom n trueno m; boom m; * vi retumbar.

boon n presente, regalo m; favor m.

boor n patán, villano/na m/f.

boorish adj rústico/ca, agreste.

boost n estímulo m; vt estimular.

booster n reinyección f.

boot n bota f; zapata f; **to ~** adv además.

booth n barraca, cabaña f.

booty n botín m; presa f; saqueo m.

booze vi emborracharse; * n bebida f.

border n orilla f; borde m; margen f; frontera f; * vt lindar con.

borderline n frontera f.

bore vt taladrar; barrenar; fastidiar; * n taladro m; calibre m; pelmazo/za m/f.

boredom n aburrimiento m.

borehole n barreno m.

boring adj aburrido/da, Lat Am abu-rrido/ra.

born adj nacido/da; destinado/da.

borrow vt pedir prestado/da.

borrower n prestamista m.

bosom n seno, pecho m.

bosom friend n amigo/ga íntimo/ma m/f.

boss n jefe m; patrón/ona m/f.

botanic(al) adj botánico/ca.

botanist n botánico m.

botany n botánica f.

botch vt chapuzar.

botch-up n mamarracho m.

both adj ambos, entrambos; ambas, entrambas; * conj tanto como.

bother vt preocupar; fastidiar; * n molestia f.

bottle n botella f; * vt embotellar.

bottleneck n embotellamiento m.

bottle-opener n abrebotellas m invar.

bottom n fondo m; fundamento m; * adj más bajo/ja; último/ma.

bottomless adj insondable; excesivo/va; impenetrable.

bough n brazo del árbol m; ramo m.

boulder n canto rodado m.

bounce vi rebotar; ser rechazado/da; * n rebote m.

bound n límite m; salto m; repercusión f; * vi resaltar; * adj destinado/da.

boundary n límite m; frontera f.

boundless adj ilimitado/da, infinito/ta.

bounteous, bountiful adj liberal, generoso/sa, bienhechor.

bounty n liberalidad, bondad f.

bouquet n ramillete de flores m.

bourgeois adj burgués/esa.

bout n ataque m; encuentro m.

bovine adj bovino/na.

bow[1] vt encorvar, doblar; * vi encorvarse; hacer una reverencia; * n reverencia, inclinación f.

bow[2] n arco m; arco de violín; corbata f; *Lat Am* bow m; nudo m.

bowels npl intestinos mpl; entrañas fpl.

bowl n taza; bola f; * vi jugar a las bochas.

bowling n bolos mpl.

bowling alley n bolera f.

bowling-green n campo m para jugar a las bochas.

bowstring n cuerda del arco f.

bow tie n pajarita f.

box n caja, cajita f; palco de teatro m; ~ **on the ear** bofetada f; * vt encajonar; * vi boxear.

boxer n boxeador m.

boxing n boxeo m, *Lat Am* box m.

boxing gloves npl guantes de boxeo mpl.

boxing ring n cuadrilátero m.

box office n taquilla f.

box-seat n asiento de palco m.

boy n muchacho m; niño m; zagal m.

boycott vt boicotear; * n boicot m.

boyfriend n novio m.

boyish adj pueril; frívolo.

bra n sujetador m.

brace n abrazadera f; corrector m.

bracelet n brazalete m.

bracing adj vigorizante.

bracken n (*bot*) helecho m.

bracket n puntal m; paréntesis m; corchete m; * **to ~ with** vt unir, ligar.

brag n jactancia f; * vi jactarse, fanfarronear.

braid n trenza f; * vt trenzar.

brain n cerebro m; seso, juicio m; * vt descerebrar, matar a uno.

brainchild n parto del ingenio m.

brainwash vt lavar el cerebro.

brainwave n idea luminosa f.

brainy adj inteligente.

brainless adj tonto/ta, insensato/ta.

brake n freno m; * vt, vi frenar.

brake fluid n liquido de frenos m.

brake light n luz de frenado f.

brake shoe n (*auto*) zapata de freno f.

bramble n zarza, espina f.

bramble patch n zarzal m.

bran n salvado m.

branch n ramo m; rama f; * vt (vi) ramificar(se).

branch line n (*rail*) empalme, ramal m.

brand n marca f; hierro m; * vt marcar (con un hierro incandescente).

brandish vt blandir, ondear.

brand-new adj flamante.

brandy n coñac m.

brash adj tosco/ca; descarado/da.

brass n bronce m.

brassiere n sujetador m.

brat n crío m.

bravado n baladronada f.

brave adj bravo/va, valiente, atrevi-do/da; * vt desafiar; * n bravo m; **~ly** adv bravamente.

bravery n valor m; magnificencia f.

brawl n pelea, camorra f; * vi pelearse.

brawn n fuerza muscular f; carne de verraco f.

bray vi rebuznar; * n rebuzno (del asno) m.

braze vt soldar con latón; broncear.

brazen adj de latón; desvergonzado/da; impudente; * vi hacerse desca-rado/da.

brazier n brasero m.

breach n rotura f; brecha f; violación f.

bread n pan m; (*fig*) sustento m; **brown ~** pan moreno m.

breadbox n panera f.

breadcrumbs npl migajas fpl.

breadth n anchura f.

breadwinner n sostén de la familia m.

break vt romper; quebrantar; violar; arruinar; interrumpir; * vi romperse; **to ~ into** forzar; **to ~ out** abrirse salida; * n rotura, abertura f; interrupción f; **~ of day** despuntar del día m, aurora f.

breakage n rotura f.

breakdown n avería f; descalabro m.

breakfast n desayuno m; * vi desayunar.

breaking n rompimiento m; principio de las vacaciones en las escuelas m; fractura f.

breakthrough n avance m.

breakwater n rompeolas m invar.

breast n pecho, seno m; pechuga f corazón m.

breastbone n esternón m.

breastplate n peto m; pectoral m; coraza f.

breaststroke n braza f, *Lat Am* pecho m.

breath n aliento m, respiración f; soplo de aire m.

breathe vt, vi respirar; exhalar.

breathing n respiración f; aliento m.

breathing space n descanso, reposo m.

breathless adj falto/ta de aliento; desalentado/da.

breathtaking adj pasmoso/sa.

breed n casta, raza f; * vt procrear, engendrar; producir; educar; * vi multiplicarse.

breeder n criador/a m/f.

breeding n crianza f; buena educación f.

breeze n brisa f.

breezy adj refrescado/da con brisas.

brethren n pl de **brother** hermanos mpl (en estilo grave).

breviary n breviario m.

brevity n brevedad, concisión f.

brew vt hacer; tramar, mezclar; * vi hacerse; tramarse; * n brebaje m.

brewer n cervecero m.

brewery n cervecería f.

briar, brier n zarza f, espino m.

bribe n cohecho, soborno m; * vt cohechar, corromper, sobornar.

bribery n cohecho, soborno m.

bric-a-brac *n* baratijas *fpl.*

brick *n* ladrillo *m;* * *vt* enladrillar.

bricklayer *n* albañil *m.*

bricklaying *n* albañilería *f.*

bridal *adj* nupcial.

bride *n* novia *f.*

bridegroom *n* novio *m.*

bridesmaid *n* madrina de boda *f.*

bridge *n* puente *m/f;* caballete de la nariz *m;* puente de violín *m;* **to build a ~ (over)** *vt* construir un puente (sobre).

bridle *n* brida *f* freno *m;* * *vt* embridar; reprimir, refrenar.

brief *adj* breve, conciso/sa, sucinto/ta; * *n* compendio *m;* breve *m.*

briefcase *n* cartera *f.*

briefly *adv* brevemente, en pocas palabras.

brier *n* = **briar**.

brigade *n* (*mil*) brigada *f.*

brigadier *n* (*mil*) general de brigada *m.*

brigand *n* bandido *m.*

bright *adj* claro/ra, luciente, brillante; **~ly** *adv* espléndidamente.

brighten *vt* pulir, dar lustre; ilustrar; * *vi* aclararse.

brightness *n* esplendor *m,* brillantez *f;* agudeza *f;* claridad *f.*

brilliance *n* brillo *m.*

brilliant *adj* brillante; **~ly** *adv* espléndidamente.

brim *n* borde extremo *m;* orilla *f.*

brimful(l) *adj* lleno/na hasta el borde.

bring *vt* llevar, traer; conducir; inducir, persuadir; **to ~ about** efectuar; **to ~ forth** producir; parir; **to ~ up** educar.

brink *n* orilla *f;* margen *m/f,* borde *m.*

brisk *adj* vivo/va, alegre, jovial; fres-co/ca.

brisket *n* pecho (de un animal) *m.*

briskly *adj* vigorosamente; alegremente; vivamente.

bristle *n* cerda, seta *f;* * *vi* erizarse.

bristly *adj* cerdoso/sa, lleno/na de cerdas.

brittle *adj* quebradizo, frágil.

broach *vt* comenzar a hablar de.

broad *adj* ancho.

broad bean *n* (*bot*) haba *f;* **~s** haba gruesa *fpl.*

broadcast *n* emisión *f;* * *vt, vi* emitir; transmitir.

broadcasting *n* radiodifusión *f.*

broaden *vt, vi* ensanchar(se).

broadly *adv* anchamente.

broad-minded *adj* tolerante.

broadness *n* ancho *m;* anchura *f.*

broadside *n* costado de navío *m;* andanada *f.*

broadways *adv* a lo ancho, por lo ancho.

brocade *n* brocado *m.*

broccoli *n* brécol *m.*

brochure *n* folleto *m.*

brogue *n* abarca *f;* acento irlandés *m.*

broil *vt* asar a la parrilla.

broken *adj* roto/ta, interrumpido/da; **~ English** inglés mal articulado *m.*

broker *n* corredor/a *m/f.*

brokerage *n* corretaje *m.*

bronchial *adj* bronquial.

bronchitis *n* bronquitis *f.*

bronze *n* bronce *m;* * *vt* broncear.

brooch *n* broche *m.*

brood *vi* empollar; meditar; * *n* raza *f;* nidada *f.*

brood-hen *n* empolladora *f.*

brook *n* arroyo *m.*

broom *n* retama *f;* escoba *f.*

broomstick *n* palo de escoba *m.*

broth *n* caldo *m.*

brothel *n* burdel *m.*

brother *n* hermano *m.*

brotherhood *n* hermandad *f;* fraternidad *f.*

brother-in-law *n* cuñado *m.*

brotherly *adj, adv* fraternal; fraternalmente.

brow *n* caja *f;* frente *f;* cima *f.*

browbeat *vt* intimidar.

brown *adj* moreno/na; castaño/ña; **~ paper** *n* papel de estraza *m;* **~ bread** *n* pan moreno *m;* **~ sugar** *n* azúcar terciado *m;* * *n* color moreno *m;* * *vt* volver moreno/na.

browse *vt* ramonear; * *vi* pacer la hierba.

browser *n* navegador *m.*

bruise *vt* magullar; * *n* magulladura, *Lat Am* magullón *m,* contusión *f;* roncha *f.*

brunch *n* desayuno-almuerzo *m.*

brunette *n* morena *f.*

brunt *n* choque *m.*

brush *n* cepillo *m;* escobilla *f;* combate *m;* * *vt* cepillar, *Lat Am* escobillar.

brushwood *n* breñal, zarzal *m.*

brusque *adj* brusco/ca.

Brussels sprout *n* col de Bruselas *f.*

brutal *adj* brutal; **~ly** *adv* brutalmente.

brutality *n* brutalidad *f.*

brutalize *vt* (*vi*) embrutecer(se).

brute *n* bruto *m;* * *adj* feroz, bestial; irracional.

brutish *adj* brutal, bestial; feroz; **~ly** *adv* brutalmente.

bubble *n* burbuja *f;* * *vi* burbujear, bullir.

bubblegum *n* chicle *m.*

bucket *n* cubo, pozal *m.*

buckle *n* hebilla *f;* * *vt* hebillar; abrochar; * *vi* encorvarse.

buckshot *n* perdigones *mpl.*

bucolic *adj* bucólico/ca.

bud *n* pimpollo, botón, capullo *m;* yema *f;* * *vi* brotar.

Buddhism *n* Budismo *m.*

budding *adj* en ciernes.

buddy *n* compañero *m.*

budge *vi* moverse, menearse.

budgerigar *n* periquito *m.*

budget *n* presupuesto *m.*

buff *n* entusiasta *m.*

buffalo *n* búfalo *m.*

buffers *npl* (*rail*) parochoques *m invar,* topes *mpl.*

buffet *n* buffet *m;* * *vt* abofetear.

buffoon *n* bufón, chocarrero *m.*

bug *n* chinche *m.*

bugbear n espantajo, coco m.

bugle(horn) n trompa de caza f.

build vt edificar; construir.

builder n constructor/a m/f; maestro/tra de obras m/f.

building n edificio m, Lat Am predio m; construcción f.

bulb n bulbo m; cebolla f.

bulbous adj bulboso/sa.

bulge vi combarse; * n bombeo m.

bulk n masa f; volumen m; grosura f; mayor parte f; capacidad de un buque f; **in ~ a granel.**

bulky adj grueso/sa, grande.

bull n toro m.

bulldog n dogo m.

bulldozer n aplanadora f.

bullet n bala f.

bulletin board n tablón de anuncios m.

bulletproof adj a prueba de balas.

bullfight n corrida de toros f.

bullfighter n torero m.

bullfighting n toreo m.

bullion n oro/plata en barras m/f.

bullock n novillo capado m.

bullring n plaza de toros f.

bull's-eye n centro del blanco m.

bully n valentón m; * vt tiranizar.

bulwark n baluarte m.

bum n vagabundo/da m/f.

bumblebee n abejorro, zángano m.

bump n hinchazón f; jiba f; bollo m; barriga f; * vt chocar contra.

bumpkin n patán m; villano/na m/f.

bumpy adj bacheado/da.

bun n bollo m; mono m.

bunch n ramo m; grupo m.

bundle n fardo m, haz m (de leña etc); paquete m; rollo m; * vt atar, hacer un lío.

bung n tapón m; * vt atarugar.

bungalow n bungalow m.

bungee-jumping n puenting m.

bungle vt chapucear; * vi hacer algo chabacanamente.

bunion n juanete m.

bunk n litera f.

bunker n refugio m; búnker m.

buoy n (mar) boya f.

buoyancy n capacidad para flotar f.

buoyant adj boyante.

burden n carga f; * vt cargar.

bureau n armario m; escritorio m.

bureaucracy n burocracia f.

bureaucrat n burócrata m/f.

burglar n ladrón/ona m/f.

burglar alarm n alarma antirrobo f.

burglary n robo en una casa m.

burial n enterramiento m; exequias fpl; sepultura f.

burial place n cementerio m.

burlesque n, adj lengua burlesca f; burlesco/ca m/f.

burly adj fornido/da.

burn vt quemar, abrasar, incendiar; * vi arder; * n quema dura f.

burner n quemador m; mechero m.

burning adj ardiente.

burrow n madriguera f; * vi esconderse en la madriguera.

bursar n tesorero/ra m/f.

burse n bolsa, lonja f.

burst vi reventar; abrirse; **to ~ into tears** prorrumpir en lágrimas; **to ~ out laughing** estallarse de risa; * vt **to ~ into** irrumpir en; * n reventón m; rebosadura f.

bury vt enterrar, sepultar; esconder.

bus n autobús m.

bush n arbusto, espinal m; cola de zorro f.

bushy adj espeso/sa, lleno/na de arbustos.

busily adv diligentemente, apresuradamente.

business n asunto m; negocios mpl; empleo m; ocupación f.

businesslike adj serio/ria.

businessman n hombre de negocios m.

business trip n viaje de negocios m.

businesswoman n mujer de negocios f.

bus lane n carril bus m.

bust n busto m.

bus stop n parada de autobuses f.

bustle vi hacer ruido; menearse; andar al retortero; * n baraúnda f; ruido m.

bustling adj animado/da.

busy adj ocupado/da; entrometido/da.

busybody n entrometido m.

but conj pero; mas; excepto, menos; solamente.

butcher n carnicero/ra m/f; * vt matar atrozmente.

butcher's (shop/store) n carnicería f.

butchery n matadero m.

butler n mayordomo m.

butt n colilla f; cabo, extremo m; * vt topar.

butter n mantequilla f; * vt untar con mantequilla.

buttercup n (bot) ranúnculo m.

butterfly n mariposa f.

buttermilk n suero de manteca m.

buttocks npl posaderas fpl.

button n botón m; * vt abotonar.

buttonhole n ojal m.

buttress n estribo m; apoyo m; * vt estribar.

buxom adj frescachona, rolliza.

buy vt comprar.

buyer n comprador/a m/f.

buzz, buzzing n susurro, zumbido m; * vi zumbar.

buzzard n ratonero m común.

buzzer n timbre m.

by prep por; a, en; de; cerca, al lado de; **~ and ~** de aquí a poco, ahora; **~ the ~** de paso; **~ much** con mucho; **~ all means** por supuesto.

bygone adj pasado/da.

by-law n ordenanza municipal f.

bypass n carretera de circunvalación f.

by-product n derivado m.
by-road n camino secundario m.
bystander n mirador m.
byte n (comput) byte m.
byword n proverbio, refrán m.

C

cab n taxi m.
cabbage n berza, col f.
cabin n cabaña, cámara de navío f.
cabinet n consejo de ministros m; gabinete m; escritorio m.
cabinet-maker n ebanista m.
cable n cable m.
cable car n teleférico m.
cable television n televisión por cable f.
caboose n (mar) cocina f.
cache n alijo m.
cackle vi cacarear, graznar; * n cacareo m; charla f.
cactus n cacto m, cactus m invar.
cadence n (mus) cadencia f.
cadet n cadete m.
cadge vt mangar.
café n café m.
cafeteria n café m.
caffeine n cafeína f.
cage n jaula f; prisión f; * vt enjaular.
cagey adj cauteloso/sa.
cajole vt lisonjear, adular; sonsacar.
cake n bollo m; tortita f.
calamitous adj calamitoso/sa.
calamity n calamidad, miseria f.
calculable adj calculable.
calculate vt calcular, contar.
calculation n cálculo m.
calculator n calculadora f.
calculus n cálculo m.
calendar n calendario m.
calf n ternero m; ternera f; carne de ternero f.
caliber n calibre m.
calisthenics n calistenia f.
call vt llamar, nombrar; llamar por teléfono; convocar, citar; apelar; **to ~ for** preguntar por, ir a buscar; **to ~ on** visitar; **to ~ attention** llamar la atención; **to ~ names** insultar; * n llamada f, Lat Am llamado m; instancia f; invitación f; urgencia f; vocación f; profesión f.
caller n visitador/a m/f.
calligraphy n caligrafía f.
calling n profesión, vocación f.
callous adj calloso/sa, endurecido/da; insensible.
calm n calma, tranquilidad f; * adj quieto/ta, tranquilo/la; * vt calmar; aplacar, aquietar; **~ly** adv tranquilamente.
calmness n tranquilidad, calma f.
calorie n caloría f.

calumny n calumnia f.
Calvary n calvario m.
calve vi parir.
Calvinist n calvinista m/f.
camcorder n videocámara f.
camel n camello m.
cameo n camafeo m.
camera n máquina fotográfica f; cámara f.
cameraman n cámara m.
chamomile n manzanilla f.
camouflage n camuflaje m.
camp n campo m; * vi acampar; **refugee ~** campo de refugiados.
campaign n campaña f; **run-up-to-the-election ~** precampaña f; * vi hacer campaña.
campaigner n defensor/a m/f.
camper n campista m/f.
camping n camping m.
camphor n alcanfor m.
campsite n camping m.
campus n ciudad universitaria f, campus m invar.
can vi poder; * n lata f.
canal n estanque m; canal m.
cancel vt cancelar; anular, invalidar.
cancellation n cancelación f.
cancer n cáncer m.
Cancer n Cáncer m (signo del zodiaco).
cancerous adj canceroso/sa.
candid adj cándido/da, sencillo/lla, sincero/ra; **~ly** adv cándidamente, francamente.
candidate n candidato/ta m/f, Lat Am postulante m/f.
candied adj azucarado/da.
candle n candela f; vela f.
candlelight n luz de candela f.
candlestick n candelero m.
candor n candor m; sinceridad f.
candy n confitería f.
cane n caña f; bastón m.
canine adj canino/na, perruno/na.
canister n bote m.
cannabis n cannabis m.
cannibal n caníbal m/f; antropófago/ga m/f.
cannibalism n canibalismo m.
cannon n cañón m.
cannonball n bala de artillería f.
canny adj cuerdo/da, discreto/ta.
canoe n canoa f.
canon n canon m; regla f; **~law** derecho canónico m.
canonization n canonización f.
canonize vt canonizar.
can opener n abrelatas m invar.
canopy n dosel, pabellón m.
cantankerous adj áspero/ra, fastidioso/sa.
canteen n cantina f.
canter n medio galope m.
canvas n cañamazo m.
canvass vt escudriñar, examinar; controvertir; * vi solicitar votos; pretender.

canvasser n solicitador/a m/f.

canyon n cañón m.

canyoning n barranquismo m.

cap n gorra f.

capability n capacidad, aptitud, inteligencia f.

capable adj capaz.

capacitate vt hacer capaz.

capacity n capacidad f; inteligencia, habilidad f.

cape n cabo, promontorio m.

caper n cabriola f; alcaparra f; * vi hacer cabriolas.

capillary adj capilar.

capital adj capital; principal; * n capital f (la ciudad principal); capital, fondo m; mayúscula f.

capitalism n capitalismo m.

capitalist n capitalista m.

capitalize vt capitalizar; **to ~ on** aprovechar.

capital punishment n pena de muerte f.

Capitol n Capitolio m.

capitulate vi capitular.

capitulation n capitulación f.

caprice n capricho m; extravagancia f.

capricious adj caprichoso/sa; **~ly** adv caprichosamente.

Capricorn n Capricornio m (signo del zodiaco).

capsize vt (mar) volcar, zozobrar.

capsizing n (mar) zozobra f.

capsule n cápsula f.

captain n capitán/ana m/f.

captaincy, captainship n capitanía f.

captivate vt cautivar.

captivation n atractivo m.

captive n cautivo/va, esclavo/va m/f.

captivity n cautividad, esclavitud f, cautiverio m.

capture n captura f; presa f; * vt apresar, capturar.

car n coche, carro m; vagón m.

carafe n garrafa f.

caramel n caramelo m.

carat n quilate m.

caravan n caravana f.

caraway n (bot) alcaravea f.

carbohydrates npl hidratos de carbono mpl.

car bomb n coche bomba m.

carbon n carbono m, carbón m.

carbon copy n copia al carbón f.

carbonize vt carbonizar.

carbon paper n papel carbón m.

carbuncle n carbúnculo, rubí m; carbunco, tumor maligno m.

carburetor n carburador m.

carcass n cadáver m.

carcinogenic adj cancerígeno/na.

card n naipe m; carta f; **pack of ~s** baraja f.

cardboard n cartón m.

card game n juego de naipes m.

cardiac adj cardíaco/ca, cardiaco/ca.

cardinal adj cardinal, principal; * n cardenal m.

card table n mesa para jugar f.

care n cuidado m; solicitud f; * vi cuidar, tener cuidado/pena, inquietarse; **what do I ~?** ¿a mí que me importa?; **to ~ for** vt cuidar a; querer.

career n carrera f; curso m; * vi correr a carrera tendida.

carefree adj despreocupado/da.

careful adj cuidadoso/sa, diligente, prudente; **~ly** adv cuidadosamente.

careless adj descuidado/da, negligente; indolente; **~ly** adv descuidadamente.

carelessness n negligencia, indiferencia f.

caress n caricia f; * vt acariciar, halagar.

caretaker n portero m, conserje m/f.

car-ferry n transbordador para coches m.

cargo n cargamento m.

car hire n alquiler de coches m.

caribou n reno m.

caricature n caricatura f, Lat Am caricato m; * vt hacer caricaturas, ridiculizar.

caries n caries f.

caring adj humanitario/ria.

Carmelite n carmelita m.

carnage n carnicería, matanza f.

carnal adj carnal; sensual; **~ly** adv carnalmente.

carnation n clavel m.

carnival n carnaval m.

carnivorous adj carnívoro/ra.

carol n villancico m, canción de alegría/piedad f.

carpenter n carpintero m; **~'s bench** banco de carpintero m.

carpentry n carpintería f.

carpet n alfombra f, Lat Am tapete m; * vt cubrir con alfombras.

carpeting n alfombrado m.

car radio n autorradio m.

carriage n porte m; coche m; vehículo m.

carriage-free adj franco de porte.

carrier n portador, carretero m.

carrier pigeon n paloma correo/mensajera f.

carrion n carroña f.

carrot n zanahoria f.

carry vt llevar, conducir; **to ~ out** ejecutar; * vi oírse; **to ~ the day** quedar victorioso/sa; **to ~ on** seguir.

cart n carro m; carreta f; * vt llevar (en carro).

cartel n cartel m.

carthorse n caballo de tiro m.

Carthusian n cartujo (monje) m.

cartilage n cartílago m.

cartload n carretada f.

carton n caja f.

cartoon n dibujo animado m; tira cómica f.

cartridge n cartucho m.

carve vt cincelar; trinchar; grabar.

carving n escultura f.

carving knife n cuchillo de trinchar m.

car wash n lavado de coches m.

case n caja f; maleta f; caso m; estuche m; vaina f; **in ~** por si acaso.

cash n dinero contante m; * vt cobrar.

cash card n tarjeta de cajero automático f.
cash dispenser, cash machine n cajero automático m.
cashier n cajero m.
cashmere n cachemira f.
casing n forro m; cubierta f.
casino n casino m.
cask n barril, tonel m.
casket n ataúd m.
casserole n cazuela f.
cassette n cassette m.
cassette player, recorder n cassette m.
cassock n sotana f.
cast vt tirar, lanzar; modelar; * n reparto m; forma f.
castanets npl castañuelas fpl.
castaway n réprobo m.
caste n casta f.
castigate vt castigar.
casting vote n voto de calidad m.
cast iron n hierro colado m.
castle n castillo m; fortaleza f.
castor oil n aceite de ricino m.
castrate vt castrar.
castration n capadura f.
cast steel n acero fundido m.
casual adj casual, fortuito/ta; ~ly adv casualmente, fortuitamente.
casualty n víctima f; baja f.
cat n gato m; gata f.
catalog n catálogo m.
catalyst n catalizador m.
catalytic converter n catalizador m.
catamaran n catamarán m.
catapult n catapulta, honda f.
cataract n cascada f; catarata f.
catarrh n catarro m; reuma f.
catastrophe n catástrofe f.
catcall n silbido m; reclamo m.
catch vt coger, agarrar, asir; atrapar; pillar; sorprender; **to ~ cold** resfriarse; **to ~ fire** encenderse; * n presa f; captura f; (mus) canon m; trampa f.
catching adj contagioso/sa.
catch phrase n lema f.
catchword n reclamo m.
catchy adj pegadizo/za.
catechism n catecismo m.
catechize vt catequizar, examinar.
categorical adj categórico/ca; ~ly adv categóricamente.
categorize vt clasificar.
category n categoría f.
cater vi abastecer, proveer.
caterer n proveedor/a, abastecedor/a m/f.
catering n alimentación f.
caterpillar n oruga f.
catgut n cuerda de violón f.
cathedral n catedral f.
catholic adj, n católico/ca m/f.
Catholicism n catolicismo m.

cattle n ganado m.
cattle show n feria de ganado f.
caucus n junta electoral f.
cauliflower n coliflor f.
cause n causa f; razón f; motivo m; proceso m; * vt causar.
causeway n arrecife m.
caustic adj, n cáustico m.
cauterize vt cauterizar.
caution n prudencia, precaución f; aviso m; * vt avisar; amonestar; advertir.
cautionary adj de escarmiento.
cautious adj prudente, circunspecto/ta, cauto/ta.
cavalier adj arrogante.
cavalry n caballería f.
cave n caverna f; bodega f.
caveat n aviso m; advertencia f; (law) notificación f.
cavern n caverna f; bodega f.
cavernous adj cavernoso/sa.
caviar n caviar m.
cavity n hueco m; caries f invar.
CD-ROM n cederrón m.
cease vt parar, suspender; * vi desistir.
cease-fire n alto el fuego m, Lat Am cese del fuego m.
ceaseless adj incesante, continuo/nua; ~ly adv perpetuamente.
cedar n cedro m.
cede vt ceder, transferir.
ceiling n techo m.
celebrate vt celebrar.
celebration n celebración f.
celebrity n celebridad, fama f.
celery n apio m.
celestial adj celeste, divino/na.
celibacy n celibato m, soltería f.
celibate adj soltero; soltera.
cell n celdilla f; célula f; cueva f.
cellar n sótano m; bodega f.
cello n violoncelo m.
Cellophane™ n celofán m.
cellular adj celular; ~ **phone** móvil m, Lat Am celular m.
cellulitis n celulitis f.
cellulose n (chem) celulosa f.
cement n cemento; (fig) vínculo m; * vt pegar con cemento.
cemetery n cementerio m.
cenotaph n cenotafio m.
censor n censor/a m/f; crítico/ca m/f.
censorious adj severo/ra, crítico/ca.
censorship n censura f.
censure n censura, reprensión f; * vt censurar; reprender; criticar.
census n censo m.
cent n centavo m.
centenarian n centenario m; centenaria f.
centenary n centena f; * adj centena-rio/ria.
centennial adj centenario/ria.

center *n* centro *m*; * *vt* centrar; concentrar; * *vi* concentrarse.

centigrade *n* centígrado *m*.

centiliter *n* centilitro *m*.

centimeter *n* centímetro *m*.

centipede *n* escolopendra *f*.

central *adj* central; **~ly** *adv* centralmente, en el centro.

centralize *vt* centralizar.

centrifugal *adj* centrífugo/ga.

century *n* siglo *m*.

ceramic *adj* cerámico/ca.

cereals *npl* cereales *fpl*.

cerebral *adj* cerebral.

ceremonial *adj, n* ceremonial *m*; rito externo *m*.

ceremonious *adj* ceremonioso/sa; **~ly** *adv* ceremoniosamente.

ceremony *n* ceremonia *f*.

certain *adj* cierto/ta, evidente; se-guro/ra; **~ly** *adv* ciertamente, sin duda.

certainty, certitude *n* certeza *f*; seguridad *f*.

certificate *n* certificado, testimonio *m*.

certification *n* certificado *m*.

certified mail *n* correo certificado *m*.

certify *vt* certificar, afirmar.

cervical *adj* cervical.

cesarean section/operation *n* (*med*) (operación de) cesárea *f*.

cessation *n* cesación *f*.

cesspool *n* cloaca *f*; sumidero *m*.

chafe *vt* frotar; enojar, irritar.

chaff *n* paja menuda *f*.

chaffinch *n* pinzón *m*.

chagrin *n* disgusto *m*.

chain *n* cadena *f*; serie, sucesión *f*; * *vt* encadenar, atar con cadena.

chain reaction *n* reacción en cadena *f*.

chain store *n* gran almacén *m*.

chair *n* silla *f*; * *vt* presidir.

chairman *n* presidente *m*.

chalice *n* cáliz *m*.

chalk *n* creta *f*; tiza *f*.

chalkboard *n* pizarra *f*, *Lat Am* pizarrón *m*.

challenge *n* desafío *m*; * *vt* desafiar, impugnar.

challenger *n* desafiador/a *m/f*.

challenging *adj* desafiante.

chamber *n* cámara *f*; aposento *m*.

chambermaid *n* moza de cámara *f*.

chameleon *n* camaleón *m*.

chamois leather *n* gamuza *f*.

champagne *n* champaña *m*.

champion *n* campeón *m*; * *vt* defender.

championship *n* campeonato *m*.

chance *n* ventura, suerte *f*; oportunidad *f*, *Lat Am* chance *m*; **by ~** por acaso; * *vt* arriesgar.

chancellor *n* canciller *m*.

chancery *n* chancillería *f*.

chandelier *n* araña de luces *f*; candelero *m*.

change *vt* cambiar; * *vi* variar, alterarse; * *n* mudanza, variedad *f*; vicisitud *f*; cambio *m*, *Lat Am* vuelto *m*.

changeable *adj* variable, inconstante; mudable.

changeless *adj* constante, inmutable.

changing *adj* cambiante.

channel *n* canal *m*; estrecho *m*; * *vt* encauzar.

channel-hopping *n* zapping *m*.

chant *n* canto (llano) *m*; * *vt* cantar.

chaos *n* caos *m*; confusión *f*.

chaotic *adj* confuso/sa.

chapel *n* capilla *f*.

chaplain *n* capellán *m*.

chapter *n* capítulo *m*.

char *vt* chamuscar.

character *n* carácter *m*; personaje *m*.

characteristic *adj* característico/ca; **~ally** *adv* característicamente.

characterize *vt* caracterizar.

characterless *adj* sin carácter.

charade *n* charada *f*.

charcoal *n* carbón de leña *m*.

chard *n* (*bot*) acelga *f*.

charge *vt* cargar; acusar, imputar; * *n* cargo *m*; acusación *f*; (*mil*) ataque *m*; depósito *m*; carga *f*.

chargeable *adj* imputable.

charge card *n* tarjeta de compra *f*.

charitable *adj* caritativo/va; benigno/na, clemente; **~bly** *adv* caritativamente.

charity *n* caridad, benevolencia *f*; limosna *f*.

charlatan *n* charlatán/tana *m/f*.

charm *n* encanto *m*; atractivo *m*; * *vt* encantar, embelesar, atraer.

charming *adj* encantado/da.

chart *n* carta de navegar *f*.

charter *n* carta *f*; privilegio *m*; * *vt* fletar un buque; alquilar.

charter flight *n* vuelo chárter *m*, charter *m*.

chase *vt* cazar; perseguir; * *n* caza *f*.

chasm *n* vacío *m*.

chaste *adj* casto/ta; puro/ra; hones-to/ta.

chasten *vt* corregir, castigar.

chastise *vt* castigar, reformar, corregir.

chastisement *n* castigo *m*.

chastity *n* castidad, pureza *f*.

chat *vi* charlar; * *n* charla, cháchara *f*.

chatter *vi* cotorrear; rechinar; charlar; * *n* chirrido *m*; charla *f*.

chatterbox *n* parlero/ra, hablador/a, gárrulo/la *m/f*.

chatty *adj* locuaz, parlanchín/china.

chauffeur *n* chófer *m*.

chauvinist *n* machista *m*.

cheap *adj* barato/ta; **~ly** *adv* a bajo precio.

cheapen *vt* regatear; abaratar.

cheaper *adj* más barato/ta.

cheat *vt* engañar, defraudar; * *n* trampa *f*; fraude, engaño *m*; tramposo/sa *m/f*.

check¹ *vt* comprobar; contar; reprimir, refrenar; regañar; registrar; * *n* restricción *f*; freno *m*.

check² *n* cheque *m*.

check account *n* cuenta corriente *f*.

checkerboard *n* tablero de damas *m*.

checkered *adj* accidentado/da.
checkers *npl* juego de damas *m*.
checkmate *n* mate *m*.
checkout *n* caja *f*.
checkpoint *n* control *m*.
checkroom *n* consigna *f*.
check-up *n* reconocimiento médico *m*.
cheek *n* mejilla *f*; (*col*) desvergüenza *f*; atrevimiento *m*.
cheekbone *n* hueso del carrillo *m*.
cheeky *adj* descarado/da.
cheer *n* alegría *f*; aplauso *m*; buen humor *m*; * *vt* animar, alentar.
cheerful *adj* alegre, vivo/va, jovial; ~**ly** *adv* alegremente.
cheerfulness, cheeriness *n* alegría *f*; buen humor *m*.
cheese *n* queso *m*.
cheese shop *n* quesería *f*.
chef *n* jefe de cocina *m*.
chemical *adj* químico/ca.
chemist *n* químico *m*.
chemistry *n* química *f*.
chemotherapy *n* quimioterapia *f*.
cherish *vt* fomentar, proteger.
cheroot *n* puro *m*.
cherry *n* cereza *f*; * *adj* bermejo/ja.
cherry tree *n* cerezo *m*.
cherub *n* querubín *m*.
chess *n* ajedrez *m*.
chessboard *n* tablero de ajedrez *m*.
chessman *n* pieza de ajedrez *f*.
chest *n* pecho *m*; arca *f*; ~ **of drawers** cómoda *f*.
chestnut *n* castaña *f*; color de castaña *m*.
chestnut tree *n* castaño *m*.
chew *vt* mascar, masticar.
chewing gum *n* chicle *m*.
chic *adj* elegante.
chicanery *n* quisquilla *f*.
chick *n* polluelo *m*; (*col*) chica *f*.
chicken *n* pollo *m*.
chickenpox *n* varicela *f*.
chickpea *n* garbanzo *m*.
chicory *n* achicoria *f*.
chide *vt* reprobar, regañar.
chief *adj* principal, capital; ~**ly** *adv* principalmente; * *n* jefe, principal *m*.
chief executive *n* director/a general *m/f*.
chieftain *n* jefe; comandante *m*.
chiffon *n* gasa *f*.
chilblain *n* sabañón *m*.
child *n* niño *m*; niña *f*; hijo *m*; hija *f*; **from a ~** desde niño/ña; **with ~** preñada, embarazada.
childbirth *n* parto *m*.
childhood *n* infancia, niñez *f*; pequeñez *f*.
childish *adj* frívolo/la, pueril; ~**ly** *adv* puerilmente.
childishness *n* puerilidad *f*.
childless *adj* sin hijos.
childlike *adj* pueril.
children *npl* de **child** niños *mpl*.

chill *adj* frío/ría, friolero/ra; * *n* frío *m*; * *vt* enfriar; helar.
chilly *adj* friolero/ra, *Lat Am* friolento/ta.
chime *n* armonía *f*; clave *m*; * *vi* sonar con armonía; concordar.
chimney *n* chimenea *f*.
chimpanzee *n* chimpancé *m*.
chin *n* barbilla *f*.
china(ware) *n* porcelana *f*.
chink *n* grieta, hendedura *f*; * *vi* resonar.
chip *vt* astillar; * *vi* picarse; * *n* astilla *f*; chip *m*; patata/papa frita *f*.
chirp *vi* chirriar, gorjear; * *n* gorjeo, chirrido *m*.
chirping *n* canto de las aves *m*.
chisel *n* cincel *m*; * *vt* cincelar, grabar.
chitchat *n* charla *f*.
chivalrous *adj* caballeresco/ca.
chivalry *n* caballería *f*.
chives *npl* cebollinos *f*.
chlorine *n* cloro *m*.
chloroform *n* cloroformo *m*.
chock-full *adj* de bote en bote, completamente lleno/na.
chocolate *n* chocolate *m*.
choice *n* elección, preferencia *f*; -selecto *m*; * *adj* selecto/ta, exquisi-to/ta, excelente.
choir *n* coro *m*.
choke *vt* sofocar; oprimir; tapar.
cholera *n* cólera *m*.
choose *vt* escoger, elegir.
chop *vt* tajar, cortar; * *n* chuleta *f*; ~**s** *pl* (*col*) quijadas *fpl*.
chopper *n* helicóptero *m*.
chopping block *n* tajo de cocina *m*.
chopsticks *npl* palillos *mpl*.
chore *n* faena *f*.
choral *adj* coral.
chord *n* cuerda *f*.
chorist, chorister *n* corista *f*.
chorus *n* coro *m*.
Christ *n* Cristo *m*.
christen *vt* bautizar.
Christendom *n* cristianismo *m*; cristiandad *f*.
christening *n* bautismo *m*.
Christian *adj*, *n* cristiano/na *m/f*; ~ **name** nombre de pila *m*.
Christianity *n* cristianismo *m*; cristiandad *f*.
Christmas *n* Navidad *f*.
Christmas card *n* tarjeta de Navidad *f*.
Christmas Eve *n* Nochebuena *f*.
chrome *n* cromo *m*.
chronic *adj* crónico/ca.
chronicle *n* crónica *f*.
chronicler *n* cronista *m*.
chronological *adj* cronológico/ca; ~**ly** *adv* cronológicamente.
chronology *n* cronología *f*.
chronometer *n* cronómetro *m*.
chubby *adj* gordo/da.
chuck *vt* lanzar.
chuckle *vi* reírse a carcajadas.

chug *vi* resoplar.

chum *n* compañero/ra, compinche *m/f*.

chunk *n* trozo *m*.

church *n* iglesia *f*.

churchyard *n* cementerio *m*.

churlish *adj* hosco/ca, grosero/ra; tacaño/ña.

churn *n* mantequera *f*; * *vt* batir la leche para hacer manteca.

cider *n* sidra *f*.

cigar *n* cigarro *m*.

cigarette *n* cigarrillo *m*.

cigarette case *n* pitillera *f*.

cigarette end *n* colilla *f*.

cigarette holder *n* boquilla *f*.

cinder *n* carbonilla *f*.

cinnamon *n* canela *f*.

cipher *n* cifra *f*.

circle *n* círculo *m*; corrillo *m*; asamblea *f*; * *vt* circundar; cercar; * *vi* circular.

circuit *n* circuito *m*; recinto *m*.

circuitous *adj* circular, tortuoso/sa.

circular *adj* circular, redondo/da; * *n* carta circular *f*.

circulate *vi* circular; moverse alrededor.

circulation *n* circulación *f*.

circumcise *vt* circuncidar.

circumcision *n* circuncisión *f*.

circumference *n* circunferencia *f*; circuito *m*.

circumflex *n* acento circunflejo *m*.

circumlocution *n* circunlocución *f*.

circumnavigate *vt* circunnavegar.

circumnavigation *n* circunnavegación *f*.

circumscribe *vt* circunscribir.

circumspect *adj* circunspecto/ta, prudente, reservado/da.

circumspection *n* circunspección, prudencia *f*.

circumstance *n* circunstancia, condición *f*; incidente *m*.

circumstantial *adj* accidental; acce-sorio/ria.

circumstantiate *vt* circunstanciar, detallar.

circumvent *vt* burlar.

circumvention *n* evasión *f*.

circus *n* circo *m*.

cistern *n* cisterna *f*.

citadel *n* ciudadela, fortaleza *f*.

citation *n* citación, cita *f*.

cite *vt* citar (a juicio); alegar; referirse a.

citizen *n* ciudadano/na *m/f*.

citizenship *n* ciudadanía *f*.

city *n* ciudad *f*.

civic *adj* cívico/ca.

civil *adj* civil, cortés; ~**ly** *adv* civilmente.

civil defense *n* protección civil *f*.

civil engineer *n* ingeniero/ra civil *m/f*.

civilian *n* paisano *m*.

civility *n* civilidad, urbanidad, cortesía *f*.

civilization *n* civilización *f*.

civilize *vt* civilizar.

civil law *n* derecho civil *m*.

civil war *n* guerra civil *f*.

clad *adj* vestido/da, cubierto/ta.

claim *vt* pedir en juicio, reclamar; * *n* demanda *f*; derecho *m*.

claimant *n* reclamante *m*; demanda-dor/a *m/f*.

clairvoyant *n* clarividente *m/f*; zahorí *m*.

clam *n* almeja *f*.

clamber *vi* gatear, trepar.

clammy *adj* viscoso/sa.

clamor *n* clamor, grito *m*; * *vi* vociferar, gritar.

clamp *n* abrazadera *f*; * *vt* afianzar; **to ~ down on** reforzar la lucha contra.

clan *n* familia, tribu, raza *f*.

clandestine *adj* clandestino/na, oculto/ta.

clang *n* rechino, sonido desapacible *m*; * *vi* rechinar.

clap *vt* aplaudir.

clapping *n* palmada *f*; aplauso, palmoteo *m*.

claret *n* clarete *m*.

clarification *n* clarificación *f*.

clarify *vt* clarificar, aclarar.

clarinet *n* clarinete *m*.

clarity *n* claridad *f*.

clash *vi* chocar; * *n* estruendo *m*; choque *m*.

clasp *n* broche *m*; hebilla *f*; abrazo *m*; * *vt* abrochar; abrazar.

class *n* clase *f*; orden *f*; * *vt* clasificar, coordinar.

classic(al) *adj* clásico/ca; * *n* autor clásico *m*.

classification *n* clasificación *f*.

classified advertisement *n* anuncio por palabras *m*, *Lat Am* clasificado *m*.

classify *vt* clasificar.

classmate *n* compañero/ra de clase *m/f*.

classroom *n* aula *f*.

clatter *vi* resonar; hacer ruido; * *n* ruido *m*.

clause *n* cláusula *f*; artículo *m*; estipulación *f*.

claw *n* garra *f*; zarpa *f*; * *vt* desgarrar, arañar.

clay *n* arcilla *f*.

clean *adj* limpio/pia; casto/ta; * *vt* limpiar.

cleaning *n* limpieza *f*.

cleanliness *n* limpieza *f*.

cleanly *adj* limpio/pia; * *adv* limpiamente, aseadamente.

cleanness *n* limpieza *f*; pureza *f*.

cleanse *vt* limpiar, purificar; purgar.

clear *adj* claro/ra; neto/ta; diáfano/na; evidente; * *adv* claramente; * *vt* clarificar, aclarar; justificar, absolver; * *vi* aclararse.

clearance *n* despeje *m*; acreditación *f*.

clear-cut *adj* bien definido/da.

clearly *adv* claramente, evidentemente.

cleaver *n* cuchillo de carnicero *m*.

clef *n* clave *f*.

cleft *n* hendedura, abertura *f*.

clemency *n* clemencia *f*.

clement *adj* clemente, benigno/na.

clenched *adj* cerrado/da.

clergy *n* clero *m*.

clergyman *n* eclesiástico *m*.

clerical *adj* clerical, eclesiástico/ca.

clerk *n* dependiente *m*; oficinista *m*.

clever *adj* listo/ta; hábil, mañoso/sa; ~**ly** *adv* diestramente, hábilmente.

click vt chasquear; * vi taconear.
client n cliente m/f.
cliff n acantilado m.
climate n clima m; temperatura f.
climatic adj climático/ca.
climax n clímax m.
climb vt escalar, trepar; * vi subir.
climber n alpinista m/f.
climbing n alpinismo m.
clinch vt cerrar; remachar.
cling vi colgar, adherirse, pegarse.
clinic n clínica f.
clink vt hacer resonar; * vi resonar; * n retintín m.
clip vt cortar; * n clip m; horquilla f.
clipping n recorte m.
clique n camarilla f.
cloak n capa f; pretexto m; * vi encapotar.
cloakroom n guardarropa m.
clock n reloj m.
clockwork n mecanismo de un reloj m; * adj sumamente exacto y puntual.
clod n terrón m.
clog n zueco m; * vi atascarse.
cloister n claustro, monasterio m.
clone n clon m.
clone vt clonar.
cloned adj clónico/ca.
cloning n clonación f.
close vt cerrar; concluir, terminar; * vi cerrarse; * n fin m; conclusión f; * adj cercano/na; estrecho/cha; ajustado/da; denso/sa; reservado/da; * adv de cerca; ~ by muy cerca; junto.
closed adj cerrado/da.
closely adv estrechamente; de cerca.
closeness n proximidad f; estrechez; reclusión f.
closet n armario m.
close-up n primer plano m.
closure n cierre m; conclusión f.
clot n grumo m; embolia f.
cloth n paño m; mantel m; vestido m; lienzo m.
clothe vt vestir, cubrir.
clothes npl ropa f; ropaje m; ropa de cama f; bed ~ cobertores mpl.
clothes basket n cesta grande f.
clotheshorse n tendedero m.
clothesline n cuerda (de tendedero) f.
clothespin n pinza f.
clothing n vestidos mpl.
cloud n nube f; nublado m; (fig) adversidad f; * vt anublar; oscurecer; * vi anublarse; oscurecerse.
cloudiness n nubosidad f; oscuridad f.
cloudy adj nubiado/da; oscuro/ra; sombrío/ría, melancólico/ca.
clout n tortazo m.
clove n clavo m.
clover n trébol m.
clown n payaso m.

club n cachiporra f.
club car n coche restaurante m.
clue n pista f, indicios m; idea f.
clump n grupo m.
clumsily adv torpemente.
clumsiness n torpeza f.
clumsy adj torpe, pesado/da, Lat Am patón/ona; sin arte.
cluster n racimo m; manada f; pelotón m; * vt agrupar; * vi arracimarse.
clutch n embrague m; apretón m; * vt empuñar.
clutter vt atestar.
coach n autocar, autobús m; vagón m; entrenador/a m/f; * vt entrenar; enseñar.
coach trip n excursión en autocar f.
coagulate vt coagular, cuajar; * vi coagularse, cuajarse, espesarse.
coal n carbón m.
coalesce vi juntarse, incorporarse.
coalfield n yacimiento de carbón m.
coalition n coalición, confederación f.
coalman n carbonero m.
coalmine n mina de carbón, carbonería f.
coarse adj basto/ta; grosero/ra; zafio/fia; ~ly adv groseramente.
coast n costa f.
coastal adj costero/ra; ribereño/ña.
coastguard n guardacostas m invar.
coastline n litoral m.
coat n chaqueta f; abrigo m, Lat Am saco m; capa f; * vt cubrir.
coat hanger n percha f.
coat hook n percha f.
coating n revestimiento m.
coax vt lisonjear.
cob n mazorca de maíz f.
cobbler n zapatero/ra m/f.
cobbles, cobblestones npl adoquines mpl.
cobweb n telaraña f.
cocaine n cocaína f.
coccyx n rabadilla f.
cock n gallo m; macho m; * vt armar el sombrero; amartillar; montar una escopeta.
cock-a-doodle-doo n quiquiriquí m.
cockcrow n canto del gallo m.
cockerel n gallito m.
cockfight(ing) n pelea de gallos f.
cockle n berberecho m.
cockpit n cabina f.
cockroach n cucaracha f.
cocktail n cóctel m.
cocoa n coco m; cacao m.
coconut n coco m.
cocoon n capullo (del gusano de seda) m.
cod n bacalao m.
code n código m; prefijo m.
cod-liver oil n aceite de hígado de bacalao m.
coefficient n coeficiente m.
coercion n coerción f.
coexistence n coexistencia f.
coffee n café m.

coffee break *n* descanso *m*.
coffee house *n* café *m*.
coffee-pot *n* cafetera *f*.
coffee table *n* mesita *f*.
coffer *n* cofre *m*; caja *f*.
coffin *n* ataúd *m*.
cog *n* diente (de rueda) *m*.
cogency *n* fuerza, urgencia *f*.
cogent *adj* convincente, urgente; ~**ly** *adv* de modo convincente.
cognac *n* coñac *m*.
cognate *adj* cognado/da.
cognition *n* conocimiento *m*; convicción *f*.
cognizance *n* conocimiento *m*; competencia *f*.
cognizant *adj* informado/da; (*law*) competente.
cogwheel *n* rueda dentada *f*.
cohabit *vi* cohabitar.
cohabitation *n* cohabitación *f*.
cohere *vi* pegarse; unirse.
coherence *n* coherencia, conexión *f*.
coherent *adj* coherente; consiguiente.
cohesion *n* coherencia *f*.
cohesive *adj* cohesivo/va.
coil *n* rollo *m*; bobina *f*; * *vt* enrollar.
coin *n* moneda *f*; * *vt* acuñar.
coincide *vi* coincidir, concurrir, convenir.
coincidence *n* coincidencia *f*.
coke[1] *n* coque *m*.
Coke[2] *n* Coca-Cola™ *f*.
colander *n* colador *m*, *Lat Am* coladera *f*, pasador *m*.
cold *adj* frío/ría; indiferente, insensible; reservado/da; ~**ly** *adv* fríamente; indiferentemente; * *n* frío *m*; frialdad *f*; resfriado *m*.
cold-blooded *adj* impasible.
coldness *n* frialdad *f*; indiferencia, insensibilidad, apatía *f*.
cold sore *n* herpes labial *m*.
coleslaw *n* ensalada de col *f*.
colic *n* cólico *m*.
collaborate *vt* cooperar.
collaboration *n* cooperación *f*.
collapse *vi* hundirse; * *n* hundimiento; (*med*) colapso *m*.
collapsible *adj* plegable.
collar *n* cuello *m*.
collarbone *n* clavícula *f*.
collate *vt* comparar, confrontar.
collateral *adj* colateral; * *n* garantía subsidiaria *f*.
collation *n* colación *f*.
colleague *n* colega, compañero/ra *m/f*.
collect *vt* recoger; coleccionar.
collection *n* colección *f*; compilación *f*.
collective *adj* colectivo/va, congre-gado/da; ~**ly** colectivamente.
collector *n* coleccionista *m/f*.
college *n* colegio *m*, *Lat Am* facultad *f*.
collide *vi* chocar.
collision *n* choque *m*, colisión *f*.

colloquial *adj* familiar; coloquial; ~**ly** *adv* familiarmente.
colloquialism *n* lengua usual *f*.
collusion *n* colusión *f*.
colon *n* dos puntos *mpl*; (*med*) colon *m*.
colonel *n* (*mil*) coronel *m*.
colonial *adj* colonial.
colonist *n* colono *m*.
colonize *vt* colonizar.
colony *n* colonia *f*.
color *n* color *m*; ~**s** *pl* bandera *f*; * *vt* colorar; pintar; * *vi* ponerse colorado/da.
color-blind *adj* daltónico/ca.
colorful *adj* lleno de color.
coloring *n* colorido *m*.
colorless *adj* descolorido/da, sin color.
color television *n* televisión en color *f*.
colossal *adj* colosal.
colossus *n* coloso *m*.
colt *n* potro *m*.
column *n* columna *f*.
columnist *n* columnista *m*.
coma *n* coma *f*.
comatose *adj* comatoso/sa.
comb *n* peine *m*; * *vt* peinar.
combat *n* combate *m*; batalla *f*; **single** ~ duelo *m*; * *vt* combatir.
combatant *n* combatiente *m*.
combative *adj* combativo/va.
combination *n* combinación, coordinación *f*.
combine *vt* combinar; * *vi* unirse.
combustion *n* combustión *f*.
come *vi* venir; **to** ~ **across/upon** *vt* topar con; dar con; **to** ~ **by** *vt* conseguir; **to** ~ **down** *vi* bajar; ser derribado/da; **to** ~ **from** *vt* ser de; **to** ~ **in for** *vt* merecer; **to** ~ **into** *vt* heredar; **to** ~ **round/to** *vi* volver en sí; **to** ~ **up with** *vt* sugerir.
comedian *n* comediante, cómico *m*.
comedienne *n* cómica *f*.
comedy *n* comedia *f*.
comet *n* cometa *m*.
comfort *n* confort *m*; ayuda *f*; consuelo *m*; comodidad *f*; * *vt* confortar; alentar, consolar.
comfortable *adj* cómodo/da.
comfortably *adv* agradablemente; cómodamente.
comforter *n* chupete *m*.
comic(al) *adj* cómico/ca, burlesco/ca; ~**ly** *adv* cómicamente.
coming *n* venida, llegada *f*; * *adj* venidero/ra.
comma *n* (*gr*) coma *f*.
command *vt* comandar, ordenar; * *n* orden *f*.
commander *n* comandante *m*.
commandment *n* mandamiento, precepto *m*.
commando *n* comando *m*.
commemorate *vt* conmemorar; celebrar.
commemoration *n* conmemoración *f*.
commence *vt*, *vi* comenzar.
commencement *n* principio *m*.
commend *vt* encomendar; alabar; enviar.

commendable *adj* recomendable.

commendably *adv* loablemente.

commendation *n* recomendación *f*.

commensurate *adj* proporcionado/da.

comment *n* comentario *m*; * *vt* comentar; glosar.

commentary *n* comentario *m*; interpretación *f*.

commentator *n* comentarista *m/f*.

commerce *n* comercio, tráfico, trato, negocio *m*.

commercial *adj* comercial.

commiserate *vt* compadecer, tener compasión.

commiseration *n* conmiseración, piedad *f*.

commissariat *n* comisaría *f*.

commission *n* comisión *f*; * *vt* comisionar; encargar.

commissioner *n* comisionado/da, delegado/da *m/f*.

commit *vt* cometer; depositar; encargar.

commitment *n* compromiso *m*.

committee *n* comité *m*.

commodity *n* comodidad *f*.

common *adj* común; bajo/ja; **in ~** comúnmente; * *n* pastos comunales *mpl*.

commoner *n* plebeyo *m*.

common law *n* derecho consuetudinario *m*.

commonly *adv* comúnmente, frecuentemente.

commonplace *n* lugar común *m*; * *adj* trivial.

common sense *n* sentido común *m*.

commonwealth *n* república *f*.

commotion *n* tumulto *m*; perturbación del ánimo *f*.

commune *vt* conversar, conferir.

communicable *adj* comunicable, impartible.

communicate *vt* comunicar, participar; * *vi* comunicarse.

communication *n* comunicación *f*.

communicative *adj* comunicativo/va.

communion *n* comunión *f*.

communiqué *n* comunicado *m*.

communism *n* comunismo *m*.

communist *n* comunista *m/f*.

community *n* comunidad *f*; colectividad *f*.

community center *n* centro social *m*.

community chest *n* arca comunitaria *f*.

commutable *adj* conmutable, cambiable.

commutation ticket *n* billete de abono *m*.

commute *vt* conmutar.

compact *adj* compacto/ta, sólido/da, denso/sa; * *n* pacto, convenio *m*; **~ly** *adv* estrechamente; en pocas palabras.

compact disc, CD *n* compact disc *m*, disco compacto *m*.

companion *n* compañero/ra, socio/cia, compinche *m/f*.

companionship *n* sociedad, compañía *f*.

company *n* compañía, sociedad *f*; compañía de comercio *f*.

comparable *adj* comparable.

comparative *adj* comparativo/va; **~ly** *adv* comparativamente.

compare *vt* comparar.

comparison *n* comparación *f*.

compartment *n* compartimento *m*.

compass *n* brújula *f*.

compassion *n* compasión, piedad *f*.

compassionate *adj* compasivo/va.

compatibility *n* compatibilidad *f*.

compatible *adj* compatible.

compatriot *n* compatriota *m/f*.

compel *vt* compeler, obligar, constreñir.

compelling *adj* convicente.

compensate *vt* compensar.

compensation *n* compensación *f*; resarcimiento *m*.

compere *n* (*rad*, *TV*) presentador/a *m/f*.

compete *vi* concurrir, competir.

competence *n* competencia *f*; suficiencia *f*.

competent *adj* competente, ade-cuado/da; **~ly** *adv* competentemente.

competition *n* competencia *f*; concurrencia *f*.

competitive *adj* competitivo/va.

competitive scheduling *n* contraprogramación *f*.

competitor *n* competidor/a *m/f*, rival *m*.

compilation *n* compilación *f*.

compile *vt* compilar.

complacency *n* autocomplacencia *f*.

complacent *adj* complaciente.

complain *vi* quejarse, lamentarse, lastimarse, dolerse.

complaint *n* queja *f*; reclamación *f*, *Lat Am* reclamo *m*.

complement *n* complemento *m*.

complementary *adj* complemen-tario/ria.

complete *adj* completo/ta, perfecto/ta; **~ly** *adv* completamente; * *vt* completar, acabar.

completion *n* terminación *f*.

complex *adj* complejo/ja.

complexion *n* tez *f*; aspecto *m*.

complexity *n* complejidad *f*.

compliance *n* complacencia, sumisión *f*.

compliant *adj* complaciente, oficio-so/sa.

complicate *vt* complicar.

complication *n* complicación *f*.

complicity *n* complicidad *f*.

compliment *n* cumplido *m*; * *vt* cumplimentar; hacer cumplidos.

complimentary *adj* elogioso/sa, ceremonioso/sa.

comply *vi* cumplir; condescender, conformarse.

component *n* componente.

compose *vt* componer; sosegar.

composed *adj* compuesto/ta, mode-rado/da.

composer *n* compositor/a *m/f*.

composite *adj* compuesto/ta.

composition *n* composición *f*.

compositor *n* cajista *m*.

compost *n* abono, estiércol *m*.

composure *n* composición *f*; tranquilidad, sangre fría *f*.

compound *vt* componer, combinar; * *adj*, *n* compuesto *m*.

comprehend *vt* comprender, contener; entender.

comprehensible *adj* comprensible; **~ly** *adv* comprensiblemente.

comprehension *n* comprensión *f*; inteligencia *f*.

comprehensive *adj* comprensivo/va; **~ly** *adv* comprensivamente.

compress *vt* comprimir, estrechar; * *n* cabezal *m*.

comprise *vt* comprender, incluir.

compromise *n* compromiso *m*; * *vt* comprometer.

compulsion *n* compulsión *f*; apremio *m*.

compulsive *adj* compulsivo/va; **~ly** *adv* compulsivamente.

compulsory *adj* obligatorio/ria.

compunction *n* compunción, contrición *f*.

computable *adj* computable, calculable.

computation *n* computación *f*, cómputo *m*.

compute *vt* computar, calcular.

computer *n* ordenador *m*.

computer graphics *n* infografía *f*.

computerize *vt* computerizar, informatizar.

computer programing *n* programación *f*.

computer science *n* informática *f*.

computing *n* informática *f*, *Lat Am* computación *f*.

comrade *n* camarada, compañero/ra *m/f*.

comradeship *n* compañerismo *m*.

con *vt* estafar; * *n* estafa *f*.

concave *adj* cóncavo/va.

concavity *n* concavidad *f*.

conceal *vt* ocultar, esconder.

concealment *n* ocultación *f*; encubrimiento *m*.

concede *vt* conceder, asentir.

conceit *n* concepto *m*; capricho *m*; pensamiento *m*; presunción *f*.

conceited *adj* afectado/da, vano/na, presumido/da.

conceivable *adj* concebible, inteligible.

conceive *vt* concebir, comprender; * *vi* concebir.

concentrate *vt* concentrar.

concentration *n* concentración *f*.

concentration camp *n* campo de concentración *m*.

concentric *adj* concéntrico/ca.

concept *n* concepto *m*.

conception *n* concepción *f*; sentimiento *m*.

concern *vt* concernir, importar; * *n* negocio *m*; asunto *m*; preocupación *f*.

concerning *prep* tocante a.

concert *n* concierto *m*.

concerto *n* concierto *m*.

concession *n* concesión *f*; privilegio *m*.

conciliate *vt* conciliar.

conciliation *n* conciliación *f*.

conciliatory *adj* conciliador/a.

concise *adj* conciso/sa, sucinto/ta; **~ly** *adv* concisamente.

conclude *vt* concluir; decidir; determinar.

conclusion *n* conclusión, determinación *f*; fin *m*.

conclusive *adj* decisivo/va, conclusivo/va; **~ly** *adv* concluyentemente.

concoct *vt* cocer, digerir; (*fig*) zurcir.

concoction *n* confección *f*; cocción *f*.

concomitant *adj* concomitante.

concord *n* concordia, armonía *f*.

concordance *n* concordancia *f*.

concordant *adj* concordante, conforme.

concourse *n* concurso *m*; multitud *f*; gentío *m*.

concrete *n* hormigón *m*, *Lat Am* concreto *m*; * *vt* concretar.

concubine *n* concubina *f*.

concur *vi* concurrir; juntarse.

concurrence *n* concurrencia *f*; unión *f*; asistencia *f*.

concurrently *adv* al mismo tiempo.

concussion *n* conmoción cerebral *f*.

condemn *vt* condenar; desaprobar; vituperar.

condemnation *n* condena *f*.

condensation *n* condensación *f*.

condense *vt* condensar.

condescend *vi* condescender; consentir.

condescending *adj* condescendiente.

condescension *n* condescendencia *f*.

condiment *n* condimento *m*; salsa *f*.

condition *vt* condicionar; * *n* situación, condición, calidad *f*; estado *m*.

conditional *adj* condicional, hipotéti-co/ca; **~ly** *adv* condicionalmente.

conditioned *adj* condicionado/da.

conditioner *n* acondicionador *m*.

condolences *npl* pésame *m*.

condom *n* condón *m*.

condominium *n* condominio *m*.

condone *vt* perdonar.

conducive *adj* conducente, opor-tuno/na.

conduct *n* conducta *f*; manejo, proceder *m*; * *vt* conducir, guiar.

conductor *n* conductor *m*; guía, director *m*; conductor de electricidad *m*.

conduit *n* conducto *m*; cano *m*.

cone *n* cono *m*.

confection *n* confitura *f*; confección *f*.

confectioner *n* confitero/ra *m/f*.

confectioner's (**shop/store**) *n* pastelería *f*; confitería *f*.

confederacy *n* confederación *f*.

confederate *vi* confederarse; * *adj*, *n* confederado/da *m/f*.

confer *vi* conferenciar; * *vt* conferir, comparar.

conference *n* conferencia *f*.

confess *vt*, *vi* confesar(se).

confession *n* confesión *f*.

confessional *n* confesionario *m*.

confessor *n* confesor *m*.

confetti *n* confeti *m*.

confidant *n* confidente, amigo/ga íntimo/ma *m/f*.

confide *vt*, *vi* confiar; fiarse.

confidence *n* confianza, seguridad *f*.

confidence trick *n* timo *m*.

confident *adj* cierto/ta, seguro/ra; confiado/da.
confidential *adj* confidencial.
configuration *n* configuración *f*.
confine *vt* limitar; aprisionar.
confinement *n* prisión *f*; confinación *f*.
confirm *vt* confirmar; ratificar.
confirmation *n* confirmación *f*; ratificación *f*; prueba *f*.
confirmed *adj* empedernido/da.
confiscate *vt* confiscar.
confiscation *n* confiscación *f*.
conflagration *n* conflagración *f*; incendio *m*.
conflict *n* conflicto *m*; combate *m*; pelea *f*.
conflicting *adj* contradictorio/ria.
confluence *n* confluencia *f*; concurso *m*.
conform *vt, vi* conformar(se).
conformity *n* conformidad, conveniencia *f*.
confound *vt* turbar, confundir.
confront *vt* afrontar; confrontar; comparar.
confrontation *n* enfrentamiento *m*.
confuse *vt* confundir; desordenar.
confusing *adj* confuso/sa.
confusion *n* confusión *f*; perturbación *f*; desorden *m*.
congeal *vt, vi* helar, congelar(se).
congenial *adj* congenial.
congenital *adj* congénito/ta.
congested *adj* atestado/da.
congestion *n* congestión *f*; acumulación *f*.
conglomerate *vt* conglomerar, aglomerar; * *adj* aglomerado/da; * *n (com)* conglomerado *m*.
conglomeration *n* aglomeración *f*.
congratulate *vt* congratular, felicitar.
congratulations *npl* felicidades *fpl*; * *interj* enhorabuena, *Lat Am* felicitaciones.
congratulatory *adj* congratulatorio/ria.
congregate *vt* congregar, reunir.
congregation *n* congregación, reunión *f*.
congress *n* congreso *m*; conferencia *f*.
congressman *n* miembro del Congreso *m*.
congruity *n* congruencia *f*.
congruous *adj* idóneo/nea, congruo/rua, apto/ta.
conic(al) *adj* cónico/ca.
conifer *n* conífera *f*.
coniferous *adj (bot)* conífero/ra.
conjecture *n* conjetura, apariencia *f*; * *vt* conjeturar; pronosticar.
conjugal *adj* conyugal, matrimonial.
conjugate *vt (gr)* conjugar.
conjugation *n* conjugación *f*.
conjunction *n* conjunción *f*; unión *f*.
conjuncture *n* coyuntura *f*; ocasión *f*; tiempo crítico *m*.
conjure *vi* conjurar, suplicar.
conjurer *n* conjurador/a, encan-tador/a *m/f*.
con man *n* timador *m*.
connect *vt* juntar, unir, enlazar.
connection *n* conexión *f*.
connivance *n* connivencia *f*.
connive *vi* tolerar.

connoisseur *n* conocedor/a *m/f*.
conquer *vt* conquistar; vencer.
conqueror *n* vencedor/a, conquis-tador/a *m/f*.
conquest *n* conquista *f*.
conscience *n* conciencia *f*; escrúpulo *m*.
conscientious *adj* concienzudo/da, escrupuloso/sa; **~ly** *adv* concienzudamente.
conscientious objector *n* objetor de conciencia *m*.
conscious *adj* sabedor, consciente; **~ly** *adv* a sabiendas.
consciousness *n* conciencia *f*.
conscript *n* conscripto *m*.
conscription *n* reclutamiento *m*.
consecrate *vt* consagrar; dedicar.
consecration *n* consagración *f*.
consecutive *adj* consecutivo/va; **~ly** *adv* consecutivamente.
consensus *n* consenso *m*.
consent *n* consentimiento *m*; aprobación *f*; * *vi* consentir; aprobar.
consequence *n* consecuencia *f*; importancia *f*.
consequent *adj* consecutivo/va, concluyente; **~ly** *adv* consiguientemente.
conservation *n* conservación *f*.
conservative *adj* conservador/a *m/f*.
conservatory *n* conservatorio *m*.
conserve *vt* conservar; * *n* conserva *f*.
consider *vt* considerar, examinar; * *vi* pensar, deliberar.
considerable *adj* considerable; importante; **~bly** *adv* considerablemente.
considerate *adj* considerado/da, prudente, discreto/ta; **~ly** *adv* juiciosamente; prudentemente.
consideration *n* consideración *f*; deliberación *f*; importancia *f*; valor, mérito *m*.
considering *conj* en vista de; **~ that** a causa de; visto que, en razón a.
consign *vt* consignar.
consignment *n* consignación *f*.
consist *vi* consistir.
consistency *n* consistencia *f*.
consistent *adj* consistente; conveniente, conforme; solido/da, estable; **~ly** *adv* conformemente.
console *n* consola *f*.
consolable *adj* consolable.
consolation *n* consolación *f*; consuelo *m*.
consolatory *adj* consolatorio/ria.
console *vt* consolar.
consolidate *vt, vi* consolidar(se).
consolidation *n* consolidación *f*.
consonant *adj* consonante, conforme; * *n (gr)* consonante *f*.
consort *n* consorte, socio *m*.
conspicuous *adj* conspicuo/cua, aparente; notable; **~ly** *adv* claramente.
conspiracy *n* conspiración *f*.
conspirator *n* conspirador/a *m/f*.
conspire *vi* conspirar, maquinar.

constancy *n* constancia, perseverancia, persistencia *f*.

constant *adj* constante; perseverante; **~ly** *adv* constantemente.

constellation *n* constelación *f*.

consternation *n* consternación *f*; -terror *m*.

constipated *adj* estreñido/da.

constituency *n* circunscripción electoral *f*.

constituent *n* constitutivo *m*; * *adj* constituyente.

constitute *vt* constituir; establecer.

constitution *n* constitución *f*; estado *m*; temperamento *m*.

constitutional *adj* constitucional.

constrain *vt* constreñir, forzar; restringir.

constraint *n* constreñimiento *m*; fuerza, violencia *f*.

constrict *vt* constreñir, estrechar.

construct *vt* construir, edificar.

construction *n* construcción *f*.

construe *vt* construir; interpretar.

consul *n* cónsul *m*.

consular *adj* consular.

consulate, consulship *n* consulado *m*.

consult *vt* (*vi*) consultar(se); aconse-jar(se).

consultant *n* asesor *m*.

consultation *n* consulta, deliberación *f*.

consume *vt* consumir; disipar; * *vi* consumirse.

consumer *n* consumidor/a *m/f*.

consumer goods *npl* bienes de consumo *mpl*.

consumerism *n* consumismo *m*.

consumer society *n* sociedad de consumo *f*.

consummate *vt* consumar, acabar, perfeccionar; * *adj* cumplido/da, consumado/da.

consummation *n* consumación, perfección *f*.

consumption *n* consumo *m*.

contact *n* contacto *m*.

contact lenses *npl* lentes de contacto *fpl*.

contagious *adj* contagioso/sa.

contain *vt* contener, comprender; caber, reprimir, refrenar.

container *n* recipiente *m*.

contaminate *vt* contaminar; corromper; **~d** *adj* contaminado/da, co-rrompido/da.

contamination *n* contaminación *f*.

contemplate *vt* contemplar.

contemplation *n* contemplación *f*.

contemplative *adj* contemplativo/va.

contemporaneous, contemporary *adj* contemporáneo/nea.

contempt *n* desprecio, desdén *m*.

contemptible *adj* despreciable, vil; **~bly** *adv* vilmente.

contemptuous *adj* desdeñoso/sa, insolente; **~ly** *adv* con desdén.

contend *vi* contender, disputar, afirmar.

content *adj* contento/ta, satisfecho/cha; * *vt* contentar, satisfacer; * *n* contenido *m*; **~s** *pl* contenido *m*; tabla de materias *f*.

contentedly *adv* de un modo satisfe-cho/cha; con paciencia.

contention *n* contención, altercación *f*.

contentious *adj* contencioso/sa, liti-gioso/sa; **~ly** *adv* contenciosamente.

contentment *n* contentamiento, placer *m*.

contest *vt* contestar, disputar, litigar; * *n* concurso *m*; contestación, altercación *f*.

contestant *n* concursante/ta *m/f*.

context *n* contexto *m*; contextura *f*.

contiguous *adj* contiguo/gua, vecino/na.

continent *adj* continente; * *n* continente *m*.

continental *adj* continental.

contingency *n* contingencia *f*; acontecimiento *m*; eventualidad *f*.

contingent *n* contingente *m*; cuota *f*; * *adj* contingente, casual; **~ly** *adv* casualmente.

continual *adj* continuo/nua; **~ly** *adv* continuamente.

continuation *n* continuación, serie *f*.

continue *vt* continuar; * *vi* durar, perseverar, persistir.

continuity *n* continuidad *f*.

continuous *adj* continuo/nua, unido/da; **~ly** *adv* continuadamente.

contort *vt* torcer.

contortion *n* contorsión *f*.

contour *n* contorno *m*.

contraband *n* contrabando *m*; * *adj* prohibido/da, ilegal.

contraception *n* contracepción *f*.

contraceptive *n* anticonceptivo *m*; * *adj* anticonceptivo/va.

contract *vt* contraer; abreviar; contratar; *vi* contraerse; * *n* contrato, pacto *m*.

contraction *n* contracción *f*; abreviatura *f*.

contractor *n* contratante *m/f*.

contradict *vt* contradecir.

contradiction *n* contradicción, oposición *f*.

contradictory *adj* contradictorio/ria.

contraption *n* artilugio *m*.

contrariness *n* contrariedad, oposición *f*.

contrary *adj* contrario/ria, opuesto/ta; * *n* contrario *m*; **on the** ~ al contrario.

contrast *n* contraste *m*; oposición *f*; * *vt* contrastar, oponer.

contrasting *adj* opuesto/ta.

contravention *n* contravención *f*.

contributory *adj* contributario/ria; contribuyente.

contribute *vt* contribuir, ayudar.

contribution *n* contribución *f*; tributo *m*.

contributor *n* contribuidor/a *m/f*.

contrite *adj* contrito/ta, arrepentido/da.

contrition *n* penitencia, contrición *f*.

contrivance *n* designio *m*; invención *f*; concepto *m*.

contrive *vt* inventar, trazar, maquinar; manejar; combinar.

control *n* control *m*; inspección *f*; * *vt* controlar; manejar; restringir; gobernar.

control room *n* sala de mando *f*.

control tower *n* torre de control *f*.

controversial *adj* polémico/ca.

controversy *n* controversia *f*.

contusion n contusión f, magullamiento m.

conundrum n problema m.

conurbation n conurbación f.

convalesce vi convalecer.

convalescence n convalecencia f.

convalescent adj convaleciente.

convene vt convocar; juntar, unir; * vi convenir, juntarse.

convenience n conveniencia, comodidad, conformidad f.

convenient adj conveniente, apto/ta, cómodo/da, propio/pia; ~ly adv cómodamente, oportunamente.

convent n convento, claustro, monasterio m.

convention n convención f; contrato, tratado m.

conventional adj convencional, esti-pulado/da.

converge vi converger.

convergence n convergencia f.

convergent adj convergente.

conversant adj versado en; íntimo/ma.

conversation n conversación f, Lat Am conversa f.

converse vi conversar; platicar.

conversely adv mutuamente, recíprocamente.

conversion n conversión, transmutación f.

convert vt (vr) convertir(se); * n converso, convertido m.

convertible adj convertible, transmutable; * n descapotable m.

convex adj convexo/xa.

convexity n convexidad f.

convey vt transportar; transmitir, transferir.

conveyance n transporte m; conducción f; escritura de traspaso f.

conveyancer n notario m.

convict vt probar un delito; * n con-victo/ta m/f.

conviction n convicción f.

convince vt convencer, poner en evidencia.

convincing adj convincente.

convincingly adv de modo convincente.

convivial adj sociable; hospitalario/ria.

conviviality n sociabilidad f.

convoke vt convocar, reunir.

convoy n convoy m.

convulse vt conmover, convulsionar.

convulsion n convulsión f; conmoción f; tumulto m.

convulsive adj convulsivo/va; ~ly adv convulsivamente.

coo vi arrullar.

cook n cocinero/ra m/f; * vt cocinar; * vi cocinar; guisar.

cookbook n libro de cocina m.

cooker n cocina f.

cookery n arte culinario m, cocina f.

cookie n galleta f.

cool adj fresco/ca; indiferente; * n frescura f; * vt enfriar, refrescar.

coolly adv frescamente; indiferentemente.

coolness n fresco m; frialdad, frescura f.

cooperate vi cooperar.

cooperation n cooperación f.

cooperative adj cooperativo/va; cooperante.

coordinate vt coordinar.

coordination n coordinación, elección f.

cop n (col) poli m.

copartner n compañero/ra, socio/cia m/f.

cope vi arreglárselas.

copier n copiadora f.

copious adj copioso/sa, abundante; ~ly adv en abundancia.

copper n cobre m.

coppice, copse n bosquecillo m.

copulate vi copular.

copy n copia f; original m; ejemplar m; * vt copiar; imitar.

copybook n copiador de cartas (libro) m.

copying machine n copiadora f.

copyist n copista m/f.

copyright n propiedad de una obra literaria f; derechos de autor mpl.

coral n coral m.

coral reef n arrecife de coral m.

cord n cuerda f; cable m.

cordial adj cordial, de corazón, amistoso/sa; ~ly adv cordialmente.

corduroy n pana f.

core n cuesco m; interior, centro, corazón m; materia f.

cork n alcornoque m; corcho m; * vt encorchar.

corkscrew n sacacorchos m invar.

corn[1] n maíz m; borona f; granos mpl.

corn[2] n callo m.

corncob n mazorca f.

cornea n córnea f.

corned beef n carne acecinada f.

corner n rincón m; esquina f.

cornerstone n piedra angular f.

cornet n corneta f.

cornfield n maizal m.

cornflakes npl copos de maíz mpl.

cornice n cornisa f.

cornstarch n harina de maíz f.

corollary n corolario m.

coronary n infarto m.

coronation n coronación f.

coroner n oficial que hace la inspección jurídica de los cadáveres m.

coronet n corona pequeña f.

corporal n cabo m.

corporate adj corporativo/va.

corporation n corporación f; gremio m.

corporeal adj corpóreo/rea.

corps n cuerpo (de ejército) m; regimiento m.

corpse n cadáver m.

corpulent adj corpulento/ta, gordo/da.

corpuscle n corpúsculo, átomo m.

corral n corral m.

correct vt corregir; enmendar; * adj correcto/ta, justo/ta; ~ly adv correctamente.

correction n corrección f; enmienda f; censura f.

corrective *adj* correctivo/va; * *n* correctivo *m*; restricción *f*.

correctness *n* exactitud *f*.

correlation *n* correlación *f*.

correlative *adj* correlativo/va.

correspond *vi* corresponder; corresponderse.

correspondence *n* correspondencia *f*.

correspondent *adj* correspondiente, conforme; * *n* corresponsal *m*.

corridor *n* pasillo *m*.

corroborate *vt* corroborar.

corroboration *n* corroboración *f*.

corroborative *adj* corroborativo/va.

corrode *vt* corroer.

corrosion *n* corrosión *f*.

corrosive *adj*, *n* corrosivo *m*.

corrugated iron *n* chapa ondulada *f*.

corrupt *vt* corromper; sobornar; * *vi* corromperse, pudrirse; * *adj* corrom-pido/da; depravado/da.

corruptible *adj* corruptible.

corruption *n* corrupción *f*; depravación *f*.

corruptive *adj* corruptivo/va.

corset *n* corsé, corpiño *m*.

cortege *n* cortejo *m*.

cosmetic *adj* cosmético/ca; * *n* cosmético *m*.

cosmic *adj* cósmico/ca.

cosmonaut *n* cosmonauta *m/f*.

cosmopolitan *adj* cosmopolita.

cosset *vt* mimar.

cost *n* coste, precio *m*; * *vi* costar.

costly *adj* costoso/sa, caro/ra.

costume *n* traje *m*.

cottage *n* casita, casucha *f*.

cotton *n* algodón *m*.

cotton candy *n* algodón azucarado *m*.

cotton mill *n* hilandería de algodón.

cotton wool *n* algodón hidrófilo *m*.

couch *n* sofá *m*.

couchette *n* litera *f*.

cough *n* tos *f*; * *vi* toser.

council *n* concilio, consejo *m*.

councilor *n* concejal/a *m/f*.

counsel *n* consejo, aviso *m*; abogado/-da *m/f*.

counselor *n* consejero/ra *m/f*; abo-gado/da *m/f*.

count *vt* contar, numerar; calcular; **to ~ on** contar con; * *n* cuenta *f*; cálculo *m*; conde *m*.

countdown *n* cuenta atrás *f*.

countenance *n* rostro *m*; aspecto *m*; (buena/mala) cara *f*.

counter *n* mostrador *m*; ficha *f*.

counteract *vt* contrariar, impedir, estorbar; frustrar.

counterbalance *vt* contrapesar; igualar, compensar; * *n* contrapeso *m*.

counterfeit *vt* contrahacer, imitar, falsear; * *adj* falsificado/da; fingi-do/da.

countermand *vt* contramandar; revocar.

counterpart *n* parte correspondiente *f*.

counterproductive *adj* contraproducente.

countersign *vt* refrendar; firmar un decreto.

countess *n* condesa *f*.

countless *adj* innumerable.

countrified *adj* rústico/ca; tosco/ca, rudo/da.

country *n* país *m*; campo *m*; región *f*; patria *f*; * *adj* rústico/ca; campestre, rural.

country house *n* casa de campo, granja *f*.

countryman *n* paisano *m*; compatriota *m*.

county *n* condado *m*.

coup *n* golpe *m*.

coupé *n* (*auto*) cupé *m*.

couple *n* par *m*; lazo *m*; yuntas *fpl*; * *vt* unir, parear; casar.

couplet *n* copla *f*; par *m*.

coupon *n* cupón *m*.

courage *n* coraje, valor *f*.

courageous *adj* corajudo/da, vale-roso/sa; **~ly** *adv* valerosamente.

courier *n* correo, mensajero/ra *m/f*, expreso *m*.

course *n* curso *m*; carrera *f*; camino *m*; ruta *f*; método *m*; **of ~** por supuesto, sin duda.

court *n* corte *f*; palacio *m*; tribunal de justicia *m*, *Lat Am* corte *f*; * *vt* cortejar; solicitar, adular.

courteous *adj* cortés; benévolo/la; **~ly** *adv* cortésmente.

courtesan *n* cortesana *f*.

courtesy *n* cortesía *f*; benignidad *f*.

courthouse *n* palacio de justicia *m*.

courtly *adj* cortesano/na, elegante.

court martial *n* consejo de guerra *m*.

courtroom *n* sala de justicia *f*.

courtyard *n* patio *m*.

cousin *n* primo *m*; prima *f*; **first ~** primo hermano *m*.

cove *n* (*mar*) ensenada, caleta *f*.

covenant *n* contrato *m*; convención *f*; * *vi* pactar, estipular.

cover *n* cubierta *f*; abrigo *m*; pretexto *m*; * *vt* cubrir; tapar; ocultar; proteger.

coverage *n* alcance *m*.

coveralls *npl* mono *m*; *Lat Am* overol *m*.

covering *n* ropa *f*; vestido *m*.

cover letter *n* carta de explicación *f*.

covert *adj* cubierto/ta; oculto/ta, se-creto/ta; **~ly** *adv* secretamente.

cover-up *n* encubrimiento *m*.

covet *vt* codiciar, desear con ansia.

covetous *adj* avariento/ta, sórdido/da.

cow *n* vaca *f*.

coward *n* cobarde *m/f*.

cowardice *n* cobardía, timidez *f*.

cowardly *adj*, *adv* cobarde; pusilánime.

cowboy, cowhand *n* vaquero *m*.

cower *vi* agacharse.

cowherd *n* vaquero *m*; vaquerizo *m*.

coy *adj* recatado/da, modesto/ta; es-quivo/va; **~ly** *adv* con esquivez.

coyness *n* esquivez, modestia *f*.

cozily *adv* cómodamente, con facilidad.

cozy *adj* cómodo/da.

crab *n* cangrejo *m*; manzana silvestre *f*.

crab apple *n* manzana silvestre *f*; ~ **tree** *n* manzano silvestre *m*.

crack *n* crujido *m*; hendedura, quebraja *f*; * *vt* hender, rajar; romper; **to ~ down on** reprimandar fuertemente;* *vi* reventar.

cracker *n* buscapiés *m invar*; galleta *f*.

crackle *vi* crujir, chillar.

crackling *n* estallido, crujido *m*.

cradle *n* cuna *f*; * *vt* acunar.

craft *n* arte *m*; artificio *m*; barco *m*.

craftily *adv* astutamente.

craftiness *n* astucia, estratagema *f*.

craftsman *n* artífice, artesano *m*.

craftsmanship *n* artesanía *f*.

crafty *adj* astuto/ta, artificioso/sa.

crag *n* despeñadero *m*.

cram *vt* embutir; engordar; empujar; * *vi* empollar.

crammed *adj* atestado/da.

cramp *n* calambre *m*; * *vt* constreñir.

cramped *adj* apretado/da.

crampon *n* crampón *m*.

cranberry *n* arándano agrio *m*.

crane *n* grulla *f*; grúa *f*.

crash *vi* estallar; * *vr* zamparse; * *n* estallido *m*; choque *m*.

crash helmet *n* casco *m*.

crash landing *n* aterrizaje forzoso *m*.

crass *adj* craso/sa, grueso/sa, basto/ta, tosco/ca, grosero/ra.

crate *n* cesta grande *f*.

crater *n* cráter *m*; boca de volcán *f*.

cravat *n* pañuelo *m*.

crave *vt* rogar, suplicar.

craving *adj* insaciable, pedigüeño/ña; * *n* deseo ardiente *m*.

crawfish *n* cangrejo de río *m*.

crawl *vi* arrastrar; **to ~ with** hormiguear.

crayon *n* lápiz *m*.

craze *n* manía *f*.

craziness *n* locura *f*.

crazy *adj* loco/ca.

creak *vi* crujir, chirriar.

cream *n* crema *f*; * *adj* color crema.

creamy *adj* cremoso/sa.

crease *n* pliegue *m*; * *vt* plegar.

create *vt* crear; causar.

creation *n* creación *f*; elección *f*.

creative *adj* creativo/va.

creator *n* creador/a *m/f*.

creature *n* criatura *f*.

credence *n* creencia, fe *f*; renombre *m*.

credentials *npl* (cartas) credenciales *fpl*.

credibility *n* credibilidad *f*.

credible *adj* creíble.

credit *n* crédito *m*; reputación *f*; autoridad *f*; * *vt* creer, fiar, acreditar.

creditable *adj* estimable, honorífico/ca; ~**bly** *adv* honorablemente.

credit card *n* tarjeta de crédito *f*.

creditor *n* acreedor *m*.

credulity *n* credulidad *f*.

credulous *adj* crédulo/la; ~**ly** *adv* con credulidad.

creed *n* credo *m*.

creek *n* arroyo *m*.

creep *vi* arrastrar, serpear; complacer bajamente.

creeper *n* (*bot*) enredadera *f*.

creepy *adj* horripilante.

cremate *vt* incinerar cadáveres.

cremation *n* cremación *f*.

crematorium *n* crematorio *m*.

crescent *adj* creciente; * *n* cuarto creciente *m*.

cress *n* berro *m*.

crest *n* cresta *f*.

crested *adj* crestado/da.

crestfallen *adj* acobardado/da, abati-do/da de espíritu.

crevasse *n* grieta (de glaciar) *f*.

crevice *n* raja, hendedura *f*.

crew *n* banda, tropa *f*; tripulación *f*.

crib *n* cuna *f*; pesebre *m*.

cricket *n* grillo *m*; críquet *m*.

crime *n* crimen *m*; culpa *f*.

criminal *adj* criminal, reo/rea; ~**ly** *adv* criminalmente; * *n* criminal *m/f*.

criminality *n* criminalidad *f*.

crimson *adj*, *n* carmesí *m*.

cripple *vt* lisiar; (*fig*) estropear.

crisis *n* crisis *f invar*.

crisp *adj* crujiente.

crispness *n* sequedad *f*.

criss-cross *adj* entrelazado/da.

criterion *n* criterio *m*.

critic *n* crítico *m*; crítica *f*.

critic(al) *adj* crítico/ca; exacto/ta; delicado/da; ~**ally** *adv* exactamente, rigurosamente.

criticism *n* crítica *f*.

criticize *vt* criticar, censurar; zaherir; (*fig*) zurrar.

croak *vi* graznar.

crochet *n* ganchillo *m*; * *vt*, *vi* hacer ganchillo.

crockery *n* loza *f*; vasijas de barro *fpl*.

crocodile *n* cocodrilo *m*.

crony *n* amigote *m*; compinche *m*.

crook *n* (*col*) ladrón *m*; cayado *m*.

crooked *adj* torcido/da; perverso/sa.

crop *n* cultivo *m*; cosecha *f*; * *vt* recortar.

cross *n* cruz *f*; carga *f*; * *adj* mal humorado/da; * *vt* atravesar, cruzar; **to ~ over** traspasar.

crossbar *n* travesaño *m*.

crossbreed *n* raza cruzada *f*.

cross-country *n* carrera a campo traviesa *f*.

cross-examine *vt* preguntar a un testigo.

crossfire *n* fuego cruzado *m*.

crossing *n* cruce *m*; paso a nivel *m*.

cross-purpose *n* disposición contraria *f*; contradicción *f*; **to be at ~s** entenderse mal.

cross-reference *n* remisión *f*.

crossroad *n* encrucijada *f*.

crosswalk *n* paso de peatones *m*.

crotch *n* entrepierna *f*.

crouch *vi* agacharse, bajarse.

crow *n* cuervo *m*; canto del gallo *m*; * *vi* cantar el gallo.

crowd *n* público *m*; muchedumbre *f*; * *vt* amontonar; * *vi* reunirse.

crown *n* corona *f*; cumbre *f*; * *vt* coronar.

crown prince *n* príncipe real *m*.

crucial *adj* crucial.

crucible *n* crisol *m*.

crucifix *n* crucifijo *m*.

crucifixion *n* crucifixión *f*.

crucify *vt* crucificar; atormentar.

crude *adj* crudo/da, imperfecto/ta; ~ly *adv* crudamente.

cruel *adj* cruel, inhumano/na; ~ly *adv* cruelmente.

cruelty *n* crueldad *f*.

cruet set/stand *n* vinagreras *fpl*.

cruise *n* crucero *m*; * *vi* hacer un crucero.

cruiser *n* crucero *m*.

crumb *n* miga *f*.

crumble *vt* desmigajar, desmenuzar; * *vi* desmigajarse.

crumple *vt* arrugar.

crunch *vt* apretar, oprimir; * *n* choque *m*.

crunchy *adj* crujiente.

crusade *n* cruzada *f*.

crush *vt* apretar, oprimir; * *n* choque *m*.

crust *n* costra *f*; corteza *f*; zoquete *m*.

crusty *adj* costroso/sa; bronco/ca, áspero/ra.

crutch *n* muleta *f*.

crux *n* lo esencial.

cry *vt* (*vi*) gritar; exclamar; llorar; * *n* grito *m*; lloro *m*; clamor *m*.

crypt *n* cripta *f*.

cryptic *adj* enigmático/ca.

crystal *n* cristal *m*.

crystal-clear *adj* claro/ra como el agua.

crystalline *adj* cristalino/na; transparente.

crystallize *vt* (*vi*) cristalizar(se).

cub *n* cachorro *m*.

cube *n* cubo *m*.

cubic *adj* cúbico/ca.

cuckoo *n* cuco *m*.

cucumber *n* pepino *m*.

cud *n*: **to ~ the chew** ~ rumiar; (*fig*) reflexionar.

cuddle *vt* abrazar; * *vi* abrazarse; * *n* abrazo *m*.

cudgel *n* garrote, palo *m*.

cue *n* taco (de billar) *m*.

cuff[1] *n* puño *m*, bocamanga *f*, vuelta *f*.

cuff[2] *n* puñada *f*.

culinary *adj* culinario/ria, de la cocina.

cull *vt* escoger, elegir.

culminate *vi* culminar.

culmination *n* colmo *m*.

culpability *n* culpabilidad *f*.

culpable *adj* culpable, criminal; ~bly *adv* culpablemente, criminalmente.

culprit *n* culpable *m/f*.

cult *n* culto *f*.

cultivate *vi* cultivar, mejorar; perfeccionar.

cultivation *n* cultivo *m*.

cultural *adj* cultural.

culture *n* cultura *f*.

cumbersome *adj* engorroso/sa, pesa-do/da, confuso/sa.

cumulative *adj* cumulativo/va.

cunning *adj* astuto/ta; intrigante; ~ly *adv* astutamente; expertamente; * *n* astucia, sutileza *f*; ~ **person** zorro *m*.

cup *n* taza, jícara *f*; (*bot*) cáliz *m*.

cupboard *n* armario *m*.

curable *adj* curable.

curate *n* teniente de cura *m*; párroco *m*.

curator *n* curador/a *m/f*; guardián/ana *m/f*.

curb *n* freno *m*; bordillo *m*; * *vt* refrenar, contener, moderar.

curd *n* cuajada *f*.

curdle *vt* (*vi*) cuajar(se), coagular(se).

cure *n* cura *f*; remedio *m*; * *vt* curar, sanar.

curfew *n* toque de queda *m*.

curing *n* curación *f*.

curiosity *n* curiosidad *f*; rareza *f*.

curious *adj* curioso/sa; ~ly *adv* curiosamente.

curl *n* rizo de pelo *m*; * *vt* rizar; ondear; * *vi* rizarse.

curling iron *n*, **curling tongs** *npl* tenacillas de rizar *fpl*.

curly *adj* rizado/da.

currant *n* pasa *f*.

currency *n* moneda *f*; circulación *f*; duración *f*.

current *adj* corriente, común; * *n* curso, progreso *m*; marcha *f*; corriente *f*.

current affairs *npl* actualidades *fpl*.

currently *adv* actualmente.

curriculum vitae *n* currículum *m*.

curry *n* curry *m*.

curse *vt* maldecir; * *vi* imprecar; blasfemar; * *n* maldición *f*.

cursor *n* cursor *m*.

cursory *adj* precipitado/da, incon-siderado/da.

curt *adj* sucinto/ta.

curtail *vt* acortar.

curtsy *n* reverencia *f*; * *vi* hacer una reverencia.

curvature *n* curvatura *f*.

curve *vt* encorvar; * *n* curva *f*.

cushion *n* cojín *m*; almohada *f*.

custard *n* natillas *fpl*.

custodian *n* custodio *m*.

custody *n* custodia *f*; prisión *f*.

custom *n* costumbre *f*, uso *m*.

customary *adj* usual, acostumbrado/da, ordinario/ria.

customer *n* cliente *m/f*.

customs *npl* aduana *f*.

customs duty *n* derechos de aduana *mpl*.

customs officer *n* aduanero/ra *m/f*.

cut *vt* cortar; separar; herir; dividir; cortar los naipes; **to ~ short** interrumpir, cortar la palabra; **to ~ teeth** nacerle los dientes (a un niño); * *vi* traspasar; cruzarse; * *n* corte *m*;

cortadura *f*; herida *f*; **~ and dried** *adj* rutinario/ria.

cutback *n* reducción *f*.

cute *adj* lindo/da.

cutlery *n* cuchillería *f*.

cutlet *n* chuleta *f*.

cut-rate *adj* a precio reducido.

cut-throat *n* asesino *m*; * *adj* encarni-zado/da.

cutting *n* cortadura *f*; * *adj* cortante; mordaz.

cyanide *n* cianuro *m*.

cyberspace *n* ciberespacio *m*.

cycle *n* ciclo *m*; bicicleta *f*; * *vi* ir en bicicleta.

cycling *n* ciclismo *m*.

cyclist *n* ciclista *m/f*.

cyclone *n* ciclón *m*.

cygnet *n* pollo del cisne *m*.

cylinder *n* cilindro *m*; rollo *m*.

cylindric(al) *adj* cilíndrico/ca.

cymbals *n* címbalo *m*.

cynic(al) *adj* cínico/ca; obsceno/na; * *n* cínico *m* (filósofo).

cynicism *n* cinismo *m*.

cypress *n* ciprés *m*.

cyst *n* quiste *m*.

czar *n* zar *m*.

D

dab *n* pedazo pequeño *m*; toque *m*.

dabble *vi* chapotear.

dad(dy) *n* papa *m*.

daddy-long-legs *n* típula *f*.

daffodil *n* narciso *m*.

dagger *n* puñal *m*.

daily *adj* diario/ria, cotidiano/na; * *adv* diariamente, cada día; * *n* diario *m*.

daintily *adv* delicadamente.

daintiness *n* elegancia *f*; delicadeza *f*.

dainty *adj* delicado/da. elegante.

dairy *n* lechería *f*.

dairy farm *n* vaquería *f*.

dairy produce *n* productos lácteos *mpl*.

daisy *n* margarita, maya *f*.

dale *n* valle *m*.

dally *vi* tardar.

dam *n* presa *f*; * *vt* represar.

damage *n* daño *m*; perjuicio *m*; * dañar; perjudicar.

damask *n* damasco *m*; * *adj* de damasco.

damn *vt* condenar; * *adj* maldito/ta.

damnable *adj* maldito/ta; **~bly** *adv* terriblemente.

damnation *n* perdición *f*.

damning *adj* irrecusable.

damp *adj* húmedo/da; * *n* humedad *f*; * *vt* mojar.

dampen *vt* mojar.

dampness *n* humedad *f*.

damson *n* damascena *f* (ciruela).

dance *n* danza *f*; baile *m*; * *vi* bailar.

dance hall *n* salón de baile *m*.

dancer *n* bailarín *m*, bailarina *f*.

dandelion *n* diente de león *m*.

dandruff *n* caspa *f*.

dandy *adj* mono/na.

danger *n* peligro, riesgo *m*.

dangerous *adj* peligroso/sa; **~ly** *adv* peligrosamente.

dangle *vi* estar colgado/da.

dank *adj* húmedo/da.

dapper *adj* apuesto/ta.

dappled *adj* rodado/da.

dare *vi* atreverse; * *vt* desafiar.

daredevil *n* atrevido *m*.

daring *n* osadía *f*; * *adj* atrevido/da; **~ly** *adv* atrevidamente, osadamente.

dark *adj* oscuro/ra; negro/gra; * *n* oscuridad *f*; ignorancia *f*.

darken *vt* (*vi*) oscurecer(se).

dark glasses *npl* gafas de sol *fpl*.

darkness *n* oscuridad *f*.

darkroom *n* cuarto oscuro *m*.

darling *n*, *adj* querido/m.

darn *vt* zurcir.

dart *n* dardo *m*.

dartboard *n* diana *f*.

dash *vi* irse de prisa; * *n* pizca *f*; **at one ~** de un golpe.

dashboard *n* tablero de instrumentos *m*.

dashing *adj* gallardo/da.

dastardly *adj* cobarde.

data *n* datos *mpl*.

database *n* base de datos *f*.

data processing *n* proceso de datos *m*.

date *n* fecha *f*; cita *f*; (*bot*) dátil *m*; * *vt* fechar; salir con.

dated *adj* anticuado/da.

dative *n* dativo *m*.

daub *vt* manchar.

daughter *n* hija *f*; **~ in-law** nuera *f*.

daunting *adj* desalentador/a.

dawdle *vi* gastar tiempo.

dawn *n* alba *f*; * *vi* amanecer.

day *n* día *m*; luz *f*; **by ~** de día; **~ by ~** de día en día.

daybreak *n* alba *f*.

day laborer *n* jornalero *m*.

daylight *n* luz del día, luz natural *f*; **~ saving time** *n* hora de verano *f*.

daytime *n* día *m*.

daze *vt* aturdir.

dazed *adj* aturdido/da.

dazzle *vt* deslumbrar.

dazzling *adj* deslumbrante.

deacon *n* diácono *m*.

dead *adj* muerto/ta. marchito/ta; **~wood** *n* lastre *m*; **~ silence** *n* silencio profundo *m*; **the ~** *npl* los muertos.

dead-drunk *adj* borracho como una cuba.

deaden *vt* amortiguar.

dead heat *n* empate *m*.

deadline *n* fecha tope *f*.

deadlock n punto muerto m.
deadly adj mortal; * adv terriblemente.
dead march n marcha fúnebre f.
deadness n inercia f.
deaf adj sordo/da.
deafen vt ensordecer.
deaf-mute n sordomudo/da m./f.
deafness n sordera f.
deal n convenio m; transacción f; **a great ~** mucho; **a good ~** bastante; * vt distribuir; dar; * vi comerciar; **to ~ in/with** tratar en/con.
dealer n comerciante m/f; traficante m/f; mano f.
dealings npl trato m.
dean n deán m.
dear adj querido/da. caro/ra, costoso/sa; **~ly** adv caro.
dearness n carestía f.
dearth n escasez f.
death n muerte f.
deathbed n lecho de muerte m.
deathblow n golpe mortal m.
death certificate n partida de defunción f.
death penalty n pena de muerte f.
death throes npl agonía f.
death warrant n sentencia de muerte f.
debacle n desastre m.
debar vt excluir, no admitir.
debase vt degradar.
debasement n degradación f.
debatable adj discutible.
debate n debate m; polémica f; * vt discutir; examinar.
debauched adj vicioso/sa.
debauchery n libertinaje m.
debilitate vt debilitar.
debit n debe m; * vt (com) cargar en una cuenta.
debt n deuda f; obligación f; **to get into ~** contraer deudas.
debtor n deudor/a m/f.
debunk vt desacreditar.
decade n década f.
decadence n decadencia f.
decaffeinated adj descafeinado/da.
decanter n garrafa f.
decapitate vt decapitar, degollar.
decapitation n decapitación f.
decay vi decaer; pudrirse; * n decadencia f; caries f.
deceased adj muerto/ta.
deceit n engaño m.
deceitful adj engañoso/sa; **~ly** adv falsamente.
deceive vt engañar.
December n diciembre m.
decency n decencia f; modestia f.
decent adj decente, razonable; **~ly** adv decentemente.
deception n engaño m.
deceptive adj engañoso/sa.
decibel n decibelio m.
decide vt, vi decidir; resolver.

decided adj decidido/da.
decidedly adv decididamente.
deciduous adj (bot) de hoja caduca.
decimal adj decimal.
decimate vt diezmar.
decipher vt descifrar.
decision n decisión, determinación f.
decisive adj decisivo/va; **~ly** adv de modo decisivo.
deck n cubierta f; * vt adornar.
deckchair n tumbona f.
declaim vi declamar.
declamation n declamación f.
declaration n declaración f.
declare vt declarar, manifestar.
declension n declinación f.
decline vt (gr) declinar; evitar; * vi decaer; * n decadencia f.
declutch vi desembragar.
decode vt descifrar.
decoder n (TV) descodificador m.
decompose vt descomponer.
decomposition n descomposición f.
decor n decoración f.
decorate vt decorar, adornar.
decoration n decoración f.
decorative adj decorativo/va.
decorator n pintor (decorador) m.
decorous adj decoroso/sa; **~ly** adv decorosamente.
decorum n decoro, garbo m.
decoy n señuelo m.
decrease vt disminuir; * n disminución f.
decree n decreto m; * vt decretar; ordenar.
decrepit adj decrépito/ta.
decry vt desacreditar, censurar.
dedicate vt dedicar; consagrar.
dedication n dedicación f; dedicatoria f.
deduce vt deducir; concluir.
deduct vt restar.
deduction n deducción f; descuento m.
deed n acción f; hecho m; hazaña f.
deem vi juzgar.
deep adj profundo/da.
deepen vt profundizar.
deep-freeze n congeladora f.
deeply adv profundamente.
deepness n profundidad f.
deer n ciervo m.
deface vt desfigurar, afear.
defacement n desfiguración f.
defamation n difamación f.
default n defecto m; falta f; * vi faltar.
defaulter n (law) moroso/sa m/f.
defeat n derrota f; * vt derrotar; frustrar.
defect n defecto m; falta f.
defection n deserción f.
defective adj defectuoso/sa.
defend vt defender; proteger.
defendant n acusado/da m/f.
defense n defensa f; protección f.

defenseless *adj* indefenso/sa.
defensive *adj* defensivo/va; **~ly** *adv* de modo defensivo.
defer *vt* aplazar.
deference *n* deferencia *f*; respeto *m*.
deferential *adj* respetuoso/sa.
defiance *n* desafío *m*.
defiant *adj* insolente.
deficiency *n* defecto *m*; falta *f*.
deficient *adj* insuficiente.
deficit *n* déficit *m*, *Lat Am* faltante *m*.
defile *vt* ensuciar.
definable *adj* definible.
define *vt* definir.
definite *adj* definido/da. preciso/sa; **~ly** *adv* no cabe duda..
definition *n* definición *f*.
definitive *adj* definitivo/va; **~ly** *adv* definitivamente.
deflate *vt* desinflar.
deflect *vt* desviar.
deflower *vt* desvirgar.
deform *vt* desfigurar.
deformity *n* deformidad *f*.
defraud *vt* estafar.
defray *vt* costear.
defrost *vt* deshelar; descongelar.
defroster *n* luneta térmica *f*.
deft *adj* diestro/tra; **~ly** *adv* hábilmente.
defunct *adj* difunto/ta.
defuse *vt* desactivar.
degenerate *vi* degenerar; * *adj* dege-nerado/da.
degeneration *n* degeneración *f*.
degradation *n* degradación *f*.
degrade *vt* degradar.
degree *n* grado *m*; título *m*.
dehydrated *adj* deshidratado/da.
de-ice *vt* deshelar.
deign *vi* dignarse.
deity *n* deidad, divinidad *f*.
dejected *adj* desanimado/da.
dejection *n* desaliento *m*.
delay *vt* demorar; * *n* retraso *m*.
delectable *adj* deleitoso/sa.
delegate *vt* delegar; * *n* delegado *m*.
delegation *n* delegación *f*.
delete *vt* tachar; borrar.
deliberate *vt* deliberar; * *adj* inten-cionado/da; **~ly** *adv* a propósito.
deliberation *n* deliberación *f*.
deliberative *adj* deliberativo/va.
delicacy *n* delicadeza *f*.
delicate *adj* delicado/da. exquisito/ta; **~ly** *adv* delicadamente.
delicious *adj* delicioso/sa. exquisito/ta; **~ly** *adv* deliciosamente.
delight *n* delicia *f*; gozo, encanto *m*; * *vt, vi* deleitar(se).
delighted *adj* encantado/da.
delightful *adj* encantador/a, **~ly** *adv* en forma encantadora.

delineate *vt* delinear.
delineation *n* delineación *f*.
delinquency *n* delincuencia *f*.
delinquent *n* delincuente *m/f*.
delirious *adj* delirante.
delirium *n* delirio *m*.
deliver *vt* entregar; pronunciar.
deliverance *n* liberación *f*.
delivery *n* entrega *f*; parto *m*.
delude *vt* engañar.
deluge *n* diluvio *m*.
delusion *n* engaño *m*; ilusión *f*.
delve *vi* hurgar.
demagog *n* demagogo/a *m/f*.
demand *n* demanda *f*; reclamación *f*; * *vt* exigir; reclamar.
demanding *adj* exigente.
demarcation *n* demarcación *f*.
demean *vi* rebajarse.
demeanor *n* conducta *f*.
demented *adj* demente.
demise *n* desaparición *f*.
democracy *n* democracia *f*.
democrat *n* demócrata *m/f*.
democratic *adj* democrático/ca.
Democratic Party *n* Partido Democrático *m*.
demolish *vt* demoler.
demolition *n* demolición *f*.
demon *n* demonio, diablo *m*.
demonstrable *adj* demostrable; **~bly** *adv* manifiestamente.
demonstrate *vt* demostrar, probar; * *vi* manifestarse.
demonstration *n* demostración *f*; manifestación *f*.
demonstrative *adj* demostrativo/va.
demonstrator *n* manifestante *m/f*.
demoralization *n* desmoralización *f*.
demoralize *vt* desmoralizar.
demote *vt* degradar.
demur *vi* objetar.
demure *adj* modesto/ta; **~ly** *adv* modestamente.
den *n* guarida *f*.
denatured alcohol *n* alcohol desnaturalizado *m*.
denial *n* negación *f*.
denims *npl* vaqueros *mpl*.
denomination *n* valor *m*.
denominator *n* (*math*) denominador *m*.
denote *vt* denotar, indicar.
denounce *vt* denunciar.
dense *adj* denso/sa, espeso/sa.
density *n* densidad *f*.
dent *n* abolladura *f*; * *vt* abollar.
dental *adj* dental.
dentifrice *n* dentífrico *m*.
dentist *n* dentista *m/f*.
dentistry *n* odontología *f*.
denture *npl* dentadura postiza *f*.
denude *vt* desnudar, despojar.
denunciation *n* denuncia *f*.
deny *vt* negar.

deodorant *n* desodorante *m*.
deodorize *vt* desodorizar.
depart *vi* partir.
department *n* departamento *m*.
department store *n* gran almacén *m*.
departure *n* partida *f*.
departure lounge *n* sala de embarque *f*.
depend *vi* depender; ~ **on/upon** contar con.
dependable *adj* seguro/ra, serio/ria.
dependant *n* dependiente *m*.
dependency *n* dependencia *f*.
dependent *adj* dependiente.
depict *vt* pintar, retratar; describir.
depleted *adj* reducido/da.
deplorable *adj* deplorable, lamentable; **~bly** *adv* deplorablemente.
deplore *vt* deplorar, lamentar.
deploy *vt* (*mil*) desplegar.
depopulated *adj* despoblado/da.
depopulation *n* despoblación *f*.
deport *vt* deportar.
deportation *n* deportación *f*; destierro *m*.
deportment *n* conducta *f*.
deposit *vt* depositar; * *n* depósito *m*; yacimiento *m*.
deposition *n* deposición *f*.
depositor *n* depositante *m*.
depot *n* depósito *m*.
deprave *vt* depravar, corromper.
depraved *adj* depravado/da.
depravity *n* depravación *f*.
deprecate *vt* lamentar.
depreciate *vi* depreciarse.
depreciation *n* depreciación *f*.
depredation *n* pillaje *m*.
depress *vt* deprimir.
depressed *adj* deprimido/da.
depression *n* depresión *f*.
deprivation *n* privación *f*.
deprive *vt* privar.
deprived *adj* necesitado/da.
depth *n* profundidad *f*.
deputation *n* diputación *f*.
depute *vt* diputar, delegar.
deputize *vi* suplir a.
deputy *n* diputado/da *m/f*.
derail *vt* descarrilar.
deranged *adj* trastornado/da.
derby *n* hongo *m*.
derelict *adj* abandonado/da.
deride *vt* burlar.
derision *n* mofa *f*.
derisive *adj* irrisorio/ria.
derivable *adj* deducible.
derivation *n* derivación *f*.
derivative *n* derivado *m*.
derive *vt, vi* derivar(se).
dermatologist *n* dermatólogo/ga *m/f*.
dermatology *n* dermatología *f*.
derogatory *adj* despectivo/va.
derrick *n* torre de perforación *f*.

desalinate *vt* desalinizar.
desalination plant *n* desalinizadora *f*.
descant *n* (*mus*) discante *m*.
descend *vi* descender.
descendant *n* descendiente *m*.
descent *n* descenso *m*.
describe *vt* describir.
description *n* descripción *f*.
descriptive *adj* descriptivo/va.
descry *vt* divisar.
desecrate *vt* profanar.
desecration *n* profanación *f*.
desert[1] *n* desierto *m*; * *adj* desierto/ta.
desert[2] *vt* abandonar; desertar; * *n* mérito *m*.
deserter *n* desertor/a *m/f*.
desertion *n* deserción *f*.
deserve *vt* merecer, *Lat Am* ameritar; ser digno/na.
deservedly *adv* merecidamente.
deserving *adj* meritorio/ria.
desideratum *n* desiderátum *m*.
design *vt* diseñar; * *n* diseño *m*; dibujo *m*.
designate *vt* nombrar; designar.
designation *n* designación *f*.
designedly *adv* a propósito.
designer *n* diseñador *m*; modisto *m*.
desirability *n* conveniencia *f*.
desirable *adj* deseable.
desire *n* deseo *m*; * *vt* desear.
desirous *adj* deseoso/sa, ansioso/sa.
desist *vi* desistir.
desk *n* escritorio *m*.
desktop publishing *n* autoedición *f*.
desolate *adj* desierto/ta.
desolation *n* desolación *f*.
despair *n* desesperación *f*; * *vi* desesperarse.
despairingly *adj* desesperadamente.
desperado *n* bandido/da *m/f*.
desperate *adj* desesperado/da; **~ly** *adv* desesperadamente; sumamente.
desperation *n* desesperación *f*.
despicable *adj* despreciable.
despise *vt* despreciar.
despite *prep* a pesar de.
despoil *vt* despojar.
despondency *n* abatimiento *m*.
despondent *adj* abatido/da.
despot *n* déspota *m/f*.
despotic *adj* despótico/ca, absoluto/ta; **~ally** *adv* despóticamente.
despotism *n* despotismo *m*.
dessert *n* postre *m*.
destination *n* destino *m*.
destine *vt* destinar.
destiny *n* destino *m*; suerte *f*.
destitute *adj* indigente.
destitution *n* miseria *f*.
destroy *vt* destruir, arruinar.
destruction *n* destrucción, ruina *f*.
destructive *adj* destructivo/va.
desultory *adj* irregular; sin método.

detach *vt* separar.

detachable *adj* desmontable; de quitapón.

detachment *n* (*mil*) destacamento *m*.

detail *n* detalle *m*; in ~ detalladamente; * *vt* detallar.

detain *vt* retener; detener.

detect *vt* detectar.

detection *n* descubrimiento *m*.

detective *n* detective *m/f*.

detector *n* detector *m*.

detention *n* detención *f*.

deter *vt* disuadir.

detergent *n* detergente *m*.

deteriorate *vt* deteriorar.

deterioration *n* deterioro *m*.

determination *n* resolución *f*.

determine *vt* determinar, decidir.

determined *adj* resuelto/ta.

deterrent *n* fuerza de disuasión *f*.

detest *vt* detestar, aborrecer.

detestable *adj* detestable, abominable.

dethrone *vt* destronar.

dethronement *n* destronamiento *m*.

detonate *vi* detonar.

detonation *n* detonación *f*.

detour *n* desviación *f*.

detract *vt* desvirtuar.

detriment *n* perjuicio *m*.

detrimental *adj* perjudicial.

deuce *n* deuce *m*.

devaluation *n* devaluación *f*.

devastate *vt* devastar.

devastating *adj* devastador.

devastation *n* devastación, ruina *f*.

develop *vt* desarrollar.

development *n* desarrollo *m*.

deviate *vi* desviarse.

deviation *n* desviación *f*.

device *n* mecanismo *m*.

devil *n* diablo, demonio *m*.

devilish *adj* diabólico/ca; ~ly *adv* diabólicamente.

devious *adj* taimado/da.

devise *vt* inventar; idear.

devoid *adj* desprovisto/ta.

devolve *vt* delegar.

devote *vt* dedicar; consagrar.

devoted *adj* fiel.

devotee *n* partidario/a *m/f*.

devotion *n* devoción *f*.

devotional *adj* devoto/ta.

devour *vt* devorar.

devout *adj* devoto/ta, piadoso/sa; ~ly *adv* piadosamente.

dew *n* rocío *m*.

dewy *adj* rociado/da.

dexterity *n* destreza *f*.

dexterous *adj* diestro/tra, hábil.

diabetes *n* diabetes *f*.

diabetic *n* diabético/ca *m/f*.

diabolic *adj* diabólico/ca; ~ally *adv* diabólicamente.

diadem *n* diadema *f*.

diagnosis *n* (*med*) diagnóstico *m*.

diagnostic *adj*, *n* diagnóstico *m*; ~s *pl* diagnóstica *f*.

diagonal *adj*, *n* diagonal *f*; ~ly *adv* diagonalmente.

diagram *n* diagrama *m*.

dial *n* cuadrante *m*; disco *m*.

dial code *n* prefijo *m*.

dialect *n* dialecto *m*.

dialog *n* diálogo *m*.

dial tone *n* tono de marcar *m*.

diameter *n* diámetro *m*.

diametrical *adj* diametral; ~ly *adv* diametralmente.

diamond *n* diamante *m*.

diamond-cutter *n* diamantista *m/f*.

diamonds *npl* (cards) diamantes *mpl*.

diaper *n* pañal *m*; disposable ~ pañal desechable.

diaphragm *n* diafragma *m*.

diarrhea *n* diarrea *f*.

diary *n* diario *m*.

dice *npl* dados *mpl*.

dictate *vt* dictar; * *n* dictado *m*.

dictation *n* dictado *m*.

dictatorial *adj* autoritativo/va, magistral.

dictatorship *n* dictadura *f*.

diction *n* dicción *f*

dictionary *n* diccionario *m*.

didactic *adj* didáctico/ca.

die[1] *vi* morir; to ~ away perderse; to ~ down apagarse.

die[2] *n* dado *m*.

diehard *n* reaccionario/ria *m/f*.

diesel *n* diesel *m*.

diet *n* dieta *f*; régimen *m*; * *vi* estar a dieta.

dietary *adj* dietético/ca.

differ *vi* diferenciarse.

difference *n* diferencia, disparidad *f*.

different *adj* diferente; ~ly *adv* diferentemente.

differentiate *vt* diferenciar.

difficult *adj* difícil.

difficulty *n* dificultad *f*.

diffidence *n* timidez *f*.

diffident *adj* desconfiado/da; ~ly *adv* desconfiadamente.

diffraction *n* difracción *f*.

diffuse *vt* difundir, esparcir; * *adj* difuso/sa.

diffusion *n* difusión *f*.

dig *vt* cavar; to ~ ditches zanjar; * *n* empujón *m*.

digest *vt* digerir.

digestible *adj* digerible.

digestion *n* digestión *f*.

digestive *adj* digestivo/va.

digit *n* dígito *m*.

digital *adj* digital.

digitize *vt* digitalizar.

dignified *adj* grave.

dignitary *n* dignatario *m*.

dignity n dignidad f.

digress vi divagar.

digression n digresión f.

dike n dique m.

dilapidated adj desmoronado/da.

dilapidation n ruina f.

dilate vt, vi dilatar(se).

dilemma n dilema m.

diligence n diligencia f.

diligent adj diligente, asiduo/dua; **~ly** adv diligentemente.

dilute vt diluir.

dim adj turbio/bia; lerdo/da; oscuro/ra; * vt bajar.

dime n moneda de diez centavos f.

dimension n dimensión, extensión f.

diminish vt, vi disminuir(se).

diminution n disminución f.

diminutive n diminutivo m.

dimly adv indistintamente.

dimmer n interruptor m.

dimple n hoyuelo m, Lat Am hoyito m.

din n alboroto m.

dine vi cenar.

diner n restaurante (económico) m.

dinghy n lancha neumática f.

dingy adj sombrío/ría.

dinner n cena f.

dinner-jacket n smoking m.

dinner time n hora de comer f.

dinosaur n dinosaurio m.

dint n: by ~ of a fuerza de.

diocese n diócesis f invar.

dip vt mojar; * n zambullida f.

diphtheria n difteria f.

diphthong n diptongo m.

diploma n diploma m.

diplomacy n diplomacia f.

diplomat n diplomático/ca m/f.

diplomatic adj diplomático/ca.

dipsomania n dipsomanía f.

dipstick n (auto) varilla de nivel f.

dire adj calamitoso/sa.

direct adj directo/ta; * vt dirigir.

direction n dirección f; instrucción f.

directly adj directamente; inmediatamente.

director n director/a m/f.

directory n guía f.

dirt n suciedad f; ~ on clothes zarpa f.

dirtiness n suciedad f.

dirty adj sucio/cia; vil, bajo/ja.

disability n discapacidad f.

disabled adj discapacitado/da.

disabuse vt desengañar.

disadvantage n desventaja f; * vt perjudicar.

disadvantageous adj desventajoso/sa.

disaffected adj descontento/ta.

disagree vi no estar de acuerdo.

disagreeable adj desagradable; **~bly** adv desagradablemente.

disagreement n desacuerdo m.

disallow vt rechazar.

disappear vi desaparecer; ausentarse.

disappearance n desaparición f.

disappoint vt decepcionar.

disappointed adj decepcionado/da.

disappointing adj decepcionante.

disappointment n decepción f.

disapproval n desaprobación, censura f.

disapprove vt desaprobar.

disarm vt desarmar.

disarmament n desarme m.

disarray n desarreglo m.

disaster n desastre m.

disastrous adj desastroso/sa, calamitoso/sa.

disband vt disolver.

disbelief n incredulidad f.

disbelieve vt desconfiar.

disburse vt desembolsar, pagar.

discard vt descartar.

discern vt discernir, percibir.

discernible adj perceptible.

discerning adj perspicaz.

discernment n perspicacia f.

discharge vt descargar; pagar (una deuda); cumplir; * n descarga f; descargo m.

disciple n discípulo/la m/f.

discipline n disciplina f; * vt disciplinar.

disclaim vt negar.

disclaimer n negación f.

disclose vi revelar.

disclosure n revelación f.

discolor vt descolorar.

discoloration n descolorimiento m.

discomfort n incomodidad f.

disconcert vt desconcertar.

disconnect vt desconectar.

disconsolate adj inconsolable; **~ly** adv desconsoladamente.

discontent n descontento/ta m/f; * adj descontento/ta.

discontented adj descontento/ta.

discontinue vt interrumpir.

discord n discordia f.

discordant adj discordante.

discotheque n disco f discoteca f.

discount n descuento m; rebaja f; * vt descontar.

discourage vt desalentar, desanimar.

discouraged adj desalentado/da.

discouragement n desaliento m.

discouraging adj desalentador/a.

discourse n discurso m.

discourteous adj descortés, grosero/ra; **~ly** adv descortésmente.

discourtesy n descortesía f.

discover vt descubrir.

discovery n descubrimiento m; revelación f.

discredit vt desacreditar.

discreditable adj ignominioso/sa.

discreet adj discreto/ta; **~ly** adv discretamente.

discrepancy n discrepancia, diferencia f.

discretion n discreción f.

discretionary adj discrecional.

discriminate *vt* distinguir.

discrimination *n* discriminación *f*.

discursive *adj* discursivo/va.

discuss *vt* discutir.

discussion *n* discusión *f*.

disdain *vt* desdeñar; * *n* desdén, desprecio *m*.

disdainful *adj* desdeñoso/sa; ~ly *adv* desdeñosamente.

disease *n* enfermedad *f*.

diseased *adj* enfermo/ma.

disembark *vt*, *vi* desembarcar.

disembarkation *n* desembarco *m*.

disenchant *vt* desencantar.

disenchanted *adj* desilusionado/da.

disenchantment *n* desilusión *f*.

disengage *vt* soltar.

disentangle *vt* desenredar.

disfigure *vt* desfigurar, afear.

disgrace *n* ignominia *f*; escándalo *m*; * *vt* deshonrar.

disgraceful *adj* ignominioso/sa; ~ly *adv* vergonzosamente.

disgruntled *adj* descontento/ta.

disguise *vt* disfrazar; * *n* disfraz *m*.

disgust *n* aversión *f*; * *vt* repugnar.

disgusting *adj* repugnante.

dish *n* fuente *f*; plato *m*; taza *f*; * *vt* servir en fuente; to ~ up servir.

dishabille *n* deshabillé *m*.

dishcloth *n* paño de cocina *m*.

dishearten *vt* desalentar.

disheveled *adj* desarreglado/da.

dishonest *adj* deshonesto/ta; ~ly *adv* deshonestamente.

dishonesty *n* falta de honradez *f*.

dishonor *n* deshonra, ignominia *f*; * *vt* deshonrar.

dishonorable *adj* deshonroso/sa; ~bly *adv* deshonrosamente.

dishtowel *n* trapo de fregar *m*.

dishwarmer *n* escalfador *m*.

dishwasher *n* lavaplatos *m/f*; lavavajillas *m invar*.

disillusion *vt* desilusionar.

disillusioned *adj* desilusionado/da.

disincentive *n* freno *m*.

disinclination *n* aversión *f*.

disinclined *adj* reacio/cia.

disinfect *vt* desinfectar.

disinfectant *n* desinfectante *m*.

disinherit *vt* desheredar.

disintegrate *vi* disgregarse.

disinterested *adj* desinteresado/da; ~ly *adv* desinteresadamente.

disjointed *adj* inconexo/xa.

disk *n* disco.

diskette *n* disco, disquete *m*.

dislike *n* aversión *f*; * *vt* tener antipatía.

dislocate *vt* dislocar.

dislocation *n* dislocación *f*.

dislodge *vt*, *vi* desalojar.

disloyal *adj* desleal; ~ly *adv* deslealmente.

disloyalty *n* deslealtad *f*.

dismal *adj* triste.

dismantle *vt* desmontar.

dismay *n* consternación *f*.

dismember *vt* despedazar.

dismiss *vt* despedir, *Lat Am* remover.

dismount *vt* desmontar; * *vi* apearse.

disobedience *n* desobediencia *f*.

disobedient *adj* desobediente.

disobey *vt* desobedecer.

disorder *n* desorden *m*; confusión *f*.

disorderly *adj* desarreglado/da, con-fuso/sa.

disorganization *n* desorganización *f*.

disorganized *adj* desorganizado/da.

disorientated *adj* desorientado/da.

disown *vt* desconocer.

disparage *vt* despreciar.

disparaging *adj* despreciativo/va.

disparity *n* disparidad *f*.

dispassionate *adj* desapasionado/da.

dispatch *vt* enviar; * *n* envío *m*; informe *m*.

dispel *vt* disipar.

dispensary *n* dispensario *m*.

dispense *vt* dispensar; distribuir.

disperse *vt* dispersar.

dispirited *adj* desalentado/da.

displace *vt* desplazar.

display *vt* exponer; * *n* ostentación *f*; despliegue *m*.

displeased *adj* disgustado/da.

displeasure *n* disgusto *m*.

disposable *adj* desechable.

disposal *n* disposición *f*.

dispose *vt* disponer; arreglar.

disposed *adj* dispuesto/ta.

disposition *n* disposición *f*.

dispossess *vt* desposeer.

disproportionate *adj* desproporcio-nado/da.

disprove *vt* refutar.

dispute *n* disputa, controversia *f*; * *vt* disputar.

disqualify *vt* incapacitar.

disquiet *n* inquietud *f*.

disquieting *adj* inquietante.

disquisition *n* disquisición *f*.

disregard *vt* desatender; * *n* desdén *m*.

disreputable *adj* de mala fama.

disrespect *n* irreverencia *f*.

disrespectful *adj* irreverente; ~ly *adv* irreverentemente.

disrobe *vt* desnudar.

disrupt *vt* interrumpir.

disruption *n* interrupción *f*.

dissatisfaction *n* descontento/ta, disgusto *m*.

dissatisfied *adj* insatisfecho/cha.

dissect *vt* disecar.

dissection *n* disección *f*.

disseminate *vt* diseminar.

dissension *n* disensión *f*.

dissent *vi* disentir; * *n* disensión *f*.

dissenter *n* disidente *m*.

dissertation *n* disertación *f*.

dissident n disidente m.

dissimilar adj distinto/ta.

dissimilarity n disimilitud f.

dissimulation n disimulo m.

dissipate vt disipar.

dissipation n disipación f.

dissociate vt disociar.

dissolute adj libertino/na.

dissolution n disolución f.

dissolve vt disolver; * vi disolverse, derretirse.

dissonance n disonancia f.

dissuade vt disuadir.

distance n distancia f; **at a ~** de lejos; * vt apartar.

distant adj distante.

distaste n disgusto m.

distasteful adj desagradable.

distend vt hinchar.

distill vt destilar.

distillation n destilación f.

distillery n destilería f.

distinct adj distinto/ta, diferente; claro/ra; ~**ly** adv distintamente.

distinction n distinción f.

distinctive adj distintivo/va.

distinctness n claridad f.

distinguish vt distinguir; discernir.

distort vt retorcer.

distorted adj distorsionado/da.

distortion n distorción f.

distract vt distraer.

distracted adj distraído/da; ~**ly** adj distraídamente.

distraction n distracción f; confusión f.

distraught adj enloquecido/da.

distress n angustia f; * vt angustiar.

distressing adj penoso/sa.

distribute vt distribuir, repartir.

distribution n distribución f.

distributor n distribuidor m.

district n distrito m.

district attorney n fiscal del distrito m/f.

distrustful adj desconfiado/da. sospechoso/sa.

disturb vt molestar.

disturbance n disturbio m.

disturbed adj preocupado/da.

disturbing adj inquietante.

disuse n desuso m.

disused adj abandonado/da.

ditch n zanja f.

dither vi vacilar.

ditto adv ídem.

ditty n cancioneta f.

diuretic adj (med) diurético/ca.

dive vi sumergirse; bucear; * vr zambullirse; * n zambullida f.

diver n buzo m.

diverge vi divergir.

divergence n divergencia f.

divergent adj divergente.

diverse adj diverso/sa, diferente; ~**ly** adv diversamente.

diversion n diversión f.

diversity n diversidad f.

divert vt desviar; divertir.

divest vt desnudar; despojar.

divide vt dividir; * vi dividirse.

dividend n dividendo m.

dividers npl (math) compás de puntas m.

divine adj divino/na.

divinity n divinidad f.

diving n salto m; buceo m.

diving board n trampolín m.

divisible adj divisible.

division n (math) división f; desunión f.

divisor n (math) divisor m.

divorce n divorcio m; * vi divorciarse.

divorced adj divorciado/da.

divulge vt divulgar, publicar.

dizziness n vértigo m.

dizzy adj mareado/da.

DJ n pinchadiscos m.

do vt hacer, obrar.

docile adj dócil, apacible.

dock n muelle m; * vi atracar.

docker n estibador m.

dockyard n (mar) astillero m.

doctor n médico/ca m/f.

doctrinal adj doctrinal.

doctrine n doctrina f.

document n documento m.

documentary adj documental.

dodge vt esquivar.

doe n gama f; ~ **rabbit** coneja f.

dog n perro m.

dogged adj tenaz; ~**ly** adv tenazmente.

dog kennel n perrera f.

dogmatic adj dogmático/ca; ~**ly** adv dogmáticamente.

doings npl hechos mpl; eventos mpl.

do-it-yourself n bricolaje m.

doleful adj lúgubre, triste.

doll n muñeca f.

dollar n dólar m.

dolphin n delfín m.

domain n campo m.

dome n cúpula f.

domestic adj doméstico/ca.

domesticate vt domesticar.

domestication n domesticación f.

domesticity n domesticidad f.

domicile n domicilio m.

dominant adj dominante.

dominate vi dominar.

domination n dominación f.

domineer vi dominar.

domineering adj dominante.

dominion n dominio m.

dominoes npl dominó m.

donate vt donar.

donation n donación f.

done adj hecho/cha; cocido/da.

donkey n asno, borrico m.

donor n donante m/f.

doodle vi garabatear.

doom n suerte f.

door n puerta f.

doorbell n timbre m.

door handle n tirador m.

doorman n portero m.

doormat n felpudo m.

doorplate n planchuela f.

doorstep n peldaño m.

doorway n entrada f.

dormant adj latente.

dormer window n buhardilla f.

dormitory n dormitorio m.

dormouse n lirón m.

dosage n dosis f invar.

dose n dosis f invar, Lat Am dosaje m; * vt disponer la dosis de.

dossier n expediente m.

dot n punto m.

dote vi adorar.

dotingly adv con cariño excesivo.

double adj doble; * vt doblar; duplicar; * n doble m.

double bed n cama matrimonial f.

double-breasted adj cruzado/da.

double chin n papada f.

double-dealing n duplicidad f.

double-edged adj de doble filo.

double entry n (com) partida doble f.

double-lock vt echar la segunda vuelta a la llave a.

double room n habitación doble f.

doubly adj doblemente.

doubt n duda, sospecha f; * vt dudar; sospechar.

doubtful adj dudoso/sa.

doubtless adv sin duda.

dough n masa f.

douse vt apagar.

dove n paloma f.

dovecot(e) n palomar m.

dowdy adj mal vestido/da.

down n plumón m; flojel m; * prep abajo; **to sit ~** sentarse; **upside ~** al revés.

downcast adj cabizbajo/ja.

downfall n ruina f.

downhearted adj desanimado/da.

downhill adv cuesta abajo/ja.

down payment n entrada f.

downpour n aguacero m.

downright adj manifiesto/ta.

downstairs adv abajo/ja.

down-to-earth adj práctico/ca.

downtown adv al centro (de la ciudad).

downward(s) adv hacia abajo.

dowry n dote f.

doze vi dormitar.

dozen n docena f.

dozy adj somnoliento/ta.

drab adj gris.

draft n borrador m; quinta f; corriente de aire f.

drafty adj expuesto/ta al aire.

drag vt arrastrar; tirar con fuerza; * n lata f.

dragnet n red barredera f.

dragon n dragón m.

dragonfly n libélula f.

drain vt desaguar; secar; * n desaguadero m.

drainage n desagüe m.

draining board n escurridor m.

drainpipe n desagüe m.

drake n ánade macho m.

dram n traguito m.

drama n drama m.

dramatic adj dramático/ca; **~ally** adv dramáticamente.

dramatist n dramaturgo/ga m/f.

dramatize vt dramatizar.

drape vt cubrir; *n cortina f; telón (en teatro) m; **~s** npl cortinas f pl.

drastic adj drástico/ca.

draw vt tirar; dibujar; **to ~ nigh** acercarse.

drawback n desventaja f.

drawer n cajón m.

drawing n dibujo m.

drawing board n tablero de dibujo m.

drawing room n salón m.

drawl vi hablar con pesadez.

dread n terror, espanto m; * vt temer.

dreadful adj espantoso/sa; **~ly** adv terriblemente.

dream n sueño m; * vi soñar.

dreary adj triste.

dredge vt dragar.

dregs npl heces f pl.

drench vt empapar.

dress vt vestir; vendar; * vi vestirse; * n vestido m.

dresser n aparador m.

dressing n vendaje m; aliño m.

dressing gown n bata f.

dressing room n tocador m.

dressing table n tocador m.

dressmaker n modista f.

dressy adj elegante.

dribble vi caer gota a gota, babear.

dribbling n regateo m.

dried adj seco/ca.

drift n montón m; ventisquero m; significado m; * vi ir a la deriva.

driftwood n madera de deriva f.

drill n taladro m; (mil) instrucción f; * vt taladrar.

drink vt, vi beber; * n bebida f.

drinkable adj potable.

drinker n bebedor/a m/f.

drinking bout n borrachera f.

drinking water n agua potable f.

drip vi gotear; * n gota f; goteo m.

drive vt conducir, Lat Am manejar; empujar; * vi conducir, Lat Am manejar; * n paseo en coche m; entrada f.

drivel n baba f; * vi babear.

driver n conductor/a m/f; Lat Am chofer m.

driver's license n carnet m de conducir, carnet m de manejar.

driveway n entrada f.

driving n conducción f, Lat Am manejo m.

driving instructor n profesor/a de autoescuela m/f.

driving school n autoescuela f.

driving test n examen de conducir, examen de manejo m.

drizzle vi lloviznar.

droll adj gracioso/sa.

drone n zumbido m; zángano m.

drool vi babear.

droop vi decaer.

drop n gota f; * vt dejar caer; * vi bajar; **to ~ out** retirarse.

drop-out n marginado m.

dropper n cuentagotas m invar.

dross n escoria f.

drought n sequía f.

drove n: **in ~s** en tropel.

drown vt anegar; * vi anegarse.

drowsiness n somnolencia f.

drowsy adj somnoliento/ta.

drudgery n trabajo monótono m; zurra f.

drug n droga f; * vt drogar.

drug addict n drogadicto/ta m/f.

drug addiction n drogadicción f.

druggist n farmacéutico/ca m/f.

drugstore n farmacia f.

drug trafficker n narcotraficante m/f.

drum n tambor m; **rural ~** zambomba f; * vi tocar el tambor.

drum majorette n batonista f.

drummer n batería m/f, Lat Am baterista m/f.

drumstick n palillo de tambor m.

drunk adj borracho/cha.

drunkard n borracho m.

drunken adj borracho/cha.

drunkenness n borrachera f.

dry adj seco/ca; * vt secar; * vi secarse.

dry-cleaning n lavado en seco m.

dry-goods store n mercería f.

dryness n sequedad f.

dry rot n podredumbre f.

dual adj doble.

dual-purpose adj de doble uso.

dubbed adj doblado/da.

dubious adj dudoso/sa.

duck n pato m; * vt (vi) zambullir(se).

duckling n patito m.

dud adj estropeado/da.

due adj debido/da, apto/ta; * adv exactamente; * n derecho m.

duel n duelo m.

duet n (mus) dúo m.

dull adj lerdo/da; insípido/da; zopen-co/ca; gris; * vt aliviar.

duly adv debidamente; puntualmente.

dumb adj mudo/da; **~ly** adv sin chistar.

dumbbell n pesa f.

dumbfounded adj pasmado/da.

dump n montón m; * vt dejar.

dumping n (com) dumping m.

dumpling n bola de masa f.

dumpy adj gordito/ta.

dunce n zopenco m.

dune n duna f.

dung n estiércol m.

dungeon n calabozo m.

dupe n bobo m; * vt engañar, embaucar.

duplex n dúplex m.

duplicate n duplicado m; copia f; * vt multicopiar.

duplicity n duplicidad f.

durability n durabilidad f.

durable adj duradero/ra.

duration n duración f.

during prep mientras, durante el tiempo que.

dusk n crepúsculo m.

dust n polvo m; * vt desempolvar.

duster n plumero m.

dusty adj polvoriento/ta.

Dutch courage n valor fingido m.

duteous adj fiel, leal.

dutiful adj obediente, sumiso/sa; **~ly** adv obedientemente.

duty n deber m; obligación f.

duty-free adj libre de derechos de aduana.

dwarf n enano m; enana f; * vt empequeñecer.

dwell vi habitar, morar.

dwelling n habitación f; domicilio m.

dwindle vi mermar, disminuirse.

dye vt teñir; * n tinte m.

dyer n tintorero/ra m/f.

dyeing n tintorería f; tintura f.

dye-works npl taller del tintorero m.

dying adj agonizante, moribundo/da; * n muerte f; **~ moments** postrimerías fpl.

dynamic adj dinámico/ca.

dynamics n dinámica f.

dynamite n dinamita f.

dynamiter n dinamitero/ra m/f.

dynamo n dinamo f, Lat Am dinamo m.

dynasty n dinastía f.

dysentery n disentería f.

dyspepsia n (med) dispepsia f.

dyspeptic adj dispéptico/ca.

E

each pn cada uno, cada una; **~ other** unos a otros, unas a otras, mutuamente.

eager adj entusiasmado/da; **~ly** adv con entusiasmo.

eagerness n ansia f; anhelo m.

eagle n águila f.

eagle-eyed adj con vista de lince.

eaglet n aguilucho m.

ear n oreja f; oído m; espiga f; **by ~** de oreja.

earache n dolor de oídos m.

eardrum n tímpano (del oído) m.
early adj temprano/na; adv temprano.
earmark vt destinar a.
earn vt ganar; conseguir.
earnest adj serio/ria; en serio; ~ly adv seriamente.
earnestness n seriedad f.
earnings npl ingresos mpl.
earphones npl auriculares mpl.
earring n zarcillo, pendiente m.
earth n tierra f; * vt conectar a tierra.
earthen adj de tierra.
earthenware n loza de barro f.
earthquake n terremoto m.
earthworm n lombriz f.
earthy adj sensual.
earwig n tijereta f.
ease n comodidad f; facilidad f; at ~ con desahogo; * vt aliviar; mitigar.
easel n caballete m.
easily adv fácilmente.
easiness n facilidad f.
east n este m; oriente m.
Easter n Pascua de Resurrección; Semana Santa f.
Easter egg n huevo de Pascua m.
easterly adj del este.
eastern adj del este, oriental.
eastward(s) adv hacia el este.
easy adj fácil; cómodo/da, ~ going acomodadizo/za.
easy chair n sillón m.
eat vt comer; * vi alimentarse.
eatable adj comestible; * ~s npl víveres mpl.
eaves npl alero m.
eau de Cologne n agua de Colonia f.
eavesdrop vt escuchar a escondidas.
ebb n reflujo m; menguar; decaer, disminuir.
ebony n ébano m.
eccentric adj excéntrico/ca.
eccentricity n excentricidad f.
ecclesiastic adj eclesiástico/ca.
echo n eco m; * vi resonar, repercutir.
eclectic adj ecléctico/ca.
eclipse n eclipse m; * vt eclipsar.
ecologist, environmentalist n ecologista m/f.
ecology n ecología f.
e-commerce n comercio electrónico m.
economic(al) adj económico/ca, frugal, moderado/da.
economics npl economía f.
economist n economista m/f.
economize vt economizar.
economy n economía f; frugalidad f.
ecosystem n ecosistema m.
ecotax n ecotasa f.
ecotourism n ecoturismo m.
ecstasy n éxtasis m; rapto m.
ecstatic adj extático/ca; ~ally adv en éxtasis.
eczema n eczema m.

eddy n reflujo de agua m; remolino m; * vi arremolinarse.
edge n filo m; punta f; margen m/f; acrimonia f; * vt ribetear; introducir.
edgeways, edgewise adv de lado.
edging n orla, orilla f.
edgy adj nervioso/sa.
edible adj comestible.
edict n edicto, mandato m.
edification n edificación f.
edifice n edificio m; fábrica f.
edify vt edificar.
edit vt dirigir; redactar; cortar.
edition n edición f; publicación f; impresión f.
editor n director/a m/f; redactor/a m/f.
editorial adj, n editorial m.
educate vt educar; enseñar.
education n educación f.
eel n anguila f.
eerie adj espeluznante.
efface vt borrar, destruir.
effect n efecto m; realidad f; ~s npl efectos, bienes mpl; * vt efectuar, ejecutar.
effective adj eficaz; efectivo/va; ~ly adv efectivamente, en efecto.
effectiveness n eficacia f.
effectual adj eficiente, eficaz; ~ly adv eficazmente.
effeminacy n afeminación f.
effeminate adj afeminado/da.
effervescence n efervescencia f; hervor m.
effete adj estéril.
efficacy n eficacia f.
efficiency n eficiencia, virtud f.
efficient adj eficaz.
effigy n efigie, imagen f; retrato m.
effort n esfuerzo, empeño m.
effortless adj sin esfuerzo.
effrontery n descaro m; impudencia, desvergüenza f.
effusive adj efusivo/va.
egg n huevo m; to ~ on vt animar.
eggcup n huevera f.
eggplant n berenjena f.
eggshell n cáscara de huevo f.
ego(t)ism n egoísmo m.
ego(t)ist n egoísta m/f.
ego(t)istical adj egotista.
eiderdown n edredón m.
eight adj, n ocho.
eighteen adj, n dieciocho.
eighteenth adj, n decimoctavo.
eighth adj, n octavo.
eightieth adj, n octogésimo/ma.
eighty adj, n ochenta.
either pn cualquiera; * conj o, sea, ya.
ejaculate vt exclamar; eyacular.
ejaculation n exclamación f; eyaculación f.
eject vt expeler, desechar.
ejection n expulsión f.
ejector seat n asiento eyectable m.

eke *vt* alargar; prolongar; hacer crecer.

elaborate *vt* elaborar; * *adj* elabora-do/da; ~**ly** *adv* cuidadosamente.

elapse *vi* pasar, correr (el tiempo).

elastic *adj* elástico/ca.

elasticity *n* elasticidad *f*.

elated *adj* regocijado/da.

elation *n* regocijo *m*.

elbow *n* codo *m*; * *vt* codear.

elbow-room *n* anchura *f*; espacio suficiente *m*; (*fig*) libertad, latitud *f*.

elder *n* saúco *m* (árbol); * *adj* mayor.

elderly *adj* anciano/na.

elders *npl* ancianos, antepasados *mpl*.

eldest *adj* el mayor, la mayor.

elect *vt* elegir; * *adj* elegido/da, esco-gido/da.

election *n* elección *f*.

electioneering *n* electoralismo *m*.

elective *adj* facultativo/va.

elector *n* elector/a *m/f*.

electoral *adj* electoral, *Lat Am* elec-cionario/a.

electorate *n* electorado *m*.

electric(al) *adj* eléctrico/ca; ~ **domestic appliance** electrodoméstico *m*.

electric blanket *n* manta eléctrica *f*.

electric cooker *n* cocina eléctrica *f*.

electric fire *n* estufa eléctrica *f*.

electrician *n* electricista *m/f*.

electricity *n* electricidad *f*.

electrify *vt* electrizar.

electrocardiogram *n* electrocardiograma *m*.

electron *n* electrón *m*.

electronic *adj* electrónico/ca; ~**s** *npl* electrónica *f*.

elegance *n* elegancia *f*.

elegant *adj* elegante, delicado/da; ~**ly** *adv* elegantemente.

elegy *n* elegía *f*.

element *n* elemento *m*; fundamento *m*.

elemental, elementary *adj* elemental.

elephant *n* elefante *m*.

elephantine *adj* inmenso/sa.

elevate *vt* elevar, alzar, exaltar.

elevation *n* elevación *f*; altura *f*; alteza (de pensamientos) *f*.

elevator *n* ascensor *m*.

eleven *adj*, *n* once.

eleventh *adj*, *n* undécimo.

elf *n* duende *m*.

elicit *vt* sacar de.

eligibility *n* elegibilidad *f*.

eligible *adj* elegible.

eliminate *vt* eliminar, descartar.

elk *n* alce *m*.

elliptic(al) *adj* elíptico/ca.

elm *n* olmo *m*.

elocution *n* elocución *f*.

elocutionist *n* profesor de elocución *m*.

elongate *vt* alargar.

elope *vi* escapar, huir, evadirse.

elopement *n* fuga, huida, evasión *f*.

eloquence *n* elocuencia *f*.

eloquent *adj* elocuente; ~**ly** *adv* elocuentemente.

else *pn* otro/ra.

elsewhere *adv* en otra parte.

elucidate *vt* explicar.

elucidation *n* elucidación, explicación *f*.

elude *vt* eludir, evitar.

elusive *adj* esquivo/va.

emaciated *adj* demacrado/da.

e-mail *n* correo electrónico *m*.

emanate (from) *vi* emanar.

emancipate *vt* emancipar; dar libertad.

emancipation *n* emancipación *f*.

embalm *vt* embalsamar.

embankment *n* terraplén *m*.

embargo *n* embargo *m*.

embark *vt* embarcar.

embarkation *n* embarque *m*.

embarrass *vt* avergonzar.

embarrassed *adj* avergonzado/da.

embarrassing *adj* violento/ta; emba-razoso/sa.

embarrassment *n* desconcierto *m*.

embassy *n* embajada *f*.

embed *vt* empotrar; clavar.

embellish *vt* hermosear, adornar.

embellishment *n* adorno *m*.

embers *npl* rescoldo *m*.

embezzle *vt* desfalcar.

embezzlement *n* desfalco *m*.

embitter *vt* amargar.

emblem *n* emblema *m*.

emblematic(al) *adj* emblemático/ca, simbólico/ca.

embodiment *n* incorporación *f*.

embody *vt* incorporar.

embrace *vt* abrazar; contener; * *n* abrazo *m*.

embroider *vt* bordar.

embroidery *n* bordado *m*; bordadura *f*.

embroil *vt* embrollar; confundir.

embryo *n* embrión *m*.

emendation *n* enmienda, corrección *f*.

emerald *n* esmeralda *f*.

emerge *vi* salir, proceder.

emergency *n* emergencia *f*; necesidad urgente *f*.

emergency cord *n* timbre de alarma *m*.

emergency exit *n* salida de emergencia *f*.

emergency landing *n* aterrizaje forzoso *m*.

emergency meeting *n* reunión extraordinaria *f*.

emery *n* esmeril *m*.

emigrant *n* emigrante *m/f*.

emigrate *vi* emigrar.

emigration *n* emigración *f*.

eminence *n* altura *f*; eminencia, excelencia *f*.

eminent *adj* eminente, elevado/da; distinguido/da; ~**ly** *adv* eminentemente.

emission *n* emisión *f*.

emit *vt* emitir; arrojar, despedir.

emolument *n* emolumento, provecho *m*.

emotion *n* emoción *f*.

emotional *adj* emocional.

emotive *adj* emotivo/va.

emperor *n* emperador *m*.

emphasis *n* énfasis *m*.

emphasize *vt* hablar con énfasis.

emphatic *adj* enfático/ca; **~ally** *adv* enfáticamente.

empire *n* imperio *m*.

employ *vt* emplear, ocupar.

employee *n* empleado/da *m/f*.

employer *n* patrón *m*; empresario/ria *m/f*.

employment *n* empleo *m*; trabajo *m*.

emporium *n* emporio *m*.

empress *n* emperatriz *f*.

emptiness *n* vaciedad *f*; futilidad *f*.

empty *adj* vacío/cía; vano/na; ignorante; * *vt* vaciar, evacuar.

empty-handed *adj* con las manos vacías.

emulate *vt* emular, competir; imitar.

emulsion *n* emulsión *f*.

enable *vt* capacitar.

enact *vt* promulgar; representar; hacer.

enamel *n* esmalte *m*; * *vt* esmaltar.

enamor *vt* enamorar.

encamp *vi* acamparse.

encampment *n* campamento *m*.

encase *vt* encajar, encajonar.

enchant *vt* encantar.

enchanting *adj* encantador/a.

enchantment *n* encanto *m*.

encircle *vt* cercar, circundar.

enclose *vt* cercar, circunvalar, circundar; incluir.

enclosure *n* cercamiento *m*; cercado *m*.

encompass *vt* abarcar.

encore *adv* otra vez, de nuevo.

encounter *n* encuentro *m*; duelo *m*; pelea *f*; * *vt* encontrar.

encourage *vt* animar, alentar.

encouragement *n* estímulo, patrocinio *m*.

encroach *vt* usurpar, avanzar gradualmente.

encroachment *n* usurpación, intrusión *f*.

encrusted *adj* incrustado/da.

encumber *vt* embarazar, cargar.

encumbrance *n* embarazo, impedimento *m*.

encyclical *adj* encíclico/ca, circular.

encyclopedia *n* enciclopedia *f*.

end *n* fin *m*; extremidad *f*; término *m*; resolución *f*; **to the ~ that** para que; **to no ~** en vano; **on ~** en pie, de pie; * *vt* terminar, concluir, fenecer; * *vi* acabar, terminar.

endanger *vt* peligrar, arriesgar.

endear *vt* encarecer.

endearing *adj* simpático/ca.

endearment *n* ternura *f*.

endeavor *vi* esforzarse; intentar; * *n* esfuerzo *m*.

endemic *adj* endémico/ca.

ending *n* conclusión; *f*; desenlace *m*; terminación *f*.

endive *n* (*bot*) endibia *f*.

endless *adj* infinito/ta, perpetuo/tua; **~ly** *adv* sin fin, perpetuamente.

endorse *vt* endosar; aprobar.

endorsement *n* endoso *m*; aprobación *f*.

endow *vt* dotar.

endowment *n* dote, dotación *f*.

endurable *adj* sufrible, tolerable.

endurance *n* duración *f*; paciencia *f*; sufrimiento *m*.

endure *vt* sufrir, soportar; * *vi* durar.

endways, endwise *adv* de punta, derecho.

enemy *n* enemigo/ga, antagonista *m/f*.

energetic *adj* enérgico/ca, vigoroso/sa.

energy *n* energía, fuerza *f*; **renewable forms of ~** energía renovables.

enervate *vt* enervar, debilitar.

enfeeble *vt* debilitar.

enfold *vt* envolver.

enforce *vt* hacer cumplir.

enforced *adj* forzoso/sa.

enfranchise *vt* emancipar.

engage *vt* llamar; abordar; contratar.

engaged *adj* prometido/da.

engagement *n* empeño *m*; combate *m*; pelea *f*; obligación *f*.

engagement ring *n* anillo de prometida *m*.

engaging *adj* atractivo/va.

engender *vt* engendrar; producir.

engine *n* motor *m*; locomotora *f*.

engine driver *n* maquinista *m/f*.

engineer *n* ingeniero/ra *m/f*; maquinista *m/f*.

engineering *n* ingeniería *f*.

engrave *vt* grabar; esculpir; tallar.

engraving *n* grabado *m*; estampa *f*.

engrossed *adj* absorto/ta.

engulf *vt* sumergir.

enhance *vt* aumentar, realzar.

enigma *n* enigma *m*.

enjoy *vt* gozar; poseer.

enjoyable *adj* agradable; divertido/da.

enjoyment *n* disfrute *m*; placer *m*; fruición *f*.

enlarge *vt* engrandecer, dilatar, extender.

enlargement *n* aumento *m*; ampliación *f*, soltura *f*.

enlighten *vt* iluminar; instruir.

enlightened *adj* iluminado/da.

Enlightenment *n*: **the ~** el Siglo de las Luces *m*, la Ilustración *f*.

enlist *vt* alistar.

enlistment *n* alistamiento *m*.

enliven *vt* animar; avivar; alegrar.

enmity *n* enemistad *f*; odio *m*.

enormity *n* enormidad *f*; atrocidad *f*.

enormous *adj* enorme; **~ly** *adv* enormemente.

enough *adv* bastante; basta; * *n* bastante *m*.

enounce *vt* declarar.

enquiry *n* pesquisa *f*.

enrage *vt* enfurecer, irritar.

enrapture *vt* arrebatar, entusiasmar; encantar.

enrich *vt* enriquecer; adornar.

enrichment *n* enriquecimiento *m*.

enroll *vt* registrar; arrollar.

enrollment *n* inscripción *f*.

en route adv durante el viaje.

ensign n (mil) bandera f; abanderado m; (mar) alférez m.

enslave vt esclavizar, cautivar.

ensue vi seguirse; suceder.

ensure vt asegurar.

entail vt suponer.

entangle vt enmarañar, embrollar.

entanglement n enredo m.

enter vt entrar; admitir; registrar; **to ~ for** presentarse para; **to ~ into** establecer; formar parte de/en; firmar.

enterprise n empresa f.

enterprising adj emprendedor/a.

entertain vt divertir; hospedar; mantener.

entertainer n artista m/f.

entertaining adj divertido/da.

entertainment n entretenimiento, pasatiempo m.

enthralled adj encantado/da.

enthralling adj cautivador/a.

enthrone vt entronizar.

enthusiasm n entusiasmo m.

enthusiast n entusiasta m/f.

enthusiastic adj entusiasta.

entice vt tentar; seducir.

entire adj entero/ra, completo/ta, perfecto/ta; **~ly** adv enteramente.

entitle vt intitular; conferir algún derecho.

entitled adj titulado/da.

entity n entidad, existencia f.

entourage n séquito m.

entrails npl entrañas fpl; asadura f.

entrance n entrada f; admisión f; principio m.

entrance examination n examen de ingreso m.

entrance fee n cuota f.

entrance hall n pórtico, vestíbulo m.

entrance ramp, on ramp n rampa de acceso f.

entrant n participante m; candidato m.

entrap vt enredar; engañar.

entreat vt rogar, suplicar.

entreaty n petición, suplica, instancia f.

entrepreneur n empresario/ria m/f.

entrust vt confiar.

entry n entrada f.

entry phone n portero automático m.

entwine vt entrelazar, enroscar, torcer.

enumerate vt enumerar, numerar.

enunciate vt enunciar, declarar.

enunciation n enunciación f.

envelop vt envolver.

envelope n sobre m.

enviable adj envidiable.

envious adj envidioso/sa; **~ly** adv envidiosamente.

environment n medio ambiente m.

environmental adj ambiental, medioambiental.

environs npl vecindad f; contornos mpl.

envisage vt prever; concebir.

envoy n enviado/da m/f; mensajero/ra m/f.

envy n envidia, malicia f; * vt envidiar.

ephemeral adj efímero/ra.

epic adj épico/ca; * n épica f.

epidemic adj epidémico/ca; * n epidemia f.

epilepsy n epilepsia f.

epileptic adj epiléptico/ca.

epilog n epílogo m.

Epiphany n Epifanía f.

episcopacy n episcopado m.

Episcopal adj episcopal.

Episcopalian n anglicano/na m/f.

episode n episodio m.

epistle n epístola f.

epistolary adj epistolar.

epithet n epíteto m.

epitome n epítome, compendio m.

epitomize vt epitomar, abreviar.

epoch n época f.

equable adj uniforme; **~bly** adv uniformemente.

equal adj igual; justo/ta; semejante; * n igual m; compañero m; * vt igualar; compensar.

equalize vt igualar.

equalizer n igualada f.

equality n igualdad, uniformidad f.

equally adv igualmente.

equanimity n ecuanimidad f.

equate vt equiparar (con).

equation n ecuación f.

equator n ecuador m.

equatorial adj ecuatorial, ecuatorio/ria.

equestrian adj ecuestre.

equilateral adj equilátero/ra.

equilibrium n equilibrio m.

equinox n equinoccio m.

equip vt equipar, pertrechar.

equipment n equipaje m.

equitable adj equitativo/va, imparcial; **~bly** adv equitativamente.

equity n equidad, justicia, imparcialidad f.

equivalent adj, n equivalente m.

equivocal adj equívoco/ca, ambiguo/gua; **~ly** adv equivocadamente, ambiguamente.

equivocate vt equivocar, usar equívocos.

equivocation n equívoco m.

era n era f.

eradicate vt desarraigar, extirpar.

eradication n extirpación f.

erase vt borrar.

eraser n goma de borrar f.

erect vt erigir; establecer; * adj derecho/ha, erguido/da, vertical.

erection n establecimiento m; estructura f; erección f.

ermine n armiño m.

erode vt erosionar; corroer.

erotic adj erótico/ca.

err vi vagar, errar; desviarse.

errand n recado, mensaje m.

errand boy n recadero m.

errata npl fe de erratas f.

erratic adj errático/ca, errante; irregular.

erroneous adj erróneo/nea; falso/sa; **~ly** adv erróneamente.

error *n* error *m*; yerro *m*.

erudite *adj* erudito/ta.

erudition *n* erudición *f*; doctrina *f*.

erupt *vi* entrar en erupción; hacer erupción.

eruption *n* erupción *f*.

escalate *vi* extenderse.

escalation *n* intensificación *f*.

escalator *n* escalera mecánica *f*.

escapade *n* travesura *f*.

escape *vt* evitar; escapar; * *vi* evadirse, salvarse; * *vr* zafarse; * *n* escapada, huida, fuga *f*; inadvertencia *f*; **to make one's** ~ poner los pies en polvorosa.

escapism *n* escapismo *m*.

eschew *vt* huir, evitar, evadir.

escort *n* escolta *f*; * *vt* escoltar.

esoteric *adj* esotérico/ca.

especial *adj* especial; ~**ly** *adv* especialmente.

espionage *n* espionaje *m*.

esplanade *n* (*mil*) esplanada *f*.

espouse *vt* desposar.

essay *n* ensayo *m*.

essence *n* esencia *f*.

essential *n* esencia *f*; * *adj* esencial, substancial, principal; ~**ly** *adv* esencialmente.

establish *vt* establecer, fundar, fijar; confirmar.

establishment *n* establecimiento *m*; fundación *f*; institución *f*.

estate *n* estado *m*; hacienda *f*; bienes *mpl*.

esteem *vt* estimar, apreciar; pensar; * *n* estima *f*; consideración *f*.

esthetic *adj* estético/ca; ~**s** *npl* estética *f*.

estimate *vt* estimar, apreciar, tasar; * *n* presupuesto *m*.

estimation *n* estimación, valuación *f*; opinión *f*.

estrange *vt* extrañar, apartar, enajenar.

estranged *adj* separado/da.

estrangement *n* enajenación *f*; extrañeza, distancia *f*.

estuary *n* estuario *m*, ría *f*.

etch *vt* grabar al aguafuerte.

etching *n* grabado al aguafuerte *m*.

eternal *adj* eterno/na, perpetuo/tua, inmortal; ~**ly** *adv* eternamente.

eternity *n* eternidad *f*.

ether *n* éter *m*.

ethical *adj* ético/ca; ~**ly** *adv* moralmente.

ethics *npl* ética *f*.

ethnic *adj* étnico/ca.

ethos *n* genio *m*.

etiquette *n* etiqueta *f*.

etymological *adj* etimológico/ca.

etymologist *n* etimólogo/ga *m/f*, etimologista *m/ f*.

etymology *n* etimología *f*.

Eucharist *n* Eucaristía *f*.

eulogy *n* elogio, encomio *m*; alabanza *f*.

eunuch *n* eunuco *m*.

euphemism *n* eufemismo *m*.

euro *n* euro *m*.

Euro MP *n* eurodiputado/da *m/f*.

Europe *n* Europa *f*.

European Community *n* Comunidad Europea *f*.

European Parliament *n* eurocámara *f*.

European Union *n* unión Europea *f*.

Euroskeptic *n* euroescéptico/ca *m/f*.

Eurotunnel, Channel Tunnel *n* eurotúnel *m*.

evacuate *vt* evacuar.

evacuation *n* evacuación *f*.

evade *vt* evadir, escapar, evitar.

evaluate *vt* evaluar; interpretar.

evangelic(al) *adj* evangélico/ca.

evangelist *n* evangelista *m*.

evaporate *vt* evaporar; * *vi* evaporarse; disiparse.

evaporated milk *n* leche evaporada *f*.

evaporation *n* evaporación *f*.

evasion *n* evasión *f*; escape *m*.

evasive *adj* evasivo/va; ~**ly** *adv* con evasivas.

eve *n* víspera *f*.

even *adj* llano/na, igual; par, semejante; * *adv* aun; aun cuando, supuesto que; no obstante; * *vt* igualar, allanar; * *vi*: **to** ~ **out** nivelarse.

even-handed *adj* imparcial, equitati-vo/va.

evening *n* tarde *f*.

evening class *n* clase nocturna *f*.

evening dress *n* traje de etiqueta *m*; traje de noche *m*.

evenly *adv* igualmente, llanamente.

evenness *n* igualdad *f*; uniformidad *f*; llanura *f*; imparcialidad *f*.

event *n* acontecimiento, evento *m*; suceso *m*.

eventful *adj* lleno de acontecimientos.

eventual *adj* final; ~**ly** *adv* por fin.

eventuality *n* eventualidad *f*.

ever *adv* siempre; **for** ~ **and** ~ siempre jamás, eternamente; ~ **since** después.

evergreen *adj* de hoja perenne; * *n* árbol de hoja perenne *m*.

everlasting *adj* eterno/na.

evermore *adv* eternamente, para siempre jamás.

every *adj* cada uno, cada una; ~ **where** en/por todas partes; ~ **thing** todo; ~ **one**, ~ **body** todos, todo el mundo.

evict *vt* desahuciar.

eviction *n* desahucio *m*.

evidence *n* evidencia *f*; testimonio *m*; prueba *f*; * *vt* evidenciar.

evident *adj* evidente; patente, mani-fiesto/ta; ~**ly** *adv* evidentemente.

evil *adj* malo/la, depravado/da, pernicioso/sa; dañoso/sa; * *n* mal *m*; maldad *f*.

evil-minded *adj* malicioso/sa, mal intencionado/ da.

evocative *adj* sugestivo/va.

evoke *vt* evocar.

evolution *n* evolución *f*.

evolve *vt*, *vi* evolucionar; desenvolver; desplegarse.

ewe *n* oveja *f*.

exacerbate *vt* exacerbar.

exact *adj* exacto/ta; * *vt* exigir.

exacting *adj* exigente.
exaction *n* exacción, extorsión *f*.
exactly *adj* exactamente.
exactness, exactitude *n* exactitud *f*.
exaggerate *vt* exagerar.
exaggeration *n* exageración *f*.
exalt *vt* exaltar, elevar; alabar; realzar.
exaltation *n* exaltación, elevación *f*.
exalted *adj* exaltado/da; muy anima-do/da.
examination *n* examen *m*.
examine *vt* examinar; escudriñar.
examiner *n* inspector/a *m/f*.
example *n* ejemplar *m*; ejemplo *m*.
exasperate *vt* exasperar, irritar, enojar, provocar; agravar; amargar.
exasperation *n* exasperación, irritación *f*.
excavate *vt* excavar, ahondar.
excavation *n* excavación *f*.
excavator *n* excavadora *f*.
exceed *vt* exceder; sobrepujar.
exceedingly *adv* extremamente, en sumo grado.
excel *vt* sobresalir, exceder; * *vi* descollar.
excellence *n* excelencia *f*; preeminencia *f*.
Excellency *n* Excelencia (título) *f*.
excellent *adj* excelente; **~ly** *adv* excelentemente.
except *vt* exceptuar, excluir; **~(ing)** *prep* excepto, a excepción de.
exception *n* excepción, exclusión *f*.
exceptional *adj* excepcional.
excerpt *n* extracto *m*.
excess *n* exceso *m*.
excessive *adj* excesivo/va; **~ly** *adv* excesivamente.
exchange *vt* cambiar; trocar, permutar; * *n* cambio *m*; bolsa *f*.
exchange rate *n* tipo de cambio *m*.
excise *n* impuestos sobre el consumo *mpl*.
excitability *n* excitabilidad *f*.
excitable *adj* excitable.
excite *vt* excitar; estimular.
excited *adj* emocionado/da.
excitement *n* estímulo, excitación *f*.
exciting *adj* emocionante.
exclaim *vi* exclamar.
exclamation *n* exclamación *f*; clamor *m*.
exclamation mark *n* punto de admiración *m*.
exclamatory *adj* exclamatorio/ria.
exclude *vt* excluir; exceptuar.
exclusion *n* exclusión, exclusiva, excepción *f*.
exclusive *adj* exclusivo/va; **~ly** *adv* exclusivamente.
excommunicate *vt* excomulgar.
excommunication *n* excomunión *f*.
excrement *n* excremento *m*.
excruciating *adj* atroz, enorme, grave.
exculpate *vt* disculpar; justificar.
excursion *n* excursión *f*; digresión *f*.
excusable *adj* excusable.
excuse *vt* disculpar; perdonar; * *n* disculpa, excusa *f*; pretexto *m*; **~ me!** *interj* ¡perdón!.

execute *vt* ejecutar.
execution *n* ejecución *f*.
executioner *n* ejecutor/a *m/f*; verdugo *m*.
executive *adj* ejecutivo/va.
executor *n* testamentario/ria, albacea *m/f*.
exemplary *adj* ejemplar.
exemplify *vt* ejemplificar.
exempt *adj* exento/ta.
exemption *n* exención *f*.
exercise *n* ejercicio *m*; ensayo *m*; tarea *f*; practica *f*; * *vi* hacer ejercicio; * *vt* ejercer; valerse de.
exercise book *n* cuaderno *m*.
exert *vt* emplear; **to ~ oneself** esforzarse.
exertion *n* esfuerzo *m*.
exhale *vt* exhalar.
exhaust *n* escape *m*; * *vt* agotar.
exhausted *adj* agotado/da.
exhaustion *n* agotamiento *m*; extenuación *f*.
exhaustive *adj* comprensivo/va.
exhibit *vt* exhibir; mostrar; * *n* (*law*) objeto expuesto *m*.
exhibition *n* exposición, presentación *f*.
exhilarating *adj* estimulante.
exhilaration *n* alegría *f*; buen humor, regocijo *m*.
exhort *vt* exhortar, excitar.
exhortation *n* exhortación *f*.
exhume *vt* exhumar, desenterrar.
exile *n* destierro *m*; * *vt* desterrar, deportar.
exist *vi* existir.
existence *n* existencia *f*.
existent *adj* existente.
existing *adj* actual, presente.
exit *n* salida *f*; * *vi* hacer mutis.
exit ramp, off ramp *n* vía de acceso *f*.
exodus *n* éxodo *m*.
exonerate *vt* exonerar, descargar.
exoneration *n* exoneración *f*.
exorbitant *adj* exorbitante, excesi-vo/va.
exorcise *vt* exorcizar, conjurar.
exorcism *n* exorcismo *m*.
exotic *adj* exótico/ca, extranjero/ra.
expand *vt* extender, dilatar.
expanse *n* extensión *f*.
expansion *n* expansión *f*.
expansive *adj* expansivo/va.
expatriate *vt* expatriar.
expect *vt* esperar, aguardar.
expectance, expectancy *n* expectación, esperanza *f*.
expectant *adj* expectante.
expectant mother *n* mujer encinta *f*.
expectation *n* expectación, expectativa *f*.
expediency *n* conveniencia, oportunidad *f*.
expedient *adj* oportuno/na, conveniente; * *n* expediente *m*; **~ly** *adv* convenientemente.
expedite *vt* acelerar; expedir.
expedition *n* expedición *f*.
expeditious *adj* pronto/ta, expedito/ta; **~ly** *adv* prontamente.
expel *vt* expeler, desterrar.
expend *vt* expender; desembolsar.

expendable *adj* prescindible.

expenditure *n* gasto, desembolso *m*.

expense *n* gasto *m*; coste *m*.

expense account *n* cuenta de gastos *f*.

expensive *adj* caro/ra; costoso/sa; ~ly *adv* costosamente.

experience *n* experiencia *f*; práctica *f*; * *vt* experimentar.

experienced *adj* experimentado/da.

experiment *n* experimento *m*; * *vt* experimentar.

experimental *adj* experimental; ~ly *adv* experimentalmente.

expert *adj* experto/ta, diestro/tra.

expertise *n* pericia *f*.

expiration *n* expiración *f*; muerte *f*.

expire *vi* expirar.

explain *vt* explanar, explicar.

explanation *n* explicación *f*.

explanatory *adj* explicativo/va.

expletive *adj* expletivo/va.

explicable *adj* explicable.

explicit *adj* explícito/ta; ~ly *adv* explícitamente.

explode *vt, vi* estallar, explotar.

exploit *vt* explotar; * *n* hazaña *f*; hecho heroico *m*.

exploitation *n* explotación *f*.

exploration *n* exploración *f*; examen *m*.

exploratory *adj* exploratorio/ria.

explore *vt* explorar, examinar; sondear.

explorer *n* explorador/a *m/f*.

explosion *n* explosión *f*.

explosive *adj, n* explosivo *m*.

exponent *n* (*math*) exponente *m*.

export *vt* exportar.

export, exportation *n* exportación *f*.

exporter *n* exportador/a *m/f*.

expose *vt* exponer; mostrar; descubrir; poner en peligro.

exposed *adj* expuesto/ta.

exposition *n* exposición *f*; interpretación *f*.

expostulate *vi* debatir, contender.

exposure *n* exposición *f*; velocidad de obturación *f*; fotografía *f*.

exposure meter *n* fotómetro *m*.

expound *vt* exponer; interpretar.

express *vt* exprimir; representar; * *adj* expreso/sa, claro/ra; a propósito; * *n* expreso, correo *m*; (*rail*) tren expreso *m*.

expression *n* expresión *f*; locución *f*.

expressionless *adj* sin expresión (cara).

expressive *adj* expresivo/va; ~ly *adv* expresivamente.

expressly *adv* expresamente.

expressway *n* autopista *f*.

expropriate *vt* expropiar (por causa de utilidad pública).

expropriation *n* (*law*) expropiación *f*.

expulsion *n* explosión *f*.

expurgate *vt* expurgar.

exquisite *adj* exquisito/ta, perfecto/ta, excelente; ~ly *adv* exquisitamente.

extant *adj* existente.

extempore *adv* de improviso.

extemporize *vi* improvisar.

extend *vt* extender; amplificar; * *vi* extenderse.

extension *n* extensión *f*.

extensive *adj* extenso/sa, dilatado/da; ~ly *adv* extensivamente.

extent *n* extensión *f*.

extenuate *vt* extenuar, disminuir, atenuar.

extenuating *adj* atenuante.

exterior *adj, n* exterior *m*.

exterminate *vt* exterminar; extirpar.

extermination *n* exterminación, extirpación *f*.

external *adj* externo/na; ~ly *adv* exteriormente; ~s *npl* exterior *m*.

extinct *adj* extinto/ta; abolido/da.

extinction *n* extinción *f*; abolición *f*.

extinguish *vt* extinguir; suprimir.

extinguisher *n* extintor *m*, *Lat Am* extinguidor *m*.

extirpate *vt* extirpar.

extoll *vt* alabar, magnificar, alzar, exaltar.

extort *vt* sacar por la fuerza.

extortion *n* extorsión *f*.

extortionate *adj* excesivo/va.

extra *adv* extra; * *n* extra *m*.

extract *vt* extraer; extractar; * *n* extracto *m*; compendio *m*.

extraction *n* extracción *f*; descendencia *f*.

extracurricular *adj* extraescolar.

extradite *vt* extraditar.

extradition *n* (*law*) extradición *f*.

extramarital *adj* extramatrimonial.

extramural *adj* extraescolar.

extraneous *adj* extraño/ña, ajeno/na.

extraordinarily *adv* extraordinariamente.

extraordinary *adj* extraordinario/ria.

extravagance *n* extravagancia *f*; gastos, excesivos *mpl*.

extravagant *adj* extravagante, exorbitante; pródigo/ga; ~ly *adv* extravagantemente.

extreme *adj* extremo/ma, supremo/ma; último/ma; * *n* extremo *m*; ~ly *adv* extremamente.

extremist *adj, n* extremista *m/f*.

extremity *n* extremidad *f*.

extricate *vt* desembarazar, desenredar.

extrinsic(al) *adj* extrínseco/ca, exterior.

extrovert *n* extrovertido *m*.

exuberance *n* exuberancia, suma abundancia *f*.

exuberant *adj* exuberante, abundan-tísimo/ma; ~ly *adv* exuberantemente.

exude *vi* transpirar.

exult *vt* exultar, regocijarse, triunfar.

exultation *n* exultación *f*; regocijo *m*.

eye *n* ojo *m*; * *vt* ojear, contemplar, observar.

eyeball *n* globo del ojo *m*.

eyebrow *n* ceja *f*.

eyelash *n* pestaña *f*.

eyelid *n* párpado *m*.

eyesight *n* vista *f*.

eyesore *n* monstruosidad *f*.

eyetooth n colmillo m.
eyewitness n testigo ocular m.
eyrie n nido de águila m.

F

fable n fábula f; ficción f.
fabric n tejido m.
fabricate vt fabricar, edificar.
fabrication n fabricación f.
fabulous adj fabuloso/sa; **~ly** adv fabulosamente.
facade n fachada f.
face n cara, faz f; superficie f; fachada f; aspecto m; apariencia f; * vt encararse; hacer frente; **to ~ up to** hacer frente a.
face cream n crema facial f.
face-lift n lifting m.
face powder n polvos mpl.
facet n faceta f.
facetious adj chistoso/sa, alegre, gra-cioso/sa; **~ly** adv chistosamente.
face value n valor nominal m.
facial adj facial.
facile adj fácil, afable.
facilitate vt facilitar.
facility n facilidad, ligereza f; afabilidad f.
facing n paramento m; * prep enfrente.
facsimile n facsímil m; fax m.
fact n hecho m; realidad f; **in ~** en efecto.
faction n facción f; disensión f.
factor n factor m.
factory n fábrica f.
factual adj basado/da en hechos reales.
faculty n facultad f; personal docente m.
fad n moda f.
fade vi decaer, marchitarse, fallecer.
fail vt suspender, Lat Am reprobar; fallar a; * vi suspender; fracasar; fallar; (fig) zozobrar.
failing n falta f; defecto m.
failure n falta f; culpa f; descuido m; quiebra, bancarrota f.
faint vi desmayarse, debilitarse; * n desmayo m; * adj débil; **~ly** adv débilmente.
fainthearted adj cobarde, medroso/sa, pusilánime.
faintness n flaqueza f; desmayo m.
fair adj hermoso/sa, bello/la; blanco/ca; rubio/bia; claro/ra, sereno/na; favorable; recto/ta, justo/ta; franco/ca; * adv limpio; * n feria f.
fairly adv justamente; completamente.
fairness n hermosura f; justicia f.
fair play n juego limpio m.
fair trade n comercio justo m.
fairy n hada f.
fairy tale n cuento de hadas m.
faith n fe f; dogma de fe m; fidelidad f.
faithful adj fiel, leal; **~ly** adv fielmente.
faithfulness n fidelidad, lealtad f.
fake n falsificación f; impostor/a m/f; * adj falso/sa; * vt fingir; falsificar.

falcon n halcón m.
falconry n cetrería f.
fall vi caer(se); perder el poder; disminuir, decrecer en precio; **to ~ asleep** dormirse; **to ~ back** retroceder; **to ~ back on** recurrir a; **to ~ behind** quedarse atrás; **to ~ down** caerse; **to ~ for** dejarse engañar; enamorarse de; **to ~ in** hundirse; **to ~ short** faltar; **to ~ sick** enfermar; **to ~ in love** enamorarse f; **to ~ off** caerse; disminuir; **to ~ out** reñir, disputar; * n caída f; otoño m.
fallacious adj falaz, fraudulento/ta; **~ly** adv falazmente.
fallacy n falacia, sofistería f; engaño m.
fallibility n falibilidad f.
fallible adj falible.
fallow adj en barbecho; **~ deer** n gamo m.
false adj falso/sa; **~ly** adv falsamente.
false alarm n falsa alarma f.
falsehood, falseness n falsedad f.
falsify vt falsificar.
falsity n falsedad, mentira f.
falter vi tartamudear; faltar.
faltering adj vacilante.
fame n fama f; renombre m.
famed adj celebrado/da, famoso/sa.
familiar adj familiar; casero/ra; **~ly** adv familiarmente.
familiarity n familiaridad f.
familiarize vt familiarizar.
family n familia f; linaje m; clase, especie f.
family business n negocio familiar m.
family doctor n médico de familia m.
famine n hambre f; carestía f.
famished adj hambriento/ta.
famous adj famoso/sa, afamado/da; **~ly** adv famosamente.
fan n abanico m; aficionado m; fan m/f; * vt abanicar; atizar.
fanatic adj, n fanático/ca m/ca.
fanaticism n fanatismo m.
fan belt n correa del ventilador f.
fanciful adj imaginativo/va, caprichoso/sa; **~ly** adv caprichosamente.
fancy n fantasía, imaginación f; capricho m; * vt tener ganas de; imaginarse.
fancy-goods npl novedades, modas fpl.
fancy-dress ball n baile de disfraces m.
fanfare n (mus) fanfarria f.
fang n colmillo m.
fantastic adj fantástico/ca; caprichoso/sa; **~ally** adv fantásticamente.
fantasy n fantasía f.
far adv lejos, a una gran distancia; * adj lejano/na, distante, remoto/ta; **~ and away** con mucho, de mucho; **~ off** lejano/na.
faraway adj remoto/ta.
farce n farsa f.
farcical adj burlesco/ca.
fare n precio m; tarifa f; comida f; viajero m; pasaje m.

farewell n despedida f; **~!** excl ¡adiós!

farm n finca f, granja f; * vt cultivar.

farmer n agricultor/a m/f; granjero/ra m/f.

farmhand n peón m.

farmhouse n casa de hacienda f, granja f.

farming n agricultura f.

farmland n tierra de cultivo f.

farmyard n corral m.

far-reaching adj de gran alcance.

fart n (col) pedo; * vi tirarse un pedo.

farther adv más lejos; más adelante; * adj más lejos, ulterior.

farthest adv lo más lejos; lo más tarde; a lo más.

fascinate vt fascinar, encantar.

fascinating adj fascinante.

fascination n fascinación f; encanto m.

fascism n fascismo.

fascist n fascista m/f.

fashion n moda f; forma, figura f; uso m; manera f; estilo m; **people of ~** gente de tono f; * vt formar, amoldar.

fashionable adj a la moda; elegante; **the ~ world** el gran mundo; **~bly** adv a/según la moda.

fashion show n desfile de modelos m.

fast vi ayunar; * n ayuno m; * adj rápido/da; firme, estable; * adv rápidamente; firmemente; estrechamente.

fasten vt abrochar; afirmar, asegurar, atar; fijar; * vi fijarse, establecerse.

fastener, fastening n cierre m; cerrojo m.

fast food n comida rápida f.

fastidious adj fastidioso/sa, desdeño-so/sa; **~ly** adv fastidiosamente.

fat adj gordo/da; * n grasa f.

fatal adj fatal; funesto/ta; **~ly** adv fatalmente.

fatalism n fatalismo m.

fatalist n fatalista m/f.

fatality n fatalidad, predestinación f.

fate n hado, destino m.

fateful adj fatídico/ca.

father n padre m; **loving (over-indulgent) ~** padrazo m.

fatherhood n paternidad f.

father-in-law n suegro m.

fatherland n patria f.

fatherly adj paternal.

fathom n braza (medida) f; * vt sondar; penetrar.

fatigue n fatiga f; * vt fatigar, cansar.

fatten vt, vi engordar.

fatty adj graso/sa.

fatuous adj fatuo/tua, tonto/ta, imbécil.

faucet n grifo m, llave f.

fault n falta, culpa f; delito m; defecto m; yerro m.

faultfinder n censurador/a m/f.

faultless adj perfecto/ta, cumplido/da.

faulty adj defectuoso/sa.

fauna n fauna f.

faux pas n metedura de pata f.

favor n favor, beneficio m; patrocinio m; blandura f; * vt favorecer, proteger.

favorable adj favorable, propicio/cia; **~bly** adv favorablemente.

favored adj favorecido/da.

favorite n favorito/ta m/f; * adj favo-recido/da.

favoritism n favoritismo m.

fawn n cervatillo m; * vi adular servilmente.

fawningly adv lisonjeramente, con adulación servil.

fax n facsímil(e) m; fax m; * vt mandar por fax.

fear vi temer; * n miedo m.

fearful adj medroso/sa, temeroso/sa; tímido/da; **~ly** adv medrosamente, temerosamente.

fearless adj intrépido/da, atrevido/da; **~ly** adv sin miedo.

fearlessness n intrepidez f.

feasibility n posibilidad f.

feasible adj factible, viable.

feast n banquete, festín m; fiesta f; * vi banquetear.

feat n hecho m; acción, hazaña f.

feather n pluma f;.

feather bed n plumón m.

feature n característica f; rasgo m; forma f; * vi figurar.

feature film n largometraje m.

February n febrero m.

federal adj federal.

federalist n federalista m/f.

federate vt, vi federar(se).

federation n federación f.

fed-up adj harto/ta.

fee n honorarios mpl; cuota f.

feeble adj flaco/ca, débil.

feebleness n debilidad f.

feebly adv débilmente.

feed vt nutrir; alimentar; **to ~ on** alimentarse de; * vi nutrirse; engordar; * n comida f; pasto m.

feedback n reacción f.

feel vt sentir; tocar; creer; **to ~ around** tantear; * n sensación f; tacto, sentido m.

feeler n antena f; (fig) tentativa f.

feeling n tacto m; sensibilidad f; corazonada f.

feelingly adv sensiblemente.

feign vt inventar, fingir; disimular.

feline adj felino/na.

fellow n tipo, tío m; socio/cia m/f.

fellow citizen n conciudadano/na m/f.

fellow countryman n compatriota m/f.

fellow feeling n simpatía f.

fellow men npl semejantes mpl.

fellowship n compañerismo m; beca (en un colegio) f.

fellow student n compañero/ra de curso m/f.

fellow traveler n compañero/ra de viaje m/f.

felon n criminal m/f.

felony n crimen m.

felt n fieltro m.

felt-tip pen, fiber-tip pen n rotulador m, Lat Am marcador m.

female n hembra f; * adj femenino/na.

feminine *adj* femenino/na.

feminism *n* feminismo *m*.

feminist *n* feminista *m/f*.

fence *n* cerca *f*, *Lat Am* cerco *m*; defensa *f*; * *vt* cercar; * *vi* esgrimir.

fencing *n* esgrima *f*.

fender *n* parachoques *m invar*.

fennel *n* (*bot*) hinojo *m*.

ferment *n* agitación *f*; * *vi* fermentar.

fern *n* (*bot*) helecho *m*.

ferocious *adj* feroz; fiero/ra; ~ly *adv* ferozmente.

ferocity *n* ferocidad, fiereza *f*.

ferret *n* hurón *m*; * *vt* huronear; **to** ~ **out** descubrir, echar fuera.

ferryboat, ferry *n* transbordador, ferry *m*; * *vt* transportar.

fertile *adj* fértil, fecundo/da.

fertility *n* fertilidad, fecundidad *f*.

fertilization *n* fertilización *f*.

fertilize *vt* fertilizar.

fertilizer *n* abono *m*.

fervent *adj* ferviente; fervoroso/sa; ~ly *adv* con fervor.

fervid *adj* ardiente, vehemente.

fervor *n* fervor, ardor *m*.

fester *vi* enconarse, inflamarse.

festival *n* fiesta *f*; festival *m*.

festive *adj* festivo/va.

festivity *n* festividad *f*.

fetch *vt* ir a buscar.

fetching *adj* atractivo/va.

fete *n* fiesta *f*.

fetid *adj* fétido/da, hediondo/da.

fetus *n* feto *m*.

feud *n* riña, contienda *f*.

feudal *adj* feudal.

feudalism *n* feudalismo *m*.

fever *n* fiebre *f*.

feverish *adj* febril, *Lat Am* afiebra-do/da.

few *adj* poco/ca; **a** ~ algunos; ~ **and far between** pocos.

fewer *adj* menor; * *adv* menos.

fewest *adj* los menos.

fiancé *n* novio *m*.

fiancée *n* novia *f*.

fib *n* mentira *f*; * *vi* mentir.

fiber *n* fibra, hebra *f*.

fiberglass *n* fibra de vidrio *f*.

fickle *adj* voluble, inconstante, mudable, ligero/ra.

fiction *n* ficción *f*; invención *f*.

fictional *adj* novelesco/ca.

fictitious *adj* ficticio/cia; fingido/da; ~ly *adv* fingidamente.

fiddle *n* violín *m*; trampa *f*; * *vi* tocar el violín.

fiddler *n* violinista *m/f*.

fidelity *n* fidelidad, lealtad *f*.

fidget *vi* inquietarse.

fidgety *adj* inquieto/ta, impaciente.

field *n* campo *m*; campaña *f*; espacio *m*.

field day *n* (*mil*) día de maniobras *m*.

fieldmouse *n* ratón de campo *m*.

fieldwork *n* trabajo de campo *m*.

fiend *n* enemigo *m*; demonio *m*.

fiendish *adj* demoniaco/ca.

fierce *adj* fiero/ra, feroz; cruel, furio-so/sa; ~ly *adv* furiosamente.

fierceness *n* fiereza, ferocidad *f*.

fiery *adj* ardiente; apasionado/da.

fifteen *adj*, *n* quince.

fifteenth *adj*, *n* decimoquinto/ta.

fifth *adj*, *n* quinto/ta; ~ly *adv* en quinto lugar.

fiftieth *adj*, *n* quincuagésimo/ma.

fifty *adj*, *n* cincuenta.

fig *n* higo *m*.

fight *vt*, *vi* reñir; batallar; combatir; * *n* batalla *f*; combate *m*; pelea *f*.

fighter *n* combatiente *m*; luchador/a *m/f*; caza *m*.

fighting *n* combate *m*.

fig-leaf *n* hoja de higuera *f*.

fig tree *n* higuera *f*.

figurative *adj* figurativo/va; ~ly *adv* figuradamente.

figure *n* figura, forma *f*; imagen *f*; cifra *f*; * *vi* figurar; ser lógico/ca; **to** ~ **out** comprender.

figurehead *n* testaferro *m*.

filament *n* filamento *m*; fibra *f*.

filch *vi* ratear.

filcher *n* ratero/ra, ladroncillo/lla *m/f*.

file *n* hilo *m*; lista *f*; (*mil*) fila, hilera *f*; lima *f*; carpeta *f*; fichero *m*; * *vt* enhilar; limar; clasificar; presentar; * *vi* **to** ~ **in/out** entrar/salir en fila; **to** ~ **past** desfilar ante.

filing cabinet *n* archivador *m*.

fill *vt* llenar; hartar; **to** ~ **in** rellenar; **to** ~ **up** llenar (hasta el borde).

fillet *n* filete *m*.

fillet steak *n* filete de ternera *m*.

fillip *n* (*fig*) estímulo *m*.

filly *n* potra *f*.

film *n* película *f*; film *m*; capa *f*; * *vt* filmar; * *vi* rodar.

film star *n* estrella de cine *f*.

film strip *n* tira de película *f*.

filter *n* filtro *m*; * *vt* filtrar.

filter-tipped *adj* con filtro.

filth(iness) *n* inmundicia, porquería *f*; fango, lodo *m*.

filthy *adj* sucio/cia, puerco/ca.

fin *n* aleta *f*.

final *adj* final, último/ma; ~ly *adv* finalmente; ~ **stages** postrimerías *fpl*.

finale *n* final *m*.

finalist *n* finalista *m/f*.

finalize *vt* concluir.

finance *n* fondos *mpl*.

financial *adj* financiero/ra.

financier *n* financiero/ra *m/f*, *Lat Am* financista *m/f*.

find *vt* hallar, descubrir, *Lat Am* ubicar; **to** ~

out averiguar; descubrir; **to ~ one's self** hallarse; * *n* hallazgo *m*.

findings *npl* fallo *m*; recomendaciones *fpl*.

fine *adj* fino/na; agudo/da, cortante; claro/ra, trasparente; delicado/da; astuto/ta; elegante; bello/la; * *n* multa *f*; * *vt* multar, *Lat Am* infraccionar.

fine arts *npl* bellas artes *fpl*.

finely *adv* con elegancia.

finery *n* adorno, atavío *m*.

finesse *n* sutileza *f*.

finger *n* dedo *m*; * *vt* tocar, manosear; manejar.

fingernail *n* uña *f*.

fingerprint *n* huella dactilar *f*.

fingertip *n* yema del dedo *f*.

finicky *adj* delicado/da.

finish *vt* acabar, terminar, concluir; **to ~ off** acabar (con); **to ~ up** terminar; * *vi*: **to ~ up** ir a parar.

finishing line *n* línea de llegada, línea de meta *f*.

finishing school *n* academia para señoritas *f*.

finite *adj* finito/ta; conjugado/da.

fir tree *n* abeto *m*

fire *n* fuego *m*; incendio *m*; * *vt* disparar; incendiar; despertar; * *vi* encenderse.

fire alarm *n* alarma de incendios *f*.

firearm *n* arma de fuego *f*.

fireball *n* bola *f* de fuego.

firebreak, fire line *n* cortafuegos *m*.

fire department *n* cuerpo de bomberos *m*.

fire engine *n* coche de bomberos *m*.

fire escape *n* escalera de incendios *f*.

fire extinguisher *n* extintor *m*.

firefly *n* luciérnaga *f*.

fireman *n* bombero *m*.

fireplace *n* hogar, fogón *m*.

fireproof *adj* a prueba de fuego.

fireside *n* chimenea *f*.

fire station, fire house *n* parque de bomberos *m*.

firewater *n* aguardiente *m*.

firewood *n* leña *f*.

fireworks *npl* fuegos artificiales *mpl*.

firing *n* disparos *mpl*.

firing squad *n* pelotón de ejecución *m*.

firm *adj* firme, estable, constante; * *n* (com) firma *f*; **~ly** *adv* firmemente.

firmament *n* firmamento *m*.

firmness *n* firmeza *f*; constancia *f*.

first *adj* primero/ra; * *adv* primeramente; **at ~** al principio; **~ly** *adv* en primer lugar.

first aid *n* primeros auxilios *mpl*.

first-aid kit *n* botiquín *m*.

first-class *adj* de primera (clase).

first-hand *adj* de primera mano.

First Lady *n* primera dama *f*.

first name *n* nombre de pila *m*.

first-rate *adj* de primera (clase).

fiscal *adj* fiscal.

fish *n* pez *m*; * *vi* pescar.

fishbone *n* espina *f*.

fisherman *n* pescador *m*.

fish farm *n* piscifactoría *f*.

fishing *n* pesca *f*.

fishing line *n* sedal *m*.

fishing rod *n* caña de pescar *f*.

fishing tackle *n* aparejo *m*.

fish market *n* lonja de pescado *f*.

fishseller *n* pescadero/ra *m/f*.

fish shop *n* pescadería *f*.

fishy *adj* (fig) sospechoso/sa.

fissure *n* grieta, hendedura *f*.

fist *n* puño *m*.

fit *n* paroxismo *m*; convulsión *f*; * *adj* en forma; apto/ta, idóneo/nea, justo/ta; * *vt* ajustar, acomodar, adaptar; **to ~ out** proveer; * *vi* convenir; **to ~ in** encajarse; llevarse bien (con todos).

fitness *n* salud *f*; aptitud, conveniencia *f*.

fitted carpet *n* moqueta *f*.

fitted kitchen *n* cocina amueblada *f*.

fitter *n* ajustador *m*.

fitting *adj* conveniente, idóneo/nea, justo/ta; * *n* conveniencia *f*; **~s** *pl* guarnición *f*.

five *adj, n* cinco.

fix *vt* fijar, establecer; **to ~ up** arreglar.

fixation *n* obsesión *f*.

fixed *adj* fijo/ja.

fixings *npl* equipajes *mpl*; pertrechos *mpl*; ajuar *m*.

fixture *n* encuentro *m*.

fizz(le) *vi* silbar.

fizzy *adj* gaseoso/sa.

flabbergasted *adj* pasmado/da.

flabby *adj* blando/da, flojo/ja, lacio/cia.

flaccid *adj* flojo/ja, flaco/ca; fláccido/da.

flag *n* bandera *f*; losa *f*; * *vi* debilitarse.

flagpole *n* asta de bandera *f*.

flagrant *adj* flagrante; notorio/ria.

flagship *n* buque insignia *m*.

flag stop *n* parada a petición *f*.

flair *n* aptitud especial *f*.

flak *n* fuego antiaéreo *m*; lluvia de críticas.

flake *n* copo *m*; lámina *f*; * *vi* romperse en láminas.

flaky *adj* escamoso/sa, desmenuzable.

flamboyant *adj* vistoso/sa.

flame *n* llama *f*; fuego (del amor) *m*.

flamingo *n* flamenco *m*.

flammable *adj* inflamable.

flank *n* ijada *f*; (mil) flanco *m*; * *vt* flanquear.

flannel *n* franela, flanela *f*.

flap *n* solapa *f*; hoja *f*; aletazo *m*; * *vt* aletear; * *vi* ondear.

flare *vi* lucir, brillar; **to ~ up** encenderse; encolerizarse; estallar; * *n* llama *f*.

flash *n* flash *m*; relámpago *m*; * *vt* **to ~ on and off** encender y apagar.

flashbulb *n* bombilla de flash *f*.

flash cube *n* cubo de flash *m*.

flashlight *n* linterna *f*; antorcha *f*.

flashy *adj* superficial.

flask n frasco m; botella f.

flat adj llano/na, plano/na; insípido/da; * n llanura f; plano m; (mus) bemol m; **~ly** adv horizontalmente; llanamente; enteramente; de plano, de nivel; francamente.

flatness n llanura f; insipidez f.

flatten vt allanar; abatir.

flatter vt adular, lisonjear.

flattering adj halagüeño/ña, zalame-ro/ra.

flattery n adulación, lisonja f; zalamería f.

flatulence n (med) flatulencia f.

flaunt vt ostentar.

flavor n sabor m; * vt sazonar.

flavored adj con sabor (a).

flavorless adj soso/sa.

flaw n falta, tacha f; defecto m.

flawless adj sin defecto.

flax n lino m.

flea n pulga f.

flea bite n picadura de pulga f.

fleck n mota f; punto m.

flee vt huir de; * vi escapar; huir.

fleece n vellón m; * vt (col) pelar.

fleet n flota f; escuadra f.

fleeting adj pasajero/ra, fugitivo/va.

flesh n carne f.

flesh wound n herida superficial f.

fleshy adj carnoso/sa, pulposo/sa.

flex n cordón m; * vt tensar.

flexibility n flexibilidad f.

flexible adj flexible.

flick n golpecito m; * vt dar un golpecito a.

flicker vt aletear; fluctuar.

flier n aviador/a m/f.

flight n vuelo m; huida, fuga f; bandada (de pájaros) f; (fig) elevación f.

flight attendant n auxiliar de vuelo m/f.

flight deck n cabina de mandos f.

flimsy adj débil; fútil.

flinch vi encogerse.

fling vt lanzar, echar.

flint n pedernal m.

flip vt arrojar, lanzar.

flippant adj petulante, locuaz.

flipper n aleta f.

flirt vi coquetear; * n coqueta f.

flirtation n coquetería f.

flit vi volar, huir; aletear.

float vt hacer flotar; lanzar; * vi flotar; * n flotador m; carroza f; reserva f.

flock n manada f; rebaño m; gentío m; * vi congregarse.

flog vt azotar; (col) zurrar.

flogging n tunda, zurra f.

flood n diluvio m; inundación f; flujo m; * vt inundar.

flooding n inundación f.

floodlight n foco m.

floor n suelo, piso m; piso (de una casa); * vt dejar sin respuesta.

floorboard n tabla f.

floor lamp n lámpara de pie f.

floor show n cabaret m.

flop n fracaso m.

floppy adj flojo/ja

floppy disk n floppy m, disquete m.

flora n flora f.

floral adj floral.

florescence n florescencia f.

florid adj florido/da.

florist n florista m/f.

florist's (shop) n floristería f.

flotilla n (mar) flotilla f.

flounder n platija (pez de mar) f; * vi tropezar.

flour n harina f.

flourish vi florecer; gozar de prosperidad; * n belleza f; lazo m; (mus) floreo, preludio m.

flourishing adj floreciente.

flout vt burlarse de.

flow vi fluir, manar; crecer la marea; ondear; * n flujo de la marea m ; abundancia f; flujo m.

flow chart n organigrama m.

flower n flor f; * vi florear; florecer.

flowerbed n parterre m.

flowerpot n tiesto m, maceta f.

flowery adj florido/da.

flower show n exposición de flores f.

fluctuate vi fluctuar.

fluctuation n fluctuación f.

fluency n fluidez f.

fluent adj fluido/da; fácil; **~ly** adv con fluidez.

fluff n pelusa f; **~y** adj velloso/sa.

fluid adj, n fluido/da m.

fluidity n fluidez f.

fluke n (col) chiripa f.

fluoride n fluoruro m.

flurry n ráfaga f; agitación f.

flush vt: **to ~ out** levantar; desalojar; * vi ponerse colorado/da; * n rubor m; resplandor m.

flushed adj ruborizado/da.

fluster vt confundir.

flustered adj aturdido/da.

flute n flauta f.

flutter vi revolotear; estar en agitación; * n confusión f; agitación f.

flux n flujo m.

fly vt pilotar; transportar; * vi volar; huir; escapar; **to ~ away/off** emprender el vuelo; * n mosca f; bragueta f.

flying n aviación f.

flying saucer n platillo volante m.

flypast n desfile aéreo m.

flysheet n doble techo m.

foal n potro m.

foam n espuma f; * vi espumar.

foam rubber n espuma de caucho f.

foamy adj espumoso/sa.

focus n foco m.

fodder n forraje m.

foe n adversario/ria m/f, enemigo/ga m/f.

fog n niebla f.

foggy adj nebuloso/sa, brumoso/sa.

fog light n faro antiniebla m.

foible n debilidad, parte flaca f.

foil vt frustrar; * n hoja f; florete m.

fold n redil m; pliegue m; * vt plegar; * vi: **to ~ up** plegarse, doblarse; quebrar.

folder n carpeta f; folleto m.

folding adj plegable.

folding chair n silla de tijera f.

foliage n follaje m.

folio n folio m.

folk n gente f.

folklore n folklore m.

folk music n folk m.

folk song n canción folklórica f.

follow vt seguir; acompañar; imitar; **to ~ up** responder a; investigar; * vi seguir, resultar, provenir.

follower n seguidor/a m/f; imitador/a m/f; secuaz, partidario/ria m/f; adherente m; compañero/ra m/f.

following adj siguiente; * n afición f.

folly n extravagancia, bobería f.

foment vt fomentar; proteger.

fond adj cariñoso/sa; **~ly** adv cariñosamente.

fondle vt acariciar.

fondness n gusto m; cariño m.

font n pila bautismal f.

food n comida f.

food mixer n batidora f.

food poisoning n intoxicación alimentaria f.

food processor n robot de cocina m.

foodstuffs npl comestibles mpl.

fool n loco/ca, tonto/ta, Lat Am sonso/sa, Lat Am zonzo/za m/f; * vt engañar.

foolhardy adj temerario/ria.

foolish adj bobo/ba, tonto/ta; **~ly** adv tontamente.

foolproof adj infalible.

foolscap n papel tamaño folio m.

foot n pie m; pata f; paso m; **on, by ~ a** pie.

footage n imágenes fpl.

football n balón m; fútbol m.

footballer n futbolista m/f; jugador/a de fútbol m/f.

footbrake n freno de pie m.

footbridge n puente peatonal m.

foothills npl estribaciones fpl.

foothold n pie firme m.

footing n base f; estado m; condición f; fundamento m.

footlights npl candilejas fpl.

footman n lacayo m; soldado de infantería m.

footnote n nota de pie f.

footpath n senda f.

footprint n huella, pisada f.

footsore adj con los pies doloridos.

footstep n paso m; huella f.

footwear n calzado m.

for prep por, a causa de; para; * conj porque, para que; por cuanto; **as ~ me** tocante a mí; **what ~?** ¿para qué?

forage n forraje m; * vt forrajear; saquear.

foray n incursión f.

forbid vt prohibir, vedar; impedir; **God ~!** ¡Dios no quiera!

forbidding adj inhóspito/ta; severo/ra.

force n fuerza f; poder, vigor m; violencia f; necesidad f; **~s** pl tropas fpl; * vt forzar, violentar; esforzar; constreñir.

forced adj forzado/da.

forced march n (mil) marcha forzada f.

forceful adj enérgico/ca.

forceps n fórceps m.

forcible adj fuerte, eficaz, poderoso/sa; **~bly** adv fuertemente, forzadamente.

ford n vado m; * vt vadear.

fore n: **to the ~** en evidencia.

forearm n antebrazo m.

foreboding n presentimiento m.

forecast vt pronosticar; * n pronóstico m.

forecourt n patio m.

forefather n abuelo, antecesor m.

forefinger n índice m.

forefront n: **in the ~ of** en la vanguardia de.

forego vt ceder, abandonar; preceder.

foregone adj pasado/da; anticipado/da.

foreground n delantera f.

forehead n frente f; insolencia f.

foreign adj extranjero/ra; extraño/ña.

foreigner n extranjero/ra, forastero/ra m/f.

foreign exchange n divisas fpl.

foreleg n pata delantera f.

foreman n capataz m; (law) presidente del jurado.

foremost adj principal.

forenoon n mañana f.

forensic adj forense; **~ scientist** n forense m/f.

forerunner n precursor/a m/f; prede-cesor/a m/f.

foresee vt prever.

foreshadow vt pronosticar; simbolizar.

foresight n previsión f; presciencia f.

forest n bosque m; selva f.

forestall vt anticipar; prevenir.

forester n guardabosque m/f.

forestry n silvicultura f.

foretaste n muestra f.

foretell vt predecir, profetizar.

forethought n providencia f; premeditación f.

forever adv para siempre.

forewarn vt prevenir de antemano.

foreword n prefacio m.

forfeit n confiscación f; * vt perder derecho a.

forge n fragua f; fábrica de metales f; * vt forjar; falsificar; inventar; * vi: **to ~ ahead** avanzar constantemente.

forger n falsificador/a m/f.

forgery n falsificación f.

forget vt olvidar; * vi olvidarse.

forgetful adj olvidadizo/za; descuida-do/da.

forgetfulness n olvido m; negligencia f.

forget-me-not n (bot) nomeolvides m.

forgive *vt* perdonar.

forgiveness *n* perdón *m*; remisión *f*.

fork *n* tenedor *m*; horca *f*, *Lat Am* horqueta *f*; * *vi* bifurcarse; **to ~ out** (*col*) desembolsar.

forked *adj* horcado/da.

fork-lift truck *n* carretilla elevadora *f*.

forlorn *adj* abandonado/da, perdido/da.

form *n* forma *f*; modelo *m*; modo *m*; formalidad *f*; método *m*; molde *m*; * *vt* formar.

formal *adj* formal, metódico/ca; ceremonioso/sa; **~ly** *adv* formalmente.

formality *n* formalidad *f*; ceremonia *f*.

format *n* formato *m*; * *vt* formatear.

formation *n* formación *f*.

formative *adj* formativo/va.

former *adj* precedente; anterior, pasado/da; **~ly** *adv* antiguamente, en tiempos pasados.

formidable *adj* formidable, terrible.

formula *n* fórmula *f*.

formulate *vt* formular, articular.

forsake *vt* dejar, abandonar.

fort *n* castillo *m*; fortaleza *f*.

forte *adj* (*mus*) fuerte *m*.

forthcoming *adj* venidero/ra.

forthright *adj* franco/ca.

forthwith *adj* inmediatamente, sin tardanza.

fortieth *adj*, *n* cuadragésimo *m*.

fortification *n* fortificación *f*.

fortify *vt* fortificar; corroborar.

fortitude *n* fortaleza *f*; valor *m*.

fortnight *n* quince días *mpl*; dos semanas *fpl*; **~ly** *adj*, *adv* cada quince días.

fortress *n* (*mil*) fortaleza *f*.

fortuitous *adj* impensado/da; casual; **~ly** *adv* fortuitamente.

fortunate *adj* afortunado/da; **~ly** *adv* felizmente.

fortune *n* fortuna, suerte *f*.

fortune-teller *n* sortílego/ga, adivino/na *m/f*.

forty *adj*, *n* cuarenta.

forum *n* foro *m*.

forward *adj* avanzado/da; delantero/ra; presumido/da; **~(s)** *adv* adelante, más allá; * *vt* remitir; promover, patrocinar.

forwardness *n* precocidad *f*; audacia *f*.

fossil *adj*, *n* fósil *m*.

foster *vt* criar, nutrir.

foster child *n* hijo/ja adoptivo/va *m/f*.

foster father *n* padre adoptivo *m*.

foster mother *n* madre adoptiva *f*.

foul *adj* sucio/cia, puerco/ca; impuro/ra, detestable; **~ copy** *n* borrador *m*; **~ly** *adv* suciamente; ilegítimamente; * *vt* ensuciar.

foul play *n* mala jugada *f*; muerte violenta *f*.

found *vt* fundar, establecer; edificar; fundir.

founder *n* fundador/a *m/f*; fundidor *m*; * *vi* (*mar*) irse a pique; zozobrar.

foundling *n* niño/ña expósito/ta *m/f*.

foundry *n* fundición *f*.

fount, fountain *n* fuente *f*.

fountainhead *n* origen de fuente *m*.

four *adj*, *n* cuatro.

fourfold *adj* cuádruple.

four-poster (**bed**) *n* cama de dosel *f*.

foursome *n* grupo de cuatro personas *m*.

fourteen *adj*, *n* catorce.

fourteenth *adj*, *n* decimocuarto/ta.

fourth *adj*, *n* cuarto/ta; * *n* cuarto *m*; **~ly** *adv* en cuarto lugar.

fowl *n* ave *f* de corral.

fox *n* zorra *f*; (*fig*) zorro *m*.

foyer *n* vestíbulo *m*.

fracas *n* riña *f*.

fraction *n* fracción *f*.

fracture *n* fractura *f*; * *vt* fracturar, romper.

fragile *adj* frágil; débil.

fragility *n* fragilidad *f*; debilidad, flaqueza *f*.

fragment *n* fragmento *m*.

fragmentary *adj* fragmentario/ria.

fragrance *n* fragancia *f*.

fragrant *adj* fragante, oloroso/sa; **~ly** *adv* con fragancia.

frail *adj* frágil, débil.

frailty *n* fragilidad *f*; debilidad *f*.

frame *n* armazón *m*; marco, cerco *m*; cuadro de vidriera *m*; estructura *f*; montura *f*; * *vt* encuadrar; componer, construir, formar.

frame of mind *n* estado de ánimo *m*.

framework *n* estructura *f*; esqueleto *m*, armazón *f*.

franchise *n* sufragio *m*; concesión *f*.

frank *adj* franco/ca, liberal.

frankly *adv* francamente.

frankness *n* franqueza *f*.

frantic *adj* frenético/ca, furioso/sa.

fraternal *adj*, **~ly** *adv* fraternal(men-te).

fraternity *n* fraternidad *f*.

fraternize *vi* hermanarse.

fratricide *n* fratricidio *m*; fratricida *m/f*.

fraud *n* fraude, engaño *m*.

fraudulence *n* fraudulencia *f*.

fraudulent *adj* fraudulento/ta; **~ly** *adv* fraudulentamente.

fraught *adj* cargado/da, lleno/na.

fray *n* riña, disputa, querella *f*.

freak *n* fantasía *f*; fenómeno *m*.

freckle *n* peca *f*.

freckled *adj* pecoso/sa.

free *adj* libre; liberal; suelto/ta; exento/ta; desocupado/da; gratis; * *vt* soltar; librar; eximir; * *vr*: **to ~ oneself from trouble** zafarse de.

freedom *n* libertad *f*.

freehold *n* propiedad absoluta *f*.

free-for-all *n* trifulca *f*.

free gift *n* prima *f*.

free kick *n* tiro libre *m*.

freelance *adj*, *adv* por cuenta propia.

freely *adv* libremente; espontáneamente; liberalmente, gratis.

freemason *n* francmasón *m*, masón *m*.

freemasonry *n* francmasonería *f*, masonería *f*.

Freepost™ *n* franqueo pagado *m*.

free-range *adj* de granja.

freethinker *n* librepensador/a *m/f*.

freethinking *n* librepensamiento *m*.

free trade *n* libre comercio *m*.

freeway *n* autopista *f*.

freewheel *vi* ir en punto muerto.

free will *n* libre albedrío *m*.

freeze *vi* helar(se); * *vt* congelar; helar.

freeze-dried *adj* liofilizado/da.

freezer *n* congelador *m*, *Lat Am* freezer *m*.

freezing *adj* helado/da.

freezing point *n* punto de congelación *m*.

freight *n* carga *f*; flete *m*.

freighter *n* fletador *m*.

freight train *n* tren de mercancías *m*.

French bean *n* judía verde *f*.

French fries *npl* patatas/papas fritas *fpl*.

French window *n* puertaventana *f*.

frenzied *adj* loco/ca, delirante.

frenzy *n* frenesí *m*; locura *f*.

frequency *n* frecuencia *f*.

frequent *adj*, **~ly** *adv* frecuente(men-te); * *vt* frecuentar.

fresco *n* fresco *m*.

fresh *adj* fresco/ca; nuevo/va, reciente; **~ water** *n* agua dulce *f*.

freshen *vt* (*vi*) refrescar(se).

freshly *adv* nuevamente; recientemente.

freshman *n* novato *m*.

freshness *n* frescura *f*; fresco *m*.

freshwater *adj* de agua dulce.

fret *vi* agitarse, enojarse.

friar *n* fraile *m*.

friction *n* fricción *f*.

Friday *n* viernes *m*; Good ~ Viernes Santo *m*.

friend *n* amigo/ga *m/f*.

friendless *adj* sin amigos.

friendliness *n* amistad, benevolencia, bondad *f*.

friendly *adj* amistoso/sa.

friendship *n* amistad *f*.

frieze *n* friso *m*.

frigate *n* (*mar*) fragata *f*.

fright *n* espanto, terror *m*.

frighten *vt* espantar.

frightened *adj* asustado/da.

frightening *adj* espantoso/sa.

frightful *adj* espantoso/sa, horrible; **~ly** *adv* espantosamente, terriblemente.

frigid *adj* frío/ría, frígido/da; **~ly** *adv* fríamente.

fringe *n* franja *f*.

fringe benefits *npl* ventajas adicionales *fpl*.

frisk *vt* cachear.

frisky *adj* juguetón/ona.

fritter *vt*: to ~ away desperdiciar.

frivolity *n* frivolidad *f*.

frivolous *adj* frívolo/la, vano/na.

frizz(le) *vt* frisar; rizar.

frizzy *adj* rizado/da.

fro *adv*: to go to and ~ ir y venir.

frog *n* rana *f*.

frolic *vi* juguetear.

frolicsome *adj* juguetón/ona, travie-so/sa.

from *prep* de; después; desde.

front *n* parte delantera *f*; fachada *f*; paseo marítimo *m*; frente *m*; apariencias *fpl*; * *adj* delantero/ra; pri-mero/ra.

frontal *adj* de frente.

front door *n* puerta principal *f*.

frontier *n* frontera *f*.

front page *n* primera plana *f*.

front-wheel drive *n* (*auto*) tracción delantera *f*.

frost *n* helada *f*; hielo *m*; * *vt* escarchar.

frostbite *n* congelación *f*.

frostbitten *adj* helado/da, con síntomas de congelación.

frosted *adj* deslustrado/da.

frosty *adj* helado/da, frío/ría como el hielo.

froth *n* espuma (de algún líquido) *f*; * *vi* espumar.

frothy *adj* espumoso/sa.

frown *vt* mirar con ceño; * *n* ceño *m*.

frozen *adj* helado/da.

frugal *adj* frugal; económico/ca; sob-rio/ria; **~ly** *adv* frugalmente.

fruit *n* fruta *f*; fruto *m*; producto *m*.

fruiterer *n* frutero/ra *m/f*.

fruitful *adj* fructífero/ra, fértil; prove-choso/sa, útil; **~ly** *adv* con fertilidad.

fruitfulness *n* fertilidad *f*.

fruition *n* realización *f*.

fruit juice *n* zumo de fruta *m*.

fruitless *adj* estéril; inútil; **~ly** *adv* vanamente, inútilmente.

fruit salad *n* ensalada de frutas *f*, macedonia *f*.

fruit seller *n* frutero/ra *m*.

fruit shop/store *n* frutería *f*.

fruit tree *n* frutal *m*.

frustrate *vt* frustrar; anular.

frustrated *adj* frustrado/da.

frustration *n* frustración *f*.

fry *vt* freír, *Lat Am* fritar.

frying pan *n* sartén *f*.

fuchsia *n* (*bot*) fucsia *f*.

fudge *n* caramelo blando *m*.

fuel *n* combustible *m*.

fuel tank *n* depósito de combustible *m*.

fugitive *adj*, *n* fugitivo/va *m/f*.

fugue *n* (*mus*) fuga *f*.

fulcrum *n* fulcro *m*.

fulfill *vt* cumplir; realizar.

fulfillment *n* cumplimiento *m*.

full *adj* lleno/na, repleto/ta, completo/ta; perfecto/ta; * *adv* enteramente, del todo.

full-blown *adj* hecho/cha y derecho/cha.

full-fledged *adj* hecho/cha y derecho/cha.

full-length *adj* de cuerpo entero/ra; completo/ta.

full moon *n* plenilunio *m*; luna llena *f*.

fullness *n* plenitud, abundancia *f*.

full-scale *adj* en gran escala; de tamaño natural.

full-time *adj* de tiempo completo.

fully *adv* llenamente, enteramente, ampliamente.

fulsome *adj* exagerado/da.

fumble *vi* manejar torpemente.

fume *vi* humear; encolerizarse.

fumes *npl* humo *m*.

fumigate *vt* fumigar, *Lat Am* humear.

fun *n* diversión *f*; alegría *f*.

function *n* función *f*.

functional *adj* funcional.

fund *n* fondo *m*; fondos públicos *mpl*; * *vt* costear.

fundamental *adj* fundamental; ~**ly** *adv* fundamentalmente.

fundamentalism *n* fundamentalismo *m*.

fundamentalist *n* fundamentalista *m/f*.

funeral service *n* misa de difuntos *f*, funeral *m*.

funeral *n* funeral *m*.

funereal *adj* funeral, fúnebre.

fungus *n* hongo *m*; seta *f*.

funnel *n* embudo *m*; cañón (de chimenea) *m*.

funny *adj* divertido/da; curioso/sa; zumbón/ona.

fur *n* piel *f*.

fur coat *n* abrigo de pieles *m*.

furious *adj* furioso/sa, frenético/ca; ~**ly** *adv* con furia.

furlong *n* estadio *m*; (octava parte de una milla).

furlough *n* (*mil*) licencia *f*; permiso *m*.

furnace *n* horno *m*; hornaza *f*.

furnish *vt* amueblar, *Lat Am* amoblar; facilitar; suministrar.

furniture *n* muebles *mpl*.

furrow *n* surco *m*; * *vt* surcar; estriar.

furry *adj* peludo/da.

further *adj* nuevo/va; más lejano/na; * *adv* más lejos, más allá; aún; además; * *vt* adelantar, promover, -ayudar.

further education *n* educación para adultos *f*.

furthermore *adv* además.

furthest *adv* lo más lejos, lo más remoto.

furtive *adj* furtivo/va; secreto/ta; ~**ly** *adv* furtivamente.

fury *n* furor *m*; furia *f*; ira *f*.

fuse *vt*, *vi* fundir; derretirse; * *n* fusible *m*, *Lat Am* tapón *m*; mecha *f*.

fuse box *n* caja de fusibles *f*.

fusion *n* fusión *f*.

fuss *n* lío *m*; alboroto *m*.

fussy *adj* jactancioso/sa.

futile *adj* fútil, frívolo/la.

futility *n* futilidad, vanidad *f*.

future *adj* futuro/ra; * *n* futuro *m*; porvenir *m*.

fuzzy *adj* borroso/sa; muy rizado/da.

G

gab *n* (*col*) charla *f*.

gabble *vi* charlar, parlotear; * *n* algarabía *f*.

gable *n* gablete *m*.

gadget *n* dispositivo *m*.

gaffe *n* plancha *f*.

gag *n* mordaza *f*; chiste *m*; * *vt* amordazar.

gage *n* calibre *m*; entrevía *f*; indicador *m*; * *vt* medir.

gaiety *n* alegría *f*.

gaily *adv* alegremente.

gain *n* ganancia *f*; interés, provecho *m*; * *vt* ganar; conseguir.

gait *n* marcha *f*; porte *m*.

gala *n* fiesta *f*.

galaxy *n* galaxia *f*.

gale *n* vendaval *m*.

gall *n* hiel *f*.

gallant *adj* galante.

gall bladder *n* vesícula biliar *f*.

gallery *n* galería *f*.

galley *n* cocina *f*; galera *f*.

gallon *n* galón *m* (medida).

gallop *n* galope *m*; * *vi* galopar.

gallows *n* horca *f*.

gallstone *n* cálculo biliar *m*.

galore *adv* en abundancia.

galvanize *vt* galvanizar.

gambit *n* estrategia *f*.

gamble *vi* jugar; especular; * *n* riesgo *m*; apuesta *f*.

gambler *n* jugador/a *m/f*.

gambling *n* juego *m*.

game *n* juego *m*; pasatiempo *m*; partido *m*; partida *f*, caza *f*; * *vi* jugar.

gamekeeper *n* guardabosques *m invar*.

gaming *n* juego *m*.

gammon *n* jamón *m*.

gamut *n* (*mus*) gama *f*.

gander *n* ganso *m*.

gang *n* pandilla, banda *f*.

gangrene *n* gangrena *f*.

gangster *n* gángster *m*.

gangway *n* pasarela *f*.

gap *n* hueco *m*; claro *m*; intervalo *m*.

gape *vi* boquear; estar con la boca abierta.

gaping *adj* muy abierto/ta.

garage *n* garaje *m*, *Lat Am* garage *m*.

garbage can *n* cubo de la basura *m*.

garbageman *n* basurero *m*.

garbled *adj* falsificado/da.

garden *n* jardín *m*.

garden-hose *n* regadera *f*.

gardener *n* jardinero/ra *m/f*.

gardening *n* jardinería *f*.

gargle *vi* hacer gárgaras.

gargoyle *n* gárgola *f*.

garish *adj* ostentoso/sa.

garland *n* guirnalda *f*.

garlic *n* ajo *m*.

garment *n* prenda *f*.

garnish *vt* guarnecer, adornar; * *n* guarnición *f*; adorno *m*.

garret *n* guardilla *f*; desván *m*.

garrison *n* (*mil*) guarnición *f*; * *vt* (*mil*) guarnecer.

garrote vt estrangular.
garrulous adj gárrulo/la, locuaz, charlador/a.
garter n liga f.
garter belt n liguero m.
gas n gas m; gasolina f.
gas burner n mechero de gas m.
gas cylinder n bombona de gas f.
gaseous adj gaseoso/sa.
gas fire n estufa de gas f.
gash n cuchillada f; raja f; * vt acuchillar.
gasket n junta de culata f.
gas mask n careta antigás f.
gas meter n contador de gas m.
gasoline n gasolina f; **four-star ~** súper f.
gasp vi jadear; * n boqueada f.
gas pedal n acelerador f.
gas ring n hornillo de gas m.
gassy adj gaseoso/sa.
gas tap n llave del gas f.
gastric adj gástrico/ca.
gastronomic adj gastronómico/ca.
gasworks npl fábrica de gas f.
gate n puerta f.
gateway n puerta f.
gather vt recoger, amontonar; entender; plegar;
    * vi juntarse.
gathering n reunión f; colecta f.
gauche adj torpe.
gaudy adj chillón/ona.
gaunt adj flaco/ca, delgado/da.
gauze n gasa f.
gay adj alegre; vivo/va; gay.
gaze vi contemplar, considerar; * n mirada f.
gazelle n gacela f.
gazette n gaceta f.
gazetteer n gacetero m; diccionario geográfico
    m.
gear n atavío m; vestido m; aparejo m; tirantes
    mpl; velocidad f.
gearbox n caja de cambios f.
gear wheel n rueda dentada f.
gel n gel m.
gelatin(e) n gelatina, jalea f.
gelignite n gelignita f.
gem n gema f.
Gemini n Géminis m (signo del zodiaco).
gender n género m.
gene n gen m.
genealogical adj genealógico/ca.
genealogy n genealogía f.
general adj general, común, usual; **in ~** por lo
    general; **~ly** adv generalmente; * n general
    m; generala f.
general delivery n lista de correos f.
generality n generalidad, mayor parte f.
generalization n generalización f.
generalize vt generalizar.
generate vt engendrar; producir; causar.
generation n generación f.
generator n generador m.
generic adj genérico/ca.

generosity n generosidad, liberalidad f.
generous adj generoso/sa.
genetic engineering n ingeniería genética f.
genetics npl genética f.
genial adj genial, natural; alegre.
genitals npl genitales mpl.
genitive n genitivo m.
genius n genio m.
genteel adj refinado/da, elegante.
gentile n gentil, pagano/na m/f.
gentle adj suave, dócil, manso/sa, moderado/da;
    benigno/na.
gentleman n caballero m.
gentleness n dulzura, suavidad f.
gently adv suavemente.
gentry n alta burguesía f.
gents n aseos mpl.
genuflection n genuflexión f, Lat Am hincada f.
genuine adj genuino/na, puro/ra; **~ly** adv
    puramente, naturalmente.
genus n género m.
geographer n geógrafo/fa m/f.
geographical adj geográfico/ca.
geography n geografía f.
geological adj geológico/ca.
geologist n geólogo/ga m/f.
geology n geología f.
geometric(al) adj geométrico/ca.
geometry n geometría f.
geranium n (bot) geranio m.
geriatric n, adj geriátrico/ca m/f.
germ n germen m.
germinate vi brotar.
gesticulate vi gesticular.
gesture n gesto, movimiento expresivo m.
get vt ganar; conseguir, obtener, alcanzar; coger;
    agarrar; * vi hacerse, ponerse; prevalecer;
    introducirse; **to ~ the better** salir vencedor/a,
    sobrepujar.
geyser n géiser m; calentador de agua m.
ghastly adj espantoso/sa.
gherkin n pepinillo, cohombrillo m.
ghetto n gueto m.
ghost n fantasma m, Lat Am espanto m; espectro
    m.
ghostly adj fantasmal.
giant n gigante m.
gibberish n jerigonza f.
gibe vi escarnecer, burlarse, mofar; * n mofa,
    burla f.
giblets npl menudillos mpl.
giddiness n vértigo m.
giddy adj vertiginoso/sa.
gift n regalo m; don m; dádiva f; talento m.
gifted adj dotado/da.
gift voucher n vale de regalo m.
gigantic adj gigantesco/ca.
giggle vi reírse tontamente.
gild vt dorar.
gilding, gilt n doradura f.
gill n cuarta parte de pinta f; **~s** pl agallas fpl.

gilt-edged *adj* de máxima garantía.

gimmick *n* truco *m*.

gin *n* ginebra *f*.

ginger *n* jengibre *m*.

gingerbread *n* pan de jengibre *m*.

ginger-haired *adj* pelirrojo/ja.

giraffe *n* jirafa *f*.

girder *n* viga *f*.

girdle *n* faja *f*; cinturón *m*.

girl *n* muchacha, chica *f*, zagala *f*.

girlfriend *n* amiga; novia *f*.

girlish *adj* de niña.

giro *n* giro postal *m*.

girth *n* cincha *f*; circunferencia *f*.

gist *n* punto principal *m*.

give *vt, vi* dar, donar; conceder; abandonar; pronunciar; aplicarse, dedicarse; **to ~ away** regalar; traicionar; revelar; **to ~ back** devolver; **to ~ in** ceder; *vt* entregar; **to ~ off** despedir; **to ~ out** distribuir; **to ~ up** *vi* rendir; *vt* renunciar a.

gizzard *n* molleja *f*.

glacial *adj* glacial.

glacier *n* glaciar *m*.

glad *adj* alegre, contento/ta, agradable; **I am ~ to see** me alegro de ver; **~ly** *adv* alegremente.

gladden *vt* alegrar.

gladiator *n* gladiador *m*.

glamor *n* encanto, atractivo *m*.

glamorous *adj* atractivo/va.

glance *n* ojeada *f*; *vi* mirar; echar una ojeada.

glancing *adj* oblicuo/cua.

gland *n* glándula *f*.

glare *n* deslumbramiento *m*; mirada feroz y penetrante *f*; * *vi* deslumbrar, brillar; echar miradas de indignación.

glaring *adj* deslumbrante; manifiesto/ta; notorio/ria.

glass *n* vidrio *m*, cristal *m*; telescopio *m*; vaso *m*; espejo *m*; **~es** *pl* gafas *fpl*; * *adj* vítreo/rea.

glassware *n* cristalería *f*.

glassy *adj* vítreo/rea, cristalino/na, vidrioso/sa.

glaze *vt* vidriar; embarnizar.

glazier *n* vidriero *m*, cristalero *m*.

gleam *n* relámpago, rayo *m*; * *vi* relampaguear, brillar.

gleaming *adj* reluciente.

glean *vt* espigar; recoger.

glee *n* alegría *f*; gozo *m*; jovialidad *f*.

glen *n* valle *m*; llanura *f*.

glib *adj* con lab; **~ly** *adv* con labia.

glide *vi* resbalar; planear.

gliding *n* vuelo sin motor *m*.

glimmer *n* vislumbre *f*; * *vi* vislumbrarse.

glimpse *n* vislumbre *m*; relámpago *m*; ojeada *f*; * *vt* entrever, percibir.

glint *vi* centellear.

glisten, glitter *vi* relucir, brillar.

gloat *vi* relamerse; saborear.

global *adj* mundial.

globalization *n* globalización *f*.

global warming *n* calentamiento global *m*.

globe *n* globo *m*; esfera *f*.

gloom, gloominess *n* oscuridad *f*; melancolía, tristeza *f*; **~ily** *adv* oscuramente; tristemente.

gloomy *adj* sombrío/ría, oscuro/ra; cubierto de nubes; triste, melancó-lico/ca.

glorification *n* glorificación, alabanza *f*.

glorify *vt* glorificar, celebrar.

glorious *adj* glorioso/sa, ilustre; **~ly** *adv* gloriosamente.

glory *n* gloria, fama, celebridad *f*.

gloss *n* glosa *f*; lustre *m*; * *vt* glosar, interpretar; **to ~ over** encubrir.

glossary *n* glosario *m*.

glossy *adj* lustroso/sa, brillante.

glove *n* guante *m*.

glove compartment *n* guantera *f*.

glow *vi* arder; inflamarse; relucir; * *n* color vivo *m*; viveza de color *f*; vehemencia de una pasión *f*.

glower *vi* mirar con ceño.

glue *n* cola *f*, *Lat Am* cemento *m*; * *vt* pegar.

gluey *adj* viscoso/sa, pegajoso/sa.

glum *adj* abatido/da, triste.

glut *n* hartura, abundancia *f*.

glutinous *adj* glutinoso/sa, viscoso/sa.

glutton *n* glotón/ona, tragón/ona *m/f*.

gluttony *n* glotonería *f*.

glycerin *n* glicerina *f*.

gnarled *adj* nudoso/sa.

gnash *vt, vi* rechinar.

gnat *n* mosquito *m*, *Lat Am* jején *m*.

gnaw *vt* roer.

gnome *n* gnomo *m*.

go *vi* ir, irse, andar, caminar; partir(se), marchar; huir; pasar; **to ~ ahead** seguir adelante; **to ~ away** marcharse; **to ~ back** volver; **to ~ by** pasar; **to ~ for** ir por; gustar; **to ~ in** entrar; **to ~ off** irse; pasarse; **to ~ on** seguir; pasar; **to ~ out** salir; apagarse; **to ~ up** subir.

goad *n* aguijada, aijada *f*, *Lat Am* picana *f*; * *vt* aguijar, *Lat Am* picanear; estimular, incitar.

go-ahead *adj* emprendedor/a; * *n* luz verde *f*.

goal *n* meta *f*; fin *m*.

goalkeeper *n* portero/ra *m/f*, *Lat Am* arquero/ra *m/f*, *Lat Am* guardavallas *m/f invar*.

goalpost *n* poste (de la portería) *m*.

goatherd *n* cabrero/ra *m/f*.

gobble *vt* engullir, tragar; **to ~ down** zampar.

go-between *n* mediador/a *m/f*.

goblet *n* copa *f*.

goblin *n* espíritu ambulante, duende *m*.

God *n* Dios *m*.

godchild *n* ahijado, hijo de pila *m*.

goddaughter *n* ahijada, hija de pila *f*.

goddess *n* diosa *f*.

godfather *n* padrino *m*.

godforsaken *adj* dejado/da de la mano de Dios.

godhead *n* deidad, divinidad *f*.

godless *adj* infiel, impío/pía, sin Dios, ateo/tea.

godlike *adj* divino/na.

godliness n piedad, devoción, santidad f.

godly adj piadoso/sa, devoto/ta, reli-gioso/sa; recto/ta, justificado/da.

godmother n madrina f.

godsend n don del cielo m.

godson n ahijado m.

goggle-eyed adj con ojos desorbitados.

goggles npl gafas fpl; gafas de bucear fpl.

going n ida f; salida f; partida f; progreso m.

gold n oro m.

golden adj áureo/rea, de oro; excelente; ~ **rule** n regla de oro f.

goldfish n pez de colores m.

gold-plated adj chapado/da en oro.

goldsmith n orfebre m.

golf n golf m.

golf ball n pelota de golf f.

golf club n club de golf m.

golf course n campo de golf m.

golfer n golfista m/f.

gondolier n gondolero/ra m/f.

gone adj ido/da; perdido/da; pasado/da; gastado/da; muerto/ta.

gong n atabal chino, gong m.

good adj bueno/na, benévolo/la, cariñoso/sa; conveniente, apto/ta; * adv bien; * n bien m; prosperidad, ventaja f; ~**s** pl bienes muebles mpl; mercaderías fpl.

goodbye ! excl adiós!

Good Friday n Viernes Santo m.

goodies npl golosinas fpl.

good-looking adj guapo/pa.

good nature n bondad f.

good-natured adj bondadoso/sa.

goodness n bondad f.

goodwill n benevolencia, bondad f.

goose n ganso m; oca f.

gooseberry n grosella espinosa f.

goose bumps, goose flesh npl carne de gallina f.

goose-step n paso de la oca m.

gore n sangre cuajada f; * vt cornear.

gorge n barranco m; * vt engullir, tragar.

gorgeous adj maravilloso/sa.

gorilla n gorila m.

gorse n aulaga f.

gory adj sangriento/ta.

goshawk n azor m.

gospel n evangelio m.

gossamer n vello m; pelusa (de frutas) f.

gossip n cotilleo m; * vi cotillear.

gothic adj gótico/ca.

gout n gota f (enfermedad).

govern vt gobernar, dirigir, regir.

governess n gobernadora f.

government n gobierno m; administración publica f.

governor n gobernador/a m/f.

gown n toga f; vestido de mujer m; bata f.

grab vt agarrar.

grace n gracia f; favor m; merced f; perdón m;

gracias fpl; **to say** ~ bendecir la mesa; * vt adornar; agraciar.

graceful adj gracioso/sa, primoroso/sa; ~**ly** adv elegantemente, con gracia.

gracious adj gracioso/sa; favorable; ~**ly** adv graciosamente.

gradation n gradación f.

grade n grado m; curso m.

grade crossing n paso a nivel m.

grade school n escuela primaria f.

gradient n (rail) pendiente.

gradual adj gradual; ~**ly** adv gradualmente.

graduate vi graduarse, Lat Am egresar.

graduation n graduación f, Lat Am egreso m.

graffiti n pintadas fpl.

graft n injerto m; * vt injertar, ingerir.

grain n grano m; semilla f; cereales mpl.

gram n gramo m (peso).

grammar n gramática f.

grammatical adj gramatical; ~**ly** adv gramaticalmente.

granary n granero m.

grand adj grande, ilustre.

grandchild n nieto/ta m/f.

granddad n abuelo m.

granddaughter n nieta f; **great** ~ bisnieta f.

grandeur n grandeza f; pompa f.

grandfather n abuelo m; **great** ~ bisabuelo m.

grandiose adj grandioso/sa.

grandma n abuelita f.

grandmother n abuela f; **great** ~ bisabuela f.

grandparents npl abuelos mpl.

grand piano n piano de cola m.

grandson n nieto m; **great** ~ bisnieto m.

grandstand n tribuna f.

granite n granito m.

grant vt conceder; **to take for** ~**ed** presuponer; * n beca f; concesión f.

granulate vt granular.

granule n gránulo m.

grape n uva f; **bunch of** ~**s** racimo de uvas m.

grapefruit n toronja f, pomelo m.

graph n gráfica f.

graphic(al) adj gráfico/ca; pintores-co/ca; ~**ally** adv gráficamente.

graphics n artes gráficas fpl; gráficos mpl.

grapnel n (mar) arpeo m.

grasp vt empuñar, asir, agarrar; * n puño m; comprensión f; poder m.

grasping adj avaro/ra.

grass n hierba f, Lat Am pasto m.

grasshopper n saltamontes m invar.

grassland n pampa, pradera f.

grass-roots adj popular.

grass snake n culebra de agua f.

grassy adj herboso/sa.

grate n reja, verja, rejilla f; * vt rallar; rechinar (los dientes); enrejar.

grateful adj grato/ta, agradecido/da; ~**ly** adv agradecidamente.

gratefulness n gratitud f.

grater n rallador m.

gratification n gratificación f.

gratify vt contentar; gratificar.

gratifying adj grato/ta.

grating n rejado m; * adj áspero/ra; ofensivo/va.

gratis adv gratis.

gratitude n gratitud f.

gratuitous adj gratuito/ta, voluntario/ria; ~ly adv gratuitamente.

gratuity n gratificación, recompensa f.

grave n sepultura f; * adj grave, serio/ria; ~ly adv con gravedad, seriamente.

grave digger n sepulturero m.

gravel n cascajo m.

gravestone n lápida f.

graveyard n cementerio m.

gravitate vi gravitar.

gravitation n gravitación f.

gravity n gravedad f.

gravy n jugo de la carne f; salsa f.

gray adj gris; cano/na; * n gris m.

gray-haired adj canoso/sa.

grayish adj grisáceo/a; entrecano/na.

grayness n color gris m.

graze vt pastorear; tocar ligeramente; * vi pacer.

grease n grasa f; * vt untar.

greaseproof adj a prueba de grasa.

greasy adj grasiento/ta, Lat Am grasoso/sa.

great adj gran, grande; principal; ilustre; noble, magnánimo/ma; ~ly adv muy, mucho.

greatcoat n sobretodo m.

greatness n grandeza f; dignidad f; poder m; magnanimidad f.

greedily adv vorazmente, ansiosamente.

greediness, greed n gula f; codicia f.

greedy adj avaro/ra, codicioso/sa, Lat Am abusador/ra; goloso/sa, glotón/ona.

Greek n griego (idioma) m.

green adj verde, fresco/ca, reciente; no maduro/ra; * n verde m; llanura verde f; ~s pl verduras fpl.

greenback n billete m.

green belt n zona verde f.

green card n carta verde f.

greenery n verdura f.

greenhouse n invernadero m

greenhouse effect n efecto invernadero m.

greenish adj verdoso/sa.

green movement n ecologismo m.

greenness n verdor, vigor m; frescura, falta de experiencia f; novedad f.

greet vt saludar, congratular.

greeting n saludo m.

greeting(s) card n tarjeta de felicitación f.

grenade n (mil) granada f.

grenadier n granadero m.

greyhound n galgo m.

grid n reja f; red f.

gridiron n parrilla f; campo de fútbol americano m.

grief n dolor m; aflicción, pena f.

grievance n pesar m; molestia f; agravio m; injusticia f; perjuicio m.

grieve vt agraviar, afligir; * vi afligirse; llorar.

grievous adj doloroso/sa; enorme, atroz; ~ly adv penosamente; cruelmente.

griffin n grifo m.

grill n parrilla f; * vt interrogar.

grille n reja f.

grim adj feo, fea; horrendo/da; ceñu-do/da.

grimace n mueca f.

grime n porquería f.

grimy adj ensuciado/da.

grin n mueca f; * vi sonreír.

grind vt moler; pulverizar; afilar; picar; rechinar los dientes.

grinder n molinero m; molinillo m; amolador m.

grip n asimiento m; asidero m; maletín m; * vt agarrar.

gripping adj absorbente.

grisly adj horroroso/sa.

gristle n tendón, cartílago m.

gristly adj tendinoso/sa, cartilagino-so/sa.

grit n gravilla f; valor m.

groan vi gemir, suspirar; * n gemido, suspiro m.

grocer n tendero/ra, abarrotero/ra m/f.

groceries npl comestibles mpl.

grocery store n tienda de comestibles f.

groggy adj atontado/da.

groin n ingle f.

groom n establero m; criado m; novio m; * vt cuidar, almohazar.

groove n ranura f.

grope vt, vi tentar, buscar a oscuras; andar a tientas.

gross adj grueso/sa, corpulento/ta, espeso/sa; grosero/ra; estúpido/da; ~ly adv enormemente.

grotesque adj grotesco/ca.

grotto n gruta f.

ground n tierra f; terreno, suelo, pavimento m; fundamento m; razón fundamental f; campo (de batalla) m; fondo m; * vt mantener en tierra; conectar con tierra.

ground floor n planta baja f.

grounding n conocimientos básicos mpl.

groundless adj infundado/da; ~ly adv sin motivo.

ground staff n personal de tierra m.

groundwork n preparación f.

group n grupo m; * vt agrupar.

grouse n lagópodo escocés m; * vi quejarse.

grove n arboleda f.

grovel vi arrastrarse.

grow vt cultivar; * vi crecer, aumentarse; ~ up crecer.

grower n cultivador/a m/f; productor/a m/f.

growing adj creciente.

growl vi regañar, gruñir; * n gruñido m.

grown-up n adulto/ta m/f.

growth n crecimiento m.

grub *n* gusano *m*.

grubby *adj* sucio/cia.

grudge *n* rencor, odio *m*; envidia *f*; * *vt, vi* envidiar.

grudgingly *adv* de mala gana.

grueling *adj* penoso/sa, duro/ra.

gruesome *adj* horrible.

gruff *adj* brusco/ca; **~ly** *adv* bruscamente.

gruffness *n* aspereza, severidad *f*.

grumble *vi* gruñir; murmurar.

grumpy *adj* regañón/ona.

grunt *vi* gruñir; * *n* gruñido *m*.

G-string *n* taparrabo *m*.

guarantee *n* garantía *f*; * *vt* garantizar.

guard *n* guardia *f*; * *vt* guardar; defender.

guarded *adj* cauteloso/sa, mesura-do/da.

guardroom *n* (*mil*) cuarto de guardia *m*.

guardian *n* tutor/ra *m/f*; curador/a *m/f*; guardián/ dana *m/f*.

guardianship *n* tutela *f*.

guerrilla *n* guerrillero/ra *m/f*.

guerrilla group *n* guerrilla *f*.

guerrilla warfare *n* guerra de guerrillas *f*.

guess *vt, vi* conjeturar; adivinar; suponer; * *n* conjetura *f*.

guesswork *n* conjeturas *fpl*.

guest *n* huésped/a, convidado/da *m/f*.

guest room *n* cuarto de huéspedes *m*.

guffaw *n* carcajada *f*.

guidance *n* gobierno *m*; dirección *f*.

guide *vt* guiar, dirigir; * *n* guía *m*.

guide dog *n* perro lazarillo *m*.

guidelines *npl* directiva *f*.

guidebook *n* guía *f*.

guild *n* gremio *m*; corporación *f*.

guile *n* astucia *f*.

guillotine *n* guillotina *f*; * *vt* guillotinar.

guilt *n* culpabilidad *f*.

guiltless *adj* inocente, libre de culpa.

guilty *adj* reo, rea, culpable.

guinea pig *n* cobaya *f*, conejillo de Indias *m*.

guise *n* manera *f*.

guitar *n* guitarra *f*.

gulf *n* golfo *m*; abismo *m*.

gull *n* gaviota *f*.

gullet *n* esófago *m*.

gullibility *n* credulidad *f*; simpleza *f*.

gullible *adj* crédulo/la.

gully *n* barranco *m*.

gulp *n* trago *m*; * *vi* tragar saliva; * *vr* tragarse.

gum *n* goma *f*; cemento *m*; encía *f*; chicle *m*; * *vt* pegar con goma.

gum tree *n* árbol gomero *m*.

gun *n* pistola *f*; escopeta *f*.

gunboat *n* cañonera *f*.

gun carriage *n* cureña *f*.

gunfire *n* disparos *mpl*.

gunman *n* pistolero *m*.

gunmetal *n* bronce de cañones *m*.

gunner *n* artillero *m*.

gunnery *n* artillería *f*.

gunpoint *n*: **at ~** a punta de pistola; a mano armada.

gunpowder *n* pólvora *f*.

gunshot *n* escopetazo *m*.

gunsmith *n* armero/ra *m/f*.

gurgle *vi* gorgotear.

guru *n* gurú *m*.

gush *vi* brotar; chorrear; * *n* chorro *m*

gushing *adj* superabundante.

gusset *n* escudete *m*.

gust *n* ráfaga *f*; soplo de aire *m*, racha *f*.

gusto *n* entusiasmo *m*.

gusty *adj* tempestuoso/sa.

gut *n* intestino *m*; **~s** *npl* valor *m*; * *vt* destripar.

gutter *n* canalón *m*; arroyo *m*.

guttural *adj* gutural.

guy *n* tío *m*; tipo *m*.

guzzle *vt* engullir.

gym(nasium) *n* gimnasio *m*.

gymnast *n* gimnasta *m/f*.

gymnastic *adj* gimnástico/ca; **~s** *npl* gimnástica *f*.

gynecologist *n* ginecólogo/ga *m/f*.

Gypsy *n* gitano/na *m/f*.

gypsum *n* yeso *m*.

gyrate *vi* girar.

H

haberdasher *n* camisero/ra *m/f*.

haberdashery *n* camisería *f*; mercería *f*; prendas de caballero *fpl*.

habit *n* costumbre *f*.

habitable *adj* habitable.

habitat *n* hábitat *m*.

habitual *adj* habitual; **~ly** *adv* por costumbre.

hack *n* corte *m*; gacetillero/ra *m/f*; * *vt* tajar, cortar.

hackneyed *adj* trillado/da.

haddock *n* especie de bacalao *f*.

hag *n* bruja *f*.

haggard *adj* ojeroso/sa.

haggle *vi* regatear.

hail *n* granizo *m*; * *vt* saludar; * *vi* granizar.

hailstone *n* piedra de granizo *f*.

hair *n* pelo; cabello *m*.

hairbrush *n* cepillo *m*.

haircut *n* corte de pelo *m*.

hairdresser *n* peluquero/ra *m/f*, *Lat Am* peinador/ra *m/f*.

hairdryer *n* secador de pelo *m*.

hairless *adj* calvo/va.

hairnet *n* redecilla *f*.

hairpiece *n* tupé *m*.

hairpin *n* horquilla *f*.

hairpin curve *n* curva muy cerrada *f*.

hair remover *n* depilatorio *m*.

hairspray *n* laca *f*.

hairstyle *n* peinado *m*.

hairy *adj* peludo/da, cabelludo/da.

hale adj sano/na, vigoroso/sa.
half n mitad f; * adj medio/dia.
half-caste adj mestizo/za.
half-hearted adj indiferente.
half-hour n media hora f.
half-moon n media luna f.
half-price adj a mitad de precio.
half step n (mus) semitono m.
half-time n descanso m.
halfway adv a medio camino.
hall n vestíbulo m; hall m, Lat Am jol m.
hallmark n contraste m.
hallow vt consagrar, santificar.
hallucination n alucinación f.
halo n halo m.
halt vi parar; * n parada f; alto m.
halve vt partir por la mitad.
ham n jamón m.
hamburger n hamburguesa f.
hammer n martillo m; * vt martillar.
hammock n hamaca f.
hamper n cesto f; * vt estorbar.
hamstring vt desjarretar.
hand n mano f; brazo m; aguja f; at ~ a mano; * vt alargar.
handbag n cartera f, Lat Am sobre m.
handbell n campanilla f.
handbook n manual m.
handbrake n freno de mano m.
handcuff n esposa f.
handful n puñado m.
handicap n desventaja f.
handicapped adj minusválido/da.
handicraft n artesanía f.
handiwork n obra f.
handkerchief n pañuelo m.
handle n mango, puño m; asa; Lat Am manija f; * vt manejar; tratar.
handlebars npl manillar m, Lat Am manubrio m.
handling n manejo m.
handrail n pasamanos m.
handshake n apretón de manos m.
handsome adj guapo/pa; ~ly adv primorosamente.
handwriting n letra f.
handy adj práctico/ca; diestro/tra.
hang vt colgar; ahorcar; * vi colgar; ser ahorcado/da.
hanger n percha f.
hanger-on n parásito m.
hangings npl tapicería f.
hangman n verdugo m.
hangover n resaca f.
hang-up n complejo m.
hanker vi ansiar, apetecer.
haphazard adj fortuito/ta.
hapless adj desgraciado/da.
happen vi pasar; acontecer, acaecer.
happening n suceso m.
happily adv felizmente.

happiness n felicidad f.
happy adj feliz.
harangue n arenga f; * vi arengar.
harass vt cansar, fatigar.
harbinger n precursor m.
harbor n puerto m; * vt albergar.
hard adj duro/ra, firme; difícil; penoso/sa; severo/ra, rígido/da; ~ of hearing medio sordo/da; ~ by muy cerca.
harden vt (vi) endurecer(se).
hard-headed adj realista.
hard-hearted adj duro de corazón, insensible.
hardiness n robustez f.
hardly adv apenas.
hardness n dureza f; dificultad f; severidad f.
hardship n penas fpl.
hard-up adj sin plata.
hardware n hardware m; quincallería f.
hardwearing adj resistente.
hardy adj fuerte, robusto/ta.
hare n liebre f.
hare-brained adj atolondrado/da.
hare-lipped adj labihendido/da.
haricot n alubia f.
harlequin n arlequín m.
harm n mal, daño m; perjuicio m; * vt dañar.
harmful adj perjudicial.
harmless adj inocuo/cua.
harmonic adj armónico/ca.
harmonious adj armonioso/sa; ~ly adv armoniosamente.
harmonize vt armonizar.
harmony n armonía f.
harness n arreos de un caballo mpl; * vt enjaezar.
harp n arpa f.
harpist n arpista m/f.
harpoon n arpón m.
harpsichord n clavicordio m.
harrow n grada f; rastro m.
harry vt hostigar.
harsh adj duro/ra; austero/ra; ~ly adv severamente.
harshness n aspereza, dureza f; austeridad f.
harvest n cosecha f; * vt cosechar.
harvester n cosechadora f.
hash n hachís m; picadillo m.
hassock n cojín de paja m.
haste n apuro m; to be in ~ estar apurado/da.
hasten vt acelerar, apresurar; * vi tener prisa.
hastily adv precipitadamente.
hastiness n precipitación f.
hasty adj apresurado/da.
hat n sombrero m.
hatbox n sombrerera f.
hatch vt incubar; tramar; to ~ a plot/scheme zurcir; * n escotilla f.
hatchback n tres puertas, cinco puertas m invar.
hatchet n hacha f.
hatchway n (mar) escotilla f.
hate n odio, aborrecimiento m; * vt odiar, detestar.

hateful adj odioso/sa.

hatred n odio, aborrecimiento m.

hatter n sombrerero m.

haughtily adv orgullosamente.

haughtiness n orgullo m; altivez f.

haughty adj altanero/ra, orgulloso/sa.

haul vt tirar; * n botín m.

hauler n transportista m/f.

haunch n anca f.

haunt vt frecuentar, rondar; * n guarida f; costumbre f.

have vt haber; tener; poseer.

haven n asilo m; puerto m.

haversack n mochila f.

havoc n estrago m.

hawk n halcón m; * vi cazar con halcón.

hawthorn n espino blanco m.

hay n heno m.

hay fever n fiebre del heno f.

hayloft n henil m.

haystack n almiar m.

hazard n riesgo m; * vt arriesgar.

hazardous adj arriesgado/da, peli-groso/sa.

haze n niebla f.

hazel n avellano m; * adj castaño/ña.

hazelnut n avellana f.

hazy adj oscuro/ra.

he pn él.

head n cabeza f; jefe m; juicio m; * vt encabezar; **to ~ for** dirigirse a.

headache n dolor de cabeza m.

headdress n cofia f; tocado m.

headland n promontorio m.

headlight n faro m, Lat Am foco m.

headline n titular m.

headlong adv precipitadamente.

headmaster n director m.

head office n oficina central f.

headphones npl auriculares mpl, Lat Am audífonos mpl.

headquarters npl (mil) cuartel general m; sede central f.

headroom n altura f.

headstrong adj testarudo/da, cabe-zudo/da.

headwaiter n maître m.

headway n progresos mpl.

heady adj cabezón/ona.

heal vt, vi curar.

health n salud f; brindis m invar.

healthiness n sanidad f.

healthy adj sano/na.

heap n montón m; * vt amontonar.

hear vt oír; escuchar; * vi oír; escuchar.

hearing n oído m.

hearing aid n audífono m.

hearsay n rumor m; fama f.

hearse n coche fúnebre m.

heart n corazón m; **by ~** de memoria; **with all my ~** con toda mi alma.

heart attack n infarto, infarto de miocardio m.

heartbreaking adj desgarrador.

heartburn n ardor de estómago m

heart failure n fallo cardíaco m.

heartfelt adj sincero/ra.

hearth n hogar m.

heartily adv sinceramente, cordialmente.

heartiness n cordialidad, sinceridad f.

heartless adj cruel; **~ly** adv cruelmente.

hearty adj cordial.

heat n calor m; * vt calentar.

heater n calentador m.

heather n (bot) brezo m.

heathen n pagano/na m/f; **~ish** adj salvaje.

heating n calefacción f.

heat wave n ola de calor f.

heave vt alzar; tirar; * n tirón m.

heaven n cielo m.

heavenly adj divino/na.

heavily adv pesadamente.

heaviness n pesadez f.

heavy adj pesado/da; opresivo/va.

Hebrew n hebreo m.

heckle vt interrumpir.

hectic adj agitado/da.

hedge n seto m; * vt cercar con seto.

hedgehog n erizo m.

heed vt hacer caso de; * n cuidado m; atención f.

heedless adj descuidado/da, negligente; **~ly** adv negligentemente.

heel n talón m; **to take to one's ~s** apretar los talones, huir.

hefty adj grande.

heifer n ternera f.

height n altura f; altitud f.

heighten vt realzar; adelantar, mejorar; exaltar.

heinous adj atroz.

heir n heredero/ra m/f; **~ apparent** heredero/ra forzoso/sa m/f.

heiress n heredera f.

heirloom n reliquia de familia f.

helicopter n helicóptero m.

hell n infierno m.

hellish adj infernal.

helm n (mar) timón m.

helmet n casco m.

help vt, vi ayudar, socorrer; **I cannot ~ it** no puedo remediarlo; no lo puedo evitar; * n ayuda f; socorro, remedio m.

helper n ayudante m/f.

helpful adj útil.

helping n ración f.

helpless adj indefenso/sa; **~ly** adv irremediablemente.

helter-skelter adv a trochemoche, en desorden.

hem n ribete m; * vt ribetear.

he-man n macho m.

hemisphere n hemisferio m.

hemorrhage n hemorragia f.

hemorrhoids npl hemorroides mpl.

hemp n cáñamo m.

hen n gallina f.

henchman *n* secuaz *m*.

henceforth, henceforward *adv* de aquí en adelante.

henhouse *n* gallinero *m*.

hepatitis *n* hepatitis *f*.

her *pn* su; ella; de ella; a ella.

herald *n* heraldo *m*.

heraldry *n* heráldica *f*.

herb *n* hierba *f*; ~s *pl* hierbas *fpl*.

herbaceous *adj* herbáceo/cea.

herbalist *n* herbolario *m*.

herbivorous *adj* herbívoro/ra.

herd *n* rebaño *m*.

here *adv* aquí, acá.

hereabout(s) *adv* aquí alrededor.

hereafter *adv* en el futuro.

hereby *adv* por esto.

hereditary *adj* hereditario/ria.

heredity *n* herencia *f*.

heresy *n* herejía *f*.

heretic *n* hereje *m/f*; * *adj* herético/ca.

herewith *adv* con esto.

heritage *n* patrimonio *m*.

hermetic *adj* hermético/ca; ~ly *adv* herméticamente.

hermit *n* ermitaño/ña *m/f*.

hermitage *n* ermita *f*.

hernia *n* hernia *f*.

hero *n* héroe *m*.

heroic *adj* heroico/ca; ~ally *adv* heroicamente.

heroine *n* heroína *f*.

heroism *n* heroísmo *m*.

heron *n* garza *f*.

herring *n* arenque *m*.

hers *pn* suyo, de ella.

herself *pn* ella misma.

hesitant *adj* vacilante.

hesitate *vt* dudar; tardar.

hesitation *n* duda, irresolución *f*.

heterogeneous *adj* heterogéneo/nea.

heterosexual *adj*, *n* heterosexual *m*.

hew *vt* tajar; cortar; picar.

heyday *n* apogeo *m*.

hi! *excl* ¡hola!

hiatus *n* (*gr*) hiato *m*.

hibernate *vi* invernar.

hiccup *n* hipo *m*; * *vi* tener hipo.

hickory *n* nogal americana *m*.

hide *vt* esconder; * *n* cuero *m*; piel *f*.

hideaway *n* escondite *m*.

hideous *adj* horrible; ~ly *adv* horriblemente.

hiding place *n* escondite, escondrijo *m*.

hierarchy *n* jerarquía *f*.

hieroglyphic *adj* jeroglífico/ca; * *n* jeroglífico *m*.

hi-fi *n* estéreo, hi-fi *m*.

higgledy-piggledy *adv* confusamente.

high *adj* alto/ta; elevado/da.

high altar *n* altar mayor *m*.

highchair *n* silla alta *f*.

high-handed *adj* despótico/ca.

highlands *npl* tierras montañosas, tierras altas *fpl*.

highlight *n* punto culminante *m*.

highly *adv* en sumo grado.

highness *n* altura *f*; alteza *f*.

high school *n* centro de enseñanza secundaria *m*; escuela secundaria *f*.

highly strung *adj* hipertenso/sa.

high water *n* marea alta *f*.

highway *n* carretera *f*.

hike *vi* ir de excursión.

hijack *vt* secuestrar.

hijacker *n* secuestrador/a *m/f*.

hilarious *adj* alegre.

hill *n* colina *f*.

hillock *n* colina *f*.

hillside *n* ladera *f*.

hilly *adj* montañoso/sa.

hilt *n* puño de espada *m*.

him *pn* le, lo, el.

himself *pn* él mismo, se, si mismo.

hind *adj* trasero/ra, posterior; * *n* cierva *f*.

hinder *vt* impedir.

hindrance *n* impedimento, obstáculo *m*.

hindmost *adj* postrero/ra.

hindquarter *n* cuarto trasero *m*.

hindsight *n*: with ~ en retrospectiva.

hinge *n* bisagra *f*.

hint *n* indirecta *f*; * *vt* insinuar; sugerir.

hip *n* cadera *f*.

hippopotamus *n* hipopótamo *m*.

hire *vt* alquilar; * *n* alquiler *m*.

his *pn* su, suyo, de él.

Hispanic *adj* hispano/na; hispánico/ca; * *n* hispanoamericano/na *m/f*.

hiss *vt*, *vi* silbar.

historian *n* historiador/a *m/f*.

historic(al) *adj* histórico/ca; ~ally *adv* históricamente.

history *n* historia *f*.

histrionic *adj* teatral.

hit *vt* golpear; alcanzar; zumbar; to ~ each other *vr* zumbarse; * *n* golpe *m*; éxito *m*.

hitch *vt* atar; * *n* problema *m*.

hitch-hike *vi* hacer autoestop.

hitch-hiker *n* autoestopista *m/f*.

hitch-hiking *n* autoestop *f*.

hitherto *adv* hasta ahora, hasta aquí.

hive *n* colmena *f*.

HIV-negative *adj* seronegativo/va.

HIV-positive *adj* seropositivo/va.

hoard *n* montón *m*; tesoro escondido *m*; * *vt* acumular.

hoarfrost *n* escarcha *f*.

hoarse *adj* ronco/ca; ~ly *adv* roncamente.

hoarseness *n* ronquera, carraspera *f*.

hoax *n* trampa *f*; * *vt* engañar, burlar.

hobble *vi* cojear.

hobby *n* pasatiempo *m*, afición *f*.

hobbyhorse *n* caballo de batalla *m*.

hobo *n* vagabundo/da *m/f*.

hockey *n* hockey *m*.

hodgepodge *n* mezcolanza *f*.

hoe n azadón m; * vt azadonar.

hog n cerdo, puerco m, LatAm chancho m; (col) cochino m.

hoist vt alzar; * n grúa f.

hold vt tener; detener; contener; celebrar; **to ~ on to** agarrarse a; * vi valer; * n presa f; poder m.

holder n poseedor/a m/f; titular m/f.

holding n tenencia, posesión f.

hold up n atraco m; retraso m.

hole n agujero m.

holiness n santidad f.

hollow adj hueco/ca; * n hoyo m; * vt excavar, ahuecar.

holly n (bot) acebo m.

hollyhock n malva hortense f.

holocaust n holocausto m.

holster n pistolera f.

holy adj santo/ta, pío, pía; consagra-do/da.

holy water n agua bendita f.

holy week n semana santa f.

homage n homenaje m.

home n casa f; patria f; domicilio m; **~ly** adj casero/ra.

home address n domicilio m.

home improvement n bricolaje m.

homeless adj sin casa.

homeliness n simpleza f.

homely adj casero/ra.

home-made adj casero/ra.

homeopathist n homeópata m/f.

homeopathy n homeopatía f.

home shopping program (TV) n teletienda f.

homesick adj nostálgico/ca.

homesickness n nostalgia f.

hometown n ciudad natal f.

homeward adj hacia casa; hacia su país.

homework n deberes mpl.

homicidal adj homicida.

homicide n homicidio m; homicida m/f.

homogeneous adj homogéneo/nea.

homosexual adj, n homosexual m.

honest adj honrado/da; **~ly** adv honradamente.

honesty n honradez f.

honey n miel f.

honeycomb n panal m.

honeymoon n luna de miel f.

honeysuckle n (bot) madreselva f.

honor n honra f; honor m; * vt honrar.

honorable adj honorable; ilustre.

honorably adv honorablemente.

honorary adj honorario/ria.

hood n capo m; capucha f.

hoodlum n matón m.

hoof n pezuña f.

hook n gancho m; anzuelo m; **by ~ or by crook** de un modo u otro; * vt enganchar.

hooked adj encorvado/da.

hooligan n gamberro/rra m/f.

hoop n aro m.

hop n (bot) lúpulo m; salto m; * vi saltar, brincar.

hope n esperanza f; * vi esperar.

hopeful adj esperanzador/a; **~ly** adv con esperanza.

hopefulness n buena esperanza f.

hopeless adj desesperado/da; **~ly** adv sin esperanza.

hopscotch n tejo m.

horde n horda f.

horizon n horizonte m.

horizontal adj horizontal; **~ly** adv horizontalmente.

hormone n hormona f.

horn n cuerno m; (auto) sirena f.

horned adj cornudo/da.

hornet n avispón m.

horny adj calloso/sa.

horoscope n horóscopo m.

horrendous adj horrendo/da.

horrible adj horrible, terrible.

horribly adv horriblemente; enormemente.

horrid adj horrible.

horrific adj horroroso/sa.

horrify vt horrorizar.

horror n horror, terror m.

horror film n película de horror f.

hors d'oeuvre n entremeses mpl.

horse n caballo m; caballete m.

horseback adv: **on ~** a caballo.

horse-breaker n domador/a de caballos m/f.

horse chestnut n castaño de Indias m.

horsefly n moscarda f; moscardón m.

horseman n jinete m.

horsemanship n equitación f.

horsepower n caballo de fuerza m.

horse race n carrera de caballos f.

horseracing n hípica f.

horseradish n rábano silvestre m.

horseshoe n herradura de caballo f.

horsewoman n jineta f.

horticulture n horticultura, jardinería f.

horticulturist n jardinero/ra m/f.

hosepipe n manguera f.

hosiery n calcetería f.

hospitable adj hospitalario/ria.

hospitably adv con hospitalidad.

hospital n hospital m.

hospitality n hospitalidad f.

host n anfitrión m; hostia f.

hostage n rehén m.

hostess n anfitriona f.

hostile adj hostil.

hostility n hostilidad f.

hot adj caliente; cálido/da.

hotbed n semillero m.

hotdog n perro caliente m.

hotel n hotel m.

hotelier n hotelero/ra m/f.

hot-headed adj exaltado/da.

hothouse n invernadero m.

hotline n línea directa f.

hotplate n hornillo m.

hotly *adv* con calor; violentamente.

hound *n* perro de caza *m*.

hour *n* hora *f*.

hour-glass *n* reloj de arena *m*.

hourly *adv* cada hora.

house *n* casa *f*; familia *f*; * *vt* alojar.

houseboat *n* casa flotante *f*.

housebreaker *n* ladrón/ona de casa *m/f*.

housebreaking *n* allanamiento de morada *m*.

household *n* familia *f*.

householder *n* amo de casa, padre de familia *m*; dueño/ña de la casa *m/f*.

housekeeper *n* ama de llaves *f*.

housekeeping *n* trabajos domésticos *mpl*.

house-warming party *n* fiesta de estreno de una casa *f*.

housewife *n* ama de casa *f*.

housework *n* faenas de la casa *fpl*.

housing *n* vivienda *f*.

housing development *n* urbanización *f*.

hovel *n* choza, cabaña *f*.

hover *vi* flotar.

how *adv* cómo, como; ~ **do you do!** ¡encantado!

however *adv* comoquiera, comoquiera que sea, aunque; no obstante.

howl *vi* aullar; * *n* aullido *m*.

hub *n* centro *m*.

hubbub *n* barullo *m*.

hubcap *n* tapacubos *m invar*.

hue *n* color *m*; matiz *m*.

huff *n*: **in a ~** picado/da.

hug *vt* abrazar; * *n* abrazo *m*.

huge *adj* vasto/ta, enorme; ~**ly** *adv* inmensamente.

hulk *n* (*mar*) casco *m*; armatoste *m*.

hull *n* (*mar*) casco *m*.

hum *vi* canturrear.

human *adv* humano/na.

humane *adv* humano/na; benigno/na; ~**ly** *adv* humanamente.

humanist *n* humanista *m/f*.

humanitarian *adj* humanitario/ria.

humanity *n* humanidad *f*.

humanize *vt* humanizar.

humanly *adv* humanamente.

humble *adj* humilde, modesto/ta; * *vt* humillar, postrar.

humbleness *n* humildad *f*.

humbly *adv* con humildad.

humbug *n* tonterías *fpl*.

humdrum *adj* monótono/na.

humid *adj* húmedo/da.

humidity *n* humedad *f*.

humiliate *vt* humillar.

humiliation *n* humillación *f*.

humility *n* humildad *f*.

humming *n* zumbido *m*.

humming-bird *n* colibrí *m*, *Lat Am* chupaflor *m*, *Lat Am* picaflor *m*.

humor *n* sentido del humor *m*, humor *m*; jocosidad *f*; * *vt* complacer.

humorist *n* humorista *m/f*.

humorous *adj* gracioso/sa; ~**ly** *adv* con gracia.

hump *n* giba, joroba *f*.

hunch *n* corazonada *f*; ~**backed** *adj* jorobado/da, jiboso/sa.

hundred *adj* ciento; * *n* centenar *m*; un ciento.

hundredth *adj* centésimo.

hundredweight *n* quintal *m*.

hunger *n* hambre *f*; * *vi* hambrear.

hunger strike *n* huelga de hambre *f*.

hungrily *adv* con apetito.

hungry *adj* hambriento/ta, *Lat Am* hambreado/da.

hunt *vt* cazar; perseguir; buscar; * *vi* andar a caza; * *n* caza *f*.

hunter *n* cazador/a *m/f*.

hunting *n* caza *f*.

huntsman *n* cazador *m*.

hurdle *n* valla *f*.

hurl *vt* tirar con violencia; arrojar.

hurricane *n* huracán *m*.

hurried *adj* hecho/cha de prisa; ~**ly** *adv* con prisa.

hurry *vt* acelerar, apresurar; * *vi* apresurarse; * *n* prisa *f*.

hurt *vt* hacer daño; ofender; * *n* mal, daño *m*.

hurtful *adj* dañoso/sa; ~**ly** *adv* dañosamente.

hurtle *vr* zamparse.

husband *n* marido *m*.

husbandry *n* agricultura *f*.

hush! ¡chitón!, ¡silencio!; * *vt* hacer callar; * *vi* estar quieto/ta.

husk *n* cáscara *f*.

huskiness *n* ronquedad *f*.

husky *adj* ronco/ca.

hustings *n* tribuna para las elecciones *f*.

hustle *vt* empujar con fuerza.

hut *n* cabaña, barraca *f*.

hutch *n* conejera *f*.

hyacinth *n* jacinto *m*.

hydrant *n* boca de incendios *f*.

hydraulic *adj* hidráulico/ca; ~**s** *npl* hidráulica *f*.

hydroelectric *adj* hidroeléctrico/ca.

hydrofoil *n* hidroala *f*.

hydrogen *n* hidrógeno *m*.

hydrophobia *n* hidrofobia *f*.

hydroplane *n* hidroavión *m*.

hyena *n* hiena *f*.

hygiene *n* higiene *f*.

hygienic *adj* higiénico/ca.

hymn *n* himno *m*.

hyperbole *n* hipérbole *f*; exageración *f*.

hypermarket *n* hipermercado *m*.

hyphen *n* (*gr*) guión *m*.

hypochondria *n* hipocondria *f*.

hypochondriac *adj*, *n* hipocondríaco/ca *m/f*.

hypocrisy *n* hipocresía *f*.

hypocrite *n* hipócrita *m/f*.

hypocritical *adj* hipócrita.

hypothesis *n* hipótesis *f*.

hypothetical *adj* hipotético/ca; ~**ly** *adv* hipotéticamente.

hysterical *adj* histérico/ca.
hysterics *npl* histeria *f.*

I

I *pn* yo; ~ myself yo mismo.
ice *n* hielo *m*; * *vt* helar.
ice-axe *n* piqueta *f.*
iceberg *n* iceberg *m.*
ice-bound *adj* rodeado/da de hielos.
icebox *n* nevera *f.*
ice cream *n* helado *m.*
ice rink *n* pista de hielo *f.*
ice skating *n* patinaje sobre hielo *m.*
icicle *n* carámbano *m.*
iconoclast *n* iconoclasta *m/f.*
icy *adj* helado/da; frío/ría.
idea *n* idea *f.*
ideal *adj* ideal; ~ly *adv* idealmente.
idealist *n* idealista *m/f.*
identical *adj* idéntico/ca.
identification *n* identificación *f.*
identify *vt* identificar.
identity *n* identidad *f.*
identity card *n* carnet *m* de identidad, *Lat Am*
cédula *f* de identidad.
ideology *n* ideología *f.*
idiom *n* idioma *m.*
idiomatic *adj* idiomático/ca.
idiosyncrasy *n* idiosincrasia *f.*
idiot *n* idiota, necio/cia *m/f.*
idiotic *adj* tonto/ta, bobo/ba.
idle *adj* desocupado/da; holgazán/zana; inútil.
idleness *n* pereza *f.*
idler *n* holgazán/zana *m/f*; zángano *m.*
idly *adv* ociosamente; vanamente.
idol *n* ídolo *m.*
idolatry *n* idolatría *f.*
idolize *vt* idolatrar.
idyllic *adj* idílico/ca.
i.e. *adv* esto es.
if *conj* si, aunque; ~ not si no.
igloo *n* iglú *m.*
ignite *vt* encender.
ignition *n* (*chem*) ignición *f*; encendido *m.*
ignition key *n* llave de contacto *f.*
ignoble *adj* innoble; bajo/ja.
ignominious *adj* ignominioso/sa; ~ly *adv*
ignominiosamente.
ignominy *n* ignominia, infamia *f.*
ignoramus *n* ignorante, tonto/ta *m/f.*
ignorance *n* ignorancia *f.*
ignorant *adj* ignorante; ~ly *adv*
ignorantemente.
ignore *vt* no hacer caso de.
ill *adj* malo/la, enfermo/ma; * *n* mal, infortunio
m; * *adv* mal.
ill-advised *adj* imprudente.
illegal *adj*, ~ly *adv* ilegal(mente).
illegality *n* ilegalidad *f.*

illegible *adj* ilegible.
illegibly *adv* de modo ilegible.
illegitimacy *n* ilegitimidad *f.*
illegitimate *adj* ilegítimo/ma; ~ly *adv*
ilegítimamente.
ill feeling *n* rencor *m.*
illicit *adj* ilícito/ta.
illiterate *adj* analfabeto/ta.
illness *n* enfermedad *f.*
illogical *adj* ilógico/ca.
ill-timed *adj* inoportuno/na.
ill-treat *vt* maltratar.
illuminate *vt* iluminar.
illumination *n* iluminación *f.*
illusion *n* ilusión *f.*
illusory *adj* ilusorio/ria.
illustrate *vt* ilustrar; explicar.
illustration *n* ilustración *f*; elucidación *f.*
illustrative *adj* explicativo/va.
illustrious *adj* ilustre, insigne.
ill-will *n* rencor *m.*
image *n* imagen *f.*
imagery *n* imágenes *fpl.*
imaginable *adj* concebible.
imaginary *adj* imaginario/ria.
imagination *n* imaginación *f.*
imaginative *adj* imaginativo/va.
imagine *vt* imaginarse; idear, inventar.
imbalance *n* desequilibrio *m.*
imbecile *adj* imbécil, necio/cia.
imbibe *vt* beber.
imbue *vt* infundir.
imitate *vt* imitar, copiar.
imitation *n* imitación, copia *f.*
imitative *adj* imitativo/va.
immaculate *adj* inmaculado/da, puro/ra.
immaterial *adj* poco importante.
immature *adj* inmaduro/ra.
immeasurable *adj* inconmensurable.
immeasurably *adv* inmensamente.
immediate *adj* inmediato/ta; ~ly *adv*
inmediatamente; ya.
immense *adj* inmenso/sa; vasto/ta; ~ly *adv*
inmensamente.
immensity *n* inmensidad *f.*
immerse *vt* sumergir.
immersion *n* inmersión *f.*
immigrant *n* inmigrante *m/f.*
immigrate *vi* inmigrar.
immigration *n* inmigración *f.*
imminent *adj* inminente.
immobile *adj* inmóvil.
immobility *n* inmovilidad *f.*
immoderate *adj* inmoderado/da, exce-sivo/va;
~ly *adv* inmoderadamente.
immodest *adj* inmodesto/ta.
immoral *adj* inmoral.
immorality *n* inmoralidad *f.*
immortal *adj* inmortal.
immortality *n* inmortalidad *f.*
immortalize *vt* inmortalizar, eternizar.

immune *adj* inmune.
immunity *n* inmunidad *f*.
immunize *vt* inmunizar.
immutable *adj* inmutable.
imp *n* diablillo, duende *m*.
impact *n* impacto *m*.
impair *vt* disminuir.
impale *vt* empalar.
impalpable *adj* impalpable.
impart *vt* comunicar.
impartial *adj*, **~ly** *adv* imparcial (mente).
impartiality *n* imparcialidad *f*.
impassable *adj* intransitable.
impasse *n* punto muerto *m*.
impassive *adj* impasible.
impatience *n* impaciencia *f*.
impatient *adj*, **~ly** *adv* impaciente (mente).
impeach *vt* acusar, denunciar.
impeccable *adj* impecable.
impecunious *adj* indigente.
impede *vt* estorbar.
impediment *n* obstáculo *m*.
impel *vt* impeler, impulsar.
impending *adj* inminente.
impenetrable *adj* impenetrable.
imperative *adj* imperativo/va.
imperceptible *adj* imperceptible.
imperceptibly *adv* imperceptiblemente.
imperfect *adj* imperfecto/ta, defec-tuoso/sa; **~ly** imperfectamente *adv*; * *n* (*gr*) pretérito imperfecto *m*.
imperfection *n* imperfección *f*, defecto *m*.
imperial *adj* imperial.
imperialism *n* imperialismo *m*.
imperious *adj* imperioso/sa; arrogante; **~ly** *adv* imperiosamente, arrogantemente.
impermeable *adj* impermeable.
impersonal *adj*, **~ly** *adv* imperso-nal(mente).
impersonate *vt* hacerse pasar por; imitar.
impertinence *n* impertinencia *f*; descaro *m*.
impertinent *adj* impertinente; **~ly** *adv* impertinentemente.
imperturbable *adj* imperturbable.
impervious *adj* impermeable.
impetuosity *n* impetuosidad *f*.
impetuous *adj* impetuoso/sa; **~ly** *adv* impetuosamente.
impetus *n* ímpetu *m*.
impiety *n* impiedad *f*.
impinge (on) *vt* tener influjo en.
impious *adj* impío/pía, irreligioso/sa.
implacable *adj* implacable.
implacably *adv* implacablemente.
implant *vt* implantar; plantear.
implement *n* herramienta *f*; utensilio *m*.
implicate *vt* implicar.
implication *n* implicación *f*.
implicit *adj* implícito/ta; **~ly** *adv* implícitamente.
implore *vt* suplicar.
imply *vt* suponer.
impolite *adj* maleducado/da.

impoliteness *n* falta de educación *f*.
impolitic *adj* imprudente; impolíti-co/ca.
import *vt* importar; * *n* importación *f*.
importance *n* importancia *f*.
important *adj* importante.
importation *n* importación *f*.
importer *n* importador/a *m/f*.
importunate *adj* importuno/na.
importune *vt* importunar.
importunity *n* importunidad *f*.
impose *vt* imponer.
imposing *adj* imponente.
imposition *n* imposición, carga *f*.
impossibility *n* imposibilidad *f*.
impossible *adj* imposible.
impostor *n* impostor *m*.
impotence *n* impotencia *f*.
impotent *adj* impotente; **~ly** *adv* sin poder.
impound *vt* embargar.
impoverish *vt* empobrecer.
impoverished *adj* necesitado/da.
impoverishment *n* empobrecimiento *m*.
impracticability *n* inviavilidad *f*.
impracticable *adj* impracticable, inviable.
impractical *adj* poco práctico/ca.
imprecation *n* imprecación, maldición *f*.
imprecise *adj* impreciso/sa.
impregnable *adj* inexpugnable.
impregnate *vt* impregnar.
impregnation *n* fecundación *f*; impregnación *f*.
impress *vt* impresionar.
impression *n* impresión *f*; edición *f*.
impressionable *adj* impresionable.
impressive *adj* impresionante.
imprint *n* sello *m*; * *vt* imprimir; estampar.
imprison *vt* encarcelar.
imprisonment *n* encarcelamiento *m*.
improbability *n* improbabilidad *f*.
improbable *adj* improbable.
impromptu *adj* de improviso.
improper *adj* impropio/pia, indecente; **~ly** *adv* impropiamente.
impropriety *n* impropiedad *f*.
improve *vt*, *vi* mejorar, *Lat Am* repuntar.
improvement *n* progreso *m*, mejora *f*.
improvident *adj* imprévido/da, imprudente.
improvise *vt* improvisar.
imprudence *n* imprudencia *f*.
imprudent *adj* imprudente.
impudence *n* impudencia *f*.
impudent *adj* impudente; **~ly** *adv* desvergonzadamente.
impugn *vt* impugnar.
impulse *n* impulso *m*.
impulsive *adj* impulsivo/va.
impunity *n* impunidad *f*.
impure *adj* impuro/ra; **~ly** *adv* impuramente.
impurity *n* impureza *f*.
in *prep* en.
inability *n* incapacidad *f*.
inaccessible *adj* inaccesible.

inaccuracy *n* inexactitud *f*.
inaccurate *adj* inexacto/ta.
inaction *n* inacción *f*.
inactive *adj* inactivo/va, perezoso/sa.
inactivity *n* inactividad *f*.
inadequate *adj* inadecuado/da, defec-tuoso/sa.
inadmissible *adj* inadmisible.
inadvertently *adv* sin querer.
inalienable *adj* inalienable.
inane *adj* necio/cia.
inanimate *adj* inanimado/da.
inapplicable *adj* inaplicable.
inappropriate *adj* impropio/pia.
inasmuch *adv* visto que; en tanto en cuanto.
inattentive *adj* desatento/ta.
inaudible *adj* inaudible.
inaugural *adj* inaugural.
inaugurate *vt* inaugurar.
inauguration *n* inauguración *f*.
inauspicious *adj* poco propicio/cia.
in-between *adj* intermedio/dia.
inborn, inbred *adj* innato/ta.
incalculable *adj* incalculable.
incandescent *adj* incandescente.
incantation *n* conjuro *m*.
incapable *adj* incapaz.
incapacitate *vt* inhabilitar.
incapacity *n* incapacidad *f*.
incarcerate *vt* encarcelar.
incarnate *adj* encarnado/da.
incarnation *n* encarnación *f*.
incautious *adj* incauto/ta; **~ly** *adv* incautamente.
incendiary *n* bomba incendiaria *f*.
incense *n* incienso *m*; * *vt* exasperar.
incentive *n* incentivo *m*.
inception *n* principio *m*.
incessant *adj* incesante, constante; **~ly** *adv* continuamente.
incest *n* incesto *m*.
incestuous *adj* incestuoso/sa.
inch *n* pulgada *f*; **~ by ~** palmo a palmo.
incidence *n* frecuencia *f*.
incident *n* incidente *m*.
incidental *adj* casual; **~ly** *adv* a propósito.
incinerator *n* incinerador *m*.
incipient *adj* incipiente.
incise *vt* tajar, cortar.
incision *n* incisión *f*.
incisive *adj* incisivo/va.
incisor *n* incisivo *m*.
incite *vt* incitar, estimular.
inclement *adj* feo, fea.
inclination *n* inclinación, propensión *f*.
incline *vt* (*vi*) inclinar(se); * *n* cuesta *f*.
include *vt* incluir, comprender.
including *prep* incluso.
inclusion *n* inclusión *f*.
inclusive *adj* inclusivo/va.
incognito *adv* de incógnito.
incoherence *n* incoherencia *f*.

incoherent *adj* incoherente, inconsecuente; **~ly** *adv* de modo incoherente.
income *n* renta *f*; ingresos *mpl*.
income tax *n* impuesto sobre la renta *m*.
incoming *adj* entrante.
incomparable *adj* incomparable.
incomparably *adv* incomparablemente.
incompatibility *n* incompatibilidad *f*.
incompatible *adj* incompatible.
incompetence *n* incompetencia *f*.
incompetent *adj*, **~ly** *adv* incompetente(mente).
incomplete *adj* incompleto/ta.
incomprehensibility *n* incomprensibilidad *f*.
incomprehensible *adj* incomprensible.
inconceivable *adj* inconcebible.
inconclusive *adj* no concluyente; **~ly** *adv* sin conclusión.
incongruity *n* incongruencia *f*.
incongruous *adj* incongruo/rua; **~ly** *adv* incongruamente.
inconsequential *adj* inconsecuente.
inconsiderate *adj* desconsiderado/da; **~ly** *adv* desconsideradamente.
inconsistency *n* inconsecuencia *f*.
inconsistent *adj* inconsecuente.
inconsolable *adj* inconsolable.
inconspicuous *adj* discreto/ta.
incontinence *n* incontinencia *f*.
incontinent *adj* incontinente.
incontrovertible *adj* incontrovertible.
inconvenience *n* incomodidad *f*; * *vt* incomodar.
inconvenient *adj* incómodo/da; **~ly** *adv* incómodamente.
incorporate *vt* (*vi*) incorporar(se).
incorporated company (inc) *n* sociedad anónima *f*.
incorporation *n* incorporación *f*.
incorrect *adj* incorrecto/ta; **~ly** *adv* incorrectamente.
incorrigible *adj* incorregible.
incorruptibility *n* incorruptibilidad *f*.
incorruptible *adj* incorruptible.
increase *vt* acrecentar, aumentar; * *vi* crecer; * *n* aumento *m*.
increasing *adj* creciente; **~ly** *adv* cada vez más.
incredible *adj* increíble.
incredulity *n* incredulidad *f*.
incredulous *adj* incrédulo/la.
increment *n* incremento *m*.
incriminate *vt* incriminar.
incrust *vt* incrustar.
incubate *vi* incubar.
incubator *n* incubadora *f*.
inculcate *vt* inculcar.
incumbent *adj* obligatorio/ria; * *n* beneficiado/da *m/f*.
incur *vt* incurrir.
incurability *n* lo incurable.
incurable *adj* incurable.
incursion *n* incursión, invasión *f*.

indebted adj agradecido/da.

indecency n indecencia f.

indecent adj indecente; **~ly** adv indecentemente.

indecision n irresolución f.

indecisive adj indeciso/sa.

indecorous adj indecente.

indeed adv verdaderamente, de veras.

indefatigable adj incansable.

indefinite adj indefinido/da; **~ly** adv indefinidamente.

indelible adj indeleble.

indelicacy n falta de delicadeza, grosería f.

indelicate adj poco delicado/da.

indemnify vt indemnizar.

indemnity n indemnidad f.

indent vt mellar.

independence n independencia f.

independent adj independiente; **~ly** adv independientemente.

indescribable adj indescriptible.

indestructible adj indestructible.

indeterminate adj indeterminado/da.

index n índice m.

index card n ficha f.

indexed adj indexado/da.

index finger n dedo índice m.

indicate vt indicar.

indication n indicación f; indicio m.

indicative adj, n (gr) indicativo m.

indicator n indicador m.

indict vt acusar.

indictment n acusación f.

indifference n indiferencia f.

indifferent adj indiferente; **~ly** adv indiferentemente.

indigenous adj indígena.

indigent adj indigente.

indigestible adj indigerible.

indigestion n indigestión f.

indignant adj indignado/da.

indignation n indignación f.

indignity n indignidad f.

indigo n añil m.

indirect adj indirecto/ta; **~ly** adv indirectamente.

indiscreet adj indiscreto/ta; **~ly** adv indiscretamente.

indiscretion n indiscreción f.

indiscriminate adj indistinto/ta; **~ly** adv sin distinción.

indispensable adj indispensable.

indisposed adj indispuesto/ta.

indisposition n indisposición f.

indisputable adj indiscutible.

indisputably adv indisputablemente.

indistinct adj indistinto/ta, confuso/sa; **~ly** adv indistintamente.

indistinguishable adj indistinguible.

individual adj individual; **~ly** adv individualmente; * n individuo m.

individuality n individualidad f.

indivisible adv indivisible; **~bly** adv indivisiblemente.

indoctrinate vt adoctrinar.

indoctrination n adoctrinamiento m.

indolence n indolencia, pereza f.

indolent adj indolente; **~ly** adv con negligencia.

indomitable adj indomable.

indoors adv dentro.

indubitably adv indudablemente.

induce vt inducir, persuadir; causar.

inducement n aliciente m.

induction n inducción f.

indulge vt, vi conceder; ser indulgente.

indulgence n indulgencia f.

indulgent adj indulgente; **~ly** adv de modo indulgente.

industrial adj industrial.

industrialist n industrial m/f.

industrialization n industrialización f.

industrialize vt industrializar.

industrial park n polígono industrial m.

industrious adj trabajador/a.

industry n industria f.

inebriated adj embriagado/da.

inebriation n embriaguez f.

inedible adj incomestible.

ineffable adj inefable.

ineffective, ineffectual adj ineficaz; **~ly** adv sin efecto.

inefficiency n ineficacia f.

inefficient adj ineficaz.

ineligible adj inelegible.

inept adj incompetente.

ineptitude n incompetencia f.

inequality n desigualdad f.

inert adj inerte, perezoso/sa.

inertia n inercia f.

inescapable adj ineludible.

inestimable adj inestimable, inapreciable.

inevitable adj inevitable.

inevitably adv inevitablemente.

inexcusable adj inexcusable.

inexhaustible adj inagotable.

inexorable adj inexorable.

inexpedient adj imprudente.

inexpensive adj económico/ca.

inexperience n inexperiencia f.

inexperienced adj inexperto/ta.

inexpert adj inexperto/ta.

inexplicable adj inexplicable.

inexpressible adj indecible.

inextricably adv indisolublemente.

infallibility n infalibilidad f.

infallible adj infalible; indefectible.

infamous adj vil, infame; **~ly** adv infamemente.

infamy n infamia f.

infancy n infancia f; pequeñez f.

infant n niño/ña m/f.

infanticide n infanticidio m; infanticida m/f.

infantile adj infantil.

infantry *n* infantería *f*.
infatuated *adj* chiflado/da.
infatuation *n* infatuación *f*.
infect *vt* infectar.
infection *n* infección *f*.
infectious *adj* contagioso/sa; infec-cioso/sa.
infer *vt* inferir.
inference *n* inferencia *f*.
inferior *adj* inferior; * *n* subordinado/da *m/f*.
inferiority *n* inferioridad *f*.
infernal *adj* infernal.
inferno *n* infierno *m*.
infest *vt* infestar.
infidel *n* infiel, pagano *m*.
infidelity *n* infidelidad *f*.
infiltrate *vi* infiltrarse.
infinite *adj* infinito/ta; **~ly** *adv* infinitamente.
infinitive *n* infinitivo *m*.
infinity *n* infinito *m*; infinidad *f*.
infirm *adj* enfermo/ma, débil.
infirmary *n* enfermería *f*.
infirmity *n* fragilidad, enfermedad *f*.
inflame *vt* (*vi*) inflamar(se).
inflammation *n* inflamación *f*.
inflammatory *adj* inflamatorio/ria.
inflatable *adj* inflable.
inflate *vt* inflar, hinchar.
inflation *n* inflación *f*.
inflection *n* inflexión *f*; modulación de la voz *f*.
inflexibility *n* inflexibilidad *f*.
inflexible *adj* inflexible; yerto/ta.
inflexibly *adv* inflexiblemente.
inflict *vt* imponer.
influence *n* influencia *f*; * *vt* influir.
influential *adj* influyente.
influenza *n* gripe *f*.
influx *n* afluencia *f*.
inform *vt* informar.
informal *adj* informal.
informality *n* informalidad *f*.
informant *n* informante *m/f*.
information *n* información *f*; **~ superhighway** autopista de la información *f*.
infraction *n* infracción *f*.
infra-red *adj* infrarrojo/ja.
infrastructure *n* infraestructura *f*.
infrequent *adj* raro/ra; **~ly** *adv* raramente.
infringe *vt* infringir; violar.
infringement *n* infracción *f*.
infuriate *vt* enfurecer.
infuse *vt* infundir.
infusion *n* infusión *f*.
ingenious *adj* ingenioso/sa; **~ly** *adv* ingeniosamente.
ingenuity *n* ingeniosidad *f*.
ingenuous *adj* ingenuo/nua, sincero/ra; **~ly** *adv* ingenuamente.
inglorious *adj* ignominioso/sa, ver-gonzoso/sa; **~ly** *adv* ignominiosamente.
ingot *n* lingote *m*.
ingrained *adj* inveterado/da.

ingratiate *vi* congraciarse.
ingratitude *n* ingratitud *f*.
ingredient *n* ingrediente *m*.
inhabit *vt*, *vi* habitar.
inhabitable *adj* habitable.
inhabitant *n* habitante *m/f*.
inhale *vt* inhalar.
inherent *adj* inherente.
inherit *vt* heredar.
inheritance *n* herencia *f*.
inheritor *n* heredero/a *m/f*.
inhibit *vt* inhibir.
inhibited *adj* cohibido/da.
inhibition *n* inhibición *f*.
inhospitable *adj* inhospitalario/ria.
inhospitality *n* inhospitalidad *f*.
inhuman *adj* inhumano/na, cruel; **~ly** *adv* inhumanamente.
inhumanity *n* inhumanidad, crueldad *f*.
inimical *adj* enemigo/ga.
inimitable *adj* inimitable.
iniquitous *adj* inicuo/cua, injusto/ta.
iniquity *n* iniquidad, injusticia *f*.
initial *adj* inicial; * *n* inicial *f*.
initially *adv* al principio.
initiate *vt* iniciar.
initiation *n* principio *m*; iniciación *f*.
initiative *n* iniciativa *f*.
inject *vt* inyectar.
injection *n* inyección *f*.
injudicious *adj* poco juicioso/sa.
injunction *n* entredicho *m*.
injure *vt* herir.
injury *n* daño *m*.
injury time *n* descuento *m*.
injustice *n* injusticia *f*.
ink *n* tinta *f*.
inkling *n* sospecha *f*.
inkstand *n* tintero *m*.
inlaid *adj* taraceado/da.
inland *adj* interior; * *adv* tierra -adentro.
in-laws *npl* suegros *mpl*.
inlay *vt* taracear.
inlet *n* ensenada *f*.
inmate *n* preso *m*.
inmost *adj* más íntimo/ma.
inn *n* posada *f*; mesón *m*.
innate *adj* innato/ta.
inner *adj* interior.
innermost *adj* más íntimo/ma.
inner tube *n* cámara *f*.
innkeeper *n* posadero/ra, mesonero/ra *m/f*.
innocence *n* inocencia *f*.
innocent *adj* inocente; **~ly** *adv* inocentemente.
innocuous *adj* inocuo/cua; **~ly** *adv* inocentemente.
innovate *vt* innovar.
innovation *n* innovación *f*.
innuendo *n* indirecta, insinuación *f*.
innumerable *adj* innumerable.
inoculate *vt* inocular.

inoculation n inoculación f.

inoffensive adj inofensivo/va.

inopportune adj inconveniente, in-oportuno/na.

inordinately adv desmesuradamente.

inorganic adj inorgánico/ca.

inpatient n paciente interno/na m/f.

input n entrada f.

inquest n encuesta judicial f.

inquire, enquire vt, vi preguntar; to ~ about informarse de; to ~ after vt preguntar por; to ~ into vt investigar, indagar, inquirir.

inquiry n pesquisa f.

inquisition n inquisición f.

inquisitive adj curioso/sa.

inroad n incursión, invasión f.

insane adj loco/ca, demente.

insanity n locura f.

insatiable adj insaciable.

inscribe vt inscribir; dedicar.

inscription n inscripción f; dedicatoria f.

inscrutable adj inescrutable.

insect n insecto m.

insecticide n insecticida m.

insecure adj inseguro/ra.

insecurity n inseguridad f.

insemination n inseminación f.

insensible adj inconsciente.

insensitive adj insensible.

inseparable adj inseparable.

insert vt introducir.

insertion n inserción f.

inshore adj costero/ra.

inside n interior m; * adv dentro; Lat Am adentro de.

inside out adv al revés; a fondo.

insidious adj insidioso/sa; ~ly adv insidiosamente.

insight n perspicacia f.

insignia npl insignias fpl.

insignificant adj insignificante, frívolo/la.

insincere adj poco sincero/ra.

insincerity n falta de sinceridad f.

insinuate vt insinuar.

insinuation n insinuación f.

insipid adj insípido/da; insulso/sa; ñoño/ña.

insipidness n ñoñería f.

insist vi insistir.

insistence n insistencia f.

insistent adj insistente.

insole n plantilla f.

insolence n insolencia f.

insolent adj insolente; ~ly adv insolentemente.

insoluble adj insoluble.

insolvency n insolvencia f.

insolvent adj insolvente.

insomnia n insomnio m.

insomuch conj puesto que.

inspect vt examinar, inspeccionar.

inspection n inspección f.

inspector n inspector, superintendente m.

inspiration n inspiración f.

inspire vt inspirar.

instability n inestabilidad f.

install vt instalar.

installation n instalación f.

installment n instalación f; plazo m, Lat Am cuota f.

installment plan n compra a plazos f.

instance n ejemplo m; for ~ por ejemplo.

instant adj inmediato/ta; ~ly adv en seguida; * n instante, momento m.

instantaneous adj instantáneo/nea; ~ly adv instantáneamente.

instead (of) prep por, en lugar de, en vez de.

instep n empeine m.

instigate vt instigar.

instigation n instigación f.

instill vt inculcar.

instinct n instinto m.

instinctive adj instintivo/va; ~ly adv por instinto.

institute vt establecer; * n instituto m.

institution n institución f.

instruct vt instruir, enseñar; illustrar.

instruction n instrucción f.

instructive adj instructivo/va.

instructor n instructor/a m/f.

instrument n instrumento m.

instrumental adj instrumental.

insubordinate adj insubordinado/da.

insubordination n insubordinación f.

insufferable adj insoportable.

insufferably adv de modo insoportable.

insufficiency n insuficiencia f.

insufficient adj insuficiente; ~ly adv insuficientemente.

insular adj insular.

insulate vt aislar.

insulating tape n cinta aislante f.

insulation n aislamiento m.

insulin n insulina f.

insult vt insultar; * n insulto m.

insulting adj insultante.

insuperable adj insuperable.

insurance n (com) seguro m.

insurance policy n póliza de seguros f.

insure vt asegurar.

insurgent n insurgente, rebelde m.

insurmountable adj insuperable.

insurrection n insurrección f.

intact adj intacto/ta.

intake n admisión f; entrada f.

integral adj íntegro/gra; (chem) integrante; * n todo m.

integrate vt integrar.

integration n integración f.

integrity n integridad f.

intellect n intelecto m.

intellectual adj intelectual.

intelligence n inteligencia f.

intelligent adj inteligente.

intelligentsia n intelectualidad f.

intelligible adj inteligible.

intelligibly adv inteligiblemente.
intemperate adj inmoderado/da; ~ly adv inmoderadamente.
intend vi tener intención de.
intendant n intendente m.
intended adj deseado/da.
intense adj intenso/sa, hondo/da; ~ly adv intensamente.
intensify vt intensificar.
intensity n intensidad f.
intensive adj intensivo/va.
intensive care unit n unidad de vigilancia intensiva, unidad de cuidados intensivos f.
intent adj atento/ta, cuidadoso/sa; ~ly adv con aplicación; * n designio m.
intention n intención f; designio m.
intentional adj intencional; ~ly adv a propósito.
inter vt enterrar.
interaction n interacción f.
intercede vi interceder.
intercept vt interceptar.
intercession n intercesión, mediación f.
interchange n intercambio m.
intercom n interfono m.
intercourse n coito m.
interest vt interesar; * n interés m.
interesting adj interesante.
interest rate n tipo de interés m.
interface n interfaz, interface f.
interfere vi entrometerse.
interference n interferencia f.
interim adj provisional.
interior adj interior.
interior design n interiorismo m.
interior designer n interiorista m/f.
interjection n (gr) interjección f.
interlock vi endentarse.
interlocutor n interlocutor/a m/f.
interloper n intruso/sa m/f.
interlude n intermedio m.
intermarriage n matrimonio mixto m.
intermediary n intermediario/ria m/f.
intermediate adj intermedio/dia.
interment n entierro m; sepultura f.
interminable adj inacabable.
intermingle vt, vi entremezclar; mezclarse.
intermission n descanso m.
intermittent adj intermitente.
intern n interno m.
internal adj interno/na; ~ly adv internamente.
international adj internacional.
Internet café n cibercafé m.
interplay n interacción f.
interpose vt interponer.
interpret vt interpretar.
interpretation n interpretación f.
interpreter n intérprete m/f.
interracial adj interracial.
interregnum n interregno m.
interrelated adj interrelacionado/da.
interrogate vt interrogar.

interrogation n interrogatorio m.
interrogative adj interrogativo/va.
interrupt vt interrumpir.
interruption n interrupción f.
intersect vi cruzarse.
intersection n cruce m.
intersperse vt esparcir.
intertwine vt entretejer.
interval n intervalo m.
intervene vi intervenir; ocurrir.
intervention n intervención f.
interview n entrevista f, Lat Am reportaje m; * vt entrevistar.
interviewer n entrevistador/a m/f.
interweave vt entretejer.
intestate adj intestado/da.
intestinal adj intestinal.
intestine n intestino m.
intimacy n intimidad f.
intimate n amigo/ga íntimo/ma m/f; * adj íntimo/ma; ~ly adv íntimamente; * vt insinuar, dar a entender.
intimidate vt intimidar.
into prep en, dentro, adentro.
intolerable adj intolerable.
intolerably adv intolerablemente.
intolerance n intolerancia f.
intolerant adj intolerante.
intonation n entonación f.
intoxicate vt embriagar.
intoxication n embriaguez f.
intractable adj intratable.
intransitive adj (gr) intransitivo/va.
intravenous adj intravenoso/sa.
in-tray n bandeja de entrada f.
intrepid adj intrépido/da; ~ly adv intrépidamente.
intrepidity n intrepidez f.
intricacy n complejidad f.
intricate adj intrincado/da, complica-do/da; ~ly adv intrincadamente.
intrigue n intriga f; * vi intrigar.
intriguing adj fascinante.
intrinsic adj intrínseco/ca; ~ally adv intrínsecamente.
introduce vt introducir.
introduction n introducción f.
introductory adj introductorio/ria.
introspection n introspección f.
introvert n introvertido/da m/f.
intrude vi entrometerse.
intruder n intruso/sa m/f.
intrusion n invasión f.
intuition n intuición f.
intuitive adj intuitivo/va.
inundate vt inundar.
inundation n inundación f.
inure vt acostumbrar, habituar.
invade vt invadir.
invader n invasor/a m/f.
invalid adj inválido/da, nulo/la; * n minusválido m.

invalidate *vt* invalidar, anular.
invaluable *adj* inapreciable.
invariable *adj* invariable.
invariably *adv* invariablemente.
invasion *n* invasión *f*.
invective *n* invectiva *f*.
inveigle *vt* seducir, persuadir.
invent *vt* inventar.
invention *n* invento *m*.
inventive *adj* inventivo/va.
inventor *n* inventor *m*.
inventory *n* inventario *m*.
inverse *adj* inverso/sa.
inversion *n* inversión *f*.
invert *vt* invertir.
invest *vt* invertir.
investigate *vt* investigar.
investigation *n* investigación, pesquisa *f*.
investigator *n* investigador/a *m/f*.
investment *n* inversión *f*.
inveterate *adj* inveterado/da.
invidious *adj* odioso/sa.
invigilate *vt* vigilar.
invigorating *adj* vigorizante.
invincible *adj* invencible.
invincibly *adv* invenciblemente.
inviolable *adj* inviolable.
invisible *adj* invisible.
invisibly *adv* invisiblemente.
invitation *n* invitación *f*.
invite *vt* invitar.
inviting *adj* atractivo/va.
invoice *n* (com) factura *f*.
invoke *vt* invocar.
involuntarily *adv* involuntariamente.
involuntary *adj* involuntario/ria.
involve *vt* implicar, *Lat Am* involucrar.
involved *adj* complicado/da.
involvement *n* compromiso *m*.
invulnerable *adj* invulnerable.
inward *adj* interior; interno/na; ~, ~s *adv* hacia
   dentro.
iodine *n* (chem) yodo *m*.
IOU (I owe you) *n* pagaré *m*.
irascible *adj* irascible.
irate, ireful *adj* enojado/da.
iris *n* iris *m*.
irksome *adj* fastidioso/sa.
iron *n* hierro *m*, *Lat Am* fierro *m*, plancha *f*; *
   adj* férreo/rea; * *vt* planchar.
ironic *adj* irónico/ca; ~ly *adv* con ironía.
ironing *n* planchado *m*.
ironing board *n* tabla de planchar *f*.
iron ore *n* mineral de hierro *m*.
ironwork *n* herraje *m*; ~s *pl* herrería *f*.
irony *n* ironía *f*.
irradiate *vt* irradiar.
irrational *adj* irracional.
irreconcilable *adj* irreconciliable.
irregular *adj*, ~ly *adv* irregular(men-te).
irregularity *n* irregularidad *f*.

irrelevant *adj* impertinente.
irreligious *adj* irreligioso/sa.
irreparable *adj* irreparable.
irreplaceable *adj* irreemplazable.
irrepressible *adj* incontenible.
irreproachable *adj* irreprensible.
irresistible *adj* irresistible.
irresolute *adj* irresoluto/ta; ~ly *adv*
   irresolutamente.
irresponsible *adj* irresponsable.
irretrievably *adv* irreparablemente.
irreverence *n* irreverencia *f*.
irreverent *adj* irreverente; ~ly *adv*
   irreverentemente.
irrigate *vt* regar.
irrigation *n* riego *m*.
irritability *n* irritabilidad *f*.
irritable *adj* irritable.
irritant *n* (med) irritante *m*.
irritate *vt* irritar.
irritating *adj* fastidioso/sa.
irritation *n* fastidio *m*; picazón *f*.
Islam *n* islam *m*.
Islamic *adj* islámico/ca.
island *n* isla *f*.
islander *n* isleño/ña *m/f*.
isle *n* isla *f*.
isolate *vt* aislar.
isolation *n* aislamiento *m*.
issue *n* asunto *m*; * *vt* expedir; publicar; repartir.
isthmus *n* istmo *m*.
it *pn* él, ella, ello, lo, la, le.
italic *n* cursiva *f*.
itch *n* picazón *f*; * *vi* picar.
item *n* artículo *m*.
itemize *vt* detallar, *Lat Am* itemizar.
itinerant *n* ambulante, errante *m*.
itinerary *n* itinerario *m*.
its *pn* su, suyo.
itself *pn* se, por sí mismo.
ivory *n* marfil *m*.
ivy *n* hiedra *f*; yedra *f*.

J

jab *vt* clavar.
jabber *vi* farfullar.
jack *n* gato *m*; sota *f*.
jackal *n* chacal *m*.
jackboots *npl* botas militares *fpl*.
jackdaw *n* grajo *m*.
jacket *n* chaqueta *f*, *Lat Am* saco *m*; funda *f*.
jack-knife *vi* colear.
jackpot *n* premio gordo *m*.
jacuzzi *n* jacuzzi *m*.
jade *n* jade *m*.
jagged *adj* dentado/da.
jaguar *n* jaguar *m*, *Lat Am* tigre *m*.
jail *n* cárcel *f*.
jailbird *n* preso/sa *m/f*.

jailer *n* carcelero/ra *m/f.*

jam *n* conserva *f*; mermelada de frutas *f*; (*auto*) embotellamiento *m*

jangle *vi* sonar.

janitor *n* portero/ra *m/f*, bedel *m.*

January *n* enero *m.*

jar *vi* chocar; (*mus*) discordar; reñir; * *n* jarra *f.*

jargon *n* jerigonza *f.*

jasmine *n* jazmín *m.*

jaundice *n* ictericia *f.*

jaunt *n* excursión *f.*

jaunty *adj* alegre.

javelin *n* jabalina *f.*

jaw *n* mandíbula *f.*

jay *n* arrendajo *m.*

jazz *n* jazz *m.*

jealous *adj* celoso/sa; envidioso/sa.

jealousy *n* celos *mpl*; envidia *f.*

jeans *npl* vaqueros *mpl*, jeans *mpl*, *Lat Am* jean *m.*

Jeep™ *n* jeep *m.*

jeer *vi* befar, mofar; * *n* burla *f.*

jelly *n* jalea, gelatina *f.*

jellyfish *n* medusa *f*, aguamar *m.*

jeopardize *vt* arriesgar, poner en riesgo.

jerk *n* sacudida *f*; * *vt* tirar.

jerky *adj* espasmódico/ca.

jersey *n* jersey *m.*

jest *n* broma *f.*

jester *n* bufón/ona *m/f.*

jestingly *adv* de burlas.

Jesuit *n* jesuita *m.*

Jesus *n* Jesús *m.*

jet *n* avión a reacción *m*; azabache *m.*

jet engine *n* motor a reacción *m*, reactor *m.*

jettison *vt* desechar.

jetty *n* muelle *m.*

Jew *n* judío/día *m/f.*

jewel *n* joya *f.*

jeweler *n* joyero/ra *m/f.*

jewelry *n* joyería *f.*

jeweler's (shop/store) *n* joyería *f.*

Jewish *adj* judío/día.

jib *n* (*mar*) foque *m.*

jibe *n* mofa *f.*

jig *n* giga *f.*

jigsaw *n* rompecabezas *m invar.*

jilt *vt* dejar.

jinx *n* gafe *m.*

job *n* trabajo *m.*

jockey *n* jinete *m/f.*

jocular *adj* jocoso/sa, alegre.

jocularity *n* jocosidad *f.*

jog *vi* hacer footing.

jogging *n* footing *m.*

join *vt* juntar, unir; (*fig*) zurcir; **to ~ in** participar en; * *vi* unirse, juntarse.

joiner *n* carpintero/ra *m/f.*

joinery *n* carpintería *f.*

joint *n* articulación *f*; * *adj* común.

jointly *adv* conjuntamente.

joint-stock company *n* (*com*) sociedad por acciones *f.*

joke *n* broma *f*; * *vi* bromear.

joker *n* comodín *m.*

jollity *n* alegría *f.*

jolly *adj* alegre.

jolt *vt* sacudir; * *n* sacudida *f.*

jostle *vt* codear.

journal *n* revista *f.*

journalism *n* periodismo *m.*

journalist *n* periodista *m/f.*

journey *n* viaje *m*; * *vt* viajar.

jovial *adj* jovial, alegre; **~ly** *adv* con jovialidad.

joy *n* alegría *f*; júbilo *m.*

joyful, joyous *adj* alegre, gozoso/sa; **~ly** *adv* alegremente.

joystick *n* palanca de control *f*, joystick *m.*

jubilant *adj* jubiloso/sa.

jubilation *n* júbilo/la, regocijo *m.*

jubilee *n* jubileo *m.*

Judaism *n* judaísmo *m.*

judge *n* juez/a *m/f*; * *vt* juzgar.

judgement *n* juicio *m.*

judicial *adj*, **~ly** *adv* judicial(mente).

judiciary *n* poder judicial *m*, judicatura *f.*

judicious *adj*, prudente.

judo *n* judo *m.*

jug *n* jarro *m.*

juggle *vi* hacer juegos malabares.

juggler *n* malabarista *m/f.*

jugular *adj* yugular.

juice *n* zumo, jugo *m.*

juicy *adj* jugoso/sa.

jukebox *n* gramola *f.*

July *n* julio *m.*

jumble *vt* mezclar; * *n* revoltijo *m.*

jump *vi* saltar, brincar; * *n* salto *m.*

jumper *n* suéter, jersey *m.*

jumpy *adj* nervioso/sa.

juncture *n* coyuntura *f.*

June *n* junio *m.*

jungle *n* selva *f.*

junior *adj* más joven.

juniper *n* (*bot*) enebro *m.*

junk *n* basura *f*; baratijas *fpl.*

junk food *n* comida basura *f.*

junkman *n* trapero *m.*

junta *n* junta *f.*

jurisdiction *n* jurisdicción *f.*

jurisprudence *n* jurisprudencia *f.*

jurist *n* jurista *m/f.*

juror, juryman *n* jurado/da *m/f.*

jury *n* jurado *m.*

just *adj* justo/ta; * *adv* justamente, exactamente; **~ as** como; **~ now** ahora mismo.

justice *n* justicia *f.*

justifiably *adv* con justificación.

justification *n* justificación *f.*

justify *vt* justificar.

justly *adv* justamente.

justness *n* justicia *f.*

jut *vi*; **to ~ out** sobresalir.
jute *n* yute *m*.
juvenile *adj* juvenil.
juxtapose *vt* yuxtaponer.
juxtaposition *n* yuxtaposición *f*.

K

kaleidoscope *n* caleidoscopio *m*.
kangaroo *n* canguro *m*.
karaoke *n* karaoke *m*.
karate *n* kárate *m*.
kebab *n* pincho *m* moruno.
keel *n* (*mar*) quilla *f*.
keen *adj* agudo/da; vivo/va.
keenness *n* entusiasmo *m*.
keep *vt* mantener; guardar; conservar.
keeper *n* guardián/ana *m/f*.
keepsake *n* recuerdo *m*.
keg *n* barril *m*.
kennel *n* perrera *f*.
kernel *n* fruta *f*; meollo *m*.
kerosene *n* queroseno *m*, *Lat Am* querosén *m*.
ketchup *n* catsup, ketchup *m*.
kettle *n* hervidor *m*.
kettle-drum *n* timbal *m*.
key *n* llave *f*; (*mus*) clave *f*; tecla *f*.
keyboard *n* teclado *m*.
keyhole *n* ojo de la cerradura *m*.
keynote *n* (*mus*) tónica *f*.
key ring *n* llavero *m*.
keystone *n* piedra clave *f*.
khaki *n* caqui *m*.
kick *vt*, *vi* patear; * *n* puntapié *m*; patada *f*.
kid *n* chico/ca *m/f*.
kidnap *vt* secuestrar.
kidnaper *n* secuestrador/a *m/f*.
kidnaping *n* secuestro *m*; rapto *m*.
kidney *n* riñón *m*.
killer *n* asesino/na *m/f*.
killing *n* asesinato *m*.
kiln *n* horno *m*.
kilo *n* kilo *m*.
kilobyte *n* kilobyte *m*.
kilogram *n* kilo *m*.
kilometer *n* kilómetro *m*.
kilt *n* falda escocesa *f*.
kin *n* parientes *mpl*; **next of ~** pariente próximo *m*, pariente próxima *f*.
kind *adj* cariñoso/sa; * *n* género *m*.
kindergarten *n* parvulario *m*.
kind-hearted *adj* bondadoso/sa.
kindle *vt*, *vi* encender.
kindliness *n* benevolencia *f*.
kindly *adj* bondadoso/sa.
kindness *n* bondad *f*.
kindred *adj* emparentado/da.
kinetic *adj* cinético/ca.
king *n* rey *m*.
kingdom *n* reino *m*.

kingfisher *n* martín pescador *m*.
king prawn *n* langostino *m*.
kiosk *n* quiosco *m*.
kiss *n* beso *m*; * *vt* besar.
kissing *n* besos *mpl*.
kit *n* equipo *m*.
kitchen *n* cocina *f*.
kitchen garden *n* huerta *f*.
kitchen maid *n* fregona *f*.
kite *n* cometa *f*.
kitten *n* gatito *m*.
knack *n* don *m*.
knapsack *n* mochila *f*.
knave *n* bribón, pícaro *m*; (cards) sota *f*.
knead *vt* amasar.
knee *n* rodilla *f*.
knee-deep *adj* metido hasta las rodillas.
kneel *vi* arrodillarse.
knell *n* toque de difuntos *m*.
knife *n* cuchillo *m*.
knight *n* caballero *m*.
knit *vt*, *vi* tejer, tricotear; **to ~ the brows** fruncir el ceño.
knitter *n* calcetero/ra, mediero/ra *m/f*.
knitting needle *n* aguja de tejer *f*.
knitwear *n* prendas de punto *fpl*.
knob *n* bulto *m*; nudo en la madera *m*; botón de las flores *m*.
knock *vt*, *vi* golpear, tocar; **to ~ down** derribar; * *n* golpe *m*.
knocker *n* aldaba *f*.
knock-kneed *adj* patizambo/ba; zambo/ba.
knock-out *n* KO *m*, *Lat Am* nocaut *m*.
knoll *n* cima de una colina *f*.
knot *n* nudo *m*; lazo *m*; * *vt* anudar.
knotty *adj* escabroso/sa.
know *vt*, *vi* conocer; saber.
know-all *n* sabelotodo *m/f*.
know-how *n* conocimientos *mpl*.
knowing *adj* entendido/da; **~ly** *adv* a sabiendas.
knowledge *n* conocimiento *m*.
knowledgeable *adj* bien informado/da.
knuckle *n* nudillo *m*.

L

label *n* etiqueta *f*.
labor *n* trabajo *m*; **to be in ~** estar de parto; * *vt* trabajar.
laboratory *n* laboratorio *m*.
laborer *n* peón *m*.
laborious *adj* laborioso/sa; difícil; **~ly** *adv* laboriosamente.
labor union *n* sindicato *m*, *Lat Am* gremial *f*.
labor unionist *n* sindicalista *m/f*, *Lat Am* gremialista *m/f*.
labyrinth *n* laberinto *m*.
lace *n* cordón; encaje *m*; * *vt* abrochar.
lacerate *vt* lacerar.
lack *vt*, *vi* faltar; * *n* falta *f*.

lackadaisical *adj* descuidado/da.
lackey *n* lacayo *m*.
laconic *adj* lacónico/ca.
lacquer *n* laca *f*.
lad *n* muchacho *m*.
ladder *n* escalera *f*.
ladle *n* cucharón *m*.
ladleful *n* cucharada *f*.
lady *n* señora *f*.
ladybug *n* mariquita *f*.
lady-killer *n* casanova *m*.
ladylike *adj* fino/na.
ladyship *n* señoría *f*.
lag *vi* quedarse atrás.
lager *n* cerveza (rubia) *f*.
lagoon *n* laguna *f*.
laid-back *adj* relajado/da.
lair *n* guarida *f*.
laity *n* laicado *m*.
lake *n* lago *m*; laguna *f*.
lamb *n* cordero *m*; * *vi* parir.
lame *adj* cojo/ja.
lament *vt* (*vi*) lamentar(se); * *n* lamento *m*.
lamentable *adj* lamentable, deplorable.
lamentation *adj* lamentación *f*.
laminated *adj* laminado/da; plastifi-cado/da.
lamp *n* lámpara *f*.
lampoon *n* sátira *f*.
lampshade *n* pantalla *f*.
lance *n* lanza *f*; * *vt* abrir con lanceta.
lancet *n* lanceta *f*.
land *n* país *m*; tierra *f*; * *vt*, *vi* desembarcar.
land forces *npl* tropas de tierra *fpl*.
land-holder *n* hacendado *m*.
landing *n* desembarco *m*.
landing strip *n* pista de aterrizaje *f*.
landlady *n* propietaria *f*.
landlord *n* propietario *m*.
landlubber *n* marinero de agua dulce *m*.
landmark *n* lugar conocido; hito *m*.
landowner *n* terrateniente *m/f*.
landscape *n* paisaje *m*.
landslide *n* corrimiento de tierras *m*, *Lat Am* deslave *m*.
lane *n* callejuela *f*.
langoustine *n* langostino *m*.
language *n* lengua *f*; lenguaje *m*.
languid *adj* lánguido/da, débil; **~ly** *adv* lánguidamente, débilmente.
languish *vi* languidecer.
lank *adj* lacio/cia.
lanky *adj* larguirucho/cha.
lantern *n* linterna *f*; farol *m*.
lap *n* regazo *m*; * *vt* lamer.
lapdog *n* perro faldero *m*.
lapel *n* solapa *f*.
lapse *n* lapso *m*; * *vi* transcurrir.
laptop *n* portátil *m*.
larceny *n* latrocinio *m*.
larch *n* alerce *m*.
lard *n* manteca de cerdo *f*.

larder *n* despensa *f*.
large *adj* grande; **at ~** en libertad; **~ly** *adv* en gran parte.
large-scale *adj* en gran escala.
largesse *n* liberalidad *f*.
lark *n* alondra *f*.
larva *n* larva, oruga *f*.
laryngitis *n* laringitis *f*.
larynx *n* laringe *f*.
lascivious *adj* lascivo/va; **~ly** *adv* lascivamente.
laser *n* láser *m*.
laser printer *n* impresora láser *f*.
lash *n* latigazo *m*, *Lat Am* cuerazo *m*; * *vt* dar latigazos, *Lat Am* cuerear; atar.
lasso *n* lazo *m*, *Lat Am* peal *m*.
last *adj* último/ma; pasado/da; **at ~** por fin; **~ly** *adv* finalmente; * *n* horma de zapatero *f*; * *vi* durar.
last-ditch *adj* último/ma.
lasting *adj* duradero/ra, permanente; **~ly** *adv* perpetuamente.
last-minute *adj* de última hora.
latch *n* picaporte *m*.
latch-key *n* llave maestra *f*.
late *adj* tarde; difunto/ta; (*rail*) **the train is ten minutes ~** el tren tiene un retraso de diez minutos; * *adv* tarde; **~ly** *adv* recientemente.
latecomer *n* recién llegado/da *m/f*.
latent *adj* latente.
lateral *adj*, **~ly** *adv* lateral(mente).
lathe *n* torno *m*.
lather *n* espuma *f*.
latitude *n* latitud *f*.
latrine *n* letrina *f*.
latter *adj* último/ma; **~ly** *adv* últimamente, recientemente.
lattice *n* celosía *f*.
laudable *adj* loable.
laudably *adv* loablemente.
laugh *vi* reir; **to ~ at** *vt* reírse de; * *n* risa *f*.
laughable *adj* absurdo/da.
laughing stock *n* hazmerreír *m*.
laughter *n* risa *f*.
launch *vt* (*vi*) lanzar(se); * *n* (*mar*) lancha *f*.
launching *n* lanzamiento *m*.
launching pad *n* plataforma de lanzamiento *f*.
launder *vt* lavar.
Launderette™ *n* lavandería automática *f*.
laundry *n* lavandería *f*.
laurel *n* laurel *m*.
lava *n* lava *f*.
lavatory *n* cuarto de baño *m*.
lavender *n* (*bot*) espliego *m*, lavanda *f*.
lavish *adj* pródigo/ga; **~ly** *adv* pródigamente; * *vt* disipar.
law *n* ley *f*; derecho *m*.
law-abiding *adj* respetuoso/sa con la ley.
law and order *n* orden público *m*.
law court *n* tribunal *m*.
lawful *adj* legal; legítimo/ma; **~ly** *adv* legalmente.

lawless *adj* anárquico/ca.
lawlessness *n* anarquía *f*.
lawmaker *n* legislador/a *m/f*.
lawn *n* pasto *m*, *Lat Am* grama *f*.
lawnmower *n* cortacésped *m*.
law school *n* facultad de derecho *f*.
lawsuit *n* proceso *m*.
lawyer *n* abogado/da *m/f*.
lax *adj* laxo/xa; flojo/ja.
laxative *n* laxante *m*.
laxity *n* laxitud *f*; flojedad *f*.
lay *vt* poner; **to ~ claim** reclamar; pretender; **to ~ into** (*col*) zurrar; * *vi* poner.
layabout *n* vago/ga *m/f*.
layer *n* capa *f*.
layette *n* ajuar de niño *m*.
layman *n* lego, seglar *m*.
layout *n* composición *f*.
laze *vi* holgazanear.
lazily *adv* perezosamente; lentamente.
laziness *n* pereza *f*.
lazy *adj* perezoso/sa.
lead[1] *n* plomo *m*.
lead[2] *vt* conducir, guiar; * *vi* mandar.
leader *n* jefe/fa *m/f*.
leadership *n* dirección *f*; liderazgo *m*.
leading *adj* principal; capital; **~ article** *n* artículo principal *m*.
leaf *n* hoja *f*, yema *f*.
leaflet *n* folleto *m*.
leafy *adj* frondoso/sa.
league *n* liga, alianza *f*; legua *f*.
leak *n* escape *m*; * *vi* (*mar*) hacer agua.
leaky *adj* agujereado/da.
lean *vt* (*vi*) apoyar(se); * *adj* magro/ra.
leap *vi* saltar; * *n* salto *m*.
leapfrog *n* pídola *f*.
leap year *n* año bisiesto *m*.
learn *vt*, *vi* aprender.
learned *adj* docto/ta.
learner *n* aprendiz *m*.
learning *n* erudición *f*.
lease *n* arriendo *m*; * *vt* arrendar.
leasehold *n* arriendo *m*.
leash *n* correa *f*.
least *adj* mínimo/ma; **at ~** por lo menos; **not in the ~** en absoluto.
leather *n* cuero *m*.
leathery *adj* correoso/sa.
leave *n* licencia *f*; permiso *m*; **to take ~** despedirse; * *vt* dejar, abandonar.
leaven *n* levadura *f*; * *vt* fermentar.
leavings *npl* sobras *fpl*.
lecherous *adj* lascivo/va.
lecture *n* conferencia *f*; * *vt* dar una conferencia.
lecturer *n* conferenciante *m/f*; profe-sor/ra *m/f*.
ledge *n* reborde *m*.
ledger *n* (*com*) libro mayor *m*.
lee *n* (*mar*) sotavento *m*.
leech *n* sanguijuela *f*.
leek *n* (*bot*) puerro *m*.

leer *vt* mirar de manera lasciva.
lees *npl* sedimento, poso *m*.
leeward *adj* (*mar*) sotavento.
leeway *n* libertad de acción *f*.
left *adj* izquierdo/da; zurdo/da; **on the ~** a la izquierda.
left-handed *adj* zurdo/da.
leftovers *npl* sobras *fpl*.
leg *n* pierna *f*; pie *m*.
legacy *n* herencia *f*.
legal *adj* legal, legítimo/ma; **~ly** *adv* legalmente.
legal holiday *n* fiesta oficial *f*.
legality *n* legalidad, legitimidad *f*.
legalize *vt* legalizar.
legal tender *n* moneda de curso legal *f*.
legate *n* legado *m*.
legatee *n* legado *m*.
legation *n* legación *f*.
legend *n* leyenda *f*.
legendary *adj* legendario/ria.
legible *adj* legible.
legibly *adv* legiblemente.
legion *n* legión *f*.
legislate *vt* legislar.
legislation *n* legislación *f*.
legislative *adj* legislativo/va.
legislator *n* legislador/a *m/f*.
legislature *n* cuerpo legislativo *m*.
legitimacy *n* legitimidad *f*.
legitimate *adj* legítimo/ma; **~ly** *adv* legítimamente; * *vt* legitimar.
leisure *n* ocio *m*; **~ly** *adj* sin prisa; **at ~** desocupado/da.
lemon *n* limón *m*.
lemonade *n* limonada *f*.
lemon tea *n* te con limón *m*.
lemon tree *n* limonero *m*.
lend *vt* prestar.
length *n* largo *m*; duración *f*; **at ~** finalmente.
lengthen *vt* alargar; * *vi* alargarse.
lengthways, lengthwise *adv* a lo largo.
lengthy *adj* largo/ga.
lenient *adj* indulgente.
lens *n* lente *f*.
Lent *n* Cuaresma *f*.
lentil *n* lenteja *f*.
leopard *n* leopardo *m*; mallas *fpl*.
leotard *n* leotardo *m*.
leper *n* leproso/sa *m/f*.
leprosy *n* lepra *f*.
lesbian *n* lesbiana *f*.
less *adj* menor; * *adv* menos.
lessen *vt* disminuir; * *vi* disminuirse.
lesser *adj* más pequeño/ña.
lesson *n* lección *f*.
lest *conj* para que no.
let *vt* dejar, permitir; alquilar.
lethal *adj* mortal.
lethargic *adj* letárgico/ca.
lethargy *n* letargo *m*.
letter *n* letra *f*; carta *f*.

letter bomb n carta bomba f.
lettering n letras fpl.
letter of credit n carta de crédito f.
lettuce n lechuga f.
leukemia n leucemia f.
level adj llano/na, igual; nivelado/da; * n nivel m; * vt allanar; nivelar.
level-headed adj sensato/ta.
lever n palanca f.
leverage n influencia f.
levity n ligereza f.
levy n leva (de tropas) f; * vt recaudar.
lewd adj obsceno/na.
lexicon n lexicón m.
liability n responsabilidad f.
liable adj sujeto/ta; responsable.
liaise vi enlazar.
liaison n enlace m.
liar n embustero m.
libel n difamación f; * vt difamar.
libelous adj difamatorio/ria.
liberal adj liberal, generoso/sa; **~ly** adv liberalmente.
liberality n liberalidad, generosidad f.
liberate vt libertar.
liberation n liberación f.
libertine n libertino m.
liberty n libertad f.
Libra n Libra f.
librarian n bibliotecario/ria m/f.
library n biblioteca f.
libretto n libreto m.
license n licencia f; permiso m; * vt autorizar, licenciar.
license plate n placa de matrícula f.
licentious adj licencioso/sa.
lichen n (bot) liquen m.
lick vt lamer.
lid n tapa f.
lie n mentira f; * vi mentir; echarse.
lie down vi yacer.
lieu n: in ~ of en vez de.
lieutenant n lugarteniente m/f; teniente m/f.
life n vida f; **for** ~ para toda la vida.
lifeboat n lancha de socorro f; bote salvavidas m.
lifeguard n socorrista m/f.
lifeless adj muerto/ta; sin vida.
lifelike adj natural.
lifeline n cordón umbilical m.
life preserver n chaleco salvavidas m.
life sentence n cadena perpetua f.
life-sized adj de tamaño natural.
life span n vida f.
lifestyle n estilo de vida f.
life-support system n sistema de respiración asistida m.
lifetime n vida f.
lift vt levantar.
ligament n ligamento m.
light n luz f; * adj ligero/ra; claro/ra; * vt encender; alumbrar.

light bulb n foco m; bombilla f.
lighten vi relampaguear; * vt iluminar; aligerar; (mar) zafar.
lighter n encendedor m.
light-headed adj mareado/da.
light-hearted adj alegre.
lighthouse n (mar) faro m.
lighting n iluminación f.
lightly adv ligeramente.
lightning n relámpago m.
lightning-rod n pararrayos m invar.
light pen n lápiz óptico m.
lightweight adj ligero/ra.
light year n año luz m.
ligneous adj leñoso/sa.
like adj semejante; igual; * adv como, del mismo modo que; * vt, vi gustar.
likeable adj simpático/ca.
likelihood n probabilidad f.
likely adj probable, verosímil.
liken vt comparar.
likeness n semejanza f.
likewise adv igualmente.
liking n agrado m.
lilac n lila f.
lily n lirio m; ~ **of the valley** lirio de los valles.
limb n miembro m.
limber adj flexible.
lime n cal f; lima f; ~ **tree** tilo m.
limestone n piedra caliza f; caliza f.
limit n límite, término m; * vt restringir.
limitation n limitación f; restricción f.
limitless adj inmenso/sa.
limousine n limusina f.
limp vi cojear; * n cojera f; * adj flojo/ja.
limpet n lapa f.
limpid adj claro/ra, transparente.
line n línea f; raya f; * vt forrar; revestir.
lineage n linaje m; filiación f.
linear adj lineal.
lined adj rayado/da; arrugado/da.
linen n lino m.
liner n transatlántico m.
linesman n juez de línea m.
linger vi persistir.
lingerie n ropa interior f.
lingering adj lento/ta.
linguist n lingüista m/f.
linguistic adj lingüístico/ca.
linguistics n lingüística f.
liniment n linimento m.
lining n forro m.
link n eslabón m; * vt enlazar.
linnet n pardillo m.
linoleum n linóleo m.
linseed n linaza f.
lint n hilas fpl.
lintel n dintel, tranquero m.
lion n león m.
lioness n leona f.
lip n labio m; borde m.

liposuction n liposucción f.
lip read vi leer los labios.
lip salve n crema protectora para labios f.
lipstick n lápiz de labios m.
liqueur n licor m.
liquid adj líquido/da; * n líquido m.
liquidate vt liquidar.
liquidation n liquidación f.
liquidize vt licuar.
liquor n licor m.
liquorice n regaliz m.
lisp vi cecear; * n ceceo m.
list n lista f; * vt hacer una lista de.
listen vi escuchar.
listless adj indiferente.
litany n letanía f.
liter n litro m.
literal adj, ~ly adv literal(mente).
literary adj literario/ria.
literate adj culto/ta.
literature n literatura f.
lithe adj ágil.
lithograph n litografía f.
lithography n litografía f.
litigation n litigio m.
litigious adj litigioso/sa.
litter n litera f; camada f; * vt parir.
little adj pequeño/ña, poco/ca; ~ by ~ poco a poco; * n poco m.
liturgy n liturgia f.
live vi vivir; habitar; **to ~ on** alimentarse de; **to ~ up to** vt cumplir con; * adj vivo/va.
livelihood n vida f.
liveliness n vivacidad f; belleza f.
lively adj vivo/va.
liven up vt animar.
liver n hígado m.
livery n librea f.
livestock n ganado m.
livid adj lívido/da, cárdeno/na.
living n vida f; * adj vivo/va.
living room n sala de estar f.
lizard n lagarto m.
load vt cargar; * n carga f.
loaded adj cargado/da.
loaf n pan m.
loafer n holgazán, gandul m.
loam n marga f.
loan n préstamo m.
loathe vt aborrecer; tener hastío; * vi fastidiar.
loathing n aversión f.
loathsome adj asqueroso/sa.
lobby n vestíbulo m.
lobe n lóbulo m.
lobster n langosta f.
local adj local.
local anesthetic n anestesia local f.
local government n gobierno municipal m.
locality n localidad f.
localize vt localizar.
locally adv en la vecindad.

locate vt localizar, Lat Am ubicar.
location n situación f.
loch n lago m.
lock n cerradura f; * vt cerrar con llave.
locker n vestuario m.
locket n medallón m.
lockout n cierre patronal m.
locksmith n cerrajero m.
locomotive n locomotora f.
locust n langosta f.
lodge n casa del guarda f; * vi alojarse.
lodger n inquilino/na m/f.
loft n desván m.
lofty adj alto/ta.
log n leño m.
logbook n (mar) diario de a bordo m.
logic n lógica f.
logical adj lógico/ca.
logo n logotipo m.
loin n lomo m.
loiter vi merodear.
loll vi repantigarse.
lollipop n pirulí m, piruleta f.
loneliness n soledad f.
lonesome adj solitario/ria; solo/la.
long adj largo/ga; * vi anhelar.
long-distance n: ~ **call** llamada interurbana f.
longevity n longevidad f.
long-haired adj de pelo largo.
longing n anhelo m.
longitude n longitud f.
longitudinal adj longitudinal.
long jump n salto de longitud m.
long-legged adj zancudo/da.
long-playing record n elepé m.
long-range adj de gran alcance.
long-term adj a largo plazo.
long wave n onda larga f.
long-winded adj prolijo/ja.
look vi mirar; parecer; **to ~ after** vt cuidar; **to ~ for** vt buscar; **to ~ forward to** vt esperar con impaciencia; **to ~ out for** vt aguardar; * n aspecto m; mirada f.
looking glass n espejo m.
lookout n (mil) centinela f; vigía f.
loom n telar m; * vi amenazar.
loop n lazo m.
loophole n escapatoria f.
loose adj suelto/ta; flojo/ja; ~ly adv aproximadamente.
loosen vt aflojar, zafar.
loot vt saquear; * n botín m.
lop vt desmochar.
lop-sided adj desequilibrado/da.
loquacious adj locuaz.
loquacity n locuacidad f.
lord n señor m.
lore n saber popular m.
lose vt perder; * vi perder; **to ~ weight** vi adelgazar.
loss n pérdida f; **to be at a ~** no saber qué hacer.

lost and found n objetos perdidos mpl.
lot n suerte f; lote m; **a ~** mucho.
lotion n loción f.
lottery n lotería, rifa f.
loud adj fuerte; **~ly** adv fuerte.
loudspeaker n altavoz m, Lat Am altoparlante m.
lounge n salón m.
louse n (pl lice) piojo m.
lousy adj vil.
lout n gamberro m.
lovable adj amable.
love n amor, cariño m; **to fall in ~** enamorarse; * vt amar; gustar.
love letter n carta de amor f.
love life n vida sentimental f.
lovely adj hermoso/sa.
lover n amante m.
lovesick adj enamorado/da.
loving adj amoroso/sa.
low adj bajo/ja; * vi mugir.
low-cut adj escotado/da.
lower adj más bajo/ja; * vt bajar.
lowest adj más bajo/ja, ínfimo/ma.
lowland n tierra baja f.
lowliness n humildad f.
lowly adj humilde.
low water, low tide n bajamar f.
loyal adj leal; fiel; **~ly** adv lealmente.
loyalty n lealtad f; fidelidad f.
lozenge n pastilla f.
lubricant n lubricante m.
lubricate vt lubricar.
lucid adj lúcido/da.
luck n suerte; fortuna f.
luckily adv afortunadamente.
luckless adj desdichado/da.
lucky adj afortunado/da.
lucrative adj lucrativo/va.
ludicrous adj absurdo/da.
lug vt arrastrar.
luggage n equipaje m.
lugubrious adj lúgubre, triste.
lukewarm adj tibio/bia.
lull vt acunar; * n tregua f.
lullaby n nana f.
lumbago n lumbago m.
lumber n trastera f.
lumberjack n maderero/ra m/f.
lumber room n trastero m.
luminous adj luminoso/sa.
lump n terrón m; bulto m; chichón m; * vt juntar.
lump sum n suma global f.
lunacy n locura f.
lunar adj lunar.
lunatic adj loco/ca.
lunch, luncheon n almuerzo m, comida f; * vt, vi almorzar.
lungs npl pulmones mpl.
lurch n sacudida f.
lure n señuelo m; cebo m; * vt inducir.

lurid adj sensacional.
lurk vi esconderse.
luscious adj delicioso/sa.
lush adj exuberante.
lust n lujuria, sensualidad f; concupiscencia f; * vi lujuriar; **to ~ after** vt codiciar.
luster n lustre m.
lustful adj lujurioso/sa, voluptuoso/sa; **~ly** adv lujuriosamente.
lustily adv vigorosamente.
lusty adj fuerte, vigoroso/sa.
lute n laúd m.
Lutheran n luterano/na m/f.
luxuriance n exuberancia, superabundancia f.
luxuriant adj exuberante, superabundante.
luxuriate vi crecer con exuberancia.
luxurious adj lujoso/sa; exuberante; **~ly** adv lujosamente.
luxury n lujo m, voluptuosidad f; exuberancia f.
lying n mentiras fpl.
lymph n linfa f.
lynch vt linchar.
lynx n lince m.
lyrical adj lírico/ca.
lyrics npl letra f.

M

macaroni n macarrones mpl.
macaroon n almendrado m.
mace n maza f; macis f invar.
macerate vt macerar; mortificar.
machination n maquinación, trama f.
machine n máquina f.
machine gun n ametralladora f.
machinery n maquinaria, mecánica f.
mackerel n caballa f.
mad adj loco/ca, furioso/sa, rabioso/sa, insensato/ta.
madam n madama, señora f.
madden vt enloquecer.
madder n (bot) rubia f.
madhouse n casa de locos f.
madly adv locamente.
madman n loco m.
madness n locura f.
magazine n revista f; almacén m.
maggot n gusano m.
magic n magia f; * adj mágico/ca; **~ally** adv mágicamente.
magician n mago/ga m/f; prestidigi-tador/a m/f.
magisterial adj magistral; **~ly** adv magistralmente.
magistracy n magistratura f.
magistrate n magistrado/da m/f.
magnanimity n magnanimidad f.
magnanimous adj magnánimo; **~ly** adv magnánimamente.
magnet n iman m.
magnetic adj magnetico/ca.
magnetism n magnetismo m.

magnificence *n* magnificencia *f*.

magnificent *adj* magnifico; **~ly** *adv* magníficamente. .

magnify *vt* aumentar; exagerar.

magnifying glass *n* lupa *f*.

magnitude *n* magnitud *f*.

magpie *n* urraca *f*.

mahogany *n* caoba *f*.

maid *n* criada *f*, *Lat Am* chinita *f*.

maiden *n* doncella *f*.

maiden name *n* nombre de soltera *m*.

mail *n* correo *m*.

mailbox *n* buzón *m*.

mailing list *n* lista de direcciones *f*.

mail order *n* venta por correo *f*.

mail train *n* (*rail*) tren correo *m*.

maim *vt* mutilar.

main *adj* principal; esencial; **in the ~** en general.

mainland *n* continente *m*.

main line *n* (*rail*) línea principal *f*.

mainly *adv* principalmente.

main street *n* calle mayor *f*.

maintain *vt* mantener; sostener.

maintenance *n* mantenimiento *m*.

maize *n* maíz *m*; borona *f*.

majestic *adj* majestuoso/sa; **~ally** *adv* majestuosamente.

majesty *n* majestad *f*.

major *adj* principal; * *n* (*mil*) coman-dante/a *m/f*.

majority *n* mayoría *f*.

make-*vt* hacer, crear; **to ~ for** dirigirse hacia; **to ~ up** inventar; **to ~ up for** compensar; **to ~ off with something** alzar; * *n* marca *f*.

make-believe *n* invención *f*.

makeshift *adj* improvisado.

make-up *n* maquillaje *m*.

make-up remover *n* desmaquillador *m*.

malady *n* enfermedad *f*.

malaise *n* malestar *m*.

malaria *n* malaria *f*.

malcontent *adj*, *n* malcontento/ta *m/f*.

male *adj* masculino/na; * *n* macho *m*.

malevolence *n* malevolencia *f*.

malevolent *adj* malévolo/la; **~ly** *adv* malignamente.

malfunction *n* mal funcionamiento, fallo *m*.

malice *n* malicia *f*.

malicious *adj* malicioso/sa; **~ly** *adv* maliciosamente.

malign *adj* maligno; * *vt* calumniar.

malignant *adj* maligno/na; **~ly** *adv* malignamente.

mall (shopping) *n* centro comercial; paseo *m*.

malleable *adj* maleable.

mallet *n* mazo *m*.

mallow *n* (*bot*) malva *f*.

malnutrition *n* desnutrición *f*.

malpractice *n* negligencia *f*.

malt *n* malta *f*.

maltreat *vt* maltratar.

mammal *n* mamífero *m*.

mammoth *adj* gigantesco/ca.

man *n* hombre *m*; * *vt* (*mar*) tripular.

manacle *n* manilla *f*; **~s** *npl* esposas *fpl*.

manage *vt*, *vi* manejar, dirigir, *Lat Am* gerenciar.

manageable *adj* manejable.

management *n* dirección *f*.

manager *n* director/a *m/f*.

manageress *n* directora *f*.

managerial *adj* directivo/va.

managing director *n* director/a general *m/f*.

mandarin *n* (*bot*) mandarina *f*; mandarín *m*.

mandate *n* mandato *m*.

mandatory *adj* obligatorio/ria.

mane *n* crines *fpl*, melena *f*.

maneuver *n* maniobra *f*.

manfully *adv* valerosamente.

manger *n* pesebre *m*.

mangle *n* rodillo *m*; * *vt* mutilar.

mangy *adj* sarnoso/sa.

manhandle *vt* maltratar.

manhood *n* madurez; hombría *f*.

man-hour *n* hora hombre *f*.

mania *n* manía *f*.

maniac *n* maníaco/ca *m/f*.

manic *adj* frenético/ca.

manicure *n* manicura *f*.

manifest *adj* manifiesto/ta, patente; * *vt* manifestar.

manifestation *n* manifestación *f*.

manifesto *n* manifiesto *m*.

manipulate *vt* manejar; manipular.

manipulation *n* manejo; manipulación *f*.

mankind *n* género humano *m*.

manlike *adj* varonil.

manliness *n* valentía, hombría *f*.

manly *adj* varonil.

man-made *adj* artificial.

manner *n* manera *f*; modo *m*; forma *f*; **~s** *pl* modales *mpl*.

manpower *n* mano de obra *f*.

mansion *n* palacio *m*, mansión *f*.

manslaughter *n* homicidio (sin premeditación) *m*.

mantelpiece *n* repisa (de chimenea) *f*.

manual *adj*, *n* manual *m*.

manufacture *n* fabricación *f*; * *vt* fabricar.

manufacturer *n* fabricante *m/f*.

manure *n* abono *m*; estiércol *m*; fiemo *m*; * *vt* abonar.

manuscript *n* manuscrito *m*.

many *adj* muchos, muchas; **~ a time** muchas veces; **how ~?** ¿cuantos?; **as ~ as** tantos como.

map *n* mapa *m*; * *vt* planear, trazar el mapa de; **to ~ out** proyectar.

maple *n* arce *m*.

mar *vt* estropear.

marathon *n* maratón *m*.

marauder *n* merodeador/a *m/f*.

marble *n* mármol *m*; * *adj* marmó-reo/rea.

March *n* marzo *m*.
march *n* marcha *f*; * *vi* marchar.
march past *n* desfile *m*.
mare *n* yegua *f*.
margarine *n* margarina *f*.
margin *n* margen *m*; borde *m*.
marginal *adj* marginal.
marigold *n* (*bot*) caléndula *f*.
marijuana *n* marihuana *f*.
marinate *vt* adobar.
marine *adj* marino/na; * *n* infante de marina *m*.
mariner *n* marinero/ra *m/f*.
marital *adj* marital.
maritime *adj* marítimo/ma.
marjoram *n* mejorana *f*.
mark *n* marca *f*; señal *f*; * *vt* marcar.
marker *n* registro *m*.
market *n* mercado *m*.
marketable *adj* vendible.
marketing *n* márketing *m*.
marketplace *n* mercado *m*.
market research *n* análisis de mercados *m invar*.
market value *n* valor de mercado *m*.
marksman *n* tirador *m*.
marmalade *n* mermelada de naranja *f*.
maroon *adj* marrón.
marquee *n* entoldado/da *m/f*.
marriage *n* matrimonio *m*; casamiento *m*.
marriageable *adj* casadero/ra.
marriage certificate *n* partida de casamiento *f*.
married *adj* casado/da; conyugal.
marrow *n* médula *f*.
marry *vi* casarse.
marsh *n* pantano *m*.
marshal *n* mariscal/a *m/f*.
marshy *adj* pantanoso/sa.
marten *n* marta *f*.
martial *adj* marcial; ~ **law** *n* ley marcial *f*.
martyr *n* mártir *m*.
martyrdom *n* martirio *m*.
marvel *n* maravilla *f*; * *vi* maravi-llar(se).
marvelous *adj* maravilloso/sa; ~**ly** *adv* maravillosamente.
marzipan *n* mazapán *m*.
mascara *n* rímel *m*.
masculine *adj* masculino/na, varonil.
mash *n* mezcla *f*.
mask *n* máscara *f*; * *vt* enmascarar.
masochist *n* masoquista *m/f*.
mason *n* albañil *m*.
masonry *n* mampostería *f*.
masquerade *n* mascarada *f*.
mass *n* masa *f*; misa *f*; montón *m*.
massacre *n* carnicería, matanza *f*; * *vt* hacer una carnicería.
massage *n* masaje *m*.
masseur *n* masajista *m*.
masseuse *n* masajista *f*.
massive *adj* enorme.
mass-media *npl* medios de comunicación de masas *mpl*.

mast *n* mástil *m*.
master *n* amo/ma, dueño/ña *m/f*; maestro/tra *m/f*; * *vt* dominar.
masterly *adj* magistral.
mastermind *vt* dirigir.
masterpiece *n* obra maestra *f*.
mastery *n* maestría *f*.
masticate *vt* masticar.
mastiff *n* mastín *m*.
mat *n* estera *f*; felpudo *m*.
match *n* fósforo *m*, cerilla *f*; partido *m*, *Lat Am* juego *m*; * *vt* igualar; * *vi* hacer juego.
matchbox *n* caja de fósforos *f*.
matchless *adj* incomparable, sin par.
matchmaker *n* casamentero/ra *m/f*.
mate *n* compañero/ra *m/f*; * *vt* acoplar.
material *adj*, ~**ly** *adv* material(men-te).
materialism *n* materialismo *m*.
maternal *adj* maternal.
maternity clothes *npl* vestido premamá *m*.
maternity hospital *n* hospital de maternidad *m*.
math *n* mates, matemáticas *fpl*.
mathematical *adj* matemático/ca; ~**ly** *adv* matemáticamente.
mathematician *n* matemático/ca *m/f*.
mathematics *npl* matemáticas *fpl*.
matinee *n* función de la tarde *f*.
mating *n* aparejamiento *m*.
matins *npl* maitines *mpl*.
matriculate *vt* matricular.
matriculation *n* matriculación *f*.
matrimonial *adj* matrimonial.
matte *adj* mate.
matted *adj* enmarañado/da.
matter *n* materia, substancia *f*; asunto *m*; cuestión *f*; **what is the ~?** ¿qué pasa?; **as a ~ of fact** en realidad; * *vi* importar.
mattress *n* colchón *m*.
mature *adj* maduro/ra; * *vt* madurar.
maturity *n* madurez *f*.
maul *vt* magullar.
mausoleum *n* mausoleo *m*.
mauve *adj* malva.
maxim *n* máxima *f*.
maximum *n* máximo *m*.
may *vi* poder; ~**be** acaso, quizá.
May *n* mayo *m*.
Mayday *n* primero de mayo *m*.
mayonnaise *n* mayonesa *f*.
mayor *n* alcalde *m*.
mayoress *n* alcaldesa *f*.
maze *n* laberinto *m*.
me *pn* me; mí.
meadow *n* pradera *f*; prado *m*.
meager *adj* pobre.
meagerness *n* escasez *f*.
meal *n* comida *f*; harina *f*.
mealtime *n* hora de comer *f*.
mean *adj* tacaño/ña; **in the ~time**, **~while** mientras tanto; ~**s** *npl* medios *mpl*; * *vt*, *vi* significar.

meander *vi* serpentear.
meaning *n* sentido, significado *m*.
meaningful *adj* significativo/va.
meaningless *adj* sin sentido.
meanness *n* tacañería *f*.
meantime, meanwhile *adv* mientras tanto, *Lat Am* intertanto.
measles *npl* sarampión *m*.
measure *n* medida *f*; (*mus*) compás *m*; * *vt* medir.
measurement *n* medida *f*.
meat *n* carne *f*.
meatball *n* albóndiga *f*.
meaty *adj* sustancioso/sa.
mechanic *n* mecánico/ca *m/f*.
mechanical *adj* mecánico; **~ly** *adv* mecánicamente.
mechanics *npl* mecánica *f*.
mechanism *n* mecanismo *m*.
medal *n* medalla *f*.
medallion *n* medallón *m*.
medallist *n* medallero/ra *m/f*.
meddle *vi* entrometerse.
meddler *n* entrometido *m*.
media *npl* medios de comunicación *mpl*.
median strip *n* mediana *f*.
mediate *vi* mediar.
mediation *n* mediación, interposición *f*.
mediator *n* intermediario/ria *m/f*.
medical *adj* médico/ca.
medicate *vt* medicar.
medicated *adj* medicinal.
medicinal *adj* medicinal.
medicine *n* medicina *f*; medicamento *m*.
medieval *adj* medieval.
mediocre *adj* mediocre.
mediocrity *n* mediocridad *f*.
meditate *vi* meditar.
meditation *n* meditación *f*.
meditative *adj* contemplativo/va.
Mediterranean *adj* mediterráneo/nea; **the ~** el Mediterráneo/nea *m*.
medium *n* medio *m*; * *adj* mediano/na.
medium wave *n* onda media *f*.
medley *n* mezcla *m*.
meek *adj* manso/sa; **~ly** *adv* mansamente.
meekness *n* mansedumbre *f*.
meet *vt* encontrar; **to ~ with** reunirse con; * *vi* encontrarse; juntarse.
meeting *n* reunión *f*; congreso *m*.
megaphone *n* megáfono *m*.
melancholy *n* melancolía *f*; * *adj* melancólico/ca.
mellow *adj* maduro/ra; suave; * *vi* madurar.
mellowness *n* madurez *f*.
melodious *adj* melodioso/sa; **~ly** *adv* melodiosamente.
melody *n* melodía *f*.
melon *n* melón *m*.
melt *vt* derretir; * *vi* derretirse.
melting point *n* punto de fusión *m*.

member *n* miembro *m/f*.
membership *n* número de miembros *m*, *Lat Am* membresía *f*.
membrane *n* membrana *f*.
memento *n* recuerdo *m*.
memo *n* memorándum *m*.
memoir *n* memoria *f*.
memorable *adj* memorable.
memorandum *n* memorándum *m*.
memorial *n* monumento conmemorativo *m*.
memorize *vt* memorizar, aprender de memoria.
memory *n* memoria *f*; recuerdo *m*.
menace *n* amenaza *f*; * *vt* amenazar.
menacing *adj* amenazador/ra.
menagerie *n* casa de fieras *f*.
mend *vt* reparar.
mending *n* reparación *f*.
menial *adj* doméstico/ca.
meningitis *n* meningitis *f*.
menopause *n* menopausia *f*.
menstruation *n* menstruación *f*.
mental *adj* mental, intelectual.
mentality *n* mentalidad *f*.
mentally *adv* mentalmente, intelectualmente.
mention *n* mención *f*; * *vt* mencionar.
mentor *n* mentor *m*.
menu *n* menú *m*; carta *f*.
mercantile *adj* mercantil.
mercenary *adj*, *n* mercenario/ria *m/f*.
merchandise *n* mercancía *f*.
merchant *n* comerciante *m/f*.
merchantman *n* navío mercante *m*.
merchant marine *n* marina mercante *f*.
merciful *adj* compasivo/va.
merciless *adj* despiadado/da; **~ly** *adv* despiadadamente.
mercury *n* mercurio *m*.
mercy *n* compasión *f*.
mere *adj* mero/ra; **~ly** *adv* simplemente.
merge *vt* fundir.
merger *n* fusión *f*.
meridian *n* meridiano *m*.
meringue *n* merengue *m*.
merit *n* mérito *m*; * *vt* merecer.
meritorious *adj* meritorio/ria.
mermaid *n* sirena *f*.
merrily *adv* alegremente.
merriment *n* diversión *f*; regocijo *m*.
merry *adj* alegre.
merry-go-round *n* tiovivo *m*.
mesh *n* malla *f*.
mesmerize *vt* hipnotizar.
mess *n* lío *m*, *Lat Am* relajo *m*; mamarracho *m*; (*mil*) comedor *m*; **to ~ up** *vt* desordenar.
message *n* mensaje *m*.
messenger *n* mensajero/ra *m/f*.
metabolism *n* metabolismo *n*.
metal *n* metal *m*.
metallic *adj* metálico/ca.
metallurgy *n* metalurgía *f*.
metamorphosis *n* metamorfosis *f invar*.

metaphor *n* metáfora *f*.
metaphoric(al) *adj* metafórico/ca.
metaphysical *adj* metafísico/ca.
metaphysics *npl* metafísica *f*.
mete (out) *vt* imponer.
meteor *n* meteoro *m*.
meteorological *adj* meteorológico/ca.
meteorology *n* meteorología *f*.
meter[1] *n* contador *m*, *Lat Am* medidor *m*.
meter[2] *n* metro *m*.
method *n* método *m*.
methodical *adj* metódico/ca; **~ly** *adv* metódicamente.
Methodist *n* metodista *m/f*.
metric *adj* métrico/ca.
metropolis *n* metrópoli *f*.
metropolitan *adj* metropolitano/na.
mettle *n* valor *m*.
mettlesome *adj* brioso/sa.
mew *vi* maullar.
mezzanine *n* entresuelo *m*.
microbe *n* microbio *m*.
microphone *n* micrófono *m*.
microchip *n* microchip *m*.
microscope *n* microscopio *m*.
microscopic *adj* microscópico/ca.
microwave *n* microondas *m invar*; **~ oven** microondas *m*.
mid *adj* medio/dia.
midday *n* mediodía *m*.
middle *adj* medio/dia; * *n* medio, centro *m*.
middle name *n* segundo nombre *m*.
middleweight *n* peso medio *m*.
middling *adj* mediano/na.
midge *n* mosquito *m*.
midget *n* enano/na *m/f*.
midi system *n* minicadena *f*.
midnight *n* medianoche *f*.
midriff *n* diafragma *m*.
midst *n* medio, centro *m*.
midsummer *n* pleno verano *m*.
midway *adv* a medio camino.
midwife *n* partera *f*.
midwifery *n* obstetricia *f*.
might *n* poder *m*; fuerza *f*.
mighty *adj* fuerte.
migraine *n* jaqueca *f*.
migrate *vi* emigrar, migrar.
migration *n* emigración, migración *f*.
migratory *adj* migratorio/ria.
mike *n* micrófono *m*.
mild *adj* apacible; suave; **~ly** *adv* suavemente.
mildew *n* moho *m*.
mildness *n* dulzura *f*.
mile *n* milla *f*.
mileage *n* kilometraje *m*.
milieu *n* ambiente *m*.
militant *adj* militante.
military *adj* militar.
militate *vi* militar.
militia *n* milicia *f*.

milk *n* leche *f*; * *vt* ordenar.
milkshake *n* batido de leche *m*, *Lat Am* malteada *f*.
milky *adj* lechoso/sa; **M~ Way** *n* Via Lactea *f*.
mill *n* molino *m*; * *vt* moler.
millennium *n* milenio *m*.
miller *n* molinero/ra *m/f*.
millet *n* (*bot*) mijo *m*.
milligram *n* miligramo *m*.
milliliter *n* mililitro *m*.
millimeter *n* milímetro *m*.
milliner *n* sombrerero/ra *m/f*.
millinery *n* sombrerería *f*.
million[1] *n* millón *m*.
millionaire *n* millonario/ria *m/f*.
millionth *adj*, *n* millonésimo/ma *m/f*.
millstone *n* piedra de molino *f*.
mime *n* mimo *m*.
mimic *vt* imitar.
mimicry *n* mímica *f*.
mince *vt* picar.
mind *n* mente *f*; * *vt* cuidar; * *vi* molestar.
minded *adj* dispuesto/ta.
mindful *adj* consciente.
mindless *adj* sin motivo.
mine *pn* mío, mía, mi; * *n* mina; * *vi* minar.
minefield *n* campo de minas *m*.
miner *n* minero/ra *m/f*.
mineral *adj*, *n* mineral *m*.
mineralogy *n* mineralogía *f*.
mineral water *n* agua mineral *f*.
minesweeper *n* dragaminas *m invar*.
mingle *vt* mezclar.
miniature *n* miniatura *f*.
minimal *adj* mínimo/ma.
minimize *vt* minimizar.
minimum *n* mínimo *m*.
mining *n* minería *f*.
minion *n* favorito/ta *m/f*.
minister *n* ministro/tro *m/f*; * *vt* servir.
ministerial *adj* ministerial.
ministry *n* ministerio *m*.
mink *n* visón *m*.
minnow *n* vario *m* (pez).
minor *adj* menor; * *n* menor (de edad) *m/f*.
minority *n* minoría *f*.
minstrel *n* juglar *m*.
mint *n* (*bot*) menta *f*; casa de la moneda *f*; * *vt* acuñar.
minus *adv* menos.
minute[1] *adj* diminuto/ta; **~ly** *adv* minuciosamente.
minute[2] *n* minuto *m*.
miracle *n* milagro *m*.
miraculous *adj* milagroso/sa.
mirage *n* espejismo *m*.
mire *n* fango *m*.
mirky *adj* turbio/bia.
mirror *n* espejo *m*.
mirth *n* alegría *f*.
mirthful *adj* alegre.

misadventure n desgracia f.

misanthrope, misanthropist n misántropo m.

misapply vt aplicar mal.

misapprehension n error m.

misbehave vi portarse mal.

misbehavior n mala conducta f.

miscalculate vt calcular mal.

miscarriage n aborto (espontáneo) m.

miscarry vi abortar (espontáneamente); malograrse.

miscellaneous adj varios, varias.

miscellany n miscelánea f.

mischief n mal, daño m.

mischievous adj dañoso/sa; travie-so/sa.

misconception n equivocación f.

misconduct n mala conducta f.

misconstrue vt interpretar mal.

miscount vt contar mal.

miscreant n malvado/da m/f.

misdeed n delito m.

misdemeanor n delito m.

misdirect vt dirigir mal.

miser n avaro/ra m/f.

miserable adj miserable, infeliz.

miserly adj mezquino/na, tacaño/ña.

misery n miseria f.

misfit n inadaptado/da m/f.

misfortune n desgracia f.

misgiving n recelo m; presentimiento m.

misgovern vt gobernar mal.

misguided adj equivocado/da.

mishandle vt manejar mal.

mishap n desgracia f.

misinform vt informar mal, Lat Am malinformar.

misinterpret vt interpretar mal.

misjudge vi juzgar mal.

mislay vt extraviar.

mislead vt engañar.

mismanage vt manejar mal.

mismanagement n mala administración f.

misnomer n nombre inapropriado m.

misogynist n misógino/na m/f.

misplace vt extraviar.

misprint vt imprimir mal; * n errata f.

misrepresent vt representar mal.

Miss n señorita f.

miss vt perder; echar de menos.

missal n misal m.

misshapen adj deforme.

missile n misil m.

missing adj perdido/da; ausente.

mission n misión f.

missionary n misionero/ra m/f.

misspent adj disipado/da.

mist n niebla f.

mistake vt entender mal; * vi equivocarse, engañarse; to be mistaken equivocarse; * n equivocación f; error m, Lat Am falla f, yerro m.

Mister n Señor m.

mistletoe n (bot) muérdago m.

mistress n amante f.

mistrust vt desconfiar; * n desconfianza f.

mistrustful adj desconfiado/da.

misty adj nebuloso/sa.

misunderstand vt entender mal.

misunderstanding n malentendido m.

misuse vt maltratar; abusar de.

miter n mitra f.

mitigate vt mitigar.

mitigation n mitigación f.

mittens npl manoplas fpl.

mix vt mezclar.

mixed adj surtido/da; mixto/ta.

mixed-up adj confuso/sa.

mixer n licuadora f.

mixture n mezcla f.

mix-up n confusión f.

moan n gemido m; * vi gemir; quejarse.

moat n foso m.

mob n multitud f.

mobile adj móvil; ~/cell phone móvil m, Lat Am celular m.

mobile home n caravana f.

mobility n movilidad f.

mobilize vt (mil) movilizar.

moccasin n mocasín m.

mock vt burlarse.

mockery n mofa f.

mode n modo m.

model n modelo m; * vt modelar.

modem n módem m.

moderate adj moderado/da; ~ly adv medianamente; * vt moderar.

moderation n moderación f.

modern adj moderno/na.

modernize vt modernizar.

modest adj modesto/ta; ~ly adv modestamente.

modesty n modestia f.

modicum n mínimo m.

modification n modificación f.

modify vt modificar.

modulate vt modular.

modulation n (mus) modulación f.

module n módulo m.

mogul n magnate m/f.

mohair n mohair m.

moist adj húmedo/da.

moisten vt humedecer.

moisture n humedad f.

molars npl muelas fpl.

molasses npl melaza f.

mold n molde m; moho m; * vt moldear.

molder vi decaer.

moldy adj enmohecido/da.

mole n topo m.

molecule n molécula f.

molehill n topera f.

molest vt importunar.

mollify vt apaciguar.

mollusk n molusco m.

mollycoddle vt mimar.

molt vt mudar.

molten adj derretido/da.

moment n momento m.

momentarily adv momentáneamente.

momentary adj momentáneo/nea.

momentous adj importante.

momentum n ímpetu m.

mommy n mamá f.

monarch n monarca m.

monarchy n monarquía f.

monastery n monasterio m.

monastic adj monástico/ca.

Monday n lunes m.

monetary adj monetario/ria.

money n dinero m, Lat Am plata f.

money box n hucha f, Lat Am alcancía f.

money laundering n blanqueo m.

money order n giro m.

Mongol n mongólico/ca m/f.

mongrel adj, n mestizo/za m/f.

monitor n monitor m.

monk n monje m.

monkey n mono m.

monochrome adj monocromo/ma.

monocle n monóculo m.

monolog n monólogo m.

monopolize vt monopolizar.

monopoly n monopolio m.

monosyllable n monosílabo m.

monotonous adj monótono/na.

monotony n monotonía f.

monsoon n (mar) monzón m.

monster n monstruo m.

monstrosity n monstruosidad f.

monstrous adj monstruoso/sa; ~ly adv monstruosamente.

montage n montaje m.

month n mes m.

monthly adj, adv mensual(mente).

monument n monumento m.

monumental adj monumental.

moo vi mugir.

mood n humor m.

moodiness n mal humor m.

moody adj malhumorado/da.

moon n luna f.

moonbeams npl rayos lunares mpl.

moonlight n luz de la luna f.

moor vt (mar) atracar.

mooring rope n amarra f.

moorland, moor n páramo m.

moose n alce m.

mop n fregona f; * vt fregar.

mope vi estar triste.

moped n ciclomotor m.

moral adj, ~ly adv moral(mente); ~s npl moralidad f.

morale n moral f.

moralist n moralista m/f.

morality n ética, moralidad f.

moralize vt, vi moralizar.

morass n pantano m.

morbid adj morboso/sa.

more adj, adv más; **never** ~ nunca más; **once** ~ otra vez; ~ **and** ~ más y más, cada vez más; **so much the** ~ cuanto más.

moreover adv además.

morgue n depósito de cadáveres m.

morning n mañana f; **good** ~ buenos días mpl.

moron n imbécil m/f.

morose adj hosco/ca.

morphine n morfina f.

morsel n bocado m.

mortal adj mortal; ~ly adv mortalmente; * n mortal m/f.

mortality n mortalidad f.

mortar n mortero m.

mortgage n hipoteca f; * vt hipotecar.

mortgage company n banco hipotecario m.

mortgager n deudor hipotecario m, deudora hipotecaria f.

mortician n director de pompas fúnebres.

mortification n mortificación f.

mortuary n depósito de cadáveres m.

mosaic n mosaico m.

mosque n mezquita f.

mosquito n mosquito m; zancudo/da m.

moss n (bot) musgo m, Lat Am lama f.

mossy adj cubierto/ta de musgo.

most adj la mayoría de; * adv sumamente; **at** ~ a lo sumo; ~ly adv principalmente.

motel n motel m.

moth n polilla f.

mothball n bola de naftalina f.

mother n madre f; **loving** ~ madraza f.

motherhood n maternidad f.

mother-in-law n suegra f.

motherless adj sin madre.

motherly adj maternal.

mother-of-pearl n nácar m.

mother-to-be n futura madre f.

mother tongue n lengua materna f.

motif n tema m.

motion n movimiento m.

motionless adj inmóvil.

motion picture n película f.

motivated adj motivado/da.

motive n motivo m.

motley adj abigarrado/da.

motor n motor m.

motorbike n moto f.

motorboat n lancha motora f.

motorcycle n motocicleta f.

motor scooter n moto f.

motor vehicle n automóvil m.

mottled adj multicolor.

motto n lema m.

mound n montón m.

mount n monte m; * vt subir.

mountain n montaña f.

mountaineer *n* montañero/ra *m/f*, alpinista *m/f*, *Lat Am* andinista *m/f.*

mountaineering *n* montañismo *m*, alpinismo *m*, *Lat Am* andinismo *m.*

mountainous *adj* montañoso/sa.

mourn *vt* lamentar.

mourner *n* doliente *m/f.*

mournful *adj* triste; **~ly** *adv* tristemente.

mourning *n* luto *m.*

mouse *n* (*pl* mice) ratón *m.*

mouse mat *n* alfombrilla *f.*

mousse *n* mousse *f.*

mouth *n* boca *f*; desembocadura *f.*

mouthful *n* bocado *m.*

mouth organ *n* harmónica *f.*

mouthpiece *n* boquilla *f.*

mouthwash *n* enjuague *m.*

mouthwatering *adj* apetitoso/sa.

movable *adj* movible.

move *vt* mover; proponer; * *vi* moverse; * *n* movimiento *m.*

movement *n* movimiento *m.*

movie *n* película *f.*

movie camera *n* cámara cinematográfica *f.*

movie theater, movie house *n* cine *m.*

moving *adj* conmovedor/a.

mow *vt* segar.

mower *n* cortacésped *m.*

Mrs *n* señora *f.*

much *adj, adv* mucho/cha; con mucho.

muck *n* suciedad *f.*

mucous *adj* mocoso/sa.

mucus *n* moco *m.*

mud *n* barro *m.*

muddle *vt* confundir *m*; confusión *f.*

muddy *adj* fangoso/sa.

mudguard *n* guardabarros *m invar.*

muffle *vt* embozar.

mug *n* jarra *f.*

muggy *adj* bochornoso/sa.

mulberry *n* mora *f*; **~ tree** morera *f.*

mule *n* mulo *m*, mula *f.*

mull *vt* meditar.

multifarious *adj* múltiple.

multimedia *adj* multimedia.

multiple *adj* múltiplo *m.*

multiplication *n* multiplicación *f*; **~ table** tabla de multiplicar *f.*

multiply *vt* multiplicar.

multitude *n* multitud *f.*

mumble *vt, vi* refunfuñar.

mummy *n* momia *f.*

mumps *npl* paperas *fpl.*

munch *vt, vi* mascar.

mundane *adj* trivial.

municipal *adj* municipal.

municipality *n* municipalidad *f.*

munificence *n* munificencia *f.*

munitions *npl* municiones *fpl.*

mural *n* mural *m.*

murder *n* asesinato *m*; homicidio *m*; * *vt* asesinar.

murderer *n* asesino/na *m/f.*

murderess *n* asesina *f.*

murderous *adj* homicida.

murky *adj* sombrío/ría.

murmur *n* murmullo *m*;* *vi* murmurar.

muscle *n* músculo *m.*

muscular *adj* muscular.

muse *vi* meditar.

museum *n* museo *m.*

mushroom *n* (*bot*) seta *f*; champiñón *m.*

music *n* musica *f.*

musical *adj* musical; melodioso/sa.

musician *n* músico/ca *m/f.*

musk *n* almizcle *m.*

muslin *n* muselina *f.*

mussel *n* mejillón *m.*

must *v aux* tener que, deber; deber de.

mustache *n* bigote *m.*

mustard *n* mostaza *f.*

muster *vt* agregar.

musty *adj* mohoso/sa, añejo/ja.

mute *adj* mudo/da, silencioso/sa.

muted *adj* callado/da.

mutilate *vt* mutilar.

mutilation *n* mutilación *f.*

mutiny *n* motin, tumulto *m*; * *vi* amotinarse, rebelarse.

mutter *vt, vi* murmurar, musitar; * *n* murmuración *f.*

mutton *n* carnero *m.*

mutual *adj* mutuo/tua, mutual, recí-proco/ca; **~ly** *adv* mutuamente, recíprocamente.

muzzle *n* bozal *m*; hocico *m*; * *vt* embozar.

my *pn* mi, mis; mío, mia; míos, mías.

myriad *n* miríada *f*; gran número *m.*

myrrh *n* mirra *f.*

myrtle *n* mirto, arrayán *m.*

myself *pn* yo mismo/ma.

mysterious *adj* misterioso/sa; **~ly** *adv* misteriosamente.

mystery *n* misterio *m.*

mystic(al) *adj* místico/ca.

mystify *vt* dejar perplejo/ja.

mystique *n* misterio *m.*

myth *n* mito *m.*

mythology *n* mitología *f.*

N

nab *vt* agarrar.

nag *n* jaca *f*; * *vt* regañar.

nagging *adj* persistente; * *npl* quejas *fpl.*

nail *n* uña *f*; garra *f*; clavo *m*; * *vt* clavar.

nailbrush *n* cepillo de uñas *m.*

nailfile *n* lima de uñas *f.*

nail polish *n* esmalte de uñas *m.*

nail scissors *npl* tijeras de manicura *fpl.*

naïve *adj* ingenuo/nua.

naked *adj* desnudo/da evidente; puro/ra, simple.

name n nombre m; fama, reputación f; * vt nombrar; mencionar.

nameless adj anónimo/ma.

namely adv a saber.

namesake n tocayo/ya m/f.

nanny n niñera f.

nap n sueño ligero m.

napalm n napalm m.

nape n nuca f.

napkin n servilleta f.

narcissus n (bot) narciso m.

narcotic adj narcótico/ca; * n narcótico m.

narrate vt narrar, relatar.

narrative adj narrativo/va; * n narrativa f.

narrow adj angosto/ta, estrecho/cha; ~ly adv estrechamente; * vt estrechar; limitar.

narrow-minded adj estrecho/cha de miras.

narrow pass n puerto m.

nasal adj nasal.

nasty adj sucio/cia, puerco/ca; obsce-no/na; sórdido/da.

natal adj nativo/va; natal.

nation n nación f.

national adj, ~ly adv nacional(men-te).

nationalism n nacionalismo m.

nationalist adj, n nacionalista m/f.

nationality n nacionalidad f.

nationalize vt nacionalizar.

nationwide adj a nivel nacional.

native adj nativo/va; * n natural m/f.

native language n lengua materna f.

Nativity n Navidad f.

natural adj natural; sencillo/lla; ~ly adv naturalmente.

natural gas n gas natural m.

naturalist n naturalista m/f.

naturalize vt naturalizar.

nature n naturaleza f; índole f.

naturopath n naturópata m/f.

naught, nought n cero m.

naughty adj malo/la, malvado/da.

nausea n náuseas fpl, gana de vomitar f.

nauseate vt dar náuseas a.

nauseous adj fastidioso/sa.

nautical, naval adj náutico/ca, naval.

nave n nave (de la iglesia) f.

navel n ombligo m.

navigate vi navegar.

navigation n navegación f.

navy n marina f; armada f.

Nazi n nazi m/f.

near prep cerca de, junto a; * adv casi; cerca, cerca de; * adj cercano/na, proximo/ma.

nearby adj cercano/na.

nearly adv casi.

near-sighted adj miope.

neat adj hermoso/sa, pulido/da; puro/ra; neto/ta; ~ly adv elegantemente.

nebulous adj nebuloso/sa.

necessarily adv necesariamente.

necessary adj necesario/ria.

necessitate vt necesitar.

necessity n necesidad f.

neck n cuello m, Lat Am cogote m; * vi besuquearse.

necklace n collar m.

nectar n néctar m.

née, nee adj: ~ Brown de soltera Brown.

need n necesidad f; pobreza f; * vt necesitar.

needle n aguja f.

needless adj superfluo/lua, inútil.

needlework n costura f; bordado de aguja m; obra de punto m.

needy adj necesitado/da, pobre.

negation n negación f.

negative adj negativo/va; ~ly adv negativamente; * n negativa f.

neglect vt descuidar, desatender; * n negligencia f.

negligee n salto de cama m.

negligence n negligencia f; descuido m.

negligent adj negligente, descuidado/da; ~ly adv negligentemente.

negligible adj insignificante.

negotiate vt, vi negociar (con).

negotiation n negociación f; negocio m.

Negress n negra f.

Negro adj negro/gra; * n negro m.

neigh vi relinchar; * n relincho m.

neighbor n vecino/na m/f; * vt confinar.

neighborhood n vecindad f; vecindario m.

neighboring adj vecino/na.

neighborly adj sociable.

neither conj ni; * pn ninguno/na, ni uno ni otro, ni una ni otra.

neon n neón m.

neon light n luz de neón f.

nephew n sobrino m.

nepotism n nepotismo m.

nerve n nervio m; valor m.

nerve-racking adj espantoso/sa.

nervous adj nervioso/sa; nervudo/da.

nervous breakdown n crisis nerviosa f.

nest n nido m; nidada f.

nest egg n (fig) ahorros mpl.

nestle vt anidarse.

net n red f.

netball n nétbol m.

net curtain n visillo m.

netting n mallado m.

nettle n ortiga f.

network n red f, malla f.

neuron n neurona f.

neurosis n neurosis f invar.

neurotic adj, n neurótico/ca m/f.

neuter adj (gr) neutro/tra.

neutral adj neutral.

neutrality n neutralidad f.

neutralize vt neutralizar.

neutron n neutrón m.

neutron bomb n bomba de neutrones f.

never adv nunca, jamás; ~ mind no importa.

never-ending *adj* sin fin.

nevertheless *adv* no obstante.

new *adj* nuevo/va, fresco/sca, reciente; **~ly** *adv* nuevamente.

newborn *adj* recién nacido/da.

newcomer *n* recién llegado/da *m*.

new-fangled *adj* inventado/da por novedad.

news *npl* novedad, noticias *fpl*.

news agency *n* agencia de noticias *f*.

newscaster *n* presentador/a *m/f*.

newsdealer *n* vendedor/a de periódicos *m/f*.

news flash *n* noticia de última hora *f*.

newsletter *n* boletín *m*.

newspaper *n* periódico *m*.

newsreel *n* noticiario *m*.

New Year *n* Año Nuevo *m*; **~'s Day** Día de Año Nuevo *m*; **~'s Eve** Nochevieja *f*.

next *adj* próximo/ma; **the ~ day** el día siguiente; * *adv* luego, inmediatamente después.

nib *n* pico *m*; punta *f*.

nibble *vt* picar, mordiscar.

nice *adj* simpático/ca; agradable; lindo/da; **~ly** *adv* bien.

nice-looking *adj* guapo/pa.

niche *n* nicho *m*.

nick *n* mella *f*; * *vt* (*col*) robar.

nickel *n* níquel *m*; moneda de cinco centavos *f*.

nickname *n* mote, apodo *m*; * *vt* poner apodos.

nicotine *n* nicotina *f*.

niece *n* sobrina *f*.

niggling *adj* insignificante.

night *n* noche *f*; velador *m*; **by ~** de noche; **good ~** buenas noches.

nightclub *n* cabaret *m*.

nightfall *n* anochecer *m*.

nightingale *n* ruiseñor *m*.

nightly *adv* por las noches, todas las noches; * *adj* nocturno/na.

nightmare *n* pesadilla *f*.

night school *n* clases nocturnas *fpl*.

night shift *n* turno de noche *m*.

night-time *n* noche *f*.

night work *n* vela *f*.

nihilist *n* nihilista *m/f*.

nimble *adj* ligero/ra, activo/va, listo/ta, ágil.

nine *adj*, *n* nueve.

ninepin *n* bolo *m*.

nineteen *adj*, *n* diecinueve.

nineteenth *adj*, *n* decimonoveno/na.

ninetieth *adj*, *n* nonagésimo/ma.

ninety *n* noventa.

ninth *adj*, *n* nono/na, noveno/na.

nip *vt* pellizcar; morder.

nipple *n* pezón *m*; tetilla *f*.

nit *n* liendre *f*.

nitrogen *n* nitrógeno *m*.

no *adv* no; * *adj* ningún, ninguno/na.

nobility *n* nobleza *f*.

noble *adj* noble; insigne; * *n* noble *m/f*.

nobleman *n* noble *m*.

nobody *n* nadie, ninguna persona *f*.

nocturnal *adj* nocturnal, nocturno/na.

nod *n* cabeceo *m*; señal *f*; * *vi* cabecear; amodorrarse.

noise *n* ruido, estruendo *m*; rumor *m*.

noisily *adv* con ruido.

noisiness *n* ruido, tumulto, alboroto *m*.

noisy *adj* ruidoso/sa, turbulento/ta.

nominal *adj*, **~ly** *adv* nominal(men-te).

nominate *vt* nombrar.

nomination *n* nominación *f*.

nominative *n* (*gr*) nominativo *m*.

nominee *n* candidato/ta *m/f*.

nonalcoholic *adj* no alcóholico/ca.

nonaligned *adj* no alineado/da.

nonchalant *adj* indiferente.

noncommittal *adj* reservado/da.

nonconformist *n* inconformista *m/f*.

nondescript *adj* no descrito/ta.

none *adj* nadie, ninguno/na.

nonentity *n* nulidad *f*.

nonetheless *adv* sin embargo.

nonexistent *adj* inexistente.

nonfiction *n* no ficción *f*.

nonplussed *adj* confuso/sa.

nonsense *n* disparate, absurdo *m*, *Lat Am* sonsera *f*.

nonsensical *adj* absurdo/da.

nonsmoker *n* no fumador/a *m/f*.

nonstick *adj* antiadherente.

nonstop *adj* directo/ta; * *adv* sin parar.

noodles *npl* fideos (chinos) *mpl*.

noon *n* mediodía *m*.

noose *n* nudo corredizo *m*.

nor *conj* ni.

normal *adj* normal.

north *n* norte *m*; * *adj* del norte.

North America *n* América del Norte, Norteamérica *f*.

northeast *n* nor(d)este *m*.

northerly, northern *adj* norteño/ña.

North Pole *n* polo norte *m*.

northward(s) *adv* hacia el norte.

northwest *n* nor(d)oeste *m*.

nose *n* nariz *f*; olfato *m*.

nosebleed *n* hemorragia nasal *f*.

nosedive *n* picado vertical *m*.

nostalgia *n* nostalgia *f*.

nostril *n* ventana de la nariz *f*.

not *adv* no.

notable *adj* notable; memorable.

notably *adv* especialmente.

notary *n* notario/ria *m/f*.

notch *n* muesca *f*; * *vt* hacer muescas.

note *n* nota, marca *f*; señal *f*; aprecio *m*; billete *m*; consecuen cia *f*; noticia *f*; indirecta *f*; * *vt* notar, marcar; observar.

notebook *n* cuaderno *m*, libreta *f*.

noted *adj* afamado/da, celebre.

notepad *n* bloc *m*.

notepaper *n* papel de cartas *m*.

nothing *n* nada *f*; **good for ~** lo que sirve para nada.

notice *n* noticia *f*; aviso *m*; * *vt* observar.

noticeable *adj* notable, reparable.

notification *n* notificación *f*.

notify *vt* notificar.

notion *n* noción *f*; opinión *f*; idea *f*.

notoriety *n* mala fama *f*.

notorious *adj* tristemente célebre; **~ly** *adv* notoriamente.

notwithstanding *conj* no obstante, aunque.

nougat *n* turrón *m*.

noun *n* (*gr*) sustantivo *m*.

nourish *vt* nutrir, alimentar.

nourishing *adj* nutritivo/va.

nourishment *n* nutrimiento, alimento *m*.

novel *n* novela *f*.

novelist *n* novelista *m/f*.

novelty *n* novedad *f*.

November *n* noviembre *m*.

novice *n* novicio/cia *m/f*.

now *adv* ya, ahora, hoy (en) día; **~ and then** de vez en cuando.

nowadays *adv* hoy (en) día.

nowhere *adv* en ninguna parte.

noxious *adj* nocivo/va, dañoso/sa.

nozzle *n* boquilla *f*.

nuance *n* matiz *m*.

nuclear *adj* nuclear; **~ power** energía nuclear *f*; **~ power station** *n* central nuclear *f*.

nucleus *n* núcleo *m*.

nude *adj* desnudo/da, en carnes, en cueros, sin vestido.

nudge *vt* dar un codazo a.

nudist *n* nudista *m/f*.

nudity *n* desnudez *f*.

nuisance *n* daño, perjuicio *m*; incomodidad *f*.

nuke *n* (*col*) bomba atómica *f*; * *vt* atacar con arma nuclear.

null *adj* nulo/la, inválido/da.

nullify *vt* anular, invalidar.

numb *adj* entorpecido/da; * *vt* entorpecer.

number *n* número *m*; cantidad *f*; * *vt* numerar.

numbness *n* entumecimiento *m*.

numeral *n* número *m*.

numerical *adj* numérico/ca.

numerous *adj* numeroso/sa.

nun *n* monja, religiosa *f*.

nunnery *n* convento de monjas *m*.

nuptial *adj* nupcial; **~s** *npl* nupcias *fpl*.

nurse *n* enfermera *f*; * *vt* cuidar; amamantar.

nursery *n* guardería infantil *f*; criadero *m*.

nursery rhyme *n* canción infantil *f*.

nursing home *n* clínica de reposo *f*.

nurture *vt* criar, educar.

nut *n* nuez *f*.

nutcrackers *npl* cascanueces *m invar*.

nutmeg *n* nuez moscada *f*.

nutritious *adj* nutritivo/va.

nutshell *n* cáscara de nuez *f*.

nylon *n* nylon, nailon *m*; * *adj* de nylon, de nailon.

O

oak *n* roble *m*.

oar *n* remo *m*.

oasis *n* oasis *f invar*.

oath *n* juramento *m*.

oatmeal *n* harina de avena *f*.

oats *npl* avena *f*.

obedience *n* obediencia *f*.

obedient *adj*, **~ly** *adv* obedien-te(mente).

obese *adj* obeso/sa, gordo/da.

obesity *n* obesidad *f*.

obey *vt* obedecer.

obituary *n* necrología *f*.

object *n* objeto *m*; * *vt* objetar.

objection *n* oposición, objeción, réplica *f*.

objectionable *adj* desagradable.

objective *adj* objetivo/va; * *n* objetivo *m*.

obligation *n* obligación *f*.

obligatory *adj* obligatorio/ria.

oblige *vt* obligar; complacer, favorecer.

obliging *adj* servicial.

oblique *adj* oblicuo/cua; indirecto/ta; **~ly** *adv* oblicuamente.

obliterate *vt* borrar.

oblivion *n* olvido *m*.

oblivious *adj* olvidadizo/za.

oblong *adj* oblongo/ga.

obnoxious *adj* odioso/sa.

oboe *n* oboe *m*.

obscene *adj* obsceno/na, impúdico/ca.

obscenity *n* obscenidad *f*.

obscure *adj* oscuro/ra; **~ly** *adv* oscuramente; * *vt* oscurecer.

obscurity *n* oscuridad *f*.

observance *n* observancia *f*; reverencia *f*.

observant *adj* observante, respetuo-so/sa.

observantly *adv* cuidadosamente, atentamente.

observation *n* observación *f*.

observatory *n* observatorio *m*.

observe *vt* observar, mirar.

observer *n* observador/a *m/f*.

obsess *vt* obsesionar.

obsessive *adj* obsesivo/va.

obsolete *adj* obsoleto/ta.

obstacle *n* obstáculo *m*.

obstinacy *n* tenacidad *f*.

obstinate *adj* obstinado/da; **~ly** *adv* obstinadamente.

obstruct *vt* obstruir; impedir.

obstruction *n* obstrucción *f*; impedimento *m*.

obtain *vt* obtener, adquirir; **~ by cunning** sonsacar.

obtainable *adj* asequible.

obtrusive *adj* intruso/sa, importuno/na.

obtuse *adj* obtuso/sa, sin punta; lerdo/da, torpe.

obvious *adj* obvio/via, evidente; **~ly** *adv* naturalmente.

occasion *n* ocasión *f*; momento oportuno *m*; * *vt* ocasionar, causar.

occasional *adj* ocasional, casual; **~ly** *adv* ocasionalmente.

occupant, occupier *n* ocupante *m/f*; poseedor/a *m/f*; inquilino/na *m/f*.

occupation *n* ocupación *f*; empleo *m*.

occupy *vt* ocupar, emplear.

occur *vi* pasar, ocurrir.

occurrence *n* incidente *m*.

ocean *n* océano *m*; alta mar *f*.

ocean-going *adj* de alta mar.

oceanic *adj* océanico/ca.

ocher *n* ocre *m*.

octave *n* octava *f*.

October *n* octubre *m*.

octopus *n* pulpo *m*.

odd *adj* impar; particular; extravagante; extraño/ña; **~ly** *adv* extrañamente.

oddity *n* singularidad, particularidad, rareza *f*.

oddness *n* desigualdad *f*; singularidad *f*.

odds *npl* probabilidades *fpl*; apuestas *fpl*.

odious *adj* odioso/sa.

odometer *n* cuentakilómetros *m invar*.

odor *n* olor *m*; fragancia *f*.

odorous, odoriferous *adj* odorífero/ra.

of *prep* de; tocante; segun.

of course! *interj* inaturalmente!

off *adv* desconectado/da; apagado/da; cerrado/da; cancelado/da; **~!** *excl* lfuera!

offend *vt* ofender, irritar; injuriar; * *vi* pecar.

offender *n* delincuente *m*.

offense *n* ofensa *f*; injuria *f*.

offensive *adj* ofensivo/va; injurioso/sa; **~ly** *adv* ofensivamente.

offer *vt* ofrecer; * *n* oferta *f*.

offering *n* sacrificio *m*; oferta *f*.

offhand *adj* descortés; * *adv* de repente.

office *n* oficina *f*; oficio, empleo *m*; servicio *m*.

office building *n* bloque de oficinas *m*.

office hours *npl* horas de oficina *fpl*.

officer *n* oficial/a, empleado/da *m/f*.

office worker *n* oficinista *m/f*.

official *adj* oficial; **~ly** *adv* de oficio; * *n* empleado *m*.

officiate *vi* oficiar.

officious *adj* oficioso/sa; **~ly** *adv* oficiosamente.

off-line *adj, adv* fuera de línea.

off-peak *adj* de temporada baja.

off-season *adj, adv* fuera de temporada, en tarifa reducida.

offset *vt* contrarrestar.

offshoot *n* ramificación *f*.

offshore *adj* costero/ra.

offside *adj* fuera de juego.

offspring *n* prole *f*; linaje *m*; descendencia *f*.

offstage *adv* entre bastidores.

off-the-peg *adj* confeccionado/da.

ogle *vt* comerse con los ojos.

oil *n* aceite *m*; óleo *m*; * *vt* engrasar.

oilcan *n* lata de aceite *f*.

oilfield *n* campo petrolífero *m*.

oil filter *n* filtro de aceite *m*.

oil painting *n* pintura al óleo *f*.

oil rig *n* torre de perforación *f*.

oil slick *n* marea negra *f*.

oil tanker *n* petrolero *m*.

oil well *n* pozo petrolífero *m*.

oily *adj* aceitoso/sa; grasiento/ta.

ointment *n* ungüento *m*.

OK, okay *excl* vale, *Lat Am* okey; * *adj* bien; * *vt* dar el visto bueno a.

old *adj* viejo/ja; antiguo/gua.

old age *n* vejez *f*.

old-fashioned *adj* pasado/da de moda.

olive *n* olivo *m*; oliva *f*.

olive oil *n* aceite de oliva *m*.

Olympic Games *npl* las Olímpicos *fpl*.

omelet *n* tortilla (francesa) *f*, *Lat Am* omelet *f*.

omen *n* agüero, presagio *m*.

ominous *adj* ominoso/sa.

omission *n* omisión *f*; descuido *m*.

omit *vt* omitir.

omnipotence *n* omnipotencia *f*.

omnipotent *adj* omnipotente, todo-poderoso/sa.

on *prep* sobre, encima, en; de; a; * *adj* encendido/da; prendido/da; abier-to/ta; puesto/ta.

once *adv* una vez; **at ~** en seguida; **all at ~** de una vez, en seguida; **~ more** otra vez.

oncoming *adj* que viene de frente.

one *adj* un, uno, una; **~ by ~** uno a uno, una a una, uno por uno, una por una.

one-day excursion *n* billete de ida y vuelta en un día *m*.

one-man *adj* individual.

onerous *adj* oneroso/sa, molesto/ta.

oneself *pn* sí mismo; sí misma.

one-sided *adj* parcial.

one-to-one *adj* de uno a uno; cara a cara.

ongoing *adj* continuo/nua.

onion *n* cebolla *f*.

on line *adj, adv* en línea.

onlooker *n* espectador/a *m/f*.

only *adj* único/ca, solo/la; * *adv* solamente.

onset, onslaught *n* acometida *f*; ataque *m*.

onus *n* responsabilidad *f*.

onward(s) *adv* adelante.

ooze *vi* manar suavemente, rezumar.

opaque *adj* opaco/ca.

open *adj* abierto/ta; patente, evidente; sincero/ra, franco/ca; **~ly** *adv* con franqueza; * *vt* (*vi*) abrir(se); descubrir(se); **to ~ on to** dar a; **to ~ up** *vt* abrir; *vi* abrirse.

opening *n* abertura *f*; (*com*) salida *f*; principio *m*.

open-minded *adj* de mentalidad abierta.

openness *n* claridad *f*; franqueza, sinceridad *f*.

opera *n* ópera *f*.

opera house *n* teatro de la ópera *m*.

operate *vi* obrar, operar.

operating theater *n* quirófano *m*.

operation *n* operación *f*; efecto *m*.

operational *adj* operacional.

operative *adj* operativo/va.

operator *n* operario/ria *m/f*; opera-dor/a *m/f*.

ophthalmic *adj* oftálmico/ca.

opine *vi* opinar, juzgar.

opinion *n* opinión *f*; juicio *m*.

opinionated *adj* testarudo/da.

opinion poll *n* sondeo *m*.

opponent *n* antagonista *m/f*; adver-sario/ria *m/f*.

opportune *adj* oportuno/na.

opportunist *n* oportunista *m/f*.

opportunity *n* oportunidad *f*.

oppose *vt* oponerse.

opposing *adj* opuesto/ta.

opposite *adj* opuesto/ta; contrario/ria; * *adv* enfrente; *prep* frente a; * *n* lo contrario.

opposition *n* oposición *f*; resistencia *f*; impedimento *m*.

oppress *vt* oprimir.

oppression *n* opresión *f*.

oppressive *adj* opresivo/va, cruel.

oppressor *n* opresor/a *m/f*.

optic(al) *adj* óptico/ca; **~s** *npl* óptica *f*.

optician *n* óptico/ca *m/f*.

optimist *n* optimista *m/f*.

optimistic *adj* optimista.

optimum *adj* óptimo/ma.

option *n* opción *f*; deseo *m*.

optional *adj* facultativo/va.

opulent *adj* opulento/ta.

or *conj* o; u.

oracle *n* oráculo *m*.

oral *adj* oral, vocal; **~ly** *adv* verbalmente, de palabra.

orange *n* naranja *f*.

orator *n* orador/a *m/f*.

orbit *n* órbita *f*.

orchard *n* huerto *m*.

orchestra *n* orquesta *f*.

orchestral *adj* orquestal.

orchid *n* orquídea *f*.

ordain *vt* ordenar; establecer.

ordeal *n* prueba rigurosa *f*.

order *n* orden *m/f*; regla *f*; mandato *m*; serie, clase *f*; * *vt* ordenar, arreglar; mandar.

order form *n* hoja de pedido *f*.

orderly *adj* ordenado/da, regular.

ordinarily *adv* ordinariamente.

ordinary *adj* ordinario/ria.

ordination *n* ordenación *f*.

ordnance *n* armamento *m*; pertrechos *mpl*.

ore *n* mineral *m*.

organ *n* órgano *m*.

organic *adj* orgánico/ca.

organic farming *n* agricultura biológica *f*.

organism *n* organismo *m*.

organist *n* organista *m/f*.

organization *n* organización *f*.

organize *vt* organizar.

orgasm *n* orgasmo *m*.

orgy *n* orgía *f*.

oriental *adj* oriental.

orifice *n* orificio *m*.

origin *n* origen, principio *m*.

original *adj* original, primitivo/va; **~ly** *adv* originalmente.

originality *n* originalidad *f*.

originate *vi* originar.

ornament *n* ornamento *m*; * *vt* ornamentar, adornar.

ornamental *adj* ornamental, decora-tivo/va.

ornate *adj* adornado/da, ataviado/da.

ornithology *n* ornitología *f*.

orphan *adj*, *n* huérfano/na *m/f*.

orphanage *n* orfanato *m*.

orthodox *adj* ortodoxo/xa.

orthodoxy *n* ortodoxia *f*.

orthography *n* ortografía *f*.

orthopedic *adj* ortopédico/ca.

Oscar *n* óscar *m*.

oscillate *vi* oscilar, vibrar.

osprey *n* águila pescadora *f*.

ostensibly *adv* aparentemente.

ostentatious *adj* ostentoso/sa.

osteopath *n* osteópata *m/f*.

ostracize *vt* condenar al ostracismo.

ostrich *n* avestruz *m*.

other *pn* otro, otra.

otherwise *adv* de otra manera, por otra parte.

otter *n* nutria *f*.

ouch *excl* ¡ay!

ought *v aux* deber, ser menester.

ounce *n* onza *f*.

our, ours *pn* nuestro, nuestra, nuestros, nuestras.

ourselves *pn pl* nosotros mismos, nosotras mismas.

oust *vt* quitar; desposeer.

out *adv* fuera, afuera; apagado/da.

outboard *adj*: **~ motor** fueraborda *m*.

outbreak *n* erupción *f*.

outburst *n* explosión *f*.

outcast *n* paria *m/f*.

outcome *n* resultado *m*.

outcry *n* clamor *m*; griterío *m*.

outdated *adj* fuera de moda.

outdo *vt* exceder a otro, sobrepujar.

outdoor *adj*, **~s** *adv* al aire libre.

outer *adj* exterior.

outermost *adj* extremo/ma; lo más exterior.

outer space *n* espacio exterior *m*.

outfit *n* vestidos *mpl*; ropa *f*.

outfitter *n* sastre *m*.

outgoing *adj* extrovertido/da.

outgrow *vt* sobrecrecer.

outhouse *n* dependencia (de una casa) *f*.

outing *n* excursión *f*.

outlandish *adj* estrafalario/ria.

outlaw *n* bandido *m*; * *vt* proscribir.

outlay *n* despensa *f*, gastos *mpl*.

outlet *n* salida *f*.

outline *n* contorno *m*; bosquejo *m*.

outlive *vt* sobrevivir.

outlook *n* perspectiva *f.*

outlying *adj* distante, lejos.

outmoded *adj* anticuado/da.

outnumber *vt* superar en número.

out-of-date *adj* caducado/da; pasado/da de moda.

outpatient *n* paciente externo/na *m/f.*

outpost *n* puesto avanzado *m.*

output *n* rendimiento *m*; salida *f.*

outrage *n* ultraje *m*; * *vt* ultrajar.

outrageous *adj* escandaloso/sa; atroz; **~ly** *adv* escandalosamente; injuriosamente; enormemente.

outright *adv* absolutamente; * *adj* completo/ta.

outrun *vt* correr más que.

outset *n* principio *m.*

outshine *vt* exceder en brillantez, eclipsar.

outside *n* superficie *f*; exterior *m*; apariencia *f*; * *adv* fuera, *Lat Am* afuera de; * *prep* fuera de.

outsider *n* forástero *m/f.*

outsize *adj* de talla grande.

outskirts *npl* alrededores *mpl.*

outspoken *adj* muy franco/ca.

outstanding *adj* excepcional; pendiente.

outstretch *vt* extenderse, alargar.

outstrip *vt* dejar atrás; superar.

out-tray *n* bandeja de salida *f.*

outward *adj* exterior, externo/na; de ida; **~ly** *adv* por fuera; exteriormente.

outweigh *vt* pesar más que.

outwit *vt* burlar.

oval *n* óvalo *m*; * *adj* oval.

ovary *n* ovario *m.*

oven *n* horno *m.*

ovenproof *adj* resistente al horno.

over *prep* sobre, encima; más de; durante; **all ~** por todos lados; * *adj* terminado/da; de sobra; **~ again** otra vez; **~ and ~** repetidas veces.

overall *adj* total; * *adv* en conjunto.

overalls *npl* mono *m*; *Lat Am* overol *m.*

overawe *vt* imponer respeto.

overbalance *vi* perder el equilibrio.

overbearing *adj* déspotico/ca.

overboard *adv* (*mar*) por la borda, al mar.

overbook *vt* sobrereservar.

overcast *adj* encapotado/da.

overcharge *vt* sobrecargar; cobrar de más.

overcoat *n* abrigo *m.*

overcome *vt* vencer; superar.

overconfident *adj* demasiado confia-do/da.

overcrowded *adj* atestado/da; super-poblado/da.

overdo *vi* hacer más de lo necesario; exagerar.

overdose *n* sobredosis *f invar.*

overdraft *n* saldo deudor, descubierto *m.*

overdrawn *adj* en descubierto.

overdress *vt* engalanar con exceso.

overdue *adj* retrasado/da.

overeat *vi* comer demasiado.

overestimate *vt* sobreestimar.

overflow *vt*, *vi* inundar; rebosar; * *n* inundación *f*; superabundancia *f.*

overgrown *adj* invadido/da.

overgrowth *n* vegetación exuberante *f.*

overhang *vt* colgar sobre.

overhaul *vt* revisar; * *n* revisión *f.*

overhead *adv* sobre la cabeza, en lo alto.

overhear *vt* oír por casualidad.

overjoyed *adj* muy gozoso/sa.

overkill *n* exceso de medios *m.*

overland *adj*, *adv* por tierra.

overlap *vi* traslaparse.

overleaf *adv* al dorso.

overload *vt* sobrecargar.

overlook *vt* mirar desde lo alto; examinar; repasar; pasar por alto, tolerar; descuidar.

overnight *adv* durante la noche; * *adj* de noche.

overpass *n* paso superior *m.*

overpower *vt* predominar, oprimir.

overpowering *adj* agobiante.

overrate *vt* sobrevalorar.

override *vt* no hacer caso de; anular.

overriding *adj* predominante.

overrule *vt* denegar.

overrun *vt* inundar; infestar; rebasar.

overseas *adv* fuera del país; * *adj* extranjero/ra.

oversee *vt* inspeccionar.

overseer *n* superintendente *m.*

overshadow *vt* eclipsar.

overshoot *vt* excederse.

oversight *n* yerro *m*; equivocación *f.*

oversleep *vi* dormir demasiado.

overspill *n* exceso de población *m.*

overstate *vi* exagerar.

overstep *vt* traspasar, exceder.

overt *adj* abierto/ta; publico/ca; **~ly** *adv* abiertamente.

overtake *vt* adelantar, sobrepasar.

overthrow *vt* trastornar; demoler; destruir; * *n* trastorno *m*; ruina, derrota *f.*

overtime *n* horas extra *fpl.*

overtone *n* trasfondo *m.*

overture *n* abertura *f*; (*mus*) obertura *f.*

overturn *vt* subvertir, trastornar.

overweight *adj* demasiado pesado/da.

overwhelm *vt* abrumar; oprimir; sumergir.

overwhelming *adj* arrollador/a; irresistible.

overwork *vi* trabajar demasiado.

owe *vt* deber, tener deudas; estar obligado/da.

owing *adj* que es debido/da; **~ to** por causa de.

owl *n* búho *m.*

own *adj* propio/pia; **my ~** mío, mía; * *vt* tener; poseer; **to ~ up** *vi* confesar.

owner *n* dueño/ña, propietario/ria *m/f.*

ownership *n* posesión *f.*

ox *n* buey *m*; **~en** *pl* ganado vacuno *m.*

oxidize *vt* oxidar.

oxygen *n* oxígeno *m.*

oxygen mask *n* máscara de oxígeno *f.*

oxygen tent *n* tienda de oxígeno *f.*

oyster *n* ostra *f*.
ozone *n* ozono *m*.

P

pa *n* papá *m*.
pace *n* paso *m*; * *vt* regular el ritmo de; * *vi* pasear.
pacemaker *n* marcapasos *m invar*.
pacific *adj* pacífico/ca; P~ Ocean el Pacífico *m*.
pacification *n* pacificación *f*.
pacifier *n* chupete *m*.
pacify *vt* pacificar.
pack *n* lío, fardo *m*; baraja (de naipes) *f*; cuadrilla *f*; * *vt* empaquetar; hacer la maleta; llenar.
package *n* paquete *m*; acuerdo *m*.
package tour *n* viaje organizado *m*.
packet *n* paquete *m*.
packing *n* embalaje *m*.
pact *n* pacto *m*.
pad *n* bloc *m*; plataforma *f*; (*col*) casa *f*; * *vt* rellenar.
padding *n* relleno *m*; paja *f*.
paddle *vi* vadear; remar; chapotear; * *n* canalete *m*.
paddle steamer *n* vapor de ruedas *m*.
paddling pool *n* piscina para niños *f*.
paddock *n* corral *m*.
paddy field *n* arrozal *m*.
pagan *adj, n* pagano/na *m/f*.
page *n* página *f*; paje *m*.
pageant *n* espectáculo público *m*.
pageantry *n* pompa *f*.
pail *n* cubo, pozal *m*.
pain *n* pena *f*; castigo *m*; dolor *m*; * *vt* afligir.
pained *adj* afligido/da.
painful *adj* dolorido/da; penoso/sa; ~ly *adv* dolorosamente, con pena.
painkiller *n* analgésico *m*.
painless *adj* sin pena; indoloro/ra.
painstaking *adj* laborioso/sa, meticu-loso/sa.
paint *vt* pintar.
paintbrush *n* pincel *m*; brocha *f*.
painter *n* pintor *m/f*.
painting *n* pintura *f*.
paintwork *n* pintura *f*.
pair *n* par *m*; yuntas *fpl*.
pajamas *npl* pijama *m*.
pal *n* compañero/ra *m/f*.
palatable *adj* sabroso/sa.
palate *n* paladar *m*; gusto *m*.
palatial *adj* palatino/na.
palaver *n* lío *m*.
pale *adj* pálido/da; claro/ra.
palette *n* paleta *f*.
paling *n* estacada, palizada *f*.
pall *n* cortina de humo *f*; * *vi* perder el sabor.
palliative *adj* paliativo/va; * *n* paliativo *m*.
pallid *adj* pálido/da.
pallor *n* palidez *f*.

palm *n* (*bot*) palma *f*.
palmistry *n* quiromancia *f*.
Palm Sunday *n* Domingo de Ramos *m*.
palpable *adj* palpable; evidente.
palpitation *n* palpitación *f*.
paltry *adj* irrisorio/ria; mezquino/na.
pamper *vt* mimar.
pamphlet *n* folleto *m*.
pan *n* cazuela *f*; sartén *f*; olla *f*.
panacea *n* panacea *f*.
panache *n* estilo *m*.
pancake *n* crepe *f*, *Lat Am* panqueque *m*.
pandemonium *n* jaleo *m*.
pane *n* cristal *m*.
panel *n* panel *m*; paño *m*.
paneling *n* paneles *mpl*.
pang *n* angustia, congoja *f*.
panic *adj, n* pánico/ca *m*.
panicky *adj* asustadizo/za.
panic-stricken *adj* preso/sa del pánico.
pansy *n* (*bot*) pensamiento *m*.
pant *vi* jadear.
panther *n* pantera *f*.
pantihose *npl* medias *fpl*.
pants *npl* bragas *fpl*.
pantry *n* despensa *f*.
papacy *n* papado *m*.
papal *adj* papal.
papaw, pawpaw, papaya *n* papaya *f*.
paper *n* papel *m*; periódico *m*; examen *m*; estudio *m*; ~s *pl* escrituras *fpl*; (*com*) fondos *mpl*; * *adj* de papel; * *vt* empape lar; tapizar.
paperback *n* libro en rústica *m*.
paper bag *n* bolsa de papel *f*.
paperclip *n* clip *m*.
paperweight *n* sujetapapeles *m invar*.
paperwork *n* papeleo *m*.
paprika *n* pimentón *m*, paprika *f*.
par *n* equivalencia *f*; igualdad *f*; par *m*; at ~ (*com*) a la par.
parable *n* parábola *f*.
parachute *n* paracaídas *m invar*; * *vi* lanzarse en paracaídas.
parade *n* ostentación, pompa *f*; (*mil*) parada *f*; * *vt, vi* desfilar; pasear; hacer gala.
paradise *n* paraíso *m*.
paradox *n* paradoja *f*.
paradoxical *adj* paradójico/ca.
paragliding *n* parapente *m*.
paragon *n* dechado *m*.
paragraph *n* párrafo *m*, *Lat Am* acápite *m*.
parallel *adj* paralelo/la; * *n* línea paralela *f*; * *vt* paralelizar; parangonar.
paralyze *vt* paralizar.
paralysis *n* parálisis *f*.
paralytic *adj* paralítico/ca.
paramedic *n* auxiliar sanitario/ria *m/f*.
paramount *adj* supremo/ma, superior.
paranoid *adj* paranoico/ca.
paraphernalia *n* parafernalia *f*.
parasite *n* parásito *m*.

parasol n parasol, quitasol m.

paratrooper n paracaidista m.

parcel n paquete m; porción, cantidad f; equipajes, bultos mpl; * vt empaquetar, embalar.

parch vt resecar.

parched adj reseco/ca; muerto/ta de sed.

parchment n pergamino m.

pardon n perdón m; * vt perdonar.

parent n padre m; madre f.

parentage n parentela f; extracción f.

parental adj de los padres.

parenthesis n paréntesis m invar.

parish n parroquia f; * adj parroquial.

parishioner n parroquiano/na m/f.

parity n paridad f.

park n parque m; * vt, vi aparcar, estacionar.

parking n aparcamiento, estacionamiento m.

parking lot n aparcamiento, estacionamiento m.

parking meter n parquímetro m.

parking ticket n multa de estacionamiento f.

parlance n lenguaje m.

parliament n parlamento m.

parliamentary adj parlamentario/ria.

parlor n salón m.

parody n parodia f; * vt parodiar.

parole n: on ~ en libertad bajo palabra.

parricide n parricidio m; parricida m/f.

parrot n papagayo m.

parry vt parar.

parsley n (bot) perejil m.

parsnip n (bot) chirivía f.

part n parte f; partido m; oficio m; papel (de un actor) m; obligación f; raya f; ~s pl partes fpl; paraje, distrito m; * vt partir, separar, desunir; * vi partirse, separarse; to ~ with entregar; pagar; deshacerse de; ~ly adv en parte.

partial adj, ~ly adv parcial(mente).

participant n concursante m.

participate vi participar (en).

participation n participación f.

participle n (gr) participio m.

particle n partícula f.

particular adj particular, singular; ~ly adv particularmente; * n particular m; particularidad f.

parting n separación, partida f; raya (en los cabellos) f.

partisan n partidario/ria m/f.

partition n partición, separación f; * vt partir, dividir en varias partes.

partner n socio/cia, compañero/ra m/f.

partnership n compañía, sociedad de comercio f.

partridge n perdiz f.

party n partido m; fiesta f.

pass vt pasar; traspasar; transferir; adelantarse a; * vi pasar, aprobar; * n permiso m; puerto m; to ~ away vi fallecer; to ~ by vi pasar; vt pasar por alto; to ~ on vt transmitir.

passable adj pasadero/ra, transitable.

passage n pasaje m; travesía f; pasadizo m.

passbook n libreta de depósitos f.

passenger n pasajero/ra m/f.

passer-by n transeúnte m/f.

passing adj pasajero/ra.

passion n pasión f; amor m; celo, ardor m.

passionate adj apasionado/da; ~ly adv apasionadamente; ardientemente.

passive adj pasivo/va; ~ly adv pasivamente.

passkey n llava maestra f.

Passover n Pascua f.

passport n pasaporte m.

passport control n control de pasaportes m.

password n contraseña f.

past adj pasado/da; gastado/da; * n (gr) pretérito m; el pasado; * prep más allá de; después de.

pasta n pasta f.

paste n pasta f; engrudo m; * vt engrudar.

pasteurized adj pasteurizado/da.

pastime n pasatiempo m; diversión f.

pastor n pastor m.

pastoral adj pastoril; pastoral.

pastry n pastelería f.

pasture n pasto m, Lat Am potrero m.

pasty adj pastoso/sa; pálido/da.

pat vt dar golpecillos.

patch n remiendo m; parche m; terreno m; * vt remendar; to ~ up reparar; hacer las paces en.

patchwork n obra de retacitos f; chapucería f.

pâté n paté m.

patent adj patente; privilegiado/da; * n patente f; * vt privilegiar.

patentee n poseedor/a de una patente m/f.

patent leather n charol m.

paternal adj paternal.

paternity n paternidad f.

path n senda f.

pathetic adj patético/ca; ~ally adv patéticamente.

pathological adj patológico/ca.

pathology n patología f.

pathos n patetismo m.

pathway n sendero m.

patience n paciencia f.

patient adj paciente, sufrido/da, Lat Am aguantador/ra; ~ly adv con paciencia; * n enfermo/ma m/f.

patio n patio m.

patriarch n patriarca m.

patriot n patriota m.

patriotic adj patriotico/ca.

patriotism n patriotismo m.

patrol n patrulla f; * vi patrullar.

patrol car n coche patrulla m.

patrolman n policía m.

patron n patrón/ona, protector m/f.

patronage n patrocinio m; patronato, patronazgo m.

patronize vt patrocinar, proteger.

patter n golpeteo m; labia f; * vi tamborilear.

pattern *n* patrón *m*; dibujo *m*; *Lat Am* molde *m*.
paunch *n* panza *f*; vientre *m*.
pauper *n* pobre *m/f*.
pause *n* pausa *f*; * *vt* pausar; deliberar.
pave *vt* empedrar; enlosar, embaldosar.
pavilion *n* pabellón *m*.
paving stone *n* ladrillo *m*; losa *f*.
paw *n* pata *f*; garra *f*; * *vt* manosear.
pawn *n* peón *m*; * *vt* empeñar.
pawnbroker *n* prestamista *m/f*.
pawnshop *n* casa de empeños *f*.
pay *vt* pagar; sufrir por; **to ~ back** *vt* reembolsar; **to ~ for** pagar; **to ~ off** *vt* liquidar; *vi* dar resultados; * *n* paga *f*; salario *m*.
payable *adj* pagadero/ra.
payday *n* día de paga *m*.
payee *n* portador/a *m/f*.
pay envelope *n* sobre (de paga) *m*.
paymaster *n* pagador/a *m/f*.
payment *n* paga *f*; pagamento, pago *m*.
payphone *n* teléfono público *m*.
payroll *n* nómina *f*.
pea *n* guisante *m*, *Lat Am* chícharro *m*.
peace *n* paz *f*.
peaceful *adj* tranquilo/la, pacífico/ca.
peach *n* melocotón *m*, *Lat Am* durazno *m*.
peacock *n* pavón, pavo real *m*.
peak *n* cima *f*.
peak hours, peak period *n* horas punta *fpl*.
peal *n* campaneo *m*; estruendo *m*.
peanut *n* cacahuete *m*; maní *m*.
pear *n* pera *f*.
pearl *n* perla *f*.
peasant *n* campesino/na *m/f*.
peat *n* turba *f*.
pebble *n* guija *f*; guijarro *m*.
peck *n* picotazo *m*; * *vt* picotear; picar.
pecking order *n* orden de jerarquía *m*.
peculiar *adj* peculiar, particular, singular; **~ly** *adv* peculiarmente.
peculiarity *n* particularidad, singularidad *f*.
pedal *n* pedal *m*; * *vi* pedalear.
pedant *n* pedante *m/f*.
pedantic *adj* pedante.
pedestal *n* pedestal *m*.
pedestrian *n* peatón/ona *m/f*; * *adj* pedestre.
pedigree *n* genealogía *f*; * *adj* de raza.
peddler *n* vendedor/a ambulante *m/f*.
peek *vi* mirar de soslayo.
peel *vt* pelar; * *vi* desconcharse; * *n* piel *f*; cáscara *f*.
peer *n* compañero/ra *m/f*; par *m*.
peerless *adj* incomparable.
peeved *adj* enojado/da.
peevish *adj* regañón/ona, bronco/ca; enojadizo/za.
peg *n* clavija *f*; gancho *m*; * *vt* clavar.
pelican *n* pelícano *m*.
pellet *n* bolita *f*; **~s** perdigones *mpl*.
pelt *n* pellejo, cuero *m*; * *vt* arrojar; * *vi* llover a cántaros.

pen *n* bolígrafo *m*; pluma *f*; redil *m*.
penal *adj* penal.
penalty *n* pena *f*; castigo *m*; multa *f*.
penance *n* penitencia *f*.
pence *n pl* de **penny**.
pencil *n* lápiz *m*; lapicero *m*.
pencil case *n* estuche *m*.
pendant *n* pendiente *m*.
pending *adj* pendiente.
pendulum *n* péndulo *m*.
penetrate *vt* penetrar.
penguin *n* pingüino *m*.
penicillin *n* penicilina *f*.
peninsula *n* península *f*.
penis *n* pene *m*.
penitence *n* penitencia *f*.
penitent *adj*, *n* penitente *m*.
penitentiary *n* penitenciaría *f*.
penknife *n* navaja *f*.
pennant *n* banderola *f*.
penniless *adj* sin dinero.
penny *n* penique *m*.
penpal *n* amigo/ga por carta *m/f*.
pension *n* pensión *f*; * *vt* dar pensión a.
pensive *adj* pensativo/va; **~ly** *adv* pensativamente.
pentagon *n*: **the P~** el Pentágono.
Pentecost *n* Pentecostés *m*.
penthouse *n* ático *m*.
pent-up *adj* reprimido/da.
penultimate *adj* penúltimo/ma.
penury *n* penuria, carestía *f*.
people *n* pueblo *m*; nación *f*; gente *f*; * *vt* poblar.
people mover *n* monovolumen *m*.
pep *n* energía *f*; **to ~ up** *vt* animar.
pepper *n* pimienta *f*; * *vt* sazonar con pimienta.
peppermint *n* menta *f*.
per *prep* por.
per annum *adv* al año.
per capita *adj*, *adv* per cápita.
perceive *vt* percibir, comprender.
percentage *n* porcentaje *m*.
perception *n* percepción, idea, noción *f*.
perch *n* percha *f*.
perchance *adv* acaso, quizá.
percolate *vt* colar; filtrar.
percolator *n* cafetera de filtro *f*.
percussion *n* percusión *f*; golpe *m*.
perdition *n* pérdida, ruina *f*.
peremptory *adj* perentorio/ria; deci-sivo/va.
perennial *adj* perenne; perpetuo/tua.
perfect *adj* perfecto/ta, acabado/da; puro/ra; **~ly** *adv* perfectamente; * *vt* perfeccionar, acabar.
perfection *n* perfección *f*.
perforate *vt* horadar.
perforated *adj* (of stamps) dentado/da.
perforation *n* perforación *f*.
perform *vt* ejecutar; efectuar; * *vi* representar, hacer papel.
performance *n* ejecución *f*; cumplimiento *m*, *Lat Am* performance *m*; obra *f*; representación teatral, función *f*.

performer *n* ejecutor/a *m/f*; actor *m*, actriz *f*.

perfume *n* perfume *m*; fragancia *f*; * *vt* perfumar.

perhaps *adv* quizá, quizás.

peril *n* peligro, riesgo *m*.

perilous *adj* peligroso/sa; ~**ly** *adv* peligrosamente.

perimeter *n* perímetro *m*.

period *n* período *m*; época *f*; regla *f*.

periodic *adj* periódico/ca; ~**ally** *adv* periódicamente.

periodical *n* periódico *m*.

peripheral *adj* periférico/ca; * *n* periférico *m*.

perish *vi* perecer.

perishable *adj* perecedero/ra.

perjure *vt* perjurar.

perjury *n* perjurio *m*.

perk *n* extra *m*.

perky *adj* animado/da.

perm *n* permanente *f*.

permanent *adj*, ~**ly** *adv* permanen-te(mente).

permeate *vt* penetrar, atravesar.

permissible *adj* lícito/ta, permiso.

permission *n* permiso *m*.

permissive *adj* permisivo/va.

permit *vt* permitir; * *n* permiso *m*.

permutation *n* permutación *f*.

perpendicular *adj*, ~**ly** *adv* perpendi-cular(mente); * *n* línea perpendicular *f*.

perpetrate *vt* perpetrar, cometer.

perpetual *adj* perpetuo/tua; ~**ly** *adv* perpetuamente.

perpetuate *vt* perpetuar, eternizar.

perplex *vt* confundir.

persecute *vt* perseguir, importunar.

persecution *n* persecución *f*.

perseverance *n* perseverancia *f*.

persevere *vi* perseverar.

persist *vi* persistir.

persistence *adj* persistencia *f*.

persistent *adj* persistente.

person *n* persona *f*.

personable *adj* atractivo/va.

personage *n* personaje *m*.

personal *adj*, ~**ly** *adv* perso-nal(mente).

personal assistant *n* secretario/ria personal *m/f*.

personal column *n* anuncios personales *mpl*.

personal computer *n* ordenador personal *m*, computadora personal *f*.

personality *n* personalidad *f*.

personification *n* personificación *f*.

personify *vt* personificar.

personnel *n* personal *m*.

perspective *n* perspectiva *f*.

perspiration *n* transpiración *f*.

perspire *vi* transpirar.

persuade *vt* persuadir.

persuasion *n* persuasión *f*.

persuasive *adj* persuasivo/va; ~**ly** *adv* de modo persuasivo.

pert *adj* listo/va, vivo/va; petulante.

pertaining: ~ **to** *prep* relacionado/da con.

pertinent *adj* pertinente; ~**ly** *adv* oportunamente.

pertness *n* impertinencia *f*; vivacidad *f*.

perturb *vt* perturbar.

perusal *n* lectura, lección *f*.

peruse *vt* leer; examinar atentamente.

pervade *vt* atravesar, penetrar.

perverse *adj* perverso/sa, depravado/da; ~**ly** *adv* perversamente.

pervert *vt* pervertir, corromper.

pessimist *n* pesimista *m*.

pest *n* plaga *f*; molestia *f*.

pester *vt* molestar, cansar.

pestilence *n* pestilencia *f*.

pet *n* animal doméstico *m*; favorito/ta *m/f*; * *vt* mimar; * *vi* besuquearse.

petal *n* (*bot*) pétalo *m*.

petite *adj* chiquito/ta.

petition *n* presentación, petición *f*; * *vt* suplicar, *Lat Am* peticionar; requerir en justicia.

petrified *adj* horrorizado/da.

petroleum *n* petróleo *m*.

petticoat *n* enaguas *fpl*.

pettiness *n* mezquindad *f*; pequeñez *f*.

petty *adj* mezquino/na; insignificante.

petty cash *n* dinero para gastos menores *m*.

petty officer *n* contramaestre *m*.

petulant *adj* petulante.

pew *n* banco *m*.

pewter *n* peltre *m*.

phantom *n* fantasma *m*.

Pharisee *n* fariseo/sea *m/f*.

pharmaceutical *adj* farmacéutico/ca.

phase *n* fase *f*.

pheasant *n* faisán *m*.

phenomenal *adj* fenomenal.

phenomenon *n* fenómeno *m*.

phial *n* vial *m*.

philanthropic *adj* filantrópico/ca.

philanthropist *n* filántropo/pa *m/f*.

philanthropy *n* filantropía *f*.

philologist *n* filólogo/ga *m/f*.

philology *n* filología *f*.

philosopher *n* filósofo/fa *m/f*.

philosophic(al) *adj* filosófico/ca; ~**ally** *adv* filosóficamente.

philosophize *vi* filosofar.

philosophy *n* filosofía *f*; **natural** ~ filosofía natural *f*.

phlegm *n* flema *f*.

phlegmatic(al) *adj* flemático/ca.

phobia *n* fobia *f*.

phone *n* teléfono *m*; * *vt* telefonear; **to** ~ **back** *vt*, *vi* volver a llamar; **to** ~ **up** llamar por teléfono.

phone book *n* guía telefónica *f*.

phone box *n* cabina telefónica *f*, *Lat Am* monedero *m*.

phone call *n* llamada (telefonica) *f*.

phosphorus *n* fosforo *m*.

photocopier n fotocopiadora f.
photocopy n fotocopia f; * vt fotografiar.
photograph n fotografía f; * vt fotografiar.
photographer n fotógrafo/fa m/f.
photographic adj fotográfico/ca.
photography n fotografía f.
phrase n frase f; estilo m; * vt expresar.
phrase book n libro de frases m.
physical adj físico/ca; ~ly adv físicamente.
physical education n educación física f.
physician n médico/ca m/f.
physicist n físico/ca m/f.
physiological adj fisiológico/ca.
physiologist n fisiólogo/ga m/f.
physiology n fisiología f.
physiotherapy n fisioterapia f.
physique n físico m.
pianist n pianista m/f.
piano n piano m.
piccolo n flautín m.
pick vt escoger, elegir; recoger; mondar, limpiar; **to ~ on** vt meterse con; **to ~ out** vt escoger; **to ~ up** vi ir mejor; recobrarse; * vt recoger; comprar; aprender; * n pico m; **the ~ of** lo más escogido de.
pickax n pico m.
picket n piquete m.
pickle n escabeche m; *vt escabechar.
pickpocket n carterista m/f.
pick-up n (auto) furgoneta f.
picnic n picnic m.
pictorial adj pictórico/ca.
picture n pintura f; retrato m; * vt pintar; figurar.
picture book n libro de dibujos m.
picturesque adj pintoresco/ca.
pie n pastel m; tarta f; empanada f.
piece n pedazo m; pieza, obra f; * vt remendar.
piecemeal adv en pedazos; * adj di-vidido/da.
piecework n destajo m; * vi **to do ~** trabajar a destajo.
pier n pilar m; muelle m.
pierce vt penetrar, agujerear, taladrar.
piercing adj penetrante.
piety n piedad, devoción f.
pig n cerdo m, Lat Am chancho m; (col) cochino m.
pigeon n paloma f; **carrier/homing ~** paloma mensajera f.
pigeonhole n casillero m.
piggy bank n hucha f.
pig-headed adj terco/ca.
pigpen n pocilga f.
pigtail n trenza f.
pike n lucio m; pica f.
pile n estaca f; pila f; montón m; pelo m; pelillo m; ~s pl almorranas fpl; *vt amontonar, apilar.
pile-up n colisión múltiple f.
pilfer vt hurtar.
pilgrim n peregrino/na m/f.
pilgrimage n peregrinación f.
pill n píldora f.

pillage vt saquear.
pillar n pilar m.
pillion n asiento trasero m.
pillow n almohada f.
pillowcase n funda de almohada f.
pilot n piloto m/f; * vt pilotar; (fig) guiar.
pilot light n piloto m.
pimp n chulo, cafiche m.
pimple n grano m.
pin n alfiler m; ~s **and needles** npl hormigueo m; * vt prender con alfileres; fijar con clavija.
pinafore n delantal m.
pinball n flíper m.
pincers n pinzas, tenazuelas fpl.
pinch vt pellizcar; (col) birlar; * vi apretar; * n pellizco m.
pincushion n acerico m.
pine¹ n (bot) pino m.
pine² vi ansiar por.
pineapple n piña f, ananás m invar.
ping n sonido agudo m.
pink n rosa f; * adj color de rosa.
pinnacle n cumbre f.
pinpoint vt precisar.
pint n pinta f.
pioneer n pionero/ra m/f.
pious adj pío, pía, devoto/ta; ~ly adv piadosamente.
pip n pepita f.
pipe n tubo, caño m; pipa f, Lat Am cachimbo m; ~s cañería f.
pipe cleaner n limpiapipas m invar.
pipe dream n sueño imposible m.
pipeline n tubería f; oleoducto m; gasoducto m.
piper n gaitero/ra m/f.
piping adj hirviente.
pique n pique m; desazón f; ojeriza f.
piracy n piratería f.
pirate n pirata m/f.
pirouette n pirueta f; vi piruetear.
Pisces n Piscis m (signo del zodiaco).
piss n (col) meada f; * vi mear.
pistol n pistola f.
piston n émbolo m.
pit n hoyo m; mina f.
pitch n lanzamiento m; tono m; campo m, Lat Am cancha f; * vt tirar, arrojar; * vi caerse; caer de cabeza.
pitch-black adj negro/gra como boca de lobo.
pitcher n cántaro m.
pitchfork n horca f.
pitfall n trampa f.
pithy adj meduloso/sa.
pitiable adj lastimoso/sa.
pitiful adj lastimoso/sa, compasivo/va; ~ly adv lastimosamente.
pittance n pitanza, ración f; porcioncilla f.
pity n piedad, compasión f; * vt compadecer.
pivot n eje m.
pizza n pizza f.
placard n pancarta f.

placate vt apaciguar.

place n lugar, sitio m; rango, empleo m; * vt colocar; poner.

placid adj plácido/da, quieto/ta; ~ly adv plácidamente.

plagiarism n plagio m.

plague n peste, plaga f; * vt atormentar; infestar, apestar.

plaice n platija f (pez).

plaid n tartán m.

plain adj liso/so, llano/na, abierto/ta; sincero/ra; puro/ra, simple, común; claro/ra, evidente, distinto/ta; ~ly adv llanamente; claramente; * n llano m.

plaintiff n (law) demandante m/f.

plait n pliegue m, trenza f; * vt plegar; trenzar.

plan n plano m; plan m; * vt proyectar.

plane n avión m; plano m; cepillo m; * vt allanar; acepillar.

planet n planeta m.

planetary adj planetario/ria.

plank n tabla f.

planner n planificador/a m/f.

planning n planificación f.

plant n planta f; fábrica f; maquinaria f; * vt plantar.

plantation n plantación f; colonia f.

plaque n placa f.

plaster n yeso m; emplasto m; * vt enyesar; emplastar.

plastered adj (col) borracho/cha.

plasterer n yesero/ra m/f.

plaster of Paris n yeso mate m.

plastic adj plástico/ca.

plastic surgery n cirugía plástica f.

plate n plato m; lámina f; placa f.

plateau n meseta f.

plate glass n vidrio cilindrado m.

platform n plataforma f.

platinum n platino m.

platitude n tópico m.

platoon n (mil) pelotón m.

platter n fuente f; plato grande m.

plaudit n aplauso m.

plausible adj plausible.

play n juego m; comedia f; * vt, vi jugar; juguetear; representar; (mus) tocar; to ~ down vt quitar importancia a.

playboy n playboy m.

player n jugador/a m/f; comediante/ta m/f, actor m, actriz f.

playful adj juguetón/ona, travieso/sa; ~ly adv juguetonamente, reto zando.

playmate n camarada m/f.

playground n patio m.

playgroup n parvulario m.

play-off n desempate m.

playpen n corral (de niños) m.

plaything n juguete m.

playwright n dramaturgo/ga m/f.

plea n defensa f; excusa f; pretexto m; * vt pretextar.

plead vt defender en juicio; alegar.

pleasant adj agradable; placentero/ra, alegre; ~ly adv alegremente, placenteramente.

please vt agradar, complacer.

pleased adj contento/ta.

pleasing adj agradable, placen-tero/ra.

pleasure n gusto, placer m; recreo m.

pleat n pliegue m.

pledge n prenda f; fianza f; * vt empeñar; prometer.

plentiful adj copioso/sa, abundante.

plenty n copia, abundancia f.

plethora n plétora f.

pleurisy n pleuresía f.

pliable, pliant adj flexible, dócil.

pliers npl alicates mpl.

plight n situación difícil f.

plinth n plinto m; zócalo m.

plod vi afanarse mucho, ajetrearse.

plot n terreno m; plano m; conspiración, trama f; estratagema f; * vi trazar; conspirar; tramar.

plow n arado m; * vt arar, labrar la tierra; to ~ back vt reinvertir; to ~ through abrirse paso; roer.

ploy n truco m.

pluck vt tirar con fuerza; arrancar; desplumar; * n ánimo m.

plucky adj gallardo/da.

plug n tapón m; enchufe m; bujía f; * vt tapar.

plum n ciruela f.

plumage n plumaje m.

plumb n plomada f; * adv a plomo; * vt aplomar.

plumber n fontanero/ra, plomero/ra m/f.

plume n pluma f.

plump adj gordo/da, rollizo/za.

plum tree n ciruelo m.

plunder vt saquear, pillar, robar; * n pillaje, botín m.

plunge vi sumergir(se), precipitarse; * n zambullida f.

plunger n desatascador m.

pluperfect n (gr) pluscuamperfecto m.

plural adj, n plural m.

plurality n pluralidad f.

plus n signo de más m; * prep más, y, además de.

plush adj de felpa.

plutonium n plutonio m.

ply vt trabajar con ahínco; * vi aplicarse; (mar) ir y venir.

plywood n madera contrachapada f.

pneumatic adj neumático/ca.

pneumatic drill n martillo neumático m.

pneumonia n pulmonía f.

poach vt escalfar; cazar en vedado; * vi cazar en vedado.

poached adj escalfado/da.

poacher n cazador furtivo m.

poaching n caza furtiva f.

pocket n bolsillo m; bolsa f; * vt embolsar.

pocketbook n cartera f.

pocket money n dinero para gastos m.

pod n vaina f.

podgy adj gordinflón/ona.

podiatrist n pedicuro/ra m/f, Lat Am pedicurista m/f.

poem n poema m.

poet n poeta m, poetisa f.

poetic adj poético/ca.

poetry n poesía f.

poignant adj punzante.

point n punta f; punto m; promontorio m; puntillo m; estado m; ~ **of view** n punto de vista m; * vt apuntar; aguzar; puntuar; **to ~ a gun** encañonar.

point-blank adv directamente.

pointed adj puntiagudo/da; epigra-mático/ca; ~**ly** adv sutilmente.

pointer n apuntador/a m/f; perro de muestra m.

pointless adj sin sentido.

poise n peso m; equilibrio m.

poison n veneno m; * vt envenenar.

poisoning n envenenamiento m.

poisonous adj venenoso/sa.

poke vt hurgar; empujar.

poker n atizador m; póker m.

poker-faced adj con cara de póker.

poky adj estrecho/cha.

polar adj polar.

pole n polo m; palo m; pértiga f.

pole bean n judía trepadora f.

pole vault n salto con pértiga m.

police n policía f.

police car n coche patrulla m.

police officer, policeman n policía m.

police station n comisaría f, Lat Am destacamento m de policía.

policewoman n mujer policía f.

policy n política f.

polio n polio f.

polish vt pulir, alisar; limar; **to ~ off** vt terminar; despachar; * n pulimento m.

polished adj elegante, pulido/da.

polite adj pulido/da, cortés; ~**ly** adv cortésmente.

politeness n cortesía f.

politic adj político/ca; astuto/ta.

political adj político/ca.

political asylum n asilo político m.

politician n político/ca m/f.

politics npl política f.

polka n polca f; ~ **dot** n lunar m.

poll n voto m; encuesta f, sondeo m.

pollen n (bot) polen m.

pollute vt contaminar.

pollution n polución, contaminación f.

polo n polo m.

polyester n poliéster m.

polyethylene, polythene n polietileno m.

polygamy n poligamia f.

polystyrene n poliestireno m.

polytechnic n politécnico m.

pomegranate n granada f.

pomp n pompa f; esplendor m.

pompom n borla f.

pompous adj pomposo/sa.

pond n estanque m.

ponder vt ponderar, considerar.

ponderous adj ponderoso/sa, pe-sado/da.

pontiff n pontífice, papa m.

pontoon n pontón m.

pony n jaca f; potro m.

ponytail n cola de caballo f.

pool n charca f; piscina, alberca f; * vt juntar; **to form a ~** remansarse.

poor adj pobre; humilde; de poco valor; ~**ly** adv pobremente; **the ~** n los pobres mpl.

pop n pop m; papá m; gaseosa f; chasquido m; * **to ~ in/out** vi entrar/salir un momento.

pop concert n concierto pop m.

popcorn n palomitas fpl.

Pope n Papa m.

poplar n álamo m.

poppy n (bot) amapola f.

populace n populacho m.

popular adj, ~**ly** adv popular(mente).

popularity n popularidad f.

popularize vt popularizar.

populate vi poblar.

population n población f.

populous adj populoso/sa.

pop video n videoclip m.

porcelain n porcelana, china, loza fina f.

porch n pórtico, vestíbulo m, zaguán m.

porcupine n puerco espín m.

pore n poro m.

pork n carne de cerdo, carne de puerco f.

pornography n pornografía f.

porous adj poroso/sa.

porpoise n marsopa f.

porridge n gachas de avena fpl.

port n puerto m; (mar) babor m; vino de Oporto m.

portable adj portátil.

portal n portal m; portada f.

porter n portero m; mozo m; conserje m/f.

portfolio n cartera f.

porthole n portilla f.

portico n pórtico, portal m.

portion n porción, parte f.

portly adj rollizo/za.

portrait n retrato m.

portray vt retratar.

pose n postura f; pose f; * vi posar; * vt plantear.

posh adj elegante.

position n posición, situación f; * vt colocar.

positive adj positivo/va, real, verda-dero/ra; ~**ly** adv positivamente; ciertamente.

posse n pelotón m.

possess vt poseer; gozar.

possession n posesión f.

possessive adj posesivo/va.

possibility n posibilidad f.

possible *adj* posible; **~ly** *adv* quizá, quizás.

post *n* correo *m*; puesto *m*; empleo *m*; poste *m*; * *vt* apostar; fijar.

postage *n* franqueo *m*.

postage stamp *n* sello de correos *m*; *Lat Am* estampilla *f*.

postal box, PO Box *n* apartado de correos *m*.

postcard, postal card *n* tarjeta *f* postal, *Lat Am* carta *f* postal.

post code *n* código postal *m*.

postdate *vt* posfechar.

poster *n* cartel *m*, *Lat Am* afiche *m*.

posterior *n* trasero *m*.

posterity *n* posteridad *f*.

postgraduate *n* posgraduado/da *m/f*.

posthumous *adj* póstumo/ma.

postman *n* cartero *m*.

postmark *n* matasellos *m*.

postmaster *n* administrador/a de correos *m/f*.

post office *n* correos *m*.

postpone *vt* diferir, suspender; posponer.

postscript *n* posdata *f*.

posture *n* postura *f*.

post-war *adj* de posguerra.

postwoman *n* cartera *f*.

posy *n* ramillete de flores *m*.

pot *n* marmita *f*; olla *f*; (*col*) marihuana *f*; * *vt* preservar en marmitas.

potato *n* patata *f*, *Lat Am* papa *f*.

potato peeler *n* pelapatatas *m invar*, *Lat Am* pelapapas *m invar*.

potbellied *adj* panzudo/da.

potent *adj* potente, poderoso/sa, eficaz.

potential *adj* potencial, poderoso/sa.

pothole *n* bache *m*.

potion *n* poción, bebida medicinal *f*.

potted *adj* en conserva; en tiesto.

potter *n* alfarero/ra *m/f*.

pottery *n* cerámica *f*.

potty *adj* chiflado/da.

pouch *n* bolsa *f*; petaca *f*; zurrón *m*.

poultice *n* cataplasma *f*.

poultry *n* aves de corral *fpl*.

pound *n* libra *f*; libra esterlina *f*; corral *m*; * *vt* machacar; * *vi* dar golpes.

pour *vt* echar; servir; * *vi* fluir con rapidez; llover a cántaros.

pout *vi* fruncir el ceño.

poverty *n* pobreza *f*.

powder *n* polvo *m*; pólvora *f*; * *vt* polvorear.

powder compact *n* polvera *f*.

powdered milk *n* leche en polvo *f*.

powder puff *n* borla *f*.

powder room *n* aseos *mpl*.

powdery *adj* polvoriento/ta.

power *n* poder *m*; potestad *f*; imperio *m*; potencia *f*; autoridad *f*; fuerza *f*; * *vt* impulsar.

powerful *adj* poderoso/sa; **~ly** *adv* poderosamente, con mucha fuerza.

powerless *adj* impotente.

power station *n* central eléctrica *f*.

practicable *adj* factible; viable.

practical *adj* práctico/ca; **~ly** *adv* prácticamente.

practicality *n* viabilidad *f*.

practical joke *n* broma pesada *f*.

practice *n* práctica *f*; uso *m*; costumbre *f*; **~s** *pl* intrigas *fpl*; * *vi* practicar, ejercer.

practice *vi* practicar, ejercer.

practitioner (medical) *n* médico/ca *m/f*.

pragmatic *adj* pragmático/ca.

prairie *n* pampa *f*.

praise *n* renombre *m*; alabanza *f*; * *vt* celebrar, alabar.

praiseworthy *adj* digno/na de alabanza; laudable.

prance *vi* cabriolar.

prank *n* travesura, extravagancia *f*.

prattle *vi* charlar; * *n* charla *f*.

prawn *n* gamba *f*.

pray *vi* rezar; rogar; orar.

prayer *n* oración, súplica *f*.

prayer book *n* devocionario *m*.

preach *vi* predicar.

preacher *n* pastor/a; predicador/a *m/f*.

preamble *n* preámbulo *m*.

precarious *adj* precario, incierto/ta; **~ly** *adv* precariamente.

precaution *n* precaución *f*.

precautionary *adj* preventivo/va.

precede *vt* anteceder, preceder.

precedence *n* precedencia *f*.

precedent *adj*, *n* precedente *m*.

precinct *n* límite, lindero *m*; barrio *m*; distrito electoral *m*.

precious *adj* precioso/sa.

precipice *n* precipicio *m*.

precipitate *vt* precipitar; * *adj* preci-pitado/da.

precise *adj* preciso/sa, exacto/ta; **~ly** *adv* precisamente, exactamente.

precision *n* precisión, limitación exacta *f*.

preclude *vt* prevenir, impedir.

precocious *adj* precoz, temprano/na, prematuro/ra.

preconceive *vt* preconcebir.

preconception *n* preconcepción *f*.

precondition *n* condición previa *f*.

precursor *n* precursor/a *m/f*.

predator *n* depredador/a *m/f*.

predecessor *n* predecesor/a, antece-sor/a *m/f*.

predestination *n* predestinación *f*.

predicament *n* aprieto *m*; dilema *m*.

predict *vt* predecir.

predictable *adj* previsible.

prediction *n* predicción *f*.

predilection *n* predilección *f*.

predominant *adj* predominante.

predominate *vt* predominar.

preen *vt* limpiarse (las plumas).

prefab *n* casa prefabricada *f*.

preface *n* prefacio *m*.

prefer *vt* preferir.

preferable *adj* preferible.

preferably *adv* de preferencia.
preference *n* preferencia *f*.
preferential *adj* preferente.
preferment *n* promoción *f*; preferencia *f*.
prefix *vt* prefijar; * *n* (*gr*) prefijo *m*.
pregnancy *n* embarazo *m*.
pregnant *adj* embarazada.
prehistoric *adj* prehistórico/ca.
prejudice *n* perjuicio, daño *m*; * *vt* perjudicar, hacer daño.
prejudiced *adj* predispuesto/ta; parcial.
prejudicial *adj* perjudicial, dañoso/sa.
preliminary *adj* preliminar.
prelude *n* preludio *m*.
premarital *adj* premarital.
premature *adj* prematuro/ra; **~ly** *adv* anticipadamente.
premeditation *n* premeditación *f*.
premier *n* primer ministro *m*, primera ministra *f*.
première *n* estreno *m*.
premise *n* premisa *f*.
premises *npl* establecimiento *m*.
premium *n* premio *m*; remuneración *f*; prima *f*.
premonition *n* presentimiento *m*.
preoccupied *adj* preocupado/da; ensimismado/da.
prepaid *adj* con el porte pagado.
preparation *n* preparación *f*; cosa preparada *f*.
preparatory *adj* preparatorio/ria.
prepare *vt* (*vi*) preparar(se).
prepared *adj* abonado/da.
preponderance *n* preponderancia *f*.
preposition *n* preposición *f*.
preposterous *adj* absurdo/da.
prerequisite *n* requisito *m*.
prerogative *n* prerrogativa *f*.
prescribe *vi* prescribir; recetar.
prescription *n* prescripción *f*; receta medicinal *f*.
presence *n* presencia *f*; asistencia *f*.
present *n* regalo *m*; * *adj* presente; **~ly** *adv* al presente; * *vt* ofrecer, presentar; regalar; acusar.
presentable *adj* decente, decoroso/sa.
presentation *n* presentación *f*.
present-day *adj* actual.
presenter *n* presentador/a *m/f*.
presentiment *n* presentimiento *m*.
preservation *n* preservación *f*.
preservative *n* preservativo *m*.
preserve *vt* preservar, conservar; poner en conserva; * *n* conserva, confitura *f*.
preside *vi* presidir; dirigir.
presidency *n* presidencia *f*.
president *n* presidente *m/f*.
presidential *adj* presidencial.
press *vt* empujar; apretar; compeler; * *vi* apretar; * *n* prensa *f*; armario *m*; apretón *m*; imprenta *f*.
press agency *n* agencia de prensa *f*.

press conference *n* rueda de prensa *f*.
pressing *adj*, **~ly** *adv* urgente(mente).
press-up *n* plancha *f*.
pressure *n* presión *f*; opresión *f*.
pressure cooker *n* olla exprés, olla a presión *f*.
pressure group *n* grupo de presión *m*.
pressurized *adj* a presión.
prestige *n* prestigio *m*.
presumable *adj* presumible.
presumably *adv* es de suponer que.
presume *vt* presumir, suponer.
presumption *n* presunción *f*.
presumptuous *adj* presuntuoso/sa.
presuppose *vt* presuponer.
pretend *vi* pretender; presumir.
pretender *n* pretendiente *m/f*.
pretense *n* pretexto *m*; pretensión *f*.
pretension *n* pretensión *f*.
pretentious *adj* presumido/da; os-tentoso/sa.
preterit *n* preterito *m*.
pretext *n* pretexto *m*; **to find a ~ for** pretextar.
pretty *adj* lindo/da, bien parecido/da; hermoso/sa; * *adv* algo, un poco.
prevail *vi* prevalecer, predominar.
prevailing *adj* dominante (uso, costumbre).
prevalent *adj* predominante, eficaz.
prevent *vt* prevenir; impedir.
prevention *n* prevención *f*.
preventive *adj* preventivo/va.
previous *adj* previo/via; antecedente; **~ly** *adv* antes.
prevue *n* preestreno *m*.
prewar *adj* de antes de la guerra.
prey *n* presa *f*.
price *n* precio *m*.
priceless *adj* inapreciable.
price list *n* tarifa, lista de precios *f*.
pricey *adj* carero/ra.
prick *vt* punzar, picar; apuntar; excitar; * *n* puntura *f*; pica dura *f*; punzada *f*.
prickle *n* pincho *m*; espina *f*.
prickly *adj* espinoso/sa.
pride *n* orgullo *m*; vanidad *f*; jactancia *f*.
priest *n* sacerdote *m*.
priestess *n* sacerdotisa *f*.
priesthood *n* sacerdocio *m*.
priestly *adj* sacerdotal.
priggish *adj* afectado/da.
prim *adj* peripuesto/ta, afectado/da.
primacy *n* primacía *f*.
primarily *adv* primariamente, sobre todo.
primary *adj* primario/ria, principal, primero/ra.
primate *n* primadoprimate *m*.
prime *n* (*fig*) flor, nata *f*; primavera *f*; principio *m*; * *adj* primero/ra; primoroso/sa, excelente; * *vt* cebar.
prime minister *n* primer ministro *m*, primera ministra *f*.
primeval *adj* primitivo/va.
priming *n* cebo *m*; imprimación *f*.
primitive *adj* primitivo/va; **~ly** *adv* primitivamente.

primrose n (bot) primavera f.

prince n príncipe m.

princess n princesa f.

principal adj, ~**ly** adv principal(men-te); * n principal, jefe m.

principality n principado/da m.

principle n principio m; causa primitiva f; fundamento, motivo m.

print vt imprimir; * n impresión, estampa, edición f; impreso m; **out of** ~ vendido/da, agotado/da.

printed matter n impresos mpl.

printer n impresor/a m/f.

printing n imprenta f.

prior adj anterior, precedente; * n prior (prelado) m.

priority n prioridad f.

priory n priorato m.

prism n prisma m.

prison n prisión, carcel f.

prisoner n prisionero/ra m/f.

pristine adj prístino/na, antiguo/gua.

privacy n soledad f.

private adj secreto/ta, privado/da; particular; ~ **soldier** n soldado raso m; ~**ly** adv en secreto.

private eye n detective privado/da m/f.

private school n instituto; colegio privado m.

privet n (bot) alheña f.

privilege n privilegio m.

prize n premio m; presa f; * vt apreciar, valuar; **to** ~ **open** abrir por fuerza.

prize-giving n entrega de premios f.

prizewinner n premiado/da m/f, Lat Am favorecido/da m/f.

pro prep para.

probability n probabilidad, verosimilitud f.

probable adj probable, verosímil; ~**bly** adv probablemente.

probation n prueba f.

probationary adj de prueba.

probe n sonda f; encuesta f; * vt sondar; investigar.

problem n problema m.

problematical adj problemático/ca; ~**ly** adv problemáticamente.

procedure n procedimiento m; progreso, proceso m.

proceed vi proceder; provenir; originarse; ~**s** npl producto m; rédito m; **gross** ~**s** producto íntegro; **net** ~**s** producto neto.

proceedings n procedimiento m; proceso m; conducta f.

process n proceso m.

procession n procesión f.

proclaim vt proclamar, promulgar; publicar.

proclamation n proclamación f; decreto m.

procrastinate vt diferir, retardar.

proctor n censor/a m/f.

procure vt procurar.

procurement n procuración f.

prod vt empujar.

prodigal adj pródigo/ga.

prodigious adj prodigioso/sa; ~**ly** adv prodigiosamente.

prodigy n prodigio m.

produce vt producir, criar; causar; * n producto m; verdura f.

produce dealer n verdulero/ra m/f.

producer n productor/a m/f.

product n producto m; obra f; efecto m.

production n producción f; producto m.

production line n línea de producción f.

productive adj productivo/va.

productivity n productividad f.

profane adj profano/na.

profess vt profesar; ejercer; declarar.

profession n profesión f.

professional adj profesional.

professor n profesor/a, catedratico/ca m/f.

proficiency n capacidad f.

proficient adj proficiente, adelanta-do/da.

profile n perfil m.

profit n ganancia f, Lat Am utilidad f; provecho m; ventaja f; * vi aprovechar.

profitability n rentabilidad f.

profitable adj provechoso/sa, venta-joso/sa.

profiteering n explotación f.

profound adj profundo/da; ~**ly** adv profundamente.

profuse adj profuso/sa, prodigo/ga; ~**ly** adv profusamente.

program n programa m.

programer n programador/a m/f.

programing n programación f.

progress n progreso m; curso m; * vi hacer progresos.

progression n progresión f; adelantamiento m.

progressive adj progresivo/va; ~**ly** adv progresivamente.

prohibit vt prohibir, vedar; impedir.

prohibition n prohibición f.

project vt proyectar, trazar; * n proyecto m.

projectile n proyectil m.

projection n proyección f; estimación f.

projector n proyector m.

proletarian adj proletario/ria.

proletariat n proletariado m.

prolific adj prolifico/ca, fecundo/da.

prolog n prólogo m.

prolong vt prolongar; diferir.

prom n baile de gala.

promenade n paseo m.

prominence n prominencia f.

prominent adj prominente, sale-dizo/za.

promiscuous adj promiscuo/cua.

promise n promesa f; * vt prometer.

promising adj prometedor/a.

promontory n promontorio m.

promote vt promover.

promoter n promotor/a, promove-dor/a m/f.

promotion n promoción f.

prompt adj pronto/ta; ~**ly** adv prontamente; * vt sugerir, insinuar; (theat) apuntar.

prompter *n* apuntador/a *m/f*.

prone *adj* inclinado/da.

prong *n* diente *m*.

pronoun *n* pronombre *m*.

pronounce *vt* pronunciar; recitar.

pronounced *adj* marcado/da.

pronouncement *n* declaración *f*.

pronunciation *n* pronunciación *f*.

proof *n* prueba *f*; * *adj* impenetrable; de prueba.

prop *vt* sostener; * *n* apoyo, puntal *m*; sostén *f*.

propaganda *n* propaganda *f*.

propel *vt* impeler.

propeller *n* hélice *f*.

propensity *n* propensión, tendencia *f*.

proper *adj* propio/pia; conveniente; exacto/ta; bien parecido/da; ~ly *adv* propiamente, justamente.

property *n* propiedad *f*.

prophecy *n* profecía *f*.

prophesy *vt* profetizar.

prophet *n* profeta *m*.

prophetic *adj* profético/ca.

proportion *n* proporción *f*; simetría *f*.

proportional *adj* proporcional.

proportionate *adj* proporcionado/da.

proposal *n* propuesta, proposición *f*; oferta *f*.

propose *vt* proponer.

proposition *n* proposición, propuesta *f*.

proprietor *n* propietario/ria *m/f*.

propriety *n* propiedad *f*.

pro rata *adv* de forma prorrateada.

prosaic *adj* prosaico/ca, en prosa.

prose *n* prosa *f*.

prosecute *vt* proseguir.

prosecution *n* prosecución *f*; acusación *f*.

prosecutor *n* fiscal *m/f*.

prospect *n* perspectiva *f*; esperanza *f*; * *vt* explorar; * *vi* buscar.

prospecting *n* prospección *f*.

prospective *adj* probable; futuro/ra.

prospector *n* explorador/a *m/f*.

prospectus *n* prospecto *m*.

prosper *vi* prosperar.

prosperity *n* prosperidad *f*.

prosperous *adj* próspero/ra, feliz.

prostitute *n* prostituta *f*.

prostitution *n* prostitución *f*.

prostrate *adj* postrado/da.

protagonist *n* protagonista *m*.

protect *vt* proteger; amparar.

protection *n* protección *f*.

protective *adj* protectorio/ria.

protector *n* protector/a, patrono/na *m/f*.

protégé(e) *n* protegido/da *m/f*.

protein *n* proteína *f*.

protest *vi* protestar; * *n* protesta *f*.

Protestant *n* protestante *m/f*.

protester *n* manifestante *m/f*.

protocol *n* protocolo *m*.

prototype *n* prototipo *m*.

protracted *adj* prolongado/da.

protrude *vi* sobresalir.

proud *adj* soberbio/bia, orgulloso/sa; ~ly *adv* soberbiamente.

prove *vt* probar, justificar; * *vi* resultar; salir (bien/mal).

proverb *n* proverbio *m*.

proverbial *adj*, ~ly *adv* prover-bial(mente).

provide *vt* proveer; **to ~ for** mantener a; tener en cuenta.

provided *conj*: **~ that** con tal que.

providence *n* providencia *f*.

province *n* provincia *f*; campo de acción *m*.

provincial *adj* provincial; * *n* provin-cial/a *m/f*.

provision *n* provisión *f*; precaución *f*.

provisional *adj* provisional, *Lat Am* provisorio/a; ~ly *adv* provisionalmente, *Lat Am* provisoriamente.

proviso *n* estipulación *f*.

provocation *n* provocación *f*; apelación *f*.

provocative *adj* provocativo/va.

provoke *vt* provocar; apelar.

prow *n* (*mar*) proa *f*.

prowess *n* proeza, valentía *f*.

prowl *vi* rondar, vagar.

prowler *n* merodeador/a *m/f*.

proximity *n* proximidad *f*.

proxy *n* poder *m*; apoderado/da *m/f*.

prudence *n* prudencia *f*.

prudent *adj* prudente, circunspecto/ta; ~ly *adv* con juicio.

prudish *adj* gazmoño/ña, mojigato/ta.

prune *vt* podar; * *n* ciruela pasa *f*.

prussic acid *n* ácido prúsico *m*.

pry *vi* espiar, acechar; **to ~ open** *vt* abrir por fuerza.

psalm *n* salmo *m*.

pseudonym *n* seudónimo *m*.

psyche *n* psique *f*.

psychiatric *adj* psiquiátrico/ca.

psychiatrist *n* psiquiatra *m/f*.

psychiatry *n* psiquiatría *f*.

psychic *adj* psíquico/ca.

psychoanalysis *n* psicoanálisis *m*.

psychoanalyst *n* psicoanalista *m/f*.

psychological *adj* psicológico/ca.

psychologist *n* psicólogo/ga *m/f*.

psychology *n* psicología *f*.

puberty *n* pubertad *f*.

public *adj* público/ca; común; noto-rio/ria; ~ly *adv* publicamente; * *n* público *m*.

public-address system *n* megafonía *f*.

publican *n* publicano *m*; tabernero/ra *m/f*.

publication *n* publicación *f*; edición *f*.

publicity *n* publicidad *f*.

publicize *vt* publicitar; hacer propaganda para.

public opinion *n* opinión pública *f*.

publish *vt* publicar.

publisher *n* editorial *f*; editor/a *m/f*.

publishing *n* industria del libro *f*.

pucker *vt* arrugar, hacer pliegues.

pudding *n* pudín *m*; morcilla *f*.

puddle n charco m.

puerile adj pueril.

puff n soplo m; bocanada f, Lat Am pitada f; resoplido m; * vt chupar; * vi bufar; resoplar.

puff pastry n hojaldre m.

puffy adj hinchado/da, entumeci-do/da.

pull vt tirar; coger; rasgar, desgarrar; **to ~ down** derribar; **to ~ in** parar; llegar a la estación; **to ~ off** cerrar; **to ~ out** vi irse; salir; * vt arrancar; **to ~ through** salir adelante; **to ~ up** vi parar; * vt arrancar; parar; * n tirón m; sacudida f.

pulley n polea, garrucha f.

pullover n jersey m.

pulp n pulpa f; pasta f.

pulpit n púlpito m.

pulsate vi pulsar, latir.

pulse n pulso m; legumbres fpl.

pulverize vt pulverizar.

pumice n piedra pómez f.

pummel vt aporrear.

pump n bomba f; zapatilla f; * vt bombear; sondear; sonsacar.

pumpkin n calabaza f.

pun n juego de palabras m; * vi hacer juegos de palabras.

punch n puñetazo m; punzón m; taladro m; ponche m; * vt golpear; perforar.

punctual adj puntual, exacto/ta; **~ly** adv puntualmente.

punctuate vi puntuar.

punctuation n puntuación f.

pundit n experto/ta m/f.

pungent adj picante, acre, mordaz.

punish vt castigar.

punishment n castigo m; pena f.

punk n punk m/f; música punk f; rufián/fiana m/ f.

punt n barco llano m.

puny adj joven, pequeño/ña; inferior.

pup n cachorro m; * vi parir (la perra).

pupil n alumno/na m/f; pupila f.

puppet n títere, muñeco m.

puppy n perrito m.

purchase vt comprar; * n compra f; adquisición f.

purchaser n comprador/a m/f.

pure adj puro/ra; **~ly** adv puramente.

purée n puré m.

purge vt purgar.

purification n purificación f.

purifier n depuradora f.

purify vt purificar.

purist n purista m/f.

puritan n puritano/na m/f.

purity n pureza f.

purl n punto del revés m.

purple adj purpúreo/rea; * n púrpura f.

purport vi: **to ~** dar a entender que.

purpose n intención f; designio, proyecto m; **to the ~** al propósito; **to no ~** inútilmente; **on ~** a propósito.

purposeful adj resuelto/ta.

purr vi ronronear.

purse n bolsa f; cartera f, Lat Am sobre m.

purser n comisario m/f.

pursue vt perseguir; seguir, acosar.

pursuit n perseguimiento m; ocupación f.

purveyor n abastecedor m.

push vt empujar; estrechar, apretar; **to ~ aside** apartar; **to ~ off** (col) largarse; **to ~ on** seguir adelante; * n impulso m; empujón m; esfuerzo m; asalto m.

pusher (drug) n traficante de drogas m/f.

put vt poner, colocar; proponer; imponer; obligar; **to ~ away** guardar; **to ~ away hurriedly** zampar; **to ~ down** poner en el suelo; sacrificar; apuntar; sofocar; **to ~ forward** adelantar; **to ~ off** aplazar; desanimar; **to ~ on** ponerse; encender; presentar; ganar; echar; **to ~ out** apagar; extender; molestar; **to ~ up** alzar; aumentar; alojar.

putrid adj podrido/da.

putt n putt m; vi hacer un putt.

putty n masilla f.

puzzle n acertijo m; rompecabezas m invar.

puzzling adj extraño/ña.

pylon n torre de alta tensión f.

pyramid n pirámide f.

python n pitón m.

Q

quack vi graznar; * n graznido m; (col) curandero/ra m/f.

quadrangle n cuadrángulo m.

quadrant n cuadrante m.

quadrilateral adj cuadrilátero/ra.

quadruped n cuadrúpedo m.

quadruple adj cuádruplo.

quadruplet n cuatrillizo/za m/f.

quagmire n barrizal m, cenagal m.

quail n codorniz f.

quaint adj pulido/da; exquisito/ta.

quake vi temblar; tiritar.

Quaker n cuáquero/ra m/f.

qualification n calificación f; título m.

qualified adj capacitado/da; titula-do/da.

qualify vt calificar; modificar; * vi clasificarse.

quality n calidad f.

qualm n escrúpulo m.

quandary n incertidumbre, duda f.

quantitative adj cuantitativo/va.

quantity n cantidad f.

quarantine n cuarentena f.

quarrel n riña, contienda f; * vi reñir, disputar.

quarrelsome adj pendenciero/ra.

quarry n cantera f.

quarter n cuarto m; cuarta parte f; **~ of an hour** cuarto de hora; * vt cuartear.

quarterly adj trimestral; * adv trimestralmente.

quartermaster n (mil) comisario/ria m/f.

quartet n (mus) cuarteto m.
quartz n cuarzo m.
quash vt fracasar; anular, abrogar.
quay n muelle m.
queasy adj nauseabundo/da.
queen n reina f; dama f.
queer adj extraño/ña; ridículo/la; * n (col) maricón m.
quell vt calmar; sosegar.
quench vt apagar; extinguir.
query n cuestión, pregunta f; * vt preguntar.
quest n pesquisa, inquisición, busca f.
question n pregunta f; cuestión f; asunto m; duda f; * vt dudar de; interrogar.
questionable adj cuestionable, dudo-so/sa.
questioner n interrogador/a m/f.
question mark n signo de interrogación m.
questionnaire n cuestionario m.
quibble vi buscar evasivas.
quick adj rapido/da; vivo/va; pronto/ta; ágil; ~ly adv rápidamente.
quicken vt apresurar; * vi darse prisa.
quicksand n arenas movedizas f/pl.
quicksilver n azogue, mercurio m.
quick-witted adj agudo/da, perspicaz.
quiet adj callado/da; ~ly adv tranquilamente.
quietness n tranquilidad f.
quinine n quinina f.
quintet n (mus) quinteto m.
quintuple adj quíntuplo.
quintuplet n quintillizo/za m/f.
quip n indirecta f; * vt echar pullas.
quirk n peculiaridad f.
quit vt dejar; desocupar; * vi renunciar; irse; * adj libre, descar-gado/da.
quite adv bastante; totalmente, enteramente, absolutamente.
quits adv ¡en paz!
quiver vi temblar.
quixotic adj quijotesco/ca.
quiz n concurso m; programa concurso m; * vt interrogar.
quizzical adj burlón/ona.
quota n cuota f.
quotation n citación, cita f.
quotation marks npl comillas f/pl.
quote vt citar.
quotient n cociente m.

R

rabbi n rabino/na m/f.
rabbit n conejo m.
rabbit hutch n conejera f.
rabble n gentuza f.
rabid adj rabioso/sa; furioso/sa.
rabies n rabia f.
race n raza, casta f; carrera f; * vt hacer correr a; competir contra; acelerar; * vi correr; competir; latir rápidamente.

racehorse n caballo de carreras m.
racial adj racial.
raciness n vivacidad f.
racing n carreras f/pl.
racist adj, n racista m/f.
rack n rejilla f; estante m; * vt atormentar; trasegar.
racket n ruido m; raqueta f.
rack-rent n alquiler abusivo m.
racy adj picante, vivo/va.
radiance n brillantez f, resplandor m.
radiant adj radiante, brillante, Lat Am radioso/sa.
radiate vt, vi radiar, irradiar.
radiation n radiación f.
radiator n radiador m.
radical adj radical; ~ly adv radicalmente.
radicalism n radicalismo m.
radio n radio f.
radioactive adj radioactivo/va; ~ fallout lluvia radioactiva f.
radish n rábano m.
radius n radio f.
raffle n rifa f (juego); * vt rifar.
raft n balsa, almadía f.
rafter n par m; viga f.
rafting n rafting m.
rag n trapo, andrajo m.
ragamuffin n granuja, galopín/ina m/f.
rage n rabia f; furor m; * vi rabiar; encolerizarse.
ragged adj andrajoso/sa.
raging adj furioso/sa, rabioso/sa.
ragpicker n trapero m.
raid n incursión f; * vt invadir.
raider n invasor/a m/f.
rail n baranda, barandilla f; (rail) raíl, carril m; * vt cercar con barandillas.
raillery n burlas f/pl.
railroad n ferrocarril m.
raiment n vestido m.
rain n lluvia f; * vi llover.
rainbow n arco iris m.
rainwater n agua de lluvia f.
rainy adj lluvioso/sa.
raise vt levantar, alzar, Lat Am parar; fabricar; edificar; elevar.
raisin n pasa f.
rake n rastro, rastrillo m; libertino/na m/f; * vt rastrillar.
rakish adj libertino/na, disoluto/ta.
rally vt (mil) reunir; * vi reunirse.
ram n carnero, morueco m; ariete m; * vt chocar con.
ramble vi divagar; salir de excursión a pie; * n excursión a pie, caminata f.
rambler n excursionista m/f.
ramification n ramificación f.
ramify vi ramificarse.
ramp n rampa f.
rampant adj exuberante.
rampart n terraplén m; (mil) muralla f.

ramrod *n* baqueta *f*; atacador *m*.
ramshackle *adj* en ruina.
ranch *n* hacienda, estancia *f*.
rancid *adj* rancio/cia.
rancor *n* rencor *m*.
random *adj* fortuito/ta, sin orden; **at ~** al azar.
range *vt* colocar, ordenar; **vi* vagar; ** n* clase *f*; orden *m*; hilera *f*; cordillera *f*; campo abierto *m*; campo de tiro *m*; reja de cocina *f*.
ranger *n* guardabosques *m invar*.
rank *adj* exuberante; rancio/cia; fétido/da; ** n* fila, hilera, clase *f*.
rankle *vi* doler.
rankness *n* exuberancia *f*; olor/gusto rancio *m*.
ransack *vt* saquear, pillar.
ransom *n* rescate *m*.
rant *vi* vociferar.
rap *vi* dar un golpecito; ** n* golpecito *m*.
rapacious *adj* rapaz; ~ly *adv* con rapacidad.
rapacity, rapaciousness *n* rapacidad *f*.
rape *n* violación *f*; estupro *m*; (*bot*) colza *f*; ** vt* violar.
rapid *adj* rápido/da; ~ly *adv* rápidamente.
rapidity *n* rapidez *f*.
rapier *n* espadín *m*.
rapist *n* violador *m*.
rapt *adj* arrebatado/da; absorto/ta.
rapture *n* rapto *m*; éxtasis *m invar*.
rapturous *adj* arrebatado/da.
rare *adj* raro/ra, extraordinario/ria; ~ly *adv* raramente.
rarity *n* raridad, rareza *f*.
rascal *n* pícaro/ra *m/f*.
rash *adj* precipitado/da, temerario/ria; ~ly *adv* temerariamente; ** n* salpullido *m*; erupción (cutánea) *f*.
rashness *n* temeridad *f*.
rasp *n* raspador *m*; ** vt* raspar, escofinar.
raspberry *n* frambuesa *f*; ~ bush frambueso *m*.
rat *n* rata *f*.
rate *n* tasa *f*, precio, valor *m*; grado *m*; ** vt* tasar, apreciar.
rather *adv* más bien; antes.
ratification *n* ratificación *f*.
ratify *vt* ratificar.
rating *n* tasación *f*; clasificación *f*; índice *m*.
ratio *n* razón *f*.
ration *n* ración *f*; (*mil*) víveres *mpl*.
rational *adj* racional; razonable; ~ly *adv* racionalmente.
rationality *n* racionalidad *f*.
rattan *n* (*bot*) rota *f*.
rattle *vi* golpear; traquetear; ** vt* sacudir; ** n* traqueteo *m*; sonajero *m*.
rattlesnake *n* serpiente de cascabel *f*.
ravage *vt* saquear, pillar; estragar; ** n* saqueo *m*.
rave *vi* delirar.
rave music *n* (*col*) bakalao *m*.
raven *n* cuervo *m*.
ravenous *adj*, ~ly *adv* voraz(mente).
ravine *n* barranco *m*.

ravish *vt* encantar; raptar.
ravishing *adj* encantador/a.
raw *adj* crudo/da; puro/ra; novato/ta.
rawboned *adj* huesudo/da; magro/gra.
rawness *n* crudeza *f*; falta de experiencia *f*.
ray *n* rayo de luz *m*; raya *f* (pez).
raze *vt* arrasar.
razor *n* navaja; máquina de afeitar *f*.
reach *vt* alcanzar; llegar hasta; ** vi* extenderse, llegar; alcan zar, penetrar; ** n* alcance *m*.
react *vi* reaccionar.
reaction *n* reacción *f*.
read *vt* leer; ** vi* estudiar.
readable *adj* legible.
reader *n* lector/a *m/f*.
readily *adv* pronto; de buena gana.
readiness *n* voluntad, gana *f*; prontitud *f*.
reading *n* lectura *f*.
reading room *n* sala de lectura *f*.
readjust *vt* reajustar.
ready *adj* listo/ta, pronto/ta; incli-nado/da; abonado/da; fácil.
real *adj* real, verdadero/ra; ~ly *adv* realmente.
reality *n* realidad *f*.
realization *n* realización *f*.
realize *adv* darse cuenta de; realizar.
realm *n* reino *m*.
ream *n* resma *f*.
reap *vt* segar.
reaper *n* segador/a *m/f*.
reappear *vi* reaparecer.
rear *n* parte trasera *f*; retaguardia *f*; zaga *f*; ** vt* levantar, alzar.
rearmament *n* rearme *m*.
reason *n* razon *f*; causa *f*; ** vt, vi* razonar.
reasonable *adj* razonable.
reasonableness *n* lo razonable.
reasonably *adv* razonablemente.
reasoning *n* razonamiento *m*.
reassure *vt* tranquilizar, alentar; (*com*) asegurar.
rebel *n* rebelde *m/f*; ** vi* rebelarse.
rebellion *n* rebelión *f*.
rebellious *adj* rebelde.
rebound *vi* rebotar.
rebuff *n* desaire *m*; ** vt* rechazar.
rebuild *vt* reedificar.
rebuke *vt* reprender; ** n* reprensión *f*.
rebut *vi* repercutir.
recalcitrant *adj* recalcitrante.
recall *vt* recordar; retirar; ** n* retirada *f*.
recant *vt* retractar, desdecirse.
recantation *n* retractación *f*.
recapitulate *vt, vi* recapitular.
recapitulation *n* recapitulación *f*.
recapture *n* recobra *f*.
recede *vi* retroceder.
receipt *n* recibo *m*; recepción *f*; ~s *npl* ingresos *mpl*.
receivable *adj* por cobrar.
receive *vt* recibir, *Lat Am* recepcionar; aceptar, admitir.

recent adj reciente, nuevo/va; **~ly** adv recientemente.

receptacle n receptáculo m.

reception n recepción f.

recess n descanso m; recreo m; hueco m.

recession n retirada f; (com) recesión f.

recipe n receta f.

recipient n recipiente m.

reciprocal adj recíproco/ca; **~ly** adv recíprocamente.

reciprocate vi reciprocar.

reciprocity n reciprocidad f.

recital n recital m.

recite vt recitar; referir, relatar.

reckless adj temerario/ria; **~ly** adv temerariamente.

reckon vt contar, computar; * vi calcular.

reckoning n cuenta f; cálculo m.

reclaim vt reformar; reclamar.

reclaimable adj reclamable.

recline vt (vi) reclinar(se); recos-tar(se).

recluse n recluso/sa m/f.

recognition n reconocimiento; recuerdo m.

recognize vt reconocer.

recoil vi recular.

recollect vt acordarse de; recordar.

recollection n recuerdo m.

recommence vt empezar de nuevo.

recommend vt recomendar.

recommendation n recomendación f.

recompense n recompensa f; * vt recompensar.

reconcilable adj reconciliable.

reconcile vt reconciliar.

reconciliation n reconciliación f.

recondite adj recóndito/ta, reser-vado/da.

reconnaissance n (mil) reconocimiento m.

reconnoiter vt (mil) reconocer.

reconsider vt reconsiderar.

reconstruct vt reedificar.

record vt registrar; grabar; * n registro, archivo m; disco; récord m; **~s** pl anales mpl.

recorder n registrador/a, archivero/ra m/f; (mus) flauta de pico f.

recount vt contar de nuevo; relatar.

recourse n recurso m; remedio m.

recover vt recobrar; recuperar; restablecer; * vi convalecer, restablecerse.

recoverable adj recuperable.

recovery n convalecencia; recuperación f.

recreation n recreación f; recreo m.

recriminate vi recriminar.

recrimination n recriminación f.

recruit vt reclutar; * n (mil) recluta m/f.

recruiting n recluta f.

rectangle n rectángulo m.

rectangular adj rectangular.

rectification n rectificación f.

rectify vt rectificar.

rectilinear adj rectilíneo/nea.

rectitude n rectitud f.

rector n rector/a m/f.

recumbent adj recostado/da, recli-nado/da.

recur vi repetirse.

recurrence n repetición f.

recurrent adj repetido/da.

recycle vt reciclar.

recycled adj reciclado/da.

red adj rojo/ja; tinto/ta; * n rojo m.

redden vt enrojecer; * vi ponerse colorado/da.

reddish adj rojizo/za.

redeem vt redimir, rescatar.

redeemable adj redimible.

redeemer n redentor/a m/f.

redemption n redención f.

redeploy vt reorganizar.

red-handed adj: **to catch somebody ~** pillar a alguien con las manos en la masa.

red-hot adj candente, ardiente.

red-letter day n día señalado m.

redness n rojez, bermejura f.

redolent adj fragante, oloroso/sa.

redouble vt (vi) redoblar(se).

redress vt corregir; reformar; rectificar; * n reparación, compensación f.

red tape n (fig) trámites mpl.

reduce vt reducir; disminuir; rebajar.

reducible adj reducible.

reduction n reducción f; rebaja f.

redundancy n despido m.

redundant adj superfluo/lua.

reed n caña f.

reedy adj lleno de canas.

reef n (mar) rizo m; arrecife m.

reek n mal olor m; * vi humear; vahear.

reel n carrete m; bobina f; rollo m; * vi tambalear(se).

re-election n reelección f.

re-engage vt empeñar de nuevo.

re-enter vt volver a entrar.

re-establish vt restablecer, volver a establecer.

re-establishment n restablecimiento m; restauración f.

refectory n refectorio; comedor m.

refer vt, vi referir, remitir; referirse.

referee n árbitro/ra m/f, Lat Am referí m/f.

reference n referencia, relación f.

refine vt refinar, purificar.

refinement n refinación f; refinadura f; cultura f.

refinery n refinería f.

refit vt reparar; (mar) reparar.

reflect vt, vi reflejar; reflexionar.

reflection n reflexión, meditación f.

reflector n reflector m; captafaros m invar.

reflex adj reflejo.

reform vt (vi) reformar(se).

reform, reformation n reformación f.

reformer n reformador/a m/f.

reformist n reformista m/f.

refract vt refractar.

refraction n refracción f.

refrain vi: **to ~ from something** abstenerse de algo.

refresh *vt* refrescar.

refreshment *n* refresco, refrigerio *m*.

refrigerator *n* nevera *f*; refrigerador *m*.

refuel *vi* repostar (combustible).

refuge *n* refugio, asilo *m*.

refugee *n* refugiado/da *m/f*.

refund *vt* devolver; * *n* reembolso *m*.

refurbish *vt* restaurar, renovar.

refusal *n* negativa *f*.

refuse¹ *vt* rehusar.

refuse² *n* basura *f*.

refuse collector *n* basurero *m*.

refute *vt* refutar.

regain *vt* recobrar, recuperar.

regal *adj* real.

regale *vt* regalar.

regalia *n* insignias *fpl*.

regard *vt* estimar; considerar; * *n* consideración *f*; respeto *m*.

regarding *pr* en cuanto a.

regardless *adv* a pesar de todo.

regatta *n* regata *f*.

regency *n* regencia *f*.

regenerate *vt* regenerar; * *adj* rege-nerado/da.

regeneration *n* regeneración *f*.

regent *n* regente *m/f*.

regime *n* régimen *m*.

regiment *n* regimiento *m*.

region *n* región *f*.

register *n* registro *m*; * *vt* registrar.

registrar *n* registrador/a *m/f*.

registration *n* registro *m*.

registry *n* registro *m*.

regressive *adj* regresivo/va.

regret *n* sentimiento *m*; remordimiento *m*; pensión *f*; * *vt* sentir.

regretful *adj* pesaroso/sa.

regular *adj* regular; ordinario/ria; ~ly *adv* regularmente; * *n* regular *m*.

regularity *n* regularidad *f*.

regulate *vt* regular, ordenar; *Lat Am* normar.

regulation *n* regulación *f*; arreglo *m*.

regulator *n* regulador *m*.

rehabilitate *vt* rehabilitar.

rehabilitation *n* rehabilitación *f*.

rehearsal *n* repetición *f*; ensayo *m*.

rehearse *vt* repetir; ensayar.

reign *n* reinado, reino *m*; * *vi* reinar; prevalecer.

reimburse *vt* reembolsar.

reimbursement *n* reembolso *m*.

rein *n* rienda *f*; * *vt* refrenar.

reindeer *n* reno *m*.

reinforce *vt* reforzar.

reinstate *vt* reintegrar.

reinsure *vt* (*com*) reasegurar.

reissue *n* reedición *f*.

reiterate *vt* reiterar.

reiteration *n* reiteración, repetición *f*.

reject *vt* rechazar.

rejection *n* rechazo *m*.

rejoice *vt* (*vi*) regocijar(se).

rejoicing *n* regocijo *m*.

relapse *vi* recaer; * *n* reincidencia *f*; recaída *f*.

relate *vt*, *vi* relatar, referirse.

related *adj* emparentado/da.

relation *n* relación *f*; pariente *m*.

relationship *n* parentesco *m*; relación *f*.

relative *adj* relativo/va; ~ly *adv* relativamente; * *n* pariente *m/f*.

relax *vt*, *vi* relajar; descansar.

relaxation *n* relajación *f*; descanso *m*; relax *m*.

relay *n* relevo *m*; * *vt* retransmitir.

release *vt* soltar, libertar; * *n* liberación *f*; descargo *m*.

relegate *vt* relegar.

relegation *n* relegación *f*, descenso *m*.

relent *vi* ablandarse.

relentless *adj* implacable.

relevant *adj* pertinente.

reliable *adj* fiable, de confianza, *Lat Am* confiable.

reliance *n* confianza *f*.

relic *n* reliquia *f*.

relief *n* relieve *m*; alivio *m*.

relieve *vt* aliviar, consolar; socorrer.

religion *n* religión *f*.

religious *adj* religioso/sa; ~ly *adv* religiosamente.

relinquish *vt* abandonar, dejar.

relish *n* sabor *m*; gusto *m*; salsa *f*; * *vt* gustar de, agradar.

reluctance *n* repugnancia *f*.

reluctant *adj* reticente.

rely *vi* confiar en; contar con.

remain *vi* quedar, restar, permanecer, durar.

remainder *n* resto, residuo *m*.

remains *npl* restos, residuos *mpl*; sobras *fpl*.

remand *vt*: to ~ in custody mantener bajo prisión preventiva.

remark *n* observación, nota *f*; * *vt* notar, observar.

remarkable *adj* notable, interesante.

remarkably *adv* notablemente.

remarry *vi* volver a casarse.

remedial *adv* curativo/va.

remedy *n* remedio, recurso *m*; * *vt* remediar.

remember *vt* acordarse de; recordar.

remembrance *n* memoria *f*; recuerdo *m*.

remind *vt* recordar.

reminiscence *n* reminiscencia *f*.

remiss *adj* negligente.

remission *n* remisión *f*.

remit *vt*, *vi* remitir, perdonar; disminuir.

remittance *n* remesa *f*.

remnant *n* resto, residuo *m*.

remodel *vt* remodelar.

remonstrate *vi* protestar.

remorse *n* remordimiento *m*; compunción *f*.

remorseless *adj* implacable.

remote *adj* remoto/ta, lejano/na; ~ly *adv* remotamente, lejos.

remote control *n* mando a distancia *m*.

remoteness *n* alejamiento *m*; distancia *f*.

removable *adj* de quita y pon, de quitapón.

removal *n* remoción *f*; mudanza *f*.
remove *vt* quitar; * *vi* mudarse.
remunerate *vt* remunerar.
remuneration *n* remuneración *f*.
render *vt* devolver, restituir; traducir; rendir.
rendezvous *n* cita *f*; lugar de encuentro *m*.
renegade *n* renegado/da *m/f*.
renew *vt* renovar, restablecer.
renewal *n* renovación *f*.
rennet *n* cuajo *m*.
renounce *vt* renunciar.
renovate *vt* renovar.
renovation *n* renovación *f*.
renown *n* renombre *m*; celebridad *f*.
renowned *adj* célebre.
rent *n* renta *f*; arrendamiento *m*; alquiler *m*; * *vt* alquilar.
rental *n* alquiler *m*.
renunciation *n* renuncia *f*.
reopen *vt* reabrir.
reorganization *n* reorganización *f*.
reorganize *vt* reorganizar.
repair *vt* reparar; resarcir; * *n* reparación *f*.
reparable *adj* reparable.
reparation *n* reparación *f*.
repartee *n* réplica aguda/picante *f*.
repatriate *vt* repatriar.
repay *vt* devolver; pagar, restituir.
repayment *n* pago *m*.
repeal *vt* abrogar, revocar; * *n* revocación, anulación *f*.
repeat *vt* repetir.
repeatedly *adv* repetidamente.
repeater *n* reloj de repetición *m*.
repel *vt* repeler, rechazar.
repent *vi* arrepentirse.
repentance *n* arrepentimiento *m*.
repentant *adj* arrepentido/da.
repertory *n* repertorio *m*.
repetition *n* repetición, reiteración *f*.
replace *vt* reemplazar; reponer.
replenish *vt* llenar, surtir.
replete *adj* repleto/ta, lleno/na.
reply *n* respuesta *f*; * *vi* responder.
report *vt* referir, contar; dar cuenta de; * *n* informe *m*; repor taje *m*; relación *f*.
reporter *n* reportero/ra *m/f*.
repose *vt*, *vi* reposar; * *n* reposo *m*.
repository *n* depósito *m*.
repossess *vt* reobrar.
reprehend *vt* reprender.
reprehensible *adj* reprensible.
represent *vt* representar.
representation *n* representación *f*.
representative *adj* representativo/va; * *n* representante *m/f*.
repress *vt* reprimir, domar.
repression *n* represión *f*.
repressive *adj* represivo/va.
reprieve *vt* suspender una ejecución; indultar; * *n* indulto *m*.

reprimand *vt* reprender, corregir; * *n* reprensión *f*; repri menda *f*.
reprint *vt* reimprimir.
reprisal *n* represalia *f*.
reproach *n* improperio, oprobio *m*; * *vt* hacer reproches a.
reproachful *adj* ignominioso/sa; ~ly *adv* ignominiosamente.
reproduce *vt* reproducir.
reproduction *n* reproducción *f*.
reptile *n* reptil *m*.
republic *n* república *f*.
republican *adj*, *n* republicano/a *m/f*.
republicanism *n* republicanismo *m*.
Republican Party *n* Partido Republicano *m*.
repudiate *vt* repudiar.
repugnance *n* repugnancia *f*.
repugnant *adj* repugnante; ~ly *adv* con repugnancia.
repulse *vt* repulsar, desechar; * *n* repulsa *f*; rechazo *m*.
repulsion *n* repúlsion, repulsa *f*.
repulsive *adj* repulsivo/va.
reputable *adj* honroso/sa.
reputation *n* reputación *f*.
repute *vt* reputar.
request *n* petición, súplica *f*, *Lat Am* pedido *m*; * *vt* rogar, suplicar.
require *vt* requerir, demandar.
requirement *n* requisito *m*; exigencia *f*.
requisite *adj* necesario/ria, indispensable; * *n* requisito *m*.
requisition *n* petición, demanda *f*.
requite *vt* recompensar.
rescind *vt* rescindir, abrogar.
rescue *vt* librar, rescatar; * *n* libramiento, recobro *m*.
research *vt* investigar; * *n* investigación *f*.
resemblance *n* semejanza *f*.
resemble *vt* asemejarse.
resent *vt* resentirse.
resentful *adj* resentido/da; vengativo/va; ~ly *adv* con resentimi ento.
resentment *n* resentimiento *m*.
reservation *n* reserva *f*.
reserve *vt* reservar; * *n* reserva *f*.
reservedly *adv* con reserva.
reservoir *n* depósito *m*; pantano *m*.
reside *vi* residir, morar.
residence *n* residencia, morada *f*.
resident *adj* residente.
residuary *adj* sobrado/da; ~ **legatee** *n* (*law*) legatario/ria universal *m/f*.
residue *n* residuo, resto *m*.
resign *vt*, *vi* resignar, renunciar, ceder; resignarse, rendirse.
resignation *n* resignación *f*; dimisión *f*.
resin *n* resina *f*.
resinous *adj* resinoso/sa.
resist *vt* resistir, oponerse.
resistance *n* resistencia *f*.

resolute *adj* resuelto/ta; **~ly** *adv* resueltamente.

resolution *n* resolución *f.*

resolve *vt* (*vr*) resolver(se); (*fig*) zanjar.

resonance *n* resonancia *f.*

resonant *adj* resonante.

resort *vi* recurrir, frecuentar; * *n* recurso *m*; resorte *m.*

resound *vi* resonar.

resource *n* recurso *m*; expediente *m.*

respect *n* respecto *m*; respeto *m*; motivo *m*; **~s** *pl* recuerdos *mpl*; * *vt* apreciar; respetar; venerar.

respectability *n* respetabilidad *f.*

respectable *adj* respetable; considerable; **~bly** *adv* notablemente.

respectful *adj* respetuoso/sa; **~ly** *adv* respetuosamente.

respecting *prep* con respecto a.

respective *adj* respectivo/va, rela-tivo/va; **~ly** *adv* respectivamente.

respirator *n* respirador *m.*

respiratory *adj* respiratorio/ria.

respite *n* suspensión *f*; respiro *m*; * *vt* suspender, diferir.

resplendence *n* resplandor, brillo *m.*

resplendent *adj* resplandeciente.

respond *vt* responder; corresponder.

respondent *n* (*law*) defensor/a *m.*

response *n* respuesta, réplica *f.*

responsibility *n* responsabilidad *f.*

responsible *adj* responsable.

responsive *adj* sensible.

rest *n* reposo *m*; sueño *m*; quietud *f*; (*mus*) pausa *f*; resto, residuo *m*; * *vt* descansar; apoyar; * *vi* dormir, reposar; descansarse.

restaurant *n* restaurante, restorán *m.*

resting place (**last**) *n* última morada *f.*

restitution *n* restitución *f.*

restive *adj* inquieto/ta; obstinado/da.

restless *adj* insomne; inquieto/ta.

restoration *n* restauración *f.*

restorative *adj* restaurativo/va.

restore *vt* restaurar, restituir.

restrain *vt* restringir, restriñir.

restraint *n* refrenamiento, constreñimiento *m.*

restrict *vt* restringir, limitar.

restriction *n* restricción *f.*

restrictive *adj* restrictivo/va.

result *vi* resultar; * *n* resultado *m.*

resume *vt* resumir; empezar de nuevo.

resurrection *n* resurrección *f.*

resuscitate *vt* resucitar.

retail *vt* vender al por menor; * *n* venta por menor *f.*

retain *vt* retener, guardar.

retainer *n* adherente, partidario/ria *m/f*; **~s** *pl* comitiva *f*; séquito *m.*

retake *vt* volver a tomar.

retaliate *vt* tomar represalias.

retaliation *n* represalias *fpl.*

retardation *n* retraso *m.*

retarded *adj* retrasado/da.

retch *vi* tener arcadas.

retention *n* retención *f.*

retentive *adj* retentivo/va.

reticence *n* reticencia *f.*

retina *n* retina *f.*

retire *vt* (*vi*) retirar(se); jubilar(se).

retired *adj* apartado/da, retirado/da; jubilado/da.

retirement *n* retiro *m*, jubilación *f.*

retort *vt* replicar; * *n* réplica *f.*

retouch *vt* retocar.

retrace *vt* volver a trazar.

retract *vt* retraer; retractar.

retrain *vt* reciclar.

retraining *n* reciclaje profesional *m.*

retreat *n* retirada *f*; * *vi* retirarse.

retribution *n* retribución, recompensa *f.*

retrievable *adj* recuperable; reparable.

retrieve *vt* recuperar, recobrar.

retriever *n* sabueso *m.*

retrograde *adj* retrógrado/da.

retrospect, retrospection *n* reflexión *f.*

retrospective *adj* retrospectivo/va.

return *vt* retribuir; restituir; devolver; * *n* retorno *m*; vuelta *f*; recompensa, rendimiento *m*; recaída *f.*

reunion *n* reunión *f.*

reunite *vt* (*vi*) reunir(se).

reveal *vt* revelar.

revel *vi* andar de juerga.

revelation *n* revelación *f.*

reveler *n* juerguista *m/f.*

revelry *n* juerga *f.*

revenge *vt* vengar; * *n* venganza *f.*

revengeful *adj* vengativo/va.

revenue *n* renta *f*; rédito *m.*

reverberate *vt, vi* reverberar; resonar, retumbar.

reverberation *n* rechazo *m*; reverberación *f.*

revere *vt* reverenciar, venerar.

reverence *n* reverencia *f*; * *vt* reverenciar.

reverend *adj* reverendo/da; venerable; * *n* padre *m.*

reverent, reverential *adj* reverencial, respetuoso/sa.

reversal *n* revocación *f*; cambio total *m.*

reverse *vt* trastrocar; abolir; poner en marcha atrás; * *n* vicisi tud *f*; contrario *m*; reverso *m* (de una moneda).

reversible *adj* revocable; reversible.

reversion *n* reversión *f.*

revert *vt, vi* trastrocar; volverse atrás.

review *vt* rever; (*mil*) revistar; * *n* revista *f*; reseña *f.*

reviewer *n* revisor/a *m/f*; crítico/ca *m/f.*

revile *vt* ultrajar; difamar.

revise *vt* rever; repasar.

reviser *n* revisor/a *m/f.*

revision *n* revisión *f.*

revisit *vt* volver a visitar.

revival *n* restauración *f*; restablecimiento *m.*

revive *vt* avivar; restablecer; * *vi* revivir.

revocation n revocación f.
revoke vt revocar, anular.
revolt vi rebelarse; * n rebelión f.
revolting adj asqueroso/sa.
revolution n revolución f.
revolutionary adj, n revolucionario/a m/f.
revolve vt revolver; meditar; * vi girar.
revolver n revólver m.
revolving adj giratorio/ria.
revue n revista f.
revulsion n revulsión f.
reward n recompensa f; * vt recompensar.
rhapsody n rapsodia f.
rhetoric n retórica f.
rhetorical adj retórico/ca.
rheumatic adj reumático/ca.
rheumatism n reumatismo m.
rhinoceros n rinoceronte m.
rhomboid n romboide m.
rhombus n rombo m.
rhubarb n ruibarbo m.
rhyme n rima f; poema m; * vi rimar.
rhythm n ritmo m.
rhythmical adj rítmico/ca.
rib n costilla f.
ribald adj escabroso/sa.
ribbon n listón m; cinta f.
rice n arroz m.
rich adj rico/ca; opulento/ta; abundante; ~ly adv ricamente.
riches npl riqueza f.
richness n riqueza f; abundancia f.
rickets n raquitismo m.
rickety adj raquítico/ca.
rid vt librar, desembarazar.
riddance n: good ~! ¡enhoramala!
riddle n enigma m; criba f; * vt cribar.
ride vi cabalgar; andar en coche; * n paseo a caballo/en coche m.
rider n caballero/ra, jinete m, amazona f.
ridge n espinazo, lomo m; cumbre f; * vt formar lomos/surcos.
ridicule n ridiculez f; ridiculo m; * vt ridiculizar.
ridiculous adj ridículo/la; ~ly adv ridículamente.
riding n equitación f.
riding habit n traje de amazona m.
riding school n picadero m.
rife adj común, frecuente.
riffraff n desecho, desperdicio m.
rifle vt robar, pillar; estriar, rayar; * n rifle m.
rifleman n fusilero m.
rig vt ataviar; (mar) aparejar; * n torre de perforación f; oil ~ plataforma petrolera f.
rigging n (mar) aparejo m.
right adj derecho/cha, recto/ta; justo/ta; honesto/ta; ~! ¡bien!, ¡bueno!; ~ly adv rectamente, justamente; * n justicia f; razón f; derecho m; mano derecha f; * vt hacer justicia.
righteous adj justo/ta, honrado/da; ~ly adv justamente.

righteousness n equidad f; honradez f.
rigid adj rígido/da; austero/ra, severo/ra; yerto/ta; ~ly adv con rigidez.
rigidity n rigidez, austeridad f.
rigmarole n galimatías m.
rigor n rigor m; severidad f.
rigorous adj riguroso/sa; ~ly adv rigorosamente.
rim n margen m/f; orilla f.
rind n corteza f.
ring n círculo, cerco m; anillo m; campaneo m; * vt sonar; * vi retiñir, retumbar; to ~ the bell pulsar el timbre.
ringer (bell) n campanero/ra m/f.
ringleader n cabecilla m/f.
ringlet n anillejo m.
ringworm n (med) tina favosa f.
rink n (also ice ~) pista de hielo f.
rinse vt lavar, limpiar.
riot n tumulto, bullicio m; * vi amotinarse.
rioter n amotinado/da m/f.
riotous adj bullicioso/sa, sedicioso/sa; disoluto/ta; ~ly adv disolutamente.
rip vt rasgar, lacerar; descoser.
ripe adj maduro/ra, sazonado/da.
ripen vt, vi madurar.
ripeness n madurez f.
rip-off n (col): it's a ~! ¡es una estafa!
ripple vi rizarse; * vt rizar; * n onda f, rizo m.
rise vi levantarse; nacer, salir; levantarse; ascender; hincharse; elevarse; resucitar; * n levantamiento m; elevación f; subida f; salida (del sol) f; causa f.
rising n salida (del sol) f; fin (de una junta/sesión) m.
risk n riesgo, peligro m; * vt arriesgar.
risky adj peligroso/sa, Lat Am riesgoso/sa.
rissole n croqueta f.
rite n rito m.
ritual adj, n ritual m.
rival adj, n rival m/f; * vt competir, emular.
rivalry n rivalidad f.
river n río m.
riverside adj ribereño/ña.
rivet n remache m; * vt remachar, roblar.
rivulet n riachuelo m.
road n camino m.
road sign n señal de trafico f.
roadstead n (mar) rada f.
roadworks npl obras fpl.
roam vt, vi corretear; vagar.
roan adj ruano/na.
roar vi rugir, aullar; bramar; * n rugido m; bramido, truendo m; mugido m.
roast vt asar; tostar.
roast beef n rosbif m.
rob vt robar, hurtar.
robber n ladrón/ona m/f.
robbery n robo m.
robe n manto m; toga f; * vt vestir de gala.
robin (redbreast) n petirrojo m.
robust adj robusto/ta.

robustness n robustez f.

rock n roca f; escollo m; rueca f; * vt mecer; arrullar; ape drear; * vi bambolear.

rock and roll n rocanrol m.

rock crystal n cuarzo m.

rocking chair n mecedora f.

rocket n cohete m, Lat Am cuete m.

rock salt n sal gema f.

rocky adj peñascoso/sa.

rod n varilla, verga, cana f.

rodent n roedor/a m/f.

roe[1] n corzo m.

roe[2] n hueva f.

roebuck n corzo m.

rogation n rogaciones fpl.

rogue n bribón/ona, pícaro/ra, villa-no/na m/f.

roguish adj pícaro/ra.

roll vt rodar; volver; arrollar; * vi rodar; girar; * n rodadura f; rollo m; lista f; catalogo m; bollo m; panecillo m.

roller n rodillo, cilindro m.

roller skates npl patines de rueda mpl.

rolling pin n rodillo de cocina m.

Roman Catholic adj, n católico/ca m/f (romano/na).

romance n romance m; ficción f; cuento m; fábula f.

romantic adj romántico/ca.

romp vi retozar.

roof n tejado m; paladar m; * vt techar.

roofing n techado, tejado m.

rook[1] n grajo m.

rook[2] n torre f (en el juego de ajedrez).

room n habitación, sala f; lugar, espacio m; aposento m.

roominess n espaciosidad, capacidad f.

roomy adj espacioso/sa.

roost n pértiga del gallinero f; * vi dormir en una pértiga.

root n raíz f; origen m; * vt, vi: **to ~ out** desarraigar; arraigar.

rooted adj inveterado/da.

rope n cuerda f; cordel m; * vi hacer hebras.

rope maker n cordelero/ra m/f.

rosary n rosario m.

rose n rosa f.

rose bed n campo de rosales m.

rosebud n capullo de rosa m.

rosemary n (bot) romero m.

rose tree n rosal m.

rosette n roseta f.

rosé wine n vino rosado m.

rosewood n palo de rosa m.

rosiness n color rosado m.

rosy adj rosado/da.

rot vi pudrirse; * n putrefacción f.

rotate vt, vi girar.

rotation n rotación f.

rote n uso m; práctica f.

rotten adj podrido/da, corrompido/da.

rottenness n podredumbre, putrefacción f.

rotund adj rotundo/da, redondo/da, circular, esférico/ca.

rouge n arrebol, colorete m.

rough adj áspero/ra, tosco/ca; bron-co/ca, bruto/ta, brusco/ca; tempes-tuoso/sa; **~-looking** zarrapastroso/sa; **~ly** adv rudamente.

roughcast n mezcla gruesa f.

roughen vt poner áspero/ra.

roughness n aspereza f; rudeza, tosquedad f; tempestad f.

roulette n ruleta f.

round adj redondo/da; cabal; franco/ca, sincero/ra; * n círculo m; redondez f; vuelta f; giro m; escalón m; ronda f; andanada de canones f; descarga f; * adv alrededor; por todos lados; **~ly** adv redondamente; francamente; * vt cercar, rodear; redondear.

roundabout adj amplio/lia; indirec-to/ta, vago/ga; * n tiovivo m.

roundness n redondez f.

rouse vt despertar; excitar.

rout n derrota f; * vt derrotar.

route n ruta f; camino m.

routine adj rutinario/ria; * n rutina f; número m.

rove vi vagar, vaguear.

rover n vagabundo/da m/f; pirata m/f.

row[1] n camorra f; rina f.

row[2] n hilera, fila f.

row[3] vt (mar) remar, bogar.

rowdy n alborotador/a, bullanguero/ra m/f.

rower n remero/ra m/f.

royal adj real; regio/gia; **~ly** adv regiamente.

royalist n realista m/f.

royalty n realeza, dignidad real f; honorarios que paga el editor al autor por cada ejemplar vendido de su obra mpl.

royalties npl regalías fpl.

rub vt estregar, fregar, frotar; raspar; * n frotamiento m; (fig) embarazo m; dificultad f.

rubber n caucho m, goma f; (col) condón m.

rubber-band n goma, gomita f.

rubbish n basura f; tonterías fpl; escombro m; ruinas fpl.

rubble n escombros mpl, cascote m.

ruble n rublo m.

rubric n rúbrica f.

ruby n rubí m.

rucksack n mochila f.

rudder n timón m.

ruddiness n tez encendida; rubicundez f.

ruddy adj colorado/da, rubio/bia.

rude adj rudo/da, brutal, rústico/ca, grosero/ra; tosco/ca; **~ly** adv rudamente, groseramente.

rudeness n descortesía f; rudeza, insolencia f.

rudiment n rudimentos mpl.

rue vi compadecerse; * n (bot) ruda f.

rueful adj lamentable, triste.

ruffian n malhechor/a, bandolero/ra m/f; * adj brutal.

ruffle vt desordenar, desazonar; rizar.

rug *n* alfombra *f.*

rugby *n* rugby *m.*

rugged *adj* áspero/ra, tosco/ca; brutal; peludo/da.

ruin *n* ruina *f*; perdición *f*; escombros *mpl*; * *vt* arruinar; destruir.

ruinous *adj* ruinoso/sa.

rule *n* mando *m*; regla *f*; regularidad *f*; dominio *m*; * *vt* gobernar; reglar, arreglar, dirigir.

ruler *n* gobernador/a *m/f*; regla *f.*

rum *n* ron *m.*

rumble *vi* crujir, rugir.

ruminate *vt* rumiar.

rummage *vt* rebuscar.

rumor *n* rumor *m*; * *vt* rumorearse.

rump *n* ancas *fpl.*

run *vt* dirigir; organizar; llevar; pasar; **to ~ the risk** aventurar, arriesgar; * *vi* correr; fluir; manar; pasar rápidamente; proceder; ir; desteñirse; ser candidato/ta; * *n* corrida, carrera *f*; paseo *m*; curso *m*; serie *f*; moda *f*; ataque *m.*

runaway *n* fugitivo/va, desertor/a *m/f.*

rung *n* escalón, peldaño *m* (de escalera de mano).

runner *n* corredor/a *m/f*; correo, mensajero/ra *m/f.*

running *n* carrera, corrida *f*; curso *m.*

runway *n* pista de aterrizaje *f.*

rupture *n* rotura *f*; hernia, quebradura *f*; * *vt* reventar, romper.

rural *adj* rural, campestre, rústico/ca.

ruse *n* astucia, maña *f.*

rush *n* junco *m*; ráfaga *f*; ímpetu *m*; * *vt* apresurar; * *vi* abalanzarse, tirarse.

rusk *n* galleta *f.*

russet *adj* bermejo/ja.

rust *n* herrumbre *f*; * *vi* oxidarse.

rustic *adj* rústico/ca; * *n* patán/ana, rústico/ca *m/f.*

rustiness *n* herrumbre *f.*

rustle *vi* crujir, rechinar; * *vt* hacer crujir.

rustling *n* estruendo *m*; crujido *m.*

rusty *adj* oriniento/ta, mohoso/sa; oxidado/da.

rut *n* celo *m*; carril *m.*

ruthless *adj* cruel, insensible; **~ly** *adv* inhumanamente.

rye *n* (*bot*) centeno *m.*

S

Sabbath *n* sábado *m.*

sable *n* cebellina *f.*

sabotage *n* sabotaje *m.*

saber *n* sable *m.*

saccharin *n* sacarina *f.*

sachet *n* sobrecito *m.*

sack *n* saco *m*; * *vt* despedir; saquear.

sacrament *n* sacramento *m*; Eucaristía *f.*

sacramental *adj* sacramental.

sacred *adj* sagrado/da, sacro/cra; inviolable.

sacredness *n* santidad *f.*

sacrifice *n* sacrificio *m*; * *vt, vi* sacrificar.

sacrificial *adj* de sacrificio.

sacrilege *n* sacrilegio *m.*

sacrilegious *adj* sacrílego/ga.

sad *adj* triste, melanólico/ca; infaus-to/ta; obscuro/ra; **~ly** *adv* tristemente.

sadden *vt* entristecer.

saddle *n* silla *f*; sillín *m*; * *vt* ensillar.

saddlebag *n* alforja *f.*

saddler *n* sillero *m/f.*

sadness *n* tristeza *f.*

safari *n* safari *m.*

safe *adj* seguro/ra; ileso/sa; fuera de peligro; de fiar; **~ly** *adv* seguramente; **~ and sound** sano y salvo; * *n* caja fuerte *f.*

safe-conduct *n* salvoconducto *m.*

safeguard *n* salvaguardia *f*; * *vt* proteger, defender.

safety *n* seguridad *f*; salvamento *m.*

safety belt *n* cinturón (de seguridad) *m.*

safety match *n* cerilla *f.*

safety pin *n* imperdible, seguro *m.*

saffron *n* azafrán *m.*

sage *n* (*bot*) salvia *f*; sabio/bia *m/f*; * *adj* sabio/bia; **~ly** *adv* sabiamente.

Sagittarius *n* Sagitario *m* (signo del zodíaco).

sago *n* (*bot*) sagú *m.*

sail *n* vela *f*; * *vt* gobernar; * *vi* dar a la vela, navegar.

sailing *n* navegación *f.*

sailing boat *n* yate *m.*

sailor *n* marinero/ra *m/f.*

saint *n* santo/ta *m/f.*

sainted, saintly *adj* santo/ta.

sake *n* causa, razón *f*; **for God's ~** por amor de Dios.

salable *adj* vendible.

salad *n* ensalada *f.*

salad bowl *n* ensaladera *f.*

salad dressing *n* aliño *m.*

salad oil *n* aceite para ensaladas *m.*

salamander *n* salamandra *f.*

salary *n* sueldo *m.*

sale *n* venta *f*; liquidación *f.*

salesman *n* vendedor *m.*

saleswoman *n* vendedora *f.*

salient *adj* saliente, saledizo/za.

saline *adj* salino/na.

saliva *n* saliva *f.*

sallow *adj* cetrino/na, pálido/da.

sally *n* (*mil*) salida, surtida *f*; * *vi* salir.

salmon *n* salmón *m.*

salmon trout *n* trucha salmonada *f.*

saloon *n* bar *m.*

salt *n* sal *f*; * *vt* salar.

salt cellar *n* salero *m.*

salting *n* saladura *f.*

saltpeter *n* salitre *m.*

saltworks *npl* salinas *fpl.*

salubrious *adj* salubre, saludable.
salubrity *n* salubridad *f*.
salutary *adj* salubre, salutífero/ra.
salutation *n* salutación *f*.
salute *vt* saludar; * *n* saludo *m*.
salvage *n* (*mar*) salvamento, rescate *m*.
salvation *n* salvación *f*.
salve *n* emplasto, ungüento *m*.
salver *n* salvilla, bandeja *f*.
salvo *n* salva, excusa *f*.
same *adj* mismo/ma, idéntico/ca.
sameness *n* identidad *f*.
sample *n* muestra *f*; ejemplo *m*; * *vt* probar.
sampler *n* muestra *f*; dechado, modelo *m*.
sanctify *vt* santificar.
sanctimonious *adj* santurrón/ona.
sanction *n* sanción *f*; * *vt* sancionar.
sanctity *n* santidad *f*.
sanctuary *n* santuario *m*; asilo *m*.
sand *n* arena *f*; * *vt* lijar.
sandal *n* sandalia *f*.
sandbag *n* (*mil*) saco de tierra *m*.
sandpit *n* arenal *m*.
sandstone *n* arenisca *f*.
sandwich *n* bocadillo, sandwich *m*, *Lat Am* sánduche *m*.
sandy *adj* arenoso/sa.
sane *adj* sano/na.
sanguinary *adj* sanguinario/ria.
sanguine *adj* sanguíneo/nea.
sanitarium *n* sanatorio *m*.
sanitary napkin *n* compresa *f*, *Lat Am* toalla *f* higiénica.
sanity *n* juicio sano, sentido común *m*.
sap *n* savia *f*; * *vt* minar.
sapient *adj* sabio/bia, cuerdo/da.
sapling *n* arbolito *m*.
sapper *n* (*mil*) zapador *m*.
sapphire *n* zafiro *m*.
sarcasm *n* sarcasmo *m*.
sarcastic *adj* sarcástico/ca; **~ally** *adv* sarcásticamente.
sarcophagus *n* sarcófago, sepulcro *m*.
sardine *n* sardina *f*.
sash *n* cíngulo *m*, cinta *f*.
sash window *n* ventana/vidriera corrediza *f*.
Satan *n* Satanás *m*.
satanic(al) *adj* diabólico/ca.
satchel *n* mochila *f*.
satellite *n* satélite *m*.
satellite dish *n* antena parabólica *f*.
satiate, sate *vt* saciar, hartar.
satin *n* raso *m*; * *adj* de raso.
satire *n* satira *f*.
satiric(al) *adj* satírico/ca; **~ly** *adv* satíricamente.
satirist *n* autor satírico *m*, autora satírica *f*.
satirize *vt* satirizar.
satisfaction *n* satisfacción *f*.
satisfactorily *adv* satisfactoriamente.
satisfactory *adj* satisfactorio/ria.
satisfy *vt* satisfacer; convencer.

saturate *vt* saturar.
Saturday *n* sábado *m*.
saturnine *adj* saturnino/na, melan-cólico/ca.
satyr *n* sátiro *m*.
sauce *n* salsa *f*; crema *f*; compota de frutas *f*; * *vt* condimentar.
saucepan *n* cazo *m*.
saucer *n* platillo *m*.
saucily *adv* desvergonzadamente.
sauciness *n* insolencia, impudencia *f*.
saucy *adj* insolente.
saunter *vi* callejear, corretear.
sausage *n* salchicha *f*.
savage *adj* salvaje, bárbaro/ra; **~ly** *adv* bárbaramente; * *n* salvaje *m/f*.
savageness *n* salvajería, *f*; crueldad *f*.
savagery *n* crueldad *f*.
savanna(h) *n* sabana *f*.
save *vt* salvar; economizar; ahorrar; evitar; conservar; * *adv* salvo, excepto; * *n* parada *f*, *Lat Am* atajada *f*.
saveloy sausage *n* chorizo *m*.
saver *n* ahorrador/a *m/f*.
saving *adj* frugal, económico/ca; * *prep* fuera de, excepto; * *n* salvamento *m*; **~s** *pl* ahorro *m*, economía *f*.
savings account *n* cuenta de ahorros *f*.
savings bank *n* caja de ahorros *f*.
Savior *n* Salvador *m*.
savior *n* libertador/a *m/f*.
savor *n* olor *m*; sabor *m*; * *vt* gustar, saborear.
savoriness *n* paladar; sabor *m*.
savory *adj* sabroso/sa.
saw *n* sierra *f*; * *vt* serrar, *Lat Am* serruchar.
sawdust *n* serrín *m*.
sawfish *n* pez sierra *m*.
sawmill *n* aserradero *m*.
sawyer *n* aserrador/a *m/f*.
saxophone *n* saxofóno *m*.
say *vt* decir, hablar.
saying *n* dicho, proverbio *m*.
scab *n* roña *f*; roñoso *m*.
scabbard *n* vaina (de espada) *f*; cobertura *f*.
scabby *adj* sarnoso/sa.
scaffold *n* tablado *m*; cadalso *m*.
scaffolding *n* andamio *m*.
scald *vt* escaldar; * *n* escaladura *f*.
scale *n* balanza *f*; escama *f*; escala *f*; gama *f*; * *vt, vi* escalar; descostrarse.
scallop *n* vieira *f*; festón *m*; * *vt* festonear.
scalp *n* cuero cabelludo *m*; * *vt* escalpar.
scamp *n* bribón/ona, ladrón/ona *m/f*.
scamper *vi* escapar, huir.
scampi *npl* gambas *fpl*.
scan *vt* escudriñar; registrar; escandir; escanear.
scandal *n* escándalo *m*; infamia *f*.
scandalize *vt* escandalizar.
scandalous *adj* escandaloso/sa; **~ly** *adv* escandalosamente.
scanner *n* escáner *m*.
scant, scanty *adj* escaso/sa, parco/ca.

scantily adv escasamente, estrechamente.
scantness n estrechez, escasez f.
scapegoat n chivo expiatorio m.
scar n cicatriz f; * vt dejar cicatriz en.
scarce adj raro/ra; **~ly** adv apenas.
scarcity n escasez f; raridad f.
scare vt espantar; * n susto m.
scarecrow n espantapájaros m invar.
scarf n bufanda f.
scarlet n escarlata f; * adj escarlata.
scarlet fever n escarlatina f.
scarp n escarpa f.
scat interj (col) ¡zape!
scatter vt esparcir; disipar.
scavenger n basurero/ra m/f; carro-ñero/ra m/f.
scenario n argumento m; guión m; (fig) escenario m.
scene n escena f; panorama m; escándalo m; paisaje m.
scenery n vista f; decoración (de teatro) f.
scenic adj escénico/ca.
scent n olfato m; olor m; rastro m; * vt oler.
scent bottle n frasco de perfume m.
scentless adj sin olfato; inodoro/ra.
scepter n cetro m.
schedule n horario m; programa m; lista f.
scheme n proyecto, plan m; esquema m; sistema m; modelo m; * vt proyectar; * vi intrigar.
schemer n proyectista, intrigante m/f.
schism n cisma m.
schismatic adj cismático/ca.
scholar n estudiante m/f; erudito/ta m/f, escolástico/ca m/f.
scholarship n ciencia f; erudición f.
scholastic adj escolástico/ca.
school n escuela f, colegio m; * vt enseñar.
schoolboy n alumno m.
schoolgirl n alumna f.
schooling n instrucción f.
schoolmaster n maestro de escuela m.
schoolmistress n maestra de niños/niñas f.
schoolteacher n maestro/tra m/f; profesor/a m/f.
schooner n (mar) goleta f.
sciatica n ciática f.
science n ciencia f.
scientific adj científico/ca; **~ally** adv científicamente.
scientist n científico/ca m/f.
scimitar n cimitarra f.
scintillate vi chispear, centellar.
scintillating adj brillante, ingenioso/sa.
scissors npl tijeras fpl.
scoff vi mofarse, burlarse.
scold vt, vi regañar, reñir, refunfuñar.
scoop n cucharón m; pala f; exclusiva f; * vt cavar, socavar.
scooter (child's) n patinete m.
scope n objeto, intento, designio, blanco, espacio m; alcance m; libertad f.
scorch vt quemar; tostar; * vi quemarse, secarse.

score n muesca, canalita f; consideración f; cuenta f; puntuación f; razón f; motivo m; veintena f; * vt ganar; señalar con una línea; * vi marcar.
scoreboard n marcador m.
scorn vt, vi despreciar; mofar; * n desdén, menosprecio m.
scornful adj desdeñoso/sa; **~ly** adv con desdén.
Scorpio n Escorpión m (signo del zodíaco).
scorpion n escorpión m.
scotch vt descartar.
Scotch n whisky escocés m.
scoundrel n pícaro/ra m/f.
scour vt fregar, estregar; limpiar; * vi corretear.
scourge n azote m; castigo m; * vt azotar, castigar.
scout n (mil) explorador/a m/f; espía m/f; * vi ir de reconocimiento.
scowl vi fruncir el ceño; * n ceño, semblante ceñudo m.
scragginess n flaqueza, aspereza f.
scraggy adj áspero/ra; macilento/ta.
scramble vi arrapar; trepar; disputar; * n disputa f; subida f.
scrap n migaja f; sobras fpl; pedacito m; riña f; chatarra f.
scrape vt, vi raer, raspar; arañar; tocar mal un instrumento; * n embarazo m; dificultad f.
scraper n rascador m.
scratch vt rascar, raspar; raer, garrapatear; * n rasguño m, Lat Am rasguñón m.
scrawl vt, vi garrapatear; * n garabatos mpl.
scream, screech vi chillar, dar alaridos; * n chillido, grito, alarido m.
screen n pantalla f; biombo m; mampara f; abanico de chimenea m; * vt abrigar, esconder; proyectar; cribar, cerner.
screenplay n guión m, Lat Am libreto m.
screw n tornillo m; * vt atornillar; forzar, apretar, estrechar.
screwdriver n destornillador m.
scribble vt escarabajear; * n escrito de poco mérito m.
scribe n escritor/a m/f; escriba m/f.
scrimmage n tumulto m, scrimmage m.
script n guión m; letra f.
scriptural adj bíblico/ca.
Scripture n Sagrada Escritura f.
scroll n rollo (de papel/pergamino) m.
scrounger n mamón/ona m/f.
scrub vt restregar; anular; * n maleza f.
scruffy adj desaliñado/da.
scruple n escrúpulo m.
scrupulous adj escrupuloso/sa; **~ly** adv escrupulosamente.
scrutinize vt escudriñar, examinar.
scrutiny n escrutinio, examen m.
scuffle n quimera, riña f; * vi reñir, pelear.
scull n barquillo m.
sculptor n escultor/a m/f.
sculpture n escultura f; * vt esculpir.

scum *n* espuma *f*; escoria *f*; canalla *m/f*.

scurrilous *adj* vil, bajo/ja; injurioso/sa; **~ly** *adv* injuriosamente.

scurvy *n* escorbuto *m*; * *adj* escorbú-tico/ca; vil, despreciable.

scuttle[1] *n* carbonera *f*.

scuttle[2] *vt* barrenar.

scythe *n* guadaña *f*.

sea *n* mar *m/f*; * *adj* de mar; **heavy ~** oleada *f*.

sea breeze *n* viento de mar *m*.

seacoast *n* costa marítima *f*.

sea fight *n* combate naval *m*.

seafood *n* mariscos *mpl*.

sea front *n* paseo marítimo *m*.

sea-green *adj* verdemar.

seagull *n* gaviota *f*.

sea horse *n* caballito de mar *m*.

seal *n* sello *m*; foca *f*; * *vt* sellar.

sealing wax *n* lacre *m*.

seam *n* costura *f*; * *vt* coser.

seaman *n* marinero *m*.

seamanship *n* pericia en la navegación *m*.

seamstress *n* costurera *f*.

seamy *adj* sórdido/da.

seaport *n* puerto de mar *m*.

sear *vt* cauterizar.

search *vt* examinar; escudriñar; inquirir; tentar; investigar, buscar; * *n* pesquisa *f*; busca *f*, *Lat Am* procura *f*; buscada *f*.

searchlight *n* reflector *m*.

seashore *n* ribera *f*, litoral *m*.

seasick *adj* mareado/da.

seasickness *n* mareo *m*.

seaside *n* orilla/ribera del mar *f*.

season *n* estación *f*; tiempo oportuno *m*; sazón *f*; * *vt* sazonar; imbuir.

seasonable *adj* oportuno/na, a propósito.

seasonably *adv* oportunamente.

seasoning *n* condimento *m*.

season ticket *n* abono *m*.

season ticket holder *n* abonado/da *m/f*.

seat *n* asiento *m*; silla *f*; escaño *m*; situación *f*; * *vt* situar; colocar; asentar.

seat belt *n* cinturón de seguridad *m*.

seaward *adj* del litoral; **~s** *adv* hacia el mar.

seaweed *n* alga marina *f*.

seaworthy *adj* en condiciones de navegar.

secede *vi* apartarse, separarse.

secession *n* secesión *f*; separación *f*.

seclude *vt* apartar, excluir.

seclusion *n* separación *f*; exclusión *f*.

second *adj* segundo/da; **~ (ly)** *adv* en segundo lugar; * *n* defensor/a *m/f*; segundo *m*; (*mus*) segunda *f*; * *vt* ayudar; segundar.

secondary *adj* secundario/ria.

secondary school *n* escuela secundaria *f*.

secondhand *adj* de segunda mano.

secrecy *n* secreto *m*, confidencialidad *f*.

secret *adj* secreto/ta; * *n* secreto *m*; **~ly** *adv* secretamente.

secretary *n* secretario/ria *m/f*.

secrete *vt* esconder; (*med*) secretar.

secretion *n* secreción *f*.

secretive *adj* misterioso/sa.

sect *n* secta *f*.

sectarian *n* sectario/ria *m/f*.

section *n* sección *f*.

sector *n* sector *m*.

secular *adj* secular, seglar.

secularize *vt* secularizar.

secure *adj* seguro/ra; salvo/va; **~ly** *adv* seguramente; * *vt* asegurar; salvar.

security *n* seguridad *f*; defensa *f*; confianza *f*; fianza *f*.

sedan, saloon *n* sedán *m*.

sedate *adj* sosegado/da, tranquilo/la; **~ly** *adv* tranquilamente.

sedateness *n* tranquilidad *f*.

sedative *n* sedativo *m*.

sedentary *adj* sedentario/ria.

sedge *n* (*bot*) juncia *f*.

sediment *n* sedimento *m*; hez *f*; poso *m*.

sedition *n* sedición *f*; tumulto, alboroto, motín *m*; revuelta *f*.

seditious *adj* sedicioso/sa.

seduce *vt* seducir; engañar.

seducer *n* seductor/a *m/f*.

seduction *n* seducción *f*.

seductive *adj* seductor/a.

sedulous *adj* asiduo/dua; **~ly** *adv* asiduamente.

see *vt, vi* ver, observar, descubrir; advertir; conocer, juzgar; comprender; **~!** ¡mira!

seed *n* semilla, simiente *f*; * *vi* granar.

seedling *n* plantón *m*.

seedsman *n* tratante en semillas *m*.

seedy *adj* desaseado/da.

seeing *conj*: **~ that** visto que, ya que.

seek *vt, vi* buscar; pretender.

seem *vi* parecer, semejarse.

seeming *n* apariencia *f*; **~ly** *adv* al parecer.

seemliness *n* decencia *f*.

seemly *adj* decente, propio/pia.

seer *n* profeta *m*, profetisa *f*.

seesaw *n* vaivén *m*; * *vi* balancear.

seethe *vi* hervir, bullir.

segment *n* segmento *m*.

seize *vt* asir, agarrar; secuestrar (bienes/efectos).

seizure *n* captura *f*; secuestro *m*.

seldom *adv* raramente, rara vez.

select *vt* elegir, escoger; * *adj* selec-to/ta, escogido/da.

selection *n* selección *f*.

self *n* uno/na mismo/ma; **the ~** el yo; * *pref* auto-.

self-command *n* autocontrol *m*.

self-conceit *n* presunción *f*.

self-confident *adj* que tiene confianza en sí mismo/ma.

self-defense *n* defensa propia *f*.

self-denial *n* abnegación de sí mis-mo/ma *f*.

self-employed *adj* autónomo/ma, *Lat Am* cuentapropista.

self-evident *adj* obvio/via.

self-governing adj autónomo/ma.
self-interest n interés propio m.
selfish adj egoísta; **~ly** adv interesadamente.
selfishness n egoísmo m.
self-medication n automedicación f.
self-pity n lástima de sí mismo/ma f.
self-portrait n autorretrato m.
self-possession n sangre fría, tranquilidad de ánimo f.
self-reliant adj independiente.
self-respect n amor propio m.
selfsame adj mismísimo/ma.
self-satisfied adj pagado/da de sí mismo/ma.
self-seeking adj egoísta.
self-service adj de autoservicio.
self-styled adj autoproclamado/da.
self-sufficient adj autosuficiente.
self-taught adj autodidacta.
self-willed adj obstinado/da.
sell vt, vi vender; traficar.
seller n vendedor/a m/f.
selling-off n privatización f.
Sellotape™ n celo m.
semblance n semejanza, apariencia f.
semen n semen m.
semester n semestre m.
semicircle n semicírculo m.
semicircular adj semicircular.
semicolon n punto y coma m.
semiconductor n semiconductor m.
semifinal n semifinal f.
seminarist n seminarista m.
seminary n seminario m.
semitone n (mus) semitono m.
senate n senado m.
senator n senador/a m/f.
senatorial adj senatorio/ria.
send vt enviar, despachar, mandar; enviar; producir.
sender n remitente m/f.
senile adj senil.
senility n senectud f; vejez f.
senior n mayor m; * adj mayor; superior.
seniority n antigüedad, ancianidad f.
senna n (bot) sena f.
sensation n sensación f.
sense n sentido m; entendimiento m; razón f; juicio m; sentimiento m.
senseless adj insensible; insensato/ta; **~ly** adv insensatamente.
senselessness n tontería, insensatez f.
sensibility n sensibilidad f.
sensible adj sensato/ta; juicioso/sa.
sensibly adv sensatamente.
sensitive adj sensible.
sensual, sensuous adj, **~ly** adv sensual(mente).
sensuality n sensualidad f.
sentence n oración f; sentencia f; * vt sentenciar, condenar.
sententious adj sentencioso/sa; **~ly** adv sentenciosamente.

sentient adj sensitivo/va.
sentiment n sentimiento m; opinión f.
sentimental adj sentimental.
sentinel, sentry n centinela m.
sentry box n garita f.
separable adj separable.
separate vt (vi) separar(se); * adj separado/da; distinto/ta; **~ly** adv separadamente.
separation n separación f.
September n septiembre m.
septennial adj sieteñal.
septuagenarian n septuagenario/ria m/f.
sepulcher n sepulcro m.
sequel n continuación f; consecuencia f.
sequence n serie, continuación f.
sequester, sequestrate vt secuestrar.
sequestration n secuestro m.
seraglio n serallo m.
seraph n serafín m.
serenade n serenata f; * vt dar serenatas.
serene adj sereno/na; **~ly** adv serenamente.
serenity n serenidad f.
serf n siervo/va, esclavo/va m/f.
serge n sarga f.
sergeant n sargento/ta m/f; alguacil m/f.
serial adj consecutivo/va, en serie; * n serial m; telenovela f.
series n serie f.
serious adj serio/ria, grave; **~ly** adv seriamente.
sermon n sermón f; oración evangélica f.
serpent n serpiente, sierpe f.
serpentine adj serpentino/na; * n (chem) serpentina f.
serrated adj serrado/da.
serum n suero m.
servant n criado m; criada f.
servant girl n criada f.
serve vt, vi servir; asistir (a la mesa); hacer; cumplir; sacar; ser a propósito; **to ~ a warrant** ejecutar un auto de prisión.
service n servicio m; servidumbre, utilidad f; culto divino m; acomodo m; * vt mantener; reparar.
serviceable adj servible; oficioso/sa.
service station n estación de servicio f; gasolinera f.
servile adj servil.
servitude n servidumbre, esclavitud f.
session n junta f; sesión f.
set vt poner, colocar, fijar; establecer, determinar; * vi ponerse (el sol/los astros); cuajarse; aplicarse; * n juego, conjunto m; servicio (de plata) m; conjunto/agregado de muchas cosas m; decorado m; set m; - cuadrilla, bandada f; * adj puesto/ta, fijo/ja; listo/ta; decidido/da.
settee n sofá m.
setter n setter m.
setting n establecimiento m; marco m; montadura f; **~ of the sun** puesta del sol f.
settle vt colocar, fijar, afirmar; arreglar; calmar; * vi reposarse; establecerse; sosegarse.

settlement n establecimiento m; domicilio m; contrato m; empleo m; poso m; colonia f.

settler n colono/na m/f.

set-to n riña f; combate m.

seven adj, n siete.

seventeen adj, n diecisiete.

seventeenth adj, n decimoséptimo/ma.

seventh adj n séptimo/ma.

seventieth adj, n septuagésimo/ma.

seventy adj, n setenta.

sever vt, vi separar.

several adj, pn varios/as, algunos/nas.

severance n separación f.

severe adj severo/ra, riguroso/sa, áspero/ra, duro/ra; ~ly adv severamente.

severity n severidad f.

sew vt, vi coser.

sewer n alcantarilla f.

sewerage n alcantarillado m.

sewing machine n máquina de coser f.

sex n sexo m.

sexist adj, n sexista m/f.

sextant n sextante m.

sexton n sepulturero/ra m/f.

sexual adj sexual.

sexy adj sexy.

shabbily adv vilmente, mezquinamente.

shabbiness n miseria f.

shabby adj desharrapado/da, zarra-pastroso/sa.

shackle vt poner grilletes; ~s npl grilletes mpl.

shade n sombra, oscuridad f; matiz m; sombrilla f; * vt dar sombra a; abrigar; proteger.

shadiness n sombraje m; umbría f.

shadow n sombra f; protección f.

shadowy adj umbroso/sa; oscuro/ra; quimerico/ca.

shady adj opaco/ca, oscuro/ra, som-brío/ría.

shaft n flecha, saeta f; fuste de columna m; pozo m; hueco m; rayo m.

shag n tabaco picado m; cormorán moñudo m.

shaggy adj lanoso/sa.

shake vt sacudir; agitar; **to ~ vigorously** zarandear; **to ~ hands** darse las manos; * vi vacilar; temblar; * n sacudida f, Lat Am sacudón m; vibración f.

shaking n temblor m.

shaky adj titubeante.

shallow adj somero/ra, superficial; trivial.

shallowness n poca profundidad f; necedad f.

sham vt engañar; * n fingimiento m; impostura f; * adj fingido/da, disi-mulado/da.

shambles npl confusión f.

shame n vergüenza f; deshonra f; * vt avergonzar, deshonrar.

shamefaced adj vergonzoso/sa, pu-doroso/sa.

shameful adj vergonzoso/sa; des-honroso/sa; ~ly adv ignominiosamente.

shameless adj desvergonzado/da; ~ly adv desvergonzadamente.

shamelessness n desvergüenza, impudencia f.

shammy, chamois n gamuza f.

shampoo vt lavar con champú; * n champú m.

shamrock n trébol m.

shank n caña f; asta (de ancla) f; cañón (de pipa) m.

shanty n chabola f.

shanty town n barrio de chabolas m, Lat Am barriada f.

shape vt, vi formar; proporcionar; concebir; * n forma, figura f; modelo m.

shapeless adj informe.

shapely adj bien hecho/cha.

share n parte, porción f; (com) acción f; reja del arado f; * vt, vi repartir; compartir.

sharer n partícipe m/f.

shark n tiburón m.

sharp adj agudo/da, aguzado/da; afilado/da, Lat Am filoso/sa; astuto/ta; perspicaz; penetrante; acre, mordaz, severo/ra, rígido/da; vivo/va, violento/ta; * n (mus) sostenido m; * adv en punto.

sharpen vt afilar, aguzar.

sharply adv con filo; severamente, agudamente, ingenios amente.

sharpness n agudeza f; sutileza, perspicacia f; acrimonia f.

shatter vt destrozar, estrellar; * vi hacerse pedazos.

shave vt afeitar, rasurar; * vi afeitarse, rasurarse; * n afeite m, Lat Am afeitada f.

shaver n máquina de afeitar f.

shaving n rasurado m.

shaving brush n brocha de afeitar f.

shaving cream n crema de afeitar f.

shawl n chal m, Lat Am rebozo m.

she pn ella.

sheaf n gavilla f; haz m.

shear vt atusar; tundir; ~s npl tijeras de podar fpl.

sheath n vaina f.

shed vt verter, derramar; esparcir; * n tejadillo m; cabaña f.

sheen n resplandor m.

sheep n oveja f.

sheepfold n redil m.

sheepish adj vergonzoso/sa; tímido/da.

sheepishness n timidez, cortedad de genio f.

sheepskin n piel de carnero m; zamarra f; ~ jacket zamarra f.

sheer adj puro/ra, claro/ra, sin mezcla; escarpado/da; * adv verticalmente.

sheet n sábana f; lámina f; pliego de papel f; (mar) escota f.

sheet anchor n áncora mayor de un navío f.

sheeting n tela para sábanas f.

sheet iron n chapa de hierro batido f.

sheet lightning n relampagueamiento m.

shelf n anaquel m; (mar) arrecife m; escollera f; **on the** ~ desecho/cha.

shell n cáscara f; proyectil m; concha f; corteza f; * vt descas carar, descortezar; bombardear; * vi descascararse.

shellfish *npl invar* crustáceo *m*; marisco *m*.

shelter *n* guardia *f*; amparo, abrigo *m*; asilo, refugio *m*; * *vt* guarecer, abrigar; acoger; * *vi* abrigarse.

shelve *vt* echar a un lado, arrinconar.

shelving *n* estantería *f*.

shepherd *n* pastor *m*.

shepherdess *n* pastora *f*.

sherbet *n* sorbete *m*.

sheriff *n* sheriff *m/f*.

sherry *n* jerez *m*.

shield *n* escudo *m*; patrocinio *m*; * *vt* defender.

shift *vi* cambiarse; moverse; * *vt* mudar, cambiar; transpor tar; * *n* cambio *m*; turno *m*.

shinbone *n* espinilla *f*.

shine *vi* lucir, brillar, resplandecer; * *vt* lustrar; * *n* brillo *m*.

shingle¹ *n* guijarros *mpl*.

shingle² *n* letrero con nombre del dueño *m*.

shingles *npl* (*med*) herpes *m invar*.

shining *adj* resplandeciente; * *vt* esplendor *m*.

shiny *adj* brillante, luciente.

ship *n* nave *f*; barco *m*; navío, buque *m*; * *vt* embarcar; transportar.

shipbuilding *n* construcción naval *f*.

shipmate *n* (*mar*) ayudante *m/f*.

shipment *n* cargamento *m*.

shipowner *n* naviero/ra *m/f*.

shipwreck *n* naufragio *m*.

shirt *n* camisa *f*.

shit *excl* (*col*) ¡mierda!

shiver *vi* tiritar de frío.

shoal *n* banco *m*.

shock *n* choque *m*; descarga *f*; susto *m*; * *vt* asustar; ofender.

shock absorber *n* amortiguador *m*.

shoddy *adj* de pacotilla.

shoe *n* zapato *m*; herradura *f*; * *vt* calzar; herrar.

shoe factory *n* zapatería *f*.

shoehorn *n* calzador *m*.

shoelace *n* cordón de zapato *m*.

shoemaker *n* zapatero/ra *m/f*.

shoemaking *n* zapatería *f*.

shoe shop/store *n* zapatería *f*.

shoestring *n* lazo de zapato *m*.

shoot *vt* tirar, arrojar, lanzar, disparar, *Lat Am* balacear, *Lat Am* balear; * *vi* brotar, germinar; sobresalir; lanzarse; * *n* vástago *m*.

shooter *n* tirador *m*.

shooting *n* caza con escopeta *f*; tiroteo *m*.

shop front, shop window *n* escaparate *m*, *Lat Am* vidriera *f*, *Lat Am* vitrina *f*.

shopkeeper *n* tendero/ra *m/f*.

shoplifter *n* ladrón/ona de tiendas *m/f*.

shopper *n* comprador/a *m/f*.

shopping *n* compras *fpl*.

shopping center *n* centro comercial *m*.

shopping mall *n* paseo *m*.

shore *n* costa, ribera, playa *f*.

short *adj* corto/ta, breve, sucinto/ta, conciso/sa;

~ly *adv* brevemente; pronto; en pocas palabras.

shortcoming *n* insuficiencia *f*; déficit *m*.

shorten *vt* acortar; abreviar.

shortness *n* cortedad *f*; brevedad *f*.

short-sighted *adj* miope, corto de vista.

short-sightedness *n* miopía *f*.

short wave *n* onda corta *f*.

shot *n* tiro *m*; alcance *m*; perdigones *mpl*; tentativa *f*; toma *f*.

shotgun *n* escopeta *f*.

shoulder *n* hombro *m*; brazuelo *m*; * *vt* cargar al hombro.

shout *vi* gritar, aclamar; * *vt* gritar; * *n* aclamación *f*, grito *m*.

shouting *n* gritos *mpl*.

shove *vt, vi* empujar; impeler; * *n* empujon *m*.

shovel *n* pala *f*; * *vt* traspalar.

show *vt* mostrar; descubrir, manifestar; probar; enseñar, explicar; * *vi* parecer; * *n* espectaculo *m*; muestra *f*; exposición, parada *f*.

show business *n* el mundo del espectaculo *m*.

shower *n* nubada *f*; llovizna *f*; ducha *f*, *Lat Am* baño *m*; (*fig*) abundancia *f*; * *vi* llover.

showery *adj* lluvioso/sa.

showjumping *n* hípica *f*.

showroom *n* sala de muestras *f*.

showy *adj* ostentoso/sa, suntuoso/sa.

shred *n* cacho, pedazo pequeño *m*; * *vt* hacer trizas.

shrew *n* mujer de mal genio *f*; musaraña *f*.

shrewd *adj* astuto/ta; maligno/gna; **~ly** *adv* astutamente.

shrewdness *n* astucia *f*.

shriek *vt, vi* chillar; * *n* chillido *m*.

shrill *adj* agudo/da, penetrante.

shrillness *n* aspereza (del sonido/de la voz) *f*.

shrimp *n* camarón *m*; enano/na *m/f*, hombrecillo *m*.

shrine *n* relicario *m*.

shrink *vi* encogerse; angostarse, acortarse.

shrivel *vi* arrugarse, encogerse; * *vt* encoger.

shroud *n* cubierta *f*; mortaja *f*; * *vt* cubrir, defender; amortajar; proteger.

Shrove Tuesday *n* martes de carnaval *m*.

shrub *n* arbusto *m*.

shrubbery *n* plantío de arbustos *m*.

shrug *vt* encogerse de hombros; * *n* encogimiento de hombros *m*.

shudder *vi* estremecerse; * *n* temblor *m*.

shuffle *vt* desordenar; barajar.

shun *vt* huir, evitar.

shunt *vt* (*rail*) maniobrár.

shut *vt* cerrar, encerrar; *vi* cerrarse.

shutter *n* contraventana *f*.

shuttle *n* lanzadera *f*.

shuttlecock *n* volante, rehilete *m*.

shy *adj* tímido/da; reservado/da; vergonzoso/sa, contenido/da; **~ly** *adv* tímidamente.

shyness *n* timidez *f*.

sibling *n* hermano/na *m/f*.

sibyl *n* sibila, profetisa *f*.
sick *adj* malo/la, enfermo/ma; dis-gustado/da.
sicken *vt* enfermar; * *vi* caer enfer-mo/ma.
sickle *n* hoz *f*.
sick leave *n* baja por enfermedad *f*.
sickliness *n* indisposición habitual *f*.
sickly *adj* enfermizo/za.
sickness *n* enfermedad *f*.
sick pay *n* subsidio por enfermedad *m*.
side *n* lado *m*; costado *m*; facción *f*; partido *m*; * *adj* lateral; oblicuo/cua; * *vi* unirse.
sideboard *n* aparador *m*; alacena *f*.
sidelight *n* luz lateral *f*.
sidelong *adj* lateral.
sidewalk *n* acera *f*.
sideways *adv* de lado, al través.
siding *n* toma de partido *f*; (*rail*) aguja *f*.
sidle *vi* ir de lado.
siege *n* (*mil*) sitio *m*.
sieve *n* tamiz *m*; criba *f*; colador *m*; * *vt* cribar.
sift *vt* cerner; cribar; examinar; investigar.
sigh *vi* suspirar, gemir; * *n* suspiro *m*.
sight *n* vista *f*; mira *f*; espectáculo *m*.
sightless *adj* ciego/ga.
sightly *adj* vistoso/sa, hermoso/sa.
sightseeing *n* excursionismo, turismo *m*.
sign *n* señal *f*, indicio *m*; letrero *m*; signo *m*; firma *f*; seña *f*; * *vt* firmar.
signal *n* señal *f*, aviso *m*; * *adj* insigne, señalado/da.
signalize *vt* señalar.
signal lamp *n* (*rail*) reflector de señales *m*.
signalman *n* (*rail*) guardavía *m*.
signature *n* firma *f*.
signet *n* sello *m*.
significance *n* importancia *f*.
significant *adj* significante.
signify *vt* significar.
signpost *n* indicador *m*.
silence *n* silencio *m*; * *vt* imponer silencio.
silent *adj* silencioso/sa; **~ly** *adv* silenciosamente.
silex *n* sílex *m*.
silicon chip *n* chip de silicio *m*.
silk *n* seda *f*.
silken *adj* hecho/cha de seda; sedeño/ña.
silkiness *n* blandura, molicie *f*.
silkworm *n* gusano de seda *m*.
silky *adj* hecho/cha de seda; sedo-so/sa.
sill *n* repisa *f*; umbral de puerta *m*.
silliness *n* simpleza, bobería, tontería, necedad *f*.
silly *adj* tonto/ta, imbécil; ñoño/ña.
silver *n* plata *f*; * *adj* de plata.
silversmith *n* platero/ra *m/f*.
silvery *adj* plateado/da.
similar *adj* similar; semejante; **~ly** *adv* del mismo modo.
similarity *n* semejanza *f*.
simile *n* símil *m*.
simmer *vi* hervir a fuego lento.
simony *n* simonía *f*.

simper *vi* sonreír; * *n* sonrisa *f*.
simple *adj* simple, puro/ra, sencillo/lla.
simpleton *n* simplón/ona, simplo-nazo/za *m/f*.
simplicity *n* sencillez *f*; simpleza *f*.
simplification *n* simplificación *f*.
simplify *vt* simplificar.
simply *adv* sencillamente; solo.
simulate *vt* simular, fingir.
simulation *n* simulación *f*.
simultaneous *adj* simultáneo/nea.
sin *n* pecado *m*; * *vi* pecar, faltar.
since *adv* desde, entonces, después; * *prep* desde; * *conj* desde que; ya que.
sincere *adj* sencillo/lla; sincero/ra; **~ly** *adv* sinceramente; **yours ~ly** le saluda atentamente.
sincerity *n* sinceridad *f*.
sinecure *n* sinecura *f*.
sinew *n* tendón *m*; nervio *m*.
sinewy *adj* nervioso/sa, robusto/ta.
sinful *adj* pecaminoso/sa, malvado/da; **~ly** *adv* malvadamente.
sinfulness *n* corrupción *f*.
sing *vi*, *vt* cantar; gorjear; (*poet*) celebrar.
singe *vt* chamuscar.
singer *n* cantante *m/f*.
singing *n* canto *m*.
single *adj* sencillo/lla, simple, solo/la; soltero/ra; * *n* billete sencillo *m*; sencillo *m*; * *vt* singularizar; separar.
singly *adv* separadamente.
singular *adj* singular, peculiar; * *n* singular *m*; **~ly** *adv* singularmente.
singularity *n* singularidad *f*.
sinister *adj* siniestro/tra, izquierdo/da; infeliz, funesto/ta.
sink *vi* hundirse; sumergirse; bajarse; arruinarse, decaer; * *vt* hundir, echar a lo hondo; destruir; * *n* fregadero *m*.
sinking fund *n* fondo de amortización *m*.
sinner *n* pecador/a *m/f*.
sinuosity *n* sinuosidad *f*.
sinuous *adj* sinuoso/sa.
sinus *n* seno *m*.
sip *vt* sorber; * *n* sorbo *m*.
siphon *n* sifón *m*.
sir *n* señor *m*.
sire *n* caballo padre *m*.
siren *n* sirena *f*.
sirloin *n* solomillo *m*.
sister *n* hermana *f*.
sisterhood *n* hermandad *f*.
sister-in-law *n* cuñada *f*.
sisterly *adj* de hermana.
sit *vi* sentarse; estar situado/da; * *vt* presentarse a.
sitcom *n* telecomedia *f*.
site *n* sitio *m*; situación *f*.
sit-in *n* ocupación *f*.
sitting *n* sesión, junta *f*; sentada *f*.
sitting room *n* sala de estar *f*.

situated *adj* situado/da.

situation *n* situación *f*.

six *adj*, *n* seis.

sixteen *adj*, *n* dieciséis.

sixteenth *adj*, *n* decimosexto/ta.

sixth *adj*, *n* sexto/ta.

sixtieth *adj*, *n* sexagésimo/ma.

sixty *adj*, *n* sesenta.

size *n* tamaño, talle *m*; calibre *m*; dimensión *f*; estatura *f*; condición *f*.

sizeable *adj* considerable.

skate *n* patín *m*; * *vi* patinar.

skateboard *n* monopatín *m*.

skating *n* patinaje *m*.

skating rink *n* pista de patinaje *f*.

skein *n* madeja *f*.

skeleton *n* esqueleto *m*.

skeleton key *n* llave maestra *f*.

skeptic *n* escéptico/ca *m/f*.

skeptic(al) *adj* escéptico/ca.

skepticism *n* escepticismo *m*.

sketch *n* esbozo *m*; esquicio *m*; * *vt* esquiciar, bosquejar.

skewer *n* aguja de lardear *f*; espetón *m*; * *vt* espetar.

ski *n* esquí *m*; * *vi* esquiar.

ski boot *n* bota de esquí *f*.

skid *n* patinazo *m*; * *vi* patinar.

skier *n* esquiador/a *m/f*.

skiing *n* esquí *m*.

skill *n* destreza, arte, pericia *f*.

skilled *adj* práctico/ca, instruido/da.

skillful *adj* práctico/ca, diestro/tra; ~**ly** *adv* diestramente.

skillfulness *n* destreza *f*.

skim *vt* espumar; tratar superficialmente.

skimmed milk *n* leche desnatada *f*.

skimmer, skimming ladle *n* espumadera *f*.

skin *n* piel *f*; cutis *m*; * *vt* desollar.

skin diving *n* buceo *m*.

skinned *adj* desollado/da.

skinny *adj* flaco/ca, macilento/ta.

skip *vi* saltar, brincar; * *vt* pasar, omitir; * *n* salto, brinco *m*; cuba *f*.

ski pants *npl* pantalones de esquí *mpl*.

skipper *n* capitán/ana *m/f*.

skirmish *n* escaramuza *f*; * *vi* escaramuzar.

skirt *n* falda, orla *f*; * *vt* orillar.

skit *n* burla, zumba *f*.

skittish *adj* espantadizo/za, retozón/ona; terco/ca; inconstante; ~**ly** *adv* caprichosamente.

skulk *vi* escuchar, acechar.

skull *n* cráneo *m*.

skullcap *n* casquete *m*.

sky *n* cielo, firmamento *m*.

skylight *n* claraboya *f*.

skyrocket *n* cohete *m*.

skyscraper *n* rascacielos *m invar*.

slab *n* losa *f*.

slack *adj* flojo/ja, perezoso/sa, negligente, lento/ta.

slack(en) *vt*, *vi* aflojar; ablandar; entibiarse; decaer; relajar; aliviar.

slacker *n* zángano *m*.

slackness *n* flojedad, remisión *f*; descuido *m*.

slag *n* escoria *f*.

slam *vt* cerrar de golpe; * *vi* cerrarse de golpe.

slander *vt* calumniar, infamar; * *n* calumnia *f*.

slanderer *n* calumniador/a, maldiciente *m/f*.

slanderous *adj* calumnioso/sa; ~**ly** *adv* calumniosamente.

slang *n* argot *m*; jerigonza *f*.

slant *vi* pender oblicuamente; * *n* sesgo *m*; interpretación *f*.

slanting *adj* sesgado/da, oblicuo/cua.

slap *n* manotazo *m*; bofetada *f*; * *adv* directamente; * *vt* golpear, dar una bofetada.

slash *vt* acuchillar; * *n* cuchillada *f*.

slate *n* pizarra *f*.

slater *n* pizarrero/ra *m/f*.

slating *n* techo de pizarras *m*.

slaughter *n* carnicería, matanza *f*; * *vt* matar atrozmente; hacer una matanza de.

slaughterer *n* matador/a, asesino/na *m/f*.

slaughterhouse *n* matadero *m*, *Lat Am* cuadro *m*.

slave *n* esclavo/va *m/f*; * *vi* trabajar como esclavo/va.

slaver *n* baba *f*; * *vi* babosear.

slavery *n* esclavitud *f*.

slavish *adj* servil, humilde; ~**ly** *adv* servilmente.

slavishness *n* bajeza, servidumbre *f*.

slay *vt* matar, quitar la vida.

slayer *n* matador/a *m/f*.

sleazy *adj* de mala fama.

sled, sleigh *n* trineo *m*.

sledgehammer *n* mazo *m*.

sleek *adj* liso/sa, brunido/da.

sleep *vi* dormir; * *n* sueño *m*.

sleeper *n* durmiente *m*.

sleepily *adv* con somnolencia/torpeza.

sleepiness *n* sueño *m*.

sleeping bag *n* saco *m* de dormir, *Lat Am* bolsa *f* de dormir.

sleeping pill *n* somnífero *m*.

sleepless *adj* desvelado/da.

sleepwalking *n* sonambulismo *m*.

sleepy *adj* soñoliento/ta.

sleet *n* aguanieve *f*.

sleeve *n* manga *f*.

sleight *n*: ~ **of hand** escamoteo *m*.

slender *adj* delgado/da, débil, pequeño/ña, escaso/sa; ~**ly** *adv* delgadamente.

slenderness *n* delgadez *f*; tenuidad *f*; pequeñez *f*.

slice *n* rebanada *f*; espátula *f*; * *vt* rebanar.

slide *vi* resbalar, deslizarse; correr por encima del hielo; * *n* resbalón *m*; corredera *f*; diapositiva *f*; tobogán *m*.

sliding *adj* corredizo/za.

slight *adj* ligero/ra, leve, pequeño/ña; * *n* descuido *m*; * *vt* despreciar.

slightly adv ligeramente.
slightness n debilidad f; negligencia f.
slim adj delgado/da; * vi adelgazar.
slime n lodo m, Lat Am lama f; substancia viscosa f.
sliminess n viscosidad f.
slimming n adelgazamiento m.
slimy adj viscoso/sa, pegajoso/sa.
sling n honda f; cabestrillo m; * vt tirar.
slink vi escaparse; esconderse.
slip vi resbalar; escapar, huirse; * vt deslizar; * n resbalón m, Lat Am resbalada f; tropiezo m; escapada f; papelito m.
slipper n zapatilla f.
slippery adj resbaladizo/za.
slipshod adj descuidado/da.
slipway n grada f, gradas fpl.
slit vt rajar, hender; * n raja, hendedura f.
slobber n baba f.
sloe n endrina f.
slogan n eslogan, lema m.
sloop n (mar) balandro m.
slop n aguachirle f; lodazal m; ~s pl gachas fpl.
slope n cuesta f; sesgo f; declivio m; escarpa f; * vt sesgar.
sloping adj oblicuo/cua; en declive.
sloppy adj descuidado/da; desaliña-do/da.
sloth n pereza f.
slouch vt, vi estar cabizbajo/ja; bambolearse pesadamente.
slovenliness n desaliño m; porquería f.
slovenly adj desaliñado/da, puerco/ca, sucio/cia.
slow adj tardío/día, lento/ta, torpe, perezoso/sa; ~ly adv lentamente, despacio.
slowness n lentitud, tardanza, pesadez f.
slowworm n lución f.
slug n holgazán/ana m/f, zángano m; babosa f; ficha f; trago m.
sluggish adj perezoso/sa; lento/ta; ~ly adv perezosamente.
sluggishness n pereza f.
sluice n compuerta f; * vt soltar la compuerta de.
slum n tugurio m; barrio bajo m.
slumber vi dormitar; * n sueño ligero m.
slump n depresión f.
slur vt ensuciar; calumniar; pronunciar mal; * n calumnia f.
slush n lodo, barro, cieno m.
slut n marrana f.
sly adj astuto/ta; ~ly adv astutamente.
slyness n astucia, maña f.
smack n sabor, gusto m; beso fuerte (que se oye) m; chasquido de latigo m; * vi saber; besar con ruido; * vt golpear.
small adj pequeño/ña, menudo/da.
smallish adj algo pequeño/ña.
smallness n pequeñez f.
smallpox n viruelas fpl.
small talk n charla, prosa f.
smart adj elegante; listo/ta, inge-nioso/sa; vivo/va; * vi escocer.

smartly adv agudamente, vivamente; elegantemente; inteli gentemente.
smartness n agudeza, viveza, sutileza f.
smash vt romper, quebrantar; estrellar; batir; * vi hacerse pedazos; estrellarse; * n fracaso m; choque m.
smattering n conocimiento superficial m.
smear n mancha f; (med) frotis m invar; ~ **test** Lat Am Papanicolau m; * vt untar; difamar.
smell vt, vi oler; * n olfato m; olor m; hediondez f.
smelly adj maloliente.
smelt n espirenque de mar m; * vt fundir (el metal).
smelter n fundidor/a m/f.
smile vi sonreír; * n sonrisa f.
smirk vi sonreír.
smite vt herir; afligir.
smith n herrero/ra m/f.
smithy n herrería f.
smock n camisa de mujer f.
smoke n humo m; vapor m; * vt, vi ahumar; humear; fumar.
smoked herring, kipper n arenque ahumado m.
smokeless adj sin humo.
smoker n fumador/a m/f.
smoking: no ~ prohibido fumar.
smoky adj humeante; humoso/sa.
smooth adj liso/sa, pulido/da, llano/na; suave; afable; * vt allanar; alisar; lisonjear.
smoothly adv llanamente; con blandura.
smoothness n lisura f; llanura f; suavidad f.
smother vt sofocar; suprimir.
smoulder vi arder debajo la ceniza.
smudge vt manchar; * n mancha f.
smug adj presumido/da.
smuggle vt pasar de contrabando.
smuggler n contrabandista m/f.
smuggling n contrabando m.
smut n tiznón m; suciedad f.
smuttiness n obscenidad f.
smutty adj tiznado/da; obsceno/na.
snack n bocado, bocadillo m, pinchito m.
snack bar n cafetería f.
snag n problema m.
snail n caracol m.
snake n serpiente, culebra f.
snaky adj serpentino/na.
snap vt, vi romper; agarrar; morder; insultar; **to ~ one's fingers** castañetear; * n estallido m; foto f.
snapdragon n (bot) boca de dragón f.
snare n lazo m; trampa f.
snarl vi regañar, gruñir.
snatch vt arrebatar; agarrar; * n arrebatamiento m; robo m; bocado m.
sneak vi arrastrar; * n soplón/ona m/f.
sneakers npl zapatillas de lona fpl.
sneer vi hablar con desprecio.
sneeringly adv con desprecio.
sneeze vi estornudar.

sniff *vt* oler; * *vi* resollar con fuerza.

snigger *vi* reír disimuladamente.

snip *vt* tijeretear; * *n* tijeretada *f*, pedazo pequeño *m*; porción *f*.

snipe *n* agachadiza *f*; zopenco *m*.

sniper *n* francotirador/a *m/f*.

snivel *n* moquita *f*; * *vi* moquear.

sniveler *n* lloraduelos *m invar*.

snob *n* (e)snob *m/f*.

snobbish *adj* esnob.

snooze *n* sueño ligero *m*; * *vi* echar una siesta.

snore *vi* roncar.

snorkel *n* (tubo)respirador *m*.

snort *vi* resoplar.

snout *n* hocico *m*; morro *m*.

snow *n* nieve *f*; * *vi* nevar.

snowball *n* bola de nieve *f*.

snowdrop *n* (*bot*) campanilla blanca *f*.

snowman *n* muñeco de nieve *m*.

snowplow *n* quitanieves *m invar*.

snowy *adj* nevoso/sa; nevado/da.

snub *vt* reprender, regañar.

snub-nosed *adj* chato/ta; ñato/ta.

snuff *n* rapé *m*.

snuffbox *n* tabaquera *f*.

snuffle *vi* ganguear, hablar gangoso.

snug *adj* abrigado/da; conveniente, cómodo/da, agradable, grato/ta.

so *adv* así; de este modo; tan.

soak *vi*,*vt* remojarse; calarse; empapar, remojar.

so-and-so *n* zutano/na *m/f*.

soap *n* jabón *m*; * *vt* jabonar.

soap bubble *n* burbuja de jabón *f*.

soap opera *n* telenovela *f*.

soap powder *n* jabón en polvo *m*.

soapsuds *n* jabonaduras *fpl*.

soapy *adj* jabonoso/sa.

soar *vi* remontarse, sublimarse.

sob *n* sollozo *m*; * *vi* sollozar.

sober *adj* sobrio/ria; serio/ria; ~ly *adv* sobriamente; juiciosamente.

sobriety *n* sobriedad *f*; seriedad, sangre fria *f*.

soccer *n* fútbol *m*.

sociability *n* sociabilidad *f*.

sociable *adj* sociable, comunicativo/va.

sociably *adv* sociablemente.

social *adj* social, sociable; ~ly *adv* sociablemente.

socialism *n* socialismo *m*.

socialist *n* socialista *m/f*.

social work *n* asistencia social *f*.

social worker *n* asistente/ta social *m/f*.

society *n* sociedad *f*; compañía *f*.

sociologist *n* sociólogo/ga *m/f*.

sociology *n* sociología *f*.

sock *n* calcetín *m*; media *f*.

socket *n* enchufe *m*, *Lat Am* tomacorriente *f*.

sod *n* césped *m*.

soda *n* sosa *f*; gaseosa *f*.

sofa *n* sofá *m*.

soft *adj* blando/da, suave; benigno/na, tierno/na; afeminado/da; mulli-do/da; ~ly *adv* suavemente; paso a paso.

soften *vt* ablandar, mitigar; enternecer.

soft-hearted *adj* compasivo/va.

softness *n* blandura, dulzura *f*.

soft-spoken *adj* de voz suave.

software *n* (*comput*) software *m*.

soil *vt* ensuciar, emporcar; * *n* mancha, porquería *f*; terreno *m*; tierra *f*.

sojourn *vi* residir, morar; * *n* morada *f*; residencia *f*.

solace *vt* solazar, consolar; * *n* consuelo *m*.

solar *adj* solar; ~ energy energía solar *f*.

solder *vt* soldar; * *n* soldadura *f*.

soldier *n* soldado/da *m/f*; militar *m*.

soldierly *adj* soldadesco/ca.

sole *n* planta (del pie) *f*; suela (del zapato) *f*; lenguado *m*; * *adj* único/ca, solo/la.

solecism *n* (*gr*) solecismo *m*.

solemn *adj*, ~ly *adv* solemne(mente).

solemnity *n* solemnidad *f*.

solemnize *vt* solemnizar.

solicit *vt* solicitar; implorar.

solicitation *n* solicitación *f*.

solicitor *n* representante, agente *m/f*.

solicitous *adj* solícito/ta, diligente; ~ly *adv* solícitamente.

solicitude *n* solicitud *f*.

solid *adj* sólido/da, compacto/ta; * *n* sólido *m*; ~ly *adv* sólidamente.

solidify *vt* solidificar.

solidity *n* solidez *f*.

soliloquy *n* soliloquio *m*.

solitaire *n* solitario *m*.

solitary *adj* solitario/ria, retirado/da; * *n* ermitaño/ña *m/f*.

solitude *n* soledad *f*; vida solitaria *f*.

solo *n* (*mus*) solo/la *m*.

solstice *n* solsticio *m*.

soluble *adj* soluble.

solution *n* solución *f*.

solve *vt* resolver.

solvency *n* solvencia *f*.

solvent *adj* solvente; *n* (*chem*) solvente *m*.

some *adj* algo de, un poco, algún, alguno, alguna, unos, pocos, ciertos.

somebody *n* alguien *m*.

somehow *adv* de algún modo.

someplace *adv* en alguna parte; a alguna parte.

something *n* alguna cosa, algo.

sometime *adv* algún día.

sometimes *adv* a veces.

somewhat *adv* algo; algún tanto, un poco.

somewhere *adv* en alguna parte; a alguna parte.

somnambulism *n* sonambulismo *m*.

somnambulist *n* sonámbulo/la *m/f*.

somnolence *n* somnolencia *f*.

somnolent *adj* somnoliento/ta.

son *n* hijo *m*.

sonata *n* (*mus*) sonata *f*.

song *n* canción *f*.

son-in-law *n* yerno *m*.

sonnet *n* soneto *m*.

sonorous *adj* sonoro/ra.

soon *adv* ya, pronto; **as ~ as** luego que.

sooner *adv* antes, más pronto.

soot *n* hollín *m*.

soothe *vt* adular; calmar.

soothsayer *n* adivino/na *m/f*.

sop *n* sopa *f*.

sophism *n* sofisma *m*.

sophist *n* sofista *m/f*.

sophistical *adj* sofístico/ca.

sophisticate *vt* sofisticar; falsificar.

sophisticated *adj* sofisticado/da.

sophistry *n* sofistería *f*.

soporific *adj* soporífero/ra.

sorcerer *n* hechicero *m*.

sorceress *n* hechicera *f*.

sorcery *n* hechizo, encanto *m*.

sordid *adj* sórdido/da, sucio/cia; asqueroso/sa.

sordidness *n* sordidez, suciedad *f*.

sore *n* llaga, úlcera *f*; * *adj* doloroso/sa, penoso/sa; resentido/da; **~ly** *adv* penosamente.

sorrel (*bot*) acedera *f*; * *adj* alazán rojo/ja.

sorrow *n* pesar *m*; tristeza *f*; * *vi* entristecerse.

sorrowful *adj* pesaroso/sa, afligido/da; **~ly** *adv* con aflicción.

sorry *adj* triste, afligido/da; arrepen-tido/da; **I am ~** lo siento.

sort *n* suerte *f*; género *m*; especie *f*; calidad *f*; manera *f*; * *vt* separar en distintas clases; escoger, elegir.

soul *n* alma *f*; esencia *f*; persona *f*.

sound *adj* sano/na; entero/ra; puro/ra; firme; **~ly** *adv* sanamente, vigo rosamente; * *n* sonido, ruido *m*; estrecho *m*; * *vt* sonar; tocar; celebrar; sondar; * *vi* sonar, resonar; parecer.

sounding board *n* diapasón *m*; sombrero de púlpito *m*.

sound effects *npl* efectos sonoros *mpl*.

soundings *npl* (*mar*) sondeo *m*; (*mar*) surgidero *m*.

soundness *n* sanidad *f*; fuerza, solidez *f*.

soundtrack *n* banda sonora *f*.

soup *n* sopa *f*.

sour *adj* agrio/ria, ácido/da; cortado/da; áspero/ra; **~ly** *adv* agriamente; * *vt, vi* agriar, acedar; agriarse.

source *n* manantial *m*; principio *m*.

sourness *n* acedía, agrura *f*; acrimonia *f*.

souse *n* (*col*) borracho/cha *m/f*; * *vt* escabechar; chapuzar.

souvenir *n* recuerdo *m*.

south *n* sur *m*; * *adj* del sur; * *adv* al sur.

southerly, southern *adj* del sur, meridional.

southward(s) *adv* hacia el sur.

southwester *n* (*mar*) viento de sudoeste *m*; sombrero grande de los marineros *m*.

sovereign *adj, n* soberano/na *m/f*.

sovereignty *n* soberanía *f*.

sow[1] *n* puerca, marrana *f*.

sow[2] *vt* sembrar; esparcir.

sowing time *n* sementera, siembra *f*.

soybean *n* semilla de soja *f*.

space *n* espacio *m*; intersticio *m*; * *vt* espaciar.

spacecraft *n* nave espacial *f*.

spaceman *n* astronauta *m*.

spacewoman *n* astronauta *f*.

spacious *adj* espacioso/sa, amplio/lia; **~ly** *adv* con bastante espacio.

spaciousness *n* espaciosidad *f*.

spade *n* laya, azada *f*; pica (en los naipes) *f*.

spaghetti *n* espaguetis *mpl*.

span *n* palmo *m*; envergadura *f*; * *vt* cruzar; abarcar.

spangle *n* lentejuela *f*; * *vt* adornar con lentejuelas.

spaniel *n* perro de aguas *m*.

Spanish *adj, n* español/a *m/f*; **~ musical comedy/light opera** zarzuela *f*.

Spanish America *n* Hispanoamérica *f*.

Spanish American *adj* hispanoame-ricano/na; * *n* hispanoamericano/na *m/f*.

spar *n* palo *m*; * *vi* entrenarse.

spare *vt, vi* ahorrar, economizar; perdonar; pasarse sin; vivir con economía; * *adj* de más; de reserva.

sparing *adj* escaso/sa, raro/ra, eco-nómico/ca; **~ly** *adv* parcamente, frugalmente.

spark *n* chispa *f*.

sparkle *n* centella, chispa *f*; * *vi* chispear; espumar.

spark plug *n* bujía *f*.

sparrow *n* gorrión *m*.

sparrowhawk *n* gavilán *m*.

sparse *adj* delgado/da; tenue; **~ly** *adv* tenuemente.

spasm *n* espasmo *m*.

spasmodic *adj* espasmódico/ca.

spatter *vt* salpicar, manchar.

spatula *n* espátula *f*.

spawn *n* freza *f*; * *vt, vi* desovar; engendrar.

spawning *n* freza *f*.

speak *vt, vi* hablar; decir; conversar; pronunciar.

speaker *n* altavoz *m*, *Lat Am* parlante *m*; bafle *m*; orador/a *m/f*.

spear *n* lanza *f*; arpón *m*; * *vt* herir con lanza.

special *adj* especial, particular; **~ly** *adv* especialmente.

specialty *n* especialidad *f*.

species *n* especie *f*.

specific *adj* específico/ca; * *n* específico *m*.

specifically *adv* específicamente.

specification *n* especificación *f*.

specify *vt* especificar.

specimen *n* muestra *f*; prueba *f*.

specious *adj* especioso/sa.

speck(le) *n* mácula, tacha *f*; * *vt* abigarrar, manchar.

spectacle *n* espectáculo *m*.

spectacles *npl* gafas *fpl*.

spectator *n* espectador/a *m/f*.

spectral *adj* espectral; ~ **analysis** *n* análisis espectral *m invar*.

specter *n* espectro *m*.

speculate *vi* especular; reflexionar.

speculation *n* especulación *f*; especulativa *f*; meditación *f*.

speculative *adj* especulativo/va, teó-rico/ca.

speculum *n* espéculo *m*.

speech *n* habla *m*; discurso *m*; lenguaje *m*; conversación *f*.

speechify *vi* arengar.

speechless *adj* sin habla.

speed *n* prisa *f*; velocidad *f*; * *vt* apresurar; despachar; * *vi* darse prisa.

speedboat *n* lancha motora *f*.

speedily *adv* aceleradamente, deprisa.

speediness *n* celeridad, prontitud, precipitación *f*.

speed limit *n* límite de velocidad *m*, velocidad maxima *f*.

speedometer *n* velocímetro *m*.

speedway *n* pista de carreras *f*.

speedy *adj* veloz, pronto/ta, diligente.

spell *n* hechizo, encanto *m*; período *m*; * *vt, vi* escribir correc tamente; deletrear; hechizar, encantar.

spelling *n* ortografía *f*.

spend *vt* gastar; pasar; disipar; consumir.

spendthrift *n* despilfarrador/a *m/f*.

spent *adj* agotado/da.

sperm *n* esperma *f*.

spermaceti *n* espermaceti *m*.

spew *vi* (*col*) vomitar.

sphere *n* esfera *f*.

spherical *adj* esférico/ca; ~**ly** *adv* en forma esférica.

spice *n* especia *f*; * *vt* especiar.

spick-and-span *adj* aseado/da, (bien) arreglado/da.

spicy *adj* aromático/ca.

spider *n* araña *f*.

spigot *n* grifo *m*.

spike *n* espiga de grano *f*; espigón *m*; * *vi* clavar con espi gones.

spill *vt* derramar, verter; * *vi* derramarse.

spin *vt* hilar; alargar, prolongar; girar; * *vi* dar vueltas; * *n* vuelta *f*; paseo (en coche) *m*.

spinach *n* espinaca *f*.

spinal *adj* espinal.

spindle *n* huso *m*; quicio *m*.

spine *n* espinazo *m*, espina *f*.

spineless *adj* ñoño/ña.

spinet *n* (*mus*) espineta *f*.

spinner *n* hilador/a *m/f*; hilandero/ra *m/f*.

spinning top *n* trompa *f*.

spinning wheel *n* rueca *f*.

spin-off *n* derivado, producto secundario *m*.

spinster *n* soltera *f*.

spiral *adj* espiral; ~**ly** *adv* en figura de espiral.

spire *n* espira *f*; pirámide *m*; aguja *f* (de una torre).

spirit *n* aliento *m*; espíritu *m*; ánimo, valor *m*; brío *m*; humor *m*; fantasma *m*; * *vt* incitar, animar; **to ~ away** quitar secretamente.

spirited *adj* vivo/va, brioso/sa; ~**ly** *adv* con espíritu.

spirit lamp *n* velón/quinque de alcohol *m*.

spiritless *adj* abatido/da, sin espíritu.

spiritual *adj*, ~**ly** *adv* espiritual(men-te).

spiritualist *n* espiritista *m/f*.

spirituality *n* espiritualidad *f*.

spit *n* asador *m*; saliva *f*; * *vt, vi* espetar; escupir.

spite *n* rencor *m*, malevolencia *f*; **in ~ of** a pesar de, a despe cho; * *vt* dar pesar.

spiteful *adj* rencoroso/sa, malicioso/sa; ~**ly** *adv* malignamente, con tirria.

spitefulness *n* malicia *f*; rencor *m*.

spittle *n* saliva *f*; baba *f*, esputo *m*.

splash *vt* salpicar, enlodar; * *vi* chapotear; * *n* chapoteo *m*; mancha *f*.

spleen *n* bazo *m*; esplín *m*.

splendid *adj* espléndido/da, magnífi-co/ca; ~**ly** *adv* espléndidamente.

splendor *n* esplendor *m*; pompa *f*.

splice *vt* (*mar*) empalmar, empleitar.

splint *n* tablilla *f*.

splinter *n* cacho *m*; astilla *f*; brisna *f*; * *vt* (*vi*) hender(se).

split *n* hendedura *f*; división *f*; * *vt* hender, rajar; * *vi* hen derse.

splutter, sputter *vi* escupir con frecuencia; babosear; barbotar.

spoil *vt* despojar; arruinar; mimar.

spoiled *adj* pasado/da; cortado/da.

spoke *n* radio (de la rueda) *m*.

spokesman *n* portavoz *m*, *Lat Am* personero *m*, *Lat Am* vocero *m*.

spokeswoman *n* portavoz *f*, *Lat Am* personera *f*, *Lat Am* vocera *f*.

sponge *n* esponja *f*; * *vt* limpiar con esponja; * *vi* meterse de mogollón.

sponger *n* mogollón *m*.

sponginess *n* esponjosidad *f*.

spongy *adj* esponjoso/sa.

sponsor *n* patrocinador/a *m/f*; padrino *m*; madrina *f*.

sponsorship *n* patrocinio *m*.

spontaneity *n* espontaneidad, voluntariedad *f*.

spontaneous *adj* espontáneo/nea; ~**ly** *adv* espontaneamente.

spool *n* carrete *m*; canilla *f*, broca *f*.

spoon *n* cuchara *f*.

spoonful *n* cucharada *f*.

sporadic(al) *adj* esporádico/ca.

sport *n* deporte *m*; juego, retozo *m*; juguete, divertimiento, recreo, pasatiempo *m*.

sports car *n* coche deportivo *m*.

sports coat, sports jacket *n* chaqueta deportiva *f*.

sportsman *n* deportista *m*.

sportswear *n* ropa de deporte/sport *f*.

sportswoman *n* deportista *f*.

spot n mancha f; borrón m; sitio, lugar m; grano m; * vt notar; manchar.

spotless adj limpio/pia, inmaculado/da.

spotlight n foco, reflector m.

spotted, spotty adj lleno/na de manchas; con granos.

spouse n esposo/a m/f.

spout vi borbotar; chorrear; * vt arrojar; vomitar; (fig) declamar; * n piton m, pico m.

sprain adj descoyuntar; * n dislocación f.

sprat n meleta, nuesa (pez) f.

sprawl vi revolcarse.

spray n rociada f; espray m; ramita f; espuma de la mar f.

spread vt extender, desplegar; esparcir, divulgar; * vi extenderse, desplegarse; * n extensión, dilatación f.

spree n fiesta f; juerga f.

sprig n ramito m.

sprightliness n alegría, vivacidad f.

sprightly adj alegre, despierto/ta, vivaracho/cha.

spring vi brotar, arrojar; nacer, provenir; dimanar, origi narse; saltar, brincar; * n primavera f; elasticidad f; muelle, resorte m; salto m; manantial m.

springiness n elasticidad f.

spring onion n cebolleta f.

springtime n primavera f.

spring water n agua de fuente f.

springy adj elástico/ca; mullido/da.

sprinkle vt rociar.

sprinkling n rociadura f.

sprout n vástago, renuevo m; ~s npl coles de Bruselas fpl; * vi brotar.

spruce adj pulido/da, gentil; ~ly adv bellamente, lindamente; * vr vestirse con afectación.

spruceness n lindeza, hermosura f.

spur n espuela f; espolón (del gallo) m; estímulo m; * vt espolear, Lat Am talonear; estimular.

spurious adj espurio/ria, falso/sa; contrahecho/cha; supuesto/ta; bastardo/da.

spurn vt despreciar.

spy n espía m/f; * vt, vi espiar.

squabble vi reñir, disputar; * n riña, disputa f.

squad n escuadra f; brigada f; equipo m.

squadron n (mil) escuadrón m.

squalid adj sucio/cia, puerco/ca.

squall n ráfaga f; chubasco m; * vi chillar.

squally adj borrascoso/sa.

squalor n porquería, suciedad f.

squander vt malgastar, disipar.

square adj cuadrado/da, cuadrángulo/la; exacto/ta; cabal; * n cuadro m; plaza f; escuadra f; * vt cuadrar; ajustar, arreglar; * vi ajustarse.

squareness n cuadratura f.

squash vt aplastar; * n squash m.

squat vi agacharse; * adj agachado/da; rechoncho/cha.

squatter n ocupante ilegal m/f; (col) okupa m/f.

squaw n mujer de un indio f.

squeak vi plañir, chillar; * n grito, plañido m.

squeal vi plañir, gritar.

squeamish adj fastidioso/sa; demasiado delicado/da.

squeeze vt apretar, comprimir; estrechar; * n presión f; apre ton m; restricción f.

squid n calamar m.

squint adj bizco/ca; * vi bizquear; * n estrabismo.

squirrel n ardilla f.

squirt vt jeringar; * n jeringa f; chorro m; pisaverde m.

stab vt apuñalar; * n puñalada f.

stability n estabilidad, solidez f.

stable n establo m; * vt poner en el establo; * adj estable.

stack n pila f; * vt hacinar.

staff n personal m, plantilla f; palo m; apoyo m.

stag n ciervo m.

stage n etapa f; escena f; tablado m; teatro m; parada f; escalón m.

stagger vi vacilar, titubear; estar incierto/ta; * vt asustar; esca lonar.

stagnant adj estancado/da.

stagnate vi estancarse.

stagnation n estancamiento m.

staid adj grave, serio/ria.

stain vt manchar; empañar la reputación de; * n mancha f; deshonra f.

stainless adj limpio/pia; inmaculado/da.

stair n escalón m; ~s pl escalera f.

staircase n escalera f.

stake n estaca f; apuesta (en el juego) f; * vt estacar; apostar.

stale adj añejo/ja, viejo/ja, rancio/cia, Lat Am zocato/ta.

staleness n vejez f; rancidez f.

stalk vi andar con paso majestuoso; * n tallo, pie, tronco m; troncho m (de ciertas hortalizas).

stall n pesebre m; puesto m; tabanco m; emplazamiento m; * vt parar; * vi pararse; buscar evasivas.

stallion n semental m; caballo entero m.

stalwart n partidario/ria leal m/f.

stamen n estambre m; fundamento m.

stamina n resistencia f.

stammer vi tartamudear; * n tartamudeo m.

stamp vt patear; estampar, imprimir; acuñar; andar con mucha pesadez; * vi patear; * n cuño m; sello m; impresión f; huella f; Lat Am estampilla f; zapatazo m.

stampede n estampida f.

stand vi estar de pie; ponerse de pie, Lat Am pararse; sostenerse; permanecer; pararse, hacer alto, estar situado/da; hallarse; erizarse (el pelo); * vt poner; aguantar; sostener, defender; * n puesto, sitio m; posición, situación f; parada f; estado m (fijo); tribuna f; stand m.

standard n estandarte m; modelo m; precio ordinario m; norma f; * adj normal.

standing adj permanente, fijado/da, establecido/da; de pie, Lat Am parado/da; estancado/da; * n posición f; posición f; puesto m.

standstill n pausa f; alto m.

staple n grapa f; * adj básico/ca, establecido/da; * vt grapar, Lat Am engrapar.

star n estrella f; asterisco m.

starboard n estribor m.

starch n almidón m; * vt almidonar.

stare vi: **to ~ at** clavar la vista en; * n mirada fija f.

stark adj fuerte, áspero/ra; puro/ra; * adv del todo.

starling n estornino m.

starry adj estrellado/da.

start vi empezar; sobrecogerse, sobresaltarse; levantarse de repente; salir; * vt empezar; causar; fundar; poner en marcha; * n principio m; salida f; sobresalto m; ímpetu m; paso primero m.

starter n estárter m; juez de salida m.

starting point n punto de partida m.

startle vt sobresaltar.

startling adj alarmante.

starvation n hambre, inanición f.

starve vi pasar hambre.

state n estado m; condición f; estado (político); pompa, gran deza f; **the S~s** los Estados Unidos mpl; * vt afirmar; exponer.

stateliness n grandeza, pompa f.

stately adj augusto/ta, majestuoso/sa.

statement n afirmación, cuenta f.

statesman n estadista, político m.

statesmanship n política f.

static adj estático/ca; * n parásitos mpl.

station n estación f; emisora f; empleo, puesto m; situación f; condición f; (rail) estación f; * vt apostar.

stationary adj estacionario/ria, fijo/ja.

stationer n papelero/a m/f.

stationery n papelería f.

station wagon n ranchera f.

statistical adj estadístico/ca.

statistics npl estadística f.

statuary n estatuario/ria, escultor/a m/f.

statue n estatua f.

stature n estatura, talla f.

statute n estatuto m; reglamento m.

stay n estancia f, Lat Am estadía f; ~**s** npl corsé, justillo m; * vi quedarse, estarse; detenerse; esperarse; **to ~ in** quedarse en casa; **to ~ on** quedarse; **to ~ up** velar.

steadfast adj firme, estable, sólido/da; ~**ly** adv firmemente, con constancia.

steadily adv firmemente; invariablemente.

steadiness n firmeza, estabilidad f.

steady adj firme, fijo/ja; * vt hacer firme.

steak n filete m; bistec m.

steal vt, vi robar.

stealth n hurto m; **by ~** a hurtadillas.

stealthily adv furtivamente.

stealthy adj furtivo/va.

steam n vapor m; humo m; * vt cocer al vapor; * vi echar humo.

steam-engine n máquina de vapor f.

steamer, steamboat n vapor, buque de vapor m.

steel n acero m; * adj de acero.

steelyard n romana f.

steep adj escarpado/da; excesivo/va; * vt empapar.

steeple n torre f; campanario m.

steeplechase n carrera de obstáculos f.

steepness n lo escarpado; lo abrupto.

steer[1] n novillo m.

steer[2] vt manejar, conducir; dirigir; gobernar; * vi conducir.

steering n dirección f.

steering wheel n volante m.

stellar adj estrellado/da.

stem n vástago, tallo m; estirpe f; pie m; cañón m; * vt cortar la corriente.

stench n hedor m.

stencil n cliché m.

stenographer n taquígrafo/fa m/f.

stenography n taquigrafía f.

step n paso, escalón m; huella f; * vi dar un paso; andar.

stepbrother n hermanastro m.

stepdaughter n hijastra f.

stepfather n padrastro m.

stepmother n madrastra f.

stepping stone n pasadera f.

stepsister n hermanastra f.

stepson n hijastro m.

stereo n estéreo m.

stereotype n estereotipo m; * vt estereotipar.

sterile adj estéril.

sterility n esterilidad f.

sterling adj esterlín/ina, genuino/na, verdadero/ra; * n libras esterlinas fpl.

stern adj austero/ra, rígido/da, seve-ro/ra; * n (mar) popa f; ~**ly** adv austeramente.

stethoscope n (med) estetoscopio m.

stevedore n (mar) estibador/a m/f.

stew vt estofar; * n estufa, olla f.

steward n mayordomo m; (mar) despensero m.

stewardess n azafata f, Lat Am aeromoza f.

stewardship n mayordomía f.

stick n palo, palillo, bastón m; vara f; * vt pegar, hincar; aguantar; picar; * vi pegarse; detenerse; perseverar; dudar.

stickiness n viscosidad, gomosidad f.

sticking plaster n esparadrapo m.

stick shift n palanca de cambios f.

stick-up n asalto, atraco m.

sticky adj viscoso/sa, tenaz.

stiff adj tieso/sa; duro/ra, torpe; rígido/da; yerto/ta; obstinado/da; ~**ly** adv obstinadamente.

stiffen vt atiesar, endurecer; * vi endurecerse.

stiff neck n tortícolis m.

stiffness n tesura, rigidez f; obstinación f.

stifle vt sufocar.

stifling adj bochornoso/sa.

stigma n estigma m.

stigmatize vt estigmatizar.

stile n portillo con escalones m (para pasar de un cercado a otro).

stiletto n estilete m; tacón de aguja m.

still vt aquietar, aplacar; destilar; * adj silencioso/sa, tranquilo/la; * n alambique m; * adv todavía; hasta ahora; no obstante; aún así.

stillborn adj nacido/da muerto/ta.

stillness n calma, quietud f.

stilts npl zancos mpl.

stimulant n estimulante m.

stimulate vt estimular, aguijonear.

stimulation n estímulo m; estimulación f.

stimulus n estímulo m.

sting vt picar/morder (un insecto); * vi escocer; * n aguijón m; punzada, picadura, picada f; timo m.

stingily adv avaramente.

stinginess n tacañería, avaricia f.

stingy adj mezquino/na, tacaño/ña, avaro/ra.

stink vi heder; * n hedor m.

stint n tarea f.

stipulate vt estipular.

stipulation n estipulación f; condición f.

stir vt remover; agitar; incitar; * vi moverse; * n tumulto m; turbulencia f.

stirrup n estribo m.

stitch vt coser; * n punzada f; punto m.

stoat n armiño m.

stock n existencias fpl; ganado m; caldo m; estirpe f, linaje m; capital, principal m; fondo m; ~s pl acciones en los fondos públicos fpl; * vt proveer, abastecer.

stockade n prisión militar f.

stockbroker n agente de bolsa m/f.

stock exchange n bolsa f.

stockholder n accionista m/f.

stocking n media f.

stock market n bolsa f.

stoic n estoico/ca m/f.

stoical adj estoico/ca; ~ly adv estoicamente.

stoicism n estoicismo m.

stole n estola f.

stomach n estómago m; apetito m; * vt aguantar.

stone n piedra f; pepita f; hueso de fruta m; * adj de piedra; * vt apedrear; deshuesar; empedrar; trabajar de albañil.

stone deaf adj sordo/da como una tapia.

stoning n apedreamiento m.

stony adj de piedra, pétreo/rea; duro/ra.

stool n banquillo, taburete m.

stoop vi encorvarse, inclinarse; bajarse; * n inclinación hacia abajo f.

stop vt detener, parar; tapar; * vi pararse, hacer alto; * n parada f; punto m; pausa f; obstáculo m.

stopover n parada; rescala f.

stoppage n obstrucción f; impedimento m.

stopwatch n cronómetro m.

storage n almacenamiento m; almacenaje m.

store n abundancia f; provisión f; almacén m, taller m, tienda f; * vt surtir, proveer, abastecer.

store front, store window n escaparate m.

store owner n tendero/ra m/f.

storm n tempestad, borrasca f; asalto m; * vt tomar por asalto; * vi rabiar.

stormily adv violentamente.

stormy adj tempestuoso/sa; violento/ta.

story[1] n historia f; chiste m.

story[2] n piso (de una casa) m.

stout adj robusto/ta, corpulento/ta, vigoroso/sa; terco/ca; ~ly adv valientemente; obstinadamente.

stork n cigüeña f.

stoutness n valor m; fuerza f; corpulencia f.

stove n cocina f; estufa f.

stow vt ordenar, colocar; (mar) estibar.

straggle vi rezagarse.

straggler n rezagado/da m/f.

straight adj derecho/cha; estrecho/cha; franco/ca; * adv directamente.

straightaway adv inmediatamente.

straighten vt enderezar.

straightforward adj derecho/cha; franco/ca; leal.

straightforwardness n derechura f, franqueza f.

strain vt colar, filtrar; apretar (a uno contra sí); forzar, violen tar; * vi esforzarse; * n tensión f; retorcimiento m; raza f; linaje m; estilo m; sonido m; armonía f.

strainer n colador m, Lat Am coladera f.

strait n estrecho m; aprieto, peligro m; penuria f.

straitjacket n camisa de fuerza f.

strand n hebra f; costa, playa f.

strange adj raro/ra; extraño/ña; ~ly adv extrañamente, extraordinariamente.

strangeness n rareza f; extrañeza f.

stranger n desconocido/da m/f; ex-tranjero/ra m/f.

strangle vt estrangular.

strangulation n estrangulamiento m.

strap n correa, tira de cuero f; tirante de bota m; * vt atar con correa.

strapping adj abultado/da, corpulen-to/ta.

stratagem n estratagema f; astucia f.

strategic adj estratégico/ca.

strategy n estrategia f.

stratum n estrato m.

straw n paja m; pajita f.

strawberry n fresa f.

stray vi extraviarse; perder el camino; * adj extraviado/da; perdido/da.

streak n raya, lista f; vena f; * vt rayar.

stream n arroyo m, río m, Lat Am quebrada f, torrente m; * vi correr.

streamer n serpentina f.

street n calle f.

strength n fuerza, robustez f; vigor m; fortaleza f.

strengthen vt fortificar; corroborar.

strenuous adj arduo/dua; ágil.

stress n presión f; estrés m; fuerza f; peso m; importancia f; acento m; * vt subrayar; acentuar.

stretch vt, vi extender, alargar; estirar; extenderse; esfor zarse; * n extensión f; trecho m; estirón m.

stretcher n camilla f.

strew vt esparcir; sembrar.

strict adj estricto/ta, estrecho/cha; exacto/ta, riguroso/sa, severo/ra; ~ly adv exactamente, con severidad.

strictness n exactitud f; severidad f, Lat Am estrictez f, estrechez f.

stride n tranco m; zancada f; * vi atrancar.

strife n contienda, disputa f.

strike vt, vi golpear; herir; castigar; tocar; chocar; sonar; cesar de trabajar; * n ataque m; descubrimiento m; huelga f, Lat Am paro m.

striker n huelguista m/f.

striking adj llamativo/va; notorio/ria; ~ly adv sorprendentemente.

string n cordón m; hilo m; cuerda f; hilera f; fibra f; * vt encordar; enhilar; estirar.

stringent adj astringente.

stringy adj fibroso/sa.

strip vt desnudar, despojar; * vi desnudarse; * n tira f; franja f; faja f; cinta f.

stripe n raya, lista f; azote m; * vt rayar.

strive vi esforzarse; empeñarse; disputar; contender; oponerse.

stroke n golpe m; toque (en la pintura) m; sonido (del reloj) m; plumada f; acaricia f; apoplejía f; * vt acariciar.

stroll n paseo; * vi dar un paseo.

strong adj fuerte, vigoroso/sa, robus-to/ta; poderoso/sa; violento/ta; ~ly adv fuertemente, con violencia.

strongbox n caja fuerte f.

stronghold n plaza fuerte f.

strophe n estrofa f.

structure n estructura f; edificio m.

struggle vi esforzarse; luchar; agitarse; * n lucha f.

strum vt (mus) rasguear.

strut vi pavonearse; * n contoneo m.

stub n talón m; colilla f; tronco m.

stubble n rastrojo m; cerda f.

stubborn adj obstinado/da, testaru-do/da, Lat Am necio/a; ~ly adv obstinadamente.

stubbornness n obstinación, pertinacia f.

stucco n estuco m.

stud[1] n corchete m; taco m.

stud[2] caballeriza f.

student n estudiante m/f; * adj estudiantil.

studio n estudio m.

studio flat n estudio m.

studious adj estudioso/sa; diligente; ~ly adv estudiosamente, diligentemente.

study n estudio m; aplicación f; meditación profunda f; * vt estudiar; observar; * vi estudiar; aplicarse.

stuff n materia f; material m; estofa f; * vt henchir, llenar; disecar.

stuffing n relleno m.

stuffy adj cargado/da; de miras estrechas.

stumble vi tropezar; * n traspié, tropiezo m.

stumbling block n tropiezo m; escollo m.

stump n tronco m; tocón m; muñón m.

stun vt aturdir, ensordecer.

stunner n cosa estupenda f.

stunt n vuelo acrobático m; truco publicitario m; * vt no dejar crecer.

stuntman n especialista m.

stuntwoman n especialista f.

stupefy vt atontar, atolondrar.

stupendous adj estupendo/da, mara-villoso/sa.

stupid adj estúpido/da; **very ~** zo-penco/ca; ~ly adv estúpidamente.

stupidity n estupidez f.

stupor n estupor m.

sturdily adv fuertemente.

sturdiness n fuerza, fortaleza f; obstinación f.

sturdy adj fuerte, tieso/sa, robusto/ta; bronco/ca, insolente.

sturgeon n esturión m.

stutter vi tartamudear.

sty n zahurda f; pocilga f.

stye, sty n orzuelo m.

style n estilo m; moda f; * vt titular; nombrar; estilizar.

stylish adj elegante, en buen estilo.

suave adj afable.

subdivide vt subdividir.

subdivision n subdivisión f.

subdue vt sojuzgar, sujetar; conquistar; mortificar.

subject adj sujeto/ta; sometido/da; * n sujeto m; súbdito/ta m/f; tema m; * vt sujetar; exponer.

subjection n sujeción f.

subjugate vt sojuzgar, subyugar.

subjugation n subyugación f.

subjunctive n subjuntivo m.

sublet vt subarrendar.

sublimate vt sublimar.

sublime adj sublime, excelso/sa; ~ly adv de modo sublime; * n sublime m.

sublimity n sublimidad f.

submachine gun n metralleta f.

submarine adj submarino/na; * n submarino m.

submerge vt sumergir.

submersion n inmersión f; zambullida f.

submission n sumisión f.

submissive adj sumiso/sa, obse-quioso/sa; ~ly adv con sumisión.

submissiveness n obsequio m; sumisión f.

submit vt (vi) someter(se).

subordinate adj subordinado/da, inferior; * vt subordinar.

subordination *n* subordinación *f.*
subpoena *n* citación *f;* * *vt* citar.
subscribe *vt, vi* suscribir, certificar con su firma; consentir.
subscriber *n* suscriptor/a *m/f.*
subscription *n* suscripción *f.*
subsequent *adj,* ~**ly** *adv* subsiguiente(mente).
subservient *adj* subordinado/da; servil.
subside *vi* sumergirse, irse a fondo.
subsidence *n* derrumbamiento *m.*
subsidiary *adj* subsidiario/ria.
subsidize *vt* subvencionar, dar subsidios.
subsidy *n* subvención *f;* subsidio, socorro *m.*
subsist *vi* subsistir; existir.
subsistence *n* existencia *f;* subsistencia *f.*
substance *n* substancia *f;* entidad *f;* esencia *f.*
substantial *adj* substancial; real, material; substancioso/sa; fuerte; ~**ly** *adv* substancialmente.
substantiate *vt* probar.
substantive *n* sustantivo *m.*
substitute *vt* sustituir; * *n* suplente *m/f.*
substitution *n* sustitución *f.*
substratum *n* sustrato *m.*
subterfuge *n* subterfugio *m;* evasión *f.*
subterranean *adj* subterráneo/nea.
subtitle *n* subtítulo *m.*
subtle *adj* sutil, astuto/ta.
subtlety *n* sutileza, astucia *f.*
subtly *adv* sutilmente.
subtract *vt* (*math*) sustraer.
suburb *n* zona residencial *f.*
suburban *adj* suburbano/na.
subversion *n* subversión *f.*
subversive *adj* subversivo/va.
subvert *vt* subvertir, destruir.
succeed *vt, vi* seguir; conseguir, lograr, tener exito.
success *n* éxito *m.*
successful *adj* exitoso/sa; próspero/ra, dichoso/sa; ~**ly** *adv* con éxito; prósperamente.
succession *n* sucesión *f;* descendencia *f;* herencia *f.*
successive *adj* sucesivo/va; ~**ly** *adv* sucesivamente.
successor *n* sucesor/a *m/f.*
succinct *adj* sucinto/ta, compendio-so/sa; ~**ly** *adv* con brevedad.
succulent *adj* suculento/ta, jugoso/sa.
succumb *vi* sucumbir.
such *adj* tal, semejante; ~ **as** tal como.
such and such a one *n* zutano/na y fulano *m/f.*
suck *vt, vi* chupar; mamar.
suckle *vt* amamantar.
suckling *n* mamantón/ona *m/f.*
suction *n* (*med*) succión *f.*
sudden *adj* repentino/na, no previs-to/ta; ~**ly** *adv* de repente, súbitamente.
suddenness *n* precipitación *f.*
sue *vt* demandar.

suede *n* ante *m,* gamuza *f.*
suet *n* sebo *m.*
suffer *vt, vi* sufrir, padecer; tolerar, permitir.
suffering *n* pena *f;* dolor *m.*
suffice *vi* bastar, ser suficiente.
sufficiency *n* suficiencia *f;* capacidad *f.*
sufficient *adj* suficiente; ~**ly** *adv* bastante.
suffocate *vt* asfixiar; sofocar; * *vi* asfixiarse.
suffocation *n* asfixia *f.*
suffrage *n* sufragio, voto *m.*
suffuse *vt* difundir, derramar.
sugar *n* azúcar *m;* * *vt* azucarar.
sugar beet *n* remolacha *f.*
sugar cane *n* caña de azúcar *f.*
sugar loaf *n* pan de azúcar *m.*
sugary *adj* azucarado/da.
suggest *vt* sugerir.
suggestion *n* sugestión *f.*
suicidal *adj* suicida.
suicide *n* suicidio *m;* suicida *m/f.*
suit *n* conjunto *m;* petición *f;* traje *m;* pleito *m;* surtido *m;* * *vt* convenir; sentar a; adaptar.
suitable *adj* conforme, conveniente.
suitably *adv* convenientemente.
suitcase *n* maleta, valija *f.*
suite *n* suite *f;* serie *f;* tren *m,* comitiva *f.*
suitor *n* suplicante *m;* amante, cortejo *m;* pleiteante *m/f;* galanteador *m.*
sulkiness *n* mal humor *m.*
sulky *adj* regañón, terco/ca.
sullen *adj* hosco/ca; intratable; ~**ly** *adv* de mal humor; tercamente.
sullenness *n* hosquedad *f;* obstinación, pertinacia, terquedad *f.*
sulfur *n* azufre *m.*
sulfurous *adj* sulfureo, azufroso/sa.
sultan *n* sultán *m.*
sultana *n* sultana *f;* pasa *f.*
sultry *adj* caluroso/sa; sofocante.
sum *n* suma *f;* total *m;* * **to** ~ **up** *vt* sumar; recopilar; * *vi* hacer un resumen.
summarily *adv* sumariamente.
summary *adj* sumario/ria; * *n* sumario *m.*
summer *n* verano, estío *m.*
summerhouse *n* glorieta de jardín *f.*
summit *n* ápice *m;* cima *f.*
summon *vt* citar, requerir por auto de juez; convocar, convidar; (*mil*) intimar la rendición.
summons *n* citación *f;* requerimiento *m.*
sumptuous *adj* suntuoso/sa; ~**ly** *adv* suntuosamente.
sun *n* sol *m.*
sunbathe *vi* tomar el sol.
sunburnt *adj* quemado/da por el sol.
Sunday *n* domingo *m;* * *adj* dominical; **done/worn on** ~ dominguero/ra.
Sunday driver *n* dominguero/ra *m/f.*
sundial *n* reloj de sol, cuadrante *m.*
sundry *adj* diversos/sas.
sunflower *n* girasol *m.*

sunglasses *npl* gafas de sol *fpl*.

sunless *adj* sin sol; sin luz.

sunlight *n* luz del sol *f*.

sunny *adj* soleado/da; brillante.

sunrise *n* salida del sol *f*; amanecer *m*.

sunroof *n* techo corredizo *m*.

sunset *n* puesta del sol *f*.

sunshade *n* quitasol *m*.

sunshine *n* solana *f*; claridad del sol *f*.

sunstroke *n* insolación *f*.

suntan *n* bronceado *m*.

suntan oil *n* aceite bronceador *m*.

super *adj* (col) bárbaro/ra.

superannuated *adj* añejado/da; pen-sionado/da.

superannuation *n* pensión, jubilación *f*; retiro *m*.

superb *adj* magnífico/ca; **~ly** *adv* magníficamente.

supercargo *n* (*mar*) sobrecargo *m*.

supercilious *adj* arrogante, altanero/ra; **~ly** *adv* con altivez.

superficial *adj*, **~ly** *adv* superfi-cial(mente).

superfluity *n* superfluidad *f*.

superfluous *adj* superfluo/lua.

superhuman *adj* sobrehumano/na.

superintendent *n* superintendente *m/f*.

superior *adj* superior; * *n* superior/a *m/f*.

superiority *n* superioridad *f*.

superlative *adj* superlativo/va; * *n* superlativo *m*; **~ly** *adv* superlativamente, en sumo grado.

supermarket *n* supermercado *m*.

supernatural *adj* sobrenatural.

supernumerary *adj* supernumerario/ria.

superpower *n* superpotencia *f*.

supersede *vt* sobreseer; sustituir; invalidar.

supersonic *adj* supersónico/ca.

superstition *n* superstición *f*.

superstitious *adj* supersticioso/sa; **~ly** *adv* supersticiosamente.

superstructure *n* superestructura *f*.

supertanker *n* superpetrolero *m*.

supervene *vi* sobrevenir.

supervise *vt* supervisar, revistar.

supervision *n* supervisión *f*.

supervisor *n* supervisor/a *m/f*.

supine *adj* supino/na; negligente.

supper *n* cena *f*.

supplant *vt* suplantar.

supple *adj* flexible, manejable; blan-do/da.

supplement *n* suplemento *m*.

supplementary *adj* adicional.

suppleness *n* flexibilidad *f*.

supplicant, suppliant *n* suplicante *m/f*.

supplicate *vt* suplicar.

supplication *n* súplica, suplicación *f*.

supplier *n* proveedor/a *m/f*.

supply *vt* suministrar; suplir, completar; surtir; * *n* provisión *f*; suministro *m*.

support *vt* sostener; soportar, asistir; * *n* apoyo *m*.

supportable *adj* soportable.

supporter *n* partidario/ria *m/f*; afi-cionado/da *m/f*.

suppose *vt*, *vi* suponer.

supposition *n* suposición *f*.

suppress *vt* suprimir.

suppression *n* supresión *f*.

supremacy *n* supremacía *f*.

supreme *adj* supremo/ma; **~ly** *adv* supremamente.

surcharge *vt* sobrecargar; * *n* sobretasa *f*.

sure[1] *adj* seguro/ra, cierto/ta; firme; estable; **to be ~** estar seguro/ra; **~ly** *adv* ciertamente, seguramente, sin duda.

sure![2] *interj* ¡ya!

sureness *n* certeza, seguridad *f*.

surety *n* seguridad *f*; fiador *m/f*.

surf *n* (*mar*) resaca *f*.

surface *n* superficie *f*; * *vt* revestir; * *vi* salir a la superficie.

surfboard *n* plancha de surf *f*.

surfeit *n* exceso *m*.

surge *n* ola, onda *f*; * *vi* avanzar en tropel.

surgeon *n* cirujano/na *m/f*.

surgery *n* cirugía *f*.

surgical *adj* quirúrgico/ca.

surliness *n* mal humor *m*.

surly *adj* hosco/ca.

surmise *vt* sospechar; * *n* sospecha *f*.

surmount *vt* sobrepujar; (*fig*) zanjar.

surmountable *adj* superable.

surname *n* apellido, sobrenombre *m*.

surpass *vt* sobresalir, sobrepujar, exceder, aventajar.

surpassing *adj* sobresaliente.

surplice *n* sobrepelliz *f*.

surplus *n* excedente *m*; sobrante *m*; * *adj* sobrante.

surprise *vt* sorprender; * *n* sorpresa *f*.

surprising *adj* sorprendente.

surrender *vt*, *vi* rendir; ceder; rendirse; * *n* rendición *f*.

surreptitious *adj* subrepticio/cia; **~ly** *adv* subrepticiamente.

surrogate *vt* subrogar; * *n* subro-gado/da *m/f*.

surrogate mother *n* madre de alquiler *f*.

surround *vt* circundar, cercar, rodear.

surrounding area *n* inmediaciones *fpl*.

survey *vt* inspeccionar, examinar; apear; * *n* inspección *f*; apeo (de tierras) *m*.

survive *vi* sobrevivir; * *vt* sobrevivir a.

survivor *n* superviviente *m/f*.

susceptibility *n* susceptibilidad *f*.

susceptible *adj* susceptible.

suspect *vt*, *vi* sospechar; * *n* sospe-choso/sa *m/f*.

suspend *vt* suspender.

suspense *n* suspense *m*, *Lat Am* suspenso *m*; detención *f*; incertidumbre *f*.

suspension *n* suspensión *f*.

suspension bridge *n* puente colgante *m*.

suspicion *n* sospecha *f*.

suspicious *adj* suspicaz; **~ly** *adv* sospechosamente.

suspiciousness *n* suspicacia *f*.

sustain *vt* sostener, sustentar, mantener; apoyar; sufrir.

sustenance *n* sostenimiento, sustento *m*.

suture *n* sutura, costura *f*.

swab *n* algodón *m*; frotis *m invar*.

swaddle *vt* fajar.

swaddling-clothes *npl* pañales *mpl*.

swagger *vi* baladronear.

swallow *n* golondrina *f*; * *vt* tragar, engullir.

swamp *n* pantano *m*.

swampy *adj* pantanoso/sa.

swan *n* cisne *m*.

swap *vt* canjear; * *n* intercambio *m*.

swarm *n* enjambre *m*; gentío *m*; hormiguero *m*; * *vi* enjambrar; hormiguear de gente; abundar.

swarthy *adj* atezado/da.

swarthiness *n* tez morena *f*.

swashbuckling *adj* fanfarrón/ona.

swathe *vt* fajar.

sway *vt* mover; * *vi* ladearse, inclinarse; * *n* balanceo *m*; poder, imperio, influjo *m*.

swear *vt, vi* jurar; hacer jurar; juramentar.

sweat *n* sudor *m*; * *vi* sudar; trabajar con fatiga.

sweater, sweatshirt *n* suéter *m*.

sweep *vt, vi* barrer; arrebatar; deshollinar; pasar/tocar liger amente; oscilar; * *n* barredura *f*; vuelta *f*; giro *m*.

sweeping *adj* rápido/da; **~s** *pl* barreduras *fpl*.

sweepstake *n* lotería *f*.

sweet *adj* dulce, grato/ta, gustoso/sa; suave; oloroso/sa; melodioso/sa; hermoso/sa; amable; * *adv* dulcemente, suavemente; * *n* dulce, caramelo *m*.

sweetbread *n* mellejas de ternera *fpl*.

sweeten *vt* endulzar; suavizar; aplacar; perfumar.

sweetener *n* edulcorante *m*.

sweetheart *n* novio/via *m/f*; querida *f*.

sweetmeats *npl* dulces secos *mpl*.

sweetness *n* dulzura, suavidad *f*.

swell *vi* hincharse; ensoberbecerse; embravecerse; * *vt* hinchar, inflar, agravar; * *n* marejada *f*; * *adj* (*col*) estupendo/da, fenomenal.

swelling *n* hinchazón *f*; tumor *m*.

swelter *vi* ahogarse de calor.

swerve *vi* vagar; desviarse.

swift *adj* veloz, ligero/ra, rápido/da; * *n* vencejo *m*.

swiftly *adv* velozmente.

swiftness *n* velocidad, rapidez *f*.

swill *vt* beber en exceso; * *n* bazofia *f*.

swim *vi* nadar; abundar en; * *vt* pasar a nado; * *n* nadada *f*.

swimming *n* natación *f*.

swimming pool *n* piscina *f*.

swimsuit *n* traje de baño *m*.

swindle *vt* estafar.

swindler *n* estafador/a *m/f*.

swine *n* puerco, cochino *m*.

swing *vi* balancear, columpiarse; vibrar; agitarse; * *vt* colum piar; balancear; girar; * *n* vibración *f*; balanceo *m*.

swinging *adj* (*col*) alegre.

swing (ing) door *n* puerta giratoria *f*.

swirl *n* remolino *m*.

switch *n* varilla *f*; interruptor *m*; (*rail*) agúja *f*; * *vt* cambiar de; **to ~ off** apagar; parar; **to ~ on** encender, *Lat Am* prender.

switchboard *n* centralita *f*, *Lat Am* conmutador *m*.

swivel *vt* girar.

swoon *vi* desmayarse; * *n* desmayo, deliquio, pasmo *m*.

swoop *vi* calarse; * *n* calada; redada *f*; **in one ~** de un golpe.

sword *n* espada *f*.

swordfish *n* pez espada *f*.

swordsman *n* guerrero, espadachín *m*.

sycamore *n* sicomoro *m* (árbol).

sycophant *n* sicofante *m*.

syllabic *adj* silábico/ca.

syllable *n* sílaba *f*.

syllabus *n* programa de estudios *m*.

syllogism *n* silogismo *m*.

sylph *n* silfio *m*; sílfide *f*.

symbol *n* símbolo *m*.

symbolic(al) *adj* simbólico/ca.

symbolize *vt* simbolizar.

symmetrical *adj* simétrico/ca; **~ly** *adv* con simetría.

symmetry *n* simetría *f*.

sympathetic *adj* simpático/ca; **~ally** *adv* simpáticamente.

sympathize *vi* compadecerse.

sympathy *n* simpatía *f*.

symphony *n* sinfonía *f*.

symposium *n* simposio *m*.

symptom *n* síntoma *m*.

synagogue *n* sinagoga *f*.

synchronism *n* sincronismo *m*.

syndicate *n* sindicato *m*.

syndrome *n* síndrome *m*.

synod *n* sínodo *m*.

synonym *n* sinónimo *m*.

synonymous *adj* sinónimo/ma; **~ly** *adv* con sinonimia.

synopsis *n* sinopsis *f invar*; sumario *m*.

synoptic *adj* sinóptico/ca.

syntax *n* sintaxis *f*.

synthesis *n* síntesis *f invar*.

syringe *n* jeringa, lavativa *f*; * *vt* jeringar.

system *n* sistema *m*.

systematic *adj* sistemático/ca; **~ally** *adv* sistemáticamente.

systems analyst *n* analista de sistemas *m/f*.

T

tab n lengüeta f; etiqueta f.
tabernacle n tabernáculo m.
table n mesa f; tabla f; * vt someter a discusión; poner sobre la mesa; ~ d'hôte menu m.
tablecloth n mantel m.
tablespoon n cuchara para comer f.
tablet n tableta f; pastilla f; comprimido m.
table tennis n ping-pong, tenis de mesa m.
taboo adj tabú; * n tabú m; * vt interdecir.
tabular adj tabular.
tachometer n cuentarrevoluciones m invar.
tacit adj tácito/ta; ~ly adv tácitamente.
taciturn adj taciturno/na, callado/da.
tack n bordo m; n tachuela f; * vt atar; pegar; * vi virar.
tackle n equipo m, aparejos mpl; placaje m; (mar) cordaje m, jarcia f.
tact n tacto m.
tactician n táctico/ca m/f.
tactics npl táctica f.
tadpole n renacuajo m.
taffeta n tafetán m.
tag n herrete m; * vt herretear.
tail n cola f; rabo m; * vt vigilar a.
tailgate, tailboard n puerta trasera f.
tailor n sastre m.
tailoring n corte m.
tailor-made adj hecho/cha a la medida.
tailwind n viento de cola m.
taint vt tachar, manchar; viciar; * n mancha f.
tainted adj contaminado/da; man-chado/da.
take vt tomar, coger, asir; recibir, aceptar; pillar; prender; admitir; entender; * vi prender el fuego; to ~ apart vt descoser; to ~ away quitar; llevar; to ~ back devolver; retractar; to ~ down derribar; apuntar; to ~ in entender, abarcar; acoger; to ~ off vi despegar, Lat Am decolar; vt quitar; imitar; to ~ on aceptar; contratar; desafiar; to ~ out sacar; quitar; to ~ to encariñarse con; to ~ up acortar; ocupar; dedicarse a; * n toma f.
takeoff n despegue m, Lat Am decolaje m.
takeover n absorción f; ~ bid opa f.
takings npl ingresos mpl.
talc n talco m.
talent n talento m; capacidad f.
talented adj con talento.
talisman n talismán m.
talk vi hablar, conversar; charlar; * n habla f; charla f, Lat Am conversa f; fama f.
talkative adj locuaz.
talk show n programa de entrevistas m.
tall adj alto/ta, elevado/da; robusto/ta.
tally vi corresponder.
talon n garra f.
tambourine n pandereta f.
tame adj amansado/da, domado/da,

domesticado/da; ~ly adv mansamente; bajamente; * vt domar, domesticar.
tameness n domesticidad f; sumisión f.
tamper vi tocar.
tampon n tampón m.
tan vt broncear; * vi broncearse, ponerse moreno/na; * n bronceado m.
tang n sabor fuerte m.
tangent n tangente f.
tangerine n mandarina f.
tangible adj tangible.
tangle vt enredar, embrollar.
tank n cisterna f; aljibe m.
tanker n petrolero m; camión cisterna m.
tanned adj bronceado/da.
tantalizing adj tentador/a.
tantamount adj equivalente.
tantrum n rabieta f.
tap vt tocar ligeramente; utilizar; intervenir; zapatear; * n grifo m; palmada suave f; toque ligero m; espita f.
tape n cinta f; * vt grabar.
tape measure n metro m.
taper n cirio m.
tape recorder n grabadora f.
tapestry n tapiz m; tapicería f.
tar n brea f.
target n blanco m (para tirar).
tariff n tarifa f.
Tarmac™ n alquitranado m.
tarnish vt deslustrar.
tarpaulin n alquitranado m.
tarragon n (bot) estragón m.
tart adj acedo/da, acre; * n tarta, torta f; (col) zorra f.
tartan n tela escocesa f.
tartar n tártaro m.
task n tarea f.
tassel n borlita f.
taste n gusto m; sabor m; saboreo m; ensayo m; * vt, vi gustar; probar; experimentar; agradar; tener sabor.
tasteful adj sabroso/sa; ~ly adv sabrosamente.
tasteless adj insípido/da, sin sabor.
tasty adj sabroso/sa.
tattoo n tatuaje m; * vt tatuar.
taunt vt mofar; ridiculizar; * n mofa, burla f.
Taurus n Tauro m (signo del zodíaco).
taut adj tieso/sa.
tautological adj tautológico/ca.
tautology n tautología f.
tawdry adj jarifo/fa, vistoso/sa, cha-bacano/na.
tax n impuesto m; contribución f; * vt gravar; poner a prueba.
taxable adj sujeto/ta a impuestos.
taxation n imposición de impuestos f.
tax collector n recaudador/a m/f de impuestos.
tax-free adj libre de impuestos.
taxi n taxi m; * vi rodar por la pista.
taxi driver n taxista m/f.
taxi rank n parada de taxis f.

tax payer *n* contribuyente *m/f*.
tax relief *n* desgravación fiscal *f*.
tax return *n* declaración de la renta *f*.
tea *n* té *m*.
teach *vt* enseñar, instruir, *Lat Am* dictar; * *vi* enseñar.
teacher *n* profesor/a *m/f*; maestro/tra *m/f*.
teaching *n* enseñanza *f*.
teacup *n* taza de té *f*.
teak *n* teca *f* (árbol).
team *n* equipo *m*.
teamster *n* camionero/ra *m/f*.
teamwork *n* trabajo de equipo *m*.
teapot *n* tetera *f*.
tear[1] *vt* despedazar, rasgar; **to ~ up** hacer trizas.
tear[2] *n* lágrima *f*; gota *f*.
tearful *adj* lloroso/sa; **~ly** *adv* con lloro.
tear gas *n* gas lacrimógeno *m*.
tease *vt* tomar el pelo.
tea service, tea set *n* servicio para té *m*.
teasing *adj* zumbón/ona; * *n* zumba *f*.
teaspoon *n* cucharita *f*.
teat *n* ubre, teta *f*.
technical *adj* técnico/ca.
technicality *n* detalle técnico *m*.
technician *n* técnico/ca *m*
technique *n* técnica *f*.
technological *adj* tecnológico/ca.
technology *n* tecnología *f*.
teddy (bear) *n* osito de felpa *m*.
tedious *adj* tedioso/sa, fastidioso/sa; **~ly** *adv* fastidiosamente.
tedium *n* tedio, fastidio *m*.
tee *n* tee *m*.
teem *vi* rebosar de.
teenage *adj* juvenil; **~r** *n* adolescente *m/f*.
teens *npl* adolescencia *f*.
tee-shirt, T-shirt *n* camiseta *f*.
teeth *npl* de tooth.
teethe *vi* echar los dientes.
teetotal *adj* abstemio/mía, sobrio/ria.
teetotaler *n* abstemio/mia *m/f*.
telegram *n* telegrama *m*.
telegraph *n* telégrafo *m*.
telegraphic *adj* telegráfico/ca.
telegraphy *n* telegrafía *f*.
telepathy *n* telepatía *f*.
telephone *n* teléfono *m*.
telephone banking *n* telebanca *f*.
telephone booth *n* cabina telefónica *f*.
telephone call *n* llamada telefónica *f*, *Lat Am* telefonema *m*.
telephone directory *n* guía *f* telefónica.
telephone number *n* número de teléfono *m*.
telescope *n* telescopio *m*.
telescopic *adj* telescópico/ca.
televise *vt* televisar.
television *n* televisión *f*.
television news *n* telediario *m*.
television set *n* televisor *m*.
teleworker *n* teletrabajador/ra *m/f*.

teleworking *n* teletrabajo *m*.
telex *n* télex *m*; *vt*, *vi* enviar un télex.
tell *vi* decir; informar, contar.
teller *n* cajero/ra *m/f*.
telling *adj* contundente; revelador/a.
telltale *adj* indicador/a.
temper *vt* templar, moderar; * *n* mal genio *m*.
temperament *n* temperamento *m*.
temperance *n* templanza, moderación *f*.
temperate *adj* templado/da, modera-do/da, sobrio/ria.
temperature *n* temperatura *f*.
tempest *n* tempestad *f*.
tempestuous *adj* tempestuoso/sa.
template *n* plantilla *f*.
temple *n* templo *m*; sien *f*.
temporarily *adv* temporalmente, *Lat Am* temporariamente.
temporary *adj* temporal, *Lat Am* temporario/ria.
tempt *vt* tentar; provocar.
temptation *n* tentación *f*.
tempting *adj* tentador/a.
ten *adj*, *n* diez.
tenable *adj* defendible.
tenacious *adj*, **~ly** *adv* tenaz(mente).
tenacity *n* tenacidad *f*; porfía *f*.
tenancy *n* tenencia *f*.
tenant *n* arrendatario/ria, inquilino/na *m/f*.
tend *vt* guardar, velar; * *vi* tener tendencia a.
tendency *n* tendencia *f*.
tender *adj* tierno/na, delicado/da; sensible; **~ly** *adv* tiernamente; * *n* oferta *f*; * *vt* ofrecer; estimar.
tenderness *n* ternura *f*.
tendon *n* tendón *m*.
tendril *n* zarcillo *m*.
tenement *n* casa de pisos *f*.
tenet *n* dogma *m*; aserción *f*.
tennis *n* tenis *m*.
tennis court *n* cancha de tenis *f*.
tennis player *n* tenista *m/f*.
tennis racket *n* raqueta de tenis *f*.
tennis shoes *npl* zapatillas de tenis *fpl*.
tenor *n* (*mus*) tenor *m*; contenido *m*; substancia *f*.
tense *adj* tieso/sa, tenso/sa; * *n* (*gr*) tiempo *m*.
tension *n* tensión, tirantez *f*.
tent *n* tienda de campaña *f*, *Lat Am* carpa *f*.
tentacle *n* tentáculo *m*.
tentative *adj* de ensayo, de prueba; **~ly** *adv* como prueba.
tenth *adj*, *n* décimo/ma.
tenuous *adj* tenue.
tenure *n* tenencia *f*.
tepid *adj* tibio/bia.
term *n* término *m*; dicción *f*; vocablo *m*; condición, estipulación *f*; * *vt* nombrar, llamar.
terminal *adj* mortal; * *n* terminal *m*; terminal *f*.
terminate *vt* terminar.
termination *n* terminación, conclusión *f*.
terminus *n* terminal *f*.

terrace *n* terraza *f.*
terrain *n* terreno *m.*
terrestrial *adj* terrestre, terreno/na.
terrible *adj* terrible.
terribly *adv* terriblemente.
terrier *n* terrier *m.*
terrific *adj* fantástico/ca; maravillo-so/sa.
terrify *vt* aterrar, espantar.
territorial *adj* territorial.
territory *n* territorio, distrito *m.*
terror *n* terror *m.*
terrorism *n* terrorismo *m.*
terrorist *n* terrorista *m/f.*
terrorist attack *n* atentado *m.*
terrorize *vt* aterrorizar.
terse *adj* tajante.
test *n* examen *m*; prueba *f*; * *vt* probar; examinar.
testament *n* testamento *m.*
tester *n* ensayador/a *m/f.*
testicles *npl* testículos *mpl.*
testify *vt* testificar, atestiguar.
testimonial *n* atestación *f.*
testimony *n* testimonio *m.*
test pilot *n* piloto de pruebas *m/f.*
test tube *n* probeta *f.*
testy *adj* tétrico/ca.
tetanus *n* tétanos *m invar.*
tether *vt* atar.
text *n* texto *m.*
textbook *n* libro de texto *m.*
textiles *npl* textiles *mpl.*
textual *adj* textual.
texture *n* textura *f*; tejido *m.*
than *adv* que, de.
thank *vt* agradecer, dar las gracias a.
thankful *adj* grato/ta, agradecido/da; ~ly *adv* con gratitud.
thankfulness *n* gratitud *f.*
thankless *adj* ingrato/ta.
thanks *npl* gracias *fpl.*
Thanksgiving *n* día de acción de gracias *m.*
that *pn* aquel, aquello, aquella; que; este; * *conj* porque; para que; **so ~** de modo que.
thatch *n* techo de paja *m*; * *vt* techar con paja.
thaw *n* deshielo *m*; * *vi* deshelarse.
the *art* el, la, lo; los, las.
theater *n* teatro *m.*
theatergoer *n* aficionado/da al teatro *m/f.*
theatrical *adj* teatral.
theft *n* robo *m.*
their *pn* su, suyo, suya; de ellos, de ellas; **~s** el suyo, la suya, los suyos, las suyas; de ellos, de ellas.
them *pn* los, las, les; ellos, ellas.
theme *n* tema *m.*
themselves *pn pl* ellos mismos, ellas mismas; sí mismos; se.
then *adv* entonces, después; en tal caso; * *conj* en ese caso; * *adj* entonces; **now and ~** de vez en cuando.
theologian *n* teólogo/ga *m/f.*
theological *adj* teológico/ca.

theology *n* teología *f.*
theorem *n* teorema *m.*
theoretic(al) *adj* teórico/ca; ~ly *adv* teóricamente.
theorist *n* teórico/ca *m/f.*
theorize *vt* teorizar.
theory *n* teoría *f.*
therapeutics *n* terapéutica *f.*
therapist *n* terapeuta *m/f.*
therapy *n* terapia *f.*
there *adv* allí, allá.
thereabout(s) *adv* por ahí, acerca de.
thereafter *adv* después; según.
thereby *adv* así; de ese modo.
therefore *adv* por eso, por lo tanto.
thermal *adj* termal.
thermal printer *n* impresora térmica *f.*
thermometer *n* termómetro *m.*
thermostat *n* termostato *m.*
thesaurus *n* diccionario de sinónimos *m.*
these *pn pl* éstos, éstas; *adj* estos, estas.
thesis *n* tesis *f invar.*
they *pn pl* ellos, ellas.
thick *adj* espeso/sa, denso/sa; grueso/sa; torpe.
thicken *vi* espesar, condensar; condensarse.
thicket *n* espesura *f.*
thickness *n* espesor *m.*
thickset *adj* grueso/sa; rechoncho/cha.
thick-skinned *adj* duro/ra de pellejo.
thief *n* ladrón/ona *m/f.*
thigh *n* muslo *m.*
thimble *n* dedal *m.*
thin *adj* delgado/da, delicado/da, flaco/ca; claro/ra; * *vt* atenuar; adelga zar; aclarar.
thing *n* cosa *f*; objeto *m*; chisme *m.*
think *vi* pensar, imaginar, meditar, considerar; creer, juzgar; **to ~ over** reflexionar; **to ~ up** imaginar.
thinker *n* pensador/a *m/f.*
thinking *n* pensamiento *m*; juicio *m*; opinión *f.*
third *adj* tercero/ra; * *n* tercio *m*; ~ly *adv* en tercer lugar.
third rate *adj* mediocre.
thirst *n* sed *f.*
thirsty *adj* sediento/ta.
thirteen *adj, n* trece.
thirteenth *adj, n* decimotercero/ra.
thirtieth *adj, n* trigésimo/ma.
thirty *adj, n* treinta.
this *adj* este, esta; * *pn* éste, ésta, esto.
thistle *n* cardo *m.*
thorn *n* espino *m*; espina *f.*
thorny *adj* espinoso/sa; arduo/dua.
thorough *adj* entero/ra, perfecto/ta; ~ly *adv* enteramente, profundamente.
thoroughbred *adj* de sangre, de casta.
thoroughfare *n* paso, tránsito *m.*
those *pn pl* ésos, ésas; aquéllos, aquéllas; * *adj* esos, esas; aquellos, aquellas.
though *conj* aunque, no obstante; * *adv* sin embargo.

thought *n* pensamiento, juicio *m*; opinión *f*; cuidado *m*.

thoughtful *adj* pensativo/va.

thoughtless *adj* descuidado/da; in-sensato/ta; **~ly** *adv* descuidadamente, sin reflexión.

thousand *adj, n* mil.

thousandth *adj, n* milésimo/ma.

thrash *vt* golpear; derrotar.

thread *n* hilo *m*; rosca *f*; * *vt* enhebrar.

threadbare *adj* raído/da, muy usado/da.

threat *n* amenaza *f*.

threaten *vt* amenazar.

three *adj, n* tres.

three-dimensional *adj* tridimensional.

three-monthly *adj* trimestral.

three-ply *adj* triple.

threshold *n* umbral *m*.

thrifty *adj* económico/ca.

thrill *vt* emocionar; * *n* emoción *f*.

thriller *n* película/novela de suspense *f*.

thrive *vi* prosperar; crecer.

throat *n* garganta *f*.

throb *vi* palpitar; vibrar; dar punzadas.

throne *n* trono *m*.

throng *n* tropel de gente *m*; * *vt* venir en tropel.

throttle *n* acelerador *m*; * *vt* estrangular.

through *prep* por; durante; mediante; * *adj* directo/ta; * *adv* completamente.

throughout *prep* por todo; * *adv* en todas partes.

throw *vt* echar, arrojar, tirar, lanzar; * *n* tiro *m*; golpe *m*; **to ~ away** tirar; **to ~ off** desechar; **to ~ out** tirar; **to ~ up** vomitar, devolver.

throwaway *adj* desechable.

thrush *n* tordo (ave) *m*.

thrust *vt* empujar, introducir; * *vr* zamparse; * *n* empuje *m*.

thud *n* ruido sordo *m*; zarpazo *m*.

thug *n* gamberro/rra *m/f*.

thumb *n* pulgar *m*.

thumbtack *n* chincheta *f*, *Lat Am* chinche *f*.

thump *n* golpe *m*; * *vt, vi* golpear.

thunder *n* trueno *m*; * *vi* tronar.

thunderbolt *n* rayo *m*.

thunderclap *n* trueno *m*.

thunderstorm *n* tormenta *f*.

thundery *adj* tormentoso/sa.

Thursday *n* jueves *m invar*.

thus *adv* así, de este modo.

thwart *vt* frustrar.

thyme *n* (*bot*) tomillo *m*.

thyroid *n* tiroides *m invar*.

tiara *n* tiara *f*.

tic *n* tic *m*.

tick *n* tictac *m*; palomita *f*; marca *f*; * *vt* marcar; **to ~ over** girar en marcha; ir tirando.

ticket *n* billete, *Lat Am* boleto *m*; etiqueta *f*; tarjeta *f*.

ticket collector *n* (*rail*) revisor/a *m/f*.

ticket office *n* taquilla *f*, *Lat Am* boletería *f*; *Lat Am* despacho *m* de boletos.

tickle *vt* hacer cosquillas.

ticklish *adj* con cosquillas, *Lat Am* cosquilloso/sa.

tidal *adj* de marea.

tidal wave *n* maremoto *m*.

tidbit *n* golosina *f*; pedazo *m*.

tide *n* curso *m*; marea *f*.

tidy *adj* ordenado/da; arreglado/da; aseado/da.

tie *vt* anudar, atar; * *vi* empatar; **to ~ up** envolver; atar; amarrar; concluir; * *n* atadura *f*; lazo *m*; corbata *f*; empate *m*.

tier *n* grada *f*; piso *m*.

tiger *n* tigre *m*.

tight *adj* tirante, tieso/sa, tenso/sa; cerrado/da; apretado/da; * *adv* con fuerza.

tighten *vt* tirar, estirar.

tightfisted *adj* tacaño/ña.

tightly *adv* muy fuerte.

tightrope *n* cuerda floja *f*.

tigress *n* tigresa *f*.

tile *n* teja *f*; baldosa *f*; azulejo *m*; * *vt* tejar.

tiled *adj* embaldosado/da.

till[1] *n* caja registradora *f*.

till[2] *vt* cultivar, labrar.

tiller *n* cana del timón *f*.

tilt *vt* inclinar; * *vi* inclinarse.

timber *n* madera de construcción *f*; árboles *mpl*.

time *n* tiempo; época *f*; hora *f*; momento *m*; (*mus*) compás *m*; **in ~** a tiempo; **from ~ to ~** de vez en cuando; * *vt* medir el tiempo; cronometrar.

time bomb *n* bomba de relojería *f*.

time lag *n* desfase *m*.

timeless *adj* eterno/na.

timely *adj* oportuno/na.

time off *n* tiempo libre *m*.

timer *n* interruptor *m*; programador horario *m*.

time scale *n* escala de tiempo *f*.

time trial *n* contrarreloj *f*.

time zone *n* huso horario *m*.

timid *adj* tímido/da, temeroso/sa; **~ly** *adv* con timidez.

timidity *n* timidez *f*.

timing *n* cronometraje *m*; oportunidad *f*.

tin *n* estaño *m*; hojalata *f*.

tinder *n* yesca *f*.

tinfoil *n* papel de estaño *m*.

tinge *n* matiz *m*.

tingle *vi* zumbar; latir, punzar.

tingling *n* zumbido *m*; latido *m*.

tinker *n* calderero remendón *m*; gitano/na *m/f*.

tinkle *vi* tintinear.

tin plate *n* hojalata *f*.

tinsel *n* oropel *m*.

tint *n* tinte *m*; * *vt* teñir.

tinted *adj* teñido/da; ahumado/da.

tiny *adj* pequeño/ña, chico/ca.

tip[1] *n* punta, extremidad *f*.

tip[2] *propina f*; consejo *m*; * *vt* dar una propina a.

tip[3] *vt* inclinar; vaciar.

tip-off *n* advertencia *f*.

tipsy *adj* alegre.

tiptop *adj* excelente, perfecto/ta.

tirade *n* invectiva *f.*

tire[1] *vt* cansar, fatigar; * *vi* cansarse; fastidiarse.

tire[2] *n* neumático *m*; llanta *f.*

tireless *adj* incansable.

tire pressure *n* presión de los neumáticos *f.*

tiresome *adj* tedioso/sa, molesto/ta.

tiring *adj* cansado/da.

tissue *n* tejido *m*; pañuelo de papel *m.*

tissue paper *n* papel de seda *m.*

titillate *vt* estimular.

title *n* título *m.*

title deed *n* derecho de propiedad *m.*

title page *n* portada *f.*

titter *vi* reírse disimuladamente; * *n* risa disimulada *f.*

titular *adj* titular.

to *prep* a; para; por; de; hasta; en; con; que.

toad *n* sapo *m.*

toadstool *n* (*bot*) seta venenosa *f.*

toast *vt* tostar; brindar; * *n* tostada *f*; brindis *m.*

toaster *n* tostadora *f.*

tobacco *n* tabaco *m.*

tobacconist *n* tabaquero/ra, estan-quero/ra *m/f.*

tobacconist's (shop) *n* estanco *m*, tabaquería *f*, *Lat Am* cigarrería *f.*

tobacco pouch *n* petaca *f.*

toboggan *n* tobogán *m.*

today *adv* hoy.

toddler *n* niño/ña (que empieza a andar) *m/f.*

toddy *n* ponche *m.*

toe *n* dedo del pie *m*; punta *f.*

toffee *n* caramelo *m.*

together *adv* juntamente, juntos; al mismo tiempo.

toil *vi* fatigarse, trabajar mucho; afanarse; * *n* trabajo *m*; fatiga *f*; afán *m.*

toilet *n* servicios *mpl*; sanitario *m*; * *adj* de aseo.

toilet bag *n* bolsa de aseo *f.*

toilet bowl *n* taza del retrete *f.*

toilet paper *n* papel higiénico *m.*

toiletries *npl* artículos de aseo *mpl.*

token *n* senal *f*; muestra *f*; recuerdo *m*; vale *m*; ficha *f.*

tolerable *adj* soportable; pasable.

tolerance *n* tolerancia *f.*

tolerant *adj* tolerante.

tolerate *vt* tolerar.

toll[1] *n* peaje *m*; número de victimas *m.*

toll[2] *vi* doblar.

tomato *n* tomate *m.*

tomb *n* tumba *f*; sepulcro *m*, sepultura *f.*

tomboy *n* muchachota *f.*

tombstone *n* piedra sepulcral *f.*

tomcat *n* gato *m.*

tomorrow *adv* mañana; * *n* mañana *f.*

ton *n* tonelada *f.*

tone *n* tono *m*; acento *m*; * *vi* armonizar; **to ~ down** suavizar.

tone-deaf *adj* sin oído musical.

tongs *npl* tenacillas *fpl.*

tongue *n* lengua *f.*

tongue-tied *adj* mudo/da.

tongue-twister *n* trabalenguas *m invar.*

tonic *n* (*med*) tónico *m.*

tonight *adv, n* esta tarde (*f*).

tonnage *n* tonelaje *m.*

tonsil *n* amígdala *f*; **~s** *npl* agallas *fpl.*

tonsillitis *n* agalla *f.*

tonsure *n* tonsura *f.*

too *adv* demasiado; también.

tool *n* herramienta *f*; utensilio *m.*

tool box *n* caja de herramientas *f.*

toot *vi* tocar la bocina.

tooth *n* diente *m.*

toothache *n* dolor de muelas *m.*

toothbrush *n* cepillo de dientes *m.*

toothless *adj* desdentado/da.

toothpaste *n* pasta de dientes *f.*

toothpick *n* palillo *m.*

top *n* cima, cumbre *f*; último grado *m*; lo alto; superficie *f*; tapa *f*; cabeza *f*; * *adj* de arriba; primero/ra; * *vt* elevarse por encima; sobrepujar, exceder; **to ~ off** llenar.

topaz *n* topacio *m.*

top floor *n* último piso *m.*

top-heavy *adj* inestable.

topic *n* tema *m*; **~al** *adj* actual.

topless *adj* topless.

top-level *adj* al más alto nivel.

topmost *adj* lo más alto.

topographic(al) *adj* topográfico/ca.

topography *n* topografía *f.*

topple *vt* derribar; * *vi* volcarse.

top-secret *adj* de alto secreto.

topsy-turvy *adv* al revés.

torment *vt* atormentar; * *n* tormento *m.*

tornado *n* tornado *m.*

torrent *n* torrente *m.*

torrid *adj* apasionado/da.

tortoise *n* tortuga *f.*

tortoiseshell *adj* de carey.

tortuous *adj* tortuoso/sa, sinuoso/sa.

torture *n* tortura *f*; * *vt* torturar.

toss *vt* tirar, lanzar, arrojar; agitar, sacudir.

total *adj* total, entero/ra; **~ly** *adv* totalmente.

totalitarian *adj* totalitario/ria.

totality *n* totalidad *f.*

totter *vi* vacilar.

touch *vt* tocar, palpar; **to ~ on** aludir a; **to ~ up** retocar; * *n* contacto *m*; tacto *m*; toque *m*; prueba *f.*

touch-and-go *adj* arriesgado/da.

touchdown *n* aterrizaje *m*; ensayo *m.*

touched *adj* conmovido/da; chiflado/da.

touching *adj* patético/ca, conmove-dor/a.

touchstone *n* piedra de toque *f.*

touchwood *n* yesca *f.*

touchy *adj* quisquilloso/sa.

tough *adj* duro/ra; difícil; resistente; fuerte; * *n* gorila *m.*

toughen vt endurecer.
toupee n tupé m.
tour n viaje m; visita f; * vt visitar.
touring n viajes turísticos mpl.
tourism n turismo m; **bicycle ~** cicloturismo;
　rural ~ turismo rural.
tourist n turista m/f.
tourist office n oficina de turismo f.
tournament n torneo m.
tow n remolque m; * vt remolcar.
toward(s) prep, adv hacia, con dirección a; cerca
　de, respecto a.
towel n toalla f.
toweling n toalla f.
towel rack n toallero m.
tower n torre m.
towering adj imponente.
town n ciudad f.
town clerk n secretario/ria del ayuntamiento m/
　f.
town hall n ayuntamiento m.
towrope n cable de remolque m.
toy n juguete m.
toy store n juguetería f.
trace n huella, pisada f; * vt trazar, delinear;
　encontrar.
track n vestigio m; huella f; camino m; vía f; pista
　f; canción f; * vt rastrear.
tracksuit n chándal m.
tract n región, comarca f; serie f; tratado m.
traction n tracción f.
trade n comercio, tráfico m; negocio, trato m;
　ocupación f; * vi comerciar, traficar.
trade fair n feria de muestras f.
trademark n marca comercial f.
trade name n nombre comercial m.
trader n comerciante, traficante m.
tradesman n tendero m.
trading n comercio m; * adj comercial.
tradition n tradición f.
traditional adj tradicional.
traffic n tráfico m; tránsito m; * vi traficar,
　comerciar.
traffic circle n glorieta f.
traffic jam n embotellamiento m, aglomeración
　f de tráfico.
trafficker n traficante, comerciante m/f.
traffic lights npl semáforo m.
tragedy n tragedia f.
tragic adj trágico/ca; **~ally** adv trágicamente.
tragicomedy n tragicomedia f.
trail vt, vi rastrear; arrastrar; * n rastro m; pista
　f; cola f.
trailer n tráiler m; remolque m; avance m.
train vt entrenar; amaestrar, enseñar, criar,
　adiestrar; disciplinar; * vr ejercitarse; * n tren
　m; cola f; serie f; **high-speed ~** tren de alta
　velocidad m.
trained adj cualificado/da; amaes-trado/da.
trainee n aprendiz/a m/f.
trainer n entrenador/a m/f.

training n entrenamiento m; formación f.
trait n rasgo m.
traitor n traidor/a m/f.
tram n tranvía f.
tramp n vagabundo/da m/f; (col) puta f; * vi andar
　pesadamente; * vt pisotear.
trample vt pisotear.
trampoline n cama elástica f.
trance n rapto m; éxtasis m.
tranquil adj tranquilo/la.
tranquilize vt tranquilizar.
tranquilizer n tranquilizante m.
transact vt negociar.
transaction n transacción f; negociación f.
transatlantic adj transatlántico/ca.
transcend vt trascender, pasar; exceder.
transcription n transcripción f.
transfer vt transferir, trasladar; * n transferencia
　f; traspaso m; calcomanía f.
transform vt transformar.
transformation n transformación f.
transfusion n transfusión f.
transient adj pasajero/ra, transitorio/ria.
transit n tránsito m.
transition n tránsito m; transición f.
transitional adj de transición.
transitive adj transitivo/va.
translate vt traducir.
translation n traducción f.
translator n traductor/ra m/f.
transmission n transmisión f.
transmit vt transmitir.
transmitter n transmisor m; emisora f.
transparency n transparencia f.
transparent adj transparente, diáfa-no/na.
transpire vi resultar; ocurrir.
transplant vt trasplantar; * n trasplante m.
transport vt transportar; * n transporte m.
transportation n transporte m.
trap n trampa f; * vt atrapar, bloquear.
trap door n trampilla f; escotillón m.
trapeze n trapecio m.
trappings npl adornos mpl.
trash n basura f; tonterías fpl.
trash can n cubo de la basura m.
trashy adj vil, despreciable, de ningún valor.
travel vi viajar; * vt recorrer; * n viaje m.
travel agency n agencia de viajes f.
travel agent n agente de viajes m.
traveler n viajante, viajero/ra m/f.
traveler's check n cheque de viaje m.
travel-sickness n mareo m.
travesty n parodia f.
trawler n arrastrero m.
tray n bandeja f; cajón m.
treacherous adj traidor/a, perfido/da.
treachery n traición f.
tread vi pisar; pistoear; * n pisada f; ruido de
　pasos m; banda de rodadura f.
treason n traición f; **high ~** alta traición f.
treasure n tesoro m; * vt atesorar.

treasurer *n* tesorero/ra *m/f*.

treat *vt* tratar; regalar; * *n* regalo *m*; placer *m*.

treatise *n* tratado *m*.

treatment *n* trato *m*.

treaty *n* tratado *m*.

treble *adj* triple; * *vt* (*vi*) triplicar(se); * *n* (*mus*) tiple *m*.

treble clef *n* clave de sol *f*.

tree *n* árbol *m*.

trek *n* caminata *f*; expedición *f*.

trellis *n* enrejado *m*.

tremble *vi* temblar.

trembling *n* temor *m*; trino *m*.

tremendous *adj* tremendo/da; enorme; estupendo/da.

tremor *n* temblor *m*.

trench *n* foso *m*; (*mil*) trinchera *f*; zanja *f*.

trend *n* tendencia *f*; curso *m*; moda *f*.

trendy *adj* de moda.

trepidation *n* inquietud *f*.

trespass *vt* transpasar, violar.

tress *n* trenza *f*; rizo de pelo *m*.

trestle *n* caballete de serrador *m*.

trial *n* proceso *m*; prueba *f*; ensayo *m*; desgracia *f*.

triangle *n* triángulo *m*.

triangular *adj* triangular.

tribal *adj* tribal.

tribe *n* tribu *f*; raza, casta *f*.

tribulation *n* tribulación *f*.

tributary *adj*, *n* tributario/ria *m/f*.

tribute *n* tributo *m*.

trice *n* momento, tris *m*.

trick *n* engaño, fraude *m*; burla *f*; baza *f*; zancadilla *f*; * *vt* engañar.

trickery *n* engaño *m*.

trickle *vi* gotear; * *n* reguero *m*.

tricky *adj* difícil; delicado/da.

tricycle *n* triciclo *m*.

trifle *n* bagatela, niñería *f*; * *vi* bobear; juguetear.

trifling *adj* frívolo/la, inútil.

trigger *n* gatillo *m*; **to ~ off** *vt* desencadenar.

trigonometry *n* trigonometría *f*.

trill *n* trino *m*; * *vi* trinar.

trillion *n* billón *m*.

trim *adj* aseado/da; en buen estado; arreglado/da; * *vt* arreglar; recortar; adornar.

trimester *n* trimestre *m*.

trimmings *npl* accesorios *mpl*.

Trinity *n* Trinidad *f*.

trinket *n* joya, alhaja *f*; adorno *m*.

trio *n* (*mus*) trío *m*.

trip *vt* hacer caer; * *vi* tropezar; resbalar; * *n* resbalón *m*; viaje corto *m*, *Lat Am* paseo *m*; zancadilla *f*.

tripe *n* callos *mpl*; bobadas *fpl*.

triple *adj* triple; * *vt* triplicar.

triplets *npl* trillizos/zas *m/fpl*.

triplicate *n* triplicado *m*.

tripod *n* trípode *m*.

trite *adj* trivial; usado/da.

triumph *n* triunfo *m*; * *vi* triunfar.

triumphal *adj* triunfal.

triumphant *adj* triunfante; victorio-so/sa; **~ly** *adv* en triunfo.

trivia *npl* trivialidades *fpl*.

trivial *adj* trivial, vulgar; **~ly** *adv* trivialmente.

triviality *n* trivialidad *f*.

trolley *n* carrito *m*.

trombone *n* trombón *m*.

troop *n* grupo *m*; **~s** *npl* tropas *fpl*.

trooper *n* soldado a caballo *m*.

trophy *n* trofeo *m*.

tropical *adj* trópico/ca.

trot *n* trote *m*; * *vi* trotar.

trouble *vt* afligir; molestar; * *n* problema *m*; disturbio *m*; inquietud *f*; aflicción, pena *f*.

troubled *adj* preocupado/da; agita-do/da.

troublemaker *n* agitador/a *m/f*.

troubleshooter *n* conciliador/a *m/f*.

troublesome *adj* molesto/ta.

trough *n* abrevadero *m*; comedero *m*.

troupe *n* grupo *m*.

trousers *npl* pantalones *mpl*.

trout *n* trucha *f*.

trowel *n* paleta *f*.

truce *n* tregua *f*.

truck *n* camión *m*; vagón *m*.

truck driver *n* camionero/a *m/f*.

truculent *adj* truculento/ta, cruel.

trudge *vi* andar fatigosamente, andar con dificultad.

true *adj* verdadero/ra, cierto/ta; sincero/ra; exacto/ta.

truelove *n* amor verdadero *m*.

truffle *n* trufa *f*.

truly *adv* en verdad; sinceramente.

trump *n* triunfo (en el juego de naipes) *m*.

trumpet *n* trompeta *f*.

trunk *n* baúl, cofre *m*; trompa *f*.

truss *n* braguero *m*; * *vt* atar; espetar.

trust *n* confianza *f*; trust *m*; fideicomiso *m*; * *vt* tener confianza en; confiar algo a.

trusted *adj* de confianza.

trustee *n* fideicomisario/ria, cura-dor/a *m/f*.

trustful *adj* fiel; confiado/da.

trustily *adv* fielmente.

trusting *adj* confiado/da.

trustworthy *adj* digno/na de confianza.

trusty *adj* fiel, leal; seguro/ra.

truth *n* verdad *f*; fidelidad *f*; realidad *f*; **in ~** en verdad.

truthful *adj* verídico/ca; veraz.

truthfulness *n* veracidad *f*.

try *vt* examinar, ensayar, probar; experimentar; tentar; inte ntar; juzgar; * *vi* probar; **to ~ on** probarse; **to ~ out** probar; * *n* tentativa *f*; ensayo *m*.

trying *adj* pesado/da; cansado/da.

tub *n* balde *m*, barreño *m*, cubo *m*; tina *f*.

tuba *n* tuba *f*.

tube n tubo, cañon, canuto m.

tuberculosis n tuberculosis f invar.

tubing n caería f.

tuck n pliegue m; * vt poner.

Tuesday n martes m invar.

tuft n mechón m; manojo m.

tug vt remolcar; * n remolcador m.

tuition n matrícula f; enseñanza f.

tulip n tulipán m.

tumble vi caer, hundirse; revolcarse; * vt revolver; volcar; * n caída f; vuelco m.

tumbledown adj destartalado/da.

tumbler n vaso m.

tummy n barriga f.

tumor n tumor m.

tumultuous adj tumultuoso/sa.

tuna n atún m.

tune n tono m; armonia f; aria f; * vt afinar; sintonizar.

tuneful adj armonioso/sa, acorde, melodioso/sa.

tuner n sintonizador/a m.

tunic n túnica f.

tuning fork n (mus) diapasón m.

tunnel n túnel m; * vt construir un tunel por.

turban n turbante m.

turbine n turbina f.

turbulence n turbulencia, confusión f.

turbulent adj turbulento/ta, tumul-tuoso/sa.

tureen n sopera f.

turf n césped m; * vt cubrir con césped.

turgid adj pesado/da.

turkey n pavo m.

turmoil n disturbio m; baraúnda f.

turn vi volver; cambiar; girar; dar vueltas; volverse a, mudarse, transformarse; **to ~ around** volverse; girar; **to ~ back** volverse; **to ~ down** rechazar; doblar; **to ~ in** acostarse; **to ~ off** vi desviarse; vt apagar; parar; **to ~ on** encender, prender; poner en marcha; **to ~ out** apagar; **to ~ over** vi volverse; vt volver; **to ~ up** vi llegar; aparecer; vt subir; * n vuelta f; giro m; rodeo m; turno m; vez f; inclinación f.

turncoat n desertor/a, renegado/da m/f.

turning n vuelta f.

turnip n nabo m.

turn-off n salida f.

turnout n concurrencia f.

turnover n facturación f.

turnpike n autopista de peaje f.

turnstile n torniquete m.

turntable n plato m.

turpentine n trementina f.

turquoise n turquesa f.

turret n torrecilla, torreta f.

turtle n tortuga marina f.

turtledove n tórtola f.

tusk n colmillo m.

tussle n pelea f.

tutor n tutor/a m/f; profesor/a m/f; * vt enseñar, instruir.

tuxedo n smoking m.

twang n gangueo m; sonido agudo m.

tweezers npl tenacillas fpl.

twelfth adj, n duodécimo/ma.

twelve adj, n doce.

twentieth adj, n vigésimo/ma.

twenty adj, n veinte.

twice adv dos veces.

twig n ramita f; * vi caer en la cuenta.

twilight n crepúsculo m.

twin n gemelo/la m/f.

twine vi entrelazarse; caracolear; * n bramante m.

twinge vt punzar, pellizcar; * n dolor agudo/ punzante m; punzada f.

twinkle vi centellear; parpadear.

twirl vt dar vueltas a; * vi piruetear; * n rotación f.

twist vt torcer, retorcer; entretejer; * vi serpentear; * n torsión f; vuelta f; doblez f.

twit n (col) tonto/ta m/f.

twitch vi moverse nerviosamente; * n tirón; tic m.

twitter vi gorjear; * n gorjeo m.

two adj, n dos.

two-door adj de dos puertas.

two-faced adj falso/sa.

twofold adj doble, duplicado/da; * adv al doble.

two-seater n avión/coche de dos plazas m.

twosome n pareja f.

tycoon n magnate m.

type n tipo m; letra f; modelo m; * vt escribir a máquina, Lat Am tipear.

typecast adj encasillado/da.

typeface n tipo m.

typescript n texto mecanografiado m.

typewriter n máquina de escribir f.

typewritten adj mecanografiado/da.

typical adj típico/ca.

typographer n tipógrafo m.

typographical adj tipográfico/ca

typography n tipografía f.

tyrannical adj tiránico/ca.

tyranny n tiranía f; crueldad f.

tyrant n tirano/na m/f.

U

ubiquitous adj ubicuo/cua.

udder n ubre f.

ugh excl ¡puaj!

ugliness n fealdad f.

ugly adj feo, fea; peligroso/sa.

ulcer n úlcera f.

ulterior adj ulterior.

ultimate adj último/ma; ~ly adv al final; a fin de cuentas.

ultimatum n ultimátum m.

ultramarine n ultramar m; * adj ultramarino/na.

ultrasound n ultrasonido m.

ultrasound scan n ecografía f.

umbilical cord n cordón umbilical m.

umbrella n paraguas m invar.

umpire n árbitro/tra m/f.

umpteen adj enésimos/mas.

unable adj incapaz.

unaccompanied adj solo/la, sin acompañamiento.

unaccomplished adj incompleto/ta, no acabado/da.

unaccountable adj inexplicable, extraño/ña.

unaccountably adv extrañamente.

unaccustomed adj desacostumbrado/da, desusado/da.

unacknowledged adj desconocido/da; negado/da.

unacquainted adj desconocido/da; ignorado/da.

unadorned adj sin adorno.

unadulterated adj genuino/na, puro/ra; sin mezcla.

unaffected adj sincero/ra, sin afectación.

unaided adj sin ayuda.

unaltered adj invariado/da.

unambitious adj poco/ca ambicioso/sa.

unanimity n unanimidad f.

unanimous adj unánime; **~ly** adv unánimemente.

unanswerable adj incontrovertible, incontestable.

unanswered adj no contestado/da.

unapproachable adj inaccesible.

unarmed adj inerme, desarmado/da.

unassuming adj nada presuntuoso/sa, modesto/ta.

unattached adj independiente; disponible.

unattainable adj inasequible.

unattended adj sin atender.

unauthorized adj no autorizado/da.

unavoidable adj inevitable.

unavoidably adv inevitablemente.

unaware adj ignorante.

unawares adv inadvertidamente; de improviso.

unbalanced adj desequilibrado/da; trastornado/da.

unbearable adj insoportable.

unbecoming adj indecente, indeco-roso/sa.

unbelievable adj increíble.

unbend vi relajarse; * vt enderezar.

unbiased adj imparcial.

unblemished adj sin mancha, sin tacha, irreprensible.

unborn adj no nacido/da.

unbreakable adj irrompible.

unbroken adj intacto/ta; indómito/ta; entero/ra; no batido/da.

unbutton vt desabotonar.

uncalled-for adj fuera de lugar.

uncanny adj extraordinario/ria.

unceasing adj sin cesar, continuo/nua.

unceremonious adj brusco/ca.

uncertain adj incierto/ta, dudoso/sa.

uncertainty n incertidumbre f.

unchangeable adj inmutable.

unchanged adj no alterado/da.

unchanging adj inalterable, immutable.

uncharitable adj nada caritativo/va, duro/ra.

unchecked adj desenfrenado/da, incontrolado/da.

unchristian adj poco cristiano/na.

uncivil adj grosero/ra, descortés.

uncivilized adj tosco/ca, salvaje, incivilizado/da.

uncle n tío.

uncomfortable adj incómodo/da; molesto/ta.

uncomfortably adv incómodamente; inquietantemente.

uncommon adj raro/ra, extraordina-rio/ria.

uncompromising adj irreconciliable.

unconcerned adj indiferente.

unconditional adj sin condiciones, incondicional.

unconfined adj libre, ilimitado/da.

unconfirmed adj no confirmado/da.

unconnected adj inconexo/xa.

unconquerable adj invencible, insuperable.

unconscious adj inconsciente; **~ly** adv inconscientemente.

unconstrained adj libre, voluntario/ria.

uncontrollable adj incontrolable; desenfrenado/da.

unconventional adj poco convencional.

unconvincing adj no convincente.

uncork vt destapar.

uncorrected adj sin corregir, no corregido/da.

uncouth adj grosero/ra, zafio/fia.

uncover vt descubrir.

uncultivated adj inculto/ta.

uncut adj no cortado/da, entero/ra.

undamaged adj ileso/sa, libre de daño.

undaunted adj intrépido/da.

undecided adj indeciso/sa.

undefiled adj impoluto/ta, puro/ra.

undeniable adj innegable, incontestable; **~bly** adv indubitablemente.

under prep debajo de; menos de; segun; * adv debajo.

under-age adj menor de edad.

undercharge vt cobrar de menos.

underclothing n ropa íntima f.

undercoat n primera mano f.

undercover adj clandestino/na.

undercurrent n corriente subyacente f.

undercut vt vender más barato que.

underdeveloped adj subdesarrolla-do/da.

underdog n desvalido/da m/f.

underdone adj poco cocido/da.

underestimate vt subestimar.

undergo vt sufrir; sostener.

undergraduate n estudiante univer-sitario/ria m/f.

underground n movimiento clandestino m.

undergrowth n soto m, maleza f.

underhand adv clandestinamente; * adj secreto/ta, clandestino/na.

underlie vi estar debajo.

underline vt subrayar.

undermine vt minar.

underneath adv debajo; * prep debajo de.

underpaid *adj* mal pagado/da.

underpants *npl* calzoncillos *mpl*.

underprivileged *adj* desvalido/da.

underrate *vt* menospreciar.

undersecretary *n* subsecretario/ria *m/f*.

undershirt *n* camiseta *f*.

underside *n* revés *m*.

understand *vt* entender, comprender.

understandable *adj* comprensible.

understanding *n* entendimiento *m*; inteligencia *f*; conocimiento *m*; correspondencia *f*; * compren-sivo/va.

understatement *n* subestimación *f*; modestia *f*.

undertake *vt, vi* emprender.

undertaking *n* empresa *f*; empeño *m*.

undervalue *vt* menospreciar.

underwater *adj* submarino/na; * *adv* bajo el agua.

underwear *n* ropa íntima *f*.

underworld *n* hampa *f*.

underwrite *vt* suscribir; asegurar contra riesgos.

underwriter *n* asegurador/a *m/f*.

undeserved *adj* inmerecido/da; ~ly *adv* sin haberlo merecido.

undeserving *adj* indigno/na.

undesirable *adj* indeseable.

undetermined *adj* indeterminado/da, indeciso/sa.

undigested *adj* no digerido/da.

undiminished *adj* entero/ra, no dis-minuido/da.

undisciplined *adj* indisciplinado/da.

undisguised *adj* sin disfraz, cándido/da, sincero/ra.

undismayed *adj* intrépido/da.

undisputed *adj* incontestable.

undisturbed *adj* quieto/ta, tranquilo/la.

undivided *adj* indiviso/sa, entero/ra.

undo *vt* deshacer, destar, descoser.

undoing *n* ruina *f*.

undoubted *adj* indudable; ~ly *adv* indudablemente.

undress *vi* desnudarse.

undue *adj* indebido/do; injusto/ta.

undulating *adj* ondulante.

unduly *adv* indebidamente.

undying *adj* inmortal.

unearth *vt* desenterrar.

unearthly *adj* inverosímil.

uneasiness *n* inquietud *f*; zozobra *f*.

uneasy *adj* inquieto/ta, desasosega-do/da, incomodo/da.

uneducated *adj* ignorante.

unemployed *adj* desmpleado/da, pa-rado/da; ~ person parado/da *m/f*.

unemployment *n* desempleo, paro *m*.

unending *adj* interminable.

unenlightened *adj* no iluminado/da.

unenviable *adj* poco envidiable.

unequal *adj*, ~ly *adv* desigual(men-te).

unequaled *adj* incomparable.

unerring *adj*, ~ly *adv* infalible(men-te).

uneven *adj* desigual; impar; ~ly *adv* desigualmente.

unexpected *adj* inesperado/da; ino-pinado/da; ~ly *adv* de repente; inopinadamente.

unexplored *adj* inexplorado/da, no descubierto/ta.

unfailing *adj* infalible, seguro/ra.

unfair *adj* falso/sa; injusto/ta; ~ly *adv* injustamente.

unfaithful *adj* infiel, pérfido/da.

unfaithfulness *n* infidelidad, perfidia *f*.

unfaltering *adj* firme, asegurado/da.

unfamiliar *adj* desacostumbrado/da, poco común.

unfashionable *adj* pasado/da de moda; ~bly *adv* contra la moda.

unfasten *vt* desatar, soltar, aflojar.

unfathomable *adj* insondable, impenetrable.

unfavorable *adj* desfavorable.

unfeeling *adj* insensible, duro/ra de corazón.

unfinished *adj* imperfecto/ta, no acabado/da.

unfit *adj* indispuesto/ta; incapaz.

unfold *vt* desplegar; revelar; * *vi* abrirse.

unforeseen *adj* imprevisto/ta.

unforgettable *adj* inolvidable.

unforgivable *adj* imperdonable.

unforgiving *adj* implacable.

unfortunate *adj* desafortunado/da, infeliz; ~ly *adv* por desgracia, infelizmente.

unfounded *adj* sin fundamento.

unfriendly *adj* antipático/ca.

unfruitful *adj* estéril; infructuoso/sa.

unfurnished *adj* sin muebles; des-provisto/ta.

ungainly *adj* desmañado/da.

ungentlemanly *adj* indigno/na de un hombre bien criado.

ungovernable *adj* indomable, ingobernable.

ungrateful *adj* ingrato/ta; desagradable; ~ly *adv* ingratamente.

ungrounded *adj* infundado/da.

unhappily *adv* infelizmente.

unhappiness *n* infelicidad *f*.

unhappy *adj* infeliz.

unharmed *adj* ileso/sa, sano/na y salvo/va.

unhealthy *adj* malsano/na; enfermi-zo/za.

unheard-of *adj* inaudito/ta, extraño/ña, sin ejemplo.

unheeding *adj* negligente; distraído/da.

unhitch *vt* desaparejar.

unhook *vt* desenganchar; descolgar; desabrochar.

unhoped (for) *adj* inesperado/da.

unhurt *adj* ileso/sa.

unicorn *n* unicornio *m*.

uniform *adj*, ~ly *adv* uniforme(men-te); * *n* uniforme *m*.

uniformity *n* uniformidad *f*.

unify *vt* unificar.

unimaginable *adj* inimaginable.

unimpaired *adj* no disminuido/da, no alterado/da.

unimportant *adj* poco importante.

uninformed *adj* desinformado/da.

uninhabitable *adj* inhabitable.

uninhabited *adj* inhabitado/da, desierto/ta.

uninjured *adj* ileso/sa, no dañado/da.

unintelligible *adj* ininteligible.

unintelligibly *adv* de modo ininteligible.

unintentional *adj* involuntario/ria, no intencionado/da.

uninterested *adj* desinteresado/da.

uninteresting *adj* poco interesante.

uninterrupted *adj* sin interrupción, continuo/nua.

uninvited *adj* no convidado/da.

union *n* unión *f*; sindicato *m*.

unionist *n* sindicalista *m/f*.

unique *adj* único/ca, uno/na, singular.

unison *n* unísono *m*.

unit *n* unidad *f*.

Unitarian *n* unitario/ria *m/f*.

unite *vt* (*vi*) unir(se), juntarse; (*fig*) zurcir.

unitedly *adv* unidamente, de acuerdo.

United States (of America) *npl* Estados Unidos (de América) *mpl*.

unity *n* unidad, concordia, conformidad *f*.

universal *adj*, **~ly** *adv* univer-sál(mente).

universe *n* universo *m*.

university *n* universidad *f*.

unjust *adj* injusto/ta; **~ly** *adv* injustamente.

unkempt *adj* despeinado/da; descui-dado/da.

unkind *adj* poco amable; severo/ra.

unknowingly *adv* sin saberlo.

unknown *adj* incógnito/ta.

unlawful *adj* ilegal; **~ly** *adv* ilegalmente.

unlawfulness *n* ilegalidad *f*.

unleash *vt* desencadenar.

unless *conj* a menos que, si no.

unlicensed *adj* sin licencia.

unlike, unlikely *adj* diferente; improbable; inverosímil.

unlikelihood *n* inverisimilitud *f*.

unlimited *adj* ilimitado/da.

unlisted *adj* que no viene en la guía.

unload *vt* descargar.

unlock *vt* abrir.

unluckily *adv* desafortunadamente.

unlucky *adj* desafortunado/da.

unmanageable *adj* inmanejable, intratable.

unmannered *adj* rudo/da, brutal, grosero/ra.

unmannerly *adj* malcriado/da, descortés.

unmarried *adj* soltero/ra.

unmask *vt* desenmascarar.

unmentionable *adj* que no se puede mencionar.

unmerited *adj* desmerecido/da.

unmindful *adj* olvidadizo/za, negligente.

unmistakable *adj* inconfundible; **~ly** *adv* indudablemente.

unmitigated *adj* absoluto/ta.

unmoved *adj* inmoto, firme.

unnatural *adj* antinatural; perverso/sa; afectado/da.

unnecessary *adj* inútil, innecesario/ria.

unneighborly *adj* poco atento/ta con sus vecinos; descortés.

unnoticed *adj* inadvertido/da.

unnumbered *adj* innumerable.

unobserved *adj* no observado/da.

unobtainable *adj* inconseguible; inexistente.

unobtrusive *adj* modesto/ta.

unoccupied *adj* desocupado/da.

unoffending *adj* sencillo/lla, inocente.

unofficial *adj* no oficial.

unorthodox *adj* heterodoxo/xa.

unpack *vt* desempacar; desenvolver.

unpaid *adj* no pagado/da, *Lat Am* impago/ga.

unpalatable *adj* desabrido/da, desgradable.

unparalleled *adj* sin paralelo; sin par.

unpleasant *adj*, **~ly** *adv* desagra-dable(mente).

unpleasantness *n* desagrado *m*.

unplug *vt* desconectar.

unpolished *adj* que no está pulido/da; rudo/da, grosero/ra.

unpopular *adj* impopular.

unpracticed *adj* inexperto/ta, no versado/ta.

unprecedented *adj* sin precedentes.

unpredictable *adj* imprevisible.

unprejudiced *adj* imparcial.

unprepared *adj* no preparado/da.

unprofitable *adj* inútil, vano/na; poco lucrativo/va.

unprotected *adj* desvalido/da, sin protección.

unpublished *adj* no publicado/da; inédito/ta.

unpunished *adj* impune.

unqualified *adj* sin títulos; total.

unquestionable *adj* indubitable, indisputable; **~ly** *adv* sin duda, sin disputa.

unquestioned *adj* incontestable, no preguntado/da.

unravel *vt* desenredar.

unread *adj* no leído/da; ignorante.

unreal *adj* irreal.

unrealistic *adj* poco realista.

unreasonable *adj* poco razonable; disparatado/da.

unreasonably *adv* poco razonablemente; disparatadamente.

unrelated *adj* sin relación; inconexo/xa.

unrelenting *adj* implacable.

unreliable *adj* poco fiable.

unremitting *adj* constante, incansable.

unrepentant *adj* impenitente.

unreserved *adj* sin restricción; franco/ca; **~ly** *adv* abiertamente.

unrest *n* malestar *m*; disturbios *mpl*.

unrestrained *adj* desenfrenado/da; ilimitado/da.

unripe *adj* inmaduro/ra.

unrivaled *adj* sin rival, sin igual.

unroll *vt* desenrollar.

unruliness *n* turbulencia *f*; desenfreno *m*.

unruly *adj* desenfrenado/da.

unsafe *adj* inseguro/ra, peligroso/sa.

unsatisfactory *adj* insatisfactorio/ria.

unsavory *adj* desabrido/da, insípido/da.
unscathed *adj* ileso/sa.
unscrew *vt* destornillar.
unscrupulous *adj* sin escrúpulos.
unseasonable *adj* intempestivo/va, fuera de propósito.
unseemly *adj* indecente.
unseen *adj* invisible.
unselfish *adj* desinteresado/da.
unsettle *vt* perturbar.
unsettled *adj* inquieto/ta; inestable; variable.
unshaken *adj* firme, estable.
unshaven *adj* sin afeitar.
unsightly *adj* desagradable a la vista, feo/a.
unskillful *adj* inhábil, poco mañoso/sa.
unskilled *adj* no cualificado/da.
unsociable *adj* insociable, intratable.
unspeakable *adj* inefable, indecible.
unstable *adj* instable, inconstante.
unsteadily *adv* ligeramente, inconstantemente.
unsteady *adj* inestable.
unstudied *adj* no estudiado/da; no premeditado/da.
unsuccessful *adj* infeliz, desafortu-nado/da; ~**ly** *adv* sin éxito.
unsuitable *adj* inapropiado/da; in-oportuno/na.
unsure *adj* ineguro/ra.
unsympathetic *adj* poco compren-sivo/va.
untamed *adj* indomado/da.
untapped *adj* sin explotar.
untenable *adj* insostenible.
unthinkable *adj* inconcebible.
unthinking *adj* desatento/ta, irre-flexivo/va.
untidiness *n* desaliño *m*.
untidy *adj* desordenado/da; sucio/cia.
untie *vt* desatar, deshacer, soltar, zafar.
until *prep* hasta; * *conj* hasta que.
untimely *adj* intempestivo/va.
untiring *adj* incansable.
untold *adj* nunca dicho/cha; indecible; incalculable.
untouched *adj* intacto/ta.
untoward *adj* impropio/pia; adverso/sa.
untried *adj* no ensayado/da/probado/da.
untroubled *adj* no perturbado/da, tranquilo/la.
untrue *adj* falso/sa.
untrustworthy *adj* indigno/na de confianza.
untruth *n* falsedad, mentira *f*.
unused *adj* sin usar, no usado/da.
unusual *adj* inusual, inusitado/da, raro/ra; ~**ly** *adv* inusitadamente, raramente.
unveil *vt* quitar el velo, descubrir.
unwavering *adj* inquebrantable.
unwelcome *adj* desagradable, in-oportuno/na.
unwell *adj* enfermizo/za, malo/la.
unwieldy *adj* pesado/da.
unwilling *adj* desinclinado/da; ~**ly** *adv* de mala gana.
unwillingness *n* mala gana, repugnancia *f*.
unwind *vt* desenredar, desenmarañar; * *vi* relajarse.

unwise *adj* imprudente.
unwitting *adj* inconsciente.
unworkable *adj* poco práctico/ca.
unworthy *adj* indigno/na.
unwrap *vt* desenvolver.
unwritten *adj* no escrito/ta.
up *adv* arriba, en lo alto; levantado/da; * *prep* hacia; hasta.
upbraid *vt* zaherir.
upbringing *n* educación *f*.
update *vt* poner al día.
upheaval *n* agitación *f*.
uphill *adj* difícil, penoso/sa; * *adv* cuesta arriba.
uphold *vt* sos tener, apoyar.
upholstery *n* tapicería *f*.
upkeep *n* mantenimiento *m*.
uplift *vt* levantar.
upon *prep* sobre, encima.
upper *adj* superior; más elevado/da.
upper-class *adj* de la clase alta.
upper-hand *n* (*fig*) superioridad *f*.
uppermost *adj* más alto/ta, supremo/ma; **to be ~** predominar.
upright *adj* derecho/cha, perpendicular, recto/ta; puesto/ta en pie; honrado/da.
uprising *n* sublevación *f*.
uproar *n* tumulto, alboroto *m*.
uproot *vt* desarraigar.
upset *vt* trastornar; derramar, volcar; * *n* revés *m*; trastorno *m*; * *adj* molesto/ta; revuelto/ta.
upshot *n* remate *m*; fin *m*; conclusión *f*.
upside-down *adj* al revés.
upstairs *adv* arriba.
upstart *n* advenedizo/za *m/f*.
uptight *adj* nervioso/sa.
up-to-date *adj* al día.
upturn *n* mejora *f*.
upward *adj* ascendente; ~**s** *adv* hacia arriba.
urban *adj* urbano/na.
urbane *adj* cortés.
urchin *n* golfillo/lla *m/f*.
urge *vt* animar; * *n* impulso *m*; deseo *m*.
urgency *n* urgencia *f*.
urgent *adj* urgente.
urinal *n* orinal *m*.
urinate *vi* orinar.
urine *n* orina *f*.
urn *n* urna *f*.
us *pn* nos; nosotros, nosotras.
usage *n* tratamiento *m*; uso *m*.
use *n* uso *m*; utilidad, práctica *f*; * *vt* usar, emplear.
used *adj* usado/da.
useful *adj* , ~**ly** *adv* útil(mente).
usefulness *n* utilidad *f*.
useless *adj* inútil; ~**ly** *adv* inútilmente.
uselessness *n* inutilidad *f*.
user-friendly *adj* fácil de utilizar.
usher *n* ujier *m/f*; acomodador/a *m/f*.
usherette *n* acomodadora *f*.
usual *adj* usual, común, normal; ~**ly** *adv* normalmente.

usurer *n* usurero/ra *m/f.*

usurp *vt* usurpar.

usury *n* usura *f.*

utensil *n* utensilio *m.*

uterus *n* útero *m.*

utility *n* utilidad *f.*

utilize *vt* utilizar.

utmost *adj* extremo/ma, sumo/ma; último/ma.

utter *adj* total; todo; entero/ra; * *vt* proferir; expresar; publicar.

utterance *n* expresion *f.*

utterly *adv* enteramente, del todo.

V

vacancy *n* cuarto libre *m*, vacante *f.*

vacant *adj* vacío/cía; desocupado/da; vacante.

vacant lot *n* solar *m.*

vacate *vt* desocupar; dejar.

vacation *n* vacaciones *fpl.*

vaccinate *vt* vacunar.

vaccination *n* vacunación *f.*

vaccine *n* vacuna *f.*

vacuous *adj* vacío/cía, vacuo/cua.

vacuum *n* vacío *m.*

vacuum flask *n* termo *m.*

vagina *n* vagina *f.*

vagrant *n* vagabundo/da *m/f.*

vague *adj* vago/ga; ~**ly** *adv* vagamente.

vain *adj* vano/na, inútil; vanidoso/sa.

valet *n* criado *m.*

valiant *adj* valiente, valeroso/sa.

valid *adj* válido/da.

valley *n* valle *m.*

valor *n* valor, aliento, brío, esfuerzo *m.*

valuable *adj* valioso/sa; ~**s** *npl* objetos de valor *mpl.*

valuation *n* tasa, valuación *f.*

value *n* valor, precio *m*; * *vt* valuar, *Lat Am* avaluar; estimar, apreciar.

valued *adj* apreciado/da.

valve *n* válvula *f.*

vampire *n* vampiro *m.*

van *n* camioneta *f.*

vandal *n* gamberro/rra *m/f.*

vandalism *n* vandalismo *m.*

vandalize *vt* dañar.

vanguard *n* vanguardia *f.*

vanilla *n* vainilla *f.*

vanish *vi* desvanecerse, desaparecer.

vanity *n* vanidad *f.*

vanity case *n* neceser *m.*

vanquish *vt* vencer, conquistar.

vantage point *n* punto panorámico *m.*

vapor *n* vapor *m*; exhalación *f.*

variable *adj* variable; voluble.

variance *n* discordia, desavenencia *f.*

variation *n* variación *f.*

varicose vein *n* variz *f*, *Lat Am* várice *f.*

varied *adj* variado/da.

variety *n* variedad *f.*

variety show *n* espectáculo de variedades *m.*

various *adj* vario/ria, diverso/sa, diferente.

varnish *n* barniz *m*; * *vt* barnizar.

vary *vt*, *vi* variar; cambiar.

vase *n* florero, jarrón *m.*

vast *adj* vasto/ta; inmenso/sa.

vat *n* tina *f.*

vault *n* bóveda *f*; cueva *f*; caverna *f*; * *vt* saltar.

veal *n* ternera *f.*

veer *vi* (*mar*) virar.

vegetable *adj* vegetal; * *n* vegetal *m*; ~**s** *pl* verduras *fpl.*

vegetable garden *n* huerta *f.*

vegetarian *n* vegetariano/na *m/f.*

vegetate *vi* vegetar.

vegetation *n* vegetación *f.*

vehemence *n* vehemencia, violencia *f.*

vehement *adj* vehemente, violento/ta; ~**ly** *adv* vehementemente.

vehicle *n* vehículo *m*; **all-terrain** ~ todoterreno *m.*

veil *n* velo *m*; * *vt* encubrir, ocultar.

vein *n* vena *f*; cavidad *f*; inclinación del ingenio *f.*

velocity *n* velocidad *f.*

velvet *n* terciopelo *m.*

vending machine *n* máquina expendedora *f.*

vendor *n* vendedor/a *m/f.*

veneer *n* chapa *f*; barniz *m.*

venerable *adj* venerable.

venerate *vt* venerar, honrar.

veneration *n* veneración *f.*

venereal *adj* venéreo.

vengeance *n* venganza *f.*

venial *adj* venial.

venison *n* (carne de) venado *f.*

venom *n* veneno *m.*

venomous *adj* venenoso/sa; ~**ly** *adv* venenosamente.

vent *n* respiradero *m*; salida *f*; * *vt* desahogar.

ventilate *vt* ventilar.

ventilation *n* ventilación *f.*

ventilator *n* ventilador *m.*

ventriloquist *n* ventrílocuo/cua *m/f.*

venture *n* empresa *f*; * *vi* aventurarse; * *vt* aventurar, arriesgar.

venue *n* lugar de reunión, local *m.*

veranda(h) *n* terraza *f*, porche *m.*

verb *n* (*gr*) verbo *m.*

verbal *adj* verbal, literal; ~**ly** *adv* verbalmente.

verbatim *adv* literalmente.

verbose *adj* verboso/sa.

verdant *adj* verde.

verdict *n* (*law*) veredicto *m*; opinión *f.*

verification *n* verificación *f.*

verify *vt* verificar.

veritable *adj* verdadero/ra.

vermicelli *npl* fideos *mpl.*

vermin *n* bichos *mpl.*

vermouth *n* vermut *m.*

versatile *adj* versátil; polifacético/ca.
verse *n* verso *m*; versículo *m*.
versed *adj* versado/da.
version *n* versión *f*.
versus *prep* contra.
vertebra *n* vértebra *f*.
vertebral, vertebrate *adj* vertebral.
vertex *n* cenit, vértice *m*.
vertical *adj*, **~ly** *adv* vertical(mente).
vertigo *n* vértigo *m*.
verve *n* brío *m*.
very *adj* idéntico/ca, mismo/ma; * *adv* muy, mucho, sumamente.
vessel *n* vasija *f*; vaso *m*; barco *m*.
vest *n* chaleco *m*.
vestibule *n* vestíbulo *m*.
vestige *n* vestigio *m*.
vestment *n* vestido *m*; vestidura *f*.
vestry *n* sacristía *f*.
veteran *adj*, *n* veterano/na *m/f*.
veterinarian, vet *n* veterinario/ria *m/f*.
veterinary *adj* veterinario/ria.
veterinary science *n* veterinaria *f*.
veto *n* veto *m*; * *vt* vetar.
vex *vt* molestar.
vexed *adj* molesto/ta; controvertido/da.
via *prep* por.
viaduct *n* viaducto *m*.
vial *n* ampolla *f*, vial *m*.
vibrate *vi* vibrar.
vibration *n* vibración *f*.
vicarious *adj* sustituto/ta.
vice *n* vicio *m*; culpa *f*; tornillo *m*.
vice-chairman *n* vice-presidente *m*.
vice-chancellor (of a university) *n* rector/ra *m/f*.
vice-chancellorship *n* rectorado *m*.
vice versa *adv* viceversa.
vicinity *n* vecindad, proximidad *f*; **immediate ~** inmediaciones *fpl*.
vicious *adj* vicioso/sa; **~ly** *adv* de manera viciosa.
victim *n* víctima *f*.
victimize *vt* victimizar.
victor *n* vencedor/a *m/f*.
victorious *adj* victorioso/sa.
victory *n* victoria *f*.
video *n* vídeo *m*, *Lat Am* video *m*.
video camera *n* videocámara *f*.
video cassette *n* videocasete *m*.
video game *n* videojuego *m*.
video tape *n* cinta de vídeo *f*.
vie *vi* competir.
view *n* vista *f*; perspectiva *f*; aspecto *m*; opinión *f*; paisaje *m*; * *vt* mirar, ver; examinar.
viewer *n* televidente *m/f*.
viewfinder *n* visor *m*.
viewpoint *n* punto de vista *m*.
vigil *n* vela *f*, vigilia *f*.
vigilance *n* vigilancia *f*.
vigilant *adj* vigilante, atento/ta.

vigorous *adj* vigoroso/sa; **~ly** *adv* vigorosamente.
vigor *n* vigor *m*; energía *f*.
vile *adj* vil, bajo/ja; asqueroso/sa.
vilify *vt* envilecer.
villa *n* chalet *m*; casa de campo *f*.
village *n* aldea *f*.
villager *n* aldeano/na *m/f*.
villain *n* malvado/da *m/f*.
vindicate *vt* vindicar, defender.
vindication *n* vindicación *f*; justificación *f*.
vindictive *adj* vengativo/va.
vine *n* vid *f*.
vinegar *n* vinagre *m*.
vineyard *n* viña *f*.
vintage *n* vendimia *f*.
vinyl *n* vinilo *m*.
viola *n* (*mus*) viola *f*.
violate *vt* violar.
violation *n* violación *f*.
violence *n* violencia *f*.
violent *adj* violento/ta; **~ly** *adv* violentamente.
violet *n* (*bot*) violeta *f*.
violin *n* (*mus*) violín *m*.
violinist *n* violinista *m/f*.
violoncello, cello *n* (*mus*) violoncelo, violonchelo *m*.
VIP *n* vip *m/f*.
viper *n* víbora *f*.
virgin *n* virgen *f*; * *adj* virgen.
virginity *n* virginidad *f*.
Virgo *n* Virgo *f* (signo del zodiaco).
virile *adj* viril.
virility *n* virilidad *f*.
virtual *adj*, **~ly** *adv* virtual(mente).
virtue *n* virtud *f*.
virtuous *adj* virtuoso/sa.
virulent *adj* virulento/ta.
virus *n* virus *m invar*.
visa *n* visado *m*, visa *f*.
vis-à-vis *prep* con respecto a.
viscous *adj* viscoso/sa, glutinoso/sa.
visibility *n* visibilidad *f*.
visible *adj* visible.
visibly *adv* visiblemente.
vision *n* vista *f*; visión *f*.
visit *vt* visitar; * *n* visita *f*.
visitation *n* visitación, visita *f*.
visiting hours *npl* horas de visita *fpl*.
visitor *n* visitante *m/f*; turista *m/f*.
visor *n* visera *f*.
vista *n* vista, perspectiva *f*.
visual *adj* visual.
visual aid *n* medio visual *m*.
visualize *vt* imaginarse.
vital *adj* vital; esencial; imprescindible; **~ly** *adv* vitalmente; **~s** *npl* partes vitales *fpl*.
vitality *n* vitalidad *f*.
vital statistics *npl* medidas vitales *fpl*.
vitamin *n* vitamina *f*.
vitiate *vt* viciar, corromper.
vivacious *adj* vivaz.

vivid *adj* vivo/va; gráfico/ca; intenso/sa; **~ly** *adv* vivamente; gráficamente.

vivisection *n* vivisección *f*.

vixen *n* zorra *f*.

vocabulary *n* vocabulario *m*.

vocal *adj* vocal.

vocation *n* vocación *f*; oficio *m*; carrera, profesión *f*; **~al** *adj* profesional.

vocative *n* vocativo *m*.

vociferous *adj* vocinglero/ra, clamo-roso/sa.

vodka *n* vodka *m*.

vogue *n* moda *f*; boga *f*.

voice *n* voz *f*; * *vt* expresar.

void *adj* nulo* *n* vacio *m*.

volatile *adj* volátil; voluble.

volcanic *adj* volcánico/ca.

volcano *n* volcán *m*.

volition *n* voluntad *f*.

volley *n* descarga *f*; salva *f*; rociada *f*; volea *f*.

volleyball *n* voleibol *m*, *Lat Am* vóleibol *m*.

volt *n* voltio *m*.

voltage *n* voltaje *m*.

voluble *adj* locuaz.

volume *n* volumen *m*; libro *m*.

voluntarily *adv* voluntariamente.

voluntary *adj* voluntario/ria.

volunteer *n* voluntario/ria *m/f*; * *vi* ofrecerse voluntariamente.

voluptuous *adj* voluptuoso/sa.

vomit *vt, vi* vomitar; * *n* vómito *m*.

voracious *adj*, **~ly** *adv* voraz(mente).

vortex *n* remolino, torbellino *m*.

vote *n* voto, sufragio *m*; votación *f*; * *vt* votar, *Lat Am* sufragar.

voter *n* votante *m/f*.

voting *n* votación *f*.

voucher *n* vale *m*.

vow *n* voto *m*; * *vi* jurar.

vowel *n* vocal *f*.

voyage *n* viaje *m*; travesía *f*.

vulgar *adj* vulgar, ordinario/ria; de mal gusto.

vulgarity *n* vulgaridad *f*, grosería *f*; mal gusto *m*.

vulnerable *adj* vulnerable.

vulture *n* buitre *m*.

W

wad *n* fajo *m*; bolita *f*.

waddle *vi* anadear.

wade *vi* vadear.

wafer *n* galleta *f*; oblea *f*.

waffle *n* gofre *m*.

waft *vt* hacer flotar; * *vi* flotar.

wag *vt* menear; * *vi* menearse.

wage *n* salario *m*.

wage earner *n* asalariado/da *m/f*.

wager *n* apuesta *f*; * *vt* apostar.

wages *npl* salario *m*.

waggish *adj* zumbón/ona.

waggle *vt* menear.

wagon *n* carro *m*; (*rail*) vagón *m*.

wail *n* lamento, gemido *m*; * *vi* gemir.

waist *n* cintura *f*.

waistline *n* talle *m*.

wait *vi* esperar; * *n* espera *f*; pausa *f*.

waiter *n* camarero *m*.

waiting list *n* lista de espera *f*.

waiting room *n* sala de espera *f*.

waive *vt* suspender.

wake[1] *vi* despertarse; * *vt* despertar; * *n* vela *f*.

wake[2] *n* (*mar*) estela *f*.

wakefulness *n* vela *f*.

waken *vt (vi)* despertar(se).

walk *vt, vi* pasear, ir; andar, caminar; * *n* paseo *m*; caminata *f*.

walker *n* paseante *m/f*.

walkie-talkie *n* walkie-talkie *m*.

walking *n* paseos *mpl*.

walking stick *n* bastón *m*.

walkout *n* huelga *f*.

walkover *n* (*col*) pan comido *m*.

walkway *n* paseo *m*.

wall *n* pared *f*; muralla *f*; muro *m*.

walled *adj* amurallado/da.

wallflower *n* (*bot*) alhelí *m*.

wallow *vi* revolcarse.

wallpaper *n* papel pintado *m*.

walnut *n* nogal *m*; nuez *f*.

walrus *n* morsa *f*.

waltz *n* vals *m* invar.

wan *adj* pálido/da.

wand *n* varita mágica *f*.

wander *vt, vi* errar; vagar.

wane *vi* menguar.

want *vt* querer; necesitar; faltar; * *n* necesidad *f*; falta *f*.

wanting *adj* falto/ta, defectuoso/sa.

wanton *adj* lascivo/va; juguetón/ona.

war *n* guerra *f*.

ward *n* sala *f*; pupilo/la *m/f*.

wardrobe *n* guardarropa *f*, ropero *m*.

warehouse *n* almacén *m*.

warfare *n* guerra *f*.

warhead *n* ojiva *f*.

warily *adv* prudentemente.

wariness *n* cautela, prudencia *f*.

warm *adj* cálido/da; caliente; efusivo/va; * *vt* calentar; **to ~ up** *vi* calentarse; entrar en calor; acalorarse; *vt* calentar.

warm-hearted *adj* afectuoso/sa.

warmly *adv* con calor, ardientemente.

warmth *n* calor *m*.

warn *vt* avisar; advertir.

warning *n* aviso *m*.

warning light *n* luz de advertencia *f*.

warp *vi* torcerse; * *vt* torcer; pervertir.

warrant *n* orden judicial *f*; mandamiento judicial *m*.

warranty *n* garantía *f*.

warren *n* conejero *m*.

warrior *n* guerrero/ra, soldado/da *m/f*.

warship n barco de guerra m.

wart n verruga f.

wary adj cauto/ta, prudente.

wash vt lavar; bañar; * vi lavarse; * n lavado m; baño m.

washable adj lavable.

washbowl, washbasin n lavabo m.

washcloth n manopla f.

washer n arandela f.

washing n ropa sucia f; colada f.

washing machine n lavadora f.

washing-up n fregado m.

wash out n (col) fracaso m.

washroom n aseos mpl.

wasp n avispa f.

wastage n desgaste m; pérdida f.

waste vt malgastar; destruir, arruinar; perder; * vi gastarse; * n desperdicio m; destrucción f; despilfarro m; basura f; yermo m.

wasteful adj destructivo/va; pródigo/ga; ~ly adv pródigamente.

wasteland n yermo m.

waste paper n papel usado m.

waste pipe n tubo de desagüe m.

watch n reloj m; centinela f; guardia f; * vt mirar; ver; vigilar; tener cuidado; * vi ver; montar guardia.

watchdog n perro guardián m.

watchful adj vigilante; ~ly adv vigilantemente.

watchmaker n relojero/ra m/f.

watchman n sereno m; vigilante m.

watchtower n atalaya f, garita f.

watchword n santo y seña m.

water n agua f; * vt regar, humedecer, mojar; * vi hacerse agua.

water closet, WC n váter m.

watercolor n acuarela f.

waterfall n cascada f.

water heater n calentador de agua m.

watering-can n regadera f.

water level n nivel del agua m.

water lily n ninfea f.

water line n línea de flotación f.

waterlogged adj anegado/da.

water main n cañería del agua f.

watermark n filigrana f.

water melon n sandía f.

watershed n momento crítico m.

watertight adj impermeable.

waterworks npl depuradora de agua f.

watery adj aguado/da, Lat Am agua-chento/ta; desvaído/da; lloroso/sa.

watt n vatio m.

wave n ola, onda f; oleada f; senal f; * vi agitar la mano; ondear; * vt agitar.

wavelength n longitud de onda f.

waver vi vacilar, balancear.

wavering adj inconstante.

wavy adj ondulado/da.

wax n cera f; * vt encerar; * vi crecer.

wax paper n papel de cera m.

waxworks n museo de cera m.

way n camino m; vía f; ruta f; modo m; recorrido m; **to give** ~ ceder.

waylay vt salir al paso.

wayward adj caprichoso/sa.

we pn nosotros, nosotras.

weak adj, ~ly adv débil(mente).

weaken vt debilitar.

weakling n enclenque m/f.

weakness n debilidad f; punto débil m.

weal, wheal n roncha f.

wealth n riqueza f; bienes mpl.

wealthy adj rico/ca.

wean vt destetar.

weapon n arma f.

wear vt gastar, consumir; usar, llevar; * vi consumirse; **to** ~ **away** vt gastar; vi desgastarse; **to** ~ **down** gastar; agotar; **to** ~ **off** pasar; **to** ~ **out** desgastar; agotar; * n uso m; desgaste m.

weariness n cansancio m; fatiga f; enfado m.

wearisome adj tedioso/sa.

weary adj cansado/da, fatigado/da; tedioso/sa.

weasel n comadreja f.

weather n tiempo m; * vt (out) sufrir, superar.

weather-beaten adj curtido/da.

weather cock n gallo de campanario m; veleta f.

weather forecast n boletín meteorológico m.

weave vt tejer; trenzar; (fig) zurcir.

weaving n tejido m.

web n telaraña f; membrana f; red f.

wed vt (vi) casar(se).

wedding n boda f; nupcias fpl; casamiento m.

wedding day n día de la boda m.

wedding dress n traje de novia m.

wedding present n regalo de boda m.

wedding ring n alianza f.

wedge n cuña f; * vt acuñar; apretar.

wedlock n matrimonio m.

Wednesday n miércoles m invar.

wee adj pequeñito/ta.

weed n mala hierba f; * vt escardar.

weedkiller n herbicida m.

weedy adj lleno/na de malas hierbas.

week n semana f; **tomorrow** ~ mañana en una semana; **yesterday** ~ ayer hace ocho días.

weekday n día laborable m.

weekend n fin de semana m.

weekly adj semanal; * adv semanalmente, por semana.

weep vt, vi llorar; lamentar.

weeping willow n sauce llorón m.

weigh vt, vi pesar.

weight n peso m.

weightily adv pesadamente.

weightlifter n levantador/a m/f de pesas, Lat Am fierrero/ra m/f.

weighty adj ponderoso/sa; importante.

welcome adj bienvenido/da; ~! ¡bienvenido!; * n bienvenida f; * vt dar la bienvenida a.

weld vt soldar; * n soldadura f.

welfare n prosperidad f; bienestar m; subsidio de paro m.

welfare state n estado del bienestar m.

well n fuente f; manantial m; pozo m; * adj bueno/na, sano/na; * adv bien, felizmente; favorablemente; suficientemente; convenientemente; **as ~ as** así como, además de, lo mismo que.

well-behaved adj bien educado/da.

wellbeing n felicidad, prosperidad f.

well-bred adj bien criado/da, bien educado/da.

well-built adj fornido/da.

well-deserved adj merecido/da.

well-dressed adj bien vestido/da.

well-known adj conocido/da.

well-mannered adj educado/da.

well-meaning adj bien intencionado/da.

well-off adj acomodado/da.

well-to-do adj acomodado/da.

well-wisher n partidario/ria m/f.

wench n mozuela, cantonera f.

west n oeste, occidente m; * adj occidental; * adv hacia el oeste.

westerly, western adj occidental.

westward adv hacia el oeste.

wet adj húmedo/da, mojado/da; * n humedad f; * vt mojar, hume decer.

wet-nurse n ama de leche f.

wet suit n traje de buzo m.

whack vt aporrear; * n golpe m.

whale n ballena f.

wharf n muelle m.

what pn que, ¿qué?, el que, la que, lo que; * adj ¿qué?; * excl ¡cómo!

whatever pn cualquier, cualquiera cosa que, lo que sea.

wheat n trigo m.

wheedle vt halagar, engañar con lisonjas, sonsacar.

wheedler n zalamero/ra m/f.

wheel n rueda f; volante m; timón m; * vt (hacer) rodar; volver, girar; * vi rodar.

wheelbarrow n carretilla f.

wheelchair n silla de ruedas f.

wheel clamp n cepo m.

wheeze vi jadear.

when adv ¿cuándo?; mientras que; * conj cuando.

whenever adv cuando; cada vez que.

where adv ¿dónde?; * conj donde; **any~** en cualquier parte; **every~** en todas partes.

whereabout(s) adv ¿dónde?

whereas conj mientras que; pues que, ya que.

whereby pn por lo cual, con lo cual.

whereupon conj con lo cual.

wherever adv dondequiera que.

wherewithal npl recursos mpl.

whet vt excitar.

whether conj si.

which pn qué; lo que; el que, el cual; cuál; * adj ¿qué?; cuyo.

whiff n bocanada de humo f.

while n rato m; vez f; * conj durante; mientras; aunque.

whim n antojo, capricho m.

whimper vi sollozar, gemir.

whimsical adj caprichoso/sa, fantás-tico/ca.

whine vi llorar, lamentar; * n quejido, lamento m.

whinny vi relinchar.

whip n azote m; látigo m, Lat Am chicote m, Lat Am cuero m; * vt azotar; batir.

whipped cream n nata montada f.

whirl vt, vi girar; hacer girar; mover(se) rápidamente.

whirlpool n remolino m.

whirlpool bath n hidromasaje m.

whirlwind n torbellino m.

whisky n whisky m.

whisper vi cuchichear; susurrar.

whispering n cuchicheo m; susurro m.

whistle vi silbar; * n silbido m.

white adj blanco/ca, pálido/da; cano/na; puro/ra; * n color blanco m; clara del huevo f.

white elephant n maula f.

white-hot adj incandescente.

white lie n mentirijilla f.

whiten vt, vi blanquear; emblanquecerse.

whiteness n blancura f; palidez f.

whitewash n enlucimiento m; * vt encalar; jalbegar.

whiting n pescadilla f.

whitish adj blanquecino/na.

who pn ¿quién?, que.

whoever pn quienquiera, cualquiera.

whole adj todo/da, total; sano/na, entero/ra; * n total m; conjunto m.

wholehearted adj sincero/ra.

wholesale n venta al por mayor f, Lat Am mayoreo m.

wholesome adj sano/na, saludable.

wholewheat adj integral.

wholly adv enteramente.

whom pn ¿quién?; que.

whooping cough n tos ferina f.

whore n puta f; (col) zorra f.

why n ¿por qué?; * conj por qué; * excl ¡hombre!

wick n mecha f.

wicked adj malvado/da, perverso/sa; **~ly** adv malamente.

wickedness n perversidad, malignidad f.

wicker n mimbre m; * adj tejido/da de mimbre.

wide adj ancho/cha, vasto/ta; grande; **~ly** adv muy; **far and ~** por todos lados.

wide-awake adj despierto/ta.

widen vt ensanchar, extender.

wide open adj de par en par.

widespread adj extendido/da.

widow n viuda f.

widower n viudo m.

width n anchura f.

wield vt manejar, empuñar.

wife n esposa f; mujer f.
wig n peluca f; tupé m.
wiggle vt menear; * vi menearse.
wild adj silvestre, feroz; desierto/ta; descabellado/da; salvaje.
wilderness n desierto m; yermo m.
wild life n fauna f.
wildly adv violentamente; locamente; desatinadamente.
willful adj deliberado/da; testarudo/da.
willfulness n obstinación f.
wiliness n fraude, engaño m.
will n voluntad f; testamento m; * vt querer, desear.
willing adj inclinado/da, dispuesto/ta; ~ly adv de buena gana.
willingness n buena voluntad, buena gana f.
willow n sauce m (árbol).
willpower n fuerza de voluntad f.
wilt vi marchitarse.
wily adj astuto/ta.
win vt ganar, conquistar; alcanzar; lograr.
wince vi encogerse, estremecerse.
winch n torno m.
wind n viento m; aliento m; flatulencia f.
wind vt enrollar; envolver; dar cuerda a; * vi serpentear.
windfall n golpe de suerte m.
wind farm n parque eólico m.
winding adj tortuoso/sa.
windmill n molino de viento m.
window n ventana f.
window box n jardinera de ventana f.
window cleaner n limpiacristales m invar.
window ledge n repisa f.
windowpane n cristal m.
windowsill n repisa f.
windpipe n tráquea f.
windshield n parabrisas m invar.
windshield washer n lavaparabrisas m invar.
windshield wiper n limpiaparabrisas m invar.
windsurfer n windsurfista m/f.
windsurfing n windsurf m.
wind turbine n aerogenerador m.
windy adj de mucho viento.
wine n vino m.
wine cellar n bodega f.
wine glass n copa de vino f.
wine list n carta de vinos f.
wine merchant n vinatero/ra m/f.
wine-tasting n degustación de vinos f.
wing n ala f.
winged adj alado/da.
winger n extremo m.
wink vi guiñar; * n pestañeo m; guino m.
winner n ganador/a m/f; vencedor/a m/f.
winning post n meta f.
winter n invierno m; * vi invernar.
winter sports npl deportes de invierno mpl.
wintry adj invernal.
wipe vt limpiar; borrar.

wire n alambre m; telegrama m; * vt instalar el alambrado en; conectar.
wiring n alambrada m, Lat Am alambrado m.
wiry adj delgado/da y fuerte.
wisdom n sabiduría, prudencia f.
wisdom teeth npl muelas del juicio fpl.
wise adj sabio/bia, docto/ta, juicioso/sa, prudente.
wisecrack n broma f.
wish vt querer, desear, anhelar; * n anhelo, deseo m.
wishful adj deseoso/sa.
wisp n mechón m; voluta f.
wistful adj pensativo/va, atento/ta.
wit n entendimiento, ingenio m.
witch n bruja, hechicera f.
witchcraft n brujería f; sortilegio m.
with prep con; por, de, a.
withdraw vt quitar; privar; retirar; * vi retirarse, apartarse.
withdrawal n retirada f.
withdrawn adj reservado/da.
wither vi marchitarse, secarse.
withhold vt detener, impedir, retener.
within prep dentro de, adentro; * adv interiormente; en casa.
without prep sin.
withstand vt resistir.
witless adj necio/cia, tonto/ta, falto/ta de ingenio.
witness n testimonio m; testgo m/f; * vt atestiguar, testificar.
witness stand n estrado de los testigos m.
witticism n ocurrencia f.
wittily adv ingeniosamente.
wittingly adv adrede, de propósito.
witty adj ingenioso/sa, agudo/da, chistoso/sa.
wizard n brujo, hechicero m.
wobble vi tambalearse.
woe n dolor m; miseria f.
woeful adj triste, funesto/ta; ~ly adv tristemente.
wolf n lobo m; **she ~** loba f.
woman n mujer f.
womanish adj mujeril.
womanly adj mujeril, mujeriego/ga.
womb n útero m.
women's lib n la liberación de la mujer f.
wonder n milagro m; maravilla f; asombro m; * vi maravi llarse de; preguntarse si.
wonderful adj maravilloso/sa; ~ly adv maravillosamente.
wondrous adj maravilloso/sa.
won't abbrev will not.
wont n uso m; costumbre f.
woo vt cortejar.
wood n bosque m; selva f; madera f; leña f.
wood alcohol n alcohol metílico m.
wood carving n tallado en madera m.
woodcut n estampa de madera f.
woodcutter n leñador/a m/f; grabador en láminas de madera, xilógrafo m/f.

wooded adj arbolado/da.
wooden adj de madera.
wood engraver n xilógrafo m.
wooden shoe n zueco m.
woodland n arbolado m.
woodlouse n cochinilla f.
woodpecker n pájaro carpintero m.
woodsman n cazador m; guardabosque m.
woodwind n intrumento de viento de madera m.
woodwork n carpintería f.
woodworm n carcoma f.
wool n lana f.
woolen adj de lana.
woolens npl géneros de lana mpl.
woolly, wooly adj lanudo/da, lanoso/sa.
word n palabra f; noticia f; * vt expresar; componer en escri tura.
wordiness n verbosidad f.
wording n redacción f.
word processing n tratamiento de textos m.
word processor n procesador de textos m.
wordy adj verboso/sa.
work vi trabajar; obrar; estar en movimiento/en acción; fermentar; * vt trabajar, labrar; fabricar, manufacturar; **to ~ out** vi salir bien; * vt resolver; * n trabajo m; fábrica f; obra f; empleo m.
workable adj práctico/ca.
workaholic n trabajador obsesivo m, trabajadora obsesiva f.
worker n trabajador/a m/f; obrero/ra m/f.
workforce n mano de obra f.
working-class adj obrero/ra, de clase trabajadora.
workman n labrador m.
workmanship n manufactura f; destreza del artífice f.
workmate n compañero/ra de trabajo m/f.
workshop n taller, obrador m.
world n mundo m; * adj del mundo; mundial.
worldliness n mundanería f.
worldly adj mundano/na, terreno/na.
worldwide adj mundial.
worm n gusano m; (tec) rosca de tornillo f.
worn-out adj gastado/da; rendido/da.
worried adj preocupado/da.
worry vt preocupar; * n preocupación f; pensión f.
worrying adj inquietante.
worse adj, adv peor; **~ and ~** cada vez peor; * n lo peor.
worship n culto m; adoración f; **your ~** su señoría; * vt adorar, venerar.
worst adj el/la peor; * adv peor; * n lo peor m.
worth n valor, precio m; mérito m.
worthily adv dignamente, convenientemente.
worthless adj sin valor; inútil.
worthwhile adj que vale la pena; valioso/sa.
worthy adj digno/na; respetable; honesto/ta.
would-be adj aspirante.

wound n herida, llaga f; * vt herir, llagar.
wrangle vi reñir; * n riña f.
wrap vt envolver.
wrath n ira, rabia, cólera f.
wreath n corona, guirnalda f.
wreck n naufragio m; ruina f; destrucción f; navío naufragado m; * vt naufragar; arruinar.
wreckage n restos mpl; escombros mpl.
wren n chochín m.
wrench vt arrancar; dislocar; torcer; * n llave inglesa f; tirón m.
wrest vt arrancar, arrebatar.
wrestle vi luchar; disputar.
wrestling n lucha f.
wretched adj infeliz, miserable.
wriggle vi menearse, agitarse.
wring vt torcer; arrancar; estrujar.
wrinkle n arruga f; * vt arrugar; * vi arrugarse.
wrist n muñeca f.
wristband n puno de camisa m.
wristwatch n reloj de pulsera m.
writ n escrito m; escritura f; orden f.
write vt escribir; componer; **to ~ down** apuntar; **to ~ off** borrar; desechar; **to ~ up** redactar.
write-off n pérdida total f.
writer n escritor/a, m/f; autor/a m/f.
writhe vi retorcerse.
writing n escritura f; letra f; obras fpl; escrito m.
writing desk n escritorio m.
writing paper n papel para escribir m.
wrong n injuria f; injusticia f; perjuicio m; error m; * adj malo/la; injusto/ta; equivocado/da, inopor-tuno/na; falso/sa; * adv mal, equivocadamente; * vt agraviar, injuriar.
wrongful adj injusto/ta.
wrongly adv injustamente.
wry adj irónico/ca.

X

xenophobia n xenofobia f.
Xmas n Navidad f.
X-ray n radiografía f.
xylographer n xilógrafo m.
xylophone n xilófano m.

Y

yacht n yate m.
yachting n vela f.
Yankee n yanqui m/f.
yard n corral m; yarda f.
yardstick n criterio m.
yarn n estambre m; hilo de lino m.
yawn vi bostezar; * n bostezo m.
yawning adj muy abierto/ta.
yeah adv sí.
year n año m.
yearbook n anuario m.

yearling *n* añal *m*.

yearly *adj* anual; * *adv* anualmente, todos los años.

yearn *vi* añorar.

yearning *n* añoranza *f*.

yeast *n* levadura *f*.

yell *vi* aullar; * *n* aullido *m*.

yellow *adj* amarillo/lla; * *n* amarillo *m*.

yellowish *adj* amarillento/ta.

yelp *vi* latir, gañir; * *n* aullido *m*.

yes *adv* sí; * *n* sí *m*.

yesterday *adv* ayer; * *n* ayer *m*.

yet *conj* sin embargo; pero; * *adv* todavía.

yew *n* tejo *m*.

yield *vt* dar, producir; rendir; * *vi* rendirse; ceder el paso; * *n* producción *f*; cosecha *f*; rendimiento *m*.

yoga *n* yoga *m*.

yogurt *n* yogur *m*.

yoke *n* yugo *m*; yunta *f*.

yolk *n* yema (de huevo) *f*.

yonder *adv* allá.

you *pn* vosotros/tras, tú, usted, *Lat Am* vos, ustedes.

young *adj* joven, mozo/za; ~**er** *adj* menor.

youngster *n* jovencito/ta *m/f*; joven *m/f*.

your(s) *pn* tuyo, tuya, vuestro, vuestra, suyo, suya.

yourself *pn* tú mismo, tú misma, usted mismo, usted misma.

yourselves *pn pl* vosotros mismos, vosotras mismas, ustedes mismos, ustedes mismas.

youth *n* juventud, adolescencia *f*; joven *m/f*.

youthful *adj* juvenil.

youthfulness *n* juventud *f*.

yuppie *adj*, *n* yupi *m/f*.

Z

zany *adj* estrafalario/ria.

zap *vt* borrar.

zeal *n* celo *m*; ardor *m*.

zealous *adj* celoso/sa.

zebra *n* cebra *f*.

zenith *n* cénit *m*.

zero *n* zero, cero *m*.

zest *n* ánimo *m*.

zigzag *n* zigzag *m*; * *adj* zigzag; * *vi* zigzaguear.

zinc *n* zinc *m*.

zipper *n* cremallera *f*; cierre de cremallera *m*.

zodiac *n* zodíaco *m*.

zone *n* banda, faja *f*; zona *f*.

zoo *n* zoo, zoológico *m*.

zoological *adj* zoológico/ca.

zoologist *n* zoólogo/ga *m/f*.

zoology *n* zoología *f*.

zoom *vi* zumbar.

zoom lens *n* zoom *m*.